Mexico's
Pacific Coast

Danny Palmerlee
Sandra Bao

LONELY PLANET PUBLICATIONS
Melbourne • Oakland • London • Paris

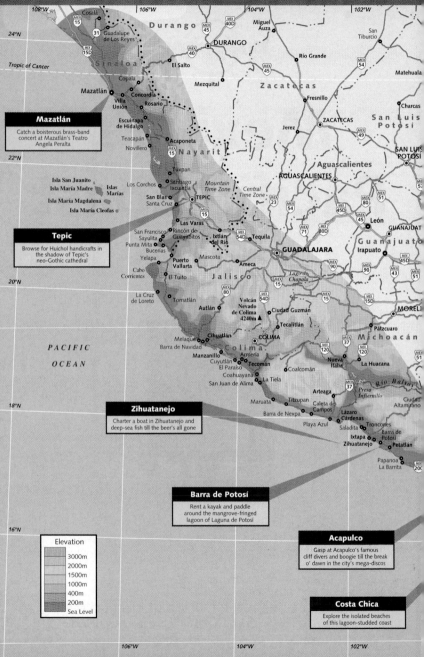

MEXICO'S PACIFIC COAST

Mazatlán
Catch a boisterous brass-band concert at Mazatlán's Teatro Angela Peralta

Tepic
Browse for Huichol handicrafts in the shadow of Tepic's neo-Gothic cathedral

Zihuatanejo
Charter a boat in Zihuatanejo and deep-sea fish till the beer's all gone

Barra de Potosí
Rent a kayak and paddle around the mangrove-fringed lagoon of Laguna de Potosí

Acapulco
Gasp at Acapulco's famous cliff divers and boogie till the break o' dawn in the city's mega-discos

Costa Chica
Explore the isolated beaches of this lagoon-studded coast

Elevation
3000m
2000m
1500m
1000m
400m
200m
Sea Level

PACIFIC OCEAN

Tropic of Cancer

Gulf of Mexico

PACIFIC OCEAN

Laguna de Manialtepec
Bird-watch your brains out among the mangrove forests of this stunning lagoon

Zipolite
Relax in a hammock and sleep for cheap at this laid-back beach hangout

Oaxaca
Explore the colonial streets and enjoy the fabulous cuisine of this vibrant city

Mexico's Pacific Coast
1st edition – February 2003

Published by
Lonely Planet Publications Pty Ltd ABN 36 005 607 983
90 Maribyrnong St, Footscray, Victoria 3011, Australia

Lonely Planet offices
Australia Locked Bag 1, Footscray, Victoria 3011
USA 150 Linden St, Oakland, CA 94607
UK 10a Spring Place, London NW5 3BH
France 1 rue du Dahomey, 75011 Paris

Photographs
Many of the images in this guide are available for licensing from
Lonely Planet Images.
w www.lonelyplanetimages.com

Front cover photograph
Baroque sculpture on the Malecón, Puerto Vallarta (Mark Gibson)

ISBN 1 74059 273 5

Printed by SNP SPrint Pte Ltd Singapore

Although the authors
and Lonely Planet try
to make the informa-
tion as accurate as
possible, we accept
no responsibility for
any loss, injury or
inconvenience sus-
tained by anyone
using this book.

Contents – Text

Contents – Maps

MAP INDEX

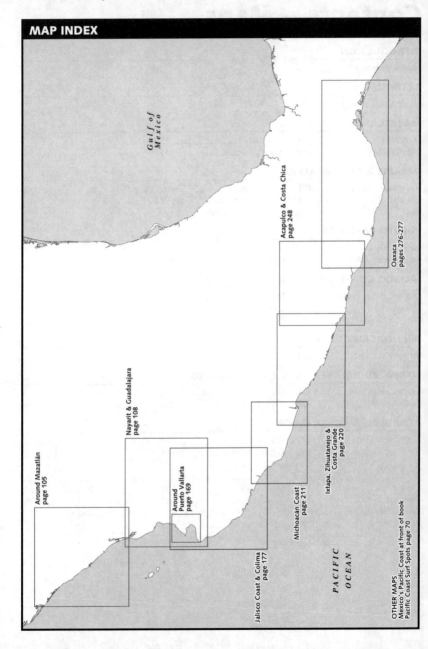

Gulf of Mexico

Around Mazatlán
page 105

Nayarit & Guadalajara
page 108

Around Puerto Vallarta
page 169

Jalisco Coast & Colima
page 177

Michoacán Coast
page 211

Ixtapa, Zihuatanejo &
Costa Grande
page 220

Acapulco & Costa Chica
page 248

Oaxaca
pages 276–277

PACIFIC OCEAN

OTHER MAPS
Mexico's Pacific Coast at front of book
Pacific Coast Surf Spots page 70

The Authors

Danny Palmerlee
Born and raised in Gilroy, California, Danny began traveling at age 12, when he and a friend floated down Uvas Creek in an abandoned bathtub. Since then he has trekked through Montana and Wyoming, traveled extensively throughout Latin America, Europe and Morocco, and spent a debauched year running a hostel in Scotland. At some point he received a Sociology degree from UC Santa Cruz, though most of his travels were funded by a lucrative body jewelry business he co-owned with an entrepreneurial friend. Over the years, he has filled the gaps of freelance writing with woodworking, house painting and substitute teaching to keep himself joyfully broke. Danny was the coordinating author of this book and researched and wrote the introductory chapters as well as the Ixtapa, Zihuatanejo & Costa Grande; Acapulco & Costa Chica; and Oaxaca chapters.

Sandra Bao
Sandra Bao was born in Buenos Aires, Argentina, to Chinese parents. She emigrated, kicking and screaming, to the United States when she was nine. Her introduction to America was Toledo, Ohio – in winter. It had been summer in Argentina. Sandra eventually forgave her parents and attended liberal UC Santa Cruz with a BA in psychology, which she finds useful, except when seeking employment. She's spent years traveling extensively around the world, and even taught introductory English to a 90-student class at Cheju University in Korea. These days she spends her time rock climbing, trying to establish good taste in music, and hanging out in her cute Oakland pad with her husband and fellow Lonely Planet writer Ben Greensfelder. Sandra's future avocations may include bass-playing rock star, glass-blowing pipe maker and perhaps ass-kicking policewoman. Sandra researched and wrote the Mazatlán, Nayarit & Guadalajara; Puerto Vallarta; Jalisco Coast & Colima; and Michoacán Coast chapters.

5

FROM THE AUTHORS

Danny Palmerlee This project was truly rockin', and I lift my glass to Sandra Bao, co-author *par excellence*. The Oaktown crew – Michele Posner, Sean Brandt and Annette Olson – were wonderful to work with. Ben, thanks for the tips. I owe my sanity to my eternal support crew: Dan, Leslie, Ellen, Mick, Julie and Pete – you guys are the best. Spears, thanks for the Chacahua tips.

In Mexico, I owe every one of the following people a shot of tequila and a world of thanks: Henry Wangeman of Amate Books, whose tips, leads and conversation kept me going for weeks; Dewey McMillin and Mike Bensal in Troncones who provided me loads of information and made my visit superb; Marcela Franco of Pinotepa Don Luis for her great generosity and help; the Bird Man of Manialtepec, Mike Malone; Juan Barnard and Mago Arizmendi of Zihuatanejo; Leo at Catcha L'Ola in Ixtapa; Jaíme Sandoval, Alejandro Flores Hernandez and Javier Acevedo Garcia in Huatulco; Christine and Valerie Truncali; Lic. José Pedano Galera and Ydalia Cortés Visairo of Acapulco; and Pedro Martinez and Pilar Cabrera of Oaxaca. For helping me push my car out of the sand, a warm thanks to Esteban Sanchez, Guillermina Blancas and Felipe Torrez of Boca de Lagunillas (you saved my day!).

Sandra Bao The most help I received for this project came from all the travelers, expatriots and Mexican people I met on the road. Thanks to them for enduring my prodding questions, banal contradictions and quirky personality. Certain individuals have also contributed to the final product held within; these would be Robert Hudson of Mazatlán, John McCrady of Puerto Vallarta, Laura del Valle and Emily Spielman of Chacala, and Dave Collins of La Manzanilla. My co-author Danny Palmerlee has been the coolest dude to work with, both on this book and on past South American projects. And my husband Ben Greensfelder managed to join me on this trip, acting as chauffeur, dining buddy and soul mate. Thanks for it all, honey bunny.

A special thanks to all the editors, designers and cartographers who worked at LP Oakland, having given their best until the year 2002. They were one of the most creative, enthusiastic and wonderful bunch of folks I've ever worked with and probably ever will. Most have now gone on to other things in other companies, and I wish them the best the world can offer.

This Book

This 1st edition of *Mexico's Pacific Coast* was coordinated by Justin Flynn at Lonely Planet's Melbourne office. He had expert editorial help from Rebecca Chau, David Andrew, Greg Alford, Sally O'Brien, Thalia Kalkipsakis, Kalya Ryan, Susannah Farfor and Kate James. The mapping was coordinated from Lonely Planet's Oakland office with assistance from Alison Lyall and Karen Fry in the Melbourne office. Project manager Huw Fowles oversaw the entire book production and kept things on track when they looked like going astray while commissioning editor Elaine Merrill worked tirelessly getting things in ship shape before the manuscript came in-house. Thanks to Vicki Beale, who did a grand job laying out the book. Special thanks to Barbara Benson for the climate charts, Quentin Frayne for the Language chapter, Anna Judd for her work during pre-layout and Pepi Bluck for organising the illustrations. Illustrations were provided by Hugh D'Andrade, Hannah Reineck and Rini Keagy.

Foreword

ABOUT LONELY PLANET GUIDEBOOKS

The story begins with a classic travel adventure: Tony and Maureen Wheeler's 1972 journey across Europe and Asia to Australia. There was no useful information about the overland trail then, so Tony and Maureen published the first Lonely Planet guidebook to meet a growing need.

From a kitchen table, Lonely Planet has grown to become the largest independent travel publisher in the world, with offices in Melbourne (Australia), Oakland (USA), London (UK) and Paris (France).

Today Lonely Planet guidebooks cover the globe. There is an ever-growing list of books and information in a variety of media. Some things haven't changed. The main aim is still to make it possible for adventurous travellers to get out there – to explore and better understand the world.

At Lonely Planet we believe travellers can make a positive contribution to the countries they visit – if they respect their host communities and spend their money wisely. Since 1986 a percentage of the income from each book has been donated to aid projects and human rights campaigns, and, more recently, to wildlife conservation.

Although inclusion in a guidebook usually implies a recommendation we cannot list every good place. Exclusion does not necessarily imply criticism. In fact there are a number of reasons why we might exclude a place – sometimes it is simply inappropriate to encourage an influx of travelers.

UPDATES & READER FEEDBACK

Things change – prices go up, schedules change, good places go bad and bad places go bankrupt. Nothing stays the same. So, if you find things better or worse, recently opened or long-since closed, please tell us and help make the next edition even more accurate and useful.

Lonely Planet thoroughly updates each guidebook as often as possible – usually every two years, although for some destinations the gap can be longer. Between editions, up-to-date information is available in our free, quarterly *Planet Talk* newsletter and monthly email bulletin *Comet*. The *Scoop* section of our website covers news and current affairs relevant to travellers. Lastly, the *Thorn Tree* bulletin board and *Postcards* section carry unverified, but fascinating, reports from travellers.

Tell us about it! We genuinely value your feedback. A well-travelled team at Lonely Planet reads and acknowledges every email and letter we receive and ensures that every morsel of information finds its way to the relevant authors, editors and cartographers.

Everyone who writes to us will find their name listed in the next edition of the appropriate guidebook, and will receive the latest issue of *Comet* or *Planet Talk*. The very best contributions will be rewarded with a free guidebook.

We may edit, reproduce and incorporate your comments in Lonely Planet products such as guidebooks, websites and digital products, so let us know if you don't want your comments reproduced or your name acknowledged.

How to contact Lonely Planet:
Online: ⓔ talk2us@lonelyplanet.com.au, Ⓦ www.lonelyplanet.com
Australia: Locked Bag 1, Footscray, Victoria 3011
UK: 10a Spring Place, London NW5 3BH
USA: 150 Linden St, Oakland, CA 94607

Introduction

Let's face it – life's better at the beach, and Mexico's Pacific coast has some of the best beaches in the world. This coast is a land of giant sunsets, mangrove-fringed lagoons, pristine bays, ramshackle fishing villages and friendly folks. It's a world where sea turtles crawl ashore by the thousand on moonlit nights to lay their eggs. Just lounging around in the sand, you might look up to spot humpback whales breaching on the horizon, or a pod of dolphins surfacing just outside the waves.

One of the world's top tourist destinations, the coast is also a land of mega-resorts, cruise ships, camera-clad tourists and rowdy spring-breakers on weekend drinking binges. You may find yourself two beers into a mellow evening in a Puerto Vallarta bar, and a *mariachi* (ensemble of street musicians) band strolls in with trumpets and guitars, the entire place turns into a party, and you finally end up teetering back to your hotel room with tequila-vision.

The beauty of Mexico's Pacific coast is that it can be whatever you want it to be. You can spend a week in a fabulous beachfront guesthouse, where food and drink are prepared fresh daily, and you don't have to think about anything beyond who gets the green hammock that day. It can be a harebrained road trip where you turn your rented VW Beetle into a dusty mess bouncing down back-roads to deserted beaches. You can take months exploring the coast on the cheap, roaring along the coastal highway in 2nd-class buses, or hanging onto the back of a pickup packed with locals on your way to a fishing village where they

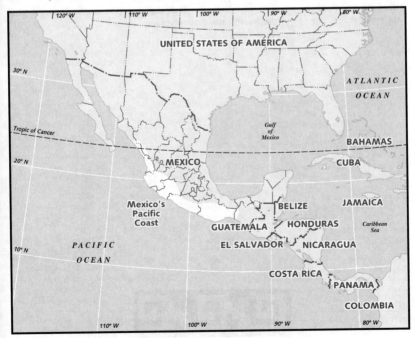

still string fishing nets by hand. You can fly into Bahías de Huatulco or Manzanillo and be whisked off in a private taxi to a luxury resort with five-star restaurants, in-house discos, theme bars and meandering swimming pools. There are opportunities to surf, scuba dive, snorkel, sail, ride horses along the beach, explore lagoons by boat, mountain bike along ocean cliffs, and drink yourself silly at the end of the day.

If you have a little time, inland destinations make excellent complements to those salty days on the coast. Guadalajara is Mexico's second-biggest city, the birthplace of mariachi music and a city of impressive architecture. Parque Nacional Volcán de Colima, near Colima, has two volcanoes, one of them still burping steam and soot. In the south, the city of Oaxaca has one of the country's most vibrant indigenous crafts scenes, magnificent colonial architecture, outstanding cuisine and colorful traditional markets.

And the food! Mexicans work wonders with seafood that the rest of the world can only dream about. Digging into a giant plate of grilled lobster or red snapper cooked in some spicy sauce and then soothing the fiery flavors with a cold beer is simply orgasmic. Then you just swim it off in the ocean.

The heart and soul of the Pacific coast, however, are the people. It's astounding that even after decades of heavy tourism they're still so damn friendly. Even the restaurant-touts, who swing menus at hundreds of tourists a day, will soften up to give directions to a confused visitor (though probably not without a quick joke at their expense). Spend some time in the many villages that are trickier to reach, and you'll soon ease into local life like a spoon into a cup of *ceviche*. Mexicans love their beaches too. In the big tourist towns, Mexican vacationers seem to have an entirely different view of what makes a good day at the beach – like, 'the more the merrier!' Join them on the sand and you might get sucked into the family fun yourself.

But whatever you do, don't forget your swimsuit.

Facts about Mexico's Pacific Coast

HISTORY

Historians traditionally divide Mexico's history before the Spanish conquest (the pre-Hispanic era) into four periods: Archaic, before 1500 BC; Preclassic, 1500 BC–AD 250; Classic, AD 250–900; and Postclassic, AD 900 to the fall of the Aztec empire in 1521. For the most part, these periods define the rise and fall of the great civilizations of central and southeast Mesoamerica, primarily the Olmecs, the civilization of Teotihuacán, the Maya and the Aztecs. These periods are less defined for western Mexico and the southern state of Guerrero, which lacked large-scale civilizations until the rise of the Tarascan empire; the Tarascans ruled Michoacán and the nearby regions of western Mexico between approximately AD 900 and the 1520s.

The First Americans

It's accepted that, barring a few Vikings in the north and some possible direct trans-Pacific contact with southeast Asia, the pre-Hispanic inhabitants of the Americas arrived from Siberia. They came in several migrations between perhaps 60,000–8000 BC, during the last Ice Age, crossing land now submerged beneath the Bering Strait. The earliest human traces in Mexico date from about 20,000 BC. These first Mexicans hunted big animal herds in the grasslands of the highland valleys. When temperatures rose at the end of the Ice Age the valleys became drier, ceasing to support such animal life and forcing the people to derive more food from plants.

Archaeologists have traced the slow beginnings of agriculture in the Tehuacán valley in Puebla state, where, soon after 6500 BC, people were planting seeds of chili and a kind of squash. Between 5000–3500 BC they started to plant mutant forms of a tiny wild maize and to grind the maize into meal. After 3500 BC a much better variety of maize, and also beans, enabled the Tehuacán valley people to live semipermanently in villages and spend less time in seasonal hunting camps. Pottery appeared around 2500 BC, and some of the oldest finds in Mexico are from sites near Acapulco.

Preclassic Period (1500 BC–AD 250)

The Olmecs Perhaps the oldest Mesoamerican culture of dramatic scale belongs to the Olmecs, who lived near the Gulf Coast in the humid lowlands of southern Veracruz and neighboring Tabasco from 1500 to around 200 BC. Their civilization is famed for the awesome 'Olmec heads,' stone sculptures up to 3m high with grim, pug-nosed faces combining the features of human babies and jaguars, a mixture referred to as the 'were-jaguar', and wearing curious helmets.

Olmec sites found far from the Gulf Coast, including some in Guerrero, may well have been trading posts or garrisons to ensure the supply of jade, obsidian and other luxuries for the Olmec elite. The two great Olmec centers, San Lorenzo in Veracruz and La Venta in Tabasco, were destroyed violently. But Olmec art and religion, and quite possibly Olmec social organization, strongly influenced later Mexican civilizations.

Pacific Mexico Western Mexico, and the southern states of Michoacán and Guerrero, are very much shrouded in mystery. Until the 1940s the area was all but ignored by archaeologists, probably because it lacked the grand architecture, writing systems, and dramatic religious deities that attracted researchers to the rest of Mesoamerica. Archaeological sites went unexcavated and unprotected for decades, and most were looted down the years by nonarchaeologists who sold their findings – primarily ceramics – to collectors. When study of the region's ancient past began in earnest, archaeologists faced the challenges of drawing conclusions from sites that no longer existed as left by their original inhabitants.

From Sinaloa south to the state of Guerrero, people lived in small, independent villages and chiefdoms, most, it is believed, with a distinct culture and language. Except for Guerrero, western Preclassic Mexico remained relatively isolated from the rest of Mesoamerica. The areas of present-day Nayarit, Jalisco and Colima – collectively referred to as West Mexico – have a distinct history, however, which is unique to all of Mesoamerica. Archaeologists and art historians treat West Mexico as a unified region, defined by its tradition of shaft or chamber tombs, underground burial chambers at the base of a deep shaft. The oldest of these have been dated as far back as 1900 BC, but the most significant were probably built between 1500–800 BC.

Much of what is known of the cultures of West Mexico is based on the excavation of these tombs and analysis of the clay sculptures and vessels found within. The ceremonial centers around the tombs suggest a fairly developed spiritual and religious life. The presence of female figurines, especially in Nayarit and Jalisco, suggest women were venerated and that their cultures may have been matriarchal. The people of West Mexico hunted in the foothills and mountains of the Sierra Madre Occidental and, toward the end of the Preclassic period, cultivated the upland valleys and coastal plains. Little is known of their political system.

Shaft tombs are found nowhere else in Mesoamerica, but they *are* found in Ecuador and Colombia. Ceramic vessels found in Colima are nearly identical to those found in Ecuador, some of which date to 1500 BC. It's therefore quite likely that maritime exchange between West Mexico and northern South America began some 3000 years ago. The West Mexican cultures probably had as much in common with Ecuador as they did with their immediate neighbors in the Mexico. Whether the shaft tomb tradition originated in Mexico or South America is still unknown.

The Chontal and Sultepec cultures (collectively referred to as the Mezcalas), who inhabited the Río Balsas region of Guerrero at the beginning of the Preclassic period, produced stone sculptures with obvious Olmec influences, suggesting contact between the Mezcalas and the Olmecs on a fairly significant scale. Throughout the Preclassic and Classic periods, Guerrero's coastline was dotted with small fishing communities that probably rarely exceeded more than a few thousand people. Little is known of Guerrero's ancient cultures, however, because many of its archaeological sites remain unexcavated.

Early Monte Albán

By 300 BC settled village life, based on agriculture and hunting, had developed throughout the southern half of Mexico. Monte Albán, the hilltop center of the Zapotecs of Oaxaca, was growing into a town of perhaps 10,000. Many carvings here have hieroglyphs or dates in a dot-and-bar system, which quite possibly means that the elite of Monte Albán invented writing and the written calendar in Mexico.

Classic Period (AD 250–900)

Teotihuacán The first great civilization in central Mexico emerged in a valley about 50km northeast of the center of modern Mexico City. Teotihuacán grew into a city of an estimated 125,000 people during its apogee between AD 250–600, and it controlled what was probably the biggest pre-Hispanic Mexican empire. Teotihuacán had writing and books, the bar-and-dot number system and the 260-day sacred year. The building of a magnificent planned city began about the time of Christ and took some 600 years to complete.

It's possible Teotihuacán could have controlled the southern two-thirds of Mexico, all of Guatemala and Belize, and some parts of Honduras and El Salvador. It possibly had hegemony over the Zapotecs of Oaxaca during the zenith of their capital, Monte Albán, which grew into a city of perhaps 25,000 people between about AD 300–600. Artifacts have been found in Guerrero, which suggests Teotihuacán had at least loose ties to the region.

Teotihuacán was burned, plundered and then abandoned during the 7th century. It is likely that the state had already been weakened by the rise of rival powers in central Mexico or by environmental desiccation caused by the deforestation of the surrounding hillsides.

Classic Maya By the close of the Preclassic period, in AD 250, the Maya people of the Yucatán Peninsula and the Petén forest of Guatemala were already building stepped temple pyramids. During the Classic period, these regions produced pre–Hispanic America's most brilliant civilization, with the great cities of Tikal, in Guatemala's Petén, the most splendid of all.

Pacific Mexico The shaft tomb tradition that so defined Nayarit, Jalisco and Colima begin to die out in the early Classic period. Objects from Teotihuacán have been found in Nayarit, Jalisco, Colima and Michoacán which suggest that Teotihuacán was probably absorbing the West Mexican cultures into its sphere. Teotihuacán was probably interested in the area for the region's precious stones and minerals.

The collapse of Teotihuacán in the 7th century was felt all throughout western Mexico and Guerrero – as it was throughout Mesoamerica – but the scattered, independent chiefdoms that characterized the coastal states continued well into the Postclassic period. The fertile coastal ecology provided plentifully for the people who hunted and farmed the coastal plains and upland valleys, and fished the coastal waters.

Around the close of the Classic period, a curious tradition made its appearance in West Mexico and Michoacán – metal working. Like the shaft tombs and ceramics of centuries past, this new tradition was tied not to Mesoamerica, but, most likely, to Ecuador. Examination of copper artifacts from both West Mexico and Ecuador show similarities far too striking to be coincidental. Archaeologists conclude that contact between west Mexico and northern

South America continued well into the Postclassic period.

Postclassic Period (AD 900–1521)

Aztecs The Aztecs were the monumental Postclassic civilization. The Aztec capital, Tenochtitlán, was founded on a lake-island in the Valle de México (site of present-day Mexico City) in the first half of the 14th century. In the mid-15th century the Aztecs formed the Triple Alliance with two other valley states and brought most of central Mexico from the Gulf Coast to the Pacific under its control. The total population of the empire's 38 provinces may have been about five million. The empire's main concern was exacting resources absent from the heartland. Jade, turquoise, cotton, paper, tobacco, rubber, lowland fruits and vegetables, cacao and precious feathers were needed for the glorification of the Aztec elite and to support the many nonproductive servants of its war-oriented state.

Much of Aztec culture was drawn from earlier Mexican civilizations. They had writing, bark-paper books and the Calendar Round, and observed the heavens for astrological purposes. Celibate priests performed cycles of great ceremonies, typically including sacrifices and masked dances or processions enacting myths.

The Tarascos The only empire to exist in western Mexico were the Tarascos and, being fierce warriors, were the only group to successfully resist Aztec invasions. After the Aztecs, they were the largest and most powerful empire in Mesoamerica. Called the Purépecha until the Spanish labeled them Tarascos, they ruled present-day Michoacán and parts of Jalisco, Guanajuato and Guerrero from the 12th century until the arrival of the Spanish in 1521. Their capital was Tzintzuntzan ('place of the hummingbirds') near Lake Pátzcuaro, about 200km west of Mexico City. Tarascan expansion throughout Michoacán was probably compelled by the desire to bring more commodities and precious metals under their control.

At Tzintzuntzan and other sites on Lake Pátzcuaro, the Tarascos built enormous stepped *yácatas* (pyramids) with pillared roofs. These ceremonial centers were the religious heart of a stratified society composed of high priests, nobility, commoners and slaves. The Tarascos were skilled artisans and jewelers, and Tarascan pottery and metalworking techniques – probably inherited directly or indirectly from Ecuador through the earlier cultures of West Mexico – were the most advanced in Mesoamerica. In contrast to the highly decorative ceramic burial figurines of Jalisco and Nayarit, Tarascan ceramics were mostly utilitarian, more similar, perhaps, to the effigy vessels of Colima.

The origin of the Tarascos themselves is unknown. Purépecha, the Tarascan language, has no linguistic similarities in Mexico, but is similar to the Quechua language of Ecuador and Peru.

Oaxaca & Guerrero After about 1200 the remaining Zapotec settlements of Oaxaca, such as Mitla and Yagul, were increasingly dominated by the Mixtecs, famed metalsmiths and potters from the uplands around the Oaxaca–Puebla border. Mixtec and Zapotec cultures became entangled before much of their territory fell to the Aztecs in the 15th and 16th centuries. Around the same time, the Aztecs were establishing small strategic presences along the Guerrero coast. The Yopes, who lived around the Bahía de Acapulco, were one of the few groups who successfully resisted the expansionist Aztecs.

Enter the Spanish

Ancient Mexican civilization, nearly 3000 years old, was shattered in the two short years from 1519–21 by a tiny group of invaders. These conquerors destroyed the Aztec and Tarascan empires, brought a new religion and reduced the native people to second-class citizens and slaves.

The Spaniards had been in the Caribbean since Christopher Columbus arrived in 1492, with their main bases on the islands of Hispaniola and Cuba. Realizing that they had not reached the East Indies, they began looking for a passage through the land mass to the west, but were distracted by tales of gold, silver and a rich empire. On February 15, 1519, Hernán Cortés set sail from Cuba with 11 ships, 550 men and 16 horses. They landed first at Cozumel, off the Yucatán Peninsula, then sailed around the coast to Tabasco, where they defeated local resistance. The expedition next put in near the present city of Veracruz.

In the Aztec capital of Tenochtitlán, tales of 'towers floating on water' bearing fair-skinned beings, reached Moctezuma II, the Aztec god-king. According to the Aztec calendar, 1519 would see the legendary god-king Quetzalcóatl return from the east. Unsure if Cortés really was the god returning, Moctezuma sent messengers to attempt to discourage Cortés from traveling to Tenochtitlán.

The Spaniards were well received at Gulf Coast communities which resented Aztec dominion. Cortés thus gained his first indigenous allies. He set up a coastal settlement called Villa Rica de la Vera Cruz and then apparently scuttled his ships to stop his men from retreating. Leaving about 150 men at Villa Rica, Cortés set off for Tenochtitlán. On the way he won over the Tlaxcalan people, who became valuable allies.

After much vacillation, Moctezuma eventually invited Cortés to meet him. The Spaniards and 6000 indigenous allies thus approached the Aztecs' lake-island capital, a city bigger than any in Spain. Entering Tenochtitlán on November 8, 1519, Cortés was met by Moctezuma, who was carried by nobles in a litter with a canopy of feathers and gold. The Spaniards were lodged, as befitted gods, in the palace of Axayácatl, Moctezuma's father.

Fall of Empires When the Spaniards had been in Tenochtitlán about six months, Moctezuma informed Cortés that another fleet had arrived on the Veracruz coast. It was led by Pánfilo de Narváez, sent by Diego Velázquez to arrest Cortés. Cortés left 140 Spaniards under Pedro de Alvarado in Tenochtitlán and sped to the coast with the others. They routed Narváez's much bigger force and most of the defeated men joined Cortés.

After six months in Tenochtitlán, and apparently fearing an attack, the Spaniards struck first and killed about 200 Aztec nobles trapped in a square during a festival. Cortés and his enlarged force returned to the Aztec capital and were allowed to rejoin their comrades – only then to come under fierce attack. Trapped in Axayácatl's palace, Cortés persuaded Moctezuma to try to pacify his people. According to one version of the events, the king went up to the roof to address the crowds but was wounded by missiles and died soon afterward; other versions have it that the Spaniards killed him.

The Spaniards fled on the night of June 30, 1520, but several hundred of them, and thousands of their indigenous allies, were killed on this Noche Triste (Sad Night). The survivors retreated to Tlaxcala, where they prepared for another campaign by building boats in sections, which could be carried across the mountains for a waterborne assault on Tenochtitlán. When the approximately 900 Spaniards re-entered the Valle de México they were accompanied by some 100,000 native allies. For the first time the odds were in their favor.

The attack started in May 1521. Cortés had to resort to razing Tenochtitlán building by building. By August 13, 1521, the resistance had ended. The Spanish captured Moctezuma's successor, Cuauhtémoc, who asked Cortés to kill him, but was kept alive until 1525 as a hostage.

In 1522, shortly after the fall of Tenochtitlán, the Spanish advanced on Tzintzuntzan. The Tarascan king, Tangoxoán II, had learned the fate of the Aztec empire and, in hopes of striking a deal to keep control of his own kingdom, cooperated with the Spanish. The king, however, was besieged and taken by the Spanish, and afterwards the majority of the Tarascan territories peacefully acquiesced to Spanish control.

Nueva España

The Spaniards renamed Tenochtitlán 'México' and rebuilt it as the capital of Nueva España (New Spain), the name they gave their new colony. Cortés granted his soldiers *encomiendas*, which were rights to the labor or tribute of groups of indigenous people.

By 1524 virtually all the Aztec empire, plus other Mexican regions such as Colima, the Huasteca area and the Isthmus of Tehuantepec, had been brought under at least loose control of the colony. In 1527 Spain set up Nueva España's first *audiencia*, a high court with government functions. Its leader, Nuño de Guzmán, was among the worst of Mexican history's long list of corrupt, violent leaders. After leading a bloody expedition to western Mexico, from Michoacán up to Sonora, he was eventually recalled to Spain.

Throughout the 1520s Cortés sent numerous expeditions to the Pacific coast to establish ship-building facilities on the most promising natural harbors. During the next 40 years the Spanish fought to wrest control of the Pacific shores from its native inhabitants, waging war against several nations, from the Yopes near Acapulco to the Totorames who lived at Mazatlán.

From several bays along the coast, including those at Acapulco, Zihuatanejo, Zacatula, Puerto Vallarta and Manzanillo, Spanish ships sailed west to Asia, traded American for Asian goods, and continued around South Africa up to Europe. Many of the expeditions that set out from Mexico hoped to navigate a return route from Asia to the Americas to avoid the dangerous journey around Africa's southern cape. Not until 1565 was a route discovered, after which all trade from Asia came back through Mexico via Acapulco. From Acapulco, goods were transported overland to Veracruz on the Gulf, where they were loaded onto ships and sent to Spain.

Plague & Place The number of native peoples in Nueva España declined disastrously, mainly due to plagues from diseases introduced by the Spaniards. The population of Nueva España fell from an estimated 25 million at the conquest to little more than one million by 1605.

In colonial times a person's place in society was determined by their skin color, parentage and birthplace. Spanish-born colonists – known as *peninsulares* or, derisively, *gachupines* – were a minuscule part of the population but were at the top of the tree and considered nobility, no matter what their origins in Spain. Next on the ladder were *criollos*, people born of Spanish parents in Nueva España. Below the criollos were the *mestizos,* people of mixed indigenous and Spanish descent. At the bottom of the pile were the indigenous people and African slaves.

Independence

Aware of the threat to Nueva España from British and French expansion in North America, King Carlos III (1759–88) sought to bring the colony under firmer control and improve the flow of funds to the Spanish crown. He expelled the Jesuits – most of them criollos – and decreed the transfer of many church assets to the royal coffers, both creating widespread discontent among criollos.

The catalyst for rebellion came in 1808, when France's Napoleon Bonaparte occupied most of Spain and direct Spanish control over Nueva España evaporated. Rivalry between peninsulares and criollos in the colony intensified.

In September, 1810 Miguel Hidalgo y Costilla, a criollo priest of the town of Dolores, Guanajuato, summoned his parishioners and issued his now-famous call to rebellion, the Grito de Dolores. A mob formed and marched quickly on San Miguel, Celaya and Guanajuato, massacring peninsulares in Guanajuato. On October 30 their army, numbering about 80,000, defeated loyalist forces at Las Cruces outside Mexico City. The rebels occupied Guadalajara, but then were pushed northward by their opponents; their numbers shrank and in 1811 their leaders, including Hidalgo, were captured and executed.

José María Morelos y Pavón, a former student of Hidalgo and also a parish priest, assumed the rebel leadership, blockading Mexico City for several months. He convened a congress at Chilpancingo, Guerrero, that adopted guiding principles for the independence movement including universal male suffrage, popular sovereignty and the abolition of slavery. Morelos was captured and executed in 1815, and his forces split into several guerrilla bands, the most successful of which was led by Vicente Guerrero in the state of Oaxaca.

In 1821 the royalist general Agustín de Iturbide defected during an offensive against Guerrero and conspired with the rebels to declare independence from Spain. Iturbide and Guerrero worked out the Plan de Iguala, which won over all influential sections of society, and the incoming Spanish viceroy in 1821 agreed to Mexican independence. Iturbide, who had command of the army, soon arranged his own nomination to the throne, which he ascended as Emperor Agustín I in 1822.

The Mexican Republic

Iturbide was deposed in 1823 by a rebel army led by another opportunistic soldier, Antonio López de Santa Anna. A new constitution in 1824 established a federal Mexican republic of 19 states and four territories. Guadalupe Victoria, a former independence fighter, became its first president.

Vicente Guerrero stood as a liberal candidate in the 1828 presidential elections and was defeated, but was eventually awarded the presidency after another Santa Anna-led revolt. Guerrero abolished slavery, but was deposed and executed by his conservative vice president, Anastasio Bustamante. The struggle between liberals, who favored social reform, and conservatives, who opposed it, would be a constant theme in 19th-century Mexican politics.

Intervention in politics by ambitious military men was also becoming a habit. Santa Anna overthrew Bustamante and was elected president in 1833, beginning 22 years of chronic instability in which the presidency changed hands 36 times; 11 of those terms went to Santa Anna. Economic decline and corruption became entrenched, and the megalomaniacal Santa Anna quickly turned into a conservative.

Santa Anna's ground became shaky after the Mexican–American war (1846–48) in which Mexico lost Texas, California, Utah, Colorado, and most of New Mexico and Arizona to the USA. The Santa Anna government sold the remainder of New Mexico and Arizona to the USA in 1853 for US$10 million, in the Gadsden Purchase. The loss precipitated the liberal-led Revolution of Ayutla, which ousted Santa Anna for good in 1855.

Juárez & the French Intervention By the time Benito Juárez, a liberal Zapotec from Oaxaca, became president in 1861, Mexico was heavily in debt to Britain, France and Spain. These three countries sent a joint force to collect their debts, but France's Napoleon III decided to go further and take over Mexico, leading to yet another war.

At the close of 1863 the French captured Mexico City and in 1864 Napoleon invited the Austrian archduke, Maximilian of Hapsburg, to become emperor of Mexico. The French army drove Juárez and his government into the provinces. Maximilian's reign was brief. In 1866, under pressure from the USA, Napoleon began to withdraw the troops who sustained Maximilian's rule. Maximilian refused to abandon his task, but was defeated at Querétaro in 1867 by forces loyal to Juárez and executed there by firing squad.

Juárez immediately set an agenda of economic and educational reform. For the first time, schooling was made mandatory, a railway was built between Mexico City and Veracruz, and a rural police force, the *rurales*, was organized to secure the transport of cargo through Mexico. Juárez died in 1872.

The Porfiriato When Juárez' successor, Sebastián Lerdo de Tejada, stood for re-election in 1876, Porfirio Díaz, an ambitious liberal, launched a rebellion and stole the elections the following year. For the next 33 years he ran Mexico with an iron fist. Díaz brought Mexico into the industrial age and kept Mexico free of the civil wars that had plagued it for more than 60 years, but at a cost: Political opposition, free elections and a free press were banned. Many of Mexico's resources went into foreign ownership,

peasants were cheated out of their land by new laws, workers suffered appalling conditions, and the country was kept quiet by a ruthless army and the now-feared rurales. Land and wealth became concentrated in the hands of a small minority.

Very early in the 20th century a liberal opposition formed, but it was forced into exile in the USA. In 1906 the most important group of exiles issued a new liberal plan for Mexico from St Louis, Missouri. Their actions precipitated strikes throughout Mexico – some violently suppressed – that led, in late 1910, to the Mexican Revolution.

From Revolution to Reform
The Mexican Revolution was a 10-year period of shifting allegiances between a spectrum of leaders, in which successive attempts to create stable governments were wrecked by continued outbreaks of fighting. The basic divide that would dog the whole revolution was between liberal reformers like Madero and more radical leaders such as Emiliano Zapata from the state of Morelos. A decade of violent civil war cost an estimated 1.5 to two million lives – roughly one in eight Mexicans – and shattered the economy.

After the revolution, former revolutionary leader Alvaro Obregón became president (1920–24) and steered the country toward national reconstruction. More than 1000 rural schools were built and some land was redistributed from big landowners to the peasants.

Obregón's successor, Plutarco Elías Calles, built more schools and distributed more land. He also closed monasteries, convents and church schools, and prohibited religious processions. These measures precipitated the bloody Cristero Rebellion by Catholics, which lasted until 1929.

At the end of President Calles' term, in 1928, Obregón was elected president again but was assassinated by a Cristero. Calles reorganized his supporters to found the Partido Nacional Revolucionario (PNR, National Revolutionary Party), precursor of today's PRI (Partido Revolucionario Instucional).

Lázaro Cárdenas, former governor of Michoacán, won the presidency in 1934 with the PNR's support and stepped up the reform programme. Cárdenas redistributed almost 200,000 sq km of land, mostly through the establishment of *ejidos* (peasant landholding cooperatives). The land was nearly double the amount distributed since 1920 and nearly one-third of the population received holdings.

Modern Mexico

The Mexican economy expanded in the two decades after WWII. By 1952 the country's population had doubled from what it was two decades earlier. Civil unrest appeared again in 1968, in the months preceding the Olympic Games in Mexico City. More than 500,000 people rallied in Mexico City's zócalo on August 27 to express their outrage with the conservative Díaz Ordaz (1964–70) administration. On October 2, with the Olympics only a few days away, a rally was organized in Tlatelolco plaza, Mexico City. The government sent in heavily armed troops and police who opened fire on the crowd, killing several hundred people.

The oil boom of the late 1970s increased Mexico's oil revenues and financed industrial and agricultural investments, but the oil glut in the early 1980s deflated petroleum prices and led to Mexico's worst recession in several decades. The population continued to escalate at Malthusian rates through the 1980s; the economy made only weak progress. In 1985 an earthquake shook Mexico City and killed at least 10,000 people and caused more than US$4 billion in damage. In a climate of economic helplessness and rampant corruption, dissent grew on both the left and the right, and even within the PRI.

Salinas, Nafta & the EZLN The Harvard-educated Carlos Salinas de Gortari took the presidency in 1988 (fraudulently, it's widely believed) and set about transforming Mexico's state-dominated economy into one of private enterprise and free trade. The apex of his programme was Nafta, the North American Free Trade Agreement, which came into effect on January 1, 1994. The same day a group of 2000 or so indigenous-peasant

rebels calling themselves Ejército Zapatista de Liberación Nacional (EZLN, Zapatista National Liberation Army) shocked Mexico by taking over San Cristóbal de Las Casas and three other towns in the country's southernmost state, Chiapas.

Though the EZLN was driven out of the towns within a few days (about 150 people were killed in the uprising), the uprising struck a chord nationally among all who felt that Salinas and Nafta were merely widening the gap between rich and poor, and who believed that the Mexican system prevented real social or political change.

During Salinas' term, drug trafficking grew into a huge business in Mexico and many Mexicans believe President Salinas and his brother Raúl and other PRI high-ups were deeply involved in drug business. Vilified also for the economic crisis into which Mexico plunged after he left office, Carlos Salinas ended up as the ex-president that Mexicans most love to hate.

After the EZLN uprising, Salinas pushed through electoral reforms against ballot-stuffing and double voting, and the 1994 presidential election was regarded as the cleanest to date. But they were hardly spotless. In March 1994 Luis Donaldo Colosio, Salinas' chosen successor as PRI presidential candidate, was assassinated in Tijuana. Colosio's replacement as PRI candidate, 43-year-old Ernesto Zedillo, won the election with 50% of the vote.

Zedillo Within days of President Zedillo taking office in late 1994, Mexico's currency, the peso, suddenly collapsed, bringing on a rapid and deep economic recession that hit everyone hard, and the poor hardest. It led to, among other things, a big increase in crime, intensified discontent with the PRI, and large-scale Mexican emigration to the USA. Zedillo's policies pulled Mexico gradually out of recession and by the end of his term in 2000, Mexicans' purchasing power was again approaching what it had been in 1994.

Zedillo was an uncharismatic figure, but was perceived as more honest than his predecessors. He set his sights on democratic reform and set up a new, independent electoral apparatus that achieved in 1997 Mexico's freest and fairest elections since 1911. Voting took place for the federal Chamber of Deputies – of which the PRI lost control for the first time. Zedillo also introduced a primary-election system for the selection of the party's candidate for the 2000 presidential elections, which replaced the traditional method by which each president personally chose his successor.

The PRI refrained from its traditional strongarm, corrupt methods in many local elections. By 1999 10 of Mexico's 31 states had elected non-PRI governors and Mexico City had a non-PRI mayor. The party remained at its most unreconstructed and antediluvian in southern states, such as Guerrero and Chiapas, both, hardly surprisingly, scenes of armed left-wing insurgency. When, for instance, Guerrero's famed Pacific resort Acapulco elected a PRD mayor in 1999, several prominent PRD figures and members of their families suddenly found themselves arrested, kidnapped, tortured and, in one case, killed.

Rebels In Chiapas, Zedillo at first negotiated with the EZLN, but then in February 1995 he sent in the army to 'arrest' Subcomandante Marcos and other leaders. The rebels escaped deeper into the jungle. On-and-off negotiations eventually brought an agreement on indigenous rights in 1996,

but Zedillo balked at turning the agreement into law.

Another left-wing rebel movement, the Ejército Popular Revolucionario (EPR, People's Revolutionary Army), emerged in 1996 in two other impoverished southern states, Guerrero (where 17 peasant political activists had been killed by police in the 1995 Aguas Blancas massacre) and Oaxaca. After a wave of attacks against police and military posts in several states, in which some 20 people died, the EPR reverted to mainly propaganda and publicity activities.

The Drug Trade Mexico has long been a marijuana and heroin producer, but a huge impetus to its drug gangs was given by a mid-1980s US crackdown on drug shipments from Colombia through the Caribbean to Florida. As a result, drugs being transported from South America to the USA went through Mexico instead. Three main Mexican cartels emerged: the Pacific or Tijuana cartel, headed by the Arellano Félix brothers; the (Ciudad) Juárez cartel, run by Amado Carrillo Fuentes; and the Matamoros-based Gulf cartel of Juan García Ábrego. These cartels bought up politicians, top antidrug officials and entire police forces. By 1997 most illegal drugs entering the USA were coming through Mexico, and the drug gangs' profits amounted to US$15 billion or more a year.

Zedillo brought the armed forces into the fight against the drug mobs. There were some successes (the biggest being the arrest of Juan García Ábrego of the Gulf cartel), but the Juárez mob and the Tijuana cartel emerged as the two big smuggling rings. The increasing power and violence of criminal organizations was attributed by some to the weakening of the PRI's strong centralized hold over Mexican life in general and over organized crime in particular. While some high-profile drug hoodlums were arrested or convicted, many others stayed free.

The Fox Presidency In 2000, Vicente Fox became the first non-PRI president since the PRI (or, strictly speaking, its predecessor the PNR) was established in 1929. Rancher, former chief of Coca-Cola's Mexican operation

Ernesto Zedillo

and former state governor of Guanajuato, Fox stands at almost 2m tall and has a penchant for wearing jeans and cowboy boots. Although Fox represents the right-of-center PAN, he is more of a centrist social democrat himself, and he entered office with the goodwill of a wide range of Mexicans who hoped a change of ruling party would betoken real change in the country. Fox picked a broad-based ministerial team ranging from ex-PRI officials to left-wing academics, and did not, as incoming Mexican administrations traditionally do, replace the entire governing apparatus with his own mates and hangers-on.

He made an early, though unsuccessful, attempt to resolve the Zapatista conflict in Chiapas and tried to resolve some of the problems of the Mexico/USA border and Mexican immigration to the USA. One year into Fox's term he was being criticized for having achieved little. His popularity ratings soured, and people questioned how committed he really was to human rights and to rooting out corruption.

He had been bequeathed a booming economy by President Zedillo, only to have things seriously complicated by the recession of 2001. Fox wanted to raise taxes to pay for better education and social programmes, increase the time an average Mexican spends in school from seven to 10 years, and reduce the number of Mexicans living in poverty by one-third. He was not being helped by tensions with the orthodox establishment of his own party, nor by the PAN's lack of overall majority in Congress, which made it harder for him to push through reforms.

GEOGRAPHY & GEOLOGY

Spectacular beaches and coastal lagoons line most of the Pacific coast. It's nearly 2000km by road from Mazatlán, the northernmost destination in this book, to Bahías de Huatulco in Oaxaca. Mazatlán sits about midway down a dry coastal plain which stretches south from Mexicali, on the US border, almost to Tepic, in Nayarit state. Inland from the flats stands the rugged, volcanically formed Sierra Madre Occidental, which is crossed by only two main transport routes – the Barranca del Cobre (Copper Canyon) railway, from Chihuahua to Los Mochis, and the dramatic Hwy 40 from Durango to Mazatlán.

South of Cabo Corrientes (that lip of land protruding into the Pacific near Puerto Vallarta), the Pacific lowlands narrow to just a thin strip and the mountains rise abruptly from the sea. The Sierra Madre Occidental widens near Nayarit and finishes in Jalisco, where it meets the Cordillera Neovolcánica, a volcanic range running east-west across the middle of Mexico. The Cordillera Neovolcánica, known in English as the Trans-Mexican Volcanic Belt, includes the active volcanoes Popocatépetl (5452m) and Volcán de Fuego de Colima (3960m), as well as Pico de Orizaba (5610m), the nation's highest peak.

The main mountain range in southern Mexico is the Sierra Madre del Sur, which stretches across the states of Guerrero and Oaxaca and separates the Oaxacan coast from its capital city. As the crow flies, it's only about 160km from Puerto Ángel, the southernmost town in Oaxaca, north to Oaxaca city; but crossing the crinkled back of the Sierra takes about six hours by car.

CLIMATE

The tropic of Cancer cuts across Mexico just north of Mazatlán, so this stretch of coast is officially tropical. The driest months, when it may not rain at all, are from November to April. These months are also the coolest, with temperatures averaging a comfortable 26° to 29°C.

The hottest months, May to October, are also the wettest, and the hottest and wettest of all are June, July and August. Rainfall increases as you move south from Mazatlán toward Acapulco (Acapulco receives twice as much rain as Mazatlán). The Oaxaca coast is drier, but closer in average rainfall to Acapulco than Mazatlán. May to October are also extremely humid, and it's generally more humid the further south you move. Temperatures are similar along the entire coast, though the southern coast is always slightly warmer than the north.

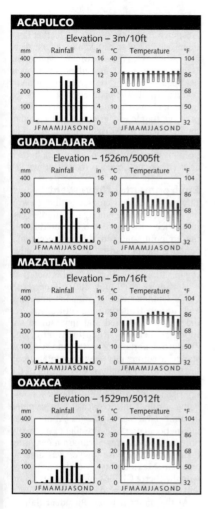

Inland, at higher elevations such as in Guadalajara or Oaxaca, the climate is drier and temperate, and winter nights can be very chilly. Descriptions of both these cities often include the classic 'city of eternal spring,' which is very near the mark.

ECOLOGY & ENVIRONMENT

The coastal plains, deciduous and mangrove forests, wetlands and lagoons of Pacific Mexico support incredible biodiversity. The rugged, mountainous topography lying just inland adds to the variety of coastal ecology by creating countless microclimates that support a diverse array of plant and animal species. As in the rest of Mexico, many of the coastal region's species are endangered. The human impact on the environment has been enormous, and the coast has a litany of problems that threaten not only the fauna and flora but people too.

Problems

Mexico's environmental crises, including those of the coast, are typical of a poor country with an exploding population struggling to develop. From early in the 20th century, urban industrial growth, intensive chemical-based agriculture, and the destruction of forests for logging and to permit grazing and development were seen as paths to prosperity, and little attention was paid to their environmental effects. A growth in environmental awareness since the 1970s has managed to achieve only very limited changes.

Forest Depletion Deforestation has increased considerably on the coast since the passage of Nafta in 1994, which gave international corporations access to vast *ejido* (communal) land holdings. For example, in the Sierra de Petatlán and Coyuca de Catalán regions of Guerrero's Costa Grande, 40% of its forests have been logged in less than a decade. The vast stands of white and sugar pine logged in the region (mostly by subsidiaries of Idaho-based Boise Cascade) were sold primarily in the USA. Local community protests against logging policies have been met with numerous human rights violations. Deforestation has caused massive erosion and has contributed to increased flooding, local climate changes, and over-silting of rivers.

Wetland Depletion Mexico's rich coastal lagoons and wetlands have experienced considerable harm in recent years from shrimp farming. Shrimp farms contribute to the destruction of mangroves, permanent flooding of lagoons, the privatization of communal fishing waters, and the introduction of massive amounts of fertilizers and chemicals. The industry is booming in Sinaloa, Nayarit and Oaxaca, and receives heavy investment from the Mexican government and the World Bank. The biggest market for Mexican farmed shrimp is the USA.

Cattle grazing has a devastating impact on wetlands where they are drained to create pastureland. Laguna Manialtepec in Oaxaca was being reduced at an alarming rate until local fishing communities were able to stop it with considerable protest.

Erosion & Water Contamination Erosion is mainly the result of deforestation followed by cattle grazing or intensive agriculture on unsuitable terrain. In the Mixteca area of Oaxaca, around 80% of the arable land is gone.

Some rural areas and watercourses have been contaminated by excessive use of chemical pesticides and defoliants. Agricultural workers have suffered health problems related to these chemicals. Sewage, and industrial and agricultural wastes contaminate most Mexican rivers. One of the rivers from which Mexico City and other cities take water is the Lerma, which receives raw sewage and industrial effluent from 95 towns on its way into poor old Lago de Chapala, Mexico's biggest natural lake, near Guadalajara. Chapala itself is shrinking because Guadalajara takes more water out of it than its feeder rivers now bring in.

Tourism In some places in Mexico it's hoped that ecologically sensitive tourism will benefit the environment by providing a less harmful source of income for local people. An example is Mazunte, Oaxaca, a village that lived by slaughtering sea turtles until the practice was banned in 1990. Villagers turned to slash-and-burn farming, threatening forest survival, before a low-key and successful tourism programme was launched.

In other cases, despite official lip service paid to conservation, large-scale tourism developments have wrecked fragile ecosystems. Acapulco grew at such a rate and pumped so much sewage into the Bay of Acapulco in the 1970s and 1980s that drastic measures had to be taken to reverse damage to the bay. In the case of now-developing Bahías de Huatulco, the federal government has taken steps to prevent water pollution by resorts, limited construction heights on hotels and even created a national park to preserve fragile ecosystems. But local communities have been displaced, and inland lagoons critical to the local ecosystem have been mysteriously drawn out of park boundaries (where golf courses may be drawn in).

Environmental Movement

Environmental consciousness first grew in the 1970s, initially among the middle class in Mexico City where nobody could ignore the air pollution. Today nongovernmental action is carried out by a growing number of groups around the country, mainly small organizations working on local issues.

Between 1999 and 2001, Guerrero's Costa Grande made continuous headlines and attracted international criticism after the military arrested and imprisoned antilogging activists Rodolfo Montiel and Teodoro Cabrera. Montiel and Cabrera started a community environmental group in 1997, which fought heavy logging of the Costa Grande. Montiel and Cabrera were imprisoned for 16 months after reportedly being tortured into confessing to trumped up drug and weapons charges. After intense international pressure, President Fox finally ordered their release – it came a month after their original defense lawyer was assassinated in Mexico City. Montiel has since won the Sierra Club's Chico Mendes award and other international prizes.

At the national level, President Salinas banned the hunting of sea turtles in 1990 and set up an important conservation and research agency, Conabio (National Commission for the Knowledge and Use of Biodiversity). President Zedillo in 1994 placed most government environmental agencies under one secretariat, currently called Semarnat (Secretaría de Medio Ambiente y Recursos Naturales, Department of Environment & Natural Resources).

FLORA & FAUNA
Flora
The Sierra Madre Occidental, the Cordillera Neovolcánica, and the Sierra Madre del Sur still have some big stretches of pine forest and, at lower elevations, oak forest.

Tropical forest covers much of the lowest western slopes of the Sierra Madre Occidental and the Cordillera Neovolcánica, and can also be found in the Oaxaca. These forests lose their leaves during the dry winter and are lush and verdant in the summer rainy season. Pink trumpet, cardinal sage, spider lily, *mala ratón* (literally 'rat killer') and *matapalo* (strangler fig) bloom in these forests during the rainy season. Much of this plant community, however, has been turned into ranches and cropland.

Along the dry Pacific coastal plain, from the southern end of the Desierto Sonorense to the state of Guerrero, the predominant vegetation is thorny bushes and small trees, including morning glory and acacias, and savanna. Some of this flora occurs naturally, some on overgrazed grassland or abandoned slash-and-burn farmland. Patches of semi-deciduous tropical forest reach almost to the sea near the Guerrero–Michoacan border.

The coastal lagoons that dot the Pacific coast are home to dense mangrove forests that have thick leathery leaves and small seasonal flowers.

Fauna
Land Life Raccoons, armadillos, skunks, rabbits and snakes are common. One critter you'll encounter is the gecko, a harmless, tiny green lizard that loves to crawl across walls and squawk at night. Michoacán and Guerrero are home to the most species of scorpions and spiders anywhere in Mexico.

Black iguanas and green iguanas are common along the entire coast. Both are prized for their meat and have been over-hunted, especially in Guerrero and Oaxaca. Boa constrictors are sometimes spotted in lagoons.

Rarer animals – that you'll be lucky to see – include spider monkeys and the beautiful, endangered jaguar that once inhabited much of the coast.

Marine Life The Pacific coast is among the world's chief sea turtle breeding grounds (see the boxed text 'Mexico's Turtles' in the Oaxaca chapter).

Dolphins can be seen off the coast, as can gray, humpback and blue whales, especially from November to March when a whale-watching trip is recommended. Early in the year, even while lying on the beach you'll probably spot whales. Sting rays and the larger Pacific manta rays can often be seen when they burst from the water with wild abandon. Tide pools harbor sea anemones, urchins, octopi, starfish, sea slugs and an array of crabs. Spend any time *under* water and you'll probably see such beauties as the Cortez angelfish, seahorses, moray eels, rays, puffers and even whale sharks. Jellyfish are abundant at the beginning of the rainy season. See under Fishing in the Activities chapter for information on the larger Pacific fish.

Coastal lagoons, especially in the south, once harbored thousands of crocodiles – they've been hunted almost to extinction.

Birdlife The lagoons and wetlands of Pacific Mexico host hundreds of species of native and migratory bird, and any break-of-dawn boat trip will send bird lovers squawking. Birds from as far north as Alaska migrate here each winter – the best season for racking up your species-spotted list. You may see parrots and parakeets, loons, grebes, frigatebirds, herons, hawks, falcons, sandpipers, plovers, ibises, swifts and boobies (to name only a handful).

In Oaxaca, it's not uncommon to spot ospreys soaring above the ocean cliffs. Of course, the bird you'll see most, wherever you are, is the *zopilote* (vulture). For the best birding locations, see Wildlife & Bird-Watching in the Activities chapter.

Parks & Reserves With all the spectacular beaches and accessible lagoons, you don't have to search for a park to experience the natural elements. Fortunately, federal, state and local governments have created a handful of protected areas to preserve some of the coast's fragile ecosystems. Some are easily accessible with private transport while others require the use of local guides (who also greatly increase your chances of spotting any wildlife).

The largest national park in this book is Parque Nacional Volcán Nevado de Colima (21,930 hectares), where you'll find two volcanoes: the extinct Volcán Nevado de Colima and the active Volcán de Fuego. The smallest national park is the 192-hectare Isla Isabel, a volcanically formed island just off Mazatlán. Parque Nacional Lagunas de Chacahua, in Oaxaca, protects 14,000 hectares comprised of two mammoth lagoons, mangroves, fishing communities and more than 13km of coastline. Mexico's newest national park, created in 1998, is the 12,000-hectare Parque Nacional de Huatulco. The park encompasses nine pristine bays, tropical deciduous forest, sea and shoreline.

The ancient Zapotec city of Monte Albán in Oaxaca is a protected archaeological zone of 2078 hectares.

The website for **Eco Travels in Latin America** (w *www.planeta.com)* brims with information and links about Mexican flora and fauna. For readers of Spanish, the site of **Conabio** (w *www.conabio.gob.mx)*, Mexico's national biodiversity commission, is another excellent resource.

GOVERNMENT & POLITICS

Mexico's Pacific coast, for this book, consists of seven of the 31 states that comprise the Federal Republic of Mexico. The states are divided into *municipios* (municipalities). A two-chambered federal congress makes the laws. A directly elected president carries out the laws, and an independent judiciary resolves disputes according to Napoleonic law. Women gained the vote in 1954 and an Equal Rights Amendment was added to the constitution in 1974. The legislatures and governors of Mexico's states are elected, as are the *ayuntamientos* (town councils) and their presidents.

That's the theory anyway. In practice, Mexican political life was dominated for most of the 20th century by one party, the Partido Revolucionario Institucional (PRI, Institutional Revolutionary Party), and its predecessors. Accusations of fraud, corruption, bribery, intimidation and violence long accompanied the PRI's election tactics and style of governing at every level.

In 2000 the country's three main parties – the PRI, the PAN (National Action Party) and the PRD (Party of the Democratic Revolution) – broke new ground by implementing a primary-election system to choose presidential candidates. This was particularly significant in the case of the PRI, whose candidates had previously been picked by the *'dedazo'* (fingering) method, by which the outgoing president, who is forbidden by law from serving more than one *sexenio* (six-year term), chose a candidate, who invariably won, to succeed him from within PRI ranks.

That year, Mexican politics celebrated its equivalent of the dismantling of the Berlin wall, when Vicente Fox Quesada of the PAN was elected president with 43% of the vote. Fox took office in December 2000 and was the first non-PRI president since the PRI was invented in 1929 – the biggest event in Mexican politics since the forming of the PRI in the chaotic aftermath of the Revolution.

Defeat did not cause the PRI to split between 'modern' free-marketeers and 'old-guard' statists, as some had predicted, but did leave it with a serious identity crisis. Without power, its *raison-d'être* for 70 years, it also lacked a niche from which to operate as opposition, now that the PRD represented the left of the political spectrum, the PAN the right, and President Fox the social democratic center.

Democratization, meanwhile, continued at other levels of Mexican politics too; by 2002 there were 15 state governorships in non-PRI hands (eight PAN, five PRD and two PAN–PRD alliance).

ECONOMY

Tourism is the second-largest employer in Mexico and one of the economic mainstays of the Pacific coast. This is especially true for Sinaloa, Jalisco and Guerrero, which are home to the coast's three biggest resort towns: Mazatlán, Puerto Vallarta and Acapulco.

Most of the Pacific coast, however, relies heavily on livestock and agriculture, especially the states of Jalisco, Nayarit and Colima. Jalisco is Mexico's primary grain producer and Nayarit accounts for most of the country's tobacco production. Vegetable and tropical fruit crops are grown throughout Jalisco and Colima as well as in Michoacán, Guerrero and Oaxaca. Sinaloa's main export is shrimp.

Timber products have been a rapidly growing sector of the Pacific economy since the passage of Nafta in 1994, which opened *ejidos* (peasant landholding cooperatives) to multinational corporations. The country's best coffee is produced in Colima and especially Oaxaca; in both states it forms a significant sector of the economy.

POPULATION & PEOPLE

In 1997 Mexico's population was estimated at 93.7 million – nearly 4½ times what is was in 1940. About 20% of the population lives in the seven Pacific states from Sinaloa to Oaxaca, most of them in cities. Guadalajara is Mexico's second-biggest city (after Mexico City) with a total urban population estimated at five million. The biggest city on the coast is Acapulco with some 800,000 people in its total urban area, followed by Mazatlán with 550,000 and Puerto Vallarta with 161,000.

By official figures, the nation's population is growing by about 1.4% a year, which is down from rates of more than 3% between 1950 and 1980. Of serious concern is the growth of the cities, which attract thousands of newcomers from the poorer countryside every day.

Ethnic Groups

The major ethnic division is between mestizos and *indígenas* or *indios* (indigenous people). Mestizos are of mixed ancestry – usually Spanish and indigenous. The Costa Chica of Guerrero and Oaxaca has a large population of Afro-mestizos (or *morenos,* as they refer to themselves), people of mixed African, European and indigenous descent. Mestizos are the overwhelming majority and, together with the few people of supposed pure Spanish descent, they hold most positions of power in Mexico. Indigenous people in general remain second-class citizens, often restricted to the worst land or forced to migrate to city slums or the USA in search of work. Their main wealth is traditional and spiritual.

Mexico's biggest indigenous group is the Nahua, descendants of the Aztecs. At least 1.7 million Náhuatl speakers are spread around central Mexico, many in Guerrero. There are approximately 500,000 Zapotecs, mainly in Oaxaca; 500,000 Mixtecs, mainly in Oaxaca, Guerrero and Puebla; and 130,000 Purépecha (Tarascos) in Michoacán. All these groups are descended from a well-known pre-Hispanic people.

The descendants of lesser-known pre-Hispanic peoples living near the coast include the approximately 29,000 Amuzgos of Oaxaca and Guerrero; 29,000 Chatinos, who live in Oaxaca, mostly around Puerto Escondido; and 19,000 Huichol of Jalisco and Nayarit.

EDUCATION

The Mexican government boasts 91% of the population can read and write. Throughout Mexico, school attendance is compulsory for children aged six to 14; attendance is lowest among indigenous people and rural communities.

ARTS
Dance

Colorful traditional indigenous dances are part of many Mexican fiestas, and many bear traces of pre-Hispanic ritual. There are hundreds, some popular in many parts of the country, others danced only in a single town. Nearly all require special costumes, among them the superb Zapotec Danza de las Plumas (Feather Dance), from Oaxaca state.

Some dances have evolved from fertility rites. Others tell stories of Spanish or colonial origin. The comical Danza de Los Viejitos (Dance of the Old Men) originated in Michoacán in mockery of the Spanish, whom the local Tarasco people thought aged very fast.

Some dances are now performed outside their religious context as simple spectacles.

The country's most famous dance festival is the Guelaguetza in Oaxaca, occurring on the last two Mondays of July.

Caribbean and South American dance and dance music – broadly described as *música afroantillana* or *música tropical* – have become highly popular in Mexico. This is tropical-style ballroom dancing, to percussion-heavy music that often includes electric guitars or brass. *Cumbia, danzón, salsa* and *merengue* are the most prominent styles.

Music

In Mexico live music may start up at any time on streets, plazas or even buses. The musicians play for a living and range from marimba (wooden xylophone) teams and *mariachi* (ensemble of street musicians) bands (trumpeters, violinists, guitarists and a singer, all dressed in smart cowboy costumes) to ragged buskers with out-of-tune guitars and sandpaper voices. Mariachi music (perhaps the most 'typical' Mexican music of all) originated in the Guadalajara area but is played nationwide (see the boxed text 'Mariachis' in the Nayarit & Guadalajara chapter).

Rock & Pop Mexican rock was pretty raw until the late 1980s, when more sophisticated music began to emerge. El Tri headed the earlier generation and the changes of the 1980s were spearheaded by the mystical Def Leppard-type rockers Caifanes. Foreign rock acts were not allowed to play in Mexico until the late 1980s. Their arrival broadened rock's appeal, and today Mexico is arguably the world's most important hub of *rock en español* (Spanish-language rock).

Talented, versatile Mexico City bands such as Café Tacuba and Maldita Vecindad took *rock en español* to new heights and new audiences (well beyond Mexico) in the 1990s, mixing a huge range of influences – from rock and roll, ska and punk to traditional Mexican *son*, bolero or mariachi. Tacuba's *Re* (1994), *Avalancha de Éxitos* (1996) and *Tiempo Transcurrido* (2001) all offer great songs. The 1999 double album *Revés/YoSoy* is a more instrumental piece of work. Significant late-1990s arrivals were mostly from Monterrey, notably the politically minded hip-hop trio Control Machete; crude, rude rappers Molotov; and the twosome Plastilina Mosh, a kind of Mexican Beastie Boys whose 1998 debut album *Aquamosh* was huge. El Gran Silencio, also from Monterrey, blend similar musical styles for some addictive sounds; their *Libres y Locos* (1999) and *Chuntarnos Radio Poder* (2001) are excellent pieces of work. Tijuana-born singer/songwriter Julieta Venegas got her start in Mexico City in the 1990s and won an MTV award for her acoustic guitar-based debut album *Aqui* (1998).

Mexican Regional Music The deepest-rooted Mexican folk music is *son* ('sound'), a term covering a range of country styles that grew out of indigenous, Spanish and African musical cultures. Son is essentially guitars plus harp or violin, often played for a foot-stamping dance audience, with witty, often improvised lyrics. The independent label Discos Corasón is doing much to promote these most traditional of Mexican musical forms.

The most celebrated brand of son, *son jaliscense,* comes from Jalisco. Son in the Costa Chica is called *chilena,* referring to the musical influences brought to the coast by Chileans stopping in Acapulco on their way to the California gold rush in the mid-19th century.

Ranchera is Mexico's urban 'country music.' Developed in the expanding cities of the 20th century, it's mostly vocalist-and-combo music with a nostalgia for rural roots. The music spawned an energetic new dance, *la quebradita.*

Norteño, now the highest selling music in the Spanish-speaking world, is country ballad and dance music with accordion backbone. Though originally from northern Mexico it now blares from stereos from Los Angeles to San Salvador. Its roots lie in *corridos,* traditional ballads about Latino/Anglo strife in the 19th century borderlands and about the Mexican Revolution. Until the 1980s, Latino youth considered corridos outdated throwbacks best left for the turntables of old-timers. That changed in the 1980s with the birth of *narcocorridos,* music about crooks, drug-runners, drug lords, dope deals and corrupt politicians that draws comparisons to US gangsta rap. Their popularity is attributed to Chalino Sanchez, a Sinaloan country kid with a raspy voice and a penchant for posing on his album covers with his pearl-handle pistol. He was shot and dumped on a Sinaloa roadside and soon became a legend. The first *narcocorridos* were recorded in the late 1970s by superstars Los Tigres del Norte, who later turned to *cumbia* and mainstream styles. The biggest current names are Los Tucanes de Tijuana, Grupo Exterminador, El As de la Sierra and Los Originales de San Juan.

Banda is a 1990s development of norteño, substituting large brass sections for guitars and accordion, playing Latin and more traditional Mexican rhythms. Banda del Recodo, who hails from Mazatlán, is the biggest name in banda.

Grupera, a feebler blend of ranchera, norteño and cumbia, is popular, especially at rural Mexican fiestas. Límite and Banda Machos are star exponents.

Música Tropical Cumbia and other forms of *música tropical* are blasted everywhere on the coast. Though originating elsewhere, they have become integral parts of the Mexican musical scene.

Literature

Mexico's best-known novelist internationally is probably Carlos Fuentes (1928–), and his most highly regarded novel is *Where the Air is Clear,* written in the 1950s. Like his *Death of Artemio Cruz,* it's an attack on the failure of the Mexican Revolution. Fuentes' *Aura* and *The Old Gringo* are both highly regarded.

In Mexico, Juan Rulfo (born in Sayula, Jalisco) is generally regarded as the country's supreme novelist. His *Pedro Páramo* (1955), in revolution times, has been called '*Wuthering Heights* set in Mexico and written by Kafka.' Among younger writers, Laura Esquivel (from Mexico City) achieved success with *Like Water for Chocolate*

(1989), a love story interwoven with both fantasy and recipes set in rural revolutionary Mexico.

Also from Mexico City, Octavio Paz (1914–98), poet, essayist and winner of the 1990 Nobel Prize for Literature, wrote a probing examination of Mexico's myths and Mexican character in *The Labyrinth of Solitude* (1950).

For information on fiction and books about Mexico by non-Mexican authors, see Books in the Facts for the Visitor chapter.

Visual Arts

Between about 200 BC and AD 800, the shaft-tomb cultures of Nayarit, Jalisco and Colima (known as West Mexico by archaeologists and art historians) produced some of the most complex ceramic sculpture in Mexico. Rarely taller than 50cm, the sculptures were usually painted red and black. In beautiful, often bizarre distortion, they depict dogs, musicians, houses, 'thinkers,' warriors, lovers and kings. Entire village scenes have been found. Though most of these West Mexican funerary sculptures were looted and sold internationally before their importance was realized, there are still some great exhibits. Excellent collections are housed at Guadalajara's Museo de Arqueología del Occidente de México, Oaxaca's Museo Rufino Tamayo and the Museo Universitario de Arqueología in Colima.

Mexicans have also had a talent for painting – and an excitement about bright colors – since pre-Hispanic times. Early Mexican murals are found at Monte Albán, in Oaxaca – themselves inherited from the styles developed earlier in Teotihuacán. The modern mural tradition blossomed in the 1920s with the work of Diego Rivera (1885–1957), José Clemente Orozco (1883–1949) and David Alfaro Siqueiros (1896–1974). Orozco was from Guadalajara and many of his murals are there. Other prominent 20th century artists include Frida Kahlo (1907–54) and Oaxacans Francisco Toledo (1940–) and Rodolfo Morales (1925–2001).

Oaxaca city is a hotbed of contemporary painting and sculpture, its vibrant scene driven by the region's thriving indigenous arts.

Oaxaca galleries and museums house some of the country's best contemporary art.

Indigenous Arts

Mexican art would be nothing without its rich heritage of indigenous art and craftsmanship. The work of indigenous artisans graces elaborate altarpieces, and sculpted walls and ceilings of churches and monasteries throughout the country. The pervasive use of brilliant, bold colors in contemporary art owes itself to indigenous Mexico. For more information on Mexican crafts see the Shopping section in the Facts for the Visitor chapter.

Cinema

Mexican cinema has a rich history, from its 'golden age' in the 1920s to the Aztec mummies, death-robots and masked wrestlers of the B-run horror flicks of the 1950s and 1960s. Of special interest to anyone reading *this* book is Alfonso Cuarón's *Y tu mamá, también* (*And Your Mother, Too*; 2001), a hilarious, erotic and often troubling roadtrip-flick to the coast of Oaxaca. It was released internationally in 2002 and is a great way to get inspired to take a trip to the coast. Other Mexican films enjoying recent international success include Alejandro González Iñárritu's award-winning *Amores Perros* (*Love is a Bitch*, 2000); *Sexo, pudor y lágrimas* (Sex, Shame and Tears, 1999) by Antonio Serrano; and Alfonso Arau's *Como agua para chocolate* (*Like Water for Chocolate*, 1993), based on Laura Esquivel's novel.

SOCIETY & CONDUCT

Mexicans in general are friendly, humorous and helpful to visitors, especially if you address them in Spanish, however rudimentary.

Traditional Culture

Roman Catholicism is one deep fount of traditional culture. Its calendar is filled with saints' days and festivals including Semana Santa (Holy Week), Día de los Muertos (Day of the Dead, November 2), Día de la Virgen de Guadalupe (December 12) and Christmas, creating processions and rituals, dances, costumes and special handicrafts year after year in traditions that evolve slowly and go back hundreds of years.

Another deep well of tradition is Mexico's indigenous heritage. The cultures of many surviving indigenous peoples are still governed by pre-Hispanic traditions, from colorful costumes and traditional crafts to the agricultural calendar and communalist society.

Many Mexican traditions interweave indigenous and Hispanic influences. El Día de los Muertos is in Catholic terms All Souls' Day, yet the Mexican celebration has strong overtones of ancestor-worship. The faith of so many Mexicans in their traditional medicine – a mixture of charms, chants, herbs, candles, incense – is evidence of the strength of pre-Hispanic tradition.

For more information on Mexican traditional culture, see the Music and Dance sections under Arts and the Religion section later in this chapter; Public Holidays & Special Events in the Facts for the Visitor chapter; and details on local traditions in each regional chapter.

The Family & Machismo Family ties remain very strong in Mexico. An invitation to a Mexican home is an honor for an outsider; as a guest you will be treated royally and will enter a part of Mexico to which few outsiders are admitted.

Connected to Mexican family dynamics is the phenomenon of machismo, an exaggerated masculinity aimed at impressing other males as well as women. Its manifestations range from driving aggressively and carrying weapons to drinking heavily. The macho image has roots in Mexico's often-violent past and seems to hinge on a network of family relationships. Since it's not uncommon for Mexican husbands to have mistresses, wives in response lavish affection on their sons, who end up idolizing their mothers and, unable to find similar perfection in a wife, take a mistress. The strong mother-son bond also means that it's crucial for a Mexican wife to get along with her mother-in-law. And while the virtue of daughters and sisters has to be protected at all costs, other women – including foreign tourists without male companions – may be seen as fair game by Mexican men. The other side of the machismo coin is women who emphasize their femininity.

Such stereotyping, however, is not universally borne out, and is under pressure from more modern influences. Machismo is much less overt among many younger Mexicans today.

Social Graces

Most tourists and travelers in Mexico are assumed to be citizens of the USA. Away from tourist destinations, your presence may evoke curiosity, wonder, fear or, occasionally, brusqueness. But negative responses will usually evaporate as soon as you act friendly.

Language may be the biggest barrier to friendly contact: some people will ignore you because they don't imagine a conversation is possible; a few words of Spanish can bring smiles and warmth, probably followed by questions.

Some indigenous peoples adopt a cool attitude: they have learned to mistrust outsiders after five centuries of exploitation. They don't like being gawked at by tourists; if in doubt about whether it's OK to take a photo, always ask first.

Dress is more casual on the coast – shorts, sleeveless tops and sandals are common – than inland (where it also happens to be a little cooler). Lean toward the more respectful end of the dress spectrum when visiting churches.

Nationalism

Most Mexicans are fiercely proud of their country, although at the same time they despair of its ever being governed well. Their independent-mindedness has roots in Mexico's 11-year war for independence from Spain in the early 19th century and subsequent struggles against US and French invasions. Any threat of foreign economic domination – as some fear will result from Nafta – is deeply resented. The classic attitude toward the USA is a combination of the envy and resentment that a poor neighbor feels for a rich one. The word *gringo*

isn't exactly a compliment, but it's not an insult either: the term can simply be – and often is – a simple synonym for 'American' or 'citizen of the USA.'

Time

'Mañana, mañana...' the Mexican attitude toward time, has probably become legendary simply from comparison with the USA. But it's true, especially outside the cities, that the urgency Europeans and North Americans are used to is often lacking. Most Mexicans value *simpatía* (congeniality) over promptness. If something is worth doing, it gets done. If not, it can wait. Life shouldn't be a succession of pressures and deadlines. Many Mexicans feel life in the 'businesslike' cultures has been de-sympathized. You may come away from Mexico convinced that they're right!

RELIGION
Roman Catholicism

About 90% of Mexicans profess Catholicism. Though its grip over emerging generations today is less strong than over their predecessors, Catholicism's dominance is remarkable considering the rocky history that the Catholic Church has had in Mexico, particularly in the last two centuries.

The church was in Mexico from the first days of the Spanish conquest. Until independence it remained the second most important institution (after the crown) and was the only unifying force in Mexican society. Everyone belonged to the church because it was the principal provider of social services and education.

The Jesuits' expulsion from the Spanish empire in the 18th century brought stormy church-state relations in Mexico. In the 19th and 20th centuries (up to 1940), Mexico passed numerous measures restricting the church's power. The bottom line was money and property, both of which the church was amassing faster than the generals and political bosses. The 1917 Mexican constitution prevented the church from owning property or running schools or newspapers, and banned clergy from voting, from wearing clerical garb and from speaking out on government policies. These provisions ceased to be enforced after 1950; in the early 1990s President Salinas had them removed from the constitution. In 1992 Mexico established diplomatic relations with the Vatican.

The Mexican church's unifying symbol is *Nuestra Señora de Guadalupe,* the dark-skinned Virgin of Guadalupe, who appeared to an indigenous Mexican in 1531 on a hill near Mexico City. The Virgin became a crucial link between Catholic and indigenous spirituality, and as Mexico grew into a mestizo society, she became the most potent symbol of Mexican Catholicism. Today she is the country's patron, her blue-cloaked image is ubiquitous, and her name is invoked in religious ceremonies, political speeches and literature.

Protestantism

Around 6% of Mexicans profess various forms of Protestantism. Many Protestant religions started in Mexico with American missionaries in the 19th century. Another wave of North American missionaries – these of evangelical leanings – gained converts in the 20th century. Evangelical churches continue to gain ground throughout Mexico today.

Indigenous Religion

The missionaries of the 16th and 17th centuries won the indigenous people over to Catholicism as much by grafting it on to pre-Hispanic religions as by deeper conversion.

Often old gods were identified with Christian saints, and the old festivals continued to be celebrated on the nearest saint's day.

Today, despite modern inroads into indigenous life, indigenous Christianity is still fused with more ancient beliefs. In some remote regions Christianity is only a veneer. The Huichol people of Jalisco have two Christs, neither a major deity. Much more important is Nakawé, the fertility goddess. The hallucinogenic drug peyote is a crucial source of wisdom in the Huichol world. Elsewhere, drunkenness is an almost sacred element at festival times.

Even among the more orthodox Christian indigenous peoples it is not uncommon for spring saints' festivals, or the pre-Lent carnival, to be accompanied by remnants of fertility rites. The carnival celebrations of Pinotepa Don Luis and San Juan Colorado in Oaxaca are as much indigenous in content as Catholic. The huge Oaxaca Guelaguetza dance festival has roots in pre-Hispanic maize-god rituals.

In the traditional indigenous world almost everything has a spiritual dimension – trees, rivers, plants, wind, rain, sun, animals and hills have their own gods.

Witchcraft, magic and traditional medicine survive today. Illness is sometimes seen as a 'loss of soul' resulting from the sufferer's wrongdoing or from the malign influence of someone with magical powers. A soul can be 'regained' if the appropriate ritual is performed by a *brujo* (witch doctor) or *curandero* (curer).

Facts for the Visitor

HIGHLIGHTS

Reducing the marvels of Mexico's Pacific coast to a finite 'best of' list is a tough task and any result is bound to be subjective. Travel highlights are personal and much depends on the company you're in, the food you just ate and so on.

Villages

Laid-back, dusty and friendly, they're the essence of the coast. They're the places you'll encounter beachside *palapa* (thatched-roof shelter) restaurants, stray chickens, thatch-roofed bars, beached fishing skiffs and friendly folks. Chacala, Mexcaltitán, Boca de Apiza, Tenacatita, Yelapa, La Ticla, Majahua and Pie de la Cuesta are all fishing villages where you can spend a day or longer doing absolutely nothing. Cruz de Huanacaxtle and El Tuito, both near Puerto Vallarta, lack the fishing skiffs and palapas, but are well worth visiting.

Then there are the villages that have turned into small hamlets for North American expats and offer a completely different feel. They're still just as dusty, but often have hip little eateries, bars or cafés. San Blas, Bucerías, Sayulita, Troncones, Puerto Ángel, Zipolite, and Mazunte, to name a few, are groovy little towns that can be really difficult to leave.

Near the Guerrero–Oaxaca border, the mostly Mixtec villages of Huazolotitlán, Jamiltepec and, up in the hills, Pinotepa Don Luis and San Juan Colorado, give a different flavor of small town life on the Pacific coast. If you're down that way, don't miss them.

Cities

Days spent on the beach can get you itching for city life, and the three coastal heavyweights – Acapulco, Puerto Vallarta and Mazatlán – are big, busy and a lot of fun. Acapulco's glitzy Zona Dorada has multilevel discos with sweeping bay views, outrageous outdoor bars and live music venues.

Hitting the Beach

With all the fabulous *playas* (beaches) along this coast – desolate beaches, party beaches, busy beaches, nude beaches, endless beaches, empty beaches and itty bitty sheltered beaches – it's almost silly to attempt to name the best. But here are some of our favorites:

- Chacahua, Oaxaca
- Playa Maruata, Michoacán
- Zipolite, Oaxaca
- Boca de Iguanas, Jalisco
- Barra de Potosí, Guerrero
- Tenacatita, Jalisco
- Playa Ventura, Guerrero
- Barra de Navidad, Jalisco
- Playa Manzanilla (Troncones), Guerrero

Puerto Vallarta rivals Acapulco for nightlife, yet its cobblestoned streets and old-fashioned buildings keep it relaxed and manageable. The streets, plazas and 19th-century buildings of old Mazatlán offer wonderful strolls before a night on the town.

Don't miss Guadalajara if you have the time for a jaunt inland: Mexico's second-biggest city and birthplace of *mariachi* (ensemble of street musicians) music, it has excellent museums and art galleries, historic architecture, and exciting nightlife. It prides itself on being the most Mexican of all Mexican cities. And Oaxaca city, with its colonial architecture, impressive churches and imaginative foods and crafts, should top the list of any trip south.

Coastal Wildlife

Teeming with birdlife, lined with mangroves and sometimes even crawling with crocodiles, the coastal lagoons of Pacific Mexico are wonderful spots to see wildlife. Many of them are flanked by a small village or two and have docks where you can hire a local fisher to buzz you around in the cool of the morning. They'll point out birds and iguanas, crocs and turtles, maybe even a boa or two, and they'll let you fish, or stop at an island beach for a swim and a snack. Mexcaltitán, Tenacatita, Cuyutlán, La Manzanilla, Playa Azul, the San Cristóbal and El Pozo estuaries near San Blas, Laguna de Potosí (at Barra de Potosí), the giant Laguna de Coyuca, Laguna Manialtepec and Lagunas de Chacahua – these are some of the lagoons you can visit.

Seven of the world's eight sea turtle species are found in Mexican waters, and four of those make it to the Pacific shores of mainland Mexico (the others are found around Baja California and the Gulf of Mexico). Getting a glimpse of these majestic creatures is truly a highlight. For more information, refer to the Wildlife & Bird-Watching section in the Activities chapter. For sea turtle species, see the boxed text 'Mexico's Turtles' in the Oaxaca chapter.

Hammocks

No trip to Mexico's Pacific coast is complete without time spent in a hammock – the more the better. Mexicans love their hammocks and nearly every beach-front palapa restaurant in every fishing village or beachside getaway has them strung for you to use (provided you patronize their place). They're easy to come by if you want your own, and easy to string up between a couple of trees for a cheap night's sleep on an isolated beach. Some of our favorite hammock hangouts are Playa Maruata in Michoacán, Barra de Potosí in Guerrero, and Mazunte and Zipolite in Oaxaca.

PLANNING
When to Go

A bad day at the beach is hard to imagine – any time of the year. Picking the *best* time to visit Mexico's Pacific coast, however, depends on your interests.

The peak holiday periods are July and August, mid-December to early January, and a week either side of Easter. Then, resorts attract big tourist crowds, room prices go up, and rooms and public transport are heavily booked, making reservations recommended.

Grab Bag

We couldn't help but mention a handful of highlights that make traveling Mexico's Pacific coast unforgettable:

- **Sunsets** Mazatlán and Pie de la Cuesta were our favorites.
- **Margaritas** The best way kick off the night (or day) anywhere on the coast.
- **Seafood** It's everywhere and it's excellent.
- **Hwy 200** Through tropical forest and thorn forest, palm plantations and fishing villages, it's a nonstop adventure to drive.
- **Taco Stands** We couldn't have survived without them.
- **Pozole** Guerrero's famous soup is our favorite too.
- **Music** In bars and restaurants, on buses and plazas, Mexico's music is as infectious as it is diverse.
- **Handicrafts** No trip to Mexico is complete without shopping for these.
- **Fiestas** Oaxaca's Guelaguetza, Guadalajara's Fiestas de Octubre, Carnaval in Mazatlán and Day of the Dead just about anywhere are all magnificent.

November to April, reliably dry, warm and blissful, are popular months for travel among North Americans and Europeans. The hottest, rainiest months are May to October. February, March and November, when weather and crowds are both moderate, can be excellent times to travel along the coast.

The water is perfect for swimming all year long. Diving and snorkeling can be good year round, but visibility is usually highest (except during plankton blooms) in the dry winter months. Fun surf can be reasonably expected year round, but waves are biggest from May to November. Deep-sea fishing, also practiced all year, has its own species-specific seasons (see Fishing in the Activities chapter). Bird-watchers often prefer winter visits when birds migrate down to the coastal lagoons from North America. Whale-watching is best from January to March.

Maps

Nelles Verlag, Hallwag, Rand McNally and AAA (American Automobile Association) all produce decent country maps of Mexico at scales of around 1:2,500,000 (1cm:25km) or 1:3,675,000 (1cm:36.75km). **ITMB** *(International Travel Maps and Books;* Ⓦ *www.itmb.com)* publishes a good map of the Mexican Pacific coast at a 1:100,000 (1cm: 10km) scale; you can order it on the website. For information on road atlases, see the Car & Motorcycle section in the Getting Around chapter.

City, town and regional maps of varying quality are often available free from local tourist offices in Mexico, or for about US$3 at bookstores, newsstands and department stores like Sanborn's.

Inegi (Instituto Nacional de Estadística, Geografía e Informática) publishes a large-scale series of topographical maps covering all of Mexico. Inegi has an office in every Mexican state capital.

US-based **Maplink** *(*Ⓦ *www.maplink.com)* is an excellent source for mail-order maps; it stocks nearly all the above maps, including Inegi topo maps. Also check out **Maps of Mexico** *(*Ⓦ *www.maps-of-mexico.com).*

What to Bring

The coast is casual. Shorts, sandals and T-shirts are appropriate just about everywhere. Thin, cotton, loose-fitting, button-front shirts are be the most comfortable in the heat. Many women swear by sarongs. A light rain jacket is indispensable from May to October. A light sweater or jacket is handy for evening boat rides and overnight buses, though you'll rarely need it in summer. Warmer clothing is

---

What? No Number?

Many small towns along Mexico's Pacific coast do not use address numbering systems, or do so only in certain parts of town. Establishments found on numberless (or partially numbered) streets are then identified by their street name followed by the abbreviation 's/n,' short for *sin numero* (without number). The abbreviation is used throughout this book. In larger towns and cities, knowing the cross-street (even when there *is* a building number) is often very helpful for locating the place you're heading to.

---

usually only necessary if you travel inland to places such as Oaxaca city or Guadalajara; night buses through the mountains can be brutally cold in winter. Bring smarter clothing if you plan to dine in fine restaurants or hit the discos at night – discos often enforce a dress code, and door policies can be based on how stylish you look. Mexicans dress more conservatively further inland, where long pants and skirts or dresses are usually the norm.

A hat, sunglasses and sunscreen are saviors from the harsh coastal sun. General toiletries are readily available, but outside the resort towns items like contact lens solution, tampons, contraceptives and insect repellent can be difficult to find.

Other useful items include a small flashlight (torch), a pocketknife, a traveler's alarm clock, some cord (especially handy for drying your clothes), a sewing kit, a money belt or pouch that you can wear underneath your clothes, a handkerchief, insect repellent (especially during the rainy season), a sink-plug for washing your dirty clothes, a small padlock and a pocket Spanish dictionary and/or phrasebook. See the Activities chapter for things to bring for specific pursuits.

For carrying it all, a backpack is most convenient if you'll be on the road much. You can make it reasonably theft-proof with small padlocks. A light daypack, too, is useful. And don't forget a swimsuit!

Tape It!

Duct tape is probably the best fix-all, patch-all, hang-all (tape-your-travel-mate's-mouth-shut-all) ever invented. Travel with it once and you'll never leave it home again. Make your own pocket-size roll by wrapping it around a pencil stub or a cigarette lighter, and you're good to go.

RESPONSIBLE TOURISM

A responsible tourist is one who treats the visited place as if it were home. Would you wander into your hometown church or temple during a service and start taking flash photos? If the drains at your home were blocked, would you put toilet paper down them to clog them further? Would you like your photo taken without being asked? Be conscious of Mexican traditions, particularly indigenous ones, which can seem foreign to outsiders.

As for Mexico's environment, everyone has an obligation to help stop it from deteriorating. Don't buy turtle, iguana or black coral products, all sold along the coast. Help prevent over-fishing by not exceeding daily catch quotas or by practicing catch-and-release. When hiking or camping on the beach take out everything you bring in and make an effort to carry out trash left by others. Before you rent a 4WD vehicle, seriously consider the damaging effects they have on riverbeds, trails and beaches. Don't dig up plants, destroy tide pool organisms or pick up artifacts. Patronize ecotourism projects that aim to preserve or restore the environments they visit. Many ecologically conscious tourism enterprises in Mexico are community-run, and community initiatives enable you also to ensure that any profit made from you goes to the people you have visited. Another way to do this is to buy crafts and commodities direct from producer cooperatives, producing villages or from artisans themselves.

As the saying goes, take only photos, leave only footprints – but don't leave footprints on the coral!

TOURIST OFFICES
Local Tourist Offices

All the major coastal resorts and larger inland cities have both state and municipal tourist offices. The better offices can be helpful, with maps, brochures and someone on hand who speaks English. Smaller towns often lack tourist offices altogether.

You can call the Mexico City office of the national tourism ministry **Sectur** (☎ 55-5250-0123, 800-903-92-00) at any time – 24 hours a day, seven days a week – for information or help in English or Spanish.

Tourist Offices Abroad

In the USA and Canada call **Mexico Tourism Board** (☎ 800-446-3942, 800-44-MEXICO) for Mexican tourist information. You can also contact a Mexico Tourism Board office at the following locations:

Chicago (☎ 312-606-9252) 300 North Michigan Ave, 4th floor, IL 60601
Houston (☎ 713-772-2581) 4507 San Jacinto, Suite 308, TX 77004
Los Angeles (☎ 213-351-2075) 2401 W 6th St, 5th floor, CA 90057
Miami (☎ 305-718-4095) 1200 NW 78th Ave, No 203, FL 33126
Montreal (☎ 514-871-1052) 1 Place Ville Marie, Suite 1931, H3B 2C3, Quebec
New York (☎ 212-821-0314) 21 East 63rd St, NY 10021
Toronto (☎ 416-925-0704 ext 22 or 23) 2 Bloor St West, Suite 1502, M4W 3E2, Ontario
Vancouver (☎ 604-669-2845) 999 West Hastings St, Suite 1110 V6C 2W2, BC

Look for the following Mexico Tourism Board offices in Europe:

France (☎ 01 42 86 96 12) 4 rue Notre Dame des Victoires, 75002 Paris
Germany (☎ 069-253 509) Taunusanlage 21, 60325 Frankfurt-am-Main
Spain (☎ 91-561 18 27) Calle Velázquez 126, Madrid 28006
UK (☎ 020-7488 9392) 41 Trinity Square, Wakefield House, London EC3N 4DJ

VISAS & DOCUMENTS

Visitors to Mexico should have a valid passport. Visitors of some nationalities have to obtain visas, but others (when visiting as tourists) need have only the easily obtained Mexican government tourist card. Because the regulations sometimes change, it's wise to confirm them at a Mexico Tourism Board office or Mexican embassy or consulate before you go. Several Mexican embassies and consulates, and foreign embassies in Mexico, have websites with useful information on tourist permits, visas and so on (see Embassies & Consulates, later), but they don't all agree with each other, so you should back up any Internet findings with some phone calls. The **Lonely Planet** website (ⓦ *www.lonelyplanet.com*) has links to updated visa information.

Travelers under 18 who are not accompanied by *both* parents need special documentation (see Under-18 Travelers later in this section).

Passports

Though it's not recommended, US tourists can enter Mexico without a passport if they have official photo identification plus some proof of their citizenship, such as a birth certificate certified by the issuing agency or their original certificate of naturalization (not a copy). Citizens of other countries who are permanent residents in the USA need a passport and Permanent Resident Alien Card.

Canadian tourists may enter Mexico with official photo identification plus proof of citizenship, such as a birth certificate. Naturalized Canadian citizens, however, require a valid passport.

It is better to have a passport anyway, because officials can immediately identify with them. Same goes for officials you'll meet on re-entry to the USA or Canada as well as to Mexican officials: the only proof of citizenship recognized by USA or Canadian immigration is a passport or (for non-naturalized citizens) a certified copy of your birth certificate. In Mexico you may need your passport when you change money.

Citizens of other countries need to show a passport valid for at least six months after they arrive in Mexico.

Mexicans with dual nationality must carry proof of both citizenships and must identify themselves as Mexican when entering or leaving Mexico.

Visas

Citizens of the USA, Canada, EU countries, Australia, New Zealand, Argentina, Brazil, Chile, the Czech Republic, Hungary, Iceland, Israel, Japan, Norway, Poland, Singapore, Slovenia, Switzerland and Uruguay are among those who do not require visas to enter Mexico as tourists. The list changes from time to time; check well ahead of travel with your local Mexican embassy or consulate. Visa procedures, for those who need them, can sometimes take several weeks.

All tourists must obtain a Mexican government tourist card (see Travel Permits).

Non-US citizens passing through the USA on the way to or from Mexico, or visiting Mexico from the USA, should check their USA visa requirements.

Travel Permits

The Mexican tourist card – the Forma Migratoria para Turista (FMT) – is a small paper that you must get stamped by Mexican immigration and keep until you leave. The card is available free at official border crossings, international airports and ports, and often from airlines, travel agencies, Mexican consulates and Mexico Tourism Board offices. At the USA–Mexico border you won't be given one automatically – you have to ask for it.

At many USA–Mexico border crossings you don't *have* to get the card stamped at the border itself, as the Instituto Nacional de Migración (INM, National Immigration Institute) has control points on the highways into the interior where it's also possible to do it – but it's advisable to do it at the border itself.

One section of the card – to be completed by the immigration officer – deals with the length of your stay. You may be asked about how long you want to stay and what you'll be doing, but normally you'll be given the maximum 180 days if you ask for it. It's always advisable to put down more days than you think you'll need, in case you are delayed or change your plans. If you arrive by air, the immigration officer will ask to see your plane ticket and stamp your card according to your return date. Look after your tourist card – it will probably be checked when you leave the country.

Since 1999, foreign tourists and business travelers visiting Mexico have been charged a fee of about US$20 called the Derecho para No Inmigrante (DNI, Nonimmigrant Fee). If you enter Mexico by air, the fee is included in the price of your plane ticket.

If you enter by land you must pay the fee at any of 27 Mexican banks listed on the back of your tourist card, at any time before you re-enter the frontier zone on your way out of Mexico (or before you check in at an airport to fly out of Mexico). Some Mexican border crossings have on-the-spot bank offices to do this. When paying at a bank, your tourist card or business visitor card will be stamped, showing you paid.

Tourists have to pay the fee once in any 180-day period. You are entitled to leave and re-enter Mexico as many times as you like within 180 days without paying again. A similar multi-entry rule applies to business travelers, but the limit is 30 days, after which they have to pay again. If you are going to return within the stipulated period, retain your stamped tourist/business visitor's card when you leave Mexico.

If the number of days given on your tourist card is less than the 180-day maximum, its validity may be extended free one or more times up to the maximum. To get a card extended you have to apply to the INM, which has offices in many towns and cities. The procedure is usually accomplished in a few minutes; you'll need your passport, tourist card, photocopies of the important pages of these documents, and – at some offices – evidence of 'sufficient funds.' A major credit card is usually OK for the latter, or an amount in traveler's checks, which could vary from US$100 to US$1000 depending on the office. Most INM offices will not extend a card until a few days before it is due to expire.

If you lose your card or need information, contact the **Sectur tourist office** in Mexico City (☎ 55-5250-01-23, 800-903-92-00) or your embassy or consulate. Your embassy or consulate may be able to give you a letter enabling you to leave Mexico without your card, or at least an official note to take to your local INM office, which will have to issue a duplicate.

Travel Insurance

Travel insurance to cover theft, loss and medical problems is a good idea. It's good to buy insurance as early as possible. If you buy it the week before you fly, you may find, for example, that you're not covered for delays to your flight caused by strikes.

Mexican medical treatment is inexpensive for common diseases and minor treatment, but if you suffer some serious medical problem, you may want to find a private hospital or fly out for treatment. Travel insurance can cover the costs of that. Some US health insurance policies stay in effect for a limited time if you travel abroad, but it's worth checking exactly what you'll be covered for in Mexico. For people whose medical insurance or national health systems don't extend to Mexico – which includes most non-Americans – a travel policy is a smart idea.

Some policies offer lower and higher medical-expense options; the higher ones are chiefly for countries, such as the USA, that have high medical costs. There are many policies available, so check the small print. Some specifically exclude 'dangerous activities' that can include scuba diving, motorcycling and even trekking. Check that the policy covers ambulances or an emergency flight home.

Driver's License & Permits

If you're thinking of renting a vehicle in Mexico, take your driver's license and a major credit card with you. For more information on rentals, see the Getting Around chapter. For the paperwork involved in taking your own vehicle into Mexico, see the Getting There & Away chapter.

Hostel, Student & Teacher Cards

The ISIC student card, the GO25 card for any traveler aged 12 to 25, and the ITIC card for teachers can help you buy reduced-price air tickets to or from Mexico at student- and youth-oriented travel agencies. In Mexico, the ISIC card will sometimes get you a discount at museums, archaeological sites and so on; the GO25 and ITIC are less recognized, but worth taking along if you have one. An HI (Hostelling International) card might save you US$1 or so in HI hostels, but don't rush out to get one specially for Mexico.

Under-18 Travelers

Every year numerous parents try to run away from the USA or Canada to Mexico with their children to escape the legal machinations of the children's other parent. To prevent this, minors (people under 18 years of age) entering Mexico without one or both of their parents may be – and often are – required to show a notarized consent form, signed by the absent parent or parents, giving permission for the young traveler to enter Mexico. A form available for this purpose can be obtained from Mexican consulates. In the case of divorced parents, a custody document may be acceptable instead. If one or both parents are deceased, or if the traveler has only one legal parent, a notarized statement stating this could be required.

These rules are aimed primarily at visitors from the USA and Canada but apparently apply to all nationalities. Procedures vary from country to country; contact a Mexican consulate to find out exactly what you need to do.

Copies

All important documents (passport data pages and visa pages, birth certificate, vehicle papers, credit or bank cards, insurance papers, air tickets, driver's license, traveler's check receipts or serial numbers etc) should be photocopied before you leave home. Leave one copy with someone at home and keep another with you, separate from the originals. When you get to Mexico, add a photocopy of your tourist permit and, if you're driving, vehicle import papers.

EMBASSIES & CONSULATES
Mexican Embassies & Consulates

Updated details can be found at **W** www .sre.gob.mx, which also has links to the embassies' and consulates' own websites. Some of these sites, such as the Mexican consulates in New York, San Diego and Los Angeles, and the Mexican embassy in London, are useful sources on visas and related matters.

Australia
Embassy: (☎ 02-6273 3963, **W** www .embassyofmexicoinaustralia.org) 14 Perth Ave, Yarralumla, Canberra, ACT 2600

Canada
Embassy: (☎ 613-233 9917/9272, **W** www .embamexcan.com) 45 O'Connor St, Suite 1500, Ottawa, ON K1P 1A4
Consulate: (☎ 514-288 2502) 2000 rue Mansfield, Suite 1015, Montreal, PQ H3A 2Z7
Consulate: (☎ 416-368 8490) Commerce Court West, 199 Bay St, Suite 4440, Toronto, ON M5L 1E9
Consulate: (☎ 604-684 3547) 710-1177 West Hastings St, Vancouver, BC V6E 2K3

France
Embassy: (☎ 01 53 70 27 70, **W** www.sre.gob .mx/francia) 9 rue de Longchamps, 75116 Paris
Consulate: (☎ 01 42 86 56 20) 4 rue Notre Dame des Victoires, 75002 Paris

Germany
Embassy: (☎ 030-269 3230, **W** www.embamex .de) Klingelhoferstrasse 3, 10785 Berlin
Consulate: (☎ 069-299 8750) Taunusanlage 21, 60325 Frankfurt-am-Main
Consulate: (☎ 040-450 1580) Hallerst 76, 20146 Hamburg

Ireland
Embassy: (☎ 01-260 0699) 43 Ailesbury Rd, Ballsbridge, Dublin 4

Italy
Embassy: (☎ 06-441151, **W** www.target .it/messico) Via Lazzaro Spallanzani 16, 00161 Rome
Consulate: (☎ 02-7602 0541) Via Cappuccini 4, 20122 Milan

New Zealand
Embassy: (☎ 04-472 0555, **W** www.mexico .org.nz) 111 Customhouse Quay, Wellington

Spain
Embassy: (☎ 91-369 2814, **W** www.embamex .es) Carrera de San Jerónimo 46, 28014 Madrid
Consulate: (☎ 93-201 1822) Avinguda Diagonal 626, 08021 Barcelona

UK
Embassy: (☎ 020-7235 6393, **W** www.embamex .co.uk) 8 Halkin St, London SW1X 7DW

USA
Embassy: (☎ 202-728 1600, **W** www.sre.gob .mx/eua) 1911 Pennsylvania Ave NW, Washington, DC 20006
Consulate: (☎ 202-736 1000) 2827 16th St NW, Washington, DC 20009

Other Mexican Consulates in the USA

There are consulates in many other US cities, especially those in the border states. For a complete listing, check online at W www .embassyofmexico.org.

Arizona
Phoenix: (☎ 602-242-7398)
Tucson: (☎ 520-882-5595)
California
Los Angeles: (☎ 213-351-6800,
W www.consulmex-la.com)
San Diego: (☎ 619-231-8414,
W www.sre.gob.mx/sandiego)
San Francisco: (☎ 415-392-5554)
Colorado
Denver: (☎ 303-331-1110)
Florida
Miami: (☎ 305-716-4977)
Orlando: (☎ 407-422-0514)
Georgia
Atlanta: (☎ 404-266-2233)
Illinois
Chicago: (☎ 312-855-1380)
Louisiana
New Orleans: (☎ 504-522-3596)
Massachusetts
Boston: (☎ 617-426-4181)
Michigan
Detroit: (☎ 313-964-4515)
Missouri
St Louis: (☎ 314-436-3233)
New Mexico
Albuquerque: (☎ 505-247-2139)
New York
New York: (☎ 212-217-6400,
W www.consulmexny.org)
Oregon
Portland: (☎ 503-274-1450)
Pennsylvania
Philadelphia: (☎ 215-922-3834)
Texas
Austin: (☎ 512-478-2866)
Dallas: (☎ 214-252-9250)
Utah
Salt Lake City: (☎ 801-521-8502)
Washington state
Seattle: (☎ 206-448-3526)

Embassies & Consulates in Mexico

All embassies are in Mexico City. Many countries also have consulates in other cities. Embassies and consulates often keep limited business hours (typically 9am or 10am to 1pm or 2pm Monday to Friday); they usually close on both Mexican and their own national holidays. Many embassies provide 24-hour emergency telephone contact. All telephone numbers given include area codes.

It's important to realize what your embassy can and can't do to help you if you get into trouble. Generally, it won't be much help in emergencies if the trouble you're in is remotely your own fault. You are bound by the laws of the country you are in. Your embassy will not be sympathetic if you end up in jail after committing a crime locally, even if such actions are legal in your own country. In genuine emergencies you might get some assistance, but only if other channels have been exhausted. For example, if you need to get home urgently, a free ticket home is very unlikely – the embassy would expect you to have insurance. If you have all your money and documents stolen, it might assist with getting a new passport, but a loan for onward travel is out of the question.

Australia
Mexico City: (☎ 55-5531-5225)
Guadalajara: (☎ 33-3615-7418) Privada Vista Alegre 945, Colonia Lomas Valle
W www.mexico.embassy.gov.au
Canada
Mexico City: (☎ 55-5724-7900, 800-706-29-00)
Acapulco: (☎ 744-484-13-05) Centro Comercial Marbella, Local 23
Guadalajara: (☎ 33-3616-5642) Hotel Fiesta Americana, Local 31, Aceves 225, Colonia Vallarta Poniente
Mazatlán: (☎ 669-913-73-20) Hotel Playa Mazatlán, Loaiza 202, Zona Dorada
Oaxaca: (☎ 951-513-37-77) Pino Suárez 700, Local 11B
Puerto Vallarta: (☎ 322-222-53-98) Zaragoza 160, Interior 10, Colonia Centro
W www.canada.org.mx
France
Mexico City: (☎ 55-5280-9700)
Acapulco: (☎ 744-469-12-08) Hyatt Regency Hotel, La Costera 1
Guadalajara: (☎ 33-3616-5516) López Mateos Nte 484
Mazatlán: (☎ 669-985-12-28) Belisario Domínguez 1008 Sur, Colonia Centro
W www.francia.org.mx

Germany
Mexico City: (☎ 55-5283-2200)
Acapulco: (☎ 744-484-18-60) Alaminos 26,
Casa Tres Fuentes, Colonia Costa Azul
Guadalajara: (☎ 33-3613-9623, 800-021-11-
70) Corona 202
Mazatlán: (☎ 669-982-28-09) Jacarandas 10,
Colonia Loma Linda
w www.embajada-alemana.org.mx

Italy
Mexico City: (☎ 55-5596-3655)
Guadalajara: (☎ 33-3616-1700) Av López
Mateos Nte 790, 1st floor, fracc.
Ladrón de Guevara
w www.embitalia.org.mx

Netherlands
Mexico City: (☎ 55-5258-9921)
Acapulco: (☎ 744-486-82-10) Hotel Costa
Club Acapulco, La Costera 159
Guadalajara: (☎ 33-3673-2211) Av Vallarta
5500, Lomas Universidad

New Zealand
Mexico City: (☎ 55-5283-9460)

Spain
Mexico City: (☎ 55-5282-2974)
Acapulco: (☎ 744-485-72-05) Llantera del
Pacífico, Av Universidad 2, fracc. Magallanes
Guadalajara: (☎ 33-3630-0450) Torre Sterling,
mezzanine izquierdo, Francisco de Quevedo
117, Sector Juárez
Oaxaca: (☎ 951-518-00-31) Calzada Porfirio
Díaz 340, Colonia Reforma

UK
Mexico City: (☎ 55-5207-85-00)
Acapulco: (☎ 744-481-17-70) Casa Consular,
Centro Internacional Acapulco, La Costera
4455
Guadalajara: (☎ 33-3343-2296) Paseo del
Eden 2449-4, Prolongación Colinas de San
Javier
w www.embajadabritanica.com.mx

USA
Mexico City: (☎ 55-5080-2000)
Acapulco: (☎ 744-469-05-56) Hotel Acapulco
Continental, La Costera 121, Local 14
Guadalajara: (☎ 33-3825-2700) Progreso 175
Ixtapa: (☎ 755-553-21-00) Plaza Ambiente,
Office 9
Mazatlán: (☎ 669-916-58-89) Hotel Playa
Mazatlán, Loaiza 202, Zona Dorada
Oaxaca: (☎ 951-514-30-54) Alcalá 407
(Plaza Santo Domingo) Interior 20
Puerto Vallarta: (☎ 322-223-00-69) Zaragoza
160, Colonia Centro
w www.usembassy-mexico.gov

CUSTOMS

Things that visitors are allowed to bring
into Mexico duty free include items for personal use, such as clothing; medicine (with
prescription in the case of psychotropic
drugs); a camera and video camera; up to 12
rolls/reels of film or video cassettes; a lap-
top computer; a cellular phone; 3L of wine,
beer or liquor; 400 cigarettes; and, if arriving by air, US$300 worth of other goods, or
US$50 worth if arriving by land. What cus-
toms officials are looking for in the case of
'other goods' are new items that are likely
to be resold, eg, 10 pairs of Levi's with the
tags still on them.

MONEY
Currency

Mexico's currency is the peso. The peso is
divided into 100 centavos. Coins come in
denominations of five, 10, 20 and 50 centavos and one, two, five, 10, 20 and 50
pesos. Bills come in denominations of 10,
20, 50, 100, 200 and 500 pesos.

The $ sign is used to refer to pesos in
Mexico. Prices quoted in US dollars will
normally be written 'US$5,' '$5 Dlls' or '5
USD' to avoid misunderstanding.

Since the peso's exchange value is un-
predictable, prices in this book are given in
US dollar equivalents.

Exchange Rates

Exchange rates as this book went to press
were:

country	unit		pesos
Australia	A$1	=	5.65
Belize	BZ$1	=	5.17
Canada	C$1	=	6.54
euro zone	€1	=	10.09
Guatemala	Q1	=	1.32
Japan	¥100	=	8.32
New Zealand	NZ$1	=	4.95
UK	UK£1	=	15.94
USA	US$1	=	10.19

Exchanging Money

The most convenient form of money in
Mexico is a major international credit card
or debit (ATM) card. Cards such as Visa,

American Express (AmEx) and MasterCard can be used to obtain cash from ATMs and are accepted for payment by most airlines, car rental companies and travel agents in Mexico, and by many hotels, restaurants and shops.

If you have a credit card or bank card, as a backup you should take some major-brand traveler's checks (denominated in US dollars) and a little US cash. If you don't have a credit or bank card, use US-dollar traveler's checks. AmEx, recognized everywhere, is a good brand. **AmEx** in Mexico City maintains a **24-hour hotline** (☎ 800-828-0366, 801-964-6665 collect to USA) for lost traveler's checks and cards.

You should be able to change Canadian dollars, British pounds and euros in cash and checks in main cities, but it can be time consuming.

You can exchange money in banks or at *casas de cambio* (exchange houses). Banks go through a more time-consuming procedure than *casas de cambio* and have shorter exchange hours (typically 9am to 3pm or 4pm Monday to Friday). *Casas de cambio* can be found in most large or medium-sized towns. They are very quick and often open evenings or weekends, but may not accept traveler's checks. If you cannot find a place to change money, particularly on a weekend, try a hotel – though the exchange rate won't be the best.

Exchange rates vary a little from one bank or *casa de cambio* to another. Different rates are also often posted for *efectivo* (cash) and *documento* (traveler's checks).

You can use major credit cards and bank cards to withdraw pesos from ATMs (common everywhere in Mexico) and over the counter at banks. ATMs are the easiest source of cash and the best value, despite the handling fee usually charged to your account. They offer the best exchange rates and no commission charges.

Mexican banks call their ATMs by a variety of names – usually something like *caja permanente* or *cajero automático*.

Should you need money wired to you, an easy method is the Western Union 'Dinero en Minutos' (Money in Minutes) service.

Western Union (☎ 800-12-13-13, 800-325-6000; ⓦ www.westernunion.com) has offices worldwide (all listed on the website) and offers this service at the numerous Elektra electronics stores around Mexico (most are open 9am to 9pm daily), at the *telégrafos* (telegraph) offices in many cities, and at some other shops – all are identified by black-and-yellow signs reading 'Western Union' and 'Dinero en Minutos'. Your sender pays money (along with a fee) at their Western Union branch, or online with a credit card, and lists who is to receive it and where. When you pick it up, take along photo identification.

Costs

On Mexico's Pacific coast, a frugal budget traveler can pay about US$15 to US$25 a day by camping or staying in budget accommodations and eating two to three meals a day in the cheapest restaurants. Add in other costs (snacks, purified water, entry to archaeological sites, long-distance buses etc), and you'll be up to US$20 to US$35 a day. If you share rooms, costs per person drop considerably.

In the mid-range you can live well for US$45 to US$60 per person per day. In most places two people can easily find a clean, modern room with private bathroom and TV for US$30 to US$50.

At the top of the scale are hotels and resorts charging anywhere from US$100 to US$300, and restaurants where you pay US$30 to US$50 per person. However, you can still get a plush room for US$50 to US$75 and eat well for US$20 to US$40 per person per day.

These figures do not take into account expenses like internal airfares or car rentals – not to mention heavy tequila consumption, disco admissions and shopping, which you should certainly budget for.

Tipping & Bargaining

Workers in cheap restaurants don't expect much in the way of tips, while those in expensive resort establishments expect you to be lavish in your largesse. Tipping in the resorts (Mazatlán, Puerto Vallarta, Acapulco) is up to US levels of 15%; elsewhere 10% is plenty. If you stay a few days in one place, leave up to 10% of your room costs for the housekeepers. A porter in a mid-range hotel would be happy with US$1 for carrying two bags. Taxi drivers don't expect tips unless they provide some special service, but gas station attendants do (US$0.25 to US$0.50).

Hotel rates are fairly firm along the coast, though you might bargain down the price in cheaper places, especially during the low season or if you stay more than a few days. In *mercados* (markets), bargaining is the rule, and you'll probably pay much more than the going rate if you accept the first price quoted. Also bargain with drivers of unmetered taxis (before you get in the cab).

Taxes

Mexico's *impuesto de valor agregado* (IVA, **ee**-bah, value-added tax), is levied at 15%. By law the tax must be included in any price quoted and should not be added afterward. Notices in shops and on menus often say *IVA incluido*. Occasionally they state instead that IVA must be added to quoted prices.

Impuesto sobre hospedaje (ISH, ee-**ess**-e-**ahch**-e, the lodging tax) is levied on the price of hotel rooms. Each Mexican state sets its own rate, but in most it's 2%, bringing the total room tax to 17%.

Most budget accommodations include both IVA and ISH in quoted prices. In top-end hotels a price may be given as, say, 'US$100 *más impuestos*' ('plus taxes'), in which case you must add about 17% to the figure. When in doubt, ask, *'án incluidos los impuestos?'* ('Are taxes included?').

Prices in this book include IVA and ISH. See the Getting There & Away and Getting Around chapters for details of departure taxes on air travel. For details of the tourist fee see Visas & Documents earlier in this chapter.

POST & COMMUNICATIONS
Post

An airmail letter or postcard weighing up to 20g costs US$0.55 to North America, US$0.65 to Europe and US$0.75 to Australa or New Zealand. Items weighing between 20g and 50g will set you back US$0.90, US$1.10 and US$1.35, respectively.

Almost every Mexican town has a *correos* (post office) where you can buy stamps and send or receive mail. They're usually open Saturday mornings as well as Monday to Friday.

Delivery times are elastic, and packages in particular sometimes go missing. If you're sending something by airmail, clearly mark it 'Vía Aérea.' Registered *(certificado* or *registrado)* service helps ensure delivery and costs just US$0.90 extra for international mail. An airmail letter from Mexico to the USA or Canada can take four to 14 days to arrive (sometimes longer). Mail to Europe may take between one and three weeks, to Australasia a month or more.

If you're sending a package internationally from Mexico, be prepared to open it for customs inspection at the post office – take packing materials with you, or don't seal it until you get there.

Mexpost express-mail service supposedly takes three working days to anywhere in the world; it costs US$12 to send up to 500g to the USA or Canada, or US$15.50 to Europe.

For assured and speedy delivery, you can use an expensive international courier service such as **UPS** (☎ 800-902-92-00; w *www.ups.com*), **FedEx** (☎ 800-900-11-00; w *www.fedex.com*) or **DHL** (☎ 5-345-70-00; w *www.dhl.com*). Packages weighing up to 500g cost about US$23 to the USA or Canada or US$25 to Europe.

You can receive letters and packages at a post office if they're addressed as follows (for example):

Jane SMITH (last name in capitals)
Lista de Correos
Acapulco
Guerrero 00000 (post code)
MEXICO

When the letter reaches the post office, the name of the addressee is placed on an alphabetical list, which is then updated daily. To claim your mail, present identification. There's no charge; the snag is that many post offices return 'Lista' mail to sender after 10 days. If you think it will be more than 10 days before you claim it, have it sent to (for example):

Jane SMITH
Poste Restante
Correo Central
Acapulco
Guerrero 00000 (post code)
MEXICO

Poste Restante may hold mail for up to one month, but there is no posted list. Again, there's no charge for collection.

Telephone

Local calls are cheap. International calls can be expensive, but not if you call from the right place at the right time.

Internet telephony (calls carried through an Internet server line instead of a phone line) has appeared at some Internet cafés along the coast. At around US$0.35 per minute to the USA or US$0.50 per minute to Canada or Europe, it's cheaper than a normal phone call.

Internet telephony aside, there are three main types of place you can call from. The cheapest are public pay phones and *casetas de teléfono* or *casetas telefónicas*. The latter are usually in a shop or restaurant, where an on-the-spot operator connects your call. The third option is calling from your hotel, but hotels can charge what they like for this service. It's nearly always cheaper to go elsewhere.

Pay Phones These are common and usually work fine. Pay phones are operated by a number of different companies: the most common, and most reliable on costs, are those marked Telmex, the name of the country's biggest phone company. Telmex pay phones work on *tarjetas telefónicas* or *tarjetas Ladatel* (phone cards), which come in denominations of 30, 50 or 100 pesos (about US$3.30, US$5.50 and US$11). These cards are sold at many kiosks and shops – look for the blue-and-yellow sign reading *'De Venta Aquí Ladatel.'* 'Ladatel'

means *teléfono de larga distancia* (long-distance telephone), but these phones work for both local and long-distance calls.

You may notice other pay phones advertising that they accept credit cards or that you can make easy collect calls to the USA on them. While some might be fair value, others charge extremely high rates. We suggest being sure about what you'll pay before making a call on a non-Telmex phone.

Casetas *Casetas de teléfono* can be more expensive than the streetside Telmex pay phones, but are not always so. You don't need a phone card to use them and because they're indoors, there is far less street noise. Many offer the same off-peak discounts offered through pay phones. *Casetas* usually have a telephone symbol outside or a sign reading 'Larga Distancia,' *'teléfono'* or 'Lada.'

Prefixes & Codes When making a call in Mexico, you need to know the *prefijo* (prefix) and *claves* (country or area code).

If you're calling a number in the town or city you're in, simply dial the local number (eight digits in Guadalajara, Monterrey and Mexico City, seven elsewhere).

To call another town in Mexico, dial the long-distance prefix ☎ 01, followed by the area code (two digits for Mexico City, Guadalajara and Monterrey; three digits elsewhere) and then the local number. You'll find area codes listed immediately underneath city and town headings in this book. If calling from one town to another that has the same area code, you still have to dial 01 and the area code.

For international calls, dial the international prefix ☎ 00, followed by the country code, area code and local number. For example, to call the New York City number ☎ 987-6543 from Mexico, dial ☎ 00, then the US country code ☎ 1, then the New York City area code ☎ 212, then ☎ 987-6543.

Mexicans may present their phone numbers and area codes in varying arrangements of digits (a consequence of having all their numbers changed once, and all their area codes twice, in the three years from

International Country Codes

Australia	☎ 61	Italy	☎ 39
Belize	☎ 501	Mexico	☎ 52
Canada	☎ 1	New Zealand	☎ 64
Cuba	☎ 53	Spain	☎ 34
France	☎ 33	UK	☎ 44
Germany	☎ 49	USA	☎ 1
Guatemala	☎ 502		

1999–2001); but if you remember that the area code and the local number always total 10 digits, you shouldn't go wrong.

To call a number in Mexico from another country, dial your international access code, then the Mexico country code (☎ 52), then the area code and number. Calls beginning with ☎ 800 are toll free.

North American Calling Cards

If you have an AT&T, MCI or Sprint card, or a Canadian calling card, you can use them for calls from Mexico to the USA or Canada by dialing the following access numbers:

AT&T	☎ 001-800-462-4240
MCI	☎ 001-800-674-7000
Sprint	☎ 001-800-877-8000
AT&T Canada	☎ 001-800-123-0201
Bell Canada	☎ 001-800-010-1990

Collect Calls

A *llamada por cobrar* (collect call) can cost the receiving party much more than if *they* call *you,* so you may prefer to pay for a quick call to the other party to ask them to call you back.

If you need to make a collect call, you can do so from pay phones without a card. Call an operator on ☎ 020 for domestic calls, or ☎ 090 for international calls, or use a Home Country Direct service. Mexican international operators usually speak English.

Some *casetas de teléfono* and hotels will make collect calls for you, but charge for the service. We've also come across *casetas* and shops that proudly announce that you can place collect calls for free, but then charge exorbitant rates to the receiving party (for example, US$24 per minute to the USA).

Home Country Direct service, for making international collect calls via an operator in the country you're calling, is available for several countries. Get information on Home Direct services from your phone company before you leave for Mexico, and you can make the calls from pay phones without any card. For Home Direct calls to the USA through AT&T, MCI or Sprint, and to Canada via AT&T Canada or Bell Canada, dial the numbers given above under North American Calling Cards. The Mexican term for Home Country Direct is *País Directo.*

Cellular Phones

When calling to Mexican cellular phone numbers starting with 044, always dial the area code after the 044, even if it is a local call.

Few cellular phones from the USA, Canada, Europe or Australasia will work in Mexico; and are probably expensive if they do. You can rent Mexican cell phones at some large airports, or purchase them at department stores like Sanborn's. At the time of writing a phone with good national and international coverage and clear connections cost around US$250 including a little airtime. Cards for additional airtime in some local areas are sold at newsstands and minimarts in denominations of 100, 200 and 400 pesos (approximately US$11, US$22 and US$44, respectively).

Fax

Public fax service is offered in many Mexican towns by the public *telégrafos* (telegraph), Telecomm and Computel offices. Also look for 'Fax' signs on shops, businesses and *casetas de teléfono,* and in bus stations and airports. You'll pay US$1 to US$2 per page to the USA or Canada.

Email & Internet Access

Internet cafés are an easy way of accessing the Internet and email while you're on the road. They're in just about every Mexican town and city, and many are listed in this book. Costs are usually US$1 to US$3 an hour. Free web-based email accounts are available through **Yahoo!** (Ⓦ *www.yahoo .com*) or **Hotmail** (Ⓦ *www.hotmail.com*).

Traveling with a portable computer is a great way to stay in touch with the rest of the world, but it has potential problems. The power supply may differ from that at home (see Electricity, later in this chapter), risking damage to your equipment. The best investment is a universal AC adapter, which will enable you to plug it in anywhere without frying the innards. You'll also need a plug adapter, which is easier to buy before leaving home.

Your PC-card modem may not work outside your home country, and you won't know for sure until you try. The safest option is to buy a reputable 'global' modem before leaving home, or buy a local PC-card modem if you're spending an extended time away. Telephone sockets in Mexico may differ from those at home, so ensure that you have at least a US RJ-11 telephone adapter that works with your modem. You can almost always find an adapter that will convert from RJ-11 to the local variety. For more information on traveling with a portable computer, check out **teleadapt** (W *www.teleadapt.com*).

Some Mexican hotel rooms have direct-dial lines that allow you to unplug the phone and insert a phone jack that runs directly to your computer. In others you're confronted with switchboard phone systems and/or room phones with a cord running directly into the wall, both of which make it impossible to go online from your room. In such cases reception will often let you borrow a line for a couple of minutes.

It's also possible to plug in your computer at some *casetas de teléfono*.

Major global Internet service providers (ISPs), such as **AOL** (W *www.aol.com*) and **CompuServe** (W *www.compuserve.com*) have dial-in nodes throughout Mexico. It's best to download a list of the dial-in numbers before you leave home. If you access an email account through a smaller ISP or your office or school network, and you want to use it on the road, your best option is to rely on Internet cafés or other public Internet access points; and you'll need three pieces of information: your incoming (POP or IMAP) mail server name, your account name and your password. Your ISP or network supervisor will be able to give you these.

DIGITAL RESOURCES

The Internet is a rich resource for travelers. You can research your trip, hunt down bargain airfares, book hotels, check on weather conditions or chat with locals and other travelers about the best places to visit (or to avoid!).

Lonely Planet

There are few better places to start your Web explorations than the **Lonely Planet website** (W *www.lonelyplanet.com*). Here you'll find succinct summaries on traveling to most places on earth, postcards from other travelers, and the Thorn Tree bulletin board where you can ask questions before you go or dispense advice when you get back. You can also find travel news, updates to many of our most popular guidebooks, and the subway section that links you to the most useful travel resources elsewhere on the web.

Mexico-Specific Sites

Dozens of Mexico-specific sites can help you prepare your trip or assist you while you're there. Those with a broad scope are mentioned here; websites focusing on specific areas or aspects of Mexico are covered in specific sections of this book.

Mexico Connect (W *www.mexconnect.com*) and **Mexico Online** (W *www.mexonline.com*) are packed with news, message and chat boards, accommodation information, articles and an endless variety of other content and links. The website of the **Mexico Tourism Board** (W *www.visitmexico.com*) is worth a peek.

Planeta.com: Ecotravels in Latin America (W *www.planeta.com*) is a marvelous resource for responsible and ecologically minded tourism. You'll find articles, lists and links covering birds, butterflies, books, language schools, protected areas and more on this constantly growing site.

The Gay Mexico Network (W *www.gaymexico.net*) houses all sorts of information, mostly for gay men, for the resorts of

Puerto Vallarta, Acapulco, Bahías de Huatulco, Guadalajara and Manzanillo.

For fun, quirky and extensive information about the coasts of Colima, Jalisco and Oaxaca, check out **Tomzap's Pacific Coast of Mexico** (W *www.tomzap.com*).

The University of Texas' **Lanic Mexico page** (W *lanic.utexas.edu/la/mexico*) has a great collection of Mexico links.

BOOKS

You can find some books in English along the coast, but only Oaxaca city has an extensive choice. The Mexican-published titles mentioned here are widely available, but it's wise to obtain other books before going to Mexico.

Many books are published in different editions by different publishers in different countries. As a result, a book might be a hardcover rarity in one country while it's readily available in paperback in another. **Bookfinder** (W *www.bookfinder.com*) is a great website for purchasing used and rare books around the world.

Lonely Planet

Lonely Planet's comprehensive country guide *Mexico* is an excellent investment. A handy companion for anyone traveling in Mexico is Lonely Planet's *Latin American Spanish phrasebook*, which contains up-to-date words and expressions in Latin American Spanish. Lonely Planet's *Read This First: Central & South America* offers great tips on preparing for a trip to Mexico.

Lonely Planet's *World Food Mexico* is an intimate, full-color guide to Mexico and its cuisine. This book covers every food or drink the traveler could encounter and plots the evolution of Mexican cuisine. Its language section includes a culinary dictionary and useful phrases to help you on your eating adventure.

Guidebooks & Travel Writing

The People's Guide to Mexico by Carl Franz (motto: 'Wherever you go...there you are') has for a quarter of a century been an invaluable, amusing resource for anyone on an extended trip. It doesn't attempt hotel,

transport, or sightseeing specifics but does provide a great all-round introduction to Mexico. In a similar vein, *Western Mexico: A Traveller's Treasury* by Tony Burton is packed with travel routes and writings on the history, nature, art and archaeology of Nayarit, Jalisco and Colima.

Few travel books stick solely to the subject of Pacific Mexico, but several books deal with the country as a whole and make great reading on any trip to Mexico. Graham Greene's *Lawless Roads* traces Greene's 1930s wanderings down eastern Mexico to Chiapas.

In *Sliced Iguana: Travels in Unknown Mexico* (2001), young travel writer Isabella Tree takes peyote with the Huicholes and meets the matriarchs of Juchitán. It's a warm and perceptive account of Mexico and its indigenous cultures, old and new. In *In Search for Captain Zero,* photojournalist Allan C Weisbecker recounts his adventure-packed surf odyssey down Mexico's Pacific coast and into Central America.

History

Michael C Meyer & William L Sherman's *The Course of Mexican History* is one of the best general accounts of Mexican history and society.

Mexico: From the Olmecs to the Aztecs by Michael D Coe gives a concise, learned and well-illustrated picture of ancient Mexico's great cultures. William Henry Prescott's mammoth *History of the Conquest of Mexico* remains a classic, although it was published in 1843 by an author who never visited Mexico. Not until 1993 did the 20th century produce an equivalent tome: Hugh Thomas' *Conquest: Montezuma, Cortes & The Fall of Old Mexico* (called *The Conquest of Mexico* in Britain).

Society & Culture

In *Narcocorrido: A Journey into the Music of Drugs, Guns and Guerrillas* North American musician-author Elijah Wald hitch-hikes through Mexico interviewing top *narcocorrido* musicians and songwriters. Sam Quinones' *True Tales from Another*

Mexico is a peek into marginalized Mexico (on both sides of the border), from Mazatlán's most famous transvestite club to the Sinaloan shrine of Narcosaint Jesús Malverde. *The Mexicans* by Patrick Oster is an interesting account of the daily lives of 20 individuals.

Art, Architecture & Crafts

The Art of Mesoamerica by Mary Ellen Miller is a good survey of pre-Hispanic art and architecture. Two excellent books on the ancient ceramic traditions of Nayarit, Jalisco and Colima are *Ancient West Mexico: Art and Architecture of the Unknown Past*, edited by Richard F Townsend; and *Companions of the Dead* by Jacki Gallagher. The most important colonial architecture book is George Kubler's *Mexican Architecture of the Sixteenth Century* (1948).

Good books on Mexico's 20th-century artists include Diego Rivera's autobiography *My Art, My Life*; Patrick Marnham's 1998 biography of Rivera, *Dreaming with his Eyes Open; Frida: A Biography of Frida Kahlo* by Hayden Herrera; *Frida Kahlo* by Malka Drucker; and *The Mexican Muralists* by Alma M Reed.

Mask Arts of Mexico by Ruth D Lechuga and Chloe Sayer is a finely illustrated work by two experts in the field – Guerrero especially has a rich mask tradition. Sayer has also written two fascinating books tracing the evolution of crafts from pre-Hispanic times to the present, with beautiful photos: *Arts & Crafts of Mexico* and *Mexican Textiles* (originally published in Britain as *Mexican Costume*).

Flora, Fauna & Environment

Joel Simon's *Endangered Mexico: An Environment on the Edge* examines Mexico's varied environmental crises with the benefit of excellent first-hand journalistic research. *Defending the Land of the Jaguar* by Lane Simonian is the absorbing story of Mexico's long, if weak, tradition of conservation.

Dedicated birders should seek out the Spanish-language *Aves de México* by Roger Tory Peterson and Edward L Chalif, published by Mexico's Editorial Diana. The English-language version of this book, *A Field Guide to Mexican Birds*, omits pictures of birds that also appear in Peterson's guides to US birds. An alternative is *A Guide to the Birds of Mexico & Northern Central America* by Steve NG Howell and Sophie Webb.

Fiction

Many foreign novelists have been inspired by Mexico. *The Power and the Glory* by Graham Greene dramatizes the state-church conflict that followed the Mexican Revolution. DH Lawrence's *Mornings in Mexico* is a collection of short stories set in both Mexico and New Mexico.

B Traven is best known as the author of that classic 1935 adventure story of gold and greed, *The Treasure of the Sierra Madre* (made into an equally classic John Huston/Humphrey Bogart film in 1948).

Carlos Castaneda's *Don Juan* series, which reached serious cult status in the 1970s, tells of a North American's experiences with a peyote guru in northwestern Mexico.

The 1990s brought some excellent new English-language novels set in Mexico. Cormac McCarthy's *All the Pretty Horses* is the laconic, tense, poetic tale of three young latter-day cowboys riding south of the border. James Maw's *Year of the Jaguar* takes its youthful English protagonist in search of the father he has never met, from the US border to Chiapas – a book that catches the feel of Mexican travel superbly.

For information on Mexican literature, see the Arts section in the Facts about Mexico's Pacific Coast chapter.

Books Published in Mexico

Mexican publisher Minutiae Mexicana produces some interesting booklets, including *A Guide to Tequila, Mezcal & Pulque; A Guide to Mexican Mammals & Reptiles; The Maya World; A Guide to Mexican Ceramics* and even *A Guide to Mexican Witchcraft*. They're widely available at around US$5 each. A similar Mexican-produced paperback series with many English titles is Panorama.

NEWSPAPERS & MAGAZINES

The English-language daily paper *The News* is published in Mexico City and distributed in all of the coast's large resort towns. It covers Mexican and foreign news, stocks and sports. You can find US newspapers and magazines, and sometimes Canadian and European ones, all at least a day old, on sale in the bigger resorts. Mazatlán, Puerto Vallarta and Puerto Escondido all have English language tourist newspapers to keep you up to date on local happenings.

Mexico has a thriving local press, as well as national newspapers such as *La Crónica*, *Reforma*, *Excelsior*, *El Universal* and *Uno más Uno*. In theory the press is free. In practice it's subject to pressure from politicians and even drug barons. *La Jornada* is a good national daily with a nonestablishment viewpoint.

México Desconocido (Unknown Mexico) is a colorful monthly magazine with intelligent coverage of many interesting places. Buy it at newsstands for US$2.

You can access about 300 Mexican newspapers and magazines on the Internet at **Zona Latina** (W *www.zonalatina.com*).

RADIO & TV

Mexico has approximately 1000 AM and FM radio stations that offer a variety of mostly mainstream Mexican music, often that of the region or area from where you're listening.

Mexican television is dominated by Televisa, the latgest TV company in the Spanish-speaking world, which runs four of the six main national channels. Its rival, TV Azteca, has two channels. Mexican airtime is devoted mainly to ads, low-budget *telenovelas* (soaps), football, game/chat/variety shows, movies and comedy. Better than the commercial channels, but not available everywhere, are the two cultural channels: Once TV (Eleven TV), operated by Mexico City's Instituto Politécnico Nacional; and Canal 22, operated by Conaculta, the National Culture & Arts Council. Cable and satellite TV (primarily Sky TV) are fairly widespread.

PHOTOGRAPHY & VIDEO

Film & Equipment

Camera and film processing shops, pharmacies and hotels all sell film. Most types of film are available in larger cities and resorts. A 36-exposure 100-ISO print film costs US$6 to US$7. Film being sold at lower prices may be outdated. If the date on the box is obscured by a price sticker, look under the sticker. Avoid any film from sun-exposed shop windows. If your camera breaks down, you'll be able to find a repair shop in most sizable towns, and prices will be agreeably low.

Mexico is a photographer's paradise. The Lonely Planet book *Travel Photography* is a mine of information on travel-related photographic techniques and equipment.

Be sensitive about photographing people; if in doubt, ask first. Indigenous people in particular can be reluctant to be photographed. It also isn't a good idea to photograph soldiers.

TIME

Most of the country, including Jalisco, Michoacan, Guerrero and Oaxaca, are on Hora del Centro, the same as US Central Time (GMT minus six hours in winter, and GMT minus five hours during daylight saving). Five western states, including Nayarit and Sinaloa, are on Hora de las Montañas, the same as US Mountain Time (GMT minus seven hours in winter, GMT minus six hours during daylight saving); if you're traveling south, set your watch forward one hour as you cross from Nayarit state into Jalisco state. *Horario de verano* (daylight saving time) runs from the first Sunday in April to the last Sunday in October.

ELECTRICITY

Electrical current in Mexico is the same as in the USA and Canada: 110V, 60 Hz. Though most plugs and sockets are the same as in the USA, Mexico has three different types of sockets. If your plug doesn't fit the Mexican socket, get an adapter or change the plug. Mexican electronics stores have a variety of adapters and extensions that should solve the problem.

WEIGHTS & MEASURES

Mexico uses the metric system. For conversion between metric and US or Imperial measures, see the Metric Conversion table at the back of this book.

LAUNDRY

Most Mexican towns have *lavanderías* (laundries) where you can take in a load of laundry and have it washed and dried the same or next day. A 3kg load costs between US$3 and US$5. At some laundries you can do your own washing, which reduces the cost.

TOILETS

Baños públicos (public toilets) can be found in some towns. While some are filthy, others are nearly clean, thanks to the caretakers, who you're required to tip (usually about US$0.10) in exchange for *papel higiénico* (toilet paper). If there's a bin beside the toilet, put used paper etc in it, because the drains can't cope otherwise.

HEALTH

Travel health depends on your predeparture preparations, your daily health care while traveling and how you handle medical problems that develop. While the potential dangers can seem quite frightening, in reality few travelers experience anything more than upset stomachs.

Predeparture Planning

Immunizations Plan ahead for vaccinations: some require more than one injection, while some should not be given together. It's recommended that you seek medical advice at least six weeks before travel.

Discuss your requirements with your doctor (there is often a greater risk of disease with children and with women during pregnancy), but vaccinations you should consider for this trip include the following (for more details about the diseases themselves, see the individual disease entries later in this section). Carry proof of your vaccinations, especially yellow fever, as this is needed for travelers arriving in Mexico from infected countries.

Diphtheria & Tetanus Vaccinations for these two diseases are usually combined and are recommended for everyone. After an initial course of three injections (usually given in childhood), boosters are necessary every 10 years.

Hepatitis A The vaccine for hepatitis A (eg, Avaxim, Havrix 1440 or VAQTA) provides long-term immunity (possibly more than 10 years) after an initial injection and a booster at six to 12 months. Alternatively, an injection of gamma globulin can provide short-term protection against hepatitis A (two to six months, depending on the dose given). It is not a vaccine, but it is a ready-made antibody collected from blood donations. It is reasonably effective and, unlike the vaccine, it is protective immediately, but because it is a blood product, there are current concerns about its long-term safety. Hepatitis A vaccine is also available in a combined form, Twinrix, with hepatitis B vaccine. Three injections over a six-month period are required, the first two providing substantial protection against hepatitis A.

Hepatitis B Travelers who should consider vaccination against hepatitis B include those on a long trip and those visiting developing countries (like Mexico) where there are high levels of hepatitis B infection, where blood transfusions may not be adequately screened or where sexual contact or needle sharing is a possibility. Vaccination involves three injections, with a booster at 12 months. More rapid courses are available if necessary.

Yellow Fever This disease is not present in Mexico, but the country requires travelers arriving from areas infected with the disease (which are all in tropical South America or Africa) to have had yellow fever vaccination and to carry a yellow fever certificate. Discuss this with your doctor if necessary.

Malaria Medication Antimalarial drugs do not prevent you from being infected, but kill the malaria parasites during a stage in their development and significantly reduce the risk of becoming very ill or dying. Expert advice on medication should be sought, as there are many factors to consider, including the area to be visited, the risk of exposure to malaria-carrying mosquitoes, the side effects of medication, your medical history and whether you are a child or an adult or pregnant. In western Mexico at the time of writing there was malaria risk in rural areas of Guerrero, Michoacán, Nayarit, Oaxaca and Sinaloa states. There is no malarial risk in any of the major Pacific coast resort destinations.

Health Insurance Make sure that you have adequate health insurance. See Travel Insurance under Visas & Documents earlier in this chapter for details.

Travel Health Guides Lonely Planet's *Healthy Travel Central & South America* is a handy pocket-size book packed with useful information including pretrip planning, emergency first aid, immunization and disease information, and what to do if you get sick on the road. *Travel with Children* from Lonely Planet includes advice on travel health for younger children.

There are a number of excellent travel health sites on the Internet. There are links to the World Health Organization and the US Centers for Disease Control & Prevention from the **Lonely Planet** website (Ⓦ *www .lonelyplanet.com/weblinks/wlheal.htm)*.

Other Preparations Make sure you're healthy before you start traveling. If you are going on a long trip, make sure your teeth are OK. If you wear glasses, take a spare pair and your prescription.

If you require a particular medication, take an adequate supply, as it may not be available locally. Take part of the packaging showing the generic name rather than the brand, which will make getting replacements easier. It's a good idea to have a legible prescription or letter from your doctor to show that you use the medication legally.

Basic Rules

Food A colonial adage goes: 'If you can cook it, boil it or peel it you can eat it...otherwise forget it.' Vegetables and fruit should be washed with purified water or peeled where possible. Beware of ice cream that's melted and refrozen. Mussels, oysters and clams should be avoided, as should undercooked meat, particularly mince. Steaming does not make shellfish safe for eating. If a place looks clean and well run, and the vendor looks clean and healthy, then the food is probably safe.

Water The number one rule is be careful of the water, especially ice. If you're not certain the water is safe, assume the worst. Reputable brands of bottled water or sodas are fine. Use water only from containers with a serrated seal – not tops or corks. Many Mexican hotels have large bottles of purified water from which you can fill a water bottle or canteen. Take care with fruit juice, particularly if water may have been added. Watch out for milk, as it might be unpasteurized, though boiled milk is fine if it is kept hygienically. Coffee and tea should also be OK.

Nutrition

If your diet is poor or limited in variety, if you're travelling hard and fast and therefore missing meals or if you simply lose your appetite, you can soon start to lose weight and place your health at risk.

Make sure your diet is well balanced. Cooked eggs, tofu, beans, lentils and nuts are all safe ways to get protein. Fruit you can peel (bananas, oranges or mandarins, for example) is usually safe and a good source of vitamins. Melons can harbour bacteria in their flesh and are best avoided. Try to eat plenty of grains (including rice) and bread. Remember that although food is generally safer if it is cooked well, overcooked food loses much of its nutritional value. If your diet isn't well balanced or if your food intake is insufficient, it's a good idea to take vitamin and iron pills.

In hot climates make sure you drink enough – don't rely on feeling thirsty to indicate when you should drink. Not needing to urinate or voiding small amounts of very dark yellow urine is a danger sign. Always carry a water bottle with you on long trips. Excessive sweating can lead to loss of salt and therefore muscle cramping. Salt tablets are not a good idea as a preventative, but in places where salt is not used much, adding salt to food can help.

The simplest way of purifying water is to boil it thoroughly. For a long trip, consider purchasing a water filter. There are two main kinds of filter. Total filters remove all parasites, bacteria and viruses. They are often expensive, but can be more cost-effective than buying bottled water. Simple filters (even a nylon mesh bag) remove dirt and larger foreign bodies from the water so that chemical solutions work more effectively; if water is dirty, chemical solutions may not work at all.

When buying a filter, read the specifications, so that you know exactly what it does and doesn't remove from the water. A simple filter will not remove all dangerous organisms, so if you cannot boil your water, then it should be treated chemically. Chlorine tablets will kill many pathogens, but not parasites. Iodine is more effective in purifying water and is available in tablets. Follow the directions, and remember too much iodine can be harmful. The Spanish term for 'water purification tablets/drops' is *'pastillas/gotasparapurificaragua'*.

Medical Problems & Treatment

We know from experience that it is possible to take dozens of journeys in every region of Mexico, climbing, trekking, camping out, staying in cheap hotels and eating in all sorts of markets and restaurants without getting anything worse than occasional traveler's diarrhea. But some of us *have* experienced hepatitis, dysentery and giardiasis, so we know that these things can happen.

Self-diagnosis and treatment can be risky, so always seek medical help. An embassy, consulate or hotel can usually recommend a local doctor or medical clinic. Most Mexican towns and cities have a hospital and/or a clinic, as well as Cruz Roja (Red Cross) emergency facilities.

In big cities and major tourist resorts you should be able to find an adequate hospital; care in remote areas is limited. In serious cases it may be best to fly elsewhere for treatment.

Hospitals are inexpensive for common ailments (diarrhea, dysentery) and minor treatments (stitches, sprains). Most have to

---

Everyday Health

Normal body temperature is up to 37°C (98.6°F); more than 2°C (4°F) higher indicates a high fever. The normal adult pulse rate is 60 to 100 per minute (children 80 to 100, babies 100 to 140). As a general rule the pulse increases about 20 beats per minute for each 1°C (2°F) rise in fever.

Respiration (breathing) rate is also an indicator of illness. Count the number of breaths per minute: Between 12 and 20 is considered normal for adults and older children (up to 30 for younger children, 40 for babies). People with a high fever or serious respiratory illness breathe more quickly than normal. More than 40 shallow breaths a minute may indicate pneumonia.

---

be paid at the time of service, and doctors usually require cash payment. Some facilities may accept credit cards.

Note that drug dosages given in this section are for emergencies only. Correct diagnosis is vital. The names for medications are generic – check with a pharmacist for brands available.

Antibiotics should ideally be administered only under medical supervision. Take only the recommended dose at the prescribed intervals and use the whole course, even if the illness seems to be cured. Stop immediately if there are serious reactions and don't use the antibiotic at all if you are unsure that you have the correct one.

Environmental Hazards

Heat Exhaustion Dehydration and salt deficiency can cause heat exhaustion. Take time to acclimatize to high temperatures, drink sufficient liquids and do not do anything too physically demanding.

Salt deficiency is characterized by fatigue, lethargy, headaches, giddiness and muscle cramps; salt tablets may help, but adding extra salt to your food is better.

Anhydrotic heat exhaustion, caused by an inability to sweat, is rare. It usually affects people who have been in a hot climate for some time, rather than newcomers. It can progress to heatstroke. Treatment involves removal to a cooler climate.

Heatstroke This serious, occasionally fatal, condition can occur if the body's heat-regulating mechanism fails and body temperature rises to dangerous levels. Long periods of exposure to high temperatures and insufficient fluids can leave you vulnerable.

Symptoms are feeling unwell, not sweating much (or at all) and a high body temperature (39° to 41°C, 102° to 106°F). Where sweating has ceased, the skin becomes flushed and red. Severe, throbbing headaches and lack of coordination also occur, and the sufferer may be confused or aggressive. Eventually the victim becomes delirious or convulses. Hospitalization is essential, but in the interim get victims out of the sun, remove their clothing, cover them with a wet sheet or towel and then fan continually. Give fluids if they are conscious.

Prickly Heat This is an itchy rash caused by excessive perspiration trapped under the skin. It usually strikes people who have just arrived in a hot climate. Keeping cool, bathing often, drying the skin and using a mild talcum or prickly-heat powder, or resorting to air-conditioning may help.

Infectious Diseases

Diarrhea Simple things such as a change of water, food or climate can cause a mild bout of diarrhea, but a few rushed toilet trips with no other symptoms are not indicative of a major problem.

Dehydration is the main danger with any diarrhea, particularly in children or the elderly. Fluid replacement is the most important thing to remember. Weak black tea with a little sugar, soda water, or soft drinks allowed to go flat and diluted 50% with clean water are all good. With severe diarrhea, a rehydrating solution is preferable to replace minerals and salts lost. Commercially available oral rehydration salts (ORS) are useful; add them to water. In an emergency, you can make a solution of six teaspoons of sugar and a half teaspoon of salt to 1L of boiled or bottled water. You need to drink at least the same volume of fluid that you are losing in bowel movements and vomiting. Urine is the best guide to the adequacy of replacement – if you have small amounts of concentrated urine, you need to drink more. Keep drinking small amounts often.

Gut-paralyzing drugs such as loperamide or diphenoxylate can be used to bring relief from the symptoms, although they do not cure the problem. Use these drugs only if you do not have access to toilets, eg, if you *must* travel. They are not recommended for children under 12 years.

Sometimes antibiotics may be required: diarrhea with blood or mucus (dysentery), any diarrhea with fever, profuse watery diarrhea, persistent diarrhea not improving after 48 hours, and severe diarrhea. These suggest a more serious cause of diarrhea and gut-paralyzing drugs should be avoided.

In these situations, a stool test may be necessary to diagnose what bug is causing your diarrhea, so you should seek medical help urgently. Where this is not possible the recommended drugs for bacterial diarrhea (the most likely cause of severe diarrhea in travelers) are norfloxacin (400mg twice daily for three days) or ciprofloxacin (500mg twice daily for five days). These are not recommended for children or pregnant women. The drug of choice for children would be co-trimoxazole with the dosage dependent on weight. A five-day course is given. Ampicillin or amoxycillin may be given in pregnancy, but medical care is necessary.

Two other causes of persistent diarrhea in travelers are giardiasis and amoebic dysentery.

Giardiasis is caused by a common parasite, *Giardia lamblia*. Symptoms include stomach cramps, nausea, a bloated stomach, watery, foul-smelling diarrhea and frequent gas. Giardiasis can appear several weeks after you have been exposed to the parasite. The symptoms may disappear for a few days and then return; this can go on for several weeks.

Amoebic dysentery, caused by the protozoan *Entamoeba histolytica*, is characterized by a gradual onset of low-grade diarrhea, often with blood and mucus.

Cramping abdominal pain and vomiting are less likely than in other types of diarrhea, and fever may not be present. It will persist until treated and can recur and cause other health problems.

You should seek medical advice if you think you have giardiasis or amoebic dysentery, but where this is not possible, tinidazole or metronidazole are the recommended drugs. Treatment is a 2g single dose of tinidazole or 250mg of metronidazole three times daily for five to 10 days.

Fungal Infections These occur more commonly in hot weather and are usually found on the scalp, between the toes (athlete's foot) or fingers, in the groin and on the body (ringworm). You can get ringworm (which is not a worm) from infected animals or other people. Moisture encourages these infections.

To prevent fungal infections, wear loose, comfortable clothes, avoid artificial fibers, wash frequently and dry carefully. If you get an infection, wash the infected area daily with a disinfectant or medicated soap and water, and rinse and dry well. Apply an antifungal cream or powder like tolnaftate. Expose the infected area to air or sunlight as much as possible, and wash towels and underwear in hot water, change them often and let them dry in the sun.

Hepatitis This is a general term for inflammation of the liver. Several different viruses can cause hepatitis and they differ in the ways they are transmitted. The symptoms are similar in all forms of the illness, and include fever, chills, headache, fatigue, feelings of weakness, and aches and pains, followed by loss of appetite, nausea, vomiting, abdominal pain, dark urine, light-colored feces, jaundiced (yellow) skin and yellowing of the whites of the eyes. People who have had hepatitis should avoid alcohol for some time after the illness, as the liver needs time to recover.

Hepatitis A is transmitted by contaminated food and drinking water. You should seek medical advice, but there is not much you can do apart from rest, drink lots of fluids, eat lightly and avoid fatty foods. Hepatitis E is transmitted in the same way as hepatitis A; it can be particularly serious in pregnant women.

The incidence of hepatitis B is low in Mexico, although it's classed as intermediate in neighboring Guatemala. Hepatitis B is spread through contact with infected blood, blood products or body fluids – for example through sexual contact, unsterilized needles, blood transfusions or contact with blood via small breaks in the skin. Other risk situations include shaving, tattoos or body piercing with contaminated equipment. The symptoms of hepatitis B may be more severe than type A and the disease can lead to long-term problems such as chronic liver damage, liver cancer or a long-term carrier state. Hepatitis C and D are spread in the same ways as hepatitis B and can also lead to long-term complications.

There are vaccines against hepatitis A and B, but there are currently no vaccines against the other types of hepatitis. Following the basic rules about food and water (hepatitis A and E) and avoiding risk situations (hepatitis B, C and D) are important preventative measures.

HIV & AIDS Infection with the human immunodeficiency virus (HIV) may lead to acquired immune deficiency syndrome (AIDS), which is a fatal disease. By the end of 2000 an estimated 64,000 people had contracted AIDS in Mexico (a much lower percentage of the population than in any of its three neighbors: the USA, Guatemala and Belize) and there were around 150,000 people with HIV. Any exposure to blood, blood products or body fluids may put the individual at risk. The disease is often transmitted through sexual contact or dirty needles – vaccinations, acupuncture, tattooing and body piercing can be potentially as dangerous as intravenous drug use. HIV/AIDS can also be spread through infected blood transfusions; in developing countries such as Mexico it is possible that transfusion blood will not have been screened for HIV. If you need an injection, you can request to see the syringe unwrapped in front of you, or take a needle and syringe pack with you.

Fear of HIV infection should never preclude treatment for any serious medical condition.

Intestinal Worms These parasites are most common in rural, tropical areas. Different worms have different ways of infecting people. Some may be ingested on food such as undercooked meat (eg, tapeworms) and some enter through your skin (eg, hookworms). Infestations may not show up for some time and, although they are not serious, if left untreated some can cause severe health problems later. Consider having a stool test when you return home to check for these and determine the appropriate treatment.

Insect-Borne Diseases

Malaria This serious, potentially fatal disease is spread by mosquito bites. When in endemic areas, it is extremely important to avoid mosquito bites and to take tablets to prevent malaria. Symptoms range from fever, chills and sweating, headache, diarrhea and abdominal pains to a vague feeling of ill health. Seek medical help immediately if malaria is suspected. Without treatment, malaria can rapidly become more serious and can be fatal.

If medical care is unavailable, malaria tablets can be used for treatment. You need to use a different malaria tablet than the one you were taking when you contracted malaria in the first place. The standard treatment dose of mefloquine is two 250mg tablets and another two six hours later. For Fansidar, it's a single dose of three tablets. If you were previously taking mefloquine and cannot obtain Fansidar, alternatives are Malarone (atovaquone-proguanil; four tablets once daily for three days), halofantrine (three doses of two 250mg tablets every six hours) or quinine sulphate (600mg every six hours). There is a greater risk of side effects with these dosages than in normal use if used with mefloquine, so medical advice is preferable. Halofantrine is no longer recommended by the WHO as emergency standby treatment, because of side effects,

and should only be used if no other drugs are available.

Travelers are advised to prevent mosquito bites at all times. In general, mosquitoes in Mexico are most bothersome from dusk to dawn and during the rainy season (May to October in most places). To avoid being bitten by a mosquito, follow these precautions:

- Wear light-colored clothing.
- Wear long trousers and long-sleeved shirts.
- Use mosquito repellents containing the compound DEET on exposed areas (prolonged overuse of DEET may be harmful, especially to children, but use is considered preferable to being bitten by disease-transmitting mosquitoes).
- Avoid perfumes or aftershave.
- Impregnate clothes and mosquito nets with repellent (permethrin); it may be worth taking your own net.

Cuts, Bites & Stings

See Less Common Diseases for details of rabies, which is passed through animal bites.

Cuts & Scratches Wash any cut well and treat it with an antiseptic, such as povidone-iodine. When possible, avoid bandages and Band-Aids, which can keep wounds wet. Coral cuts are notoriously slow to heal and, if they are not adequately cleaned, small pieces of coral can become embedded in the wound.

Bites & Stings Bedbugs live in various places, but particularly in dirty mattresses and bedding, evidenced by spots of blood on bedclothes or on the wall. Bedbugs leave itchy bites in neat rows. Calamine lotion or a sting relief spray may help.

All lice cause itching and discomfort. They make themselves at home in your hair (head lice), your clothing (body lice) or in your pubic hair (crabs). You catch lice through direct contact with infected people or by sharing combs, clothing and the like. Powder or shampoo treatment will kill the lice, and infected clothing should then be washed in hot, soapy water and left in the sun to dry.

Bee and wasp stings are usually painful rather than dangerous. However, in people who are allergic to them severe breathing difficulties may occur and require urgent medical care. Calamine lotion or a sting relief spray will give relief, and ice packs will reduce the pain and swelling. Some spiders have dangerous bites, but antivenins are usually available. Scorpion stings are notoriously painful and in some parts of Central America can be fatal. Scorpions often shelter in shoes or clothing. For more information see the boxed text 'Scorpions' in the Michoacán chapter.

Jellyfish, Sea Urchins & Stingrays Stings from all three of these sea creatures are usually 'only' excruciatingly painful; severe stings, punctures and lacerations, however, can result in infection and more serious medical problems. If symptoms persist more than a few days, seek medical attention.

Anyone can chance upon a jellyfish while swimming and get zapped. Jellyfish stings can be treated by dousing the wound in vinegar or alcohol to deactivate any stingers that have not 'fired.' Calamine lotion, antihistamines and analgesics may relieve the pain.

Sea urchins have long, black or purple venomous spines and are found in reefs, rocks and tidepools. People usually get jabbed when they step on one, pick one up, or get dashed while surfing onto the rocks or coral where urchins live. Punctures result in severe pain, swelling, redness and sometimes numbness or tingling. Immediately remove all spines from the wound. Those that break off usually work their way out within a few weeks if they're not too deep. Soak the wound in very hot water for up to 1½ hours to relieve the pain.

Stingrays have long, stinging barbs on their tails. Most stings occur when swimmers step on them in the sand. Reactions depend on the severity of the wound. Most are only severely painful, though nausea, difficulty breathing and even shock can follow a serious sting. Again, soak the wound in hot water for up to 1½ hours to relieve pain.

Leeches & Ticks Leeches may be present in rainforests; they attach themselves to your skin to suck blood. An insect repellent may keep them away. Salt or a lighted cigarette end will make them fall off. Don't pull them off, as the bite is then more likely to become infected. Clean and apply pressure if the point of attachment is bleeding.

You should always check all over your body if you have been walking through a potentially tick-infested area, as ticks can cause skin infections and more serious diseases. If a tick is found attached, press down around its head with tweezers, grab the head and gently pull upwards. Avoid pulling the rear of the body as this may squeeze the tick's gut contents through the attached mouth parts into the skin, increasing the risk of infection and disease. Smearing chemicals on the tick will not make it let go and is not recommended.

Snakes To minimize your chances of being bitten, wear boots, socks and long trousers when walking through undergrowth. Don't put your hands into holes and crevices, and be careful when collecting firewood.

Snake bites do not cause instantaneous death, and antivenins are usually available. Immediately wrap the bitten limb tightly, as you would for a sprained ankle, and then attach a splint to immobilize it. Keep the victim still and seek medical help. Tourniquets and sucking out the poison are now comprehensively discredited.

Less Common Diseases

The following diseases pose only a small risk to travelers, and so are only mentioned in passing. Seek medical advice if you think you may have either of them.

Rabies This fatal viral infection occurs throughout Latin America. Many animals can be infected (such as dogs, cats, bats and monkeys). This horrible disease is transmitted through the infected animal's saliva and any bite, scratch or even lick from an animal should be cleaned immediately and thoroughly. Scrub with soap and running water, and then apply alcohol or iodine solution.

Medical help should be sought promptly to receive a course of injections to prevent the onset of symptoms and death.

Tetanus This disease is caused by a germ that lives in the soil and in the feces of horses and other animals. It enters the body via breaks in the skin. The first symptom may be discomfort in swallowing, or stiffening of the jaw and neck; this is followed by painful convulsions of the jaw and whole body. The disease can be fatal, but it can be prevented by vaccination.

WOMEN TRAVELERS
In this land that invented machismo, women have to make some concessions to local custom – but don't let that put you off. In general, Mexicans are great believers in the difference (rather than the equality) between the sexes. Lone women must expect some catcalls and attempts to chat them up. It is possible to turn uninvited attention into a worthwhile conversation by making it clear that you *are* willing to talk, but no more.

Don't put yourself in peril by doing things Mexican women would not do, such as challenging a man's masculinity, drinking in a cantina, hitchhiking without a male companion, or going alone to isolated places.

Wearing a bra will spare you a lot of unwanted attention. A wedding ring and talk of your husband may help, too. Along the coast, and especially in the larger beach resorts, women regularly wear shorts, swimsuits of all sizes, tank tops etc. Mexicans are used to it and Mexican women do the same (at least on the beach). In inland cities like Guadalajara or Oaxaca, however, dressing more conservatively will help keep unwanted attention at bay.

GAY & LESBIAN TRAVELERS
Though it might ostensibly be one of the world's more heterosexual countries, Mexico is more broad-minded than visitors might expect. Gays and lesbians tend to keep a low profile, but in general rarely attract open discrimination or violence. Gay and lesbian travelers will find active scenes in cities such as Puerto Vallarta, Acapulco and Guadalajara.

A good source of information on the Internet is **The Gay Mexico Network** (see Internet Resources earlier). *Sergay* (w www .sergay.com.mx) is a Spanish-language magazine, focused on Mexico City but with bar and disco listings for the whole country.

The *Damron Women's Traveller*, with listings for lesbians, and *Damron Address Book*, for men, are both published annually by Damron Company of San Francisco, USA. *Men's Travel in Your Pocket*, *Women's Travel in Your Pocket* and *Gay Travel A to Z* (for men and women), all published by Ferrari Publications, and *Gay Mexico: The Men of Mexico* by Eduardo David are also useful. They can be obtained at any good bookstore, as well as on the Internet.

DISABLED TRAVELERS
Mexico's buildings and public places are not, in general, disabled-friendly, though the major tourist resorts are beginning to catch on. Hotels and restaurants that provide wheelchair access, however, are almost entirely at the top end of the market. Public transportation is mainly hopeless; flying, taxi and car are easiest.

Mobility International USA (☎ 541-343-1284; w www.miusa.org; PO Box 10767, Eugene, OR 97440, USA) runs exchange programmes (including in Mexico) and publishes *A World of Options: A Guide to International Educational Exchange, Community Service & Travel for People with Disabilities*. In Europe, there's **Mobility International** (☎ 02-201 5608; e mobint@ arcadis.be; blvd Baudouin 18, Brussels B-1000, Belgium).

Twin Peaks Press (☎ 360-694-2462; w www.pacifier.com/~twinpeak; PO Box 129, Vancouver, WA 98666-0129, USA) publishes some useful material for disabled travelers.

In the UK, **Radar** (☎ 020-7250 3222; w www.radar.org.uk; 250 City Rd, London EC1V 8AF) is run by and for disabled people. Its excellent website has links to good travel-specific sites, as does the Australian site **Acrod** (w www.acrod.org.au). Another excellent information source is **Access-able Travel Source** (w *www.access-able.com*).

SENIOR TRAVELERS

The **American Association of Retired Persons** (AARP; ☎ *800-424-3410*; w *www.aarp.org; 601 E St NW, Washington, DC 20049, USA*), is an advocacy and service group for Americans 50 years and older and a good resource for travel bargains. Membership is US$12.50 per year.

Elderhostel (☎ *877-426-8056*; w *www.elderhostel.org; 11 Ave de Lafayette, Boston, MA 02111, USA*) is a nonprofit organization providing educational travel programmes to people over age 55. It has many fascinating programmes in Mexico, typically costing around US$1000 to US$1200 a week including airfares from the USA.

Grand Circle Travel (☎ *800-597-3644*; w *www.gct.com; 347 Congress St, Boston, MA 02210, USA*) offers escorted tours and travel information in a variety of formats.

TRAVEL WITH CHILDREN

In Mexico any child whose hair is less than jet black will get called *güera* (blonde) if she's a girl, *güero* if he's a boy. Children are welcome at all kinds of hotels and in virtually every café and restaurant.

Children are likely to be more affected than adults by heat or disrupted sleeping patterns. They need time to acclimatize and extra care to avoid sunburn. Take care to replace fluids if a child gets diarrhea (see the Health section). Diapers are widely available, but you may not easily find creams, lotions, baby foods or familiar medicines outside larger cities and tourist towns. Bring what you need.

Many top-end hotels allow two children up to age 10 or 12 to stay free with paying adults. It's usually not hard to find an inexpensive babysitter if the grown-ups want to go out on their own; just ask at your hotel.

On flights to and within Mexico children under two generally travel for 10% of the adult fare, and those between two and 12 normally pay 67%. Children under 13 pay half-price on many Mexican long-distance buses and if they're under three, and small enough to sit on your lap, they will usually go free.

DANGERS & ANNOYANCES

Mexico – especially its big cities and above all Mexico City – experienced a big increase in crime after the economic crisis of the mid-1990s, which gave the entire country a bad reputation. By the end of the decade the authorities were finally taking steps to counter this, especially in the Pacific coast resorts where tourism is a major money-maker. With a few precautions you can minimize danger to your physical safety. But lone women, and even pairs of women, should always be cautious about going to remote beach spots. Your possessions are most at risk, particularly what you carry around with you.

Information from embassies and foreign affairs departments sometimes makes Mexico sound like a more alarming place to visit than it actually is. That said, you can still obtain useful information on travel to Mexico, including potential risks, by contacting your country's **foreign affairs department** by telephone or on the Internet: **Australia** (☎ *1300 555 135*; w *www.dfat.gov.au*); **Canada** (☎ *613-944-6788, 800-267-6788*; w *www.dfait-maeci.gc.ca*); **UK** (☎ *020-7238 4503*; w *www.fco.gov.uk*); **USA** (☎ *202-647-5225*; w *www.travel.state.gov*). If you're already in Mexico, you can contact your embassy.

Theft & Robbery

Tourism on the Pacific coast is a *major* source of income, both locally and nationally, and Mexico has a vested interest in keeping it safe for visitors. Major coastal resorts have a large and visible police presence, so violent crimes are rare. Remote beach spots and dark streets are the places where muggings are most likely to occur.

Purse- or bag-snatching and pickpocketing can occur in crowded buses, bus stops, bus stations, airports, markets, thronged streets and plazas.

On the Beach One concern is how to spend a day on the beach and swim in the ocean without your possessions sprouting legs and walking off as soon as you head for the water. The easiest way is to take nothing of significant value and only the money you'll need that day. Wear cheap sandals and beach clothing that won't attract sticky fingers or that you won't mind leaving unattended. Leave all your valuables in the *caja fuerte* (safe) at the hotel desk before you leave (or lock them in your baggage in your room). All hotels, except the cheapest, provide safekeeping for valuables. Leave your room key at the reception desk. Also, buy a cheap beach bag so you don't have to leave an attractive day pack on the sand.

Do not camp overnight on lonely beaches unless you can be sure they're safe. If you need to park your car in a remote area, don't leave anything of value in sight; even open the glove box so it's clear there's nothing of value inside.

In the City To avoid being robbed in cities, steer clear of lonely places like empty streets or little-used pedestrian underpasses where there are few other people. Use ATMs only in secure locations and not those that open to the street.

Pickpockets often work in teams: one may 'drop' something as a crowd jostles onto a bus and as he or she 'looks for it,' a pocket will be picked or a bag slashed. The operative principle is to distract you and get you off balance. If your valuables are *underneath* your clothing (in a money belt, shoulder wallet, or a pouch on a string around your neck) the chances of losing them are greatly reduced. Visible round-the-waist money belts are an invitation to thieves. Carry a small amount of ready-money in a pocket.

Highway Robbery Bandits occasionally hold up buses, cars and other vehicles on intercity routes, especially at night. Sometimes buses are robbed by people who board as passengers. The best way to avoid highway robbery is not to travel at night. Deluxe and 1st-class buses usually use toll highways (where they exist), which are safer than free roads.

Nontoll Hwy 200, which has had an up-and-down safety record, is now mostly safe for travel. The stretch through Guerrero and Oaxaca still has a reputation for being unsafe at night. If you're driving, remember that everything on Hwy 200 – service stations, stores, tire shops – closes around sundown; you do not want to be stranded after dark, especially in Guerrero and Oaxaca.

LEGAL MATTERS
Mexican Law
Mexican law is based on the Napoleonic code, presuming an accused person is guilty until proven innocent.

The minimum jail sentence for possession of more than a token amount of any narcotic, including marijuana and amphetamines, is 10 years. As in most other countries, the purchase of controlled medication requires a doctor's prescription.

It's against Mexican law to take any weapon or ammunition into the country (even unintentionally) without a permit from a Mexican embassy or consulate.

Road travelers should expect occasional police or military checkpoints. They are normally looking for drugs, weapons or illegal migrants. Drivers found with drugs or weapons on board may have their vehicle confiscated and may be detained for months while their cases are investigated.

See the Getting Around chapter for information on legal aspects of road accidents.

Useful warnings on Mexican law are found on the **US State Department's** website (W *www.travel.state.gov*).

Help
If arrested, you have the right to notify your embassy or consulate. Consular officials can tell you your rights and provide lists of local lawyers. They can also monitor your case, make sure you are treated humanely, and notify your relatives or friends – but they can't get you out of jail.

Most states in Mexico have a Protección al Turista (Tourist Protection) department, often found in the same building as the state tourist office (and contactable through tourist offices). It exists to help you with legal problems such as complaints, or reporting crimes or lost articles. The national tourism ministry, **Sectur** (☎ 55-5250-0123, 800-903-92-00) offers 24-hour telephone advice on tourist protection laws and where to obtain help.

If you are the victim of a crime, your embassy or consulate, or Sectur, can give advice. In some cases, you may feel there is little to gain by going to the police, unless you need a statement to present to your insurance company. If you go to the police and your Spanish is poor, take a more fluent speaker. Also take your passport and tourist card, if you still have them. If you just want to report a theft for purposes of an insurance claim, say you want to *'poner una acta de un robo'* (make a record of a robbery). This makes it clear that you merely want a piece of paper, and you should get it without too much trouble.

If Mexican police wrongfully accuse you of an infraction (as they have been known to do in the hope of obtaining a bribe), you can ask for the officer's identification or to speak to a superior, or to be shown documentation about the law you have supposedly broken. You can also note the officer's name, badge number, vehicle number and department (federal, state or municipal). Pay any traffic fines at a police station and get a receipt. Then make your complaint to Protección al Turista or to Sectur. Otherwise, pay the 'fine' on the spot.

BUSINESS HOURS

On the coast, shops are generally open from 9am or 10am to around 9pm Monday to Saturday. Because of the heat they close for siesta between 2pm and 4pm. Inland, shops will generally skip the siesta and close around 7pm. Shops in malls and tourist resorts often open on Sunday.

Offices have similar Monday to Friday hours, often with the 2pm to 4pm lunch break. Those with tourist-related business might open for a few hours on Saturday.

Some Mexican churches – particularly those with valuable works of art – are locked when not in use. But most churches are in frequent use.

Archaeological sites are usually open daily (except sometimes on Monday) from 8am or 9am to about 5pm. Museums are usually closed on Monday. On Sunday, nearly all archaeological sites and museums are free, and the major ones can get crowded.

PUBLIC HOLIDAYS & SPECIAL EVENTS

Mexico's frequent fiestas are full-blooded, highly colorful affairs that often last for days. There's a national holiday or celebration almost every month, to which towns add many local saints' days, fairs and arts festivals.

Christmas–New Year and Semana Santa, the week leading up to Easter, are the chief Mexican holiday periods. It is wise to try and book transport and accommodations well in advance.

National Holidays

Banks, post offices, government offices and many shops throughout Mexico are closed on the following days:

Año Nuevo (New Year's Day) January 1
Día de la Constitución (Constitution Day) February 5
Día de la Bandera (Day of the [national] Flag) February 24
Día de Nacimiento de Benito Juárez (anniversary of Benito Juárez's birth) March 21
Día del Trabajo (Labor Day) May 1
Cinco de Mayo (anniversary of Mexico's 1862 victory over the French at Puebla) May 5
Día de la Independencia (commemoration of the start of Mexico's war for independence from Spain) September 16
Día de la Raza (commemorating Columbus' discovery of the New World and the founding of the Mexican people) October 12
Día de la Revolución (anniversary of the Mexican Revolution of 1910) November 20
Día de Navidad (Christmas Day) December 25

Other National Celebrations

Though not official holidays, some of these are among the most important festivals on the Mexican calendar. Many offices and businesses close.

Día de los Reyes Magos (Three Kings' Day)
January 6
Mexican children traditionally receive gifts this day, rather than at Christmas (but some get two loads of presents!).

Día de la Candelaría (Candlemas) February 2
Processions, bullfights, and dancing in many towns commemorate the presentation of Jesus in the temple 40 days after his birth.

Carnaval (Carnival) late February or early March
Observed the week before Ash Wednesday (which falls 46 days before Easter Sunday), this is the party preceding the 40-day penance of Lent; it's celebrated festively in Mazatlán. Indigenous celebrations in Pinotepa Don Luis, San Juan Colorado and Oaxacan villages near Pinotepa Nacional are more religious and very impressive.

Semana Santa (Holy Week) March or April
Starting on Palm Sunday (Domingo de Ramos); business closures are usually from Good Friday (Viernes Santo) to Easter Sunday (Domingo de Resurrección); most of Mexico seems to be on the move at this time.

Informe Presidencial September 1
The president's state of the nation address to the legislature

Día de Todos los Santos (All Saints' Day)
November 1

Día de los Muertos (Day of the Dead)
November 2
Mexico's most characteristic fiesta; the souls of the dead are believed to return to earth this day. Families build altars in their homes and visit graveyards to commune with their dead on the night of November 1–2 and the day of November 2, taking garlands and gifts of, for example, the dead one's favorite foods. A happy atmosphere prevails. The souls of dead children, called *angelitos* because they are believed to have automatically become angels, are celebrated the previous day, All Saints' Day. Like many Mexican rituals, these events have pre-Hispanic roots.

Día de Nuestra Señora de Guadalupe (Day of Our Lady of Guadalupe) December 12
Mexico's national patron, the manifestation of the Virgin Mary who appeared to an indigenous Mexican, Juan Diego, in 1531; a week or more of celebrations throughout Mexico leads up to the big day, with children taken to church dressed as little Juan Diegos or indigenous girls.

Posadas December 16–24
Candlelit parades of children and adults, re-enacting the journey of Mary and Joseph to Bethlehem; held for nine nights, more in small towns. The events in Oaxaca city are marvelous.

Local Fiestas

Every city, town, *barrio* (neighborhood) and village has its own fiestas, often in honor of its patron saint(s). Street parades of holy images, special costumes, fireworks, dancing, lots of music and plenty of drinking are all part of the scene.

COURSES

Mexico's best, most popular language schools are inland: Guadalajara and Oaxaca (both covered in this book) are excellent places to study Spanish, and they give an inside angle on local life and culture. Lonely Planet's *Mexico* guide is good for finding schools in cities like Cuernavaca, Guanajuato, Mexico City, San Miguel de Allende and Taxco. Then take your Spanish to the beach!

Two good US sources on study possibilities in Mexico are the University of Minnesota's **International Service and Travel Center** (ISTC; ☎ 612-626-4782; Ⓦ *www.istc.umn.edu*) and **The Council on International Educational Exchange** (CIEE; ☎ 888-268-6245; Ⓦ *www.ciee.org*). There are also links on the **Lonely Planet** website (Ⓦ *www.lonelyplanet.com*).

Eco Travels in Latin America (Ⓦ *www.planeta.com*), and **Mexico Online** (Ⓦ *www.mexonline.com*) both have listings for Mexican language schools. Information on language study is also available from the **National Registration Center for Study Abroad** (☎ 414-278-0631; Ⓦ *www.nrcsa.com*; 823 North 2nd St, PO Box 1393, Milwaukee, WI 53201, USA).

See Courses under Oaxaca City in the Oaxaca chapter for one of Mexico's great little cooking schools for foreigners.

WORK

Mexicans themselves need jobs, and people who enter Mexico as tourists are not legally allowed to take employment. The many expats working in Mexico have usually been posted there by their companies with all the right papers.

English speakers may find teaching jobs in language schools, *preparatorias* (high schools) or universities, or can offer personal tutoring. Guadalajara is good for English-teaching work. The pay is low, but you can live on it. The *News* and cities' telephone Yellow Pages are job opportunity sources. A foreigner working in Mexico normally needs a permit or government license, but schools often find ways around this. It's helpful to know a little Spanish, even though some institutes insist that only English be spoken while in class.

You might find a little low-pay bar or restaurant work in tourist areas, where English-speaking touts or bartenders are sometimes desirable.

Volunteer Work

The website of the ISTC (see Courses earlier) has a volunteer work database with many possibilities in Mexico. *Volunteer Vacations* by Bill McMillon lists lots of volunteer work organizations and information sources.

Amigos de las Americas (☎ 800-231-7796 in the USA; ⓦ www.amigoslink.org) sends paying volunteers to work on summer public-health projects in Sinaloa and Oaxaca, among other places. Volunteers receive prior training.

AmeriSpan (ⓦ www.amerispan.com) offers a range of volunteer opportunities in Mexico, including several in Oaxaca. For most you must be at least 25 years old and speak fluent Spanish.

The Grupo Ecologico de la Costa Verde (ⓦ www.vallartaonline.com/costaverde), based north of Puerto Vallarta in San Francisco, takes volunteers to help protect olive ridley sea turtles during their nesting season (from around June 15 to around November 15). One- to five-month stays are preferred.

Earthwatch (ⓦ www.earthwatch.org) runs environmental projects in Mexico that you pay to take part in (usually US$1000-plus for one to two weeks).

ACCOMMODATIONS

Accommodations on the Pacific coast range from hammocks, palm-thatched huts and camping grounds to hostels, *casas de huéspedes* (guesthouses) and budget hotels, to world-class luxury resorts. Just about any

tourism-related Internet site can connect you to plenty of Mexican hotel websites and provide hotel information.

Seasons & Reservations

The normal tourist high season is November to April, when many North Americans and Europeans travel to Mexico for the winter. Reservations are advisable for popular places during this time. Tourism peaks during the Christmas–New Year holidays, Semana Santa (the week before Easter and up to a week after it), and the July/August summer holidays. During these periods, reservations are a must. Low season lasts from May to October, with the exception of the holiday jolt in July and August.

Some places require a deposit for a reservation during peak season, though it's less common with cheaper hotels.

Prices

Prices quoted throughout this book, unless specified, are for the November to April winter high season. Peak season rates may rise 10% to 20% above the high season rate. Low season rates are often 10% to 40% lower than those we quote. Rates at budget accommodations tend to fluctuate the least. You can often avoid paying the IVA and ISH taxes (totaling 17%) on your room price if you pay cash and don't require a receipt. To the best of our knowledge, all of our price quotes include tax.

Camping

Camping grounds are common on Mexico's Pacific coast. Most organized camping grounds are trailer parks set up for RVs (camper vans) and trailers (caravans), but they accept tent campers at lower rates. Some are basic, others luxurious. Expect to pay about US$3 to US$5 to pitch a tent and use the toilets, and US$8 to US$15 for two people to use the full facilities of a good camping ground. Restaurants or guesthouses in small beach spots will often let you pitch a tent on their land for around US$2 to US$3, or for free if you patronize their restaurant.

All Mexican beaches are public property. You can camp for nothing on most of them, but always assess the safety of the beach before spending the night on it.

For additional information, read *The People's Guide to RV Camping in Mexico* by Carl Franz or *Traveler's Guide to Mexican Camping* by Mike & Terri Church.

Hammocks & Cabanas

These options are found mainly in low-key beach spots.

You can rent a hammock and a place to hang it – usually under a palm roof outside a small *casa de huéspedes* or beach restaurant – for US$2 to US$5 per night. If you have your own hammock the cost might drop a bit. It's easy to buy hammocks throughout Mexico. Oaxaca has excellent hammocks, though the best come from the Yucatán and are sold nationwide. In hammocks, mosquito repellent is handy.

Cabanas are cabins or huts – usually with a palm-thatched roof. Some have sand floors and nothing inside but a bed; others are deluxe, with electric light, mosquito nets, fans, fridge and decor. Prices for simple cabanas range from US$5 to US$25; luxury cabanas can set you back as much as US$100. Simple cabanas are sometimes called palapa*s*.

Hostels

Hostels are less common along the Pacific coast than they are in cities like Oaxaca, Mexico City and San Miguel de Allende. When you do find them – and you will if you visit Oaxaca city – they typically have small dormitories, a relaxed atmosphere, breakfast or café service and often a guest kitchen. A bunk in a dorm can cost US$5 to US$11 and a private double can cost US$13 to US$20.

Hostels offer an alternative to budget or mid-range hotels. For single travelers in particular, they are a good value and a good place to meet other travelers.

Casas de Huéspedes & Posadas

The cheapest, most congenial accommodations are often at a *casa de huéspedes*, a home converted into a simple guesthouse. Good *casas de huéspedes* are family-run, with a relaxed and friendly atmosphere. Rooms may contain a private bathroom or not. A double typically costs US$10 to US$15, though a few places are more comfy and more expensive. Some *posadas* (inns) are like *casas de huéspedes*; others are small hotels.

Hotels

Cheap hotels exist in every Mexican town. There are many clean, friendly ones; there are also dark, dirty, smelly ones. You can get a decent double room with private shower and hot water for less than US$20. Fortunately for small groups of travelers, many hotels have rooms for three, four or five people that cost little more than a double.

Mexico specializes in good mid-range hotels where two people can usually get a room with private bathroom, TV and air-con for US$25 to US$50. Often there's a restaurant and bar.

Among the most charming lodgings are the many old mansions, inns, even convents, turned into hotels. Some date from colonial times, others from the 19th century. Most are atmospheric, with fountains gurgling in old stone courtyards. Some are a bit Spartan (but lower in price), others have been modernized and can be posh and expensive. These are often the lodgings you will remember fondly after your trip.

The coast has plenty of large, modern hotels, especially in the resort towns. They offer the expected levels of luxury at lofty prices. If you like to stay in luxury but also enjoy saving some money, choose a Mexican hotel, not one that's part of an international chain.

Note that *cuarto sencillo* (single room) means a room with one bed, which is often a *cama matrimonial* (double bed). One person can usually occupy such a room for a lower price than two people. A *cuarto doble* is usually a room with two beds, often both 'matrimonial.'

Apartments

Larger, more touristy towns often have short-term *departamentos* or *apartamentos* (both meaning apartments) with fully equipped kitchens. They can be good value for two to four people; you save by cooking your own food. Tourist offices and ads in local papers (especially English-language papers) are good sources of information on apartments.

FOOD

Mexican cuisine is enormously varied, full of regional differences and subtle surprises. You'll eat well in Mexico, and the choice is wide in all sizable towns. In addition to the Mexican fare that we describe here, there's all sorts of international food too, even some good vegetarian restaurants. For inexpensive fresh fruit, vegetables, tortillas, cheese and bread, pop into the local market. See the Food section in the Language chapter for more food information.

In restaurant listings throughout this book we include a price range in terms of 'mains.' By 'mains' we mean main courses only – not full, multicourse meals – and we try to give the average price of dishes on the menu.

Staples

Mexicans eat three meals a day: *desayuno* (breakfast), *comida* (lunch) and *cena* (supper). Each includes one or more of three national staples: *tortillas, frijoles* and *chiles.*

Tortillas are thin round patties of pressed *maíz* (corn) or *harina* (wheat-flour) dough cooked on griddles. Both can be wrapped around or served under any type of food. Frijoles are beans, eaten boiled, fried or refried in soups, on tortillas, or with just about anything.

Chiles are spicy-hot chili peppers; they come in dozens of varieties and can be consumed in hundreds of ways. Some types, such as the *habanero* and *jalapeño*, are always very hot, while others, such as the *poblano*, vary in spiciness according to when they were picked. If you are unsure about your tolerance for hot chili, ask if they are *dulce* (sweet), *picante* (hot), or *muy picante* (very hot).

Street & Market Meals

The cheapest food in Mexico is served up by the thousands of street stands selling all manner of hot and cold food and drinks. At these places you can often get a taco or a glass of orange juice for less than US$0.50. Many are popular and well patronized, but hygiene can be a risk. Deciding whether to use them is a matter of judgment; those with a lot of customers are likely to be the best and safest.

A notch up from street fare are the *comedores* found in many markets. They offer Mexico's cheapest sit-down meals – you sit on benches at long tables and the food is prepared in front of you. Usually comedores serve typical local fare, and – at the best ones – it's like home cooking. It's best to go at lunchtime, when ingredients are fresher; and pick a *comedor* that's busy, which usually means it's good.

Breakfast

The simplest breakfast is coffee or tea and *pan dulce* (sweet rolls), a basket of which is set on the table; you pay for the number consumed. Many restaurants offer combination breakfasts for about US$2 to US$4, typically composed of *jugo de fruta* (fruit juice), *café* (coffee), *bolillo* (bread roll) or *pan tostado* (toast) with *mantequilla* (butter) and *mermelada* (jam), and *huevos* (eggs, which are served in a variety of ways) and frijoles. You can usually substitute tortillas for toast.

Mexicans often eat meat for breakfast, but in many places frequented by travelers, granola, *ensalada de frutas* (fruit salad), *avena* (porridge) and even Corn Flakes are available.

Lunch

La comida, the main meal of the day, is usually served between 1pm and 4pm or 5pm. Most restaurants offer not only a la carte fare but also special fixed-price menus called *comida corrida, cubierto* or *menú del día*. These menus constitute the best food bargains because you get several courses (often with some choice) for much less than such a meal would cost a la carte. Prices may range from US$1.50 at a market comedor for a simple meal of soup, a meat dish, rice and coffee, to US$10 or more for elaborate meals beginning with oyster stew and finishing with cream-puffs. Typically you'll get four or five courses for US$2.50 to US$4.50. Drinks usually cost extra.

Dinner/Supper

La cena, the evening meal, is usually lighter than the comida. Fixed-price meals are rarely offered, so you can usually save money by eating your principal meal at lunchtime.

Snacks

Antojitos, or 'little whims' – nowadays called *especialidades mexicanas* or *platillos mexicanos* on some menus – are traditional Mexican snacks or light dishes. Some are actually small meals in themselves. They can be eaten at any time, on their own or as part of a larger meal. There are many, many varieties, some of which are peculiar to local areas.

Soup

There are many *sopas* (soups) made from meats, vegetables and seafoods. Some are light and served as starters, such as *caldo de pollo* (chicken broth soup). Others are meals in themselves such as *pozole,* a hearty hominy stew with meat, vegetables and lots of garnishing (see 'Holy Pozole!' in the Ixtapa & Zihuatanejo city section). Note that *sopa de arroz* (literally 'rice soup') is not soup at all but rice pilaf.

Seafood

Seafood, in its infinite variety, is a principal attraction of Mexico's Pacific coast. It's almost always fresh along the coast (though you should turn your bad-fish-radar on around slow restaurants in the low season) and served in whopping portions.

It is often eaten as a *filete* (filet), *frito* (fried whole fish), or – the coastal classic – *al mojo de ajo* (fried in oil or butter and garlic). Fish served *al mojo de ajo* is often excellent, almost always on the menu, and often the least expensive, depending, of course, on the type of fish you request.

Ceviche, the popular Mexican cocktail, is raw seafood (fish, shrimp etc) marinated in lime and mixed with onions, chilis, garlic and tomatoes. In some ceviches the lime marinade is light and fresh; in other recipes

a thicker tomato base is used, giving it a different flavor altogether. There are countless other seafood *cocteles* (cocktails) as well.

Meat & Poultry

Meat and poultry are often listed separately as *carnes* and *aves* on Mexican menus.

Bistec or *bistec de res* are generic terms for beefsteak. *Tasajo* is a thin slice of pounded beef that is usually grilled and sometimes fried. *Carne asada* is almost always grilled beef, often chopped and served in tacos or other *antojitos*.

Cerdo or *puerco* (pork) is served in countless ways, a favorite being *carnitas,* a specialty of Michoacán that involves slow-roasting an entire pig and selling it by the kilogram or serving it in tacos and such.

Chicken is popular and is served with a variety of sauces, from *salsa de cacahuete* (peanut sauce) to one of the seven delicious Oaxacan *moles* (sauces; see the boxed text 'Cocina Oaxaqueña' in the Oaxaca chapter for more information). Rotisserie and barbequed chicken are often sold cheaply at *rosticerías* (roast chicken eateries). You can order a *pechuga de pollo* (chicken breast), a *cuarto de pollo* (quarter chicken) or, if you're hungry, a *pollo entero* (an entire chicken).

Vegetables

Legumbres (legumes) and *verduras* (vegetables) are usually mixed into salads, soups and sauces or used as garnishes. But there are still plenty of options for vegetarians, and many Mexican towns have good vegetarian restaurants.

DRINKS

In a country with a climate as warm as Mexico's, quenching your thirst is an important activity, and Mexicans have invented some delicious ways of doing it. A huge variety of *bebidas* (drinks) are imbibed in Mexico. Don't drink any water, ice or drinks made with water unless you know the water has been purified or boiled (see the Health section, earlier in this chapter). You can buy bottles of inexpensive purified or mineral water everywhere.

Nonalcoholic Drinks

Ordinary Mexican *café*, grown mostly near Córdoba and Orizaba and in Chiapas, is flavorful but often served weak. Those addicted to stronger caffeine shots should ask for 'Nescafé' – unless they're lucky enough to be in one of the real coffeehouses that are now appearing. A few of these serve Mexican organic coffee, from Oaxaca or Chiapas. *Té* (tea), invariably in bags, is a profound disappointment to any real tea drinker, except in its herbal variations.

Pure fresh *jugos* (juices) are popular in Mexico and readily available from streetside stalls and juice bars. If you see the fruit being squeezed in front of you, as is often the case, it will almost certainly be safe to drink. Every fruit and a few of the squeezable vegetables are used.

Licuados are blends of fruit or juice with water and sugar. *Licuados con leche* use milk instead of water. The delicious combinations are practically limitless. In juice bars you can expect that *agua purificada* (purified water) is used, but don't assume the same for streetside juice stalls.

Aguas de fruta (also called *aguas frescas* or *aguas preparadas*) are made by adding sugar and water to fruit juice or a syrup made from mashed grains or seeds. You'll often see them in big glass jars on the counters of juice stands. *Horchata* is a delicious sweetened rice drink cooked with cinnamon and milk or water and served chilled.

Atole is a sweet, hot drink thickened with *masa* (corn dough) and flavored with chocolate, cinnamon or various fruits. It is often consumed at breakfast with *tamales*.

Refrescos are bottled or canned sodas, and there are some interesting and tasty local varieties.

Many brands of *agua mineral* (mineral water) are derived from Mexican springs – Tehuacán and Garci Crespo are two of the best and can sometimes be obtained with refreshing flavors, as well as plain.

Alcoholic Drinks

Mexico produces a fascinating variety of alcoholic drinks made from grapes, grains and – in the case of mezcal – lilies. Foreign liquors are widely available, too.

Mezcal, Tequila & Pulque Mezcal can be made from the sap of several species of the maguey plant, a member of the lily family with long, thick spikes sticking out of the ground. Tequila is a type of mezcal made only from the maguey *Agave tequilana weber*, grown in Jalisco and a few other states. The production method for both is similar, except that for mezcal the chopped up *piña* (core) of the plant is baked, whereas for tequila it's steamed. The final product is a clear liquid (sometimes artificially tinted) which is at its most potent as tequila. The longer the aging process, the smoother the drink and the higher the price. A *gusano* (worm) is added to many bottles of mezcal.

For foreigners who are not used to the potency of straight tequila, Mexican bartenders invented the margarita, a concoction of tequila, lime juice and liqueur served in a salt-rimmed glass. *Sangrita* is a sweet, nonalcoholic, tomato, citrus, chile and spice drink often downed as a tequila chaser.

Pulque is a cheap drink derived directly from the sap of several species of maguey, different from those that produce tequila and mezcal. Far less potent than tequila or mezcal, it is a foamy, milky, slightly sour liquid, which spoils quickly and cannot easily be bottled and shipped. Most pulque is produced around Mexico City and served in male-dominated, working-class *pulquerías*.

Beer & Wine Breweries were established in Mexico by German immigrants in the late 19th century. Mexico's several large brewing companies produce more than 25 brands of *cerveza* (beer), some of which are excellent. Each major company has a premium beer, such as Bohemia and Corona de Barril (usually served in bottles); several standard beers, such as Carta Blanca, Superior and Dos Equis ('Two Xs'); and 'popular' brands, such as Corona, Tecate and Modelo. Brands that are popular along the coast include Sol, Pacífico (from Mazatlán) and Indio. All are blond lagers meant to be served chilled. Each of the large companies also produces an *oscura* (dark) beer, such as Negra Modelo or Dos Equis Oscura. There are some regional beers, too, brewed to similar tastes.

Wine is far less popular than beer and tequila. The country's most significant wineries – LA Cetto, Pedro Domecq and Bodegas de Santo Tomás – are all around Ensenada in Baja California. Their wines can be found on menus in upscale restaurants and stores. Wine mixed with fruit juice is the basis of the tasty *sangría*.

Drinking Places Everyone knows about Mexican cantinas, those pits of wild drinking and wilder displays of machismo, where a man might draw his pistol and fire several rounds into the ceiling without anyone taking notice – well...cantinas are generally loud but not quite that loud. They are usually for men only – no women or children are allowed. They rarely have 'Cantina' signs outside, but can be identified by Wild West-type swinging half-doors, signs prohibiting minors, and a raucous atmosphere. Those who enter must be prepared to drink hard. They might be challenged by a local to go one-for-one at a bottle of tequila, mezcal or brandy. If you're not up to that, excuse yourself and beat it.

Some of the nicer 'cantinas' don't get upset about the presence of a woman if she is accompanied by a regular patron. Leave judgment of the situation up to a local, though.

Apart from cantinas, Mexico has lots of bars, lounges, 'pubs' and cafés where all are welcome.

In fact most Mexican drinking establishments are far less daunting than cantinas. A relatively recent innovation is the 'pub' – usually a place with recorded rock or dance music and a themed decor of some kind, geared to a young social crowd.

ENTERTAINMENT

Little beats a Mexican fiesta for entertainment, but if none is being celebrated you have plenty of alternatives. In larger cities and especially the resorts like Acapulco, the range of entertainment is vast. You'll find throbbing mega-discos with space-age light shows and music bars with live rock, toe-tappin' jazz or fiery *salsa* jams. Country-western theme bars with straw-covered floors and blaring *norteño, banda* and *ranchera* music are all the rage (though usually ignored by the wealthy). Mariachi bands make their rounds through busy restaurants, meaning you'll rarely lack for dinner entertainment if you pay for a song or two. *'Canta-bars'* (karaoke bars) are everywhere. Drag shows and *travesti* (transvestite) clubs are outrageously popular in cities like Mazatlán and Acapulco (which have a few famous ones). *Trova,* a word that now means folk music, can be heard live at many cafés and bars. And people-watching from a café on a plaza is tough to beat.

In the big cities you'll find Spanish-language theater, ballet and classical concerts. Cinemas screen many foreign movies, always in their original language (usually English), with Spanish subtitles. Seeing a matinee movie in a small-town theater full of bouncy, food-chomping children is a blast.

Try not to leave Mexico without seeing a performance of Mexican folk dance. If you can't catch a dance in its natural setting – at a fiesta – you can see one at a major hotel in most coastal resorts; though these can be touristy, they're always colorful and interesting and allow you to witness an essence of Mexican culture. Called *ballet folklórico* or *danza folkórica* they're often part of a *Fiesta Mexicana* if performed at a resort. A Fiesta Mexicana is a party for tourists, usually with dinner, drinks, dancing, bloodless cockfighting demonstrations, and dance performances. They cost anywhere from US$20 without dinner to US$40 with dinner and an open bar. See Arts in the Facts about Mexico's Pacific Coast chapter for more about folk dance.

SPECTATOR SPORTS

Events such as soccer games, bullfights and *charreadas* (rodeos) can be fascinating; if the action doesn't enthrall you, the crowd probably will.

Fútbol (football, soccer) is the country's favorite sport. Mexico has an 18-team national Primera División, and some rather impressive stadiums. Mexico City's Estadio Azteca (Aztec Stadium) hosted the 1970 and 1986 World Cup finals.

The two most popular teams in the country are América, of Mexico City, nicknamed Las Águilas (the Eagles), and Guadalajara (Las Chivas, the Goats). They attract large followings wherever they play. The biggest games of the year are when they play each other, an event known as 'Los Clásicos.' Games are spaced over the weekend from Friday to Sunday; details are printed in the *News* and the Spanish-language press. Attending a game is fun and rivalry between opposing fans is good-humored. Tickets can be bought at the gate and can cost from less than US$1 to US$10, depending on the quality of your seat.

Professional *béisbol* (baseball) is fairly popular. The winner of the October to January Liga Mexicana del Pacífico (W www .ligadelpacifico.com.mx), with teams from the northwest, represents Mexico in the February Serie del Caribe (the biggest event in Latin American baseball) against the champions of Venezuela, Puerto Rico and the Dominican Republic. The Liga Mexicana de Béisbol (W www.lmb.com.mx), with 16 teams spread down the center and east of the country from Monclova to Cancún, plays from March to September.

A charreada is a rodeo, held particularly in the northern half of the country during fiestas and at regular venues that are often called *lienzos charros*.

SHOPPING

Mexico is so richly endowed with appealing *artesanías* (handicrafts) that few visitors can make it home without at least one pair of earrings or a little wooden animal. Because the Pacific coast is a popular tourist destination, you'll find all sorts of shops and *mercados de artesanías* (artisans' markets) selling handicrafts from all over the country, often at good prices. If you buy crafts from individual vendors on the streets, then a lot more of the profit will go to the (usually poor) people who make them, instead of to entrepreneurs. If you're traveling throughout the states of Guerrero,

Michoacán, Nayarit and Oaxaca – which produce some of the country's finest crafts – you can even purchase *artesanías* in the villages where they are made, often directly from the artisans themselves.

Regardless of where you buy crafts, always inspect their quality and never be afraid to bargain. From around Mexico here are just a few of the many crafts to keep an eye out for:

Animalitos & Alebrijes Animalitos are tiny, light-brown and rust-colored ceramic animals from Chiapas. Alebrijes are little multicolored figurines from Oaxaca.

Baskets & Hats Colorful, homemade baskets of multifarious sizes are great for carrying other souvenirs home. The Mexican straw *sombrero* (literally 'shade maker') is a classic souvenir.

Ceramics The Guadalajara suburbs of Tonalá and Tlaquepaque are renowned pottery centers. Watch for the distinctive black pottery from San Bartolo Coyotepec, Oaxaca.

Hammocks The best are the tightly woven, cotton, thin-string ones from the Yucatán and Oaxaca.

Huaraches Sandals! Can't spend any time on the coast without a pair of these. Guadalajara is known for good huaraches.

Huipiles Sleeveless tunics for women, mostly made in the southern states. They're often embroidered and wonderfully colorful. Coastal Mixtec and Amuzgos of Oaxaca are famous for them.

Jewelry Silverwork from the central Mexican town of Taxco is sold everywhere.

Masks Guerrero is famous for its masks, as are the villages of San Juan Colorado and Huazolotitlán, Oaxaca.

Rug weavings Those from Teotitlán del Valle, Oaxaca are most famous.

Serapes An indigenous men's garment worn over the shoulders – essentially a blanket with an opening for the head.

Skulls & Skeletons These crafty creations come in all shapes, sizes and materials, and have their origin in the November 2 Día de los Muertos (Day of the Dead) festival. Now they're everywhere.

For everyday purchases, wealthier urban Mexicans like to shop in glitzy modern malls, big supermarkets and department stores. These are usually in residential districts. In city centers you're more likely to find smaller, older shops and markets, which are probably more fun in any case.

Activities

Mexico's Pacific coast is an orgy of outdoor fun. Sport fishing, diving, snorkeling, sailing, jet skiing, water-skiing, parasailing and swimming have allured sun-seekers to this spectacular shoreline for decades. But in recent years people have started to realize there's even *more* to do: kayaking, surfing, hiking, mountain biking, river rafting and wildlife viewing are becoming increasingly popular. To help plan your travels, we've compiled a brief introduction to where and how you can get active on the coast. None of them should distract you, however, from putting some serious hours in under the sun, flat on your back, down on the beach.

Refer to this book's destination sections for details on equipment rentals, and availability and advisability of guides. The Books section in the Facts for the Visitor chapter mentions some useful guidebooks for hikers, divers and nature lovers.

Good Internet sources on active-tourism agencies in Mexico are **Eco Travels in Latin America** (**w** www.planeta.com) and **Mexico Online** (**w** www.mexonline.com). **Amtave** (**w** www.amtave.com) is a grouping of more than 80 Mexican adventure-travel and ecotourism operators. Its website is packed with information.

DIVING & SNORKELING

Though it's tough to compete with the azure waters and coral reefs of the Caribbean, there are some outstanding dive sites unique to the Pacific coast – and plenty of dazzling snorkel spots. Mazatlán, Puerto Vallarta, Barra de Navidad, Manzanillo, Zihuatanejo, Playa Manzanillo (Troncones), Faro de Bucerías, Puerto Escondido, Puerto Ángel and Bahías de Huatulco all have highly praised dive sites nearby, as well as some first-rate outfitters that will tank you up and take you out. Operators generally charge around US$50 for a guided one-tank dive, around US$80 for a two-tank dive and around US$60 for a night dive.

Many outfitters are affiliates of the international dive-instructor organizations **PADI** (**w** www.padi.com) or **NAUI** (**w** www.naui.org) and post their certifications in plain view. Both organizations' websites allow you to search for their affiliated dive shops in Mexico. **FMAS** (*Federación Mexicana de Actividades Subacuáticas;* **w** www.fmas.org.mx), also internationally recognized, is the Mexican equivalent of PADI and NAUI. Be wary of unlicensed dive shops that promise certification after just a few hours' tuition.

Most dive shops offer guided snorkeling excursions, or rent snorkel equipment so you can go it alone. On beaches with good snorkeling nearby, restaurants and booths usually rent equipment, though you should check gear carefully for quality and comfort before heading out for the day. There are plenty of places to snorkel without a guide, but with a guide, you're usually taken by boat to better, hard-to-reach spots.

Safety Guidelines for Diving

Before embarking on a scuba-diving trip, carefully consider the following points to ensure a safe and enjoyable experience:

- Obtain a current diving certification card from a recognized scuba-diving instructional agency, either at home or from one of many in Mexico.
- Make sure that you are comfortable diving.
- Obtain reliable information about physical and environmental conditions at the dive site (eg, from a reputable local dive operation).
- Be aware of local laws, regulations and etiquette about marine life and the environment.
- Dive only at sites within your realm of experience; if available, hire a competent, professionally trained instructor or dive master.
- Be aware that underwater conditions vary significantly from one region, or even site, to another. Seasonal changes can significantly alter any site and dive conditions. These differences influence the way divers dress for a dive and what diving techniques they use.
- Ask about the environmental characteristics that can affect your diving and how local trained divers deal with these considerations.

The **Divers Alert Network** *(DAN;* W *www .diversalertnetwork.org)* has a comprehensive divers' health section on its website that is well worth a peek before your plunge.

FISHING

Mexico's Pacific coast has world-famous billfishing (marlin, swordfish, sailfish) and outstanding light-tackle fishing year-round. Many deep-sea charters now practice catch-and-release for billfish, a practice we highly recommend because these majestic lords of the deep are being disastrously overfished.

When & Where to Fish

You can catch fish in these waters year round, but what, how many, where and when depend on such variables as water temperature, currents, bait supply and fish migrations. In general, the biggest catches occur from April to July and between October and December. Keep in mind that summer and late fall is also prime tropical storm and hurricane season.

Mazatlán, 'the billfish capital of the world,' is famous for marlin, and Puerto Vallarta is known for sailfish; both offer big catches of yellowfin tuna, *dorado* (dolphinfish or mahi mahi), red snapper and black sea bass. In Zihuatanejo, sailfish, marlin, dorado, roosterfish and wahoo are caught most of the year, and the biggest tuna catches are in spring. In Bahías de Huatulco swordfish, sailfish and dorado are caught year-round, while marlin are caught mostly from October to May; roosterfish season is April to August.

Plenty of other light-tackle fish are caught year-round along the entire coast, including yellowtail, grouper, sierra, corvina, halibut and wahoo.

Charters

Fishing charters are available in all major resort towns and you'll find reputable local companies listed throughout this book. Always ask what's included in the rates. Fishing licenses, tackle, crew and ice are standard, but sometimes charters also include bait, cleaning and freezing, meals, drinks and tax. Live bait – usually available dockside for a few dollars – should be checked for absolute freshness. Tips for the crew are at your discretion, but US$15 to US$20 (per angler) for a successful eight hours is considered adequate. Bring along a hat, sunscreen, polarized sunglasses and Dramamine (or equivalent) if you suffer from seasickness. Make sure the toilet situation is up to your standards of privacy.

Prices depend on boat type and size. The most comfortable is the cruiser, usually 26 to 42 feet (8.6m to 14m) in length and equipped with everything from fighting chairs (to reel in the big fish) to fish-finders and a full head. Prices range from US$350 to US$500 per boat for an eight-hour day.

The cheapest boats are *pangas*, the vessel of choice of Mexican commercial fishermen, as they put you right up close with the sea. About 18 to 24 feet (6m to 8m) long, these sturdy skiffs hold three to four people and cost between US$150 and US$200. Super *pangas* are larger, accommodate four to six fishers comfortably and often feature toilets and a canvas top for shade. Rates start around US$300 per day per boat.

Licenses & Bag Limits

Anyone aboard a private vessel carrying fishing gear, on the ocean and in estuaries, must have a Mexican fishing license whether they're fishing or not. Licenses are almost always included on charters, but you'll need your own if you choose to hire a local fisherman to take you out. In Mexico, licenses are issued by the **Oficina de Pesca**, which has offices in most towns. They can also be obtained in the USA from the **Mexican Fisheries Department** *(☎ 619-233-6956, fax 233-0344; 2550 5th Ave, Suite 101, San Diego, CA 92103)*. The cost of the license at the time of research was US$11 per day, US$22 per week and US$30 per month. Prices are subject to change every six months.

The daily bag limit is 10 fish per person with no more than five of any one species. Billfish (like marlin, sailfish and swordfish) are restricted to one per day per boat, while for dorado, tarpon, roosterfish and halibut it's two.

Surf Fishing

Surf fishing is a fun – though not always easy – way to put food in your stomach, *especially* when you're camping. No license is required when fishing from land, as many Mexicans still make their livelihood this way. You don't have to bring a pole, just find a local tackle shop (they're in any sizable fishing town, and some are listed in this book) and purchase a hand-reel (a small piece of wood wrapped with fishing line) or

Here, Fishy Fishy Fish...

Who's gonna believe you if you can't even tell 'em what kind of fish you caught? This little angler's glossary should help. It will also help you communicate with Mexican guides and captains, who can usually tell you what you're most likely to catch. Keep in mind, some terms are regional. Sea bass, for instance might be called 'robalo', 'cabrilla' or 'corvina', depending on who you talk to.

barracuda	*picuda*
black marlin	*marlín negro*
blue marlin	*marlín azul*
bonito	*bonito*
dolphin fish (mahi mahi)	*dorado*
grouper	*garropa, mero*
halibut	*lenguado*
mullet	*lisa*
red snapper	*huachinango, pargo*
roosterfish	*pez gallo*
sailfish	*pez vela*
sea bass	*robalo, cabrilla, corvina*
shark	*tiburón*
sierra	*Spanish mackerel*
striped marlin	*marlín rayado*
swordfish	*pez espada*
tuna	*atún*
wahoo	*peto, guahu*
yellowtail	*jurel*
yellowfin tuna	*atún de aleta*

The phrase that will serve you most, however, may turn out to be: *'se me fue'* – 'it got away.' Then throw your hands up and say *'lo juro!'* ('I swear it!').

rollo de nylon (spool of nylon) and some hooks, lures and weights. Some tackle shops sell live bait and *carnada* (raw bait), and it's often sold near the town pier. Shrimp and other raw baits are sold cheaply in the central markets.

Surf fishing is almost always better from rocks than it is from the sand. With your hand reel in one hand let out some line, grab it with the other hand, swing it around your head (this takes practice) and let it go. Even if you fail horribly, it's a good way to meet local fishers who might give you a few tips.

SURFING

Describing all the epic surf spots on Mexico's Pacific coast would be as arduous as paddling out against a double-overhead set at Zicatela Beach – well, almost. From the 'world's longest wave' near San Blas, to the screaming barrels of Puerto Escondido's 'Mexican Pipeline,' the Pacific coast is bombarded with surf. Sayulita, Barra de Navidad, Manzanillo, Boca de Pascuales, Playa La Ticla, Barra de Nexpa, Playa Azul, Playa Troncones, Saladita, Ixtapa, Playa Revolcadero, Chacahua, Barra de la Cruz – the list goes on and on.

Most beach breaks receive some sort of surf all year, but wave season is really May to October/November. Spring and fall can see excellent conditions with fewer people, while the biggest months are June, July and August, when waves can get *huge,* and the sets roll like clockwork.

Shipping a surfboard to Mexico is not a problem, but most airlines charge at least US$50, and some will hit you for another US$50 on your way home – even if they told you they wouldn't; be ready.

A good board-bag is advisable, but a better one doesn't necessarily guarantee fewer mishaps on the aircraft. We've talked to people who've shipped their boards in what amounted to socks and escaped ding-free, while others have blown half their vacation funds on a super-bag to open it to the tune of a broken skeg. They're usually fine, however. You'll rarely, if ever, need a wetsuit, but a rashguard is highly recommended for protection against the sun. Bring plenty

PACIFIC COAST SURF SPOTS

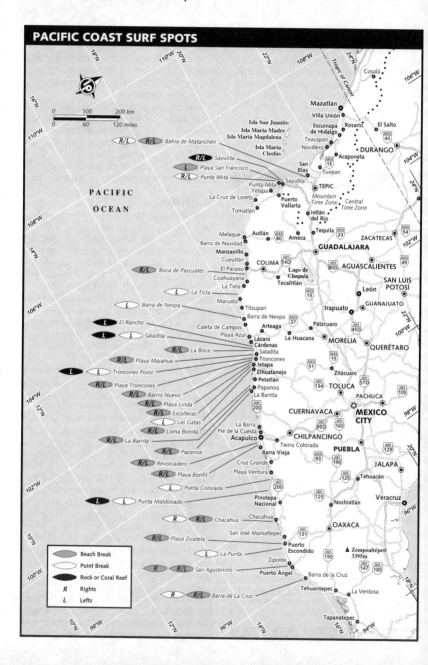

of warm-water wax, as it's tough to find south of the border. Soft racks (or some sort of packable tie-downs) are easy to carry and indispensable if you plan to do any driving (or want to secure your board to a taxi). Unless you plan to surf one spot only, renting a car (or driving your own) makes everything much easier.

KAYAKING, CANOEING & RAFTING

The coastal lagoons and sheltered bays of the Pacific coast are magnificent waters for kayaks and canoes. If you have your own boat you'll be in heaven. If you don't, don't worry – many places rent kayaks and provide guides and transportation to boot. Lagunas de Chacahua National Park, Laguna de Manialtepec, Barra de la Cruz (near Bahías de Huatulco), La Manzanilla, and Barra de Navidad are all places with brackish, bird-filled, mangrove-fringed lagoons just waiting to be paddled. Outfitters in Puerto Escondido, Sayulita and Puerto Vallarta take folks for some excellent kayaking trips. You can also rent kayaks and/or canoes and paddle off on your own at these and other places, including Bucerías, Cruz de Huanacaxtle (both near Puerto Vallarta) and Pie de la Cuesta, near Acapulco.

White-water rafting is practiced from June to November on the Copalita and Zimatán Rivers near Bahías de Huatulco; several outfitters there offer excursions.

WILDLIFE & BIRD-WATCHING

Observing the varied and exotic fauna of Mexico's Pacific coast is an increasingly popular and increasingly practicable pastime. See Flora & Fauna in the Facts about Mexico's Pacific Coast chapter for additional information on the creatures that inhabit the coast.

Sea Turtles

There are numerous places to spy on sea turtles, but you have to know where and when to go looking. One of the best places to see black sea turtles is Playa Maruata, Michoacan, where they come ashore nightly from June to December to lay their eggs. Open

June to February, the sea turtle protection project at La Cruz de Loreto, near Puerto Vallarta, is a great place to get up close to sea turtles. So is the interesting Centro Mexicano de la Tortuga, a turtle museum in Mazunte, Oaxaca. You might spot a giant leatherback turtle on one of several Oaxacan beaches or from a skiff during a snorkeling trip – especially the trips offered in Puerto Ángel. The small olive ridley turtle migrates to Oaxacan beaches by the hundreds of thousands. For protection reasons some beaches (most notably Playa Ventanilla) are guarded during nesting season and off-limits to tourists. But chances of seeing them at other beaches are still quite high. See the boxed text 'Mexico's Turtles' in the Oaxaca chapter for tips on avoiding disrupting nesting turtles if you happen to find yourself on a nesting beach.

Whale-Watching

Between November and March, humpback whales migrate to Pacific Mexico to mate and calve. Puerto Vallarta's Bahía de Banderas is one of their most-popular stomping grounds, and a whale-watching trip from one of the city's many operators can bring you almost within kissing distance. Other great places for whale-watching (which all have outfits offering seasonal trips out to sea) include Chacala, Rincón de Guayabitos and Bucerías, all near Puerto Vallarta. Even from the shore, it's not uncommon to see breaching whales along the entire coast during the first few months of the year.

Bird-Watching

If you're not a bird-watcher, this is the perfect place to experience the rush that makes birders so fanatical. A morning float around one of the coast's many lagoons, with abundant birdlife, is an unforgettable experience. And if you do it in winter, not only will you see the native waterfowl, you'll see the North American and Alaskan species that migrate here as well. See Flora & Fauna in the Facts about Mexico's Pacific Coast chapter for some of the birds you might see.

The swamp forests and lagoons around San Blas are ideal for bird-watching, and there's a bird sanctuary in the nearby San Cristóbal estuary. The island of Isla Isabel, four hours from San Blas by boat, is a bird-watcher's dream. Laguna de Manialtepec in Oaxaca is another wetland bird habitat that will truly send you over the edge. There are estuary wetlands flapping with birds near La Cruz de Loreto (south of Puerto Vallarta), Playa La Ticla (Michoacán) and Barra de Potosí in Guerrero. In Oaxaca, the pair of giant lagoons in Lagunas de Chacahua National Park, and the tiny lagoon of Barra de la Cruz near Bahías de Huatulco, are two other places offering plenty of chances to sneak up on birds. Inland, Laguna Santa María del Oro, a lake at 750m elevation near Tepic, is home to some 250 species of bird, and its mountainous surroundings make a wonderful contrast to coastal ecology.

Most outfitters offering bird-watching tours do not provide binoculars – pack your own if this activity is on your agenda.

HIKING

Mexico's beaches make outstanding places in which to hike. The 13km beach in Parque Nacional Lagunas de Chacahua, Oaxaca; Playa Larga near Zihuatanejo; and the endless, empty beaches of Michoacán are great for stretching the legs. Many villages on the coast have back roads or nearby trails you can explore by foot.

Some great hikes can be had inland too (if you can drag yourself away from the beach). Near Tepic, Nayarit, Laguna Santa María del Oro, an idyllic lake in a 50m-deep volcanic crater, and the terrain around the extinct Volcán Ceboruco, both offer superb settings for various levels of hike. Parque Nacional Volcán Nevado de Colima, in Colima, has more good hiking. The Valles Centrales of Oaxaca are popular for guided hikes between mountain villages; they're offered by several operators based in Oaxaca city.

MOUNTAIN BIKING

Shops rent mountain bikes up and down the coast, but you're usually left to your own intuition about where to explore. Troncones, Zihuatanejo, Manzanillo, Playa Azul, San Blas, Sayulita, La Crucecita (Bahías de Huatulco) and many other coastal towns have bike rentals and are small enough places that you can navigate through town and into open terrain without the fear of being run down. You can often ride from one fishing village to another, stopping in each for a beer or a bite to eat (Troncones to Saladita comes to mind here). Oaxaca has become very popular for mountain biking and several Oaxaca city operators listed in the Oaxaca chapter will take you for some beautiful rides along old mountain roads to visit tiny villages.

On the Internet, **Eco Travels in Latin America** (**w** www.planeta.com) has a 'Mexico Biking Guide.' Also see Organized Tours in the Facts for the Visitor chapter for outfitters offering some great multiday cycling trips.

HORSE RIDING

Its hard to beat a trot down the beach on a rusty, old trusty Mexican stud. Horses are rented on countless beaches along the coast. Puerto Vallarta, Troncones, Zihuatanejo, Pie de la Cuesta and Bahías de Huatulco are just a few of the places where you can mount up for about US$15 to US$30 per person for a two- to three-hour guided ride. Some places will allow you to take horses on your own if you leave a small deposit and an ID. Mexican horses tend to be a bit smaller, more worn out and less inclined to run than their North American and European counterparts, but they can still be fun. Keep in mind that if a guide accompanies you, the money he or she makes is often primarily what riders tip them; around US$5 per person is usually sufficient.

GOLF & TENNIS

Mazatlán, Puerto Vallarta, Ixtapa, Acapulco and Bahías de Huatulco all have world-class golf courses where you can swing the old irons to some spectacular views. But you'll pay a pretty price to do it: green fees run anywhere from US$60 to US$200. Carts and caddies – which are often required – can cost an additional US$30 to US$50, depending on the course.

These same resorts all have numerous tennis clubs, many of which are found in the luxury hotels. Nonhotel guests are almost always welcome to use the courts for about US$15 per hour and can rent racquets on the spot.

OTHER ACTIVITIES

Water-skiing, parasailing and 'banana' riding are widespread resort activities, especially in Acapulco, Puerto Vallarta, Zihuatanejo, Mazatlán and Bahías de Huatulco. Many of the larger resort hotels – if they're located on a bay – rent sailboats and catamarans too. Laguna de Coyuca, at Pie de la Cuesta, is famous for water-skiing and has several operators that will zip you around the lagoon. Always cast an eye over the equipment before taking off.

Adrenaline junkies can bungee jump from a platform over sea cliffs near Puerto Vallarta or from a crane-top in the middle of the hotel district in Acapulco – great for those margarita hangovers!

Getting There & Away

AIR

Most visitors to Mexico's Pacific coast arrive by air.

Airports & Airlines

Acapulco, Mazatlán, Puerto Vallarta, Ixtapa/Zihuatanejo and Manzanillo all receive direct flights from North America. To Bahías de Huatulco, the main airport on the Oaxacan coast, and to Oaxaca city, connections are via Mexico City. Many direct flights from North America also fly to Guadalajara.

Airlines with the most services from the north to the coastal resorts are Air Canada, Alaska Airlines, American Airlines, America West, Continental Airlines, Delta Air Lines, Northwest Airlines, and the Mexican airlines Aeroméxico and Mexicana. You can fly to Mexico's Pacific coast without changing planes from at least a dozen US cities, and get a single-connection flight from just about anywhere in the country. There are also direct flights (most of them charters) from at least six Canadian cities.

There are no direct flights from Europe – most connect through Mexico City or Los Angeles. Aeroméxico, Air France, British Airways, Iberia, KLM–Royal Dutch Airlines and Lufthansa Airlines are among the airlines with connections via Mexico City; US airlines connect via Los Angeles.

From Central American and South American countries, you generally have to change planes in Mexico City.

Buying Tickets

The cost of flying to Mexico's Pacific coast depends on where you are flying from and to, what time of year you fly (you pay more around Christmas and New Year's and during the summer holidays), how long you're traveling (usually the longer the trip, the more expensive) and whether you have access to discount or advance-purchase fares or special offers.

Shop for airfares as soon as you can; the cheapest tickets often have to be bought months in advance, and popular flights sell out early. There is little to be gained by buying a ticket direct from the airline. Discounted tickets are released to discount agencies and travel agencies, and these are usually the cheapest deals going. Airlines sometimes have promotional fares and special offers, but generally they sell fares at the official listed price. An exception to this is on the Internet; some airlines offer excellent online fares.

Many travel agencies have websites too, which can make the Internet an easy way to compare prices. There is also an increasing number of online agencies. Online ticket sales work well for a simple one-way or return trip on specified dates. But they're no substitute for a travel agent who knows about special deals and can offer advice on other aspects of your trip.

You may find the cheapest flights are advertised by obscure agencies. Most are honest and solvent, but there are some rogue outfits around. Paying by credit card generally offers protection, as most card issuers provide refunds if you can prove you didn't get what you paid for. Similar protection can be obtained by buying from a bonded agency, such as one covered by the Air Travel Organisers' License (ATOL) scheme (W www.atoll.org.uk) in the UK. Agents who accept only cash should hand over the tickets straight away. After you've made a booking or paid your deposit, call the airline and confirm that the booking was made. To avoid rip-offs, it's not advisable to send money (even checks) through the mail.

If you purchase a ticket and later want to make changes to your route or get a refund, you need to contact the original travel agency. Airlines only issue refunds to the purchaser of a ticket, usually the travel agent who bought the ticket on your behalf.

Full-time students, people under 26 and some teachers have access to deals by showing a document proving their date of birth or a valid International Student Identity Card (ISIC) when buying a ticket and boarding the plane.

Travelers with Special Needs

If notified early enough, airlines often make special arrangements, such as wheelchair assistance at airports, vegetarian meals, or 'Skycots' or baby food for infants. The disability-friendly website W www.allgohere .com has an airline directory providing information on the facilities offered by various airlines.

Departure Tax

A departure tax equivalent to about US$25 is levied on international flights from Mexico. It's usually included in your ticket cost, but if it isn't, you must pay with cash during airport check-in. Ask your travel agent in advance.

The USA & Canada

Discount travel agencies in the USA and Canada are known as consolidators (although you won't see a sign on the door saying 'Consolidator'). You can locate them through the Yellow Pages or advertisements in newspapers and magazines. San Francisco is the ticket consolidator capital of the USA, although good deals can also be found in Los Angeles, New York and other big cities.

The *New York Times*, *Los Angeles Times*, *Chicago Tribune* and *San Francisco Chronicle* all produce weekly travel sections in which you'll find travel agency ads. In Canada, the *Globe & Mail*, *Toronto Star*, *Montreal Gazette* and *Vancouver Sun* are good places to look for cheap fares.

STA Travel (☎ 800-777-0112; W *www.sta travel.com*) has offices in most major cities throughout the USA.

Travel CUTS (☎ 800-667-2887; W *www .travelcuts.com*) is Canada's national student travel agency and has offices in all major cities.

The following websites post excellent fares (mostly for flights originating in the USA) and are great places to begin research:

Expedia	W www.expedia.com
Onetravel.com	W air.onetravel.com
Orbitz	W www.orbitz.com
Smarter Living	W www.smarterliving.com
Travelocity.com	W www.travelocity.com

Here are some typical return trip, mid-season fares found at one week's notice:

from	to Mazatlán	to Puerto Vallarta	to Acapulco
Chicago	US$485	US$390	US$450
Dallas/ Fort Worth	US$750	US$600	US$605
Los Angeles	US$460	US$355	US$400
Miami	US$658	US$674	US$585
New York	US$1085	US$945	US$1010
Toronto	C$1325	C$1050	C$1010

A possibility is a package-tour flight. Check newspaper travel ads and call a package-tour agency, asking if you can buy 'air only' (just the return air ticket, not the hotel or other features). This is often cheaper than buying a discounted return ticket.

Australia & New Zealand

There are no direct flights from Australia or New Zealand to Mexico. The cheapest way to get there is usually via the USA (normally

Los Angeles). Typical mid-season, return fares from Sydney/Melbourne to any of the three major resorts are A$2200 to A$2700. Check US visa requirements if you're traveling via the USA.

It may be cheaper to keep going round the world on a Round-the-World (RTW) ticket rather than do a U-turn on a return ticket. RTW fares from Sydney or Melbourne, including Mexico, can be had for little more than A$2000.

Two well-known agencies for cheap fares are **STA Travel** (ⓦ *www.statravel.com.au)*, with offices in most major Australian cities and on many university campuses; and **Flight Centre** (ⓦ *www.flightcentre.com.au for Australia;* ⓦ *www.flightcentre.com.nz for New Zealand)*, with offices throughout Australia and New Zealand.

Some discount ticket agencies, particularly smaller ones, advertise cheap airfares in the weekend newspapers, such as the *Age* in Melbourne and the *Sydney Morning Herald*.

The *New Zealand Herald* has a travel section in which travel agencies advertise fares.

Good websites for fares are ⓦ www .travel.com.au and ⓦ www.travel.co.nz.

Europe

Typically, a discounted or advance-purchase return fare from anywhere in Western Europe to Mazatlán, Puerto Vallarta or Acapulco costs between €750 and €850, the cheapest flights being from Paris. Mid-season flights from the UK cost around UK£550.

With a normal return ticket, you can often change the date of the return leg, subject to seat availability, at little or no cost – it's worth checking before you buy the ticket. One-way and open-jaw tickets can be useful if you want to hop from one part of Mexico to another, or between Mexico and elsewhere in the Americas, without backtracking.

Most ticket types are available at discount rates from cheap ticket agencies in Europe's bargain flight centers, like London, Paris

Airline Contact Details

Many airlines have toll-free 800 telephone numbers that you can call from anywhere in Mexico:

airline	website (ⓦ)	telephone (☎)
Aero California	–	55-5207-1392
Aerocaribe	www.aerocaribe.com	800-502-20-00
Aerolíneas Internacionales	–	800-004-17-00
Aerolitoral	www.aeromexico.com	800-021-40-00
Aeromar	www.aeromar.com.mx	800-704-29-00
Aeroméxico	www.aeromexico.com	800-021-40-00
Air Canada	www.aircanada.ca	55-5207-6611
Alaska Airlines	www.alaska-air.com	55-5533-1747
America West	www.americawest.com	800-533-68-62
American Airlines	www.aa.com	800-904-60-00
Aviacsa	–	800-006-22-00
Aviateca	www.grupotaca.com	55-5553-3366
British Airways	www.britishairways.com	800-006-57-00
Continental Airlines	www.continental.com	800-900-50-00
Delta Airlines	www.delta-air.com	55-5279-0909
Iberia	www.iberia.com	55-5130-3030
KLM–Royal Dutch Airlines	www.klm.com	800-900-08-00
Mexicana	www.mexicana.com	800-502-20-00
Northwest Airlines	www.nwa.com	800-225-25-25
United Airlines	www.ual.com	800-003-07-70

and Amsterdam. **STA Travel** (☎ *www.sta travel)* has offices throughout Europe, or you can purchase tickets on its website. Though it specializes in student/youth travel, it can usually find good fares for anyone.

If you're traveling via the USA, remember to check US visa requirements.

The UK Discount air travel is big business in London. Advertisements for many travel agencies appear in the travel pages of the weekend broadsheets (such as the *Sunday Times,* the *Independent* and the *Daily Telegraph*), in *Time Out,* the *Evening Standard* and in the free magazine *TNT.*

An excellent place to start your fare inquiries for Mexico is **Journey Latin America** (☎ *020-8747-3108;* ⓦ *www.journeylat inamerica.co.uk; 12-13 Heathfield Terrace, Chiswick, London W4 4JE).*

Another popular travel agency is **STA Travel** (☎ *020-7361-6262;* ⓦ *www.statravel .co.uk; 86 Old Brompton Rd, London SW7),* which has branches across the country. It sells tickets to all travelers, but caters especially to those aged less than 26 and also to students.

One Internet site well worth investigating for good fares is ⓦ www.ebookers.com.

Continental Europe Agencies specializing in cheap tickets and student/youth travel include the following:

France
Nouvelles Frontières (☎ 08 25 00 08 25; ⓦ www .nouvelles-frontieres.fr) Dozens of offices around the country
OTU Voyages (☎ 01 40 29 12 12; ⓦ www.otu.fr) 39 ave Georges Bernanos, 75005. Paris Youth/ student agency with branches across the country

Germany
STA Travel (☎ 030-311 0950; ⓦ www.statravel.de) Youth/student agency with branches in major cities across the country

Italy
CTS Viaggi (☎ 06-462 0431; ⓦ www.cts.it) Via Genova 16, Rome. Youth/student agency with branches all over Italy

Spain
Halcon Viajes (ⓦ www.halcon-viajes.com) More than 500 branches

Viajes Zeppelin (☎ 902-384 253; ⓦ www.v-zep elin.es) Plaza Santo Domingo 2, 28013 Madrid

A website for airfares from France, Switzerland or Belgium is ⓦ www.degrif tour.com.

South America
For airfares from Argentina, Brazil, Chile, Uruguay or Venezuela, try ⓦ www.viajo.com. Return flights to Acapulco start at US$670 from Caracas, US$950 from Buenos Aires, US$1005 from São Paulo or US$1200 from Lima. Get student/youth fares from:

Argentina
Asatej (☎ 011-4511 8700; ⓦ www.asatej.org) Florida 835, 3rd floor, oficina 320, 1005, Buenos Aires. With 15 other offices in Argentina
Brazil
Student Travel Bureau (☎ 55-21-2512 8577, ⓦ www.stb.com.br) Rua Visconde de Pirajá 550, Ipanema, Rio de Janeiro. With 28 other branches around Brazil
Venezuela
IVI Tours (☎ 02-993 6082, ⓦ www.ividiomas.com) Residencia La Hacienda, Piso Bajo, Local 1-4T, Final Av Principal de las Mercedes, Caracas.

LAND
Border Crossings
There are about 40 crossings on the USA–Mexico border, including the following:

Arizona Douglas–Agua Prieta, Nogales-Nogales, San Luis–San Luis, Río Colorado and Naco–Naco (all open 24 hours); Sasabe–El Sásabe (open 8am to 10pm); Lukeville-Sonoita (open 8am to midnight)
California Calexico-Mexicali (two crossings, one open 24 hours); San Ysidro–Tijuana (open 24 hours); Otay Mesa–Mesa de Otay (near Tijuana airport; open 6am to 10pm); Tecate-Tecate (open 6am to midnight)
New Mexico Columbus–General Rodrigo M Quevedo (also called Palomas; open 24 hours)
Texas Brownsville-Matamoros, McAllen-Reynosa, Laredo–Nuevo Laredo, Del Rio–Ciudad Acuña, Eagle Pass–Piedras Negras, Presidio-Ojinaga and El Paso–Ciudad Juárez (all open 24 hours)

There are also 10 border crossings between Guatemala and Mexico and two crossings between Belize and Mexico. The following are the most frequently used:

La Mesilla–Ciudad Cuauhtémoc on the Pan-American Highway (between Huehuetenango, Guatemala and San Cristóbal de Las Casas, Mexico)

Ciudad Tecún Umán–Ciudad Hidalgo between Quetzaltenango, Guatemala and Tapachula, Mexico

Santa Elena–Subteniente López between Corozal, Belize and Chetumal, Mexico

See the following Car & Motorcycle section for more information on entering Mexico with a car.

The USA

Bus Buses are permitted to travel between the USA and Mexico, but they can suffer delays at the border. It's usually no great inconvenience to make your way to the border on one bus, cross it on foot, and then catch an onward bus on the other side. **Greyhound** (☎ 800-231-2222 in the USA; W www.greyhound.com) serves many US border cities and, through its Mexican affiliates, some Mexican cities.

The Greyhound affiliate **Golden State/Crucero** (☎ 602-269-0500 in Phoenix, 520-623-1675 in Tucson) offers a direct bus service to Mazatlán from both Phoenix (US$96, 22 hours) and Tucson, Arizona (US$83, 18 hours). From Los Angeles you can ride with the same bus company to Phoenix, where you would transfer to the Mazatlán bus.

Other farther-flung US cities (such as Denver or Chicago) sometimes offer connecting services to interior Mexican cities, but the greatest number of cross-border buses run to and from Texas. From Texas, Greyhound goes to/from Mexican border cities such as Nuevo Laredo (US$29 from Houston) and Matamoros (US$39 to US$49 from Austin, Texas) where you then have to switch to a Mexican bus line (such as Turistar, Futura/Estrella Blanca or Cinco Estrellas) to get to the west coast.

Autobuses de Oriente runs daily from McAllen or Brownsville, Texas to Oaxaca for US$92.

Car & Motorcycle Driving into Mexico and down the Pacific coast can be wonderful, harrowing, adventurous and frustrating all at once. Its challenges are made easier if you know some Spanish and have basic mechanical aptitude, reserves of patience and access to extra cash for emergencies.

You should also consider the danger of highway robbery (see Dangers & Annoyances in the Facts for the Visitor chapter) and avoid intercity driving at night.

Cars are most useful for travelers who have plenty of time; plan to go to remote places; will be camping a lot; or have surfboards, diving equipment or other cumbersome luggage.

Don't take a car if you are on a tight schedule, have a small budget, plan to spend most of your time in urban areas or will be traveling alone.

Cars are expensive to rent or buy in Mexico. If you plan to spend more than a few weeks, it can be cheaper to take one in from the USA, even if that means buying one there. Good cars to take to Mexico are Volkswagen, Nissan, General Motors and Ford, which have plants in Mexico as well as dealers in most big Mexican towns. Volkswagen campervans are economical, and parts and service are easy to find.

Mexican mechanics are resourceful, and most repairs can be done quickly and inexpensively, but it still pays to take spare parts and know what to do with them (spare fuel filters are very useful). Tires (including a spare), shock absorbers and suspension should be in good condition. For security, have something to immobilize the steering wheel, such as 'the Club.'

Motorcycling in Mexico is not for the faint-hearted. Roads and traffic can be rough, and parts and mechanics difficult to come by. The only parts you'll find will be for Kawasaki, Honda and Suzuki bikes.

The rules for taking a vehicle into Mexico change from time to time. The **Mexican Tourism Board** (☎ 800-446-3942 in the USA) will fax you updated rules and regulations. For more on driving and motorcycling in Mexico, see the Getting Around chapter.

Auto Insurance It is foolish to drive in Mexico without Mexican liability insurance. If you are involved in an accident, you can be jailed and have your vehicle impounded while responsibility is assessed. If you are to blame for an accident causing injury or death, you can be held until you guarantee restitution to the victims and payment of any fines. This could take weeks or months. A valid Mexican insurance policy is regarded as a guarantee that restitution will be paid, and it will also expedite release of the driver. Mexican law recognizes only Mexican motor insurance *(seguro)*, so a US or Canadian policy is of no use.

Mexican insurance is sold in US border towns, and agencies are listed in the Yellow Pages. As you approach the border from the USA you will see billboards advertising offices selling Mexican policies. At the busiest border crossings (to Tijuana, Mexicali, Nogales, Agua Prieta, Ciudad Juárez, Nuevo Laredo, Reynosa and Matamoros), there are insurance offices open 24 hours a day. It is wise to shop around.

Two organizations worth looking into, both of which also offer lots of useful travel information, are **Sanborn's** (☎ *800-222-0158 in the USA;* 🗔 *www.sanbornsinsurance .com*) and **American Automobile Association** (AAA; 🗔 *www.aaa.com*). Short-term insurance is about US$8 to US$15 a day for full coverage on a car worth less than US$10,000; for periods of more than two weeks it's often cheaper to get an annual policy. Liability-only insurance costs approximately 50% of full coverage. AAA can provide its members with Mexican insurance and the forms needed for taking a vehicle into Mexico.

Driver's License To drive a motor vehicle in Mexico, you need a valid driver's license from your home country. Mexican police are familiar with USA and Canadian licenses. Those from other countries may be scrutinized more closely, but they are still legal.

Vehicle Permit You need a *permiso de importación temporal de vehículos* (temporary vehicle import permit) to take a vehicle beyond the frontier zones along the USA, Guatemala and Belize borders. You must get this at the *aduana* (customs) office at a border crossing (see the following Sea section if you're entering mainland Mexico by ferry from La Paz).

Customs officials at the Instituto Nacional de Migración (INM; National Immigration Institute) posts in the border zones along the USA, Guatemala and Belize borders, and at the Baja California ports for ferries to mainland Mexico, will request the permit for your vehicle.

The person importing the vehicle will need originals and at least one photocopy of each of the following documents, which must all be in his/her own name:

• tourist card (FMT) – go to *migración* before you go to the aduana
• certificate of title or registration certificate for the vehicle
• a Visa, MasterCard or AmEx credit card, issued by a non-Mexican institution; if you don't have one you must pay a very large cash bond
• proof of citizenship or residency such as passport, birth certificate, voter's registration card or residency card
• driver's license

If the vehicle is financed or leased or is a rental car or company car, you need a notarized letter of permission from the lender, lien-holder or rental company; and, in the case of leased or rented vehicles, the original contract (plus a copy), which must be in the name of the person importing the car. In practice few US rental firms allow their vehicles to be taken into Mexico.

One person cannot bring in two vehicles. If you have a motorcycle attached to your car, you'll need another adult traveling with you to obtain a permit for the motorcycle, and he/she will need to have all the correct papers for it. If the motorcycle is registered in your name, you'll need a notarized affidavit authorizing the other person to take it into Mexico. A special type of import permit is needed for vehicles weighing more than 3000kg (about 3.3 US tons).

At the border there will be a building with a parking area for vehicles awaiting permits.

Go inside and find the correct counter to present your papers. After some signing and stamping of papers, you sign a promise to take the car out of the country, the Banco del Ejército (also called Banjército; it's the army bank) charges a US$22 taxable fee to your credit card (you cannot pay cash), and you go and wait with your vehicle. Make sure you get back the originals of all documents. Eventually someone will come out and give you your vehicle permit and a sticker to be displayed on your windshield.

If you don't have an international credit card, you will have to pay a large refundable cash deposit or bond to the Banco del Ejército or an authorized Mexican *afianzadora* (bonding company) at the border. The required amounts are determined by official tables of vehicle values and range from US$500 to US$20,000 depending on the age and type of the vehicle. The bond (minus administrative charges) or the deposit should be refunded when the vehicle finally leaves Mexico and the temporary import permit is canceled. If you plan to leave Mexico at a different border crossing, make sure you will be able to obtain a refund there. There are offices for Banco del Ejército and authorized Mexican bonding companies at or near all the major border points.

Your vehicle permit entitles you to take the vehicle in and out of Mexico for the period shown on your tourist card. If the car is still in Mexico after that time, the aduana may start charging fines to your credit card and the car can be confiscated. The permit allows the vehicle to be driven by other people if the owner is in the vehicle.

When you leave Mexico for the last time, you must have the permit canceled by the Mexican authorities. An official may do this as you enter the border zone, usually 20km to 30km before the border itself. If not, you'll have to find the right official at the border crossing. If you leave Mexico without having the permit canceled, once the permit expires the authorities may assume you've left the vehicle in the country illegally and start charging fines to your credit card.

Only the owner may take the vehicle out of Mexico. If the vehicle is completely wrecked, you must contact your embassy or consulate or a Mexican customs office to make arrangements to leave without it.

Guatemala & Belize

Lonely Planet's *Mexico*, *Guatemala* and *Belize* guides are excellent resources on travel between the three countries.

The Mexico–Guatemala borders on the Pacific slope at Ciudad Hidalgo–Ciudad Tecún Umán and Talismán–El Carmen are both a short distance from Tapachula, the nearest Mexican city. From Tapachula regular buses run up the Pacific coast and inland to Oaxaca, or to Juchitán where you can continue west along the coast. Direct international bus services also operate on a daily basis between Tapachula and Guatemala City.

Inland, the Pan-American Highway connects Mexico with Guatemala at Ciudad Cuauhtémoc–La Mesilla. Frequent buses or *combis* link this crossing with the Mexican towns of Comitán and San Cristóbal de Las Casas, and with the Guatemalan towns of Huehuetenango, Quetzaltenango and Guatemala City. A couple of agencies in San Cristóbal de Las Casas run shuttle services to Quetzaltenango, Panajachel and Antigua (US$60, 9½ hours) in Guatemala. Travelling west, it's about a 15-hour bus journey from Ciudad Cuauhtémoc to Oaxaca city via San Cristóbal de Las Casas and Tuxtla Guiterrez.

See the River section later in this chapter for other routes between Mexico and Guatemala.

Frequent buses run between Chetumal, Mexico, and Belize City (US$5 to US$6.75, three to four hours) via Orange Walk and Corozal in northern Belize.

Drivers entering Mexico from the south must go through the same procedures as those entering from the USA. Some 'border-zone' checkpoints of the INM are a lot farther from the border than they are in the north – up to 70km.

Note that when crossing from Mexico into Belize or Guatemala you must carry both the vehicle's certificate of title *and* the registration document.

SEA

From Baja California **Sematur** (w *www .ferrysematur.com.mx*) runs daily ferries between La Paz (Baja California Sur) and Mazatlán. The main terminal in La Paz is at Pichilingue, about 22km north of central La Paz, with a service to Mazatlán (17 hours) at 3pm. If you're shipping a vehicle, you must get a vehicle permit (see that section under Car & Motorcycle earlier) in Pichilingue, as you cannot put your car aboard without it. Permits are not available at Santa Rosalía, the other Baja ferry port. Passenger fares cost from US$50 for a seat to US$160 for a 'suite.' Shipping a car up to 5m long costs US$390. RVs can be shipped. See the website for more fares and to make online reservations.

Anyone arriving in Mexico by cruise ship is allowed to disembark without a tourist card and stay up to 72 hours in the port city without one; no tourist fee is required.

RIVER

River routes through the jungle across the Mexico–Guatemala border are fun for the mildly adventurous. There are three main routes: The busiest and easiest route – which also enables you to visit the Mayan ruins at Yaxchilán and Bonampak, Mexico – is via a short boat ride on the Río Usumacinta between Frontera Corozal in Mexico and Bethel in Guatemala. The others (each with a river ride of four hours or so) are between Benemérito de las Américas, Chiapas and Sayaxché, Guatemala; and between La Palma, Tabasco, Mexico and El Naranjo, Guatemala. In each case, bus services reach the start and end of the river sections.

TRAIN

Mexico's passenger train system, after being in decline for decades, has pretty much ceased to exist. The only passenger train with a service to anywhere remotely close to the region covered in this book is the Ferrocarril Chihuahua al Pacífico. Known in English as the Copper Canyon Railway, it runs between Chihuahua, in northwest Mexico, and Los Mochis, about 420km north of Mazatlán.

ORGANIZED TOURS

If you want a short, easy holiday on Mexico's Pacific coast, sign up for one of the many package deals offered by travel agencies and in newspaper travel sections. Mexican government tourist offices can give armfuls of brochures about these trips. Costs depend on where and when you go (peak time is usually December to February), but some packages give you flights and accommodation for little more than the cost of an individual airfare. For example, a seven-night low-season package trip from New York to Acapulco can cost as little as US$500. Some packages also include a rental car and airport transfers in the price.

If you are looking for an adventure- or activity-focused group trip to Mexico, you'll find a wide selection, mainly from North America but also from Europe. Websites to check include **Eco Travels in Latin America** (w *www.planeta.com*) and **GORP** (*Great Outdoor Recreation Pages;* w *www.gorp.com*). **STA Travel** (w *www.statravel.com*) posts all sorts of interesting tours online.

The following is a partial list of tour operators dealing with Mexico's Pacific coast.

Adventure Center (☎ 800-228-8747; w www .adventurecenter.com) 1311 63rd St, Suite 200, Emeryville, CA 94608, USA. This company offers ecologically-minded, small-group camping/hotel trips through Sierra Madre del Sur to Oaxaca coast.

El Tour (e basily@rocketmail.com; w eltour.itgo .com) A Canadian/Mexican outfit offering two-week cycling trips from Puerto Vallarta to Lázaro Cárdenas (price is about US$765), including most expenses except airfare. There is an option to combine this with a three-week ride through Sierra Madre (an additional US$995). Camping is optional. This outfit is small, personal and very well-received.

Explore Worldwide (☎ 800-227-8747 in the USA, 01252-760 000 in the UK, 02-8913 0755 in Australia; w www.explore.com) Offers small-group treks through Sierra Madre del Sur to the Oaxaca coast.

Field Guides (☎ 800-728-4953; w www.field guides.com) 9433 Bee Cave Rd, Bldg 1, Suite 150, Austin, TX 78733, USA. Field Guides offers bird-watching trips along Colima coast and inland to Jalisco and other trips visit Oaxaca.

Global Exchange (☎ 415-255-7296, 800-497-1994; W www.globalexchange.org) 2017 Mission St No 303, San Francisco, CA 94110, USA. This company offers 'reality tours' to Mexico; participants get an in-depth look at the conditions of life in problem regions, meeting community leaders, peace and social justice workers and other folk. One trip visits the Acapulco region and inland Guerrero. A one-week trip typically costs around US$550 to US$750.

Outland Adventures (☎ 206-932-7012 in the USA; W www.outlandadventures.natureavenue.com) PO Box 16343, Seattle, WA 98116. Outland Adventures offers seven-day hotel-based tours exploring the Jalisco and Colima coasts and its villages by kayak, mountain bike, boat, van, snorkel and foot. One trip is a 'Snorkel & Village Odyssey;' another is a mountain bike tour. Prices are US$795 to US$1195 depending on group size.

Suntrek (☎ 800-786-8735; W www.suntrek.com) Sun Plaza, 77 W Third St, Santa Rosa, CA 95401, USA; (☎ 08024-474490, W www.suntrek.de) Marktplatz 17, 83607 Holzkirchen, Germany. Suntrek offers small international-group camping tours. Two trips include fun Pacific coast destinations.

TrekAmerica (☎ 800-221-0596 in the USA, 01295-256 777 in the UK; W www.trekamerica.com) PO Box 189, Rockaway, NJ 07866 USA. This company has small-group camping expeditions; most participants are in their early 20s. The 'Mexican Adventure' heads from Mexico City to the Pacific coast.

Getting Around

The peak travel periods on Mexico's Pacific coast are Semana Santa (the week before Easter and a few days after it); the Christmas–New Year holiday period of about two weeks; and the July/August school holidays. These periods are hectic and heavily booked. Try to book transport three to five days in advance.

AIR

You generally cannot fly from one coastal destination to another without changing planes in Mexico City or Guadalajara. Most flights to/from the Pacific coast are flights to/from Mexico City, Guadalajara and Oaxaca city. Mazatlán, Tepic, Guadalajara, Puerto Vallarta, Manzanillo, Colima, Lázaro Cárdenas, Acapulco, Ixtapa-Zihuatanejo, Oaxaca, Puerto Escondido and Bahías de Huatulco all have passenger airports.

Aeroméxico and Mexicana are the country's two largest airlines. There are also smaller ones, often flying to/from smaller cities on the coast that the big two don't bother with. These include Aero California, Aerolitoral, Aerocaribe, Aeromar, Aviacsa, and Aerolíneas Internacionales. See the boxed text 'Airline Contact Details' in the Getting There & Away chapter for websites and telephone numbers in Mexico. Information on specific flights can be found within the Getting There & Away sections of individual city sections.

Most of these airlines are included in travel agencies computerized reservation systems in Mexico and abroad, but you may find it hard to get information on smal airlines until you reach a city served by them.

Aerolitoral and Aeromar are feeder airlines for Aeroméxico and normally share its ticket offices and booking networks. A similar arrangement exists between Aerocaribe and Mexicana.

Fares

Flying is much cheaper between an inland city (Mexico City, Guadalajara or Oaxaca)

and a coastal destination, than from one coastal destination to another. This is because nearly all flights head to/from Mexico City and Guadalajara, making it necessary to purchase two fares to get from coastal-point A to coastal-point B (via the inland city). Fares can vary between airlines and according to the time of year. Booking and paying at least a few days in advance will often save you some money.

High season corresponds to the Mexican holiday seasons (see this chapter's opening paragraph). Aeroméxico and Mexicana – theoretically competitors but both government controlled – work in tandem, with identical fare structures, but cheaper fares may be offered by other airlines. Return fares are often simply twice the price of one-way tickets.

Here are examples of one-way fares to/from Mexico City, including taxes:

Acapulco	US$170
Bahías de Huatulco	US$162
Ixtapa-Zihuatanejo	US$190
Manzanillo	US$211
Mazatlán	US$209
Guadalajara	US$177
Oaxaca	US$185
Puerto Vallarta	US$184

Small-time operators (we're talking seven- to 14-seat Cessna planes) fly from Oaxaca to/from Huatulco and Puerto Escondido for around US$100.

Domestic Departure Tax

There are two taxes on domestic flight fares: IVA, the consumer tax (15% of the fare), and TUA, an airport tax of about US$16. Taxes are normally included in quoted fares and paid when you buy the ticket.

BUS

Mexico has a good intercity road and bus network. Intercity buses are frequent and go almost everywhere, typically for around US$4 or US$6 per hour (60km to 80km) on deluxe or 1st-class buses. For trips of up to three or four hours on busy routes, you can usually go to the bus terminal, buy a ticket and head out without much of a delay. For longer trips, or routes with infrequent service, book a ticket a day or three in advance. During the peak holiday periods, book your ticket up to five days in advance to guarantee a seat.

Seats on many 1st-class lines (including UNO, ADO, Cristóbal Colón, and Plus) can be booked and purchased through **Ticket Bus** (☎ 800-702-80-00; ⓦ *www.ticketbus .com.mx*), a reservations service with offices in larger cities. You can make reservations on Ticket Bus's toll-free national reservations line.

Immediate cash refunds of 80% to 100% are available from many bus companies if you cancel your ticket more than a couple of hours before the listed departure time and if you purchased your ticket in cash. Be prepared to show some identification (such as your passport). To check whether refunds apply, ask *'Hay cancelaciones?'*.

All deluxe and most 1st-class buses are air-conditioned, so bring a jacket. Most have computerized ticket systems that allow you to select your seat from an on-screen diagram when you buy your ticket. Try to avoid the back of the bus, which is where the toilets are and also tends to give a bumpier ride. On nonair-conditioned 2nd-class buses, it's a good idea to get a window seat so that you have some control over the window. See Classes of Service later for the differences between classes.

Baggage is safe if stowed in the bus's baggage hold, but try to get a receipt for it when you hand it over. Keep your most-valuable documents (passport, money etc) with you – and protect them closely.

Food and drinks in bus stations are overpriced; bringing your own is cheaper. Drinks and snacks are provided on some deluxe services. The better buses have toilets, but carry some toilet paper.

Highway robbery happens very occasionally. The risk is higher at night, on isolated highways far from the cities, and in 2nd-class buses. See Classes of Service later in this section and Dangers & Annoyances in the Facts for the Visitor chapter for more information.

Terminals & Schedules

Most cities and towns have a single, modern, main bus station where all long-distance buses arrive and depart. It's usually called the Central Camionera, Central de Autobuses, Terminal de Autobuses, Central de Camiones or simply El Central, and it is usually far from the center of town. Frequent local buses link bus stations with town centers. Be aware of the crucial difference between the Central (bus station) and the Centro (city center).

If there is no single main terminal, bus companies will have their own terminals scattered around town.

Most bus lines have schedules posted at their ticket desks in the bus station, but the schedules aren't always comprehensive. If your destination isn't listed, ask – it may be en route to one that is. From big towns, many different bus companies may run on the same routes, so compare fares and classes of service.

Classes of Service

Long-distance buses range enormously in quality, from comfortable, nonstop, air-con deluxe services to decaying, suspensionless ex-city buses grinding out their dying years on dirt roads to remote settlements. The differences among the classes are not hard and fast, and terms such as *de lujo* (deluxe) and *primera clase* (1st class) can cover quite a wide range of comfort levels. Broadly, buses fall into three categories:

De lujo Deluxe services run mainly on the busy routes. Some bear names such as Plus, GL or Ejecutivo, and are swift, modern, comfortable and air-conditioned. They cost just 10% or 20% more than 1st class, or double for the most luxurious lines, such as UNO and Turistar Ejecutivo, which offer reclining seats, extra leg room, few or no stops, snacks, hot and cold drinks, videos and toilets on board. Some people regard these latter super-deluxe buses as a class of their own – *ejecutivo* (executive). For simplicity, this book groups them with other deluxe services.

Primera (1a clase) 1st-class buses have a comfortable numbered seat for each passenger and often show videos. Their standards of comfort are perfectly adequate. They usually have air-conditioning and a toilet, may show videos, and stop infrequently. All sizable towns have a 1st-class bus service. As with deluxe buses, you buy your ticket at the bus station before boarding.

Segunda (2a clase) 2nd-class buses serve small towns and villages and offer cheaper, slower travel on some intercity routes. A few are almost as quick and comfortable as 1st-class buses; others are old, tatty, uncomfortable and mechanically unsound. Second-class buses may be less safe than 1st-class or de lujo due to poor maintenance, driver standards and vulnerability to robbery. They will stop anywhere for someone to get on or off, which can add hours to a journey. Except on some major runs, there's no passenger limit, so if you board mid-route you might have to stand. When you board mid-route, pay your fare to the conductor. Fares are about 10% or 20% lower than 1st class. *Microbuses,* or '*micros,*' are 2nd-class buses with around 25 seats, usually running short routes between towns.

How Many Stops?

It is important to know the types of service offered:

Sin escalas Nonstop

Directo Very few stops

Semi-directo A few more stops than directo

Ordinario Stops wherever passengers want to get on or off; deluxe and 1st-class buses are never ordinario

Express Nonstop on short to medium-length trips; very few stops on long trips

Local Bus that starts its journey at the bus station you're in and usually leaves on time; preferable to de paso

De paso Bus that started its journey somewhere else, but is stopping to let off and take on passengers. A de paso bus may be late or early and may or may not have seats available; unless the bus company has a computer booking system, you also may have to wait until it arrives before any tickets are sold. If the bus is full, you may have to wait for the next one.

Viaje redondo Return trip

Vans, Combis, Pickups & Trucks

In some areas (mainly rural), a variety of other vehicles performs the service of moving people from A to B. Volkswagen combis (minivans) and more-comfortable passenger-carrying vans, such as Chevrolet Suburbans, operate shuttle services between some towns. Some vans, such as Autotransportes Atlántida's from Oaxaca to the Pacific coast, are air-conditioned, comfortable and have assigned seating. Fares are similar to 1st-class bus fares.

More primitive are passenger-carrying *camiones* (trucks) and *camionetas* (pickups). Standing in the back of a truck with a couple of dozen *campesinos* (farm workers) and their machetes and animals is at least an experience to remember. Fares are usually cheaper than a 2nd-class bus fare.

TRAIN

The only train you'll find here is the *Tequila Express,* a tourist train from Guadalajara to the nearby town of Tequila (see the Guadalajara city section in the Nayarit & Guadalajara chapter for details). In the last decade, most of the country's passenger train service has ceased to exist.

CAR & MOTORCYCLE

Driving in Mexico is not as easy as it is in North America and Europe (some of Europe anyway), but little can replace the experience of dodging donkeys and homemade speed bumps as you buzz along coastal Hwy 200 or chug up mountain roads in a VW Beetle. It's often the only way to reach those isolated beaches and tiny villages.

See Dangers & Annoyances in Facts for the Visitor for a warning about risks of highway robbery in some areas, and the Getting There & Away chapter for information about the requirements for bringing a vehicle into Mexico. The Language chapter at the back of the book has some useful Spanish words and phrases for drivers.

Two useful websites for people wishing to drive throughout Mexico are **The People's Guide to Mexico** site (Ⓦ *www.peoplesguide.com*) and the **Sanborn's Insurance** site (Ⓦ *www.sanbornsinsurance.com*).

Maps

Town and country roads are often poorly signposted. It pays to get the best road maps. The Mexican *Guía Roji Por Las Carreteras de México* road atlas is excellent. In Mexico it costs US$11 from most bookstores and city newsstands. In the USA or from Internet booksellers, it's US$18 to US$20. This atlas is updated annually and includes new highways, though minor roads may be overlooked or imperfect. Guía Roji also publishes state road maps that cost about US$9 each abroad and about US$3 from bookstores or newsstands in Mexico.

Road Rules

Drive on the right-hand side of the road.

Traffic laws and speed limits rarely seem to be enforced on the highways. Obey the laws strictly in the cities so the police have no excuse to hit you with a payable-on-the-spot 'fine'. Speed limits are usually 100km/h on highways and 40km/h or 30km/h in towns and cities.

Accidents

Under Mexico's legal system, all drivers involved in a road accident are detained, and their vehicles impounded, while responsibility is assessed. For minor accidents, drivers will probably be released if they have insurance to cover any damage they may have caused. But the culpable driver's vehicle may remain impounded until damages are paid. If the accident causes injury or death, the responsible driver will be jailed until he or she guarantees restitution to the victims and payment of any fines. Determining responsibility *could* take weeks or even months. (Mexican drivers often *don't* stop after accidents.) Adequate insurance coverage is the only real protection.

Fuel & Service

All *gasolina* (gasoline) and diesel fuel in Mexico is sold by the government monopoly, Pemex (Petróleos Mexicanos), for cash (no credit cards). Most towns, even small ones, have a Pemex station, and the stations are pretty common on most major roads.

Nevertheless, in remote areas it's better to fill up when you can.

Road Conditions

Mexican highways, even some toll highways, are not up to the standards of European or North American ones. That said, Hwy 15D and Hwy 200, the main coastal highways, are in good condition.

Driving at night is best avoided, as unlit vehicles, rocks, pedestrians and animals on the roads are common. Hijacks and robberies do occur.

Army checkpoints are common, especially on Hwy 200, and vehicles are searched randomly and regularly. It's slightly nerve-racking but no call for panic (though some people say you should keep an eye on your valuables).

Perhaps the most dangerous things you'll come across (as slowly as possible) are *topes* (speed bumps). On toll-free roads like the southern stretches of Hwy 200, they're cemented to the highway on the outskirts of *every* village and town. They'll jolt the hell out of you and severely damage your car's suspension if you don't spot them and slow almost to a stop.

Autopistas (toll roads) are usually four lanes and smooth sailing. They are generally in much better condition and a lot quicker than the alternative free roads. *Cuotas* (tolls) vary: on average you pay about US$1 for every 10km to 20km.

Free roads can suddenly become toll roads when a group of *campesinos* (farmers) or a local village decide – for whatever reason – that it's time to take up a collection. This can be anything from a pair of schoolgirls with a rope across the road to a group of farmers claiming retribution for unfulfilled government promises. They are usually never more than US$1 and you should pay like everybody else to avoid problems.

Certain aspects of Mexican roads make them particularly hazardous for bikers; watch for poor signage of road closures; dogs, donkeys and cattle on the roads; debris and deep potholes; vehicles without tail lights and a lack of highway lighting.

Breakdown Assistance

The Mexican tourism ministry, Sectur, maintains a network of Ángeles Verdes (Green Angels). These are bilingual mechanics in green uniforms and green trucks, who patrol major stretches of highway during daylight hours looking for motorists in trouble. They make minor repairs, change tires, provide fuel and oil, and arrange towing and other assistance. Service is free; parts, gasoline and oil are provided at cost. If you are near a telephone when your car has problems, call the 24-hour hot line in Mexico City (☎ 55-5250-8221); or the national 24-hour tourist assistance numbers in Mexico City (☎ 55-5250-0123, 800-903-92-00). Local numbers, when they exist, are listed in the city sections of this book.

Most serious mechanical problems can be fixed efficiently and inexpensively by mechanics in towns and cities as long as the parts are available.

Driving in the City

In towns and cities you must be especially wary of *alto* (stop) signs, *topes* and potholes. They are often not where you'd expect, and missing one can cost you in traffic fines or car damage. One-way streets are the rule in towns; usually, alternating streets run in opposite directions.

It's usually not a good idea to park on the street overnight in bigger cities. If you're just overnighting and moving on in the morning, often you can find decent motels, with easy parking, on highways just outside cities.

Rental

Auto rental in Mexico is expensive by US and European standards, but it can be worthwhile if you want to visit several places in a short time and have three or four people to share the cost. It can also be useful for getting off the beaten track, where public transport is slow or scarce. Cars can be rented in most cities and resorts, at airports and sometimes at bus and train stations. Most big hotels can arrange a car.

Renters must have a valid driver's license, passport and major credit card, and usually need to be at least 21 (sometimes 25) years old. You should get a signed rental agreement and read its small print.

In addition to the basic daily or weekly rental rate, you must pay for insurance, tax and fuel. It definitely pays to shop around. You can usually find a Volkswagen Beetle for around US$60 a day including unlimited kilometers, insurance and tax. Weekly rates are usually equivalent to six single days. The extra charge for drop-off in another city, when available, is usually about US$0.40 per kilometer.

For cheaper rates, you can book cars from outside Mexico through the large international agencies. Contact information (phone numbers are all US-based) for some major firms operating in Mexico are as follows:

Alamo (☎ 800-462-5266; **W** www.goalamo.com)
Avis (☎ 800-230-4898; **W** www.avis.com)
Budget (☎ 800-472-3325; **W** www.drivebudget .com)
Dollar (☎ 800-300-3665; **W** www.dollar.com)
Europcar (☎ 877-940-6900; **W** www.europcar .com)
Hertz (☎ 800-654-3001, 800-709-50-00; **W** www.hertz.com)
Thrifty (☎ 800-847-4389; **W** www.thrifty.com)

See Getting There & Away sections in individual chapters for details and local contact information on car rental agencies.

BICYCLE

Cycling is not a common way to tour Mexico's Pacific coast, but people do it. Reports of highway robbery, poor road surfaces and road hazards are deterrents. However, this method of moving up or down the coast is not impossible if you're prepared for the challenges. You should be very fit, use the best equipment you can muster and be able to handle your own repairs. Take the mountainous topography and hot climate into account when planning your route.

A valuable resource on cycling in Mexico is *Bicycling Mexico* by Erica Weisbroth and Eric Ellman, published in 1990 but still applicable.

It's possible to rent bikes in many resort towns for short excursions, and the same places often offer guided rides. **El Tour** and **Outland Adventures** (see Organized Tours in the Getting There & Away chapter) offer guided tours along the Pacific coast that are a great way to cycle with some experienced folks.

HITCHHIKING

Hitching is never entirely safe in any country in the world, and we don't recommend it. Travelers who decide to hitch should understand that they are taking a small but potentially serious risk. People who do choose to hitch will be safer if they travel in pairs and let someone know where they are planning to go. A woman traveling alone certainly should not hitchhike in Mexico, and even two women alone is not advisable.

However, some people do choose to hitch, and it's not an uncommon way of getting to some of the off-the-beaten-track places that tend to be poorly served by bus.

If the driver is another tourist or a private motorist, you may get the ride for free. If it is a work or commercial vehicle, you should offer to pay.

LOCAL TRANSPORT

Mexican street naming and numbering can be confusing. When asking directions, it's best to ask for a specific place, such as Hotel Central or Museo Regional, than the street it's on. To achieve a degree of certainty, ask three people (consider it triangulation).

Bus

Known as *camiones*, local buses are the cheapest way to get around cities and to nearby villages. They run everywhere, frequently, and are cheap. Fares in cities rarely cost more than US$0.50. Older buses are often noisy, dirty and crowded, but in some cities there are fleets of small, modern, more pleasant microbuses.

City buses usually halt only at specific *paradas* (bus stops), which may or may not be marked.

Colectivos, Combis & Micros

Colectivos are minibuses that have loosely fixed routes and leave when they're full. A *taxi colectivo* functions similarly but looks like a taxi. *Combis* or *micros* are VW minibuses which run along set routes – usually displayed on the windshield – and will pick you up or drop you off on any corner along their route. They're cheaper than taxis and quicker and less crowded than buses. If you're not at the start of a *colectivo's* route, go to the curb and wave your hand when you see one. Tell the driver where you want to go; you normally pay at the end of the trip, and the fare (rarely more than US$0.65) usually depends on how far you go.

Metro

Guadalajara is the only city covered in this book with a metro (subway, underground railway) system. It's quick and comfortable.

Taxi

Taxis are common in towns and cities. They're often economical, and useful if you have a lot of baggage or need to get from A to B quickly. If a taxi has a meter, ask the driver if it's working (*'el taxímetro?'*). If it's not, or if the taxi does not have a meter, establish the price of the ride *before* getting in (this usually involves a little bit of good natured haggling).

Some airports and big bus stations have taxi *taquillas* (kiosks), where you buy a fixed-price ticket to your destination and then hand it to the driver instead of paying cash. This can save haggling and rip-offs, but fares are usually higher than what you could get on the street.

Boat

You'll have plenty of opportunities to travel by boat on Mexico's Pacific coast. *Lanchas* (motor boats) and *pangas* (slightly smaller outboard fishing boats) will zip you off to isolated beaches, across lagoons or out to snorkel spots. You may have to haggle a bit, but fares are usually fixed. In places like Pie de la Cuesta or Lagunas de Chacahua, where lanchas are used regularly for transport, you'll find water shuttles. These are referred to as *colectivos* and depart from a *colectivo* dock.

ORGANIZED TOURS

Not only can guided tours be quick introductions to big cities like Guadalajara or Mazatlán, they can get you places (like into the luxury homes of Puerto Vallarta) that you wouldn't be able to go on your own. Tours are sometimes the most practical method of visiting remote natural attractions where public transportation isn't the greatest – places such as Lagunas de Chacahua and Laguna Manialtepec in Oaxaca, or the giant limestone caves near Troncones, Guerrero. Snorkeling may seem easy enough to go it alone, but a guide can get you to the best spots, often accessible only by boat, and show you sea creatures you might otherwise swim straight past.

A knowledgeable local guide can add much to your understanding and enjoyment of a place, especially if the focus of interest is, say, ethnological or cultural, such as visits to the indigenous villages around Oaxaca. A guide is a necessity in some protected areas where unaccompanied access is not allowed, such as the Los Naranjos and Palmazola coastal lagoons in Oaxaca.

A new generation of adventure/activity tourism is emerging in some parts of the coast, as throughout the country, with enthusiastic guides offering the chance to hike, bike, climb, raft and meet local people (in areas you'd probably never even know about without them). Trips run by, or in cooperation with, local community tourism organizations have the additional attraction that they channel funds directly to local people.

You'll find details on all these tours, and others, in the regional chapters. Most are best arranged locally. See Organized Tours in the Getting There & Away chapter for information on longer tours.

Good websites to look at are **EarthFoot** (W *www.earthfoot.org*), **Eco Travels in Latin America** (W *www.planeta.com*), and **Amtave** (W *www.amtave.com*). The 'Activities & Adventure' section of **Mexico Online** (W *www.mexonline.com*) posts heaps of local tour operators.

Before signing up for any tour, ask if the price includes tariffs and taxes *(tarifas y impuestos)*, or refunds.

Mazatlán

☎ 669 • pop 550,000

Around 20km south of the tropic of Cancer, Mazatlán is Mexico's principal Pacific coast port for fishing and trade, as well as a prime beach resort. It's famous for sport fishing, with thousands of sailfish and marlin tagged and released each year, and docks Latin America's largest fleet of commercial shrimp vessels. It's also home to more than half a million 'Mazatlecos,' as the residents of Mazatlán are called.

In pre-Hispanic times Mazatlán ('place of deer' in Náhuatl) was populated by Totorames, who existed by hunting, gathering, fishing and agriculture. A group of 25 Spaniards led by Nuño de Guzmán officially founded a settlement here on Easter Sunday in 1531, but almost three centuries elapsed before a permanent colony was established in the early 1820s. The port was blockaded by US forces in 1847, and by the French in 1864, but Mazatlán remained not much more than a large fishing village. Visitors first started coming in the 1930s, and some hotels appeared on Playa Olas Altas, Mazatlán's first tourist beach, in the 1950s. From the 1970s, a long strip of modern hotels and tourist facilities spread north along the coast.

Today's visitors have a choice of a luxury package-tour resort, old-style Mexican ambience, or the very basic beach-bum option. One big attraction is free for all – the daily spectacle of rocky islands silhouetted against the tropical sunset, as the fiery red fades into the sea, and another starry night begins.

Orientation

Old Mazatlán, the city center, is near the southern end of a peninsula, bounded by the Pacific Ocean on the west and the Bahía Dársena channel on the east. The center of the 'old' city is the cathedral, on Plaza Principal, surrounded by a rectangular street grid. At the southern tip of the peninsula, El Faro (the lighthouse) stands on a rocky prominence, overlooking Mazatlán's sport-fishing fleet and the La Paz ferry terminal.

Highlights

- Wandering around the streets, plazas and 19th-century buildings of Old Mazatlán

- Hiking up to the top of El Faro, the world's second-highest lighthouse after Gibraltar's

- Cruising Mazatlán's coast and visiting Isla de Venados or toasting the fiery sunset

- Taking a day trip to the mountain hamlets of Concordia, Copala or Cosalá

- Snorkeling around Isla de la Piedra's rocky point after strolling its long beach

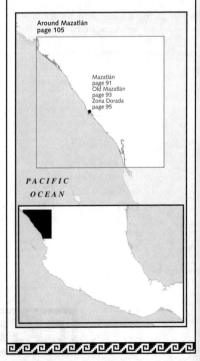

Around Mazatlán
page 105

Mazatlán
page 91
Old Mazatlán
page 93
Zona Dorada
page 95

PACIFIC
OCEAN

MAZATLÁN

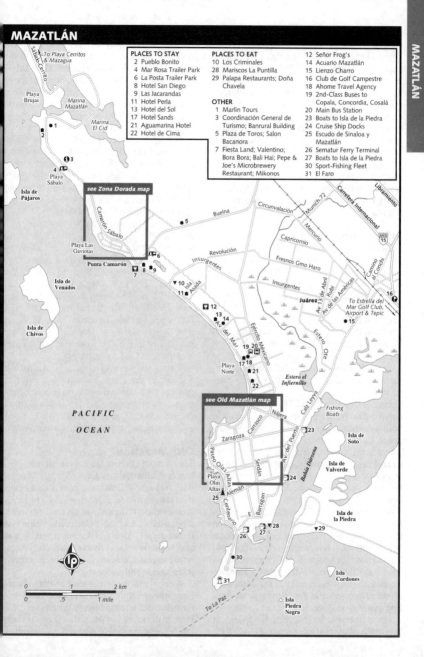

PLACES TO STAY
2 Pueblo Bonito
4 Mar Rosa Trailer Park
6 La Posta Trailer Park
8 Hotel San Diego
9 Las Jacarandas
11 Hotel Perla
13 Hotel del Sol
17 Hotel Sands
21 Aguamarina Hotel
22 Hotel de Cima

PLACES TO EAT
10 Los Criminales
28 Mariscos La Puntilla
29 Palapa Restaurants; Doña Chavela

OTHER
1 Marlin Tours
3 Coordinación General de Turismo; Banrural Building
5 Plaza de Toros; Salon Bacanora
7 Fiesta Land; Valentino; Bora Bora; Bali Hai; Pepe & Joe's Microbrewery Restaurant; Mikonos

12 Señor Frog's
14 Acuario Mazatlán
15 Lienzo Charro
16 Club de Golf Campestre
18 Ahome Travel Agency
19 2nd-Class Buses to Copala, Concordia, Cosalá
20 Main Bus Station
23 Boats to Isla de la Piedra
24 Cruise Ship Docks
25 Escudo de Sinaloa y Mazatlán
26 Sematur Ferry Terminal
27 Boats to Isla de la Piedra
30 Sport-Fishing Fleet
31 El Faro

see Zona Dorada map

see Old Mazatlán map

PACIFIC
OCEAN

To Playa Cerritos & Mazagua
Playa Brujas
Marina Mazatlán
Marina El Cid
Playa Sábalo
Isla de Pájaros
Camarón Sábalo
Playa Las Gaviotas
Punta Camarón
Isla de Venados
Isla de Chivos
Buelna
Circunvalación
Capricornio
Revolución
Insurgentes
Insurgentes
Fresnos Gmo Haro
Munich 72
Mercurio
Carretera Internacional
Libramiento
MEX 15
Camino al Conchi
Av 13 de Abril
Av de las Américas
Av del Rubí
Estero Ote
Juárez
To Estrella del Mar Golf Club, Airport & Tepic
Isla Asada
Av del Mar
Ejército Mexicano
Playa Norte
Estero el Infiernillo
Fishing Boats
see Old Mazatlán map
Carrasco
Nájera
Calz Leyva
Zaragoza
Paseo Olas Altas
Serdán
Av del Puerto
Isla de Soto
Isla de Valverde
Bahía Dársena
Playa Olas Altas
Alemán
Centenario
Barragán
E
Isla de la Piedra
Isla Cordones
To La Paz
Isla Piedra Negra

0   1   2 km
0   .5   1 mile

MAZATLÁN

A sculpture-studded, beachside boulevard (which changes names frequently) runs about 5km on the Pacific side of the peninsula from Playa Olas Altas, around some rocky outcrops, and north around the wide arc of Playa Norte to the Zona Dorada (Golden Zone), a concentration of hotels, bars, and businesses catering mainly to package tourists. Further north are more hotels, a marina and some time-share condominiums.

East of the Mazatlán peninsula (and a separate municipality), Isla de la Piedra is a short boat ride from town, though it's not really an island anymore – landfill from the construction of the airport has joined it to the mainland.

Information

Coordinación General de Turismo (☎ 916-51-60/65; e tursina@prodigy.net.mx; w www .sinaloa.gob.mx; *Camarón Sábalo s/n; open 8am-3pm Mon-Sat*) is on the 4th floor of the Banrural building, north of the Zona Dorada.

The El Cid Mega Resort's information booth, at the north end of the Zona Dorada, mainly sells boat trips, water sports and time-share presentations, but the staff can be helpful about all sorts of things to see and do.

Note that any hours listed following reflect winter schedules; summer hours may be more limited.

Banks (most with ATMs) and *casas de cambio* (exchange houses) are plentiful in both Old Mazatlán and the Zona Dorada. Some *casas de cambio* stay open Sunday. There are Bancomer and Banamex offices near Plaza Principal. **American Express** *(AmEx; ☎ 913-06-00; open 9am-6pm Mon-Fri, 9am-1pm Sat)* is on Camarón Sábalo near Las Gaviotas.

The **main post office** *(Juárez; open 8am-6pm Mon-Fri, 9am-1pm Sat)* is located on the east side of Plaza Principal. Next door, **Telecomm** has telegraph, telex, fax and Internet services, as well as pay phones, and opens similar hours. **Miscelánea Hermes** *(Serdán 1510)*, a block east of the cathedral, offers telephone and fax services, as does **Computel** next door.

Good Internet access can be found at **Telefonía Automática** *(Ángel Flores 810;*

US$1.25 per hour; open 9am-9:30pm daily) and **AhorraNet** *(Ángel Flores 508; US$2 per hour; open 8:30am-8:30pm Mon-Sat)*. In the Zona Dorada, there's **Netscape Café Internet** *(Camarón Sábalo; US$3.50 per hour; open 8am-midnight daily)*, but there's a better connection at **Cyber Café Mazatlán** *(Camarón Sábalo 204; US$3.50 per hour; open 9:15am-10pm Mon-Sat, 10am-10pm Sun)*.

If you've got some used books to trade, check out **Mazatlán Book & Coffee Company** *(☎ 916-78-99; Camarón Sábalo; open 9am-7pm daily)*, just across from the Costa de Oro Hotel and in the minimall behind Banco Santander. It's got a wide selection and serves decent coffee to boot.

The free bilingual tourist newspapers – *Pacific Pearl* and *Viejo Mazatlán* – are available at the tourist office and at many hotels and tourist-oriented businesses.

Got some sweaty duds to put through the wringer? Try **Lavandería La Blanca** *(Camarón Sábalo 357; open 8am-7pm Mon-Sat, 8am-2pm Sun)*, which charges about US$5 for 3kg of threads. **Lavamar** *(Playa Gaviotas 214; open 8am-6pm Mon-Sat)* is another possibility in the Zona Dorada, but it costs lots more at US$5 per kilogram.

There are several clinics on Camarón Sábalo, in the Zona Dorada, that cater to gringos who come down with a case of indigestion or worse. One is **Clínica Balboa** *(☎ 916-79-33; Camarón Sábalo 4480; open 24 hours daily)*, just north of Las Gaviotas.

Old Mazatlán

The heart of Old Mazatlán is the large 19th-century **cathedral** *(cnr Juárez & 21 de Marzo)*, with its high, yellow twin towers and beautiful statues inside. Built from 1875 to 1890, it faces **Plaza Principal**, which has lush trees, a bandstand, and the **Palacio Municipal** on its west side. Two blocks north, on Juaréz and Valle, is a local **market** full of clothes, housewares, fruits and vegetables, meats, juice stands and shoppers.

A couple blocks southwest of Plaza Principal, the attractive **Plazuela Machado** *(cnr Carnaval & Constitución)* is the center of a large historic area of Mazatlán that has been undergoing a massive renewal programme.

It's surrounded by historic buildings and attractive sidewalk cafés, restaurants and bars. Half a block south of the Plazuela Machado, **Teatro Angela Peralta** was built in 1860, and reopened in 1992 after a five-year restoration project. Cultural events of all kinds are presented here (see Entertainment later in this chapter), and the opulent interior is open for viewing most days.

Four blocks toward Playa Olas Altas, **Museo Arqueológico** (☎ 981-14-55; Sixto Osuna 76; admission free; open 10am-3pm Mon-Fri) is an interesting little archaeological museum with some labels in English.

Opposite, **Museo de Arte** (☎ 985-35-02; cnr Sixto Osuna & Venustiano Carranza; admission US$1.25; open 4pm-7pm Tues-Sun) has permanent and changing exhibits of work by Mexican and foreign artists.

West of the center is **Playa Olas Altas**, a small beach in a small cove. The seafront road, Paseo Olas Altas, has a few faded 1950s hotels facing the water. Look for two of the town's many seafront monuments: **Escudo de Sinaloa y Mazatlán** (Sinaloa and Mazatlán Shield) at the south end of the cove and the small **Monumento al Venado** (Monument to Deer) located in the traffic

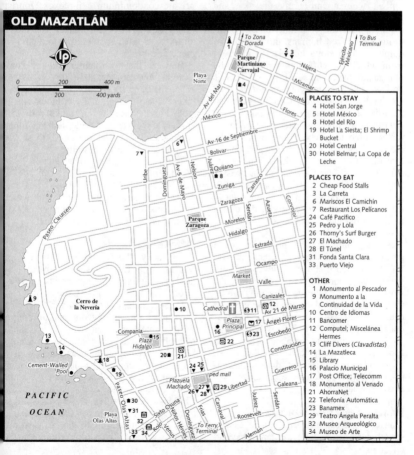

OLD MAZATLÁN

PLACES TO STAY
4 Hotel San Jorge
5 Hotel México
8 Hotel del Río
19 Hotel La Siesta; El Shrimp Bucket
20 Hotel Central
30 Hotel Belmar; La Copa de Leche

PLACES TO EAT
2 Cheap Food Stalls
3 La Carreta
6 Mariscos El Camichín
7 Restaurant Los Pelícanos
24 Café Pacífico
25 Pedro y Lola
26 Thorny's Surf Burger
27 El Machado
28 El Túnel
31 Fonda Santa Clara
33 Puerto Viejo

OTHER
1 Monumento al Pescador
9 Monumento a la Continuidad de la Vida
10 Centro de Idiomas
11 Bancomer
12 Computel; Miscelánea Hermes
13 Cliff Divers (Clavadistas)
14 La Mazateca
15 Library
16 Palacio Municipal
17 Post Office; Telecomm
18 Monumento al Venado
21 AhorraNet
22 Telefonía Automática
23 Banamex
29 Teatro Ángela Peralta
32 Museo Arqueológico
34 Museo de Arte

circle at the north end (a tribute to the city's Náhuatl name).

Farther north, on a rocky point in the water, you'll see a cement-walled, rectangular pool where locals take a dip and divers clean oysters. Just inland is the small hill **Cerro de la Nevería** (Icebox Hill), which in the mid-19th century stored ice shipped in from San Francisco. It also served as an ammunitions bunker during the revolution, and was the second place in history targeted by aerial bombs (Tripoli in Libya was first).

Sculpture along this part of the *malecón* (waterfront street) includes **La Mazatleca**, a topless woman embracing the sky, and **Monumento a la Continuidad de la Vida** (Monument to the Continuity of Life), featuring two naked humans and a group of dolphins. Also along here is the platform from which the **cliff divers** *(clavadistas)* plunge into the ocean swells below. There's no fixed schedule, but you're most likely to see the divers perform around lunchtime on Saturday and Sunday and on holidays.

Paseo Olas Altas continues around another rocky promontory, where the cannons of the old fort point out to the ocean past one of Mazatlán's best surf breaks. Changing its name to Av del Mar, the seafront road passes Playa Norte, a sunset fishing spot for pelicans and other birds, and the incongruously named **Monumento al Pescador** (Monument to the Fisherman), another of Mazatlán's nude statues.

At the south end of the peninsula, a prominent rocky outcrop provides the base for **El Faro**, 157m above sea level and supposedly the second-highest lighthouse in the world (after Gibraltar's). You can climb up there for a spectacular view of the city and coast. The hill, called Cerro del Creston, was once an island, but a causeway built in the 1930s now joins it to mainland. Mazatlán's sport-fishing fleet, the ferry to La Paz, cruise ships and some tourist boats dock in the marina on the east side of the causeway (see Boat Trips later).

Beaches & Zona Dorada

Mazatlán has 16km of sandy beaches that stretch north from Old Mazatlán to beyond the Zona Dorada. **Playa Norte** begins just north of Old Mazatlán and arcs toward Punta Camarón, a rocky point dominated by the conspicuous white walls and turrets of the FiestaLand nightclub complex. The traffic circle here marks the south end of the Zona Dorada, an unashamedly touristy precinct of hotels, restaurants, bars and souvenir shops. The fanciest hotels face the excellent beaches of **Playa Las Gaviotas** and **Playa Sábalo**.

North of the Zona Dorada, past the marina, lie a couple more beaches, **Playa Brujas** and **Playa Cerritos**, dotted mostly with private condominium complexes. Tourist services here, such as restaurants, are minimal. The Sábalo–Centro buses pass along all of these beaches, so getting to them is a piece of cake.

Between the town center and the Zona Dorada, **Acuario Mazatlán** *(☎ 981-78-15; Av de los Deportes s/n; child/adult US$3/6; open 9:30am-5:30pm daily)*, a block inland from Playa Norte, has 52 tanks with 250 species of fresh and saltwater fish and other creatures; diving, sea lion and bird shows are presented four times daily.

North of the marina, **MazAgua** *(☎ 988-00-41; Entroque Habal-Cerritos s/n; admission US$9; open 10am-6pm daily, closed Jan & Feb)* is a family aquatic park with water toboggans, wave pool and other entertainment. Take the Cerritos–Juárez bus.

Offshore Islands

Three rocky islands are clearly seen from Mazatlán's beaches – **Isla de Chivos** (Island of Goats) is on the left, and **Isla de Pájaros** (Island of Birds) is on the right.

In the middle, **Isla de Venados** (Island of Deer) has been designated a natural reserve for the protection of native flora and fauna; petroglyphs have been found on the island. Secluded beaches on the island are wonderful for a day trip, and the clear waters offer great snorkeling. Boats depart from the **Aqua Sport Centre** on the beach just south of El Cid Mega Resort *(☎ 913-33-33 ext 3341; Camarón Sábalo s/n; return trip US$9)*, at 10am, noon and 2pm daily, with the last boat returning at 4pm. Snorkeling equipment is

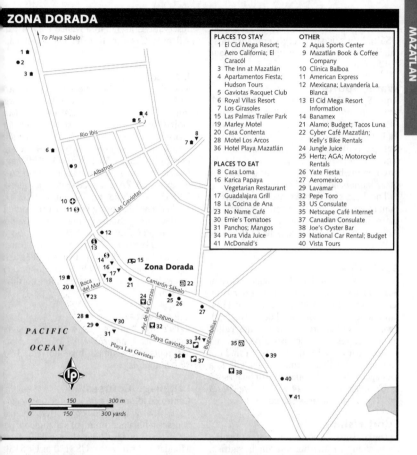

ZONA DORADA

To Playa Sábalo

PACIFIC OCEAN

Rio Ibis

Albatros

Las Gaviotas

Zona Dorada

Camarón Sábalo

Boca del Mar

Av de las Garzas

Laguna

Playa Gaviotas

Playa Las Gaviotas

Buganbilias

0   150   300 m
0   150   300 yards

PLACES TO STAY
1 El Cid Mega Resort;
  Aero California; El
  Caracól
3 The Inn at Mazatlán
4 Apartamentos Fiesta;
  Hudson Tours
5 Gaviotas Racquet Club
6 Royal Villas Resort
7 Los Girasoles
15 Las Palmas Trailer Park
19 Marley Motel
20 Casa Contenta
28 Motel Los Arcos
36 Hotel Playa Mazatlán

PLACES TO EAT
8 Casa Loma
16 Karica Papaya
  Vegetarian Restaurant
17 Guadalajara Grill
18 La Cocina de Ana
23 No Name Café
30 Ernie's Tomatoes
31 Panchos; Mangos
34 Pura Vida Juice
41 McDonald's

OTHER
2 Aqua Sports Center
9 Mazatlán Book & Coffee
  Company
10 Clínica Balboa
11 American Express
12 Mexicana; Lavandería La
  Blanca
13 El Cid Mega Resort
  Information
14 Banamex
21 Alamo; Budget; Tacos Luna
22 Cyber Café Mazatlán;
  Kelly's Bike Rentals
24 Jungle Juice
25 Hertz; AGA; Motorcycle
  Rentals
26 Yate Fiesta
27 Aeromexico
29 Lavamar
32 Pepe Toro
33 US Consulate
35 Netscape Café Internet
37 Canadian Consulate
38 Joe's Oyster Bar
39 National Car Rental; Budget
40 Vista Tours

available for US$9. For a more fancy cruise, check out the boat *Kolonahe* (☎ 916-34-68; US$42 per person).

Isla de la Piedra

'Stone Island' is actually a long, thin peninsula with its tip opposite El Faro (the lighthouse), at the south end of the city. Its sandy beach goes on as far as the eye can see, and is ideal for jogging. Bordering this beach are coconut groves and a row of *palapa* (thatched-roof shelter) restaurants, some of which have music and dancing on Sunday afternoons and holidays, when the beach is

popular with locals. Horse riding is possible, and snorkeling is good around the rocky point. Good surf breaks offshore attract surfers, as do some cheap accommodations. (See Places to Stay later in this chapter.)

To get to Isla de la Piedra, take a small boat from one of two docks. One is near the **ferry terminal** *(boats operate 9:30am-6pm)*, and boats from there will drop you at a jetty just a short walk from the Isla de la Piedra beach. The **other dock** *(boats operate 6am-midnight)* is further north, near the end of Nájera, and boats from there will leave you in the village on Isla de la Piedra, slightly further from the beach (but a *pulmonía*, a special type of taxi, will take you for about US$2). Boats depart every 10 minutes or so for the five-minute ride out to the island (US$1 return).

Water Sports

Aqua Sport Centre (☎ 913-33-33 ext 3341; just south of El Cid Mega Resort; Camarón Sábalo) is one place to go for water sports, including scuba diving, water-skiing, Hobie cats, parasailing, boogie boards and 'the banana.' Water sports equipment can also be hired on the beaches in front of most of the other large beachfront hotels.

The best **surf breaks** are the rights at Punta Camarón, and 'Cannons,' the lefts off the point near the old fort on Paseo Olas Altas, as well as the breaks just off Isla de la Piedra.

Boat Trips

As well as trips to Isla de Venados, several boats do three-hour sight-seeing trips, mostly leaving from the dock near El Faro at 11am (around US$14 including hotel transfers). Two-hour sunset cruises, sometimes called 'booze cruises,' include hors d'oeuvres and an open bar (US$16 to US$30). To find out more, look for flyers around town, talk to a tour agent, or call the operators of boats such as *Costalegre* (☎ 914-24-77) or *Yate Fiesta* (☎ 913-06-24; Camarón Sábalo 310).

Sport Fishing

Mazatlán is well known for its sport fishing – especially for marlin, swordfish, sailfish, tuna and *dorado* (dolphinfish). It's an expensive activity (around US$250 to US$360 for a day in a boat with three people fishing), though small game fishing is less expensive, especially with a group of five or six. Some of the following are based at the marina (up north), while others are at the dock near the foot of El Faro (down south).

El Cid Mega Resort (☎ 913-33-33)
Star Fleet (☎ 982-26-65; w www.starfleet.com.mx)
Flota Bibi (☎ 981-36-40)
Viking (☎ 986-34-84)
Flota Saballo (☎ 981-27-61)

For the winter high season, make fishing reservations as far in advance as you can. All operators should offer tag-and-release options.

Golf & Tennis

There's golf at **Club de Golf Campestre** (☎ 980-15-70; Hwy 15), east of town, charging US$33 for 18 holes. **Estrella del Mar Golf Club** (☎ 982-33-00; Isla de la Piedra) charges US$103 for 18 holes, golf cart and shuttle transportation. It's south of the airport by the coast. There's also **El Cid Mega Resort** (☎ 913-33-33; Camarón Sábalo s/n) north of the Zona Dorada. It costs guests US$55 for 18 holes and nonguests US$70.

You'll need to bring your own equipment to play tennis. Swing that racquet at **Gaviotas Racquet Club** (☎ 913-59-39; cnr Ibis & Bravo; US$11 per hour), with six courts (three clay), in the Zona Dorada; at El Cid Mega Resort (US$17/26 guest/nonguest); or at almost any other large hotel north of the center.

Bike Rentals

Kelly's Bike Rentals (☎ 914-11-87; Camarón Sábalo; open 10am-2pm & 4:30pm-8pm Mon-Sat) rents out mountain bikes for US$3.50/17 per hour/day.

Language Courses

Centro de Idiomas (☎ 985-56-06; Domínguez 1908; w www.spanishlink.org) offers Spanish courses with a maximum of six students per class. Two- or four-hour classes daily from Monday to Friday cost US$120 or US$150. Week-long classes are also available for homestay shared rooms (US$130) and private rooms (US$150). You can begin any Monday and study for as many weeks as you like; registration is every Saturday morning, 9am to noon. There are discounts if you sign up for four weeks. Homestays can be arranged with a Mexican family and include three meals a day (advance notice of 30 days required).

Organized Tours

Marlin Tours (☎ 913-53-01; w go2mazatlan.com/marlin/index.html; Camarón Sábalo 1504,

Local 113) offers a three-hour city tour (US$20), a colonial tour to the foothill towns of Concordia and Copala (US$35), a tour to the Tequila (US$31), and an ecological tour to Teacapan (US$44). **Vista Tours** *(☎ 986-86-10; ☒ www.vistatours.com.mx; Camarón Sábalo 51)* does at least 15 different types of tours in the area. Most cost US$28 to US$39. **AmEx** *(☎ 913-04-66; Camarón Sábalo 500)* does nine separate tours, most costing US$17 to US$28.

Robert Hudson of **Hudson Tours** *(☎ 913-17-64, 044-6699-11-68-77; ☒ www.hudsontours.com; Ibis 502)* speaks English and Spanish fluently, and does snorkeling (US$30), spearfishing (US$30), hiking (US$25), city (US$25) or shopping (US$15) tours with a minimum of two people. Robert has been doing tours in Mazatlán for more than 10 a decade.

Special Events

Mazatlán has one of Mexico's most flamboyant **Carnaval** celebrations. For the week leading up to Ash Wednesday in February or March, Mazatlán goes on a nonstop partying spree. People from around the country (and beyond) pour in for the music, dancing, parades and general revelry. If you want to brave it, be sure to reserve a hotel room in advance. The party climaxes on the Monday and Tuesday before Ash Wednesday, then abruptly ends the morning of Ash Wednesday. Catholics then go to church and receive ash marks on their foreheads for the first day of Lent.

A **fishing tournament** *(torneo de pesca)* for sailfish, marlin and *dorado* is held in mid-May and mid-November. Golf tournaments and various cultural festivals are held throughout the year; the tourist office has details.

On December 12, the **day of the Virgen de Guadalupe** is celebrated at the cathedral, to which children wearing costumes are taken.

Places to Stay – Budget

Camping The trailer parks are near the beaches toward the north end of the town, though most of them are not especially attractive for tent camping.

Mar Rosa Trailer & RV Park *(☎/fax 913-61-87; ☒ g_vanduyn@yahoo.com; Camarón Sábalo 702; sites US$14-24)* has small sites, but they're next to the beach. It's secure and offers all the basic services, but don't come in summer, when it's closed.

La Posta Trailer Park *(☎ 983-53-10; ☒ topshoes@mzt.megared.net.mx; Rafael Buelna 7; camping US$6 per person, trailer sites from US$18)* takes care of 180 grassy sites, some with shade, as well as a swimming pool and a common room. There's Internet service, and it's handy to the fleshpots of the Zona Dorada.

Las Palmas Trailer Park *(☎ 913-53-11; Camarón Sábalo 333; sites around US$17)* lies at the heart of the Zona Dorada and tends 68 palmy spaces full of gringos and their RVs. It's central but nothing special. Discounts are available for longer stays.

On **Isla de la Piedra** you can camp on the beach, though this may not be completely safe. English-speaking Victor or Chris at **Victor's** palapa restaurant can advise about security. Restaurants that may have basic rooms for rent (US$6 to US$12 per night) include **Casa Zen**, **El Palmar**, **Florencio's** and **Doña Chavela**.

Hotels Situated in a working-class 'hood, **Hotel del Río** *(☎ 982-44-30; Juárez 2410; rooms US$11)* has small rooms and a TV that blares from the lobby, but at this price who cares?

Hotel México *(☎ 981-38-06; ☒ hotelmexico@starmedia.com; México 201; 1/2 beds US$9/14)* is a good old cheapie with some personality. It's a block from the beach.

Hotel San Jorge *(☎ 981-36-95; cnr Serdán & Gastelum; rooms US$23)*, also close to the beach, though the street outside interrupts slumber. The rooms are good.

Hotel Belmar *(☎ 985-11-12; Olas Altas 166; singles/doubles US$25/29, with sea view US$28/34)* has seen better days and could use a tight face-lift, but remains a classic with a mishmash of tiles and some retro appeal. Rooms have air-con and TV – the best come with balconies and face the sea.

Hotel La Siesta *(☎ 981-26-40, fax 982-26-33; ☒ www.lasiesta.com.mx; Olas Altas 11;*

singles/doubles US$26/30, with sea views US$39/42) has a long, darkish courtyard full of tropical plants, and 51 spacious, tidy rooms with air-con, TV and a touch of character. Sunset on a private balcony facing the sea is worth the extra bucks.

Hotel Central *(☎ 982-18-88; Domínguez 2; singles/doubles with air-con & TV US$28/31)* claims a central location in the heart of Old Mazatlán. It's also friendly, clean and well kept, and there's a cafeteria downstairs.

During nonholiday periods, there are some good deals among the more expensive places along Playa Norte and the Zona Dorada.

Hotel Perla *(☎ 985-33-66; cnr Av del Mar & Isla Asada; rooms from US$13)* lies somewhat desolately on a side road about 2km south of the Zona Dorada. However, it's new, lemon yellow and cheaply built, with perfectly respectable, tidy and clean rooms.

Hotel San Diego *(☎ 983-57-03; w www .hotelsandiego.tripod.com; cnr Av del Mar & Buelna; singles/doubles US$21-25/26-31)* sits at the south end of the Zona Dorada and within stumbling distance of nightlife. Small, OK rooms come with air-con, TV and, if you're lucky, a balcony.

Las Jacarandas *(☎ 984-11-77, fax 984-10-77; Av del Mar 2500; rooms US$22, with air-con US$25)* goes for that 'unfinished' look and doesn't use its large size efficiently: it sports motel-like, forgettable rooms. But it's a bit funky and the rooms out back overlook the lagoon, while the ones in front have balconies and sea views.

Places to Stay – Mid-Range

There are some good mid-range choices on the long Av del Mar, opposite Playa Norte, with frequent buses heading north and south. All have swimming pools, car parking and air-con rooms with TV and phone, but are farther from the concentrated activity centers.

Hotel del Sol *(☎/fax 985-11-03; w www .hoteldelsol.tripod.com; Av del Mar 800; rooms with air-con from US$31, with kitchen US$53)* would be best for families that can stand the fluorescent lighting. It's not a great deal, but there's a pool.

Hotel de Cima *(☎ 982-74-00, fax 982-73-11; Av del Mar 48; rooms from US$32)* takes pride in its 140 rooms and tunnel access to the beach. It's your typical clean and pleasant digs, and a great deal when this 'sale' price is on offer.

Hotel Sands *(☎ 982-00-00, fax 982-10-25; w www.sandsarenas.com; Av del Mar 1910; singles/doubles US$40/51, singles & doubles with sea view US$62)* comes with restaurant/bar, pool area and good rooms with balcony, cable TV and fridge.

Los Girasoles *(☎ 913-52-88, fax 913-06-86; Las Gaviotas 709; apartments US$49-59)* makes your stay in Mazatlán pleasant, with beautiful, spacious and sparkling clean apartments. There's a well-tended pool in the garden, and the staff speak English.

A handful of mid-range digs are tucked away in Zona Dorada backstreets.

Apartamentos Fiesta *(☎/fax 913-53-55; w www.hudsontours.com; Ibis 502; rooms US$13-60)* coddles 12 apartments, all different in size and layout. All have kitchens and good decor and are peacefully located in or near the leafy garden area. English is spoken.

Marley Motel *(☎/fax 913-55-33; e mot marley@mzt.megared.net.mx; Playa Gaviotas 226; 1/2 beds US$77/94)* has nice kitchen apartments but only the seafront ones are really worth the price. There's a pool to take a splash in.

Motel Los Arcos *(☎/fax 913-50-66; e mlarcos@prodigy.net.mx; Playa Gaviotas 214; 1/2 beds US$79/94)* features good-value suites that have kitchenettes and sea views. They're very comfortable, spacious and clean, and the beach is right there.

Gaviotas Racquet Club *(☎/fax 913-59-39; e gaviotas@mzt.megared.net.mx; cnr Ibis & Río Bravo; suites per week/month US$440/880)* caters to long-term tennis aficionados. All pleasant suites have kitchen, there's a pool, and if you're not a guest you can play tennis for US$11 per hour. Outside areas could use a facelift.

Places to Stay – Top End

Rooms at top-end hotels can be booked most economically as part of a holiday package – see your travel agent at home.

Casa Contenta (☎ 913-49-76, fax 913-99-86; Playa Gaviotas 224; apartments US$105) has just a few intimate apartments, some with partial ocean views. There's a tiny pool and the intimate grounds are nicely tended. An oceanfront six- to eight-person house is available.

Hotel Playa Mazatlán (☎ 989-05-55; W www.playamazatlan.com.mx; Playa Gaviotas 202; rooms US$107-128) sports 425 well-appointed rooms popular with organizers of packaged vacations. It's the kind of hotel with stores on the premises, and where taxis line up outside waiting for guests to go somewhere for a vastly inflated price. Still, the pools, common areas and the sea views are terrific.

Aguamarina Hotel (☎ 981-70-80, fax 982-46-24; Av del Mar 110; rooms US$117) satisfies most picky tourists with very clean, spacious abodes. There are rooms with cable TV and phone, a pool, a restaurant-bar, a travel agency and parking. Ask for an oceanfront room.

The Inn at Mazatlán (☎ 913-55-00, fax 913-54-82; W www.innatmazatlan.com.mx; Camarón Sábalo 6291; rooms from US$175) has decent-enough rooms, suites and an eight-person penthouse. It's right on the beach, and there's a pool if you prefer chlorinated water. Rates can drop here during slow times.

El Cid Mega Resort (☎ 913-33-33, fax 914-11-34; W www.elcid.com.mx; Camarón Sábalo s/n; rooms from US$199) tries to do it all, with 1230 rooms, 10 restaurant and snack bars, tons of activities and a pool. It's the biggest luxury hotel in Mazatlán, but there are more impressive places to stay than here.

Pueblo Bonito (☎ 914-37-00, fax 914-17-23; W www.pueblobonito.com; Camarón Sábalo 2121; rooms with kitchenettes from US$206) faces a fine stretch of uncrowded beach while exuding class and sporting all the facilities that you would expect at a place in this range.

Royal Villas Resort (☎ 916-61-61, fax 914-07-77; W www.royalvillas.com.mx; Camarón Sábalo 500; rooms US$206-502) offers plenty of luxury and is one of the most

pleasant hotels in Mazatlán. All rooms are spacious and come with kitchen and dining room. The large terraced sea view balconies are simply stunning.

Places to Eat

Mazatlán is famous for fresh seafood – the shrimp is especially fantastic. Also try pescado zarandeado, a delicious charcoal-broiled fish stuffed with onion, celery and spices. A whole kilogram, feeding two people well, usually costs around US$10, while shrimp is around US$6 to US$12 per dish. The standard Mexican meat and chicken dishes are available at most places too, and generally cost much less than seafood.

Old Mazatlán There's no shortage of eateries in Old Mazatlán, and they aren't as expensive (or as fancy) as those in the Zona Dorada. For the cheapest treats head to the **food stalls** outside the local market on Nájera, toward the north. Give locally recommended, unsigned **La Carreta** a try; it's at Nájera and Carbajal. Just don't expect anything fancy.

Mariscos El Camichín (☎ 985-01-97; Paseo Claussen 97; mains US$5-11; open 10am-10pm daily) faces Playa Norte and is a palapa restaurant popular with both tourists and locals. A wide selection of delicious seafood is served, and live music often strolls by, though it's not free.

Restaurant Los Pelícanos (cnr Paseo Claussen & Uribe; meals US$4-7; open 10am-6pm Tues-Sun) is a small open-air restaurant that does some of the cheapest and tastiest seafood in Mazatlán. It has a great view of the entire arc of Playa Norte, and catches any sea breezes going by.

El Shrimp Bucket (☎ 981-63-50; Paseo Olas Altas 11; mains US$6-20; open 6am-11pm daily) serves great-sounding stuff like coconut shrimp and beer-battered shrimp (both US$20), but some think it's become indifferent and overrated. It has a large and varied menu, tables outside on the street, and a very air-conditioned interior.

La Copa de Leche (☎ 982-57-50; Paseo Olas Altas 1220; mains US$7-17; open

Taco Stands Everywhere!

Looking for a cheap, quick meal on the run? Look no farther than one of Mexico's ubiquitous taco stands, a godsend tailor-made for the busy budget traveler.

Amble on up to the counter and your choices are clear: *tripa* (intestine), *uba* (udder), *cabeza* (head meat) or *lengua* (tongue). Of course, the much more palatable and commonplace meat choices are *carne asada/res/bistek birria* (varieties of grilled beef) or chorizo. Often there will only be a few items on the menu, as different taco stands specialize in different things.

Tacos can vary in size, but are usually about three or four bites and around US$0.50 to US$0.75 each. Say *'con todo'* if you want extras such as beans, onion and cilantro. They'll be prepared to order, and put on plastic plates covered in clean plastic bags (making cleanup easy but creating unfortunate trash). The best stands are bigger and offer grilled onions, complimentary salsas and radish or cucumber slices. Unless the stand has plastic chairs or is near public seating, you'll probably have to stand to munch the tacos down. Pay for your meal after you eat.

And what about sanitary conditions? Well, have a peek at the stand itself: Does it look clean? Is it busy? Is the food piping hot or has it been hanging loose awhile? Use your instincts, but remember that many travelers (including this author) have visited heaps of these convenient treasures and never picked up a bug. There are no guarantees, but adventurous travel is all about tasting the local life, don't you think?

7:30am-11pm daily) is a covered sidewalk eatery popular with the local gentry for breakfast, a filling and economical *comida corrida* (daily special), a snack, a drink or an evening espresso. Nearby **Fonda Santa Clara** is almost identical.

Puerto Viejo (☎ 928-82-26; Olas Altas 25; meals under US$5.50; open 10:30am-11pm Mon-Fri, 10:30am-1am Sat & Sun) is a very casual, breezy and inexpensive seafood joint that also serves plenty of cheap booze, from Tom Collins to tequila sunrises (US$3 or less). Old US hits fill the air while hanging blowfish stare down from the ceilings. It's popular with expats, and local bands occasionally play.

Mariscos La Puntilla (☎ 982-88-77; Flota Playa Sur s/n; meals US$6-14; open 10am-7pm daily) is an open-air seafood spot south of town, across from Isla de la Piedra. It's especially popular on weekends – the mood is relaxed and the food good. Watch people clean their fish on the beach, while frigates and pelicans ask for a share.

In the heart of Old Mazatlán, **Plazuela Machado** is a delightful space with real Mexican tropical ambience. It's sublime in the evening when the plaza is softly lit, music plays, kids frolic, and outdoor tables offer cool drinks, snacks and meals in a very romantic atmosphere.

Café Pacífico (☎ 981-39-72; Constitución 501; meals US$6-9; open 9am-2am daily) identifies as a bar, café or restaurant, depending on your needs. It's been an anchor at this corner for years, offering solid food, stiff drinks and friendly service.

Pedro y Lola (☎ 982-25-89; Carnaval 1303; mains US$7-15) was named after old, glamorous Mexican singers Pedro Infante and Lola Beltran. It serves, among other fancy seafood things, a flambe that attracts everyone's attention at night. Seating is outdoors and romantic.

El Machado (☎ 981-13-75; Sixto Osuna 34; mains US$4.50-11; open 9am-midnight) puts out sidewalk tables perfect for a cold beer and a tasty fish taco or three.

Thorny's Surf Burger (Sixto Osuna 510B; burgers US$4; open noon-10:30pm Wed-Mon) is crammed full of gringos getting a taste of home: burgers, hot dogs and sandwiches. There are very few items on the menu, but lots on CNN.

El Túnel (Carnaval 1207; meals around US$4; open noon-midnight daily) is a cozy, traditional and friendly spot on a pedestrian street. A short hallway opens to an airy patio, where diners enjoy inexpensive traditional Mexican fare and top it off with *raspados* (flavored shaved ice).

Zona Dorada & Around Most of the Zona Dorada restaurants cater to the tourist trade.

No Name Café (☎ 913-20-31; Playa Gaviotas 417; mains US$5-13; open noon-1am daily) features a good bar area, a nice leafy patio, overly feisty waiters and lots of sports on TV. Despite its claim, the ribs aren't quite the best ones you'll ever eat – but they're good enough. Plenty of drinks help them go down easy.

Tacos Luna (Camarón Sábalo 400) is a cheap plastic chairs and tables sort of place, but once the grill gets going the US$0.75 tacos come fast and hot. Quesadillas are US$1.35 and burgers US$2.75.

Guadalajara Grill (☎ 913-50-65; Camarón Sábalo 335; meals US$5-15; open 8am-midnight daily) lives in a wildly decorated, barn-like space with nice leafy patio, bar and DJ areas. It serves safe, substantial Mexican meals at full tourist prices, and puts on some mean parties at night.

Karica Papaya Vegetarian Restaurant (☎ 922-13-75; Camarón Sábalo 333; meals US$5; open 8:30am-4:30pm Mon-Sat) rates a mention only because there aren't many veggie places in town. Limited, edgy selections of vegetarian food in a simple environment greet you here. Hopefully they've set their sights on improving quality by the time you arrive.

La Cocina de Ana (☎ 916-31-19; Laguna 49; mains US$3-7; open noon-4pm Mon-Sat) offers buffet lunch fare such as meatball soup, chili con carne and paella in a small and homey dining area. It's a good antidote for all that fancy tourist junk food.

Pura Vida Juice (☎ 916-58-15; cnr Bugambilias & Laguna; open 8am-10pm daily) squeezes out the juices for about US$2.50 per load. Some food is available, but this is mainly a place to drink up the vitamins.

Panchos (☎ 914-09-11; Playa Gaviotas 408/1B; mains US$7-17) has things on the menu like frogs' legs with garlic and 'crackaling snack squid'. The ambience is great, the music is soft, and the views are romantic. There's a wide selection of all the typical tourist fare goodies.

Mangos (☎ 916-00-44; Playa Gaviotas 404; mains US$5-14; open noon-1am Mon-Fri, noon-3am Sat-Sun), a restaurant-bar, gets wild on weekends, with dancing and plenty of heavy drinking in the tropical-themed atmosphere. The menu claims 'the mango is an aphrodisiac', so you get the idea of what's emphasized here. There's a limited selection of seafood, sandwiches, salads and Mexican dishes.

Ernie's Tomatoes (☎ 916-54-26; Playa Gaviotas 403; mains US$5.50-10; open 11:30am- idnight daily) is quite possibly the best place for a woman to get a date with one of the waiters – Ernie's not the only one with tomatoes. Seafood and meats cover most of the menu, and the atmosphere's brash and generic.

Casa Loma (☎ 913-53-98; Las Gaviotas 104; mains US$8-20; open 1:30pm-10:30pm daily) isn't your typical tourist party house

Fruit in a Bag

You'll see them in many parts of Mexico, in the city or on the beach: small cart vendors selling juicy slices of mango, cucumber and jicama, or cut squares of watermelon and papaya. Each fruit or vegetable is brightly presented in a clear plastic bag or cup (with a fork or toothpick stuck on the top), tempting you to stop, drop some spare change and take a quick refreshing snack. How can you resist?

You can often also choose a mixed bag of fruit, or ask the vendor to make up a particular combination of fruits available (this may up the price a few cents, though). The final price depends on quantity of fruit in the bag and popularity of town with tourists. Expect to pay from US$0.60 to US$1.50, with US$1.25 as the common denominator. For an extra, savory kick, have the vendor add salt, lime juice and chili powder to your package – this may sound a bit unconventional at first, but one taste of sweet mango with the opposing flavors of salt and chili and you might just get hooked. Plus, not many bugs can survive the double whammy of chili and lime. Hopefully your taste buds and tummy can, though.

but rather a more sophisticated joint that some think is the best restaurant in Mazatlán. The outdoor patio is airy, while the inside seating's darkish.

Los Criminales *(Av del Mar, near Insurgentes; open 7pm-2:20am daily)* is the home of some kick-ass quesadillas, which is the reason locals flock here. They're simply 'criminal,' one resident exclaimed. You won't see many gringos frequenting this open-air place.

Señor Frog's *(☎ 985-11-10; Av del Mar s/n; meals US$8-20; open noon-1am daily)* is situated halfway between Old Mazatlán and the Zona Dorada. The food is decent if overpriced, but folks come to Frog's mainly to party and buy those annoying T-shirts.

Isla de la Piedra Stroll along the beach here and enjoy choosing where to eat. Check what's on offer at the open kitchens under the palapas. It's hard to beat a fresh barbecued fish and a cold beer as you wiggle your toes in the sand.

Entertainment

Cultural Events The 'Nightingale of Mexico' perished in the yellow-fever epidemic that killed hundreds of Mazatlecos in the 1860s. Today she has a historic theater named after her:the **Teatro Angela Peralta** *(☎ 982-44-47; Carnaval 47, near Plazuela Machado)* showcases events of all kinds – movies, concerts, opera (Mazatlán has its own opera company), theater and more. A sign on the walkway in front of the theater announces current and upcoming cultural events here and also at other venues around the city.

If you get a chance, try to hear a rousing traditional *banda sinaloense* – a boisterous brass band unique to the state of Sinaloa and especially associated with Mazatlán.

Bars & Discos The incongruous white castle on Punta Camerón, at the south end of the Zona Dorada, is **FiestaLand** *(☎ 984-17-77; Av del Mar s/n)*, a nightlife fun zone where several of Mazatlán's major venues are concentrated. There's a central ticket office, with information about what's on at

each venue. Note that nothing really hops until after midnight.

Valentino *(☎ 984-16-66; admission US$6-8; open 9pm-4am daily)* rocks with pop, rap, disco and house music. A mixed group of well-dressed Mexican and foreign tourists, mostly 20- and 30-somethings, flock here to take in the split levels of modern decor edged by bars under dim colored lights.

Bora Bora *(☎ 984-16-66; admission after 11pm US$6; open 9pm-4am daily)* is a popular outside beach bar and disco under lit-up palm trees and open sky. There are a few separate bars and seating areas, and even a sand volleyball court.

Bali Hai bar, **Pepe & Joe's Microbrewery Restaurant** and **Mikonos** are also in the FiestaLand complex.

Jungle Juice *(☎ 913-33-15; cnr Av de las Garzas & Laguna; open 6pm-2am daily)* booms from blocks away with rock music from the 1960s to the 1990s.

Joe's Oyster Bar *(☎ 983-53-33; Playa Gaviotas 100; admission US$5.50; open 11am-2am daily)* is a beachfront bar and great hangout spot, but it goes ballistic in the evenings, when it's packed with college kids dancing on tables, chairs and each other. As one waiter put it, 'From 7pm, people come here to get drunk.'

Pepe Toro *(☎ 914-41-76; Av de las Garzas 18; admission Fri US$3.50, Sat US$5.50 including drink; open 9pm-4am Thur-Sun)* brings gays, lesbians and some straight folks into its dark and intimate dancefloor ringed by seating and a small stage. Each Saturday night there's a strip, transvestite or go-go show at 1am.

Hotel Playa Mazatlán *(☎ 989-05-55; Playa Gaviotas 202; open 7pm-midnight Sun-Thur, 7pm-1am Fri-Sat)* plays live soft rock nightly at its sophisticated beachside restaurant and bar, attracting the 30s-and-up crowd for dancing under the stars.

El Caracól *(☎ 913-33-33; El Cid Mega Resort, Camarón Sábalo s/n; open 9pm-4am daily)* caters to an upmarket crowd and gives them loud techno music and fantastic lighting. Admission charge ranges from US$6 to US$11, depending on the number of drinks included.

Señor Frog's (☎ 985-11-10; Av del Mar s/n; open noon-1am daily) attracts youthful party energy, playing loud dance music to a packed dancefloor almost every night. Expect obnoxiousness.

On Sunday afternoon there is live music and dancing at a couple of **palapas** on the beach at Isla de la Piedra, patronized mostly by hard-drinking, hot-dancing locals.

Fiestas Mexicanas Grab some sensationalized Mexican culture at a Fiesta Mexicana. Several of the largest luxury hotels run these shows, which include dinner and drinks. Summer schedules can mean fewer shows – call for exact dates and times.

Hotel Playa Mazatlán (☎ 989-05-55; Playa Gaviotas 202; admission US$28; open 7pm-10:30pm Tues, Thur & Sat) offers a Mexican buffet dinner, open bar, folkloric floor show and live Latin dance music. Call the hotel for reservations or reserve at a travel agency.

El Cid Mega Resort (☎ 913-33-33; Camarón Sábalo s/n; admission US$32) has its own offering on Wednesday and Saturday nights and other themes on other nights.

Spectator Sports

Plaza de Toros, inland from the Zona Dorada traffic circle, hosts bullfights from 4pm on Sundays from Christmas to Easter; the Sábalo–Cocos bus will drop you there. Tickets (US$33) are sold at travel agencies, major hotels, the Bora Bora shop beside Valentino disco, and the **Salon Bacanora** (☎ 986-91-55) beside Plaza de Toros.

Charreadas (rodeos) are held at **Lienzo Charro** (☎ 986-35-10; Colonia Juárez).

Shopping

Most of your tourist shopping needs will be met in the Zona Dorada, where plenty of clothes, pottery, jewelry and craft stores are located. For something more local, hop on a bus heading east to the **Tianguis de Juárez** (Juárez flea market), held every Sunday starting at 5am; the ride takes 20 minutes. You can't buy snake oil, but you can come close – snakeskins, bootleg CDs, used clothes, housewares, tools, hamsters, taco stands and other Mexican treats are for sale.

Getting There & Away

Air Situated 20km southeast of the city is **Mazatlán international airport** (☎ 982-23-99). Airlines serving the airport include:

Aero California	(☎ 916-21-95)
Aeroméxico	(☎ 914-11-11)
Alaska Airlines	(☎ 981-48-13)
America West	(☎ 981-11-84)
Mexicana	(☎ 913-07-72)

Bus The city's **main bus station** (Central de Autobuses; Av de los Deportes) is at Ejército Méxicano and Ferrusquia, about three blocks inland from the beach (Ferrusquia is marked by an old 'super scorpio V' sign on Av del Mar). Inexpensive hotels are nearby. On the other side of the block is the terminal for 2nd-class buses, which service small towns in the area (such as Concordia, Copala and Rosario). Long-distance services include those to:

Durango US$28 1st class with Estrella Blanca, seven hours, 321km, five daily; US$24 2nd class, seven daily

Guadalajara US$30 1st class with Estrella Blanca, eight hours, 506km, three daily; US$25 2nd class, hourly

Mexico City (Terminal Norte) US$68 1st class, 17 hours, 1041km, three daily; US$59 2nd class de paso, hourly

Puerto Vallarta US$32 1st class with Elite, eight hours, 459km, one daily; or take a bus to Tepic, where buses depart frequently for Puerto Vallarta

Tepic US$14 1st class with Estrella Blanca, five hours, 290km; US$12 2nd class, frequent buses

To get to San Blas (290km), go first to Tepic then get a bus from there. This involves some backtracking, but the alternative (getting off the bus at Crucero San Blas, and waiting there for a Tepic–San Blas bus) is not safe. Travelers have been accosted at Crucero San Blas.

Boat From its terminal at the south end of town, **Sematur** (☎ 981-70-20/21; w www .ferrysematur.com.mx; open 8:30am-2:30pm daily) operates ferries between Mazatlán and La Paz, Baja California (actually to the port of Pichilingue, 22km from La Paz). Ferries depart at 3pm daily in winter; summer schedules may be different. The trip costs US$51 and lasts 17 hours. For information on travel from Baja, see Sea in the Getting There & Away chapter.

Ahome Travel Agency (☎ *985-22-28;* e *vahome_mzt@hotmail.com; Ferrusquilla 149),* near the bus terminal, also sells tickets – you can book up to a month in advance.

Getting Around

To/From the Airport *Colectivos* (minibuses) operate from the airport to town, but not from town to the airport. They cost US$5.50 and run when full every five to 15 minutes from 7:30am to 10:30pm, dropping you right at your hotel. Taxis to/from the airport are about US$22.

Bus Local buses operate daily from around 5:30am to 10:30pm. Regular white buses cost US$0.40; Urban Pluss air-con green buses cost US$0.80. You can flag them down practically anywhere. Useful routes for visitors include:

Sábalo–Centro Travels from the market in the center to the beach via Juárez, then north on Av del Mar to the Zona Dorada and farther north on Camarón Sábalo

Playa Sur Travels south along Ejército Méxicano near the bus station and through the city center, passing the market, then to the ferry terminal and El Faro

To reach Old Mazatlán from the bus terminal, go to Ejército Méxicano and catch any bus going south (to your right if the bus terminal is behind you). Alternatively, walk 500m from the bus station to the beach and take a Sábalo–Centro bus heading south (left) to the center.

Car & Motorcycle Renting a car in Mexico isn't cheap; expect to pay at least US$60 per day with minimal insurance. Car rental agencies in Mazatlán include:

Aga (☎ 981-35-80) Camarón Sábalo 312
Alamo (☎ 913-10-10) Camarón Sábalo 410

Budget (☎ 913-20-00) Camarón Sábalo 402 and Camarón Sábalo Local E, Cento Comercial Camarón
Hertz (☎ 913-60-60) Camarón Sábalo 314
National (☎ 913-60-00) Camarón Sábalo 7000

Various companies on Camarón Sábalo in the Zona Dorada rent small motorcycles for getting around town – you'll see the bikes lined up beside the road. Prices are somewhat negotiable, around US$30 per day. You need a driver's license to hire one; any type of license will do.

Pulmonías & Taxis Mazatlán has both redand-white taxis and green-and-white taxis. Their standard rates for trips around town run from US$2.75 to US$5; Old Mazatlán to the Zona Dorada costs about US$3. Some locals believe the green-and-white taxis are a bit cheaper than the red-and-white ones.

There's also a special type of taxi called a *pulmonía,* a small open-air vehicle similar to a golf cart – usually a modified VW. They are just as expensive as regular taxis, if not more so – their novelty with gringos probably accounts for this.

Taxis and *pulmonías* hanging out at stands or in front of hotels charge more than those rolling along on the streets. Nighttime raises the price of your ride.

AROUND MAZATLÁN

Several small, picturesque colonial towns in the Sierra Madre foothills make pleasant day trips from Mazatlán. Note that if you visit on a Sunday, many things will be shut down.

Concordia, founded in 1565, has an 18th-century church with a baroque facade, elaborately decorated columns, a daily market around it, and hot mineral springs nearby; the village is known for its manufacture of high-quality pottery and handcarved furniture. It's about a 45-minute drive east of Mazatlán; head southeast on Hwy 15 for 20km to Villa Unión, turn inland on Hwy 40 (the highway to Durango) and go another 20km.

Also founded in 1565, the charming little town of **Copala,** 40km past Concordia on Hwy 40, was one of Mexico's first mining

AROUND MAZATLÁN

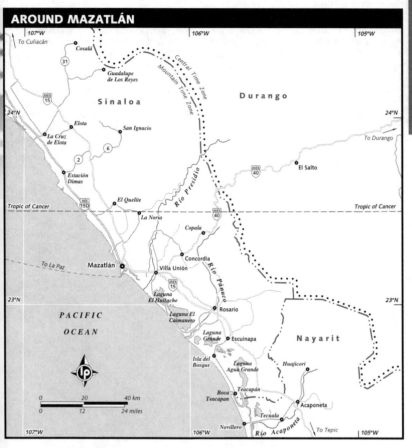

towns. It has a colonial church (1748), red-tiled houses and a tiny museum, and local urchins sell donkey rides while pigs and chickens roam the cobblestone streets. There are a couple of hotels ; try the quaint **Copala Butter Company** (☎ 985-42-25; rooms US$22) if you decide to spend the night, though you can visit both Concordia and Copala in a day – even on public transport. Take an *auriga*, or transport pickup, between the two towns (US$1.75, 30 minutes).

Rosario, 76km southeast of Mazatlán on Hwy 15, founded in 1655, is another colonial mining town. Its most famous feature is

the gold-leaf altar in its church Nuestra Señora del Rosario.

In the mountains north of Mazatlán, **Cosalá** is a beautiful colonial mining village dating from 1550. It features a 17th-century church, an even older chapel, a historical and mining museum in a colonial mansion on the leafy plaza, and four hotels. Attractions nearby include **Vado Hondo**, a *balneario* (bathing resort) with a large natural swimming pool and three waterfalls, 15km from town; **La Gruta México**, a large cave 18km from town; and the **Presa El Comedero** reservoir, 20km from town, with

MAZATLÁN

hired rowboats for fishing. To get to Cosalá, head north on Hwy 15 for 113km to the turnoff (opposite the turnoff for La Cruz de Elota on the coast) and then go about 45km up into the mountains. If taking the direct bus, consider staying the night, since bus schedules are such that you only get one hour in town before needing to head back the same day (but check and make sure this is still the case). The more adventurous can always return to Cosalá the same day by taking any bus heading to the coast highway, then another back to Mazatlán.

Buses depart from the 2nd-class terminal in Mazatlán. To Concordia they go every 15 minutes (US$1.50, 1½ hours); to Copala there are three per day (US$2.75, two hours, at 8:30am, 12:30pm and 1:30pm); to Cosalá they literally shake, rattle and roll twice daily (US$9, three hot hours; take water). Tours to these spots are available as well (see Organized Tours in this chapter).

Nayarit & Guadalajara

About 100km south of Mazatlán, Hwy 15 crosses the border into the rich state of Nayarit, which stretches south almost all the way to Puerto Vallarta. Along this length of coast, lying between occasional bird-filled marshlands or lagoons, are both isolated beaches and busy resort towns. The ocean here can kick up decent surges, making for some very attractive surfing destinations, but there are also plenty of spots in which to take it easy and do nothing. Public transportation is straightforward and simple, getting you to most destinations without much hassle. This state has much to offer, as many American and Canadian travelers have shown by settling here at least part of the year – some even establishing business enterprises to serve visitors. The capital of Nayarit, inland Tepic, is a unpretentious city with a number of museums and a pleasant center where the Huichol – one of a few indigenous peoples in Nayarit – live.

Guadalajara is further inland, east of Tepic, and the capital of neighboring Jalisco state. Rich in culture and elaborate old edifices, Mexico's second-largest city is relatively pleasant to visit. Pedestrian streets lined with trees and fountains dominate the city's center, while excellent museums and arts facilities entertain scores of Mexicans, expats and travelers. If Guadalajara is your fly-in gateway to Mexico's Pacific coastline, make sure you allow yourself some time to check this city out.

Highlights

- Boating along San Blas' mangrove jungles and spotting sunning birds and crocodiles
- Surfing killer waves at Sayulita and San Pancho, or the mile-long roller at Bahía de Matanchen
- Tripping out to Mexcaltitán, a flood-prone island believed to be the Aztec homeland
- Heading to the town of Tequila, touring a distillery and sampling the potent liquid goods
- Visiting the pleasant *zócalos* and museums of Mexico's second-largest city, Guadalajara

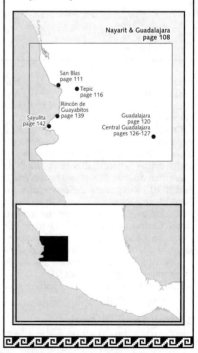

Nayarit & Guadalajara
page 108

San Blas
page 111

Tepic
page 116

Rincón de Guayabitos
page 139

Sayulita
page 142

Guadalajara
page 120
Central Guadalajara
pages 126-127

SANTIAGO IXCUINTLA
☎ 323 • pop 18,000

Santiago Ixcuintla is fairly pleasant, non-touristy town sporting a pretty little *zócalo* (main plaza) with ornate grandstand and surrounding arcaded sidewalks. Sitting inland, about 230km southeast of Mazatlán, it's mainly of interest as the jumping-off point for the historic island village of Mexcaltitán de Uribe (usually referred to as Mexcaltitán). The **tourist office** *(open 9am-3pm Mon-Fri, erratically on Sat & Sun)* and

NAYARIT & GUADALAJARA

Internet services are on the zócalo, while banks with money exchange are nearby. There's a market with cheap **food stalls** two blocks north of the zócalo.

Centro Huichol (☎ 235-11-71; Calle 20 de Noviembre 452 & Constitución; open erratically 10am-7pm Mon-Sat) is a handicrafts center where indigenous Huichols make their distinctive arts and crafts; you'll find it 10 blocks from the city center toward Mexcaltitán.

A couple of hotels are near the market. **Hotel Casino** (☎ 235-08-50; Ocampo 40; rooms from US$17) has parking, a surprisingly good restaurant and dark, modern rooms with TV. **Hotel Reforma** (Av 20 de Noviembre 89; singles/doubles US$5.50/9) is situated just off the zócalo, sporting old, very basic and clean rooms with TV.

Getting There & Away
Santiago Ixcuintla is situated about 8km west of the Hwy 15 crucero (turnoff). Three bus lines operate in town, each within a block of each other and about two blocks west of the zócalo. For transport to Mexcaltitán, see that town's Getting There & Away section.

Buses from Tepic leave frequently to Santiago Ixcuintla (US$4.50, 1½ hours). From Mazatlán, you may have to take a Tepic, Guadalajara or San Blas bus and be let off at Las Peñas, a highway town about 10km before the Santiago Ixcuintla crucero; from here there are frequent buses (US$1.50), taxis colectivos (shared taxi; US$1.75) or taxis (US$9). Avoid going all the way to the crucero and waiting there for a bus to take you in; at night it's not a safe place to hang around.

Long-distance buses leaving from Santiago include Mazatlán (Rapido del Sur, US$11, four hours), Guadalajara (Transportes del Pacífico, US$19, five hours) and San Blas (Transportes Norte de Sonora, US$3.50, 1½ hours).

MEXCALTITÁN
☎ 319 • pop 1800

A small, safe and friendly ancient island village, Mexcaltitán is also traffic-free and a fascinating place to visit – plus, getting there is half the fun. You must take a 15-minute *lancha* (motor boat) trip through mangrove channels and lagoons full of fish, shrimp, birds and mosquitoes (crocodiles used to live here too before getting hunted out). Tourism has scarcely touched this shrimp-fishing hamlet, though it does have pleasant waterside restaurants and a small museum. Birders should not miss a trip out here.

The island was originally called Aztlán (meaning 'place of egrets'), and some believe it was the original homeland of the Aztec people. Around 1116 they left the isle and began the generations-long migration that eventually led them to Tenochtitlán (modern Mexico City) about 1325.

Mexcaltitán is sometimes referred to as the 'Venice of Mexico.' It is surrounded completely by a large lagoon, and the dirt streets are sometimes covered with water after heavy rains. All travel is then done in canoes. These days, however, dikes far upstream around Durango control water flow; flooding is rare.

Orientation & Information
The island is a small oval, about 350m from east to west, 400m from north to south. The central zócalo has a church on its east side, and the museum on its north side. The hotel is a block behind the museum.

All the telephones on the island go through one operator; look for the 'larga distancia' sign one block west of the zócalo. From outside the island, phone the **switchboard** (☎ 232-02-11) and ask for the extension you want.

Things to See & Do
Museo Aztlán del Origen (*admission US$0.50; open 9am-2pm & 4pm-6pm Tues-Sun*), on the north side of the zócalo, is small but enchanting. Among the exhibits are many interesting ancient objects and a fascinating long scroll, the Codice Ruturini,

telling the story of the peregrinations of the Aztec people, with notes in Spanish.

You can arrange for **boat trips** on the lagoon for bird-watching, fishing and sightseeing (US$5.50 per hour). Ask at the pier.

Special Events
Semana Santa is celebrated in a big way. On Good Friday a statue of Christ is put on a cross in the church, then taken down and carried through the streets.

The **Fiesta de San Pedro Apóstol**, the patron saint of fishing, is celebrated on June 29. Statues of St Peter and St Paul are taken out into the lagoon in decorated *lanchas* for the blessing of the waters. Festivities start around June 20, leading up to the big day.

Places to Stay & Eat
Hotel Ruta Azteca (*☎ 232-02-11 ext 128; Venecia 5; rooms from US$11*) offers eight simple but decent rooms. The rooms at the back have lagoon views. It's the best, worst and only hotel in town.

Restaurant Alberca (*☎ 232-02-11 ext 128; mains US$5.50; open 9am-8pm daily*) is accessible by rickety wooden walkway, has a great lagoon view (see birds close up!) and specializes in shrimp dishes. Several other restaurants on the island also offer fresh seafood, but you can also take a short boat ride – free if you eat there – to **Mariscos Kika**, across the lagoon. For a local treat, try *tamales de camarón* (shrimp surrounded by corn dough and wrapped in corn husks); look for signs on houses, or women sellers walking by with bundles.

Getting There & Away
From Santiago Ixcuintla's riverside market, one block north of the Hotel Casino, take a Combi (US$1.75, one hour). They run about every two hours (mostly in the morning) to La Batanga, a small pier from where *lanchas* depart for Mexcaltitán. You can also take a bus to La Batanga, but only two per day run from the Transportes del Pacífico station in town.

Lancha arrival and departure times are coordinated with the ground transport. The boat journey takes 15 minutes and costs

US$1 per person. If you miss the boat you can hire a private *lancha* between 8am and 6pm for US$5.50.

SAN BLAS
☎ 323 • pop 16,000

The small fishing village of San Blas, 290km southeast of Mazatlán, was an important Spanish port from the late 16th to the 19th century. The Spanish built a fortress here to protect their *naos* (trading galleons) from marauding British and French pirates. Today the visitors come to enjoy isolated beaches, have a hand at surfing or check out the abundant birdlife and tropical jungle reached by riverboats.

San Blas has the amenities of a small beach resort, but retains the character of a Mexican village. One suspects that the real reason the village hasn't been developed as a major resort is the proliferation of *jejenes* (sandflies), tiny gnatlike insects with huge appetites for human flesh; their bites will leave you with irresistible itches. Mosquitoes also buzz the airspace, so bring repellant.

Orientation

San Blas sits on a tongue of land between El Pozo estuary and San Cristóbal estuary. A 36km paved road connects the town with Hwy 15. This road goes through town as Juárez, the town's main east-west street. At the small zócalo it crosses Calle Batallón de San Blas (Batallón for short), the main north-south street, which heads south to the beach, Playa El Borrego. Everything in town is within walking distance.

Information

Note that opening hours given here reflect winter schedules; summer hours may vary. The small **Secretaría de Turismo** (☎ 285-00-05, 285-03-81; open 9am-3pm Mon-Fri) is in the Casa de Gobierno, on the east side of the zócalo. It can recommend a guide or boat operator for specialized tours and boat trips. On weekends you can find them all at Matanchén village (popular mangrove tours leave from here; see Boat Trips later).

Banamex (Juárez; open 9am-4pm Mon-Fri) has an ATM. The **Agencia de Cambio** (open 8am-6pm daily) is nearby.

Next door to one another are the **post office** and **Telecomm** (cnr Sonora & Echevarría; both open 8am-2pm Mon-Fri). Upset stomachs (or worse) can head to **Centro de Salud** (☎ 285-02-32; cnr Azueta & Campeche; open 24 hours). Surf something other than waves at **Internet Explorer** (Canalizo 4; US$2.25 per hour; open 9am-9:30pm daily).

Things to See & Do

The zócalo makes a good hangout in summer; at dusk, roosting black birds screech a raucous cacophony. Meanwhile, you can join the expats and travelers who sometimes group together to chat and/or play instruments. On Saturday mornings there's a small flea market on Paredes, a block from the zócalo.

Back toward the start of town, a dirt road climbs up past a walled cemetery to the **Cerro de la Contaduría**, wherein lie the ruins of an 18th-century Spanish **fortress and church** (admission US$0.55); there's a fine view from the top.

The nearest *playa* (beach), **Playa El Borrego**, is just to the south of town. It's wide and sandy, flat and surfable, with *palapa* (thatched-roof shelter) restaurants serving seafood treats. There are reasonable **surfboard** and **boogieboard** rentals at Stoner's (see under Places to Eat), as well as surfing lessons. The waves here can occasionally be

A Path of Destruction

In October 2002, as this book was going to press, Hurricane Kenna hit the Pacific coast of Mexico. Puerto Vallarta suffered major flooding and millions of dollars' worth of damage, but San Blas was hardest hit: Most homes here were seriously damaged or destroyed in the 230km/h winds. How this will affect tourist services as you travel in this region remains to be seen, though it's likely some flimsy seaside *palapa* (thatched-roof shelter) restaurants mentioned in our guide may no longer exist as we saw them during our research time.

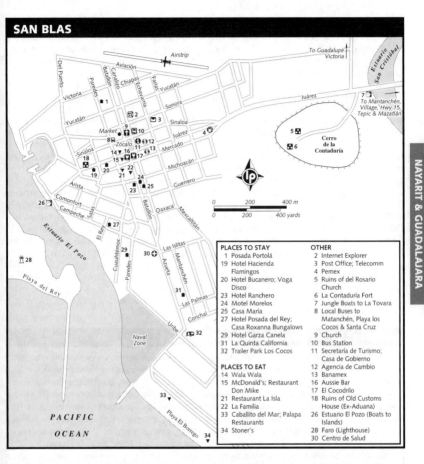

SAN BLAS

PACIFIC OCEAN

NAYARIT & GUADALAJARA

PLACES TO STAY	OTHER
1 Posada Portolá	2 Internet Explorer
19 Hotel Hacienda	3 Post Office; Telecom
Flamingos	4 Pemex
20 Hotel Bucanero; Voga	5 Ruins of del Rosario
Disco	Church
23 Hotel Ranchero	6 La Contaduría Fort
24 Motel Morelos	7 Jungle Boats to La Tovara
25 Casa María	8 Local Buses to
27 Hotel Posada del Rey;	Matanchén, Playa los
Casa Roxanna Bungalows	Cocos & Santa Cruz
29 Hotel Garza Canela	9 Church
31 La Quinta California	10 Bus Station
32 Trailer Park Los Cocos	11 Secretaría de Turismo;
	Casa de Gobierno
PLACES TO EAT	12 Agencia de Cambio
14 Wala Wala	13 Banamex
15 McDonald's; Restaurant	16 Aussie Bar
Don Mike	17 El Cocodrilo
21 Restaurant La Isla	18 Ruins of Old Customs
22 La Familia	House (Ex-Aduana)
33 Caballito del Mar; Palapa	26 Estuario El Pozo (Boats to
Restaurants	Islands)
34 Stoner's	28 Faro (Lighthouse)
	30 Centro de Salud

rough for swimming; ask locals for 'current' conditions.

The best beaches are southeast of the village around Bahía de Matanchén, starting with **Playa Las Islitas**, 7km from San Blas. To get there, take the road towards Hwy 15, and turn off to the right after about 4km. This paved road goes east past the village of Matanchén, where a dirt road goes south to Playa Las Islitas. The paved road continues past the Oceanography School to the village of Aticama, following 8km of wonderfully isolated beach. Farther on, **Playa Los Cocos** and **Playa Miramar**, also popular for surfing,

have palapas under which you can lounge and drink fresh coconut milk. Santa Cruz, about 16km from San Blas, has a pebble beach and simple accommodations. These beaches are all accessible by public bus.

A few times a year, when the swell and tides are right (usually in September and October), the world's longest surfable waves curl into Bahía de Matanchén – 1.7km according to the Guinness Book of Records.

Boat Trips

A boat trip through the jungle to the freshwater spring of **La Tovara** is a San Blas highlight. Boats chug up the Estuario San Cristóbal, passing thick jungle vegetation and mangroves; you'll see exotic birds, turtles and perhaps a few lazy crocodiles. Don't expect full ecological explanations, as trips are usually minimally guided in Spanish. Bring proper duds to swim in the clear waters of La Tovara; there's a pleasant and reasonable restaurant for lunch. For a few dollars more, you can extend the trip from Tovara to the **Cocodrilario** (crocodile nursery), where reptiles are reared in captivity for later release in the wild (crocs are fed at 10am Mondays). The extra few miles of river are especially interesting, even if the nursery doesn't grab you.

Boats, holding up to 13 passengers, leave from two different *embarcaderos* (docks). The small, untouristy one is next to the bridge into town; for a group of up to four people, it costs US$27 for Tovara (3½ hours) and US$36 to the Cocodrilario (four hours). Each extra person costs US$7/9 to Tovara/Cocodrilario. A bigger, more organized embarcadero with more services is located near Matanchén village, a short bus ride away. Since this dock is farther upriver, trips from here are one hour shorter and a few bucks cheaper. If you're alone or in a small group, and want to join a bigger group to make the trip cheaper, this may be a better place to come since it gets more tourist traffic (including large tour buses). The embarcadero near the bridge is about a 20-minute walk from the center of town, while the embarcadero near Matanchén Village is a 15-minute bus ride away. Taxis cost less than US$3.

A five-hour bird-watching trip up the Estuario San Cristóbal to the **Santuario de Aves** (Bird Sanctuary), can be arranged at the embarcadero by the bridge. Other boat trips depart from a boat dock on Estuario El Pozo, in town. They include a trip to **Piedra Blanca** to visit the statue of the Virgin; to **Estero Casa Blanca** to gather clams; to **Isla del Rey** just across from San Blas; and to **Playa del Rey**, a 20km beach on the other side of Isla del Rey (be careful if you're a lone woman).

Jejenes? What the Heck Are *Jejenes?*

Well, if you're in San Blas, it won't take long for you to find out – *jejenes* are particularly infamous here. They're a type of sand fly, sometimes called a 'no-see-um' because they're fairly small and inconspicuous. Around dusk, and often during the night and until dawn, they zero in on your bare flesh and bite down, feasting on your blood unless you manage to smack them off in time. This isn't even the worst part of getting chomped by *jejenes*: horrible, almost uncontrollable itching results and lasts for days and even weeks afterward – depending on your resistance. Small, fluid-filled bumps can develop during this period, and even scar lightly on certain types of skin. Some folks believe *jejenes* are worse during certain moon or tide cycles, bringing them out in full force.

So how do you defend yourself from these rapacious bloodsuckers? Stay indoors, away from the beach or in the waves during dusk, the worst time of day for *jejenes*. This is often no fun, however, especially if you want to catch the sunset while languidly sipping a margarita. Try applying a local repellent (ask at a nearby pharmacy) or use a DEET-based one; experiment, as different things work on different people. Some folks even dab lime juice on their skin (save those slices that come with tacos) or take PABA to limit their reaction to bites. Smoke from fires is sometimes used to keep biting insects at bay as well, though it's not pleasant to be smoked out as a human being, either.

If you're camping, make sure that the mesh protecting you is small enough for no-see-ums, as *jejenes* can easily crawl through regular mesh screens. Many unsuspecting campers have been unpleasantly surprised when they suddenly realize their tent offers little protection against these insidious little beasts. And when you do get bitten (because you probably will), try hard not to scratch, as this often makes itching worse. It's not an easy task, but this is the price you pay for hanging out near the beautiful lagoons of San Blas.

You can make an interesting trip farther afield to **Isla Isabel**, four hours northwest of San Blas by boat. The island is a bird-watcher's paradise, with colonies of many species, and there's a volcanic crater lake. Isla Isabel measures 1.5km long by 1km wide and there are no facilities, so be prepared for self-sufficient camping. Permission is required to visit the island; the boat operators can arrange it.

Special Events

Every year on January 31, the anniversary of the death of **Father José María Mercado** is commemorated with a parade, a march by the Mexican navy, and fireworks in the zócalo. Mercado lived in San Blas in the early 19th century and helped Miguel Hidalgo with the independence movement by sending him a gift set of old Spanish cannons from the village.

On February 3, festivities for **San Blas**, the town's patron saint, are an extension of those begun on January 31, with dance and musical presentations; you may hear firecrackers during this time. **Carnaval** is celebrated the weekend before Ash Wednesday. The **Virgen de Fátima** is honored on May 13. The **Día de la Marina** is celebrated on June 1 with burro races on the beach, sporting events, dances and general partying.

Places to Stay – Budget

Your cheapest camping option is the **beach**; try Stoner's (see Places to Eat) or ask at another likely palapa restaurant. Most offer free sites and minimal services if you eat some meals at their establishment. Be prepared for *jejene* nibbles, especially at sunset.

Trailer Park Los Cocos (☎ 285-00-55; *Batallón s/n; camp sites US$10, trailer sites with hookup US$11)* harbors pleasant, peaceful and grassy sites about 1km from the town center. There's a bar on the premises, and it's not too far from the beach.

Playa Amor (*Playa Los Cocos; camp sites US$9, trailer sites with hookup US$16)* is an attractive beachfront trailer park about a 15-minute drive from town. There's a fine view of the sunset and coast, no mosquitoes, and some palapa restaurants nearby.

For the cheapest accommodation ask at the palapa restaurants on Playa El Borrego; some rent very basic rooms. Note that hot water can be a luxury in this range.

Hotel Ranchero (☎ 285-08-92; *Batallón 102; rooms with shared/private bathroom US$13/17)* has eight very simple rooms around a small, dusty, parakeet-filled courtyard. Kitchen and laundry facilities are available, and there are bikes to rent.

Motel Morelos (*Batallón de San Blas 108; singles/doubles US$11/17)* is opposite the Ranchero, run by the same family and offers a similar deal: five basic rooms around a family courtyard.

Casa María (☎ 285-08-92; *Canalizo 67; rooms with 1/2 beds US$17/22)* sits a block east, still part of the same family dynasty but a step up in scale. Comfortable rooms face a shady courtyard where parakeets screech.

Posada Portolá (☎ 285-03-86; *Paredes 118;* [e] *portola_sanblas@hotmail.com; bungalows US$17-22)* features plain but very spacious bungalows, great for a family or intimate group.

Hotel Bucanero (☎ 285-01-01; *Juárez 75; singles/doubles US$17/22)* sparkles with old, salty character: a large stuffed crocodile greets you at the door, and the dark, rough-around-the-edges rooms are set around a big leafy courtyard. There's off-street parking, and a swimming pool, but beware of its weekend disco next door.

La Quinta California (☎ 285-03-10; *Matanchén 3;* [w] *www.quintacalifornia.com; bungalows US$22)* is run by US expats Chris and Rita. Four two-bedroom bungalows are roomy, simple and surround a small courtyard. Internet service and a book exchange are available.

Places to Stay – Mid-Range & Top End

The clean, modern **Hotel Posada del Rey** (☎ 285-01-23; *Campeche 10; singles/doubles with fan & air-con US$33/39)* has nicely appointed rooms and patio areas. There's a small swimming pool, and English is spoken.

Casa Roxana Bungalows (☎ 285-05-73; *El Rey 1;* [w] *www.casaroxanna.com; bungalows with air-con and TV US$44-55)* offers three wonderful bungalows and a pool on spacious manicured grounds. English is spoken.

Hotel Hacienda Flamingos (☎/fax 285-04-85; e technica@red2000com.mx; Juárez 105; singles/doubles US$65/81, more in Dec & Jan) caters to those who want class. Luxurious rooms in a wonderfully restored old building are set around wide, tiled hallways and a lovely courtyard. Nice gardens, a fountain and a swimming pool complete the deal.

Hotel Garza Canela (☎/fax 285-01-12; W www.garzacanela.com; Paredes 106 Sur; singles/doubles from US$72/90) isn't as modern or spiffy as it could be, though it offers the services of a large hotel: air-con, cable TV, pool and restaurant/bar. Look at a few rooms, as they differ in size; suites with kitchens are also available.

Places to Eat

The cheapest eats live at the local *mercado* (market) on Sonora and Batallón.

McDonald's (☎ 285-04-32; Juárez 36; mains US$4.50-9; open 7am-10pm daily) isn't related to *that* ubiquitous fast-food chain, but rather serves typical traveler's fare in a pleasant environment.

Restaurant Don Mike (☎ 285-08-32; Juárez 36; mains US$6-9; open 8am-11pm daily) is above McDonald's and features good seafood, nice open seating and occasional live music. Grab a table overlooking the street.

Wala Wala (☎ 285-08-63; Juárez 94; mains US$4.50-11; open 7:30am-10pm Mon-Sat) is another popular place, cheerfully decorated and serving inexpensive breakfasts, lunches and some very good main dishes – try the *pollo con naranja* (chicken with orange).

Restaurant La Isla (☎ 285-04-07; cnr Paredes & Mercado; mains US$6-9; open 2pm-9pm Tues-Sun) grills near-perfect seafood, but it's also worth coming in just to check out the overdone seashell decor – so tacky it's cool.

La Familia (☎ 285-02-58; Batallón 18; mains US$5-9; open 7am-10pm daily) revels in its airy, leafy, cozy inner patios. Tasty seafood and Mexican dishes supplement the pleasant decor.

There's also a good selection of places to eat at Playa El Borrego, with seafood served under shady palapas right on the sand. They all have the same languid, tropical ambience, and all charge about US$1.50 for a refreshing cold beer.

Caballito del Mar (mains US$6-8) does remarkably sophisticated seafood dishes – try the sensational *pescado con queso* (fish with cheese) or the super fresh oyster cocktails.

Stoner's (mains US$3.5-5.50) sits all by itself past the main line of palapa restaurants. It's your typical traveler's hangout, with good music, lots of hammocks and well-prepared Western food (including vegetarian). Sip a coco with tequila. It also rents surfboards, boogieboards and bikes, and tends a small book exchange.

Entertainment

El Cocodrilo (Juárez 6; open 5pm-11pm daily) is a magnet for drinking gringos, sporting an airy, colorful and piñata-decorated space.

Restaurant Don Mike (Juárez 36; open 8am-11pm daily) is perched upstairs over McDonald's restaurant. There's a good view onto the street, and often has great live music played loudly by Mike himself.

Aussie Bar (Juárez 34; open 7pm-1am Tues-Sun) is located on the 2nd floor, with six pool tables as the main focus (US$2.50 per hour). The long bar is dotted with cool youths and grungy foreigners throwing drinks back.

Voga Disco (Juárez 75; open Sat nights to 3am) is next to Hotel Bucanero and attracts the locals in hordes. An open patio and pool area serve as a dance floor.

Getting There & Around

The little **bus station** (cnr Sinaloa & Canalizo) is marked 'Norte de Sonora' but is also used by Transportes Noroeste de Nayarit. For many destinations to the south and east, it may be quicker to go to Tepic first.

Guadalajara US$19, five hours, 242km, 7am daily
Mazatlán US$19, five hours, 290km, 2:30pm daily; or go via Tepic (don't go to the highway and wait for a Tepic–Mazatlán bus at Crucero San Blas – it's not a safe place to wait at night)

Puerto Vallarta US$11, three hours, 175km, three daily
Santa Cruz US$1.25, 30 minutes, 16km, hourly
Santiago Ixcuintla US$2.75 to US$3.50, one hour, 70km, hourly
Tepic US$3.50, one hour, 62km, frequent buses

There are also small buses departing from the corner of Sinaloa and Paredes several times a day, serving all the villages and beaches on Bahía de Matanchén, including Matanchén, Playa Las Islitas, Aticama, Playa Los Cocos, Playa Miramar and Santa Cruz, at the far end of the bay.

Taxis will take you around town and to nearby beaches – a good option with two or more people. Rent bicycles at restaurants Stoner's or Wala Wala for US$1.25/5.50 per hour/day.

TEPIC

☎ 311 • pop 270,000 • elevation 900m

Tepic is the bustling capital of the small state of Nayarit, but many travelers brush past its outskirts without checking the city out. This is unfortunate, because it doesn't take long to visit Tepic – there are a few things of interest, including a large neo-Gothic cathedral and several museums. Indigenous Huichols are often seen here, wearing their colorful traditional clothing, and Huichol artwork is sold on the street and in several shops. If you want a taste of a typical, nontouristy medium-sized Mexican city, Tepic might just fit the bill.

The climate here is noticeably cooler than on the coast. Tepic is one hour behind Puerto Vallarta and Guadalajara in the neighboring state of Jalisco.

Orientation & Information

Plaza Principal, with the large cathedral at the east end, is the heart of the city. Av Mexico, the city's main artery, runs from the cathedral south to Plaza Constituyentes, past banks, restaurants, the state museum and other places of interest.

Dirección de Turismo (☎ 216-56-61; Ⓦ www.turismonayarit.gob.mx; cnr Puebla Nte & Nervo Pte; open 9am-8pm Mon-Fri, occasionally Sat mornings) has English-speaking

staff and information on Tepic and the state of Nayarit. **Secretaría de Turismo** (☎ 214-80-71; open 8am-8pm Sat-Sun) is at the Ex-Convento de la Cruz at the foot of Av Mexico.

Banks and casas de cambio (exchange houses) line Av Mexico Nte between the two plazas; they're closed on Sunday. Mail love letters home at the **post office** (cnr Durango & Morelos; open 8am-5pm Mon-Fri, 8:30am-noon Sat). **Telecomm** (Mexico 50 Nte; open 8am-7:30pm Mon-Fri, 8am-4pm Sat) has telegram, telex and fax services. Post and telephone services are also found at the bus station.

Surf the Internet at **Cafetería La Parroquia** (Hidalgo 61 Ote; US$1.75 per hour; open 8:30am-9:30pm Mon-Sat). **Publicaciones Azteca** (☎ 216-08-11, cnr Mexico & Morelos) displays some magazines in English.

Things to See & Do

The large **cathedral** (Plaza Principal), with ornate interior and glass chandeliers, was dedicated in 1750; the towers were completed in 1885. Opposite the church is the **palacio municipal** (city hall), where colorfully dressed Huichols sell handicrafts under the arches at very reasonable prices. On Av Mexico, south of Plaza Principal, look inside the **Palacio de Gobierno** and the **Cámara de Diputados** to see some impressive and colorful murals.

The 18th-century **Templo y Ex-Convento de la Cruz de Zacate** is at the end of Av Mexico on the corner of Calzada del Ejército, about 2km south of the cathedral. It was here in 1767 that Father Junípero Serra organized his expedition that established the chain of Spanish missions in the Californias; you can visit the room where he stayed, but there's not much else to see. In the southwest section of the city is the large **Parque Paseo de la Loma**.

Museums

Museo Regional de Nayarit (☎ 212-19-00; Mexico 91; admission US$3.50; open 9am-7pm Mon-Fri, 9am-3pm Sat) has a beautiful courtyard and displays a variety of exhibits on pre-Hispanic times, colonial painting and Huichol culture. **Casa y Museo Amado**

Nervo (☎ 212-29-16; Zacatecas 284 Nte; admission free; open 10am-2pm & 4pm-7pm Mon-Fri, 9am-2pm Sat) celebrates the life of the poet Amado Nervo, who was born in this house in 1870.

The rather small **Casa Museo Juan Escutia** (☎ 212-33-90; Hidalgo 71 Ote; admission free; open 9am-2pm & 4pm-7pm Mon-Fri, 10am-2pm Sat) was the home of Juan Escutia, one of Mexico's illustrious 'Niños Héroes,' who died in 1847 at age 17 defending Mexico City's Castillo de Chapultepec from US forces. Opposite, **Museo de Artes Populares** (☎ 212-17-05; Hidalgo 60 Ote; admission free; open 9am-2pm & 4pm-7pm Mon-Fri, 9am-2pm Sat & Sun) has gorgeous artwork of Nayarit's Huichol, Cora, Náhuatl and Tepehuano peoples, including clothing, yarn art, weaving, musical instruments, ceramics, and beadwork.

Museo de Artes Visuales Aramara (☎ 216-42-46; Allende 329 Pte; admission free; open 10am-2pm & 4pm-7pm Mon-Fri) is another museum of visual arts. **Museo Emilia Ortiz** (☎ 212-26-52; Lerdo 192 Pte; admission free; open 9am-7pm Mon-Sat) honors the painter Emilia Ortiz and her work.

Places to Stay

Trailer Park Los Pinos (☎ 213-12-32; Blvd Tepic-Xalisco 150; trailer sites US$12, bungalows US$18) sits some 5km south of town, offering 18 bungalows with kitchen and 27 trailer spaces with full hookups.

Hotel Tepic (☎ 213-13-77; Dr Martinez 438 Ote; singles/doubles US$10/12) is a good, modern place to stay near the bus station. Rooms are small, colorful and noisy; add US$2 for TV.

Hotel Cibrian (☎ 212-86-98; Nervo 163 Pte; singles/doubles with TV US$16/19) harbors rooms as dark as a Rembrandt painting, and they face inner patios and halls... but they're clean and cheap.

Hotel Ibarra (☎ 212-38-70; Durango 297 Nte; singles/doubles with TV US$25/27) has

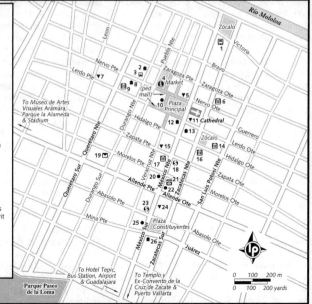

TEPIC

PLACES TO STAY
2 Hotel Ibarra
8 Hotel Cibrian
12 Hotel Fray Junípero Serra
13 Hotel Sierra de Alica
26 Hotel Real de Don Juan

PLACES TO EAT
5 Cafetería La Parroquia
7 Quetzalcoatl
11 La Gloria
15 El Trigal
24 Cafetería Diligencias

OTHER
1 2nd-Class Bus Station TNS/TNN
3 Local Buses to Bus Station & Elsewhere
4 Dirección de Turismo
6 Casa y Museo Amado Nervo
9 Museo Emilia Ortiz
10 Palacio Municipal
14 Casa Museo Juan Escutia
16 Museo de Artes Populares
17 Museo Regional de Nayarit
18 Banamex
19 Post Office
20 Publicaciones Azteca
21 Telecomm
22 Cámara de Diputados
23 Ban Crecer
25 Palacio de Gobierno

small, unmemorable rooms and sterile, institutional hallways overdone in white tile.

Hotel Sierra de Alica *(☎ 212-03-24; Mexico 180 Nte; singles/doubles US$21/26, with air-con US$33/42)* is the place to be. There are 30 spacious, bright rooms here with TV, and it's so close to Plaza Principal you can hear cathedral bells ring.

Hotel Fray Junípero Serra *(☎ 212-25-25;* W *www.frayjunipero.com.mx; Lerdo 23 Pte; singles/doubles US$54/59)* offers good, solid rooms; get one overlooking the church and Plaza Principal. The lobby (and its restaurant/bar) are pretty fancy, but halls seem bit bleak.

Hotel Real de Don Juan *(☎/fax 216-18-88; Mexico 105 Sur; rooms US$64, suites US$85)* isn't a bad deal for the best hotel in town, and it's even got some character. Comfortable modern rooms, a restaurant and parking appeal to business people and travelers alike.

Places to Eat

Surrounding Tepic are many fields of sugarcane, and around town you'll see carts selling the sweet stuff. It's cheap, so give it a try – chew it up and spit it out.

Cafetería La Parroquia *(☎ 212-95-79; Nervo 18; mains US$2-4; open 8:30am-9:30pm Mon-Sat)* sits on the north side of Plaza Principal. Find your way upstairs for breakfasts, drinks, inexpensive light meals and decent coffee.

Cafetería Diligencias *(☎ 212-15-35; Mexico 29 Sur; mains under US$4; open 7:30am-10:30pm Mon-Sat, 5pm-10pm Sun)* attracts many local males, who smoke and read newspapers with their breakfast. The *comida corrida* (daily special) is also popular, and the ambience a bit old-time.

El Trigal *(☎ 216-40-04; Veracruz 112; meals US$3; open 8:30am-9pm daily)* grills up healthy, inexpensive vegetarian food in an attractive indoor courtyard. Generous offerings include wholemeal quesadillas, veggie burgers and an excellent *menú del día* (daily set menu).

La Gloria *(☎ 217-04-22; cnr Lerdo & Mexico; mains US$5.50-11; open 7:30am-9:30pm Mon-Sat)* is perched on an airy, covered balcony overlooking Plaza Principal. Pasta, meats, seafood and salad are your lunch and dinner choices; give breakfast a shot, too. There's live music Friday to Sunday nights.

Quetzalcoatl *(☎ 212-99-66; Leon 244 Nte; mains under US$3.50; open 8:30am-6pm Mon-Sat)* is a friendly, inexpensive vegetarian restaurant with a pretty little courtyard, relaxing music and tasteful decor.

Getting There & Around

Tepic's **airport** *(☎ 214-18-50)* is in Pantanal, a 25-minute drive from Tepic, toward Guadalajara. **Aero California** *(☎ 214-23-20)* and **Aeroméxico** *(☎ 213-90-47)* offer direct flights to Mexico City and Tijuana, with connections to other cities.

The bus station is on the southeastern outskirts of town; local buses marked 'Central' and 'Centro' make frequent connections between the bus station and the city center. There are cafeterias and shops, and services for left-luggage, post, telephone, fax, telegram and telex.

The main bus companies are Elite, Futura, Estrella Blanca and Ómnibus de Mexico (all 1st-class), Transportes del Pacífico (1st and 2nd class) and TNS (2nd class). Buses include:

Guadalajara US$19/16 1st/2nd class, three hours, 216km, frequent buses 24 hours daily
Ixtlán del Río US$5.50, one hour, 88km, six daily
Mazatlán US$14/12 1st/2nd class, 4½ hours, 290km, hourly all day and night
Mexico City (Terminal Norte) US$55/50 1st/2nd class, 11 hours, 751km, hourly all day and night
Puerto Vallarta US$13/12 1st/2nd class, 3½ hours, 169km, every 30 minutes
San Blas US$4.25, 1¼ hours, 62km, hourly from 6am to 7pm
Santiago Ixcuintla US$3.75, 1½ hours, 70km, every 30 minutes from 5:30am to 8pm

Local buses scurry from 6am to 9pm (US$0.35). Combis scamper along Av Mexico from 6am to midnight (US$0.35). There are plenty of taxis chasing after them.

NAYARIT & GUADALAJARA

NAYARIT & GUADALAJARA

AROUND TEPIC
Laguna Santa María del Oro
This idyllic lake (elevation 750m), surrounded by steep, forested mountains, is in a volcanic crater 2km around and about 50m deep. The clean water reflects colors ranging from turquoise to slate. You can take some very pleasant walks around the lake and in the surrounding mountains, seeing numerous birds (some 250 species), butterflies and wildflowers along the way. You can also climb to an abandoned gold mine, bicycle, swim, row on the lake, kayak, or fish for black bass and perch. A few small restaurants serve fresh lake fish.

Koala Bungalows & RV Park (☎ 3-214-05-09; w *www.geocities.com/thetropics/reef/2688; tent sites per person US$3.50, trailer sites with hookup US$10, bungalows from US$43)* is a peaceful, grassy lakeside spot with restaurant, camp sites and good bungalows in several sizes. It's owned and operated by a Englishman who's an excellent source of information about the lake.

To get there, take the Santa María del Oro *crucero* about 40km from Tepic along the Guadalajara road; from the *crucero* it's about 10km to the village, then another 8km from the village to the lake. Buses directly to the lake depart from Tepic three times daily (US$2.50, 1½ hours, 50km). Alternatively, buses to Santa María del Oro depart from Tepic every 30 minutes; from there you can take another bus (or a taxi) to the lake.

Volcán Ceboruco
This extinct volcano, with a number of old craters, interesting plants and volcanic forms, has several short, interesting walks at the top. The 15km cobblestoned road up the volcano passes lava fields and fumaroles (steam vents), with plenty of vegetation growing on the slopes. The road begins at the village of Jala, 7km off the highway from Tepic to Guadalajara; the *crucero* is 76km from Tepic, 12km before you reach Ixtlán del Río.

Ixtlán del Río
The small town of Ixtlán del Río, about 1½ hours (88km) from Tepic along the road to Guadalajara, is unremarkable in itself, but Carlos Castaneda fans will remember that this is where Don Juan took Carlos in the book *Journey to Ixtlán*. Outside Ixtlán, the **Los Toriles** archaeological site has an impressive round stone temple, the **Templo a Quetzalcóatl** *(open 9am-5pm daily)*. Any bus between Tepic and Guadalajara will drop you at Ixtlán.

TEQUILA
☎ 374 • pop 24,000 • elevation 1219m
The town of Tequila, 50km northwest of Guadalajara, has been home to the liquor of the same name since the 17th century. Fields of blue agave, the aloe-like succulent from which tequila is distilled, surround the town. You can cop a buzz just breathing the heavily scented air that drifts from the town's distilleries. The **tourist office** (☎ 743-00-12; e *tequila@jalisco.gob.mx)*, on Plaza Principal, organizes no-frills distillery tours.

Museo del Tequila (☎ 742-24-10; *Coran 34; admission US$0.75; open 10am-3pm Tues-Sat)*, near Plaza Principal, gives a history of the industry. The two largest distilleries are also near Plaza Principal. Ask at the tourist office for details. Sauza tequila runs the **Perseverencia distillery** (☎ 742-02-43; *Francisco Javier Sauza Mora 80; tours US$3; open 9am-2pm Mon-Fri)*, noted for its tequila-inspired mural. Cuervo tequila is made in the **La Rojena distillery** (☎ 742-13-82; *José Cuervo 73; tours US$1.75; open 9am-6pm Mon-Fri)*, the biggest in town. Tours of these and other distilleries include samples of the product.

The *Tequila Express* (☎ 3-880-90-99; *US$61)* starts at Guadalajara train station at 10am. Tours include a train ride through the agave fields, a distillery visit, music, a *mariachi* (small ensemble of street musicians) show, snacks, lunch and an open bar with plenty of tequila.

The **Tequila Bus** (☎ 333-813-35-94 in *Guadalajara; US$45)* picks up tour groups from a couple of locations in Guadalajara at about 10am daily. The trip includes a walk in the agave fields, visits to distilleries and the tequila museum, a dinner with mariachi music and a folkloric show, and plentiful tastings of tequila.

Tequila

In ancient times, the *agave tequilana weber* (blue agave) was used by indigenous Mexicans as a source of food, cloth and paper. Today, the blue agave is known more widely as the source of Mexico's national drink – tequila.

To ensure quality control, by law the blue agave can be grown only in the state of Jalisco and parts of Nayarit, Michoacán, Guanajuato and Tamaulipas states. It is here, and nowhere else in Mexico, that conditions are perfect for the blue agave to produce a great-tasting tequila.

When planted, the agave heart is no bigger than an onion. Its blue-gray, sword-like leaves give the plant the appearance of a cactus, though botanists believe it has more genetically in common with the lily. By the time the agave is ready for harvesting, eight to 12 years after planting, its heart is the size of a beach ball and can weigh 50kg.

The harvested *piña* (agave heart) is chopped to bits, fed into ovens, and cooked for up to three days. After cooking the softened plants are shredded and juiced. The juice, called *aguamiel* (honeywater) for its golden, syrupy appearance, is then pumped into vats, where it typically is mixed with sugarcane and yeast, before being allowed to ferment. By law, the mixture can contain no less than 51% agave. A bottle of tequila made from 100% agave will bear a label stating so.

There are four varieties of tequila; which is best is a matter of personal taste. White (or silver) tequila is not aged, and no colors or flavors are added. The gold variety is unaged but color and flavor, usually caramel, are put in the mix. *Tequila reposado* (rested tequila) has been aged at least two months in oak barrels and coloring and flavoring agents are often added. *Añejo* (aged) tequila has spent at least one year in oak barrels, also with extra coloring and flavoring.

If you want to do this yourself, just catch one of the frequent Rojo de los Altos public buses to Tequila departing from the Antigua Central Camionera in Guadalajara (US$3, 1¾ hours, 62km).

Another option for tequila tourism is **Amatitán**, 49km from Guadalajara on the road to Tequila. This old-fashioned town is the home of Herradura brand tequila, produced at the old **San José del Refugio hacienda** (☎ 333-613-95-85 in Guadalajara; tours 9am-noon) using traditional methods. Tours of the hacienda can be arranged.

GUADALAJARA
☎ 33 • pop (metro area) 3,500,000
• elevation 1445m

Guadalajara's contributions to Mexican life include mariachi music, tequila, the broad-rimmed sombrero hat, *charreadas* (rodeos) and the Mexican Hat Dance. The second-largest city in Mexico, it's also western Mexico's biggest industrial center and has its share of museums, galleries, festivals, historic buildings, nightlife, culture and good places to stay and eat.

The renovated downtown area is grand, elegant, and full of beautiful old buildings. Attractive pedestrian streets and zócalos dotted with fountains and green shrubbery attract Guadalajara's *tapatíos* (residents) seeking a break from traffic and pollution, which doesn't even begin to approach Mexico City's. But, if you tire of the noise and congestion, surrounding suburbs like Zapopan, Tlaquepaque and Tonalá – formerly separate communities that have retained their small-town charm – and are great for a visit or shopping trip.

History
In 1532, Nuño de Guzmán founded the first Guadalajara near Nochistlán (now in Zacatecas state), naming it after Guzmán's home city in Spain. Times were tough, so the settlement moved to the pre-Hispanic

GUADALAJARA

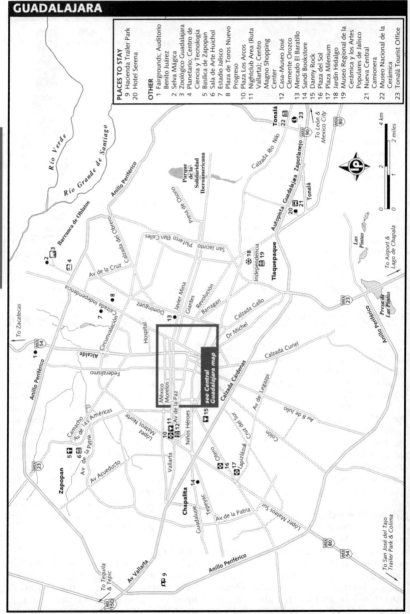

PLACES TO STAY
9 Hacienda Trailer Park
20 Hotel Serena

OTHER
1 Fairgrounds; Auditorio Benito Juárez
2 Selva Mágica
3 Zoológico Guadalajara
4 Planetario; Centro de Ciencia y Tecnología
5 Basílica de Zapopan
6 Sala de Arte Huichol
7 Estadio Jalisco
8 Plaza de Toros Nuevo Progreso
10 Plaza Los Arcos
11 Nightclub Area (Ruta Vallarta); Centro Magno Shopping Center
12 Casa-Museo José Clemente Orozco
13 Mercado El Baratillo
14 Sandi Bookstore
15 Danny Rock
16 Plaza del Sol
17 Plaza Milenium
18 Jardín Hidalgo
19 Museo Regional de la Cerámica y los Artes Populares de Jalisco
21 Nueva Central Camionera
22 Museo Nacional de la Cerámica
23 Tonalá Tourist Office

village of Tonalá, today a suburb of Guadalajara. Guzmán, however, disliked Tonalá and in 1535 had the settlement moved to nearby Tlacotán, which was destroyed by indigenous tribes in 1541. The surviving colonists wearily picked a new site in the valley of Atemajac beside San Juan de Dios Creek, which ran where Calzada Independencia is today. This new Guadalajara was founded by Oñate on February 14, 1542, near where the Teatro Degollado now stands.

The city quickly grew into one of colonial Mexico's most important population centers and the heart of a rich agricultural region. It was also the starting point for Spanish expeditions and missions to western and northern Nueva España – and as far away as the Philippines. Miguel Hidalgo, a leader in the struggle for Mexican independence, set up a revolutionary government in Guadalajara in 1810 but was defeated near the city in 1811, not long before his capture and execution in Chihuahua. The city was also the object of heavy fighting during the War of the Reform (1858–61) and between Constitutionalist and Villista armies in 1915.

By the late 19th century Guadalajara had passed Puebla as Mexico's second-biggest city. Its population has mushroomed since WWII, and now the city is a huge commercial, industrial and cultural center, and the communications hub for a large region.

Orientation

Guadalajara's giant twin-towered cathedral, at the heart of the city, is surrounded by four lovely zócalos. The zócalo east of the cathedral, Plaza de la Liberación, extends two blocks to the Teatro Degollado, also a city landmark. The area from the cathedral to the theater, and the surrounding blocks, is known as the Centro Histórico.

East of Teatro Degollado, the Plaza Tapatía pedestrian precinct extends 500m to the Instituto Cultural de Cabañas, another historically significant building. Just south of Plaza Tapatía is Mercado Libertad, a huge market.

Calzada Independencia is a major north-south central artery. From Mercado Libertad, it runs south to Parque Agua Azul and the Antigua Central Camionera (Old Bus Station), still used by short-distance regional buses. Northward, it runs to the zoo and other attractions. Don't confuse Calzada Independencia with Av Independencia, the east-west street one block north of the cathedral. In the city center, north-south streets change names at Hidalgo, the street north of the cathedral.

About 20 blocks west of the cathedral, Av Chapultepec is Guadalajara's Zona Rosa, a smart area with modern office blocks, shops and a few fine restaurants. The long-distance bus station is the Nueva Central Camionera, 9km southeast of the city center past the suburb of Tlaquepaque.

Information

The excellent, English-speaking **state tourist office** (☎ 3-668-16-00; W *vive.guadalajara.gob .mx; Morelos 102; open 9am-8pm Mon-Fri, 9am-1pm Sat & Sun*) offers information on Guadalajara and the state of Jalisco. A **tourist information booth** (*open 9am-2:30pm & 4pm-8pm Mon-Fri, 9am-1pm Sat*) nestles in the Palacio de Gobierno, facing the Plaza de Armas just south of the cathedral.

Banks are generally open from about 9am to 5pm Monday to Friday and 9am to 1pm Saturday. Most have ATMs. *Casas de cambio* on López Cotilla, in the three blocks between Av 16 de Septiembre and Molina, offer competitive exchange rates, quicker service and sometimes longer hours.

The **AmEx office** (☎ 3-818-23-19; *Vallarta 2440, open 9am-6pm Mon-Fri, 9am-1pm Sat*) is in the small Plaza Los Arcos shopping center.

The **main post office** (*Carranza s/n; open 8am-6pm Mon-Fri, 9am-1pm Sat*) is between Juan Manuel and Independencia. Computel, with long-distance telephone and fax services, has several offices around the city.

Several places around the central area offer Internet access for US$1.50 to US$2.25 per hour. Two are located in the shopping mall on Av Alcada at Juan Manuel (*locales 17 & 34; both open around 10am-9pm daily*). **Micronet** (*Juárez 811; open 8am to 11pm daily*) is 10 blocks west of center, while the most central is near the tourist office at

Degollado 128 1B (open 9am-9pm Mon-Sat, 10am-9pm Sun).

About 1km west of Av López Mateos, **Sandi Bookstore** (☎ 3-121-42-10; e sandi books@sandibooks.com; Tepeyac 718; open 9:30am-2:30pm & 3:30pm-7pm Mon-Fri, 9:30am-2pm Sat) has an extensive travel section, including many Lonely Planet guides. It takes special orders.

The Spanish-language *Público*, Guadalajara's most prominent daily newspaper, offers exhaustive entertainment listings on Friday. *Guadalajara Weekly* is a free, but not very informative, visitor newsletter, available at the tourist office and some hotels. Many of the newsstands in central Guadalajara sell English-language periodicals.

Things to See & Do

The twin-towered **cathedral** is the city's most famous symbol and a conspicuous landmark. Begun in 1558 and consecrated in 1618, the cathedral is a stylistic hodgepodge – the exterior decorations are in Churrigueresque, baroque, neoclassical and other styles. The towers date from 1848 and are much higher than the originals, which were destroyed in an earthquake. Inside there are Gothic vaults, Tuscan-style pillars and 11 richly decorated altars given to Guadalajara by King Fernando VII of Spain (1784–1833). In front of the cathedral's west facade is **Plaza de los Laureles**, and on its north side lies the **Presidencia Municipal** (City Hall), built between 1949 and 1952. Above the interior stairway is a mural by Gabriel Flores, depicting the founding of Guadalajara. Just west and across Loza is the baroque church **Templo de La Merced**, built in 1650 and home to several fine large paintings, crystal chandeliers and lots of gold decoration.

Plaza de Armas, on the south side of the cathedral, is a nice place to sit and imagine how the city was in colonial times. Free concerts of Jaliscan music are often held in the attractive central bandstand on Tuesday, Thursday and Sunday evening, starting at about 6:30pm. Nearby is the **Palacio de Gobierno**, finished in 1774, which houses state offices. Like the cathedral, it was built in a combination of styles: a mix of simple,

neoclassical features and riotous Churrigueresque decorations. Two interesting Orozco murals can be viewed inside.

The zócalo on the north side of the cathedral is ringed by 12 bronze sculptures, including a poet, a composer, a writer and an architect. Six of them are buried beneath the **Rotonda de los Hombres Ilustres**, the round pillared monument in the center. Toward the east is **Museo Regional de Guadalajara** (☎ 3-614-22-27; admission US$3.50, free Sun; open 9am-5:30pm Tues-Sat, 9am-5pm Sun), a must-see museum covering the history and prehistory of western Mexico. Displays include the skeleton of a woolly mammoth, stagecoaches, colonial paintings, a history gallery covering the area since the Spanish conquest and an ethnography section with displays about indigenous life in Jalisco.

East of the cathedral, **Plaza de la Liberación** is a lively and impressive space created by a 1980s urban renovation project involving the demolition of two whole blocks of colonial buildings. On the north side is the **Palacio Legislativo**, where the state congress meets, distinguished by massive stone columns in its interior courtyard. To the east, the imposing neoclassical-style **Teatro Degollado** (☎ 3-614-47-73; admission free; open for viewing 10am-1pm Tues-Sat) was begun in 1856, inaugurated 30 years later and reconstructed several times since. A frieze over the columns depict Apollo and the Nine Muses, while the theatre's interior is decorated with red velvet and gold, and crowned by a Gerardo Suárez mural based on the fourth canto of Dante's *Divine Comedy*. The theater hosts frequent performances of music, dance and drama.

Just north is the **Palacio de Justicia**, built in 1588 as part of the Convento de Santa María, Guadalajara's first nunnery. A 1965 mural by Guillermo Chávez, depicting Benito Juárez and other legendary Mexican lawmakers, graces the interior stairway. Nearby, the **Templo de Santa María de Gracia** served as the city's first cathedral (1549–1618).

A couple blocks behind Teatro Degollado, **Plaza Tapatía** is a modern pedestrian mall with shops, restaurants, fountains and street performers. At its east end is the **Instituto**

Cultural de Cabañas (☎ 3-668-16-40; Cabañas 8; admission US$1.25, free Sun; open 10am-6pm Tues-Sat, 10am-3pm Sun), a huge neoclassical gem originally built between 1805 and 1810 as an orphanage where up to 3000 children were housed at a time. Designed by Spanish architect Manuel Tolsá and featuring 23 separate courtyards, the building has also served as an insane asylum, military barracks and jail. Today it harbors a museum (featuring a permanent exhibition of more than 100 fine Orozco drawings and paintings), theater and school. Tours in English and Spanish are available.

Plaza de los Mariachis, a few blocks southwest on Calzada Independencia Sur, is arguably the birthplace of mariachi music. It's more like a short pedestrian street than a zócalo, but you can't miss the outdoor tables where people sit, eat and drink, while wandering mariachis offer their musical services for about US$5 per song.

A few blocks west of center, on Juárez, lies the **Santuario de Nuestra Señora del Carmen** another lovely church with lots of gold decoration, old paintings and murals in the dome. Five blocks farther west is an original building of the **Universidad de Guadalajara**, featuring a theatre hall with large, intense murals by Orozco. In this same building is the **Museo de las Artes** (☎ 3-826-91-83; admission free; open 10am-5pm Mon-Fri, noon-2pm Sat & Sun), presenting changing exhibitions on modern art. Just to the south is the gothic **Templo Expiatorio**, accented by tall, fluted stone columns and 15m-high stained-glass windows. Look up toward the ceiling in front of the small golden altar and be amazed.

South of downtown, the **Templo de Aranzazú**, built between 1749 and 1752, shows off three ornate Churrigueresque golden altars and some huge religious paintings. Beside it is the less showy **Templo de San Francisco**, built two centuries earlier.

Parque Agua Azul

About 20 blocks south of the city center, Parque Agua Azul (Calzada Independencia Sur; admission US$0.50; open 10am-6pm Tues-Sun) is a large verdant park offering pleasant

relief from the city hubbub. It features an orchid house, butterfly house, aviary and Paleontological museum (US$1.25 extra). The orchids are at their best in October, November, April and May. Bus No 60 or 62 heading south on Calzada Independencia will zoom you there from the city center.

Museo de Arqueología del Occidente de Mexico (☎ 3-619-01-01; Calzada Independencia Sur; admission US$0.40; open 10am-2pm & 5pm-7pm Tues-Sun), opposite the entrance to the park, houses a small but good collection including pre-Hispanic figurines and artefacts from Jalisco and the states of Nayarit and Colima.

The large, museum-like store **Casa de las Artesanías de Jalisco** (☎ 3-619-46-64; Calzada Gallo s/n; open 10am-6pm Mon-Fri, 10am-5pm Sat, 10am-3pm Sun) is nearby with its own separate entrance on Calzada Gallo. There's tons of gorgeous handicrafts from all over Jalisco at relatively reasonable prices.

Casa Museo José Clemente Orozco

During the 1940s, the great tapatío painter and muralist José Clemente Orozco (1883–1949) lived and worked in this house (☎ 3-616-83-29; Aurelio Aceves 29; admission free; open 9am-5pm Mon-Fri), located about 3km west of center. Personal effects, documents, photographs, a mural and a few paintings are on display.

Zoológico Guadalajara, Selva Mágica & Planetario

The zoo, Selva Mágica amusement park and the planetarium are near one another on the northern outskirts of the city. Bus No 60 and 62 (marked 'Zoológico'), heading north on Calzada Independencia, will drop you near the sites.

The decent **Zoológico Guadalajara** (☎ 3-674-43-60; admission US$3.50; open 10am-5pm Wed-Fri, 10am-6pm Sat & Sun) features large, green spaces for most of the animals. The attractions include two pyramid-shaped aviaries, a snake house, a children's petting zoo and a train that will chug you around. The north end of the site provides a view of the gorgeous gorge, Barranca de Oblatos.

The zoo opens on Monday and Tuesday during holidays.

Beside the zoo is **Selva Mágica** (☎ 3-674-12-90; admission US$4-5 depending on package; open 10am-6pm Mon-Fri, 10am-8pm Sat-Sun), a children's amusement park with a dolphin-and-seal show, a trained-bird show and mechanical rides.

About a 15-minute walk from the zoo, around a strange topiary garden, is the planetarium at the **Centro de Ciencia y Tecnología** (☎ 3-674-4106; admission US$0.50; open 9am-7pm Tues-Sun). It contains exhibits on astronomy, space, airplanes and other science-related topics. Planetarium shows (US$0.55) are scheduled hourly from 10am to 5pm.

Zapopan

About 8km from downtown, on the northwestern edge of Guadalajara, the suburb of Zapopan was a village before the Spanish arrived and an important maize-producing center in colonial times.

The **tourist police kiosk** (open 9am-9pm Tues-Fri, 10am-5pm Sat & Sun) is in front of the Zapopan basilica. Staff give out maps and informational leaflets detailing places of interest in and around the suburb. Free tours of the town are also given.

The large **Basílica de Zapopan**, constructed in 1730, is home to Nuestra Señora de Zapopan (Virgin of Zapopan), a tiny statue visited by pilgrims from near and far. On October 12, during Guadalajara's Fiestas de Octubre, the statue, after visiting some of the other churches in Jalisco before it reaches Guadalajara, is taken from Guadalajara's cathedral and returned to its home in Zapopan amid throngs of people and much merrymaking. The statue receives a new car each year for the procession, but the engine is never turned on; instead, the car is hauled along by ropes.

To the right of the basilica entrance, the small **Sala de Arte Huichol** (☎ 3-636-44-30; admission US$0.60; open 9:30am-1:30pm & 3pm-6pm Fri-Tues, 9:30am-1pm & 2:30pm-6pm Sat & Sun) exhibits some incredible yarn paintings and other fine examples of Huichol arts and crafts; there's a tiny attached store.

To the left of the basilica entrance is a 'virgin' museum that takes donations.

Bus No 275 Diagonal and TUR bus No 706, heading north on Av 16 de Septiembre or Alcalde, stop beside the basilica; the trip takes 20 minutes.

Tlaquepaque

About 7km to the southeast of downtown Guadalajara, Tlaquepaque (tlah-keh-**pah**-keh) is a major center for arts and ceramics production. In colonial times it was one of the first stops on the long road to Mexico City, and the Guadalajara gentry built substantial mansions here in the 19th century. These mansions are now stylish restaurants and galleries, and the charming zócalo is graced with flowers, small benches, monuments and a fountain. Pedestrian streets are popular with locals for long lunches, and steer tourists into fancy shops full of ceramics, bronze figures, glassware, embroidered clothing and many other beautiful items.

The Tlaquepaque **tourist office** (☎ 3-635-12-20 ext 104; Juárez 238; open 9am-8pm Mon-Fri) is on the other side of the block from the ceramic museum. There are information booths on or near the zócalo, but they're open erratically.

Museo Regional de la Cerámica y los Artes Populares de Jalisco (☎ 3-635-54-04; Independencia 237; admission free; open 10am-6pm Mon-Sat, 10am-3pm Sun) surrounds a shady courtyard and has many exhibits showing the different types and styles of ceramic work made in Tlaquepaque.

To get to Tlaquepaque, take local bus Nos 275 or 647, or TUR bus No 706 heading south on Av 16 de Septiembre. The trip takes about 30 minutes.

Tonalá

The suburb of Tonalá, beyond Tlaquepaque and about 13km southeast of the center of Guadalajara, is somewhat less touristy than Tlaquepaque. The shops here call themselves factories, not galleries – an accurate description, considering that many of them manufacture the glassware and ceramics found in other parts of Guadalajara. On Thursday and Sunday, most of the town becomes a crowded street market that takes hours to explore; you can easily eat and shop yourself into oblivion (check pieces carefully; many have slight irregularities). The best quality crafts are found in the actual factories. Other attractions in Tonalá are several old churches and the occasional *charreada* (rodeo) on Saturday.

The Tonalá **tourist office** (☎ *3-683-05-90; Tonaltecas 140; open 9am-8pm Mon-Fri)* is in the Casa de Artesanos. **Museo Nacional de la Cerámica** (☎ *3-683-0494; Constitución 110; admission free; open 10am-5pm Tues-Sun)* houses an eclectic array of pots from all over Mexico.

Local bus No 275 Diagonal or TUR bus No 706, heading south on Av 16 de Septiembre, will take you to Tonalá. The trip takes 45 minutes to an hour.

Organized Tours
During holiday periods (Easter, mid-July to late August, and the second half of December), the tourist office runs **free guided walking tours** (mostly in Spanish) of the Centro Histórico. They start at 9:30am in the Plaza de Armas and take about three hours; book at the tourist office the day before.

Panoramex (☎ *3-810-50-57; Federalismo Sur 944)* offers three tours with English-, French- and Spanish-speaking guides. The tours can be booked at the tourist office, and they start at Jardín San Francisco, on Corona, at 9:30am.

Tour No 1 (Monday to Saturday) visits some of the main sights of Guadalajara and Tlaquepaque (US$14, five hours)

Tour No 2 (three times per week) visits Chapala, Ajijic and Chula Vista (US$17, six hours)

Tour No 3 (four times per week) visits the town of Tequila, including the agave fields and a tequila distillery (US$22, 6½ hours)

Special Events
Several major festivals are celebrated in Guadalajara and its suburbs. They include the following:

Feria de Tonalá An annual handicrafts fair in Tonalá, specializing in ceramics, is held the week before and the week after Semana Santa.

Fiestas de Tlaquepaque Tlaquepaque's fiesta and handicrafts fair takes place mid-June to the first week of July.

Fiesta Internacional del Mariachi In late August and early September, mariachis come to hear, play and celebrate the latest sounds.

Fiestas de Octubre Beginning with a parade on the first Sunday in October, the October Fiestas, lasting all month, are Guadalajara's principal annual fair. Free entertainment takes place from noon to 10pm daily in Benito Juárez auditorium at the fairgrounds, while elsewhere around the city are livestock shows, art and other exhibitions and sporting and cultural events. On October 12 a religious element enters the festivities with a huge procession from the cathedral to Zapopan carrying the miniature statue of the Virgin of Zapopan (see Zapopan, earlier).

Feria Internacional del Libro This is one of the biggest book promotions in Latin America; held in the last week of November and first week of December.

Places to Stay – Budget
Guadalajara has two trailer parks, both offering full hookups and spaces for tents, trailers and motor homes.

San José del Tajo Trailer Park (☎/fax *3-686-17-38; Hwy 54/80 Km 15.5; camp sites US$22, camp sites US$18)* is a 150-site park southwest of the city center on the main road to Colima. Facilities include a pool, tennis court and laundry.

Hacienda Trailer Park (☎ *3-627-17-24; Circunvalación Pte 66, Ciudad Granja; tent & trailer sites US$18)* sits 10km west of the city center; call for directions. Amenities include a pool, laundry and plenty of trees. The communal clubhouse has a barbecue and tables for billiards and table tennis.

The city center has some budget-priced accommodation, though all places fill up during the numerous special events and whenever there's a big football game.

Hotel Hidalgo (☎ *3-613-50-67; Hidalgo 14; rooms with shared/private bathroom US$4/5.50-8)* sits on a street with all the charm of a freeway off-ramp. Expect austere, almost-clean rooms with nothing fancy attached. At least it's central and dirt cheap.

Hotel Las Américas (☎ *3-613-96-22; Hidalgo 76; singles/doubles US$16/19-22)* also

CENTRAL GUADALAJARA

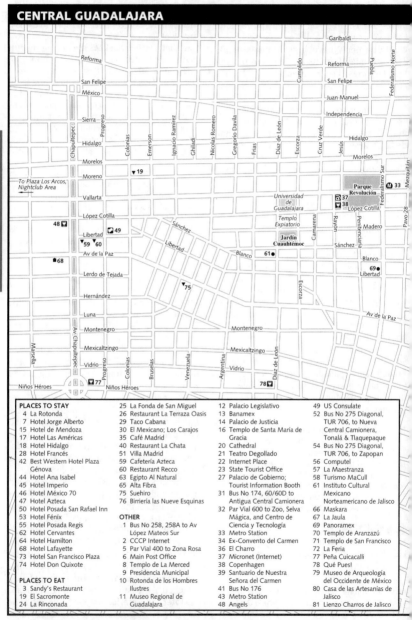

PLACES TO STAY
4 La Rotonda
7 Hotel Jorge Alberto
15 Hotel de Mendoza
17 Hotel Las Américas
18 Hotel Hidalgo
28 Hotel Francés
42 Best Western Hotel Plaza Génova
44 Hotel Ana Isabel
45 Hotel Imperio
46 Hotel México 70
47 Hotel Azteca
50 Hotel Posada San Rafael Inn
53 Hotel Fénix
55 Hotel Posada Regis
62 Hotel Cervantes
64 Hotel Hamilton
68 Hotel Lafayette
73 Hotel San Francisco Plaza
74 Hotel Don Quixote

PLACES TO EAT
3 Sandy's Restaurant
19 El Sacromonte
24 La Rinconada
25 La Fonda de San Miguel
26 Restaurant La Terraza Oasis
29 Taco Cabana
30 El Mexicano; Los Carajos
35 Café Madrid
40 Restaurant La Chata
51 Villa Madrid
59 Cafetería Azteca
60 Restaurant Recco
63 Egipto Al Natural
65 Alta Fibra
75 Suehiro
76 Birriería las Nueve Esquinas

OTHER
1 Bus No 258, 258A to Av López Mateos Sur
2 CCCP Internet
5 Par Vial 400 to Zona Rosa
6 Main Post Office
8 Templo de La Merced
9 Presidencia Municipal
10 Rotonda de los Hombres Ilustres
11 Museo Regional de Guadalajara
12 Palacio Legislativo
13 Banamex
14 Palacio de Justicia
16 Templo de Santa María de Gracia
20 Cathedral
21 Teatro Degollado
22 Internet Place
23 State Tourist Office
27 Palacio de Gobierno; Tourist Information Booth
31 Bus No 174, 60/60D to Antigua Central Camionera
32 Par Vial 600 to Zoo, Selva Mágica, and Centro de Ciencia y Tecnología
33 Metro Station
34 Ex-Convento del Carmen
36 El Charro
37 Micronet (Internet)
38 Copenhagen
39 Santuario de Nuestra Señora del Carmen
41 Bus No 176
43 Metro Station
48 Angels
49 US Consulate
52 Bus No 275 Diagonal, TUR 706, to Nueva Central Camionera, Tonalá & Tlaquepaque
54 Bus No 275 Diagonal, TUR 706, to Zapopan
56 Computel
57 La Maestranza
58 Turismo MaCull
61 Instituto Cultural Mexicano Norteamericano de Jalisco
66 Maskara
67 La Jaula
69 Panoramex
70 Templo de Aranzazú
71 Templo de San Francisco
72 La Feria
77 Peña Cuicacalli
78 Qué Pues!
79 Museo de Arqueología del Occidente de México
80 Casa de las Artesanías de Jalisco
81 Lienzo Charros de Jalisco

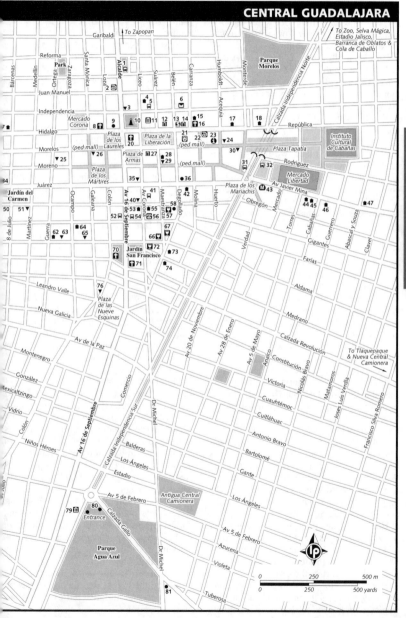

CENTRAL GUADALAJARA

NAYARIT & GUADALAJARA

lies on traffic-smothered Hidalgo, offering 49 clean and fairly modern rooms with TV, carpeting and large windows. Inside rooms are dark but outside rooms are noisy.

Hotel Hamilton *(☎ 3-614-67-26; Madero 381; singles/doubles US$9/11, TV US$2.50 extra)* features 32 small, simple and unmemorable rooms, but they are clean, generally quiet and with two beds.

Hotel Posada San Rafael Inn *(☎ 3-614-91-46; w www.sanrafael1.tripod.com/; López Cotilla 619; singles/doubles US$19-24/23-29)* exudes a homey, older, worn-around-the-edges feel, with just 11 high-ceilinged rooms facing two plant-filled, tiled and covered courtyards. Remodeled rooms cost more.

Hotel Posada Regis *(☎ 3-614-86-33; e posadaregis@usa.net; Corona 171; singles/doubles/triples US$22/27/37)* is in a converted 19th-century French-style mansion with high ceilings and ornate details. The 19 original rooms open onto a covered patio and are great value, though rooms overlooking the street can be noisy.

Hotel Jorge Alberto *(☎ 3-658-10-51; Hidalgo 656; singles/doubles US$26/33)* was originally a convent, but now it sports dingy and slightly worn charm. Almost 30 dark and slightly stuffy rooms, with TV and fan, face a courtyard.

Av Javier Mina, east of Mercado Libertad and the Plaza de los Mariachis, has a good selection of budget hotels. This part of town is more working-class and not especially pleasant, but you can often find a cheap room here when everything else is full.

Hotel Mexico 70 *(☎ 3-617-99-78; Javier Mina 230; singles/doubles US$14/17-20)* is named for the year Mexico hosted the World Cup; the receptionist wasn't confident they would ever actually win it. The bigger rooms here have two or more beds, and TV is US$2.50 extra.

Hotel Ana Isabel *(☎ 3-617-79-20; Javier Mina 164; singles/doubles with bathroom US$17/20)* has 46 clean, plain rooms on three floors of indoor halls softened by plants. TV is part of the deal.

Hotel Imperio *(☎ 3-586-57-18; e hotelimperialgdl@hotmail.com; Javier Mina 180; singles/doubles US$17/22-26)* isn't fancy, with no-view rooms that are bright but plain. Still, it's a solid, respectable budget choice.

Hotel Azteca *(☎ 3-617-74-65; Javier Mina 311; singles/doubles US$22/28-39)* is two cuts above the others and good value. Waiting for you are five stories of modern rooms with good plumbing and TV. There's a restaurant and parking too.

Places to Stay – Mid-Range

Hotel San Francisco Plaza *(☎ 3-613-89-54; Degollado 267; singles/doubles US$42/45)* presents 76 nicely done rooms with colorful furniture and surrounding a beautifully airy, plant-and-fountain-filled tropical courtyard. A restaurant and parking add to your convenience.

Hotel Don Quijote *(☎ 3-658-12-99; Heroes 91; singles/doubles US$48/54)* has beautiful, well-decorated and modern rooms with colonial touches. It's a small and cozy place, with narrow halls overlooking tables in the courtyard lobby.

La Rotonda *(☎ 3-614-10-17; e hotelesucasa@yahoo.com; Liceo 130; singles/doubles US$48/58)* comes in an old but completely renovated building, filled with friendly staff. Spacious, clean, modern and happy rooms have TV, and you can chow down at the restaurant.

Hotel Francés *(☎ 3-613-11-90, 800-853-0900 in the USA; e reserva@hotelfrances.com; Maestranza 35; rooms US$61, suites from US$64)* claims the best hotel feature in Guadalajara: balconies in the bathrooms! This historic hotel is the oldest in town (1610); the arched stone courtyard (now a bar) was originally used to keep horses. Toss back enough drinks and you can still hear them neigh.

Hotel Cervantes *(☎ 3-613-68-46; Sánchez 442; singles/doubles US$60/65)* is a swank, modern joint with 100 elegant rooms on five floors. Expect most amenities like parking, 2nd-floor pool, and a phone beside every bathtub.

If you come into town late, consider spending the night near the Nueva Central Camionera and finding a more central place in the morning.

Hotel Serena (☎ 3-600-09-10; Antigua Carretera Zapotlanejo 1500; rooms US$40-71) is situated across the road from Módulo 1 of the Nueva Central Camionera. It's not a great deal, but there's not much competition. Small rooms come with TV and fan, and the use of pools, garden and a nice lobby.

Places to Stay – Top End

Hotel de Mendoza (☎ 3-613-46-46, 800-361-2600 in the USA, fax 3-613-73-10; W www.demendoza.com.mx; Carranza 16; singles/doubles US$80/96, suites US$95/108 plus tax) sits regally near the center of town, originally built as the convent to the Santa María de Gracia church next door. Today it's a beautifully refurbished hotel with 100 modern rooms and amenities like cable TV, air-con, restaurant, bar, pool and parking.

Hotel Fénix (☎ 3-614-57-14; e ventax@ infosel.net.mx; Corona 160; rooms US$75) isn't super modern, but still attracts business clientele with services like car rental, travel agency and in-house shops. Some rooms have large balconies and nice touches like old furniture.

Best Western Hotel Plaza Génova (☎ 3-613-75-00; W www.hplazagenova.com; Juárez 123; rooms US$76 plus tax) features US-style rooms for those who miss home and its comforts. Rates include minibar, air-con, cable TV, a gym and an American breakfast.

Hotel Lafayette (☎ 3-615-02-52; e lafayete@mpsnet.com.mx; Av de la Paz 2055; rooms US$81 Mon-Thur, US$68 Fri-Sun plus tax) is an accordion-like hotel offering 200 rather small rooms with tiny baths, but they're nice – carpeting, cable TV and air-con can all be yours, along with a dip in the pool and a perch at the attractive café.

Places to Eat

Most eateries in the center of town serve up standard Mexican fare, with higher prices buying better atmosphere rather than more creative cuisine. Guadalajara's best restaurants are scattered around the suburbs, along with a surfeit of fast-food franchises.

Centro Histórico & Around The Mercado Libertad and Mercado Corona both have scores of **food stalls** serving the cheapest eats in town. Sensitive stomachs should beware: the hygiene at these spots is 'adventurous.'

La Rinconada (☎ 3-613-99-14; Morelos 86; mains US$7-12; open 9am-8:30pm daily) cooks well-prepared Mexican and US-style meals in fashionable surroundings. It's very clean and the service is good.

Taco Cabana (mains under US$3; open 9am-10:30pm daily) often has loud music and loud locals, and is a great place for cheap tacos and even cheaper (US$2.25 for two) beers. Free snacks arrive soon after your butt hits the seat, though you may have to fend off peddlers. Be patient with the service.

El Mexicano (☎ 3-658-03-45; Morelos 79; mains US$4-10; open 1pm-10pm daily) is the type of place where a young woman greets you at the door; plenty of drinks and a few dinner items comfort patrons even more. Live music often plays from 3pm.

Sandy's Restaurant (☎ 3-614-42-36; cnr Alcalde & Independencia, upstairs; mains US$6-9; open 8am-9pm daily) should be a destination for super-hungry travelers; the lunch buffet is US$4.50, and the breakfast even less. It's a chain restaurant, and food/prices are similar at all its outlets.

Café Madrid (☎ 3-614-95-04; Juárez 264; mains US$4-8; open 8am-10pm daily) sizzles up burgers, meat and Mexican dishes, along with breakfast. Professional waiters in white coats offer brisk service, and 1950s-style decor emulates a US diner.

Restaurant La Terraza Oasis (☎ 3-613-82-85; Morelos 435; mains under US$3; open 1pm-10pm daily) is a no-frills, industrial-like cafeteria with outdated furniture, but it's really cheap, serving burgers, steaks and chicken dishes. Even cigarettes are on the menu (look under 'Para la buena salud') – they're probably to accompany the nightly live music.

Restaurant La Chata (☎ 3-613-05-88; Corona 126; mains US$3-7; open 8am-midnight daily) has been cooking quality Mexican food in a homey environment for more than 50 years. Its specialty is a platillo jalisciense (chicken, potatoes, soup, an enchilada and a flauta). It also serves up pozole (hominy soup) and *chiles rellenos* (chilies stuffed with cheese, meat or other foods, deep fried and baked in sauce).

La Fonda de San Miguel *(☎ 3-613-08-09; Guerra 25; mains US$9-16)* is the kind of place you take a hot date. Gourmet dishes are served in a simply gorgeous setting: a lush courtyard filled with hanging metal stars, colorful furniture, squawking parrots and live music day and night.

The blocks southwest of the city center have a few inexpensive eateries offering healthy vegetarian fare.

Villa Madrid *(☎ 3-613-42-50; López Cotilla 223; mains under US$4; open noon-9pm Mon-Sat)* isn't exclusively a vegetarian restaurant, but does cook tasty meals like soya burgers, veg burritos and salads. The chicken burritos with *mole* (spicy sauce made with chilies), and the yogurt with fruit, are exceptionally tasty.

Alta Fibra *(☎ 3-613-69-80; Sánchez 370B; mains under US$4; open 8am-6pm Mon-Sat)* means 'high fiber' – something you need to keep you regular on the road. Soya ceviche, soya burgers, *choco de soya* (chocolate soya drink) and assorted salads will all help.

Egipto Al Natural *(☎ 3-613-62-77; Sánchez 416; mains under US$4; open 10am-6pm Mon-Sat)* is a friendly, nondescript veg restaurant popular for its filling *comida corrida*, soya-based meals, fresh vegetable juices and yogurt with fruit. It also sells some health-food products.

Plaza de las Nueve Esquinas About 10 blocks southwest of the city center, the Plaza of the Nine Corners is a small, untouristy, triangular space where several small streets intersect. It's a cute little neighborhood with a number of eateries, many specializing in *birria* (a thick stew of mutton and onions).

Birriería las Nueve Esquinas *(☎ 3-613-62-60; Colón 384; mains US$2-4; open 9am-10pm daily)* serves some of the best *birria* around, and in a charming little dining area with windows on three sides. Spotlessly clean, the classic Mexican kitchen has tiled work surfaces, suspended utensils and delicious aromas.

Near Av Chapultepec Guadalajara's Zona Rosa is basically the few blocks of Av Chapultepec north and south of Av Vallarta. It's hardly a full-on nightlife and entertainment district, but it does have some pleasant restaurants on quiet streets nearby. From the city center, catch the 'Par Vial' bus or trolley heading west on Independencia and get off at Chapultepec and Vallarta (about 10 minutes).

Cafetería Azteca *(☎ 3-825-55-99; Chapultepec 201; mains under US$4.50; open 8am-11pm daily)* is a casual, breezy place on a street corner, and in its leather chairs you feast on inexpensive burgers and Mexican specialties while watching the world zoom by on the busy avenue.

Restaurant Recco *(☎ 3-825-07-24; Libertad 1981; mains US$9-12; open 1:45pm-11:30pm Mon-Sat, 1:45pm-9:30pm Sun)* has the most inappropriate ugly sign, considering the restaurant is in an old family mansion with dim, elegant atmosphere. Excellent meat and seafood dishes, rather than pasta, dominate the Italian menu.

Suehiro *(☎ 3-826-00-94; Av de La Paz 1701; mains US$9-15; open 1:30pm-5:30pm & 7:30pm-11:30pm daily)* is situated some 500m east of Av Chapultepec and one of the best Japanese restaurants in town. A great place to visit when you're craving tempura or yakitori.

El Sacromonte *(☎ 3-825-54-47; Moreno 1398; mains US$9-17; open 1:30pm-midnight Mon-Sat)* offers fine dining in beautiful and romantic surroundings. Mexican crafts decorate the walls, soft music trembles in the air, and plenty of gringos are there to lap it all up.

Entertainment

Guadalajara is in love with music of all kinds, and live performers can be heard any night of the week. Theaters, cinemas and bars are also plentiful, but there aren't many dance venues accessible from the city center or affordable to the budget traveler.

For entertainment information, you can stop by the tourist office and view its weekly schedule of events; the bilingual staff will help you find something to suit your fancy. Or check out the Friday edition of the daily newspaper *Público*; its entertainment insert, *Ocio*, includes a cultural-events calendar for the upcoming week and is *the* place to look for information on restaurants, movies, exhibits and the club scene. *Occidental* and *Informador*, also Spanish-language dailies, have entertainment listings, as does the weekly booklet *Ciento Uno*.

Popular cultural-arts venues hosting a range of drama, dance and music performances include **Teatro Degollado** (☎ 3-614-47-73) and the **Instituto Cultural de Cabañas** (☎ 3-668-16-40), both downtown (see their respective sections, earlier), as well as the **Ex-Convento del Carmen** (☎ 3-614-71-84; *Juárez 638*).

Ballet Folklórico Grand performances by **Ballet Folklórico de la Universidad de Guadalajara** (☎ 3-614-47-73; *seats US$3-16; ticket office open 10am-1pm & 4pm-7pm daily*) at the Teatro Degollado begin at 8:30pm Thursday and 10am Sunday.

Ballet Folklórico del Instituto Cultural de Cabañas (☎ 3-668-16-40 ext 1004; *admission US$5*) performs at the Cabañas Cultural Institute at 8:30pm every Wednesday.

Mariachis Pay your respects to the mariachi tradition in its home city. Plaza de los Mariachis, just east of the historic center, is a good place to get an authentic experience. Many tourists go to one of the sanitized venues provided for the purpose.

La Feria (☎ 3-613-71-50; *Corona 291; mains US$7-10; open mainly for dinner*) asks 'Are you starving?' on its menu. Nonvegetarians can take up this offer, eating and drinking in the leather chairs of a lofty former mansion. Mariachi shows and midnight dancing follows. It's pretty touristy but a lot of fun, and many Mexicans come along for the ride.

Casa Bariachi (☎ 3-616-99-00; *Vallarta 2221; mains US$6-12; open 1pm-3am Mon-Sat*) is a restaurant/bar that comes with great atmosphere – colorful cutout paper, romantic lighting and leather chairs fill a huge barn-like space, as do the locals who like to

party here. Big margaritas and nightly mariachis entertain everyone.

Bar Bariachi (☎ 3-616-91-80; *Vallarta 2308; open 6pm-3am Mon-Sat*) is Casa Bariachi's smaller cousin, where on Tuesday nights women drink all the tequila they can for US$3.50. Guess how many men show up to watch? There's live mariachi music nightly at 11pm.

Near Tlaquepaque's main zócalo, the **El Parián** quadrangle is another mariachi magnet.

Live Music The state band presents **free concerts** of typical *música tapatía* (music typical of Jalisco state) in the Plaza de Armas at 6:30pm on most Thursdays and Sundays, and on other days as well during holiday seasons.

Instituto Cultural Mexicano Norteamericano de Jalisco (☎ 3-825-58-38; *Díaz de León 300*) often hosts classical music concerts and recitals.

Peña Cuicacalli (☎ 3-825-46-90; *Niños Héroes 1988; admission US$3-40 depending on performers; open 8:30pm-1am daily*) is a folk-music restaurant/bar/club presenting popular, varied programmes of contemporary Mexican and Latino folk ballads, rock, jazz, comedy and more. Call or go by for a schedule.

La Bodeguita del Medio (☎ 3-630-16-20; *Vallarta 2320; open 1:30pm-1am Sun-Wed, 1:30pm-2:30am Thur-Sat*) is a popular Cuban restaurant/bar with good party feel; there's 'fake' writing on the walls acting as decor, while live music rocks the place inside out Tuesday to Saturday night.

Bars The historic center has a few bars serving snacks, drinks and sometimes live music. If you stroll south of Plaza de la Liberación, down streets like Maestranza and Degollado, you'll find quite a few places that are lively at night.

La Maestranza (☎ 3-613-20-85; *Maestranza 179; open 1pm-2:30am daily*) sparkles with a great bullfighting theme. This hip cantina also attracts lots of 20- and 30-somethings with beer (pitchers US$9), salty snacks and lively Mexican music.

Mariachis

In many minds, no image captures the spirit of Mexico better than that of the proud-faced mariachis – in matching garb and broad-rimmed sombreros – belting out traditional Mexican ballads before a festive crowd. But the origin of the word 'mariachi' is something of a mystery.

Some historians contend that 'mariachi' is a corruption of the French word *mariage* (marriage) and that the name stems from the time of the French intervention in 1861–67. Mariachi bands were said to have played at wedding ceremonies during that period, hence the name.

Others say that the word was in use before the French arrived and that it had arisen from festivals honoring the Virgin Mary at which musicians performed. They note that the mariachi is indigenous to the region south of Guadalajara, probably derived from the name María with the Náhuatl diminutive '-chi' tacked on.

Still others point out that in the 1870s a Mexican poet designated as *mariache* the stage upon which dancers and musicians performed *jarabes*. A jarabe consisted of an ensemble that played and sang while a couple – a man attired as a Mexican cowboy in chaps and a wide-rimmed hat, and a woman in a handwoven shawl and full, brightly colored skirt – danced beside them.

GREG ELMS

Today's mariachi bands are of two types. The original version consists of musicians who play only string instruments and who limit their repertoire to traditional Jalisco melodies. The modern, more commercial mariachi band's main instrument is the trumpet, and they have a broader repertoire. Both types can be heard in Guadalajara's Plaza de los Mariachis and at boisterous indoor venues devoted to mariachi music.

Los Carajos (☎ 3-126-79-51; *Morelos 79; open 12:30pm-2am daily*) has imaginative tables that crowd into 2nd-floor doorway balconies and look down onto pedestrians below. Snag one and drink up.

Hotel Francés (☎ 3-613-11-90; *Maestranza 35*) has a sedate but stylish and airy courtyard piano bar, tapping out live music from 4pm to 10pm daily. It's popular with gringos and worth a look for the architecture alone.

Copenhagen (☎ 3-587-65-96; *cnr López Cotilla & Castellanos; admission US$5.50 Fri & Sat only; open 2pm-3am daily*) is a very cozy (read: tight spaces) restaurant/jazz venue serving paella (US$9), along with a few other dishes. Mostly, though, it offers live jazz music (9pm to 1:45am daily) to an older audience.

Qué Pues! (☎ 3-826-91-14; *Niños Héroes 1554; open 1pm-1am Mon-Thur, 1pm-2am Fri & Sat*) usually plays insanely loud rock videos on TV, but on Tuesdays at 10pm you get insanely loud rock music – live. The space is open, airy and somewhat intimate, and the chairs and tables tiny. Take a taxi there; it's far from the center.

Discos & Clubs West of the city center, Av Juárez becomes Av Vallarta, which has a concentration of nightspots. Discos and clubs on the 'Ruta Vallarta' attract young, affluent locals who dress to impress. No track shoes or jeans, please.

La Marcha (☎ 3-615-89-99; Vallarta 2648; admission with open bar US$16 for men & free for women Wed, US$16 for men & US$10 for women Fri & Sat; open 10pm-5am Wed, 10pm-5am Fri & Sat) perches right next to the arches on Vallarta. If you're young and gorgeous (half your luck), you'll feel right at home here, bopping to the popular beat on two floors and sipping expensive drinks from the four bars.

El Mito (☎ 3-615-28-55; Vallarta 2425; admission free-US$5.50; open 10:30pm-3am Wed-Sat) attracts mostly folks 25 years and over with music from the 1960s, '70s, '80s and '90s, as well as special shows on Friday and Saturday. It's in the huge Centro Magno shopping center.

Hard Rock Café (☎ 3-616-45-64; Vallarta 2425; admission free-US$8; open 1pm-2am daily) charges a cover that varies with time, day, and what's happening. As well as the usual slick decor and black-clad clientele, this popular joint regularly features local bands doing polished covers of rock classics. It's also located in the Centro Magno shopping mall.

More nightlife venues cluster around Plaza del Sol, on López Mateos Sur south of Vallarta.

Danny Rock (☎ 3-121-13-63; Otero 1989; admission US$7; open 9pm-3am) is a disco and video bar drawing a mixed crowd. The music here runs the gamut from the 1960s to the '90s.

Gay & Lesbian Venues With two bars, several small pastel rooms and provocative artwork, **La Jaula** (☎ 3-120-99-31; Maestranza 233; admission free) has US$1.75 beers that liven things up a whole lot.

Maskara (☎ 3-614-81-03; Maestranza 238; admission free) is a colorful bar with stylish youths, disco music and cheap drinks. What more do you need?

Angels (☎ 3-615-25-25; López Cotilla 1495; admission US$5.50 Fri & Sat with 1 drink; free Wed-Thur) comes all glittery and

thumping with techno, pop and acid jazz. It attracts a well-dressed crowd of both gay and straight folk.

Cinemas Several cinemas show international films and classics. Check *Ocio* or the local newspapers. The big shopping centers like Plaza del Sol and Plaza Milenium have multiscreen facilities showing recent movie releases.

Spectator Sports

The bullfighting season is October to March, and the fights are held on select Sundays starting at 4:30pm. A couple of fights will almost certainly take place during the October fiestas; the rest of the schedule is sporadic. Check at the bullring **Plaza de Toros Nuevo Progreso** (☎ 3-637-99-82; north end of Calzada Independencia; admission US$3-25) or the tourist office. Bus No 60 (or anything saying 'zoologico') heading north on Independencia will take you there.

Matador in action

Charreadas are held at noon on most Sundays in the ring behind the Parque Agua Azul. *Charros* (cowboys) arrive from all over Jalisco and Mexico to show off their skills. *Escaramuzas* (cowgirls) also compete in daring displays of their sidesaddle riding. To see them, get your butt on over to **Lienzo Charros de Jalisco** (☎ 3-619-32-32; *Dr Michel 577; admission from US$3.50*).

Fútbol is Guadalajara's favorite sport. The city usually has at least three teams playing in the national top-level *primera división*: Guadalajara (Las Chivas), the second most popular team in the country (after América of Mexico City), Atlas (Los Zorros), and Universidad Autónoma de Guadalajara (Los Tecos).

The teams play at stadiums around the city, but the main venue is **Estadio Jalisco** (☎ 3-637-05-63; *Siete Colinas 1772*), which has hosted a number of World Cup games. Admission runs US$3 to US$13, more for a really big game. The summer soccer season is January to May; winter season August to December. Contact the stadium or tourist office for schedules.

Shopping

Handicrafts from Jalisco, Michoacán and other Mexican states are available in Guadalajara. (See the Tlaquepaque and Tonalá sections, earlier in this chapter, for information on these two craft-making suburbs.) The **Casa de las Artesanías de Jalisco**, 20 blocks south of the city center, has a good selection. See also Parque Agua Azul earlier in this section.

Mercado Libertad (☎ 3-658-15-14; *cnr Javier Mina & Calzada Independencia; open daily*) loafs just south of Plaza Tapatía with three floors of stalls spread over three city blocks. If you can't find it here, you can't find it.

Mercado El Baratillo is a Sunday flea market that stretches blocks in every direction on and around Javier Mina. To get there, take a 'Par Vial' bus or trolley east along Hidalgo.

El Charro (☎ 3-614-97-43; *cnr Juárez & Degollado; open 9:30am-8pm Mon-Sat*) offers those cowboy boots, the Mexican hat and

mariachi suit you've always wanted. There are several similar (and cheaper) shops on Juárez to the east.

Guadalajara's most prosperous citizens prefer to shop at one of the big shopping centers west of town; to get there, take bus Nos 258 or 258A west on San Felipe.

Getting There & Away

Air Guadalajara's **Aeropuerto Internacional Miguel Hidalgo** (*code GDL;* ☎ 3-688-52-48) is 17km south of downtown, just off the highway to Chapala. The many airlines serving the airport offer direct flights to more than 20 cities in Mexico and about 10 cities in the USA and Canada, as well as one-stop connections to many other places. You'll find a tourist office at the terminal.

Book flights with one of the many travel agencies in Guadalajara. Look in the telephone Yellow Pages under 'Agencias de Viajes.' A number of airlines and travel agencies, as well as AmEx, have offices in Plaza Los Arcos, Vallarta 2440. Airline offices in Guadalajara include:

Aero California	(☎ 3-616-25-25)
Aerolitoral	(☎ 3-688-53-41)
Aeromar	(☎ 3-615-85-11)
Aeroméxico	(☎ 3-122-02-00)
Air France	(☎ 3-630-37-07)
American Airlines	(☎ 3-616-44-02)
Continental	(☎ 3-647-01-07)
Delta	(☎ 3-630-31-30)
Mexicana	(☎ 3-112-00-11)
United Airlines	(☎ 3-616-93-93)

Bus Guadalajara has two bus stations. The long-distance bus station is the **Nueva Central Camionera**, a large, U-shaped modern terminal split into seven *módulos* (modules) or *salas* (waiting rooms). It is 9km southeast of the Guadalajara city center, past Tlaquepaque.

Each *módulo* has ticket desks for a number of bus lines, plus cafeterias and pay phones. Most *módulos* have 'left luggage' services.

Buses, often frequent, travel to and from just about everywhere in western, central and northern Mexico. The same destination can (inconveniently) be served by several companies in several different *módulos*; the companies suggested in the following list have the most frequent departures to the cities indicated.

Barra de Navidad US$22, five hours, 291km, 11 daily with Autocamiones de Cihuatlán from *Módulo* 3, three daily with Primera Plus from *Módulo* 1

Colima US$15, 2½ to three hours, 202km, regularly with Primera Plus from *Módulo* 1

Mazatlán US$30, eight hours, 506km, Elite, regularly with Pacífico from *Módulo* 3

Mexico City (Terminal Norte) US$37 to US$42, seven to eight hours, 535km, regularly with Primera Plus from *Módulo* 1, regularly with Omnibus de Mexico from *Módulo* 6

Morelia US$22, 3½ hours, 278km, regularly with Primera Plus from *Módulo* 1, regularly with La Línea from *Módulo* 2

Puerto Vallarta US$28 to US$31, five hours, 344km, regularly with Pacífico, Futura and Elite from *Módulos* 3 and 4

Tepic US$20, 3½ hours, 216km, regularly with Elite and Futura from *Módulo* 3, regularly with Omnibus de Mexico from *Módulo* 6

Uruapan US$18, 3½ hours, 305km, regularly with Primera Plus from *Módulo* 1

For deluxe buses to many of these destinations (at considerably higher fares), try ETN, *Módulo* 2.

First-class bus tickets can be bought in the city center at **Turismo MaCull** (☎ 3-614-70-14; *López Cotilla 163; open 9am-7pm Mon-Fri, 9am-2pm Sat)*. Check bus schedules here too.

Guadalajara's other bus station is the **Antigua Central Camionera** *(Old Bus Station; US$0.05 entry!)*, about 1.5km south of the cathedral, near Parque Agua Azul. This station serves 2nd-class buses to and from destinations nearer Guadalajara. There are two sides, separated approximately by destination (but not exclusively): Sala A is for destinations to the east and northeast; Sala B is for destinations northwest, southwest and south.

Transportes Guadalajara–Chapala buses leave from Sala B every half hour from 6am to 9:30pm travelling to Chapala (US$3.25,

45 minutes, 40km), Ajijic (US$3.25, one hour, 47km) Jocotepec (US$3.50, 1½ hours, 68km).

Rojo de Los Altos buses depart from Sala B every 20 minutes from 5:30am to 9:30pm for Tequila (US$3.50, two hours, 62km).

Train The only train serving Guadalajara is the *Tequila Express* – a tourist excursion to the nearby town of Tequila (see the Tequila section, earlier in this chapter).

Car Guadalajara is 344km southeast of Puerto Vallarta. Hwys 15, 15D, 23, 54, 54D, 80, 80D and 90 all converge here, combining temporarily to form the Periférico, a ring road around the city.

Guadalajara has many car rental agencies, listed in the telephone Yellow Pages under 'Automóviles – Renta de.' Several of the large US companies are represented, but you may get a cheaper deal from a local company. Agencies include:

Auto Rent de Guadalajara (☎ 3-826-20-13, 800-800-4000 in the USA)

Budget (☎ 3-613-00-27, 800-700-1700 in the USA)

Dollar (☎ 3-826-79-59, 3-688-56-59)

Hertz (☎ 3-614-61-97, 800-654-3030 in the USA)

National (☎ 3-614-71-75, 800-227-7368 in the USA)

Quick Rent A Car (☎ 3-614-60-06, 3-614-22-47)

Getting Around

To/From the Airport The airport (☎ 3-688-52-48) is 17km south of downtown Guadalajara, just off the Hwy to Chapala. Bus No 176, which goes north on Corona about every 20 minutes, will eventually wind its way to the airport. Tell the driver that you're going to the *aeropuerto,* and you'll be dropped two blocks from the airport. Allow a good hour for the trip (US$0.80).

Atasa provides shuttle service between the airport and downtown (US$1, one hour). Taxis between the airport and the city center cost about US$14 on the meter.

To/From the Bus Stations To reach the city center from the Nueva Central Camionera, you can take any 'Centro' or No 644 city bus, or the more comfortable TUR No 707 bus, from the loop road within the station (immediately outside your *módulo*; see under Bus in the Getting There & Away section earlier). These only come every 30 minutes, so it's often quicker to walk out of the station between *Módulo* 1 and the Hotel Serena and take a yellow/orange bus No 275 (US$0.40), going to the right (north) along the road outside. These run every 15 minutes from 5:30am to 10:30pm and bring you into the city center along Av 16 de Septiembre.

All the city's taxis now have meters, but most taxi drivers at the bus station prefer not to use them and will quote a flat fee to the city center. About US$8 is reasonable, but don't be afraid to haggle.

From the city centre to the Nueva Central Camionera, hop on bus No 275 'Diagonal' southward on Av 16 de Septiembre, anywhere between the cathedral and Calzada Revolución. They run frequently but tend to be crowded and can take 40 to 50 minutes to get there.

Bus Nos 60 and 60D south on Calzada Independencia will take you from the city center to the Antigua Central Camionera. Bus Nos 616 and 000 run between the two bus stations.

Bus Guadalajara has a comprehensive city bus system, but be ready for crowded, rough rides. On major routes, buses run every five minutes or so from 6am to 10pm daily; they cost US$0.40. Many buses pass through the center of town, so for an inner suburban destination you'll have a few stops to choose from. The routes diverge as they get farther from the city center, and you need to know the bus number for the suburb you want. Some bus route numbers are followed by an additional letter indicating which circuitous route they will follow in the outer suburbs.

The TUR buses, painted a distinctive turquoise color, are a more comfortable alternative on some routes. They have air-con and everyone gets a seat. The fare is US$0.80. If they roar past without stopping, they're full; this can happen several times in a row during rush hour. It's enough to drive you crazy.

Useful Bus Routes

destination	bus no	route in centro
Antigua Central Camionera	60, 62 or 174	south on Calzada Independencia
Nueva Central Camionera	275 Diagonal or TUR 706	south on Av 16 de Septiembre
Parque Agua Azul	60, 62 or 62A	south on Calzada Independencia
Plaza de Toros, Zoo, Selva Mágica	60, 62 or 62D, or Par Vial 600	north on Calzada Independencia
Plaza del Sol	258 TUR 707	west on San Felipe west on Juárez
Tlaquepaque	275 Diagonal, No 647 or TUR 706	south on Av 16 de Septiembre
Tonalá	275 Diagonal or TUR 706	south on Av 16 de Septiembre
Zapopan	any 275 or TUR 706	north on Av 16 de Septiembre
Zona Rosa	Par Vial 400	west on Independencia

The tourist office has a list of the many bus routes in Guadalajara and can help you figure out how to get anywhere you want to go. The table on the previous page lists some of the most common suburban destinations, the buses that go to those destinations, and suggestions on where to catch the buses in the Centro Histórico.

Metro The Metro (☎ 3-827-00-00) has two lines that cross the city. Stops are marked around town by a 'T' symbol. The subway is quick and comfortable enough, but does not serve many points of visitor interest. Línea 1 stretches north-south for 15km all the way from the Periférico Nte to the Periférico Sur. It runs more or less below Federalismo (seven blocks west of the city center) and Av Colón. You can catch it at Parque Revolución, on the corner of Av Juárez.

Línea 2 runs east-west for 10km below Avs Juárez and Mina.

Taxi Guadalajara's plentiful taxis have meters, but many taxi drivers will quote a flat fee for a trip instead. Generally, it's cheaper to go by the meter, though the driver may take a circuitous route to increase the fare anyway. For a flat fee, try to negotiate a discount. Typical fares from the city center are: US$3.50 to the Antigua Central Camionera or Parque Agua Azul; US$5 to Plaza del Sol; US$4.50 to Tlaquepaque or the zoo; US$5 to Zapopan; US$8 to the Nueva Central Camionera; US$8 to Tonalá; and US$14 to the airport. Settle the fare before you get into the taxi.

CHACALA
pop 400
The tiny fishing village of Chacala is about a 1½-hour drive north of Puerto Vallarta and 10km west of Las Varas. Chacala occupies a beautiful cove with a 1km beach bordered by lush green slopes. You can hang out, explore the small village and take a couple of short hikes (one trail starts just outside the Mar de Jade driveway). From January to March, try hiring a *panga* (small skiff) for whale-watching or fishing; there's even

surfing nearby at La Caleta. During the Easter holidays, Chacala is thronged with Mexican families camping on the beach.

Telephone service will arrive soon to this little town and its smattering of foreign travelers. It's a friendly, calm place to hole up and just relax, with just one main, sandy thoroughfare and a few cobbled side streets.

There's no real nightlife here, though you can buy two giant margaritas for US$5 at **Koko Bongos** during happy hour (8pm to 10pm daily).

To reach Chacala, get off the bus at Las Varas (any 2nd-class bus will stop here, as will most – but not all – 1st-class buses) and take a *taxi colectivo* to Chacala (US$1.25, 15 minutes). A private taxi sets you back US$11.

Places to Stay
If you're a camper, ask for a beach space outside **Restaurant Laguna Encantada** (☎ 327-272-03-08), toward the north end. It's free, as long as you support them by eating there a few times. There's also camping/trailer parking at **Restaurant El Delfín** (☎ 327-272-10-67; sites US$3.25), toward the south end of the beach. For more solid accommodation, try **Restaurant Las Brisas** (☎ 333-673-50-08 in Guadalajara; rooms US$33-66), **Restaurant Tres Hermanos** (☎ 327-272-10-67; rooms US$33) or **Posada Sarahi** (☎ 311-240-99-26; rooms US$28). All of these places have decent spots to lay your head.

Techos de Mexico (W www.playachacala .com; e kerry@cyberhodge.com; rooms US$22-55) is a worthy cooperative of six local families that each rent out one to three modern, spacious rooms on their own properties. Find them by walking around town until you find a brown 'Techos de Mexico' sign. That house will (hopefully) have a pamphlet with a simple map and locations of all the houses. Or, email a reservation in advance.

Casa Pacifica (W www.playachacala.com; doubles US$50 including breakfast) is one mid-range option, where two large, beautiful suites come with views, queen-size beds and a kitchen. A smaller room is also available. Adults are preferred, and the owner encourages creative folks, such as artists and writers, to stay here. Follow the uphill road in town to its end at the Marina Chacala gate, then veer right.

Mar de Jade (*☎/fax 322-222-11-71 in Puerto Vallarta;* **W** *www.mardejade.com; singles/doubles from US$115-135/170-190 including all meals, children 7-12 US$25, under 7 free*) is located on the beach at the south end of the cove. It's a vacation retreat center and resort owned by the dynamic Dr Laura del Valle and offers a gorgeous, serene oceanfront setting for yoga (and other retreats), weddings and family reunions. You get three healthy and delicious buffet-style meals per day, plus the use of all facilities including swimming pool, Jacuzzi and exercise/meditation room. Also available are massage and spa services, Spanish classes, boat and horseback excursions, a three-week volunteer programme and a Spanish summer camp for teenagers. There are special rates for groups and for three-week stays.

Majahua (*☎ 311-212-40-11 in Tepic;* **W** *www.majahua.com; rooms 2-5 people US$110-297*) is great if you're looking for something really fancy. Head up the short driveway past Mar de Jade to five intimate, very creatively-designed suites with views. They're built close to the hillside and connected by leafy winding paths. All have a private terrace, are multileveled and come accented with original, artistic touches – such as an outdoor waterfall shower – that you won't find anywhere else. A gourmet restaurant (on the premises) and spa services are available for extra. Room discounts are given in the summer low season.

Places to Eat

You can grab a meal or snack at any of the dozen-plus palapa restaurants on the beach. For super-fresh seafood, head to the dock early in the morning and buy your own fish; some restaurants will cook it up for free (or a small fee), as long as you buy side dishes and drinks there too. Ask politely first.

Mauna Kea Café (*open 8am-3pm Mon-Sat*) is a tiny, unconventional and casual rooftop café at Casa Pacifica. It serves coffee, tea and pastries.

Majahua (*most mains US$6-9; open 8:30am daily until the last guest leaves*) is located up the driveway past Mar de Jade, at the south end of town. The small, rustic, outdoor restaurant offers international gourmet meals that change daily. Seafood (such as the lobster, US$22) and pasta are always available. Special orders are taken if they're given ahead of time.

RINCÓN DE GUAYABITOS
☎ 327 • pop 4000

On the coast about 60km north of Puerto Vallarta, Rincón de Guayabitos is a somewhat homey beach resort town that caters to vacationing Mexicans and snowbirds from Canada and the USA; it's very busy during Semana Santa, Christmas and the summer school holidays. If you show up at these times, try to reserve rooms in advance – and be prepared for crowds and higher hotel prices. At other times, you can have the beautiful, thick beach practically all to yourself. More-energetic activities include swimming, fishing, horse riding and hiking up to the cross on the hill for the fine view. You can also take a boat out to Isla Islote, where you can snorkel and snack in a restaurant. Boats do whale-watching trips from November to March. If you want to test out a different beach, try Playa Los Ayala, about 2km south of Guayabitos.

Orientation & Information

Rincón de Guayabitos is situated on the coast just west of Hwy 200. At the north entrance to town, a high water tower emulates an elongated mushroom. Turn into town here and soon you'll be on Guayabitos' main street, Av del Sol Nuevo. It's lined with shops, restaurants and hotels, and more restaurants and hotels sit along the beach, two blocks over – they're reached by side streets as there's no road along the waterfront.

Near the water tower, the **Delegación de Turismo** (*☎/fax 274-06-93; open 9am-2pm & 4pm-6pm Mon-Sat, 9am-2pm Sun*) provides information on the local area and the state of Nayarit. Close by is the **post office** (*open 8am-2pm Mon-Fri*).

For an **Internet place** (open 9am-9pm daily; US$3.50 per hour), check the ground floor of the large EquiNoxio building on Av del Sol Nuevo. Wash your duds at the **lavandería** (open 7am-9pm daily) on the Huanacaxtle pedestrian mall.

Places to Stay

Most of Guayabitos' accommodations are mid-range bungalows with kitchens, pitched at families. Single travelers will have a harder time finding cheap rooms. The following prices are for the winter high season, though the high-priced months can vary from one establishment to another. Staying a while? Negotiate discounts.

Paraíso del Pescador Trailer Park & Bungalows (☎ 274-00-14; e paraisodelpescador@hotmail.com; Ceibas; tent & trailer sites US$17, doubles US$55, suites US$110, 4/8 person bungalows US$55/165) caters to anglers, but anyone can enjoy the pool and modern sea-view rooms on the upper floors.

Reservations for trailer sites are crucial in winter.

Bungalows y Hotel Pancho Villa (☎ 324-02-46; Av del Sol Nuevo s/n; rooms US$17, bungalows US$24) has small, musty and downright smelly rooms and bungalows in motel-like digs, but they don't cost an arm or a leg. At least there's a pool.

Bungalows Las Glorias (☎ 274-06-81; Ceibas 11; 2/4 person bungalows US$18/22) is a good old cheapie a few blocks inland, with average-sized bungalows not the least bit luxurious – but good enough for peso-pinching backpackers.

Villa San Buenaventura (☎ 274-02-30; Laureles 14; 2/4 person bungalows US$28/44) needs a facelift, badly. But they're a good deal for grungy large groups who can tolerate springy beds, worn furniture, bleak walls and religious overtones.

Posada Jaltemba (☎ 274-01-65; Av del Sol Nuevo; rooms US$30-65; 4-person bungalows US$38-85) is a good deal. The attractive,

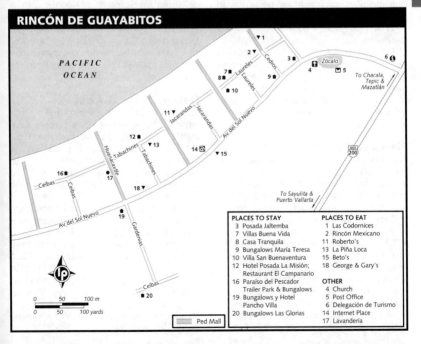

RINCÓN DE GUAYABITOS

PACIFIC OCEAN

To Chacala, Tepic & Mazatlán

To Sayulita & Puerto Vallarta

MEX 200

| 0 | 50 | 100 m |
| 0 | 50 | 100 yards |

PLACES TO STAY	PLACES TO EAT
3 Posada Jaltemba	1 Las Codornices
7 Villas Buena Vida	2 Rincón Mexicano
8 Casa Tranquila	11 Roberto's
9 Bungalows María Teresa	13 La Piña Loca
10 Villa San Buenaventura	15 Beto's
12 Hotel Posada La Misión;	18 George & Gary's
Restaurant El Campanario	
16 Paraíso del Pescador	OTHER
Trailer Park & Bungalows	4 Church
19 Bungalows y Hotel	5 Post Office
Pancho Villa	6 Delegación de Turismo
20 Bungalows Las Glorias	14 Internet Place
	17 Lavandería

Ped Mall

NAYARIT & GUADALAJARA

vine-covered stucco-and-brick buildings shine with charming rustic touches and tropical plants. Rooms fit right into this mold.

Bungalows María Teresa (☎ 324-03-92; Av del Sol Nuevo; 4/8 person bungalows US$39/88, 1 room for US$17) offers a pretty fair deal. Rustic decor gives rooms personality, while the well-maintained property enfolds a tepid pool and salmon-colored buildings.

Hotel Posada la Misión (☎/fax 274-03-57; Tabachines 6; doubles US$41; 2-person bungalows US$51) has a colonial theme going, with beautiful tiles lining open halls in front, great sea views out back, and a pretty, amoeba-shaped pool in the middle. Rooms are nice and quaint, and bungalows have balconies.

Villas Buena Vida (☎ 274-02-31; 🔳 www .villasbuenavida.com; Laureles s/n; 1-4 person villas from US$89, suites US$120-148) is true to its name, delivering the good life of lovely sea-view abodes with balconies, decent amenities and beachfront pools. Pay in cool cash and receive 5% off.

Casa Tranquila (☎ 327-03-64; 🔳 www .casatranquilamex.com; Laureles s/n; houses US$95-135, 1 week min stay high season) has two very clean, very tastefully decorated houses on beautiful, spacious, grassy and palm-dotted grounds next to the beach. It's like you never left home – your million-dollar home. Reservations are crucial in the winter high season.

Places to Eat

Beto's (☎ 274-05-75; Av del Sol Nuevo s/n; mains US$3-9; open 7am-9pm daily) is popular with large families for its simple, no-nonsense Mexican menu. Seafood, pozole and other treats help keep everyone happy.

George & Gary's (☎ 274-04-00; Av del Sol Nuevo s/n; mains under US$5; open 7am-9:30pm daily) grills up burgers, tosses chef salads and percolates fancy coffees; that's about the extent of its lunch menu. It's also popular with gringos for the breakfast waffles (US$3.50). There's a book exchange here.

El Campanario (☎ 274-03-57; Tabachines 6; mains US$5-9; open 7am-10pm daily) serves up good fish, burgers, enchiladas and

omelettes, among other menu items. Nibble on them in airy, casual and intimate surroundings, beautifully tiled and set with hanging ceramic parrots. It's at the Hotel Posada la Misión.

Roberto's (Jacarandas; mains US$5-10; open 8am-6pm Thur-Tues) caters to the breakfast and lunchtime sand-covered crowd, serving up seafood and meats in a casual, covered patio. Look for it on the beach; Roberto's also does breakfast.

Las Codornices (☎ 274-00-93; mains US$8-13; open 8am-9:30 daily) is attached to the Hotel Jacqueline, and serves burgers, steak and seafood in a lovely little patio overlooking the ocean and right next to the hotel's small pool (which can get noisy). There's also an inner covered patio.

La Piña Loca (Tabachines 7; mains US$5-9; open 7am-10pm daily) sits cute and homey, colorful and small. It's totally open and airy, serving breakfast, lunch and dinner from a Mexican menu.

Rincón Mexicano (☎ 274-06-63; cnr Cedros & Laureles; meals US$7-12; open 8am-9pm Thur-Tues) is at the beachfront Hotel Estancia San Carlos, cooking up barbecue ribs, interesting beef dishes and imaginative creations such as shrimp in mango and red wine sauce.

Getting There & Away

Rincón de Guayabitos doesn't have a bus terminal. Second-class buses coming from Puerto Vallarta (US$6, one hour) or Tepic (US$7, two hours) may drop you on the highway at the Guayabitos crucero, but 1st-class buses sometimes don't stop here. About 3km from Guayabitos, La Peñita de Jaltemba is a sure stop. Colectivo vans operate frequently between La Peñita de Jaltemba and Rincón de Guayabitos (US$0.50, eight minutes), or you can take a taxi (US$3).

Long-distance bus routes departing from La Peñita de Jaltemba include Guadalajara (US$23, four hours, hourly), Mazatlán (US$27, six hours, twice daily), Puerto Vallarta (US$6.50, one hour, every 20 minutes), Sayulita (US$3.50, 30 minutes, every 20 minutes) and Tepic (US$6.50, two hours, every 20 minutes).

PLAYAS LO DE MARCOS & SAN FRANCISCO

These are two pleasant little beach towns that make good day trips from either Rincón de Guayabitos or Puerto Vallarta. Be careful about swimming at both beaches; waves and currents are changeable, so ask locals if it's safe to enter the water during your time there.

Playa Lo de Marcos is 13km south of Guayabitos. It's a small village with a beautiful beach, and gets visited by plenty of Mexican and foreign tourists. Restaurants provide nourishment and activity, while simple bungalows are available if you decide to spend the night – one simple choice is **Padre Nuestro** (☎ 275-00-24; bungalows US$17). Just 2km to 3km south from Lo de Marcos are two more beaches with some restaurants, **Playa Los Venados** and **Playa Miñitas**. There are a few trailer parks along the side road there.

Playa San Francisco (also known as San Pancho) is 22km south of Guayabitos. The big appeal here is the beach, of course – a wide, deep and long expanse covered in thick sand and edged with crashing waves that attract surfers from miles around. Plenty of restaurants tend the more sedate tourists who'd rather lounge while sipping a margarita or three.

There are several choices for accommodation in San Pancho. Cheapest are two on the interestingly named main street, Av Tercer Mundo: **Restaurant Celia** (☎ 311-258-40-16; rooms US$22) and the nearby, no-name and depressing rooms at **number 19** (☎ 311-258-40-51; rooms US$17). For something fancier, head to **Hotel Los Amigos** (☎ 311-258-41-55; w www.losamigoshotel.com; Calle Asia; doubles/quads US$65/85-95), a modern, colorful and beautiful hotel. The snazziest choice in town is **Costa Azul Adventure Resort** (☎ 311-258-41-20; w www.costaazul.com; rooms only US$120-300, singles/doubles with meals US$118-136/190-340). Activities can be included, and sometimes the rates drop so ask.

SAYULITA
☎ 327 • pop 3000

Sayulita is a small fishing village on a pretty bay, and has a pleasant sandy beach that's popular with surfers. Its lively, well-maintained zócalo is the center of many activities and many expats now call this town home. Day-tripping tourists visit from Puerto Vallarta, an hour away by car or bus.

If surfing's your game – but you need a surfboard to play it – ask for Javier at **Papa's Palapas** (☎ 322-22-93-278; open 8am-sundown daily), on the beach. Rentals go for US$4.50/22 per hour/day; two-hour lessons cost US$26. Boogieboards are also available. Another place that rents boards is **Santa Crucecita Expediciones** (☎ 275-01-91; Navarette 14; open 9am-sunset daily), one block off the beach. Here, surfboards/boogieboards cost US$17 to US$28 per day, and repairs are also carried out. Bikes are rented for US$17 daily; snorkeling rentals cost US$2. English is spoken.

Swimming in Sayulita is fairly calm in general, but if you have any doubts ask for local advice. You can arrange bicycles, boat trips, horse riding, trekking, or kayaking from operators on the main street, including Santa Crucecita Expediciones.

One popular nearby destination is **Playa Los Muertos**, where picnics and boogieboarding top the action. It's a 15-minute walk south along coast road, past the Villa Amor terraces. The road goes through a small cemetery; the first beach you come to is Los Muertos. Follow this dirt road to other, more isolated beaches.

Information

If you're desperate for tourist information, Ian and Kerry at **Sayulita Properties** (see Places to Stay) can point you in the right direction – provided they're not too busy. There's Internet access there and at places listed below.

A tiny **caseta telefónica** (public telephone call station; cnr Revolución & Marlín) hides near the Bluebell Paletería. No banks or casas de cambio exist in Sayulita; the nearest ATM is in Bucerías, and the nearest bank in Mezcales.

An **Internet place** (open 7am-8pm daily; US$5.50 per hour) sits at the end of Delfin, on the beach. Otherwise, try the cheaper **Dot Com Internet** (Marlín 14; open 8am-8pm *daily; US$4.50 per hour)*, which also has free coffee and a book exchange. **Chocobanana Café** (see Places to Eat) has a book exchange as well.

Lava Zone *(José Mariscal; open 8am-6pm Mon-Sat; wash/dry 6kg US$5)* is the place to spin and tumble your washables.

Summer hours are more limited than winter hours in Sayulita; those listed here are winter hours. Note that there's a time difference between Sayulita and Puerto Vallarta; Sayulita is one hour behind.

Places to Stay

If you arrive during holiday periods, when everything's booked up, try the realtor **Sayulita Properties** *(☎/fax 275-02-82; **w** www.sayulitaproperties.com; Delfín 9; open 8am-8pm daily)*, which can attempt to find you something. Prices below reflect the winter high season.

El Camarón Camping *(☎/fax 275-02-82; Del Palmar s/n; camp sites per person US$4)* would be best described as 'grunge camping.' Hippies and substance-users love the beachside locale and grassy sites. Find this place by looking for the gap in the long white wall – there's no sign.

Sayulita Trailer Park & Bungalows *(☎/fax 275-02-02; **e** sayupark@prodigy.net.mx; Miramar s/n; tent/trailer sites with hookup US$12-16; bungalows US$45-65)* maintains an attractive, palm-shaded property beside the beach. A restaurant, snack bar and table tennis entertain guests.

El Punto Hideaway Cabañas *(Playa Azul 21; rooms with shared/private bathroom US$13/17)* has just five rooms around a leafy garden area. There's a cool bar/café on the premises, with occasional band/party happening.

Youth Hostel *(cnr Navarette & Caracol; per person US$11)* is very unofficial and not especially cheap, with just eight beds in a derelict old building. Still, some travelers make it here, hanging out in the small communal kitchen. Camping out on the floor might be possible for US$5.50.

Hotel Diamante *(Miramar 40; rooms US$11-22)* has downright small, basic and dirty rooms – but there's a pool and outdoor

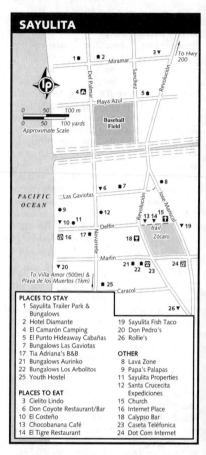

SAYULITA

0   50   100 m
0   50   100 yards
Approximate Scale

PLACES TO STAY
1 Sayulita Trailer Park & Bungalows
2 Hotel Diamante
4 El Camarón Camping
5 El Punto Hideaway Cabañas
7 Bungalows Las Gaviotas
17 Tia Adriana's B&B
21 Bungalows Aurinko
22 Bungalows Los Arbolitos
25 Youth Hostel

PLACES TO EAT
3 Cielito Lindo
6 Don Coyote Restaurant/Bar
10 El Costeño
13 Chocobanana Café
14 El Tigre Restaurant
19 Sayulita Fish Taco
20 Don Pedro's
26 Rollie's

OTHER
8 Lava Zone
9 Papa's Palapas
11 Sayulita Properties
12 Santa Crucecita Expediciones
15 Church
16 Internet Place
18 Calypso Bar
23 Caseta Telefónica
24 Dot Com Internet

covered kitchen area, which attracts thrifty backpackers.

Bungalows Las Gaviotas *(☎ 333-152-31-10 in Guadalajara; Gaviotas 12; doubles/bungalows US$22/44)* isn't very attractive, with plain but central bungalows for up to six people. However, it's friendly, central and half a block from the beach.

Tia Adriana's B&B *(☎/fax 275-01-92; **w** www.tiaadrianas.com; cnr Delfín & Navarrete; suites with breakfast US$50-120)* offers some wonderful suites with kitchenettes; top ones are open to breezes (no walls!) and have unbelievable views. Other suites also have special touches. The supreme breakfast is camaraderie-inducing, and vibrant Tia is there to make it all personal.

Bungalows Aurinko *(☎/fax 275-00-10;* **w** *www.sayulita-vacations.com; cnr Marlin, near Revolución; 1-/2-bedroom bungalows US$54-64/81-92)* has six bungalows total, all with well-designed outdoor kitchen and eating areas. They're very pleasant, comfortable and nicely decorated, with colorful paint jobs to top it all off.

Bungalows Los Arbolitos *(☎ 275-00-85;* **w** *www.sayulitabungalows.com; Marlin 20; suites US$75 plus tax)* harbors six intimate and luxurious suites right out of *Architectural Digest* magazine. Craftsman touches, creative design and lush gardens add to the paradise.

Villa Amor *(☎ 275-01-96;* **w** *www.villa amor.com; villas US$50-250 plus tax)* tumbles down the hill at the southern end of town, offering gorgeous, dream-like villas with huge private terraces (some with plunge-pool) overlooking the ocean. All are unique, with incredibly artistic touches like open showers, pipework sinks, integrated live tree branches and brick cupola ceilings. Be aware that room access can involve hiking up many stairs.

Places to Eat

The cheapest eats in town are Sayulita's wonderful taco stands: look for them in the zócalo. The most pleasant places, however, are the **palapas** on the beach, where a seafood dish, a cold beer and the salty sea breeze will cost you about US$8.

Sayulita Fish Taco *(José Mariscal s/n; open 11am-9pm Mon-Sat)* has some of the tastiest fish tacos in Mexico; American owner Albert spent years perfecting his recipe. There are only four outdoor tables and some stools.

Chocobanana Café *(☎ 275-00-43; cnr Revolución & Delfín; breakfast US$4-5; open 6am-3pm daily)* is a small shack on the zócalo with a very popular patio for breakfast. Vegetarians will find options here, and milkshake fanatics just might find heaven.

Rollie's *(Revolución 58; breakfast US$3.50-5.50; open 8am-noon daily)* is *the* place to come for filling breakfasts. Friendly Rollie

and Jeannie serve up generous portions of eggs, bacon, French toast, waffles, pancakes, potatoes and a fruit plate. Flowery menu descriptions give you a good idea of what to expect.

El Tigre Restaurant *(on the zócalo; mains US$6-15; open 5pm-10pm Mon-Sat)* sits on a small terrace upstairs, overlooking the zócalo. Some locals think the town's best seafood is grilled here; surf videos will keep you company while you wrestle with the lobster (US$15).

El Costeño *(☎ 275-00-39; Delfín; mains US$8-9; open 8am-8pm daily)* is one of Sayulita's oldest restaurants and right on the beach. The tables on the sand get packed with gringos enjoying seafood, veg side dishes and drinks.

Cielito Lindo *(☎ 275-01-80; Miramar 8; mains US$8-12; open 7:30am-12:30pm & 6pm-10pm Tues-Sun)* offers a complex fare of meats, seafood, soups and salads on the 2nd-floor, palapa terrace. It's intimate, casual and relaxing. It also does Mexican- or American-style breakfasts.

Don Coyote Restaurant/Bar *(cnr Las Gaviotas & Navarrete; mains US$5-8; open 11am-10:30pm Tue-Sat)* serves good old Western favorites like spaghetti, grilled chicken, burgers and veg dishes in an palapa patio. In the evenings events such as guitar music, firedances and fashion shows can take place.

Don Pedro's *(☎ 275-02-29; Marlin 2; meals US$11-22; upstairs restaurant open 6pm-11pm daily, downstairs bar & grill open noon-11pm daily)* is two eateries in one; a fine restaurant offering elegant dining choices, and a bar and grill serving upscale pizza and salads. Both overlook the beach.

Entertainment

Sayulita's not a place to paint the town red, but there are a few places where you can kick out the jams.

Don Pedro's (see Places to Eat) has reggae and rock on Friday nights, DJs on Saturday nights and Cuban on Monday nights. Swing your body to it all.

Don Coyote Restaurant/Bar (see Places to Eat) offers music and dancing on its open patio several nights per week. It also plans to have sports on satellite TV on weekends.

Calypso Bar *(Revolución)* is across from the zócalo and popular for its 6:30pm to 7:30pm happy hour. Surf videos liven up the TVs, and on Friday nights there's a DJ.

El Punto Café/Bar *(Playa Azul 21; open 8am-noon & 4pm-1am Thur-Tues)* is a fairly intimate joint with live music in its garden patio approximately every two weeks. Happy hour runs from 6pm to 7pm.

Getting There & Away

To reach Sayulita, take the *crucero* from Hwy 200, about 35km north of Puerto Vallarta and 25km south of Rincón de Guayabitos. Sayulita is 3km from the *crucero*. Frequent buses operate between Sayulita and the bus terminal at Puerto Vallarta (US$2.50, one hour); otherwise, any 2nd-class bus will drop you at the *crucero*. For a bus schedule, check the billboard at the *caseta telefónica*.

Puerto Vallarta

☎ 322 • pop 161,000

Many years ago, Puerto Vallarta (or PV) was a quaint seaside village nestled peacefully between the sparkling blue Bahía de Banderas and some lush, palm-covered mountain sides. Over the past 50 years, however, it's been transformed into a world-famous destination hosting millions of visitors every year, nearly half of them from other countries. Some of the most beautiful beaches, secluded and romantic just a few years ago, are now dominated by giant luxury mega-resorts. Vallarta's only industry, tourism, has also made it a bilingual city, with English almost as commonly spoken as Spanish, and the city harbors one of the largest US/Canadian expat communities in the world.

But, despite its incredible growth and commercialism, most of Puerto Vallarta maintains a pleasant and manageable feel. Cobblestoned streets, old-fashioned white adobe buildings and red tile roofs still make this one of Mexico's most picturesque coastal resort cities. And if the pretty town and its white-sand beaches aren't enough, you can venture out on day cruises, hop on horseback, sink into scuba diving or explore shops and art galleries, all the while enjoying a wild and extremely vibrant, pulsating nightlife.

History

Although indigenous peoples probably lived in this area for centuries, as they did elsewhere along the coast, the first documented settlement was in 1851, when the Sánchez family came and made their home by the mouth of the Río Cuale. Farmers and fisherfolk followed, and farmers began shipping their harvests from a small port north of the Río Cuale. In 1918 the settlement was named Vallarta, in honor of Ignacio Luis Vallarta, a former governor of the state of Jalisco.

Tourists started to visit Puerto Vallarta back in 1954 when Mexicana airlines started

Highlights

- Strolling down the cobbled streets past the red-roof-tiled buildings of pretty Puerto Vallarta
- Taking a *panga* to Yelapa, one of many surrounding beaches only accessible by boat
- Wearing yourself out with activities: scuba diving, fishing, eating, cruising or shopping
- Getting wild and partying with the crowds at one of Vallarta's many nightlife scenes
- Venturing out on a day trip north to Bucerías and Punta Mita, or south to loads of great beaches

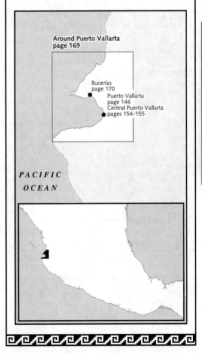

Around Puerto Vallarta
page 169

Bucerías
page 170

Puerto Vallarta
page 146
Central Puerto Vallarta
pages 154-155

*PACIFIC
OCEAN*

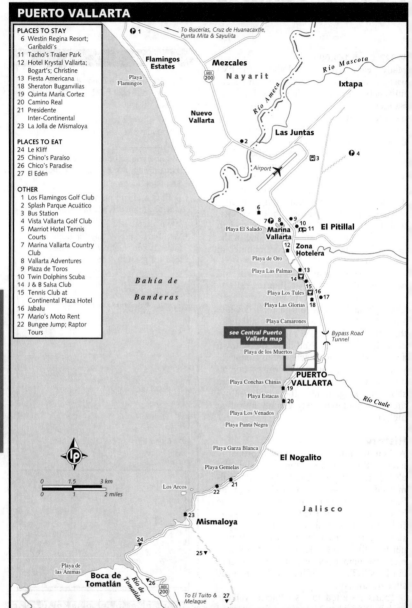

PUERTO VALLARTA

PLACES TO STAY
6 Westin Regina Resort;
   Garibaldi's
11 Tacho's Trailer Park
12 Hotel Krystal Vallarta;
   Bogart's; Christine
13 Fiesta Americana
18 Sheraton Buganvilias
19 Quinta María Cortez
20 Camino Real
21 Presidente
   Inter-Continental
23 La Jolla de Mismaloya

PLACES TO EAT
24 Le Kliff
25 Chino's Paraíso
26 Chico's Paradise
27 El Edén

OTHER
1 Los Flamingos Golf Club
2 Splash Parque Acuático
3 Bus Station
4 Vista Vallarta Golf Club
5 Marriot Hotel Tennis
   Courts
7 Marina Vallarta Country
   Club
8 Vallarta Adventures
9 Plaza de Toros
10 Twin Dolphins Scuba
14 J & B Salsa Club
15 Tennis Club at
   Continental Plaza Hotel
16 Jabalu
17 Mario's Moto Rent
22 Bungee Jump; Raptor
   Tours

To Bucerías, Cruz de Huanacaxtle, Punta Mita & Sayulita

Flamingos Estates

Mezcales

Río Mascota

Playa Flamingos

Nayarit

Ixtapa

Río Ameca

Nuevo Vallarta

Las Juntas

Airport

El Pitillal

Playa El Salado

Marina Vallarta

Zona Hotelera

Playa de Oro

Playa Las Palmas

Bahía de Banderas

Playa Los Tules

Playa Las Glorias

Playa Camarones

see Central Puerto Vallarta map

Bypass Road Tunnel

Playa de los Muertos

PUERTO VALLARTA

Playa Conchas Chinas

Playa Estacas

Río Cuale

Playa Los Venados

Playa Punta Negra

Playa Garza Blanca

El Nogalito

Playa Gemelas

Jalisco

Los Arcos

Mismaloya

0   1.5   3 km
0   1   2 miles

Playa de las Ánimas

Boca de Tomatlán

Río de Tomatlán

To El Tuito & Melaque

PUERTO VALLARTA

a promotional campaign and initiated the first flights here, landing on a dirt airstrip in Emiliano Zapata, an area that is now the center of Vallarta. A decade later, John Huston chose the nearby deserted cove of Mismaloya as a location for the film of Tennessee Williams' *The Night of the Iguana*. Hollywood paparazzi descended on the town to report on the tempestuous romance between Richard Burton and Elizabeth Taylor, and Burton's co-star Ava Gardner also raised more than a few eyebrows. Puerto Vallarta suddenly became world-famous, with an aura of steamy tropical romance. Tour groups arrived not long after the film crew left, and the rest is history.

Orientation

North of the Río Cuale lies the more modern part of town, **El Centro**, whose heart is the seaside Plaza Principal. The crown-topped steeple of Templo de Guadalupe perches nearby. On a few long blocks paralleling the beachless Malecón (waterfront street, boardwalk) lie many modern boutiques, galleries, cafés, bars and restaurants, along with a few hotels. Avs Morelos and Juárez are Puerto Vallarta's two principal thoroughfares.

South of the river, the **Zona Romantica** (also called 'Old Town' or 'Olas Altas') is another tourist district with hotels, boutiques, restaurants and bars. It has the only two beaches in the city center: Playa Olas Altas (which doesn't actually have 'high waves', despite the name) and Playa de los Muertos (Beach of the Dead), which takes its strange name from a fierce fight there sometime in the distant past. Zona Romantica has a bit more personality than El Centro, and contains some older streets and buildings.

In between these two zones is the Río Cuale, which splits to straddle the long and narrow Isla Cuale. Two short road bridges and one rickety suspended pedestrian bridge allow easy passage between the two sides of town. Many fine houses, quite a few owned by foreigners, are found further up the Río Cuale valley, commonly known as **Gringo Gulch**.

City traffic has been reduced quite dramatically with the opening of a *libramiento* or bypass road on the inland side of the city center, and diverting traffic away from the center.

North of the city is the **Zona Hotelera**, a strip of giant luxury hotels; Marina Vallarta, a large yachting marina (9km from the center); the airport (10km); the bus terminal (12km); and Nuevo Vallarta, a new resort area of hotel and condominium development (25km).

To the south of the city, in a more natural setting than Zona Hotelera, are more large resorts and some of the most beautiful beaches in the area.

Information

Puerto Vallarta is in Jalisco state, one hour ahead of nearby Nayarit. Also note that any opening hours or days listed in this chapter, especially for restaurants or shops, reflect the busy winter season; in other seasons, hours and days tend to be more limited, with some businesses even closing down altogether.

Tourist Offices Vallarta's busy but competent **municipal tourist office** (☎ 223-25-00 ext 230, 231 or 232, fax 223-25-00 ext 233; open 8am-4pm Mon-Fri), at the northeast corner of Plaza Principal, has free maps, multilingual tourist literature and bilingual staff.

The **state tourist office** (Dirección de Turismo del Estado de Jalisco; ☎ 221-26-76, 221-26-80, fax 221-26-78; e dirturpv@pvnet .com.mx; Plaza Marina, Local 144 & 146; open 9am-5pm Mon-Fri) is north of town in Marina Vallarta.

Money Most businesses in Vallarta accept US dollars as readily as they accept pesos, though the rate of exchange they give is usually less favorable than at banks. Several banks can be found around Plaza Principal, but they often have long queues. **Banamex** (open 9am-5pm Mon-Fri, 9am-2pm Sat) is on the south side of the plaza (Western Union is also situated here). Most of the banks also contain ATMs.

Vallarta has many *casas de cambio* (exchange houses); it may pay to shop around, since rates differ. Though their rates are less favorable than the banks, the difference may be slight, and the longer opening hours and faster service may make using them worthwhile. Most are open around 9am to 7pm daily, sometimes with a 2pm to 4pm lunch break. Look for them on Insurgentes, Vallarta, the Malecón and many other streets.

American Express *(AmEx; ☎ 223-29-55; cnr Morelos & Abasolo; open 9am-6pm Mon-Fri, 9am-1pm Sat)* is also near the center.

Post & Communications Send postcards home from the **post office** *(Mina 188; open 8am-7pm Mon-Fri, 9am-1pm Sat)*. **Telecomm** *(Hidalgo 582; open 8am-7:30pm Mon-Fri, 9am-noon Sat, Sun & holidays)*, with telegram, telex and fax, is near the corner of Aldama.

Vallarta has many *casetas telefónicas* (public telephone call stations), including one on Plaza Lázaro Cárdenas and another at Cárdenas 267. Public cardphones are plentiful everywhere in town. Calling North America isn't cheap; expect to pay at least US$1 per minute.

Internet Resources There are so many Internet places they are practically a plague, especially in the Zona Romantica.

Cyber Café Byblos near Plaza Principal; open 11am-11pm daily; US$2.75 per hour

Internet & Perfumes Insurgentes 236; US$2 per hour

Net House Vallarta 232; open 8am-1am daily; US$4 per hour

PV Café.com Olas Altas 250; open 8am-2am daily; US$4 per hour

Virtual Reality Rodríguez 112; open 9am-11pm daily; US$2 per hour

Bookstores You can buy and sell quality used books in English at **A Page in the Sun Bookshop-Café** *(☎ 222-36-08, cnr Olas Altas & Diéguez; open 7am-midnight daily)*; it also serves great coffee. There's another branch up north at Morelos and Langarica. **BookStore** *(☎ 223-11-77; Corona 172; open 10am-2pm & 4pm-8:30pm daily)* has a good

selection of magazines, newspapers and a few books (including Lonely Planet guides) in English.

Media *Vallarta Today*, *Vallarta Voice* and *PV Tribune* are among the daily English-language newspapers available free at the tourist office, hotels and elsewhere. You'll probably also see *Vallarta Lifestyles* for sale in bookstores and other spots; it's a glossy quarterly magazine glamorizing this fair town (US$3.85).

Laundry There are many places that will wash the traveling grime off your clothes. Those south of the Río Cuale include **Lavandería Quinter** *(Madero 407A; US$3.50 for 1-3kg; open 8am-8pm Mon-Sat)*, **Lavandería Elsa** *(Olas Altas 385; US$4.25 per load; open 8am-2pm & 3pm-7pm Mon-Sat)*, and **Lavandería Púlpito** *(Púlpito 141; US$5 per load; open 9am-7pm Mon-Fri, 9am-5pm Sat)*.

Gay Resources The Rainbow flag flies high (among other things) in gay Vallarta.

Club Paco Paco *(☎ 222-18-99; ⓦ www .pacopaco.com; Vallarta 278; open 1pm-6am daily; see Entertainment section)* acts as an informal center for Vallarta's gay community. Pick up its free *Paco Paco Tourist Info & Map*, with information on gay hotels, cruises, tours, entertainment etc.

Some useful gay websites for Puerto Vallarta include: ⓦ www.discoveryvallarta .com, ⓦ www.gayguidevallarta.com and ⓦ www.doinitright.com.

Museo del Cuale
This small museum *(admission free; open 10am-7pm Tues-Fri, 10am-5pm Sat)*, near the western end of Isla Cuale, has a well-displayed collection of beautiful pottery, grinding stones and clay figurines, among other ancient objects. It also plays host to occasional art exhibitions.

Beaches
Only two beaches, **Playa Olas Altas** and **Playa de los Muertos**, are located close to the city center. They're both situated south of the Río Cuale and full of vendors selling

souvenirs to gringos. Lining these beaches are plenty of seafood restaurants, hotels and other services.

Trendy gay men head to the section of beach called **Blue Chairs**, at the southern end of Playa de los Muertos (there are blue as well as green and yellow chairs here). For a more isolated gay beach, see under Cruises later.

For beaches farther north or south of town, see the Around Bahía de Banderas section, later.

Activities

Puerto Vallarta is simply chock-full of possibilities for keeping as busy as you want to be. Head towards the sea for diving, snorkeling, fishing and sailing. Turn inland to ride horses, play golf or drive off-road. For the sedate, wildlife-watching boat tours and scenic cruises are a good option: some include meals and plenty of drinks.

Scuba Diving Vallarta has several diving and snorkeling operators. All the following operators have certification courses. They also offer snorkeling trips, which usually means snorkelers tag along with divers. Note that diving locations aren't always best for snorkeling.

Most dives include transport, gear and light meals. Water is clearest from May to November, with peak clarity in October and November, though visibility should be decent all year round.

Pacific Scuba (☎/fax 222-47-41; w www .pacificscuba.com.mx; Juárez 722) will take groups of up to five divers. They speak English and offer good service. Costs range from US$65 to US$95 for two-tank dives to Los Arcos, Majahuita Beach or Islas Marietas, among other places.

Twin Dolphins (☎ 293-19-05; w www .twindolphinspv.com; Politécnico Nacional 94) is based to the north, across from the bullring. Prices for diving tours here range from US$81 to US$98, and it also has personalized service with English, French or Italian speakers.

Rick Bates (☎ 223-08-70; w www.mex online.com/oceansports.htm) is a private

scuba instructor from Canada with 12 years' experience diving in Vallarta. His certification classes are thorough and include two days' diving to two different spots. Tours range from US$60 to US$120, and snorkeling trips are available for US$40 per person.

Vallarta Adventures (☎ 221-21-11; w www .vallarta-adventures.com; Calle Mastil Local 13C, Marina Vallarta) is a huge but respected operator that does all sorts of organized tours (see that section later in this chapter). It also takes scuba divers out on a variety of dives. Charges can range from US$75 to US$120.

If you decide to use **Chico's Dive Shop** (Vallarta's largest operator) be aware that you are advised to make sure you double-check the equipment before you use it.

Deep-Sea Fishing Deep-sea fishing is popular all year, with a major international sailfish tournament held every November. Prime catches are sailfish, marlin, tuna, red snapper and sea bass. If you need gear, look for it carefully at the brilliantly named **Master Baiters**, on Morelos and Rodríguez.

Fishing with Carolina (☎ 224-72-50; 044-322-292-29-53; w www.fishingpuertovallarta .4t.com) takes folks out on a 30-foot sportfisher. Prices are US$100 per person or US$350 for the whole boat for up to four customers. Gear and hotel pickup is included.

Diana's Tours (☎ 222-15-10, 044-322-292-71-43, e dianatours2001@yahoo.ca) arranges fishing charters in pangas (small skiffs), which include gear and cost between US$22 to US$66 for the day.

See the Getting Around section for information on hiring private yachts or lanchas (motor boats).

Other Water Sports Snorkeling, windsurfing, sailing, riding the 'banana' and just plain swimming are all popular in Vallarta. Most activities can be arranged on the beaches in front of any of the large hotels. Note that parasailing is also very popular, but there have been some accidents in the past and the activity should be considered potentially hazardous.

A good, accessible and crowded spot for snorkeling is **Los Arcos**, some rocky islands in the bay just south of town (now a protected ecological zone). Most folks get there via boat tour, but if you're an excellent, strong swimmer try taking the Boca de Tomatlán bus and getting off at the rocky beach near the rocks. Easing yourself into the water is tricky and should be done with plenty of care. You can swim out to the rocks from here.

Kids will enjoy **Splash Parque Acuático** (☎ 297-07-08, admission US$9; Carretera Tepic Km 155; open 10am-7pm daily), which has 12 water slides, a lazy river, and a daily dolphin show. Any local bus heading north towards Nuevo Vallarta or Bucerías can drop you on Hwy 200 near the park; just get off at the Pemex station.

Cruises A host of daytime, sunset and evening cruises are available in Puerto Vallarta. Some emphasize beach visits and snorkeling stops, others focus on sailing and whale watching (in season), and the wildest pump for hard drinking ('booze cruises'). Boat tours to Yelapa and Las Ánimas beaches (around US$25 to US$40) are popular; other cruises go to the Islas Marietas, farther out. To pick the right cruise, ask your fellow travelers or inquire at the tourist office.

Marigalante (☎ 223-08-75; ⓦ www.mari galante.com.mx; 3rd floor, Paseo Díaz Ordaz, Local 21) is a reproduction Spanish galleon that does a daytime cruise (US$60, 9am to 3pm) culminating in a mock pirate attack on the Malecón, matey. It also sets sail on an evening cruise (US$66, 6pm to 10pm).

Diana's Tours (☎ 222-1510, 044-322-292-71-43; ⓔ dianatours2001@yahoo.ca) also arranges gay cruises for about US$60, including food and snorkeling gear.

Bloodhound (☎ 01-322-222-22-85) is a 98-foot replica of a 1874 British sailing yacht. It sails on whale-watching cruises from January to March, and at other times visits the Marieta Islands for snorkeling.

If you just want to visit the beaches, a cheaper way to get there is by water taxi (see Getting Around).

Dolphins & Whales Always wanted to paddle around with dolphins? You can do it in Vallarta at the dolphin center operated by Vallarta Adventures (see Organized Tours) for US$130. Dolphins are present in the bay all year round; with luck you'll see some if you go out on a boat.

Whale-watching trips operate from December to March, when humpback whales are frolicking in the bay mating, bearing young and caring for new calves. **Open Air Expeditions** and **Ecotours** are popular operators, and **Vallarta Adventures** also does whale-watching trips (see Organized Tours later in this chapter). Lucky visitors sunning on the beaches during season can sometimes spot humpback whales breaching just offshore.

Horse Riding There are plenty of opportunities to mount up and check out Vallarta's rivers, mountains and jungles from behind the perky ears of an equine.

Rancho El Girasol (☎ 222-03-86; Badillo 156) ponies up five-hour tours (US$45) to waterfalls; these include snack lunch and swim time. They claim you shouldn't 'saddle for less!'

Rancho Amigo (☎ 224-73-42) is run by Marco Polo, a friendly guy who speaks more Spanish than English.

Diana's Tours (☎ 222-15-10; 044-322-292-71-43; ⓔ dianatours2001@yahoo.ca) has good three-hour jungle horse rides for US$45.

Rancho El Charro (☎ 224-01-14), **Rancho Ojo de Agua** (☎ 224-06-07) and **Rancho Palma Real** (☎ 221-12-36) will provide transport from your hotel. Costs are US$100 for a full day excursion; part-day excursions run US$40 to US$60. Ask if their guides speak English.

For a short ride, suitable for children, there are sometimes horses for rent around Playa Olas Altas, near the western end of Carranza.

Golf & Tennis There are a few spots to swing your club.

Marina Vallarta Country Club (☎ 221-00-73, Paseo de la Marina s/n) is just north

PUERTO VALLARTA

f Marina Vallarta. It was designed by the well-named Joe Finger, with plenty of water traps full of wading birds and even some alligators. Green fees run at more than US$100.

Los Flamingos Golf Club (*01-329-296-50-06)* lies 13km north of town on Hwy 200. It's the poor man's golfing destination in Vallarta. Charges are US$95 in morning and US$65 in afternoon.

Vista Vallarta (*290-00-30)* is Vallarta's slick new Jack Nicklaus-designed course, and charges US$170 in the morning and US$110 in the afternoon.

Yes, some of us have that need to smash a tennis ball around. The following hotels have courts, and there are also plenty of others.

Continental Plaza Hotel (☎ *224-43-60 ext 4187; guest/nonguest per hour US$13/17)*

Sheraton Buganvilias (☎ *226-04-04 ext 5525; day/night per hour US$11/17)*

Hotel Krystal (☎ *224-02-02 ext 2030; per hour for all US$11)*

Marriott Hotel (☎ *221-00-04 ext 6244; per hour for all US$15)*

Bungee Jumping The bungee jump (☎ *228-06-70;* **w** *www.vallarta-action.com)* is a platform jutting out over the sea cliffs, about 9km south of Puerto Vallarta on the road to Mismaloya. Make the 40m plunge from 10am to 6pm daily (US$55).

Off-Road Driving Call the following operators if you want some dusty driving adventures. They'll tell you the rest.

Off-Road Tours (☎ *222-09-19; Mexico 1207A)* charges US$120 for four hours of rip-stompin', off-roadin' fun.

Mud Rats (☎ *222-38-02; Columbia 1384)* has dune buggy tours for US$130 and ATVs for US$80 to US$105.

Pathfinders (☎ *222-18-75; Paseo Díaz Ordaz 772)* also arranges three-hour dune buggy outings on rough roads, river beds and the nearby hills (US$140).

Raptor Tours (☎ *228-0670,* **w** *www.vallarta-action.com)*, based at the bungee jump south of town, does seven-hour excursions in similar terrain (US$196).

Timeshares

If you can endure a two-hour pitch for a timeshare condominium, and do a tour of the project, you can be rewarded (or compensated) with a free or discounted dinner, tour, horse trip, jeep rental or boat cruise. Touts in Puerto Vallarta's most touristy areas are eager to offer you freebies, if *only* you attend the presentation. The touts won't tell you any details about the timeshare deal – their job is just to get you to the hard-sell session. Be warned, however, that partaking in this activity can be very stressful for the weak of will, and take up half your day. And watch out for touts offering 'cheap' car rentals on the Malecón: Often they are really timeshare traps, 'hiding' behind official-looking car rental signs. They may not tell you right away what they're doing.

To attend a presentation, you generally must be over 25 years old, a US or Canadian resident, and have a major credit card. Some deals require that you be married, and that both husband and wife attend the presentation. The promoter will pay the taxi fare from your hotel to the project. You are under no obligation to buy or sign anything – very heavy pressure, yes; obligation, no.

People have mixed reactions to a timeshare presentation. Some say it's a relatively painless way to get a cheap jeep, a good meal, a tour or a cruise. Others break down crying or are still angry days later, after fending off the 'hard sell.' A few are still paying for it years later, after failing to fend off the 'hard sell'. Make sure you know what you're getting yourself into.

PUERTO VALLARTA

Cycling There are several companies that offer guided cycling tours around Puerto Vallarta.

Bike Mex (☎ *223-16-80;* **w** *www.bikemex.com; Guerrero 361; open 8am-8pm Mon-Sat)* runs quite a few hiking and mountain bike tours using experienced bilingual guides, tailored to your level of fitness and experience. Mountain bike rentals are available for US$33 per day!

B-B-Bobby's Bikes (☎ 223-00-08; ⓦ www.accessmexico.com/bbbobbys; cnr Iturbide & Miramar; open 7:30am-4pm Mon-Sat) also offers guided tours (US$50) and bicycle rentals (US$11/39 for basic/full suspension per day). The company is named after the stuttering soul who, unfortunately, is no longer with us.

Language Courses

University of Guadalajara's Foreign Student Study Center (☎ 223-20-82; ⓦ www.cepe.udg.mx; Libertad 105-1), opposite the Mercado Municipal, specializes in teaching Spanish and can arrange accommodation with a Mexican family. Beginning, intermediate and advanced courses are offered all throughout the year, plus intensive and super-intensive sessions; they also have a one-week 'basic skills for tourists' class. Summer offerings include Mexican culture, Mexican history, and Spanish summer courses for children age seven to nine and 10 to 13. University credit can be earned for most courses. Tuition fees start at US$129 per week.

Organized Tours

Vallarta is not short on organized ways to appreciate its assets. Here are some places you can try.

Casa Kimberley (☎ 222-13-36, Zaragoza 445; admission US$6; open 9am-6pm daily) caters to Richard Burton and Elizabeth Taylor freaks; this is the house he bought for her back in the 1960s.

International Friendship Club (☎ 222-54-66; Libertad 105; office open 9:30am-1:30pm Mon-Fri) offers US$30, 2½ hour tours that take you inside some of Vallarta's most luxurious private homes. They are given only in winter and start at 10am or 11am Wednesday and Thursday at the Hotel Molino de Agua; check with the club, located at the University of Guadalajara campus, for exact details.

Several tour companies specialize in nature and the outdoors.

Vallarta Adventures (☎ 221-21-11; ⓦ www.vallarta-adventures.com; Calle Mastil Local 13C, Marina Vallarta; office open 8:30am-

1:30pm & 4pm-7pm daily) is highly regarded, running the gauntlet of land and sea nature tours along with their dolphin center (see Dolphins & Whales in Activities earlier). Most tours here will set you back US$60 to US$80.

Open Air Expeditions (☎ 222-33-10, ⓦ www.vallartawhales.com; Guerrero 339, and **Ecotours** (☎ 223-31-30; ⓦ www.ecotours-mex.com; Vallarta 243) both offer up whale-watching, sea kayaking, snorkeling, bird-watching, hiking and customized tours. Costs run to approximately US$40 to US$80 per person.

Special Events

Semana Santa (Easter week) is the busiest holiday of the year in Puerto Vallarta. Hotels fill up and hundreds (or thousands) of excess visitors camp out on the beaches and party. It's a wild time.

Fiestas de Mayo, a city-wide fair with cultural and sporting events, music concerts, carnival rides and art exhibits, is held throughout May.

A big, international **Torneo de Pesca** (fishing tournament) is held each year in mid-November; dates vary according to the phase of the moon, which must be right for fishing.

Día de Santa Cecilia (November 22) honors the patron saint of mariachis, with all the city's mariachis forming a musical procession to the Templo de Guadalupe in the early evening. They come playing and singing, enter the church and sing homage to their saint, then go out into the plaza and continue to play. During the entire day one or another group of mariachis stays in the church making music.

All Mexico celebrates December 12 as the day of the country's patron saint, the **Virgen de Guadalupe**. In Puerto Vallarta the celebrations are more drawn out, with pilgrimages and processions to the cathedral day and night from December 1 until the big bash on the 12th.

Places to Stay

Vallarta has a good selection of accommodation for every price bracket. Prices here eflect the mid-December to mid-April high season; low-season rates can fall 20% to 50%. For accommodation at Vallarta's very busiest times – during Semana Santa or at Christmas and New Year's – reserve in advance, and be prepared to pay 20% to 40% more than the prices listed here. The most expensive hotels will most likely tack on almost 18% in taxes, so ask beforehand if these are included or not. And remember, if you plan on staying a week or more, negotiate for a better rate; monthly rates can cut your rent by half.

Places to Stay – Budget

Nacho's Trailer Park (☎ 224-21-63; *Camino Nuevo al Pitillal s/n) tent & trailer sites US$20),* opposite Colonia Aramara, has a swimming pool and 135 tent/trailer spaces with full hookups.

Youth Hostel (☎ 222-21-08; *Aguacate 302A; bunk beds US$8.25)* is clean and pleasant, though the five dorm rooms can get crowded. There's one double room that doesn't cost extra. The hostel's large courtyard spaces offer lots of lounging possibilities. It's closed from 11am to 4pm Saturday and Sunday (if you're residing there then, just evacuate the grounds).

Hotel Cartagena de Indias (☎/fax 222-69-14; e hotelcartagenapv.com.mx; *Madero 428; singles/doubles/triples US$18/23/29)* is basic but good, with street-facing balcony rooms more pleasant and bright. Singles are tiny, however.

Hotel Villa del Mar (☎/fax 222-07-85; e hvilladelmar@hotmail.com; *Madero 440; singles/doubles/triples US$19/24/27)* has good-sized rooms with old furniture and tasteful decor. And they are spick-and-span ('cleanness' it says on the business card) and the air is heavy with disinfectant. Drop the couple extra bucks for a balcony – it's worth it. Kitchen apartments are available, and the rooftop gives views over town.

Hotel Azteca (☎/fax 222-27-50; *Madero 473; singles/doubles/triples US$18/24/31, rooms with kitchenette & cable TV US$36)* sits in an old but well-kept space. Spacious, old-tiled rooms surround a narrow and shady palm-potted courtyard. As usual, street-facing rooms are lighter, but all offer good budget value.

Hotel Hortencia (☎ 222-24-84; w www.hotelhortencia.com; *Madero 336; singles/doubles US$22/28)* presents very good and clean rooms on three floors set around a plain, open courtyard. Front rooms have balconies and street noise, but inside rooms are bright enough and quieter. Cable TV, fan, cheap breakfasts next door and a very welcoming family make for a pleasant stay.

Café Frankfurt Hotel (☎ 222-34-03; w www.hotelfrankfurt.com; *Badillo 300; rooms US$28, bungalows US$39, single/double apartments with kitchen US$39/55)* is set in a large, jungly garden with squawking parrot; it's an urban tropical paradise. Rooms are good, a garden café sits in the middle and there's even enclosed parking.

Hotel Posada Lily (☎ 222-00-32; e lily@pvnet.com.mx; *Badillo 109; singles/doubles US$28/44-50)* has zero lobby and the stairs are bare, but it's affordable and half a block from beach action. The good, modern rooms sport refrigerators, cable TV and, for a few extra pesos, air-con. The best have balconies with fine views.

Posada Don Miguel (☎ 222-45-40; e hpdm322@prodigy.net.mx; *Insurgentes 322; singles/doubles US$20/30)* has rooms so large you can do three cartwheels down their length. They'd be better if stocked with more furniture, but this place remains a good deal. Kitchenettes, air-con and TV are available for extra, and it's clean. Have a splash in the small pool.

Places to Stay – Mid-Range

Hotel Belmar (☎/fax 222-05-72; e hotelbelar@pvnet.com.mx; *Insurgentes 161; singles/doubles/triples US$20/33/46)* offers a more upscale, colorful place to lay your head. Rooms are clean, comfy, spacious and come with TV and fan; air-con is US$5.50 extra. Snag one with a balcony; they're brighter and better.

Hotel Yazmín (☎ 222-00-87; *Badillo 168; singles/doubles/triples US$30/34/41)* comes clean and friendly, with pleasant rooms, a flowery courtyard and great location if you like to eat out – Badillo is also known as

PUERTO VALLARTA

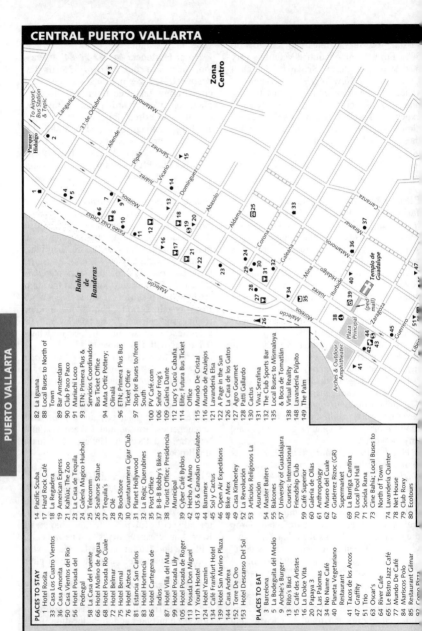

CENTRAL PUERTO VALLARTA

Zona Centro

Bahía de Banderas

PLACES TO STAY
1 Hotel Rosita
33 Casa Los Cuatro Vientos
36 Casa Amorita
50 Casa Vientos del Río
56 Hotel Posada del Pedregal
58 La Casa del Puente
66 Hotel Molino de Agua
68 Hotel Posada Río Cuale
72 Hotel Belmar
75 Hotel Bernal
76 Hotel Azteca
81 Estancia San Carlos
83 Hotel Hortencia
86 Hotel Cartegena de Indios
87 Hotel Villa del Mar
99 Hotel Posada Lily
105 Hotel Posada de Roger
113 Posada Don Miguel
117 Youth Hostel
124 Hotel Yazmin
134 Café Frankfurt Hotel
139 Hotel San Marino Plaza
144 Casa Andrea
152 Torre De Oro
153 Hotel Descanso Del Sol

PLACES TO EAT
3 Barcelona
5 La Bodeguita del Medio
9 Archie's Burger
13 Rito's Baci
15 Café des Artistes
16 La Dolce Vita
20 Papaya 3
22 Las Palomas
34 No Name Café
40 Planeta Vegetariano Restaurant
41 Tacos de los Arcos
47 Graffity
51 Trio
63 Oscar's
64 River Cafe
65 Le Bistro Jazz Café
77 Mundo De Café
84 Mariscos Polo
85 Restaurant Gilmar
92 Como Pizza

14 Pacific Scuba
17 Hard Rock Café
18 La Regadera
19 American Express
21 Kahlúa; The Zoo
23 La Casa de Tequila
24 Galería Mágico Huichol
25 Telecomm
26 Seahorse Statue
27 Tequila's
28 Olé
29 BookStore
30 Guantanamera Cigar Club
31 Planet Hollywood
32 La Reja; Querubines
35 Post Office
37 Tourist Office; Presidencia Municipal
38 B-B-B Bobby's Bikes
39 Cyber Café Byblos
42 Hecho A Mano
43 US & Canadian Consulates
44 Banamex
45 Sol y Cactus
46 Open Air Expeditions
48 Bike Mex
49 Casa Kimberley
52 La Revolución
53 Artículos Religiosos La Asunción
54 Master Baiters
55 Balcones
57 University of Guadalajara Courses; International Friendship Club
59 Café Superior
60 Galería de Ollas
61 Anthropology
62 Museo del Cuale
67 Gutiérrez Rizoc (GR) Supermarket
69 La Barriga Cantina
70 Local Pool Hall
71 Sonida Rana
73 Cine Bahía; Local Buses to North of Town
74 Lavandería Quinter
78 Net House
79 Club Roxy
80 Ecotours

82 La Iguana
88 Local Buses to North of Town
89 Bar Amsterdam
90 Club Paco Paco
91 Mariachi Loco
93 ETN; Primera Plus & Servicios Coordinados Bus Ticket Office
94 Mata Ortiz Pottery; Olinalá
96 ETN; Primera Plus Bus Ticket Office
97 Stop for Buses to/from South
100 PV Café.com
106 Señor Frog's
109 Galería Dante
112 Lucy's Cucú Cabaña
114 Elite; Futura Bus Ticket Office
115 Mundo De Cristal
116 Mundo de Azulejos
121 Lavandería Elsa
122 A Page in the Sun
126 La Casa de los Gatos
127 Agro Gourmet
128 Patti Gallardo
130 Cactus
131 Viva; Serafina
132 The Club Sports Bar
135 Local Buses to Mismaloya & Boca de Tomatlán
138 Virtual Reality
148 Lavandería Púlpito
149 The Palm

CENTRAL PUERTO VALLARTA

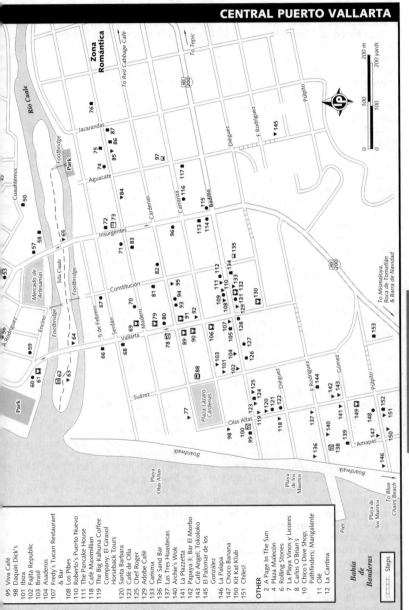

Zona Romántica

To Red Cabbage Café

To Tepic

Río Cuale

Cuauhtémoc

Footbridge

Park

Jacarandas

76

75
74
85 86 87

97

Aguacate
84

116 117

115

Carranza

Badillo

Mercado de Artesanías

Isla Cuale

57
58

65

72 73

Insurgentes

71

96

113
114

Cárdenas

83

135

Encino

Footbridge

Footbridge

64

Constitución

67
70
69

81
82

79 80

94 95
93
91 92

109 111 112
108 110
129 131 132
130

134
133

5 de Febrero

Serdán

Madero

Vallarta

78
90
89

106
105 107
102 104
101 103

128
126 127

A Rodríguez

59

60
61
62
63

Suárez

66
68

88

77

Plaza Lázaro Cárdenas

125
124
123
120 121
122

Diéguez

144

143
142
141

137

140
139
138 136

Amapas

153

150 152
151
149
148
147
146

Pulpito

F. Rodríguez

Gómez

Olas Altas

98
100
99

119
118

MEX 200

To Mismaloya, Boca de Tomatlán & Barra de Navidad

PUERTO VALLARTA

Boardwalk

Playa Olas Altas

Playa de los Muertos

Boardwalk

To Blue Chairs Beach

Playa de los Muertos

Pier

Bahía de Banderas

0   100   200 m
0   100   200 yards

Steps

'Restaurant Row'. Plus, the warm beach sands are only 1½ blocks away.

Hotel Posada del Pedregal (☎ 222-06-04; *Rodríguez 267;* **W** *www.mexonline.com/pe dregal.htm; rooms without/with kitchen US$33/ 44)* has around 15 basic yet pleasant rooms surrounding an old courtyard. Some rooms have balconies, all have TVs, and the entire place is centrally located near the handicrafts market.

Hotel Posada de Roger (☎ 222-08-36; **W** *www.posadaroger.com; Badillo 237; singles/ doubles/triples US$35/42/66)* comes with some good foreigner hangout spots, such as a 2nd-floor pool and plant-filled courtyards. Maze-like outside hallways surround clean rooms with TV, dark wood furniture and – if you're lucky – a balcony.

Casa Vientos del Rio (☎ 222-17-58; **e** *ugbug@aol.com; Cuauhtémoc 460; apartments US$55-85)* offers attractive one- or two-bedroom units with kitchen. There are nice views over the river and a swimming pool on the terrace.

Casa Los Cuatro Vientos (☎ 222-01-61; **W** *www.cuatrovientos.com; Matamoros 520; rooms & suites with breakfast US$55-69)* thrives in its hilly residential location, and harbors peaceful, decent rooms above a garden patio; the upper ones have partial views. The *best* views, however, are from the rooftop bar, which is a great, spacious hangout spot. Also on the premises are a pool and restaurant.

Hotel Posada Río Cuale (☎/fax 222-04-50; **e** *riocuale@pvnet.com.mx; Serdán 242; singles/ doubles/triples US$50/58/72)* is well located and nicely appointed, with air-con and cable TV in the cute colonial rooms, some of which are near the pretty pool area. The grounds are leafy and pleasant and, if you crave saltwater rather than the chlorinated type, the beach is only two blocks away.

Estancia San Carlos (☎/fax 222-54-84; **W** *www.accessmexico.com/sancarlos/; Constitución 210; rooms for 2-4 people US$61-83 plus tax)* gives you fully-equipped kitchens, air-con, TV and (sometimes) private balconies. Rooms are large, pleasant and modern, though small colonial touches add personality. Other perks include a courtyard

swimming pool and covered parking. Some folks stay here for months.

Torre de Oro (☎ 222-44-88; **e** *torreoro@ prodigy.net.mx; rooms US$66-88)* isn't quite the 'world-famous' hotel it claims to be, but still maintains good mid-range rooms with air-con and cable TV. Suites have kitchenettes, and all are close to the beach. The best abodes have sea views and balconies, and there's a pool for everyone.

Hotel Rosita (☎/fax 222-10-33; **W** *www .hotelrosita.com; Paseo Díaz Ordaz 901, rooms US$70-99)* naturally charges more for air-con and views, but rooms here aren't the best deal in town – a general renovation might be, ahem, in order. However, if you can't resist the beachside locale, pleasant swimming pool or attractive lobby, get yourself a view room and settle into the bar and restaurant downstairs – there's live music almost every night.

La Casa del Puente (☎ 222-07-49; **W** *www .casadelpuente.com; Libertad s/n; apartments US$81)* is unique in that there are only two apartments, both so large, comfortable and wonderfully decorated that they feel like small houses. The guesthouse's location is charming, tucked in behind the Restaurant La Fuente del Puente and next to the Río Cuale

Casa Andrea (☎ 222-12-13; **W** *www.casa-andrea.com; Francisca Rodríguez 174; apartments for 2/4 people US$83/138)* represents a haven for the handful of folks savvy enough to make their winter reservations here. What greets them are 10 beautifully decorated apartments with air-con, balconies and indoor/outdoor kitchenettes, all on spacious grounds with flowery garden patios and a gorgeous pool. There's also a library and small gym.

Blue Chairs Beach Resort (☎ 222-50-40, **W** *www.bluechairs.com; Almendro 4; rooms US$99 & US$133 plus tax)* caters to feisty gay men who esconce themselves in either full or partial-view rooms. All have balconies, and of course you *need* to get that full sea view, girlfriend. The decor is quite tasteful, of course, and the window dressing can be fabulous. Amenities are conductive to socializing: There are bars and restaurants on the beach and roof, with a pool on the roof as well. TV, air-con and kitchenettes are available.

Hotel Descanso del Sol (☎ 222-52-29; Ⓦ www.pacopaco.com; Suárez 583; rooms US$63-72, suites US$92-110) is another gay offering, but rather than being beachside is a hike or taxi ride up the hill. This makes for stunning views, especially from the killer rooftop bar, which is crammed full of shirtless gay men at sunset – what more could you ask for? The hotel also sports tidy, trim and well-dressed rooms with TV, air-con and (some) kitchenettes.

See the website Ⓦ www.pacopaco.com /hidden_paradise.html for information about staying at **Paco's Hidden Paradise**, located on a private beach near Boca de Tomatlán and accessible only by boat.

Places to Stay – Top End

At the top end of the market, Puerto Vallarta has a few small, stylish places and lots of large luxury hotels (these mostly for package tourists). From mid-April to mid-December, low-season discounts may bring some of the finest places down to a more affordable level.

Hotel Molino de Agua (☎ 222-19-07; Ⓦ www.molinodeagua.com; Vallarta 130; rooms US$74/120 plus tax) surrounds its small but cute cabin-like rooms with beautiful, lush and extensive grounds. Fancier rooms and suites sport ocean views. All come with air-con and small terrace, and there are bars, pools, jacuzzi and a restaurant for your luxurious enjoyment. A bonus: this place is about as centrally located as you could get.

Casa Kimberley (☎/fax 222-13-36; Ⓦ www .casakimberley.com; Zaragoza 445; rooms with breakfast US$90) is perhaps best for true Elizabeth Taylor and Richard Burton fans. On hand are great views from patios, a swimming pool and movie-themed decor. Daily tours pass through here so ultimate tranquility is out (see Organized Tours).

Casa Amorita (☎ 222-49-26; Ⓦ www .casaamorita.com; Iturbide 309; rooms with full breakfast US$95) is one of Vallarta's few charming B&Bs. Tucked into this two-story corner house are four beautifully decorated

rooms, three with partial sea view; a small but sparkling pool; relaxing communal spaces. It's a very pleasant and romantic place, so be sure to make reservations in winter.

Hotel San Marino Plaza (☎ 222-30-50; Ⓦ www.hotelsanmarino.com; Rodolfo Gómez 111; all-inclusive per person singles US$140; per person doubles US$121) is smack dab right on the beach, and all rooms come with balcony, comfortable decor and lots of amenities – what you'd expect at this level. Prices include all meals and recreational activities.

Many four- or five-star hotels, often with hundreds of rooms, line the beaches north and south of town. They all do big business in package tours, which can be arranged by good travel agents in your country for rates considerably lower than the 'walk-in' prices quoted here. Consequently, setting something up beforehand (call, or try the websites) will save you plenty of pesos. Note that rates vary widely with the time of year and the type of room. These four are in the Zona Hotelera, north of town:

Sheraton Buganvilias (☎ 226-04-04; Ⓦ www.sheratonvallarta.com; Fco Medina Ascencio 999; rooms US$150-200) offers pretty much what you'd expect from a Sheraton: beautiful tropical grounds, posh rooms and large pools with swim-up bars and an 'island jacuzzi' in the middle of everything.

Krystal Vallarta (☎ 224-02-02; Ⓦ www .krystal.com.mx; Las Garzas s/n; rooms US$140-300) isn't so attractively located on Zona Hotelera, but it does sport park-like grounds, fine rooms and fountains in the lobby. And if you don't want to walk, there are golf carts to speed you (and your luggage) around.

Fiesta Americana (☎ 224-20-10; Ⓦ www .fiestaamericana.com; Km 2.5 Fco Medina Ascencio; rooms from US$149) is one of the nicest in this lot, with a stunning lobby ringed by an artificial stream and sitting pretty under a giant palapa roof. Rooms are gorgeous, you can lounge on chaises in the pool, and the views are great.

Westin Regina Resort (☎ 226-11-00; Ⓦ www.westinpv.com; Paseo de la Marina Sur 205; rooms from US$128) looms like a huge white and pink structural monster in the northern harbor area of Marina Vallarta. Expansive, palm-studded grounds shelter the almost 900 balconied rooms in modern splendour. It's a little impersonal, which is saying a lot in this category.

South of town, top-end hotels have a more 'isolated' feel than their northern counterparts, since they are located on the scenic, narrow section of Hwy 200 rather than on a busy, bright-light business strip. All have fantastic views from cliff-top positions.

Camino Real (☎ 221-50-00; ⓦ www.caminoreal.com/puertovallarta/; Hwy 200 Km 3.5; rooms from US$180) has a beautiful beach and all rooms look out over it. All the luxurious basics like tennis courts, gourmet restaurants and pool with swim-up bar can be found here.

Presidente Inter-Continental (☎ 228-01-91; ⓦ www.puertovallarta.interconti.com; Hwy 200 Km 8.5; doubles including meals from US$275) is a behemoth with spectacular view from the lobby, but you'll likely spend more time in the pleasant pool area or on the fine, sandy beach.

La Jolla de Mismaloya (☎ 226-06-60; ⓦ www.lajollademismaloya.com; Hwy 200 Km 11.5; suites including meals from US$171) offers more than 300 suites with all the amenities. The set location of the old Taylor/Burton flick *Night of the Iguana* is nearby, and they'll let you know it. Also at hand are plenty of bars and restaurants, and the use of some water sports equipment is included.

Quinta Maria Cortez (☎ 221-53-17; 888-640-8100 in the USA; ⓦ www.quinta-maria.com; Calle Sagitario 132; rooms US$100-235) has to be the most atmospheric place to stay near Vallarta. The seven spacious and romantic suites, all different sizes, are furnished with antiques and eclectic decor. Most come with kitchen, fireplace and sea views, and the included breakfast is served in a terraced, palapa-covered common space. There's even a beautiful pool overlooking the sea. Try to reserve in advance.

Places to Eat

Restaurants – South of Río Cuale If you're watching your budget, look for **taco stands** that sprout in the Zona Romantica

early in the evenings – they serve some of the best and cheapest food in town. For inexpensive seafood stands, try the corner of Serdán and Constitución. There are also a few small, economical, family-run restaurants along Madero.

The following three restaurants are best for breakfast.

Choco Banana (Amapas 147; mains US$3-4; open 8am-8pm Mon-Wed, 8am-10pm Thur-Sat, 8am-6pm Sun) is a tiny shack of a place, but popular for breakfast (served all day), juices and milkshakes. Don't expect too many tables; barstools are the norm here.

Fredy's Tucan Restaurant & Bar (☎ 223-07-78; cnr Badillo & Vallarta; mains US$3-6; open 8am-2am) is a foreigner magnet for breakfast specials like pancakes, waffles and omelets. It also serves lunch, dinner, snacks and drinks, and at night this place turns into a bar. The food is fine, though the coffee has garnered some criticism (try it and let us know).

The Pancake House (☎ 222-62-72; Badillo 289; mains US$3-6; open 8am-2pm daily) aka 'Casa de Hotcakes', claims to be *'numero uno en desayuno'*. The hordes of gringos waiting for tables in the morning agree: butter pecan, chocolate chip, orange spice and Kahlua make good pancake flavors. Or go for French toast, mean waffles, fruit and yogurt or even (gads!) Mexican breakfasts.

For good Mexican cuisine there are these choices, among many:

Las Tres Huastecas (cnr Olas Altas & Rodríguez; mains US$3-8; open 8am-8:30pm daily) serves simple though somewhat greasy local favorites. The prices are good, especially for this trendy street, and inexpensive breakfasts are available. Don't expect posh fancy surroundings, however – instead, read the Spanish sayings on plaques that cover the walls.

Restaurant Gilmar (☎ 222-39-23; Madero 418; mains US$4-8; open 8am-11pm Mon-Sat) provides good tasty Mexican dishes and seafood at reasonable prices; the *comida corrida* (daily special; US$3.30) includes three courses and a drink. Expect small and homey.

Papaya 3 (☎ 223-16-92; Olas Altas 485; mains US$4-8; open 8am-10:30pm Mon-Sat,

9am-5pm Sun) is a great place for vegetarians with plenty of meat-free salads, soups, pastas and Mexican dishes. Carnivores won't get left out, as some dishes cater to them as well. Next door the operators of Papaya 3 run a sushi-bar, and there's another branch way up north at Abasolo 169.

Café de Olla (☎ 223-16-26; Badillo 168A; mains US$6-13; open 10am-11pm Wed-Mon) sometimes has lines of foreigners outside waiting to get in. The wait pays off with great Mexican fare at good prices.

Mariscos Polo (Madero 376; mains US$7-14; open noon-10pm daily) is the simple home of just seven tables with colorful tablecloths. People come here for the tasty seafood specialties – try the seafood burrito.

Fajita Republic (☎ 222-31-31; cnr Badillo & Suárez; mains US$9-14; open 8am-midnight Tues-Sun, 4pm-midnight Mon) specializes in fajitas, surprisingly enough. It's a very popular place, with jungly open seating and enchanting beehive-like lights.

Red Cabbage Café (☎ 223-04-11; Rivera Delrío 204A; mains US$8-18; open 5pm-11pm daily) is not a place to come without reservations. Though the atmosphere is casual, with fabulous eclectic and bohemian artwork, the food is serious 'alta cocina' Mexican. Order the house specialty, Chiles en Nogada, or try the 20-plus varieties of mole sauces. Vegetarians are accommodated. To get there from the Zona Romantica, begin at Insurgentes and then follow Cárdenas east five long blocks. Take a right turn before the green bridge and go approximately one more block. It's about a 10-minute walk.

If you're tired of Mexican, try the following:

Chiles! (☎ 223-03-73; Púlpito 122; mains US$4-6; open Nov-May 11am-6pm Mon-Sat) grills up good-sized servings of burgers, hotdogs, roasted chicken and veggie burgers. Get a side of potato salad, coleslaw or chili with beans and head to the beach to digest it all.

La Piazzetta (☎ 222-06-50; cnr Olas Altas & Gómez; mains US$7-9; open 4pm-midnight Mon-Sat) could just be the thing for a pasta or pizza fix. Lots of gringos, good

service and outdoor seating make for a pleasant and casual meal.

Como Pizza (☎ 222-32-72; Vallarta 279; open noon-4am Tues-Sun) belts out live tunes Friday and Saturday nights, which go well with the brick-oven, wood-fired pizza. The feel is upscale and open, the location is ground zero for hoppin' bars, and there's a pool table.

Roberto's Puerto Nuevo (☎ 222-62-10; Badillo 283; mains US$5-15; open noon-11:30pm daily) has a great business card: 'The especialty of the day depends on the appetizing whims of the waiter, don't be shy, ask him about it (sic)'. We would ask him about it.

Santa Barbara (☎ 223-20-48; Olas Altas 351; mains US$6-8) attracts gringos like gringos attract sunburn. A comfort menu of burgers, sandwiches, pizzas, seafood and margaritas help ease the hunger pangs after a day of sunning, and the 2nd floor is gorgeous. Plus, there's bingo twice a week.

Carisma (☎ 222-49-59; Badillo 284; mains US$9-17; open 5pm-midnight daily) posts its menu at the doors, but beware: one innocent peek and the eager waiters practically reel you in. Luckily, the food is good: Savor rustic octopus, hot garlic crab or rib-eye steak. Pizzas and pastas are also available, as are mixed drinks and something called 'sexy coffee.'

Archie's Wok (☎ 222-04-11; Rodríguez 130; mains US$8-19; open 2pm-11pm Mon-Sat) features Asian fusion cuisine, with dishes like Hoi Sin ribs, Thai noodles, Indian chicken-cashew curry and Philippine egg rolls. It's renowned reputation means busy tables, but if you've got the bucks it's worth sitting among the artsy handmade decor.

Ibiza (☎ 222-63-53; Suárez 321; mains US$11-20; open 5pm-11pm daily) serves up paella, Sicilian chicken and gazpacho among its Spanish repertoire. The atmosphere is airy and open, and there's live jazz Wednesday to Friday nights at 7:30pm.

Café Maximillian (☎ 222-50-58; Olas Altas 380B; mains US$5-15; open 8am-midnight Mon-Sat) tries to do it all: exotic coffees, ice-cream sundaes, salads, sandwiches, onion soup, weiner schnitzel, pasta, Austrian

PUERTO VALLARTA

pastries, tiramisu and alcoholic drinks. At least the elegant sidewalk seating's nice.

The Sand Bar (☎ 222-08-94; Diéguez & Playa de los Muertos; mains US$6-17; open 7am-11pm daily) serves salads, seafood, ribs, burgers, tacos and frog's legs. The real reason you're here, however, is to eat on the beach under a shady palapa.

Tokoloko (☎ 222-40-04; Olas Altas 443; mains US$15; open 6pm-11pm Wed-Mon) cooks a few Indonesian specialties, but it's not for large groups – the six small tables are mostly outside, sandwiched between two popular restaurants. There's a Sunday buffet for US$22.

Don't bother visiting the following places if you're a vegetarian: you won't get your money's worth.

Asaderos (☎ 044-342-957-90; Badillo 223; buffet US$8 plus tax; open 2pm-11pm Sun-Tues) grills up plenty of barbecued chicken, steak, ribs and Mexican sausage for the popular all-you-can-eat package. Salad and bread are included, but the drinks tack onto the restaurants' profits. The sidewalk or palapa seating is pleasant, and there's live music.

Los Pibes (☎ 223-20-44; Badillo 261; mains US$9-24; open 5pm-11pm Mon-Sat) proudly serves Sterling Silver meat from the USA (which one assumes is an asset). Steaks are grilled Argentine-style; try the *bife de chorizo* (sirloin), which is the most basic cut in Argentina. There's another branch up north at the yacht harbor in Marina Vallarta.

Brasil (☎ 222-29-09; Carranza 210; all-you-can-eat US$17; open 2pm-11pm daily) has the best meat in town, according to one local. It's Brazilian-style *churrasquería*, which means the skewered meats come to your table. The jungly decor is great, and comes complete with a tree in the middle and fake animal heads on the walls.

You might need to stuff your wallet and spiff your image before dining at the next six establishments.

Kit Kat Klub (☎ 223-00-93; Púlpito 120; mains US$9-19) is so hip it hurts. Sip your trendy cocktail on the modern sidewalk furniture and nibble coconut crabcakes while

catching the weekend dinner show. Thin cigarettes work well here.

El Palomar de los González (☎ 222-07-95; Aguacate 425; mains US$10-20; open 6pm-11pm daily) offers super views over the city and bay: a big draw at this terraced hillside restaurant, especially at sunset. Jumbo shrimp and fillet steak are specialties. It's a steep climb up here, so get a taxi or work up an appetite.

Chef Roger (☎ 222-59-00; Badillo 180; mains US$13-22; open 6:30pm-11pm Mon-Sat) needs to be arrived at in fancy threads, and with reservations (crucial on weekends). Only then can you enjoy the romantic outdoor fountain seating and fabulous entrées like carpaccio of ostrich with pesto and parmesan cheese. Expect elegance and bring a fat wallet.

Adobe Café (☎ 222-67-20; Badillo 252; mains US$13-20; open 6pm-11pm Wed-Mon) is an upscale, adobe-style café serving a well-prepared international menu of pastas, seafood and meat dishes. Settle into booths surrounded by dramatically lit bare sticks. No shorts or flip-flops, please.

La Palapa (☎ 222-52-25; Púlpito 103; mains US$14-36; open 9am-11pm daily) has menu selections that say it all: pan-seared scallops with mango chutney over risotto and mussel sauce. This is elegant beach dining at its best, so expect rich gringos to occupy the tables next to you.

Daiquiri Dick's (☎ 222-05-66; Olas Altas 314; mains US$12-26; open 9am-10:30pm daily) is an elegant dining establishment, despite its name. Nibble roast duck with scalloped sweet potatoes, bite into the sesame-encrusted tuna or wrestle with lobster tacos. Southwest colors, soft music and a gorgeous view help it all go down easy.

Restaurants – Isla Cuale Bring your hot and pricey date to **Le Bistro Jazz Café** (☎ 222-02-83; Isla Río Cuale 16A; mains US$8-21; open 9am-midnight Mon-Sat), which embodies high elegance while serving gourmet food like mahi mahi, shrimp Portuguese and 'lobster of desire.' Mango sour crème flan is for dessert. It's tropically romantic, overlooks the river, and plays soft, loungy music.

Oscar's (☎ 223-07-89; Isla Río Cuale 1; mains US$9-15; open 8am-11pm daily) has a menu that covers burgers, sandwiches, gourmet salads and meat dishes. All are served under an airy palapa by the sea, while soft music and ocean breezes caress you and your gringo neighbors.

River Cafe (☎ 223-07-88; Isla Río Cuale 4; mains US$9-22; open 9am-11:30pm daily) is highlighted by imaginative seafood dishes such as shrimp with pecans and orange sauce, pastas, fajitas and filet mignon. The elegant location is right next to the river, and the atmosphere is jazzy: this is a great place to be rich.

Restaurants – North of Río Cuale Just north of the river, the **Mercado Municipal RíoCuale** has simple and cheap stalls upstairs serving typical Mexican market foods. For more tourist-oriented fare, head towards **Paseo Díaz Ordaz**, the street fronting the Malecón: it's thick with restaurants and bars. Many have upstairs terraces offering fine views of the bay. Prices are considerably higher than in other parts of the city, and note that many popular night-time venues are not the best stops for a meal.

Planeta Vegetariano Restaurant (☎ 222-30-73; Iturbide 270; buffets US$4-6; open 8am-10pm daily) serves up all-you-can-eat quality buffets at every meal, and they are a vegetarians' dream. Just come; you won't be disappointed. All around are wonderfully painted murals, and the hilly pedestrian street outside is a peaceful sidedrop.

Tacos de los Arcos (Zaragoza & the beach; tacos US$0.65; open noon-2am Mon-Sat, noon-midnight Sun) is in a class by itself: really good, really cheap Mexican eats in the middle of Vallarta. Look for the 'Hooters' sign and follow it down.

Archie's Burger (☎ 222-43-83; cnr Morelos & Pipila; mains less than US$5; open noon-1am Tues-Sun) is a tiny shack of a place where budding surfers can catch some burgers, hot dogs, fries, surfer videos and reggae music. Don't bring your surfboard: there isn't much room.

Barcelona (☎ 222-05-10; cnr Matamoros & 31 de Octubre; tapas US$3.50-7; open noon-11:30pm Mon-Sat, 5:30pm-11:30pm Sun) requires a walk up a hill and some stairs, but the grand view and excellent tapas are worth it. Lamb, duck and vegetarian dishes are also served. Try to get a table on the patio up top, and order a sangria for God's sake!

Graffity (Miramar 271; mains US$5-16; open 9am-11pm daily) is a tiny, Greek-island-like place great for sunny breakfasts or lunches. It's casually located on a pedestrian street with terraced steps where three tables perch – on them international dishes are placed, sometimes by the managing Frenchman. Visit them for happy hour, from 6pm to 8pm.

La Dolce Vita (☎ 222-38-52; Paseo Díaz Ordaz 674; mains US$8-11; open noon-2am Mon-Sat, 6pm-midnight Sun) bakes up some mean wood-fired pizza and other renowned Italian specialties. Live jazz plays Thursday to Sunday for the crowded floor.

Rito's Baci (☎ 222-64-48; Domínguez 181; mains US$8-13; open 1pm-11:30pm daily) stands proud in cozy spaces filled with foreign patrons sampling delicious Italian cuisine. Moody music and small front tables make it better for romantic liaisons than large rowdy groups.

La Bodeguita del Medio (☎ 223-15-85; Paseo Díaz Ordaz 858; mains US$7-15; open 11am-2:30am daily) is a Cuban joint; test its authenticity by trying the Cuban paella or gazpacho with a Caribbean twist. A retractable roof and 2nd-floor balcony make for an open feel and good views over the Malecón. And, there's live music all day (if you're lucky).

No Name Café (☎ 223-25-08; cnr Morelos & Mina; mains US$8-18; open 9am-midnight daily) flouts very busy sports decor along with 31 (count 'em) TV sets. Obviously, a good place to catch your choice of game. It claims to serve the best ribs in Mexico: you be the judge.

Trio (☎ 222-21-96; Guerrero 264; mains US$9-22; open noon-3:30pm Nov-Apr, 6pm-11:30pm year-round) takes pride in serving gourmet food combining Mediterranean and Mexican flavors. Try the lamb ravioli, chili-roasted snapper or Lebanese salad. Dress reasonably well; this place is classy.

PUERTO VALLARTA

Las Palomas (☎ 222-36-75; cnr Paseo Díaz Ordaz & Aldama; mains US$9-28; open 8am-11pm daily) looks over the Malecón from its comfortable perch, which makes it a popular place for people-watching. The menu lists seafood, chicken crepes and Mexican specialties, and the decor is smart and festive. Soft music serenades loud and happy gringo voices; perhaps they scored a 'free margarita' coupon?

Café des Artistes (☎ 222-32-29; Sánchez 740; mains US$11-29; open 6pm-11:30pm daily) boasts exquisite French cuisine, great service and a romantic setting (including a jungly garden). It's not so elegant that 'happy birthday' songs aren't belted out every night, though. Still, expect fine gourmet food such as grilled swordfish in green tomato sauce or tuna in sesame seeds with wasabe mousse. Reservations are recommended.

Carlos O'Brian's, **Hard Rock Café** and **Planet Hollywood** all serve somewhat expensive food, but you already knew that. They're much more appreciated for music, dancing and party potential (see below under 'Wet T-Shirt'; just kidding, see the Entertainment section).

North of Puerto Vallarta, the top-end hotels in the Zona Hotelera and Marina Vallarta all have gourmet restaurants charging gourmet prices. Good examples are **Bogart's** (☎ 224-02-02 ext 2007; Hotel Krystal Vallarta) for international cuisine and **Garibaldi's** (☎ 226-11-50 ext 4419; Westin Regina Resort) for fine seafood in a beachfront setting.

Coffee Shops There are plenty of places in Vallarta to satisfy those java cravings and keep your energy levels buzzing.

Kahuna Coffee Co (☎ 222-16-93; Badillo 162; bagels US$1.50-3, coffee US$1-3) is great for when you're jonesin' for a jalapeño bagel with horseradish cream cheese. This tiny, Canadian-run coffee joint sells other bagel flavors like garlic and biali, spreadable on top with blackberry, nuts and raisins or veggie cream cheeses. Lox sandwiches are available, and they've also got good java including frozen versions.

Café Superior (☎ 222-44-23; Encino 55; mains US$3-5.50, coffee US$1-2.50; open 8am-8pm Tues-Sat, 8am-4pm Sun-Mon) brews up some great (albeit pricey) stuff, and is efficiently run by a Seattle native. Also on order are tuna salad, nachos, veggie sandwiches, milkshakes and Western-style breakfasts. The corner-store ambience is intimate and casual, with plenty of open doors for street-watching.

World of Coffee (cnr Cárdenas & Olas Altas; coffee US$1-3; open 7:30am-10:30pm daily) is where you can have your carrot cake and eat it, too; with an iced latte, even. It's not very atmospheric but there is pleasant, covered sidewalk seating, and it's across from a park. Avoid the pricey Internet service.

Viva Café (Cárdenas 292; open 8:30am-10pm Mon-Sat) perks and bubbles its java among small tables and artsy clutter. Order your usual fancy coffees; packaged grounds are also available for purchase.

Café San Angel (☎ 223-21-60; Olas Altas 449; coffee US$3-4; open 7am-1am daily) has some popular sidewalk seating, all covered with gringos sitting pretty, sipping their black and nibbling on snacks and sweets. Try coffees laced with whiskey, tequila or Kahlua (US$3.50) – they're a great way to start your day.

Cappucchino Café (Galeana 104; coffee up to US$5; open 8am-11pm daily) steams up lattes, mochas and espresso from its 2nd-story open loft. There's a great view of the little seahorse boy statue and some nice-looking desserts.

Grocery Stores Cater your own picnic and save some pesos.

Gutiérrez Rizoc (GR; cnr Constitución & Aquiles Serdán; open 6:30am-11pm daily) is a well-stocked, air-con supermarket, OK for self-catering or a small indulgence.

Agro Gourmet (☎ 222-53-57; Badillo 222; open 9am-6pm Mon-Fri, 9am-3pm Sat) actually stocks Snapple™. This small health food store also sells seasonal veggies, whole-wheat bread, grains and spices.

Entertainment

Dancing and drinking are Puerto Vallarta's main forms of night-time entertainment. In the evenings many people stroll down the

Malecón, where some wonderfully creative 'Dr Seuss-on-acid' sculpture has been placed (see the front cover of this book). Also lining the Malecón are plenty of romantic open-air restaurants and heaps of riotous bars. Entertainment is often on tap in the amphitheater by the sea (opposite Plaza Principal), and the softly lit Isla Cuale is a quiet haven for a romantic, early evening promenade.

Bars, Clubs & Discos Along the Malecón are a bunch of places where teen and 20 something (or even older) tourists get trashed and dance on tables. On a good night, they might stay open to about 5am. You can see from the street which one has the most action. Usually there's no cover charge, but drinks are on the expensive side, except during the 'happy hours' which can be any time from 8pm to 11pm.

Carlos O'Brian's (☎ 222-14-44; Paseo Díaz Ordaz 786) remains a favorite drinking hole for fun-seeking, rabble-rousing gringos in search of a good party.

Hard Rock Café (☎ 222-55-32; Paseo Díaz Ordaz 652; open 11am-2am daily) is in the same area, but gets an older, more sedate, T-shirt-collecting crowd. Spin to live music every night but Monday.

Planet Hollywood (☎ 223-27-10; cnr Morelos & Galeana) is here in Vallarta. What else do you need to know?

Kahlúa (☎ 222-24-86; cnr Paseo Díaz Ordaz & Abasolo) blares loud disco beats from its huge open windows. Inside, gringos check each other out and look for dates, while reaping the rewards of a constant happy hour.

The Zoo (☎ 222-49-45; Paseo Díaz Ordaz 638) sports an animal scene, and I'm not just talking about the decor. Grilled windows resemble cages, so if you're up for a wild time step inside – carefully. You may be greeted with all-the-margaritas-you-can-drink hour.

La Regadera (☎ 222-39-76; Morelos 664; open 8pm-4am daily) is dark, smoky and popular with young local drinkers and dancers. Come for a visit if you want to hear Mexicans singing loudly and badly.

La Cantina (☎ 222-17-34; Morelos 700; open noon-4am Wed-Sat, noon-2am Sun-Tues) also attracts the young, hip and uninhibited, sitting daintily on barstools. Again, it's a mostly Mexican crowd.

La Revolución (☎ 222-06-06; Matamoros 235; open 11am-2am Mon-Fri, 9am-2am Sat, 9am-8pm Sun) is a cool and casual local joint attracting a good mix of gringos and Mexicans. It's one of the oldest bars in Vallarta: Liz and Richard hung out here. Wednesday night there's live music, but other times there's open mike – or pick up the sax and join in.

South of the Río Cuale, a wider variety of nightspots caters to a more diverse clientele, and drink prices are generally lower than on the Malecón scene.

Señor Frog's (☎ 222-51-71; cnr Vallarta & Carranza; admission US$9-11 unless having dinner; open 11am-4am daily) employs waiters eager to recruit female patrons, and has a sign that prominently declares 'Topless women = free drinks; topless men = no service'. Nightly shows include wet T-shirt, bikini and wet boxer. You guess what kind of place this is.

Club Roxy (Vallarta 217) has a dark, crowded atmosphere while music (Santana, say) rings the air. Middle-aged and sometimes skimpily clad rockers sway and smooch in the deepest corners or in plain sight. Overheard quote outside: 'Oh, that *music*! Good exercise, though'. The live stuff (music) is pretty good.

Cactus (☎ 222-03-91; Vallarta 399; open 10pm-4am Fri-Sat, 10pm-1am Sun-Thur) is a modern disco that plays host to a bikini or wet T-shirt contest some nights. A cover charge of US$24 for men, US$14 for women (though sometimes oestrogen is so needed it gets in free) includes an open bar – which does nothing to promote responsible drinking. Isn't it great?

The Club Sports Bar & Grill (☎ 222-02-56; Badillo 286) serves Canadian/American 'cuisine' – someone was pulling this author's leg. Ice hockey dominates on the screens, and at the bar aging hippies share space with purple-haired ladies. It's friendly, modern, casual and bright.

La Barriga Cantina (Madero 259; open noon-4am daily) is expat-run but attracts both gringos and locals, which is nice. The pool table is free, the beers are just over US$1, there's a jukebox and it's cozy and friendly. This is the perfect bar, in a self-proclaimed 'spicy little neighborhood.'

The local **pool hall** (Madero 279) is not the kind of place where you'll find Tom Cruise types twirling their cues and kicking shit. It's large, full of tables and downright seedy. Get drunk and challenge the locals (all male) to a game.

North of the city, some of the large resort hotels have bars and nightclubs, but they're usually low energy, high-priced affairs. They're busier at holiday times, when well-dressed Mexicans strut their stuff. To cut the cost of the cover charge, look for discount coupons in tourist pamphlets.

Christine (☎ 224-69-90; open 10pm-3am Sun-Thur, 10pm-5am Fri-Sat) has fluctuating cover charges (free to US$11 to US$26) depending on your sex and the night. Sometimes an open bar is included. Terraced levels, spinning spotlights and hip hop music delight well-dressed dancers downing overpriced and weak drinks. Still, it's flashy, modern and lively.

Jabalu (☎ 223-40-99; Francisco Ascencio 1735; open 10pm-3am Sun-Thur, 10am-5am Fri-Sat) is just north of the Hotel Sheraton Buganvilas and stirs up some passionate salsa and merengue for a varied crowd. Balloons and colored lights add to the mix, although it's not cutting-edge cool. Cover charges are different every night, but run around US$9 on weekends.

J&B (☎ 224-46-16; Francisco Ascencio Km 2.5; admission US$9 Wed-Sun, free Mon-Tues; open 10pm-6am daily) swings with salsa, cumbia and merengue, mostly. The live stuff starts at 12:30am Wednesday to Sunday, and a somewhat tacky tropical theme encourages casual dress. The crowd runs into 40-somethings.

Gay Venues Come on 'out' – Puerto Vallarta's got the largest population of gay men, both foreign and Mexican, in the country. After a day of sunning and an afternoon of drinking, many head out for a hot night on the town.

Blue Chairs is the most popular, visible gay beach bar in PV, with droves of gay couples enjoying the ubiquitous sun rays and cool drinks. It's located at the south end of Playa de los Muertos; just keep walking south until you see the colorful chairs, which aren't just blue. Visit the hotel's rooftop bar, nearby.

Club Paco Paco (☎ 222-18-99; Vallarta 278; open 1pm-6am daily) is a popular disco bar and a good place for information on Vallarta's thriving gay scene. It's also lots of fun, with regular floor shows, strippers and drag acts. Check out the great rooftop patio.

Anthropology (Morelos 101; admission US$3.50-5.50; open 9pm-4am daily) seduces with exotic snake and Maya themes. Hot male bodies are on display for one another, and if you're lucky salsa beats will be on tap. If you're not so lucky, you'll get heavy techno thump. Check out the dark, more intimate rooftop patio.

Balcones (☎ 222-46-71; Juárez 182; admission US$2-4, special events cost more, admission free before 10pm; open 9pm-4am) has little upstairs balconies where trendy gay hipsters like to be seen. Cow covers, brick arches, great cozy spaces and colorful walls accompany DJ music and nightly strippers.

The Palm (Olas Altas 508; admission US$3.50, free before 9pm; open 7pm-2am daily) presents a different show every night, like comedy, jazz, pop Latin music or guest performers. Spinning lights, snazzy colors and palm decor make it all seem like a dream. Quote from one of the gay owners: 'No one has to be lonely here.'

Bar El Morbo (☎ 223-43-47; Olas Altas 463) glows in the dark, literally. Plus there's a free jacuzzi on the roof (open Friday to Monday nights; bring your speedo, or don't), but this author hesitated checking that out. Write in and tell me, OK?

Mariachis Vallarta has several places to enjoy this traditional Mexican music, though most will cater to tourists.

Tequila's (☎ 222-27-33; Galeana 104) 2nd-story location on the Malecón makes for an excellent backdrop to the live mariachi music every night, except for Monday, starting at around 7:30pm or 8pm. Try one of the many versions of tequila, and try visualizing Richard Burton falling off the stools here.

Mariachi Loco (☎ 223-22-05; cnr Cárdenas & Vallarta; admission US$4-5; open 1pm-late Mon-Sat, 8pm-2am Sun) is a restaurant that attracts an enthusiastic mix of nationalities. A festive and entertaining (if slightly amateur) show of music, comedy and mariachi plays daily. It's a great bit of local color, but you'll need good Spanish to enjoy it.

Fiestas Mexicanas These wonderful folkloric shows give tourists an entertaining crash course in not-very-contemporary Mexican culture.

La Iguana (☎ 222-01-05; Cárdenas 311; admission US$35; open 7pm-11pm Thur & Sun) entertains with a Mexican buffet, open bar, live music, folkloric dances, mariachis, cowboy rope tricks, bloodless cockfights and a piñata. The atmosphere is festive, familial and fine.

Hotel Krystal (☎ 224-02-02 ext 2091; Las Garzas s/n; admission US$47; shows Tues & Sat 7pm-10pm) is considered one of the best Fiestas Mexicanas, though it's not cheap. Add fireworks to the above.

Sheraton Buganvilias (☎ 226-04-04; Francisco Ascencio 999) is yet another big-name hotel that offers up a decent Mexican Fiesta night.

Cinemas Catch recent-release movies at Cine Bahía (cnr Insurgentes & Madero; admission US$3.75), often in English with Spanish subtitles.

Spectator Sports

Bullfights (US$28) are held at 5pm on Wednesdays, November to May, in the bullring opposite the marina. Any travel agency or luxury hotel worth their salt will have information or sell tickets. Or you can dial ☎ 221-04-14.

Shopping

Shops and boutiques in Puerto Vallarta sell fashion clothing, beachwear, and just about every type of handicraft made in Mexico, but prices reflect the richness of the area and are high. There are a few markets concentrating on craft stalls, and these are the places to go for cheaper prices and some hard bargaining.

Mercado Municipal RíoCuale (open 9am-8pm Mon-Sat, 9am-3pm Sun) is a honeycomb of more than 150 craft stalls offering touristy T-shirts, Taxco silver jewelry, sarapes and huaraches, wool wall-hangings, painted pottery and blown glass, among many other things. Tons of other shops line Agustín Rodríguez, facing the market. Bargain like your life depended on it: walk away and prices plummet.

Also try Plaza Malecón, up north on the Malecón near Allende. The most atmospheric handicraft district, however, is the shady and tropical strip on Isla Cuále.

For shops and boutiques, you have endless choices. The following are more upscale places:

Patti Gallardo (☎ 222-57-12; Badillo 250; open 9:30am-11pm daily) is a great place for handmade and unique 'eclectic art' (though not necessarily Mexican) made mostly by women: jewelry, sculpture, picture frames, knick-knacks and more. It's not cheap.

Viva (☎ 222-40-78; Badillo 274; open 10am-11pm daily) is the type of establishment that exclaims 'Welcome to Viva!' as you walk in. The stuff's fabulous, of course: Funky sunglasses, stylish espadrilles and excellent straw hats and beach bags. Creative and original jewelry's the specialty, though. There's a considerate sofa for the hubbies.

Ole (☎ 223-03-70; Morelos 507; open 10am-3pm, 6pm-9pm Mon-Sat) also has another branch on Vicario and Paseo Díaz Ordaz. Literally tons of wonderful metalwork and jewelry; a good selection, though its hours can be somewhat erratic (think 'Mexican Time').

Galería de Ollas (☎ 223-10-45; Morelos 101; open 10am-3pm & 4pm-9pm Mon-Fri,

PUERTO VALLARTA

10am-3pm Sat) displays more beautiful pottery, much of it intricately painted. Bring your bank account.

Galería Mata Ortiz *(☎ 222-74-07; Cárdenas 268A; open 10am-2pm & 5pm-9pm Mon-Fri, 10am-2pm Sat-Sun)* has a very small but fine collection of pottery and is for die-hard collectors only.

Olinalá *(Cárdenas 274; open 10am-2pm & 5pm-8pm Mon-Fri, 10am-2pm Sat)* offers up Mexican dance masks and other funky wood crafts.

Galería Magico Huichol *(☎ 222-30-77; Corona 179; open 10am-2pm & 4pm-8pm Mon-Sat)* presents a great selection of Huichol art.

Galería Dante *(☎ 222-24-77; Badillo 269; open 10am-5pm Mon-Fri, Sat hrs vary)* displays paintings and very creative sculpture – check out the lush garden out back.

Hecho a Mano *(☎ 223-14-55; Zaragoza 160; open 10am-10pm daily)* keeps an extensive selection of furniture and home decor, all made in Mexico and fabulous.

The following are more casual than upscale:

Sol y Cactus *(☎ 222-13-46; Independencia 231)* sells the biggest margarita glass this author has ever seen. Prices are reasonable, though there's a lot of kitsch.

La Casa de los Gatos *(☎ 222-30-76; Badillo 220; open 10am-6pm daily)* is a casual place that carries a variety of fairly priced and eccentric stuff, including some Huichol beadwork.

Serafina *(☎ 223-45-94; Badillo 260; open 9am-9pm Mon-Sat)* is a bit funky, with a good and crowded selection of pottery virgins, clothing, bags (leather, cloth, plastic) and jewelry.

La Reja *(☎ 222-22-72; Juárez 501; open 10am-7pm Mon-Sat)* competes well among the many other places for arts and crafts, as it's a good one. Next door is **Querubines** *(☎ 222-29-89; Juárez 501A; open 9am-9pm Mon-Sat)*, which is also cool.

Lucy's Cucú Cabaña *(Badillo 295; open 10am-10pm Mon-Sat)* stocks some fine, fun crafts from all over Mexico – Oaxacan wood animals, papier-mâché masks and recycled metal arts, among other things. The

owners started an animal rescue programme in Vallarta.

And, for the specialized shopper:

Mundo de Azulejos *(☎ 222-26-75; Carranza 374; open 9am-7pm Mon-Fri, 9am-2pm Sat)* has to have the best selection of artistic tiles in Vallarta. They're not cheap, but they'll custom-make whatever you can think up.

Mundo de Cristal *(☎ 222-41-57; Insurgentes 333; open 9am-7pm Mon-Fri, 9am-2pm Sat)* stocks a wide selection of hand-blown drinking glasses and other delicate crafts.

Sonido Rana *(☎ 222-72-00; Madero 325)* carries a wide selection of CDs.

Rolling Stones *(☎ 223-17-69; Paseo Díaz Ordaz 802; open 10am-11pm daily)* offers to cover you in leather or crocodile skin, and there are some wonderful styles of boots, jackets, chaps, belts, bags and wallets to custom-order. Two floors hold it all.

Guantanamera Cigar Club *(☎ 223-35-13; Corona 186B; open 10am-8pm Mon-Sat, noon-3pm Sun)* is the place to have your Cubanos rolled.

Casa de Tequila *(☎ 222-20-00; Morelos 589; open 9am-11pm daily)* pours high-quality tequila shots...for free. It also sells the stuff, so it doesn't appreciate moochers. It's a good place for information on the national drink, if you're curious.

La Playa Vinos y Licores *(☎ 223-18-18; Pipila 139; open 9am-midnight daily)* also has a branch at Olas Altas 246 and Gomez 138. Here's a good place to buy the 40% of tequila you're allowed back into the USA (that's two regular-sized bottles). By the way, airport duty prices for alcohol are comparable to town prices.

Artículos Religiosos La Asunción *(☎ 222-31-86; Libertad 319; open 10am-8pm Mon-Sat)* carries all sorts of different religious paraphernalia – check out the calendars (US$1), which make great souvenirs.

Getting There & Away

Air Puerto Vallarta's international airport (PVR), on Hwy 200 about 10km north of the city, is served by several national and international airlines. Inside are many duty-free shops (good liquor prices), exchange houses (including AmEx; good rates) and rental car stalls (again, better rates than in town). There are also some very expensive bars, restaurants, and souvenir shops; bring a small bottle of water to save yourself a couple of thirsty bucks.

Aeroméxico (☎ 224-27-77, 800-021-4010) flies to Guadalajara, León, Los Angeles, Mexico City and Tijuana, among other destinations

Alaska Airlines (☎ 221-13-50, 800-252-7522) flies to Los Angeles, San Francisco, Seattle and Phoenix

America West (☎ 221-13-33) flies to Phoenix

American Airlines (☎ 221-17-99) flies to Dallas

Continental (☎ 221-10-25, 800-900-5000) flies to Houston and Newark

Mexicana (☎ 224-89-00, 01-800-366-5400) flies to Chicago, Denver, Guadalajara and Mexico City

Bus Vallarta's **long-distance bus station** is just off Hwy 200, about 12km north of the city center and 1km to 2km north of the airport. Local buses marked 'Ixtapa,' 'Juntas' and 'Mojoneras' (or just simply 'Centro') connect the bus station with the center of town (US$0.40, 5am to 11pm). A taxi between the center and the bus station costs around US$8.25. Going into town from the bus terminal, taxis charge US$4.25 to Marina Vallarta, US$6.50 to the center, and US$8 to Olas Altas/Zona Romantica.

Most long-distance bus lines also have offices south of the Río Cuale, where you can check schedules and buy tickets without having to make a trip to the bus station. They include Elite and Futura, on the corner of Badillo and Insurgentes, and ETN, Primera Plus and Servicios Coordinados, at Cárdenas 268. ETN and Primera Plus are also at Insurgentes 282. Most these offices are open around 8am to 8pm daily.

Buses depart from the main bus station. Puerto Vallarta is a large hub, so there are fairly frequent buses to everywhere. Here are some sample fares and destinations:

Acapulco US$50 to US$72, 14 to 18 hours, 950km

Barra de Navidad US$13 to US$16, 3½ to four hours, 225km; same buses as to Manzanillo

Guadalajara US$28 to US$41, five hours, 344km

Manzanillo US$17 to US$21, five hours, 285km

Mazatlán US$28 to US$32, eight hours, 459km; also you can take a bus to Tepic, where buses go frequently to Mazatlán

Melaque US$12 to US$14, 3½ to four hours, 225km; same buses as to Manzanillo

Mexico City (Terminal Norte) US$70 to US$92, 12 to 13 hours, 880km

Rincón de Guayabitos US$7, 1½ hours, 60km; same buses as to Tepic

San Blas US$11, 3½ hours, 175km

Sayulita US$3.50, one hour, 38km

Tepic US$12, 3½ hours, 169km

Zihuatanejo US$50, 15 hours, 710km

Car & Motorcycle Renting cars in Vallarta is most definitely *not* cheap. Rates vary, but the least you can expect to pay is US$50 per day with 10% deductible. Complete coverage could cost US$60 to US$80 per day – and this is all for a decent compact car. Due to immediate competition, showing up in person at the airport car rental counters can result in the best deals (and watch out for those tricky downtown time-shares posing as rental car companies). Negotiating is always a possibility.

Check with your credit card back home to see if car insurance for a rental abroad is covered (to be covered, you must use that credit card to pay for the rental) – sometimes the coverage is limited to rentals of less than two weeks. Paying cash is often cheaper, and you won't be forced to use the rental companies self-favored rate of exchange (check the fine print on the contract).

Car rental agencies in Puerto Vallarta include:

Avis	(☎ 221-11-12)
Budget	(☎ 222-29-80)
Dollar	(☎ 223-13-54)
Hertz	(☎ 221-14-73)
MagnoCar	(☎ 222-65-45)
National	(☎ 221-12-26)
Quick	(☎ 222-00-06)

Mario's Moto Rent (☎ 044-322-229-81-42, *Francisco Ascencio 998*), opposite the Sheraton Buganvilias hotel, rents trail bikes and motor scooters at US$38 for 12 hours and

US$50 for 24 hours. It's open from 9am to 6pm Monday to Saturday.

Getting Around

To/From the Airport
The cheapest way to get to/from the airport is on a local bus for US$0.40; the 'Aeropuerto,' 'Juntas' and 'Ixtapa' buses all stop right outside the airport entrance. Getting into town from the airport, you can also take any bus with 'Centro' on the front window.

A taxi to the airport costs around US$7. From the airport to town, fixed taxi stands inside the airport ask different prices depending on where you want to go: They charge US$10/12/17 to Marina Vallarta/ Centro/Zona Romantica (also called Old Town or 'Olas Altas'). But, go outside the airport (you may need to cross the blue and orange pedestrian bridge) and passing taxis charge around US$7/11/14 for the same destinations.

Bus
Local buses operate every five minutes, 5am to 11pm, on most routes and cost US$0.40. Plaza Lázaro Cárdenas in the Zona Romantica is a major departure hub. Northbound local bus routes also stop in front of the Cine Bahía, on Insurgentes near the corner of Madero.

Northbound buses marked 'Hoteles,' 'Aeropuerto,' 'Ixtapa,' 'Pitillal' and 'Juntas' pass through the city heading north towards the airport, the Zona Hotelera and Marina Vallarta; the 'Hoteles,' 'Pitillal' and 'Ixtapa' routes can take you to any of the large hotels north of the city.

Southbound 'Boca de Tomatlán' buses pass along the southern coastal highway through Mismaloya (20 minutes) to Boca de Tomatlán (30 minutes). They cost US$0.50 and depart from Constitución near the corner of Badillo every 10 minutes, 6am to 10pm. Sit on the right side for some killer views.

Taxi
Cab prices are regulated by zones; the cost for a ride is determined by how many zones you cross. The shortest ride in town will be at least US$2.75. Some sample fares: To airport US$7; to bus terminal US$8.25; to Nuevo Vallarta US$17 (this is relatively expensive because you cross a state line and taxis can't get a fare back due to regulations). Always determine the price of the ride before you get in.

Bicycle
If you're after a two-wheeled buzz, **Bike Mex** (☎ 223-16-80; Guerrero 361) and **B-B-Bobby's Bikes** (☎ 223-00-08; cnr Miramar & Iturbide) rent mountain bikes for guided or self-guided tours, but they are not cheap. See under Organized Tours for more information.

Water Taxi
In addition to taxis on land, Vallarta also has water taxis to beautiful beaches on the south side of the bay that are accessible only by boat.

Water taxis departing from the pier at Playa de los Muertos head south around the bay, making stops at Las Ánimas (25 minutes), Quimixto (30 minutes) and Yelapa (45 minutes); fare is US$18 return for any destination. Boats depart at 10am, 11am and 4pm, and return mid-afternoon (the 4pm boat returns in the morning).

A water taxi also goes to Yelapa from the beach just south of Hotel Rosita, on the north end of the Malecón, departing at 11:30am, Monday to Saturday (US$11 one way).

Cheaper water taxis to the same places depart from Boca de Tomatlán, about 16km south of town, which is easily reachable by local bus. Water taxis to Las Ánimas (15 minutes), Quimixto (20 minutes) and Yelapa (30 minutes) depart from here daily at 10:30am and 11:30am, 1pm, 2pm, 4pm and 5:30pm, or more frequently if enough people want to make the trip; one-way fare is US$7 to any destination (double for a return trip).

If you buy a return ticket from any particular water taxi, you have to return with the same boat at the time the boatman has set to return. If you buy just a one-way ticket you can take any boat back with any boatman, though if you go to more isolated places you should probably buy a return ticket so someone knows to come back for you.

Boat
Private yachts and *lanchas* can be hired from the south side of the Playa de los Muertos pier. They'll take you to any

secluded beach around the bay; many have gear aboard for snorkeling and fishing. Lanchas can also be hired privately at Mismaloya and Boca de Tomatlán, but they are expensive.

Around Puerto Vallarta

The appeal of Puerto Vallarta is not limited to its city limits; all around the Bahía de Banderas (Bay of Flags) are many beautiful beaches some with small towns catering to visiting tourists. Many of these destinations are interesting enough to be worth a visit, and each can be seen in a day or less.

BEACHES & TOWNS NORTH OF PUERTO VALLARTA

North of town, in the Zona Hotelera, are the sandy stretches of **Camarones**, **Las Glorias**, **Los Tules**, **Las Palmas**, **Playa de Oro** and, past the Marina, **El Salado**. Nuevo Vallarta, an expansive land of all-inclusive behemoth beach hotels, is just past here. And beyond that, up towards the roof of the bay, are the

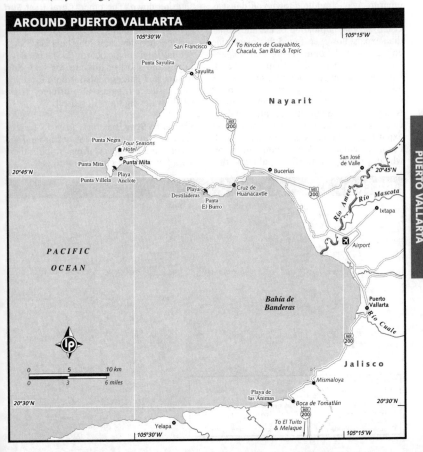

AROUND PUERTO VALLARTA

day-trip destinations of **Bucerías**, **Cruz de Huanacaxtle** and **Playa Anclote** (at Punta Mita), with more beaches dotted between.

Remember that as you travel from Jalisco state to Nayarit state (the border is between Marina Vallarta and Nuevo Vallarta) you need to set your watch back an hour. Any business hours listed in the following towns reflect winter high season hours; in summer, hours and days are often cut back, but hotel prices go down as well.

Bucerías

From the highway, Bucerías looks like another freeway-straddling town you'd just as soon zoom on by on your way to somewhere else. A sizable population of US and Canadian expats, however, found this place nice enough to call home. There's an expansively long, beautiful and surfable beach with outdoor touristy shopping stalls not far away. Some relatively traffic-free back streets make for pleasant local exploration. Naturally there are plenty of seafood palapa eateries lining the beach, and some good expat-run restaurants sit further inland. From December to March you can go on whale-watching trips. All this, along with a less-harried feel than Puerto Vallarta, makes for a worthy day trip – and there are some decent places to stay if you decide to stretch your visit a bit longer.

Bucerías consists of just a few very long blocks paralleling the beach and Hwy 200. It's a three-stoplight town. The **post office** serves the country from 8am to 3pm Monday to Friday and 8am to noon Saturday, and there's Internet service at **Sandrina's** restaurant for US$2 per 30 minutes.

Surf Shops There were two surf shops at research time, though one seemed to be shutting down. The other, **Coral Reef Surf Shop** (☎ 298-02-61; Heroes de Nacozari & Melgar; open 9am-7pm Mon-Sat) is a full service shop that rents long boards (US$22 per day) and boogie boards (US$8 per day). Long- and short-boards are for sale. Surf lessons and guides/boats for both local and long-distance trips are also offered, as are whale-watching tours in season.

Places to Stay Bucerías can easily be seen in a day, but if you want to stick around and savor some time away from Vallarta there are a few places to hang your towel.

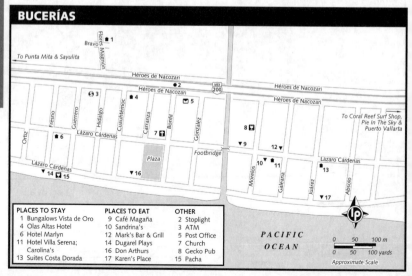

BUCERÍAS

To Punta Mita & Sayulita

Bravo

Flores Magnón

Héroes de Nacozari
Héroes de Nacozari
Héroes de Nacozari
Héroes de Nacozari

MEX 200

To Coral Reef Surf Shop,
Pie In The Sky &
Puerto Vallarta

Fresno
Guerrero
Hidalgo
Cuauhtémoc
Carranza
Bonfil
González
Ortiz
Lázaro Cárdenas
Lázaro Cárdenas
Lázaro Cárdenas
Morelos
Galeana
Juárez
Absolo

Plaza
Footbridge

PACIFIC OCEAN

PLACES TO STAY	PLACES TO EAT	OTHER
1 Bungalows Vista de Oro	9 Café Magaña	2 Stoplight
4 Olas Altas Hotel	10 Sandrina's	3 ATM
6 Hotel Marlyn	12 Mark's Bar & Grill	5 Post Office
11 Hotel Villa Serena;	14 Dugarel Plays	7 Church
Carolina's	16 Don Arthurs	8 Gecko Pub
13 Suites Costa Dorada	17 Karen's Place	15 Pacha

0   50   100 m
0   50   100 yards
Approximate Scale

PUERTO VALLARTA

Olas Altas Hotel (☎ 298-04-07; cnr Heroes de Nacozari & Cuauhtémoc; 1/2 beds US$17/28) is a very *green* (colored) hotel with good, clean, modern and large rooms.

Bungalows Vista de Oro (☎ 298-03-90; cnr Flores Magnón & Bravo; doubles/quads US$17/28) is perched a block east of the highway, on the inland side of town (look for the red pagoda and cross the highway). This friendly, funky-flavored, and pink-themed hotel is terraced up a hillside and comes with two-story pool slide. The big bungalows are good but basic; they're great for large, nonfussy groups.

Posada Don Arthur (Pacífico 6; doubles/quads US$22/44) is highlighted by the biggest sourpuss of a manager in Mexico. The location is central and rooms are large and OK for this budget. Hopefully if the place is sold it will remain a posada.

Hotel Marlyn (☎ 298-04-50; e mahesah@ prodigy.net.mx; Fresno 869; singles/doubles/ triples US$11/22/28) is home to some of the cheapest rooms in town, and despite being old and a bit funky, they're not bad. All have air-con and are sizable. There's a pool in the middle and with any luck there's water in it.

Hotel Villa Serena (☎ 298-12-88; e wwser ena@prodigy.net.mx; Cárdenas 35; rooms US$41 plus tax) provides 10 beautiful, modern rooms with kitchen around a pool courtyard.

Suites Costa Dorada (☎ 298-04-40, 333-825-86-16 in Guadalajara for reservations; w www.scostadorada.com; doubles/triples US$84/99) offers huge suites big enough for the whole family. Kitchens are included.

Bungalows Unelma (☎ 298-00-80; e naz ariocarranza@prodigy.net.mx; Cárdenas 51; doubles US$75 plus tax) is a little paradise of two beachside bungalows surrounded by lush gardens. There's a whole lot of style here; think *Architectual Digest* magazine. Kitchens are fully stocked and one unit comes with air-con. Boogie boards, sea kayaks and hammocks are part of the whole heavenly deal.

Places to Eat Many of Bucerías eateries are operated by expats, and the competition makes for some very yummy high-quality Western food.

Carolina's (☎ 298-08-89; Cárdenas 27; open 8am-2pm daily) brims with breakfasting gringos in the morning. The main attraction: coffee and donuts.

Café Magaña (☎ 298-17-62; near cnr Cárdenas & Morelos; mains US$7-18; open 11:30am-11pm Mon-Wed & Fri, 11am-6pm Thur, 10am-midnight Sat-Sun) prides itself on eight rib sauces, unique cocktails, salads and meat dishes. Californian and Spanish wines offered, there's inside and outside seating and sport is on TV.

Karen's Place (☎ 298-14-99; near Juárez at the beach; open 9am-10pm Tues-Sat, 9am-6pm Sun) spins up thirst-quenching cocktails to go along with their sushi, mahi-mahi and coconut shrimp. Salads and sandwiches are also fixed up. Western-style breakfasts start the day and Sunday brunch (US$11) ends the week.

Marks Bar & Grill (☎ 298-03-03; Cárdenas 56; mains US$9-20; open noon-10:30 daily) has a beautiful, breezy dining room, where you can enjoy a nice cocktail before tucking into that Black Angus New York steak, ricotta ravioli with goat cheese or grilled shrimp in garlic.

Dugarel Plays (☎ 298-1757; Pacífico s/n; mains US$8-17; open 10am-10pm daily) sits on a rickety-looking wooden terrace with great sea views. Most seafood and steak are served, with lots of drinks to accompany the sunset.

Sandrina's (☎ 298-02-73; Cárdenas 33; mains US$4-11; open 9am-10pm Wed-Mon) has a great backyard patio where you can savor Mediterranean chicken, Greek or Caesar salads, hummus, lasagne and souvlaki. It also bakes some great stuff: try the Kahlua flan or chocolate cream cheese brownies. This place is all-gringo – there's even Internet service.

Pie in the Sky (☎ 298-08-38; Heroes de Nacozari 202; open 9am-8pm daily) is practically on the highway at the first stoplight coming into town from Puerto Vallarta. It has established a reputation for heavenly pies, cakes and brownies; breakfast and gourmet coffees are also served.

Bars OK, Bucerías is not the place to get all wild and woolly, but it does support a couple of decent watering holes.

Gecko Pub *(Morelos near Cárdenas; open 1pm-2am daily)* is a small bar that nurses some barstools and a few tables. There's darts, pool and a jukebox. Drinks are two-for-one on some nights and ladies drink free on their nights. Wow!

Pacha *(☎ 298-15-31; Pacífico s/n; open 11am-1am daily)* has a great sea view, and is breezy and serene; not your typical obnoxious bar scene. Here also are a jukebox and pool table, but instead of darts you can talk to the parrot. Live music gets going at around 9am from Thursday to Saturday, and on Sunday it's at 5pm.

Getting There & Away There are buses every 15 minutes from Puerto Vallarta, leaving from across the Sheraton Buganvilias Hotel in Zona Hotelera. The trip takes 30 minutes and costs US$1.30; in Bucerías, get off at the second stoplight and walk inland to the plaza (unless you're only going to Bucerías for brownies at Pie in the Sky; in this case, get off at the first stoplight).

Cruz de Huanacaxtle

Cruz de Huanacaxtle is mostly a nondescript little Mexican fishing town, great for getting a good nondescript-little-Mexican-fishing-town experience. There's a pleasant yacht harbor area where many gringos anchor for free, but no good beach (try Playa Destiladeras a bit farther west). Fishermen sell their catch at the dockside every morning, and there's a village market on Wednesday from 9am to 1pm. Traffic is rare and there's hardly a dash of tourism visible for right now – enjoy it while you can.

Surf Shops If you want to try surfing, boogie boarding or sea kayaking at the beaches farther north, and need some rentals, try **Acción Tropical** *(☎ 329-295-50-87; Langosta 3; open 9am-3:30pm daily)*. Surfboard rentals are US$22 per day and kayaks cost US$33 for three hours. Snorkeling, whale-watching, boating and fishing trips are also available. If they're closed, try knocking on the gate next door (at a decent hour; they live here). There is another store branch at Punta Mita.

Places to Stay & Eat Cruz is easily seen in a couple of hours, but if you feel the need to stay try the decent **Bungalows San Angel** *(Coral 25; singles/doubles US$22)*. For something fancier, ask at the La Luna y Sol restaurant for its gorgeous beachfront casita *(W www.casarentals.com; US$80 for 2)*.

Philo's *(☎ 329-295-50-68; W www.philo hayward.com; Delfín 15; open 10am-5pm & 6pm-10pm Tues-Sun)* is a little bit of everything – restaurant, bar, music studio and cultural center. Here's the line-up: Monday is Monday Night Football; Tuesday is jam session night; Wednesday there's free pool; Thursday is open mike; on Friday and Saturday live music rocks, and Sunday there's more football. Burgers and grilled sandwiches run less than US$5, and yoga,

Bahía de Banderas

The Bay of Flags was supposedly formed by an extinct volcano slowly sinking into the ocean. It now has a depth of some 1800m and is home to an impressive variety of marine life – almost every large marine animal is found here. It's also something of a mating center and marine nursery for several species – for example, giant manta rays mate here in April. During that month they jump above the water's surface, flashing their 4m wide wings in acrobatic displays that you can sometimes see from boats or even from the shore.

Humpbacks are the bay's most numerous and oft-sighted whales – they come here from around November to the end of March to mate, and to bear the calves that were conceived the year before. Bride whales are much less numerous, but unlike humpbacks they are not a migratory whale – they remain in tropical waters all year round, so there's a chance of seeing one at any time of year. Even gray whales, which migrate between Alaska and Baja California every year, are very occasionally seen this far south.

foreign language and guitar classes are also available.

La Luna y Sol (☎/fax 329-295-52-01; Marlin 8; mains US$7-17; open 5pm-11pm daily) is an elegant Canadian-run Italian restaurant with plenty of international wines and some beautiful outdoor seating. Savor seafood cannelloni, chicken cacciatore or the half-rack of pork ribs (all around US$10). There's pizza and bar drinks too.

El Jardín del Pulpo Café (☎ 329-295-53-67; W www.hikuri.com; Coral 66; open 8am-5pm Mon-Sat) is situated in a very peaceful court-yard with gurgling fountain and shady trees. It's a great, easy-going hangout spot – and more than just a café. Wayland and Aruna are Brits who have the all-too-common story of designing and building their own boat (with money made by selling tacos on the streets of London), having a baby, then sailing around Central America for 10 years before finally settling in at Cruz de Huanacaxtle. Here they established a T-shirt printing shop, carpentry, Huichol crafts-center/store and café. Wayland also started a project of building and distributing spinning wheels for Huichol to weave more efficiently. You can see Huichol sandals being made, and a sale percentage of the Huichol-designed T-shirts sold are donated to Huichol projects in Mexico. If that isn't enough to make you feel all fuzzy inside, try the US$3 breakfasts, iced lattes or lemonades.

Getting There & Away It's easy to reach Cruz de Huanacaxtle: simply hop on a north-pointing Punta Mita bus anywhere along the Zona Hotelera (US$1.50, every 15 minutes).

Playa Anclote
Almost at the very northern tip of Bahía de Banderas is the **Punta Mita peninsula**. Here lie some creamy strands of beaches, including Playa Anclote, which is popular with surfers and boogie boarders. Ubiquitous seafood palapa restaurants on the beach offer great views of the bay and a distant Puerto Vallarta. Not a bad deal for those who also come to enjoy the beach, go on boat trips or try their balance in the surf.

If you want to get out on the water, visit **Acción Tropical**, across from the palapa restaurants on the beach road – it does boat trips in the bay (including snorkeling, and whale-watching in season). It also rents surfboards: to catch some waves, call the Cruz de Huanacaxtle **main store** (☎ 329-295-5087) ahead of time to make sure there are boards available for rent at Playa Anclote. There are a few other establishments that give tours from this beach.

There's at least one place to stay in town: **Servicios de Foto y Video** (☎ 329-291-62-84; Robalo 112). Sure, it's mainly a friendly photo store, but it also has three basic and clean bungalows (US$28) out back.

To get to Playa Anclote, simply take any Punta Mita bus roaming north on the Zona Hotelera (US$1.50, every 15 minutes) and get off at Nuevo Corral del Risco, the town above Playa Anclote.

BEACHES & TOWNS SOUTH OF PUERTO VALLARTA
South of town, off scenic Hwy 200, are the beaches of **Conchas Chinas**, **Estacas**, **Los Venados**, **Punta Negra**, **Garza Blanca** and **Gemelas**. And above this beautiful shoreline (and blessed with gorgeous sea views) perch upscale hotels, timeshare condominiums and private villas owned by some very rich and lucky types.

Near these beaches and also located further south are the hamlets of **El Nogalito**, **Playa Mismaloya**, **Boca de Tomatlán**, **Las Ánimas**, **Quimixto** and **Yelapa** – these last three are reachable only by boat. There are also quite a few upscale restaurants, both near the highway and further inland, which for some folks are a worthy destination in themselves.

El Nogalito
This small inland riverside community, about 5km south of Puerto Vallarta and 1km inland, has some good potential for exploration as well as being home to at least one three-legged dog. Hang out here, enjoy the beautiful river and surrounding jungle, and take a hike to some waterfalls. Despite its proximity to Hwy 200, tourism has not

taken a serious foothold, so don't expect too many services.

If you want to stay, try the riverside **Trailer Park & Bungalows El Nogalito** (☎ 221-54-19; sites US$11, rooms US$17). It's not unpleasant, though rooms are pretty basic. Kitchens are available for US$5 more. There are only two trailer or camp sites.

Mismaloya

The small but attractive and busy cove beach of Mismaloya, about 12km south of Puerto Vallarta, was the location for the Elizabeth Taylor/Richard Burton flick *The Night of the Iguana*. It's now dominated by the 303-room La Jolla de Mismaloya hotel (see Places to Stay in Puerto Vallarta earlier for details), and the buildings used in the film (look towards the south side of the cove) live on as seafood restaurants. There are also plenty of tourist shopping stalls and people enjoying many water activities – not quite the scene for those seeking enlightenment, at least in the traditional vein. To reach Mismaloya Beach take the coastal bus (see Puerto Vallarta's Getting Around section) and get dropped off right after the Hotel La Jolla de Mismaloya.

From Mismaloya you can head inland along a riverside dirt road to a couple of rustic yet upscale restaurants notable for lush outdoor locations and being able to function without electricity or telephone. Horses can be hired at Mismaloya for the ride up. Take insect repellant.

Chino's Paraíso (mains US$11-21; open 11am-5pm daily) is located where relaxing tiers of palapa-covered tables decorate rocky ledges on both sides of a river (cross a footbridge). It's about 1.5km from Mismaloya and there's a swimming hole – bring your swimsuit and towel. Seafood and meats are on the menu, but try to avoid being here between 1pm and 3pm, when hungry tour groups arrive for lunch. Look for iguanas; they'll be checking you out.

El Edén (mains US$10-18; open 11am-5pm daily) is worth it if you've hired a horse or taxi, or have wheels; only serious hikers will enjoy the long and dusty walk up (3km further upriver from Chino's, and about 4.5km total from Mismaloya and the highway). The trip rewards you with another pleasant restaurant overlooking the same river. It's still airy but more closed in than Chino's. There are hikes and waterfalls in the area. Also, note the helicopter skeleton lying near the stairs; it was used in Arnold's flick *Predator*.

Back on the highway, going south towards Boca de Tomatlán, is yet another noteworthy restaurant, at least for those of us with fat wallets.

Le Kliff (☎ 228-06-66; Hwy 200 Km 17.5; mains US$14-28; open noon-10pm daily) brags about being the best whale-watching spot in Vallarta...and they may be right. Its dramatic cliff-hanging locale is matched by a super seafood menu – try the tequila jumbo shrimp (US$28) or go all the way with the seafood carousel, a lobster-shrimp-fish combination (US$86 for two).

Boca de Tomatlán

About 4km past Mismaloya, Boca de Tomatlán is a peaceful, less commercialized seaside village in a small cove where the Río de Tomatlán meets the sea – a jungly place with quiet water, a nice beach and several small restaurants. *Pangas* depart from the beach here to the havens of Las Ánimas, Quimixto and Yelapa, among other places. To find an isolated paradise, pick a beach not mentioned in this guidebook.

The highway swings inland from Boca, and you can follow it 5km to the pricey restaurant **Chico's Paradise** (☎ 222-07-47; Hwy 200 Km 20; mains US$11-24; open 10am-6pm daily), which perches above the Río de Tomatlán. Dining areas under rustic palapas look down to idyllic swim holes and small waterfalls, and you can sunbath on large boulders while enjoying the lush jungle backdrop.

Las Ánimas, Quimixto & Yelapa

Farther around the southern side of the bay are the more isolated beaches and pueblos of Las Ánimas, Quimixto and Yelapa, all of which received electricity and telephone service within the past year or two. They are also accessible only by boat – wear your waterproof sandals, as landings are often wet. For transport details see under Getting Around in the Puerto Vallarta section.

Playa de las Ánimas (Beach of the Spirits) is a lovely beach with a small fishing village and some palapa restaurants offering fresh seafood – snorkeling is a popular activity here. It's possible to hike to Quimixto, via an adventurous coast trail, in about an hour.

Quimixto has a mostly thin shoreline lined with seafood restaurants, though just east past a rocky point is a pretty and deserted little beach. There's also a 10m waterfall accessible by an easy half-hour inland hike, which requires four to five shallow river crossings (wear waterproof sandals). Or hire a horse to take you up – this will cost US$6 to US$11, depending how far up the trail you are when you hire the horse. Two rustic restaurants sell pricey refreshments at the waterfall itself.

Yelapa, farthest from town, is one of Vallarta's most popular boating destinations, and it's home to a sizable colony of foreign residents. Its picturesque beach cove is crowded with restaurants, tourists and parasailers during the day, but empties out when the boats leave in late afternoon. There are plenty of hikes to beaches and waterfalls (head upriver), but just a walk around the funky little town, most of which overlooks the cove, is pleasant. There are quite a few places to stay in here, though you'll have a hard time finding anything cheaper that US$28. And remember, prices can rise if you miss that last boat.

Closest to the beach are the pleasant cabanas at **La Joya de Yelapa** (*doubles US$33*) – look behind Marlin Restaurant. Also nearby is **Hotel Luna Azul** (*☎ 329-80-840; doubles US$28-33*), which has good, bright rooms. **Hotel Lagunita** (*☎/fax 329-80-554; doubles US$77*) is the fanciest place in Yelapa, and has cute palapa cabins.

Way up in town are a couple of difficult-to-find places; try asking for directions. On the main alleyway overlooking the cove is **Casa Jiote**, which has just two rickety but romantic open-air rooms (US$40 each). Farther up the alleyway, towards the mouth of the bay, is friendly **Casa Milagros** (*☎ 329-298-14-70; singles/doubles US$30/40*), a modern spot with 10 simple rooms. The views from the terraces are unbelievable, but you'll have to climb 178 stairs just to reach the place.

El Tuito

After passing Boca de Tomatlán, Hwy 200 curves inland climbs through high pine forests. Then, about 45km south of Puerto Vallarta, it reaches the small, traditional pueblo of El Tuito. While not incredibly impressive from the highway, most of the village stretches east about 2km. It's a pleasant spot if you want to explore a completely untouristy, practically traffic-free and very Mexican place. It's also distinct in that the church is behind the cute plaza and not on it. Be prepared for curious stares, as not many gringos stop here.

There's a unique restaurant nearby, about 1km south past El Tuito and just off the Hwy. Look for signs leading to **Rancho Altamira** (*☎ 322-269-00-35; Km 167*). They're open from 10am to 6pm daily, and offer fishing and horseback tours as well. The open but covered restaurant sits on a lofty knoll overlooking green brushy hills, some agave fields and a pondfull of ducks and geese. Deer, peacocks and ostriches (that's right) scamper around in the distance, and from your aerie a gentle breeze caresses while you wolf down the very generous portions of meats and seafood (US$7 to US$20). Following, cocktails and tequila shots will wriggle and twitch your whiskers.

If you need to spend the night, there's the decent, modern **Hotel Real de Valle** (*☎ 322-269-00-11; rooms US$33-55*) back in town and on the highway. El Tuito is easily reachable by bus from Puerto Vallarta.

Jalisco Coast & Colima

South of Puerto Vallarta, Hwy 200 skirts around the Cabo Corrientes promontory and heads south to hug the coast again. Here begins the stretch of Mexico's Pacific shores known as the Costa Alegre (Happy Coast), an area of many fine, isolated beaches and some of the most luxurious resorts in Mexico. Some gung-ho developers prefer to use the more exotic term 'Mexican Riviera'. It extends all the way to the Melaque and Barra de Navidad region, and is a popular destination for Americans and Canadian 'snowbirds', full-time retirees and short-term vacationers. Despite Mexican federal laws prohibiting privatization of the shoreline, several of the coast's most pristine hideaways (such as Los Ángeles Locos or Playa Careyes) have effectively been commandeered by private interests. Thankfully, several beautiful beaches remain publicly accessible.

Just an hour's drive inland is the small but worthwhile destination of Colima, perched high and dry near two spectacular volcanoes, the active, constantly steaming Volcán de Fuego (3820m), and the extinct, snowcapped Volcán Nevado de Colima (4240m). Both can be reached relatively easily (barring eruptions) if you have a taste for adventure.

COSTA ALEGRE

Many excellent beaches stretch along the coast south of Puerto Vallarta. The Km distances mentioned for destinations are measured on Hwy 200, heading northwest from the junction of Hwys 200 and 80 (the road to Guadalajara) at Melaque.

La Cruz de Loreto

This small village, west of Hwy 200, 90km south of Puerto Vallarta, is adjacent to a wetland estuary and nature reserve. It's also the closest village to one of Mexico's most attractive, ecofriendly and *expensive* all-inclusive hotels.

Hotelito Desconocido (☎ 322-222-25-26, fax 322-223-02-93; 🆆 www.hotelito.com;

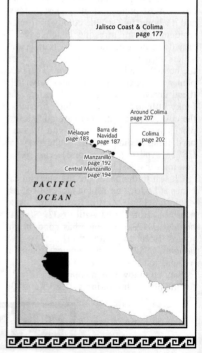

Jalisco Coast & Colima
page 177

Around Colima
page 207

Melaque
page 183

Barra de Navidad
page 187

Colima
page 202

Manzanillo
page 192

Central Manzanillo
page 194

PACIFIC OCEAN

per person US$290-565 Dec 16-Mar 31, US$215-485 Apr 1-Dec 15, plus tax) sits peacefully on a spit of land between the Pacific Ocean and an estuary. This rustic yet luxurious resort offers serenity, scenery and superb cuisine – all of this mostly without electricity. Showers and fans in the romantic waterfront *palafitos* (cabanas on short stilts) are solar-powered, and candles light up the nights. Grounds are beautifully maintained, and preservation of surrounding land is emphasized. There's 65km of beach, the bird-watching is excellent, and a sea turtle protection project operates June to

February – guests can set baby turtles free from September to December. Rates include all meals and activities such as horse riding, kayaking, windsurfing, yoga, and wildlife watching excursions. Spa services will cost you extra.

Quémaro

At Km 83 is the insignificant sign for Quémaro, a small, dusty village of dirt roads and shabby housing. Just past this village, on a short gravel road towards the coast, is one of the fanciest and priciest resorts in all of Mexico.

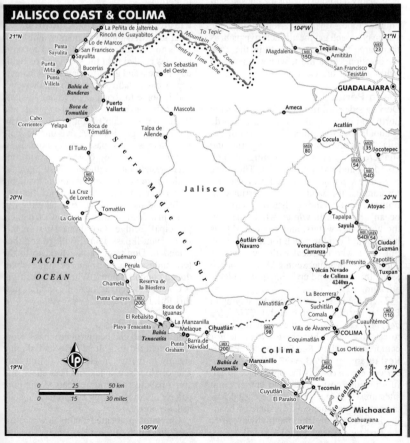

Las Alamandas (☎ 322-285-55-00, fax 322-285-50-27; W www.las-alamandas.com; doubles US$430-1320 Oct 1-May 31, US$320-1060 June 1-Sep 30, with meals add US$180-200 per day, plus tax) is the brainchild of Isabel Goldsmith, granddaughter of Don Antenor Patiño, who made his millions in the tin industry. Luxurious and colorful suites nestle in six separate adobe buildings, all simply beautiful with private terraces or patios. Most have stunning sea views and are surrounded by spacious, well-manicured and palm-studded grounds. There's a nice pool, and the gorgeous beach is basically a private one for the guests. Naturally the service is very top-notch, as is the gourmet food – if you can afford to stay here, you may as well get the all-inclusive plan, as there aren't many restaurants in the area. Reservations are a must; without them you won't get past the security gate.

Playa Pérula
Down a side road from Km 76, towards the north end of tranquil 11km-long Bahía de Chamela, lies the rather bleak town of Perula. Its beach, however, is long, flat and sheltered – great for swimming, boogie boarding and extended walks. There are only a few *palapa* (thatched-roof shelter) restaurants, the sands aren't overrun with tourists, and islands offshore break the ocean's horizon. In winter, whales bask in the warm bay waters, and you can always hire a boat from the beach for fishing trips. For those who can deal with few luxuries and services in an unexciting Mexican beach town, this could end up being quite a pleasant stop.

There are just a few options for staying in Perula: try the cheapie **Hotel CTM** (4/6 people US$22/33), on the main road into town. It's basic, but there's a pool. For campers or trailers, **Red Snapper RV Park & Restaurant** (☎ 315-333-97-84; e redsnapperrv@hotmail.com) is the only place to go: full hookups cost US$11, and gravel camp sites are US$6 per person. The casual restaurant is a good hangout. Get here by heading into town 3km from the highway; after the first *tope* (speed bump) turn left.

Back on the highway at Km 72 is a small cluster of buildings (including a decent restaurant) called 'The Super'. From here a beach road runs 1km to **Paraiso Costa Alegre** (☎ 315-333-97-77; doubles US$65), a deserted-looking hotel pretending to be a resort. The cabanas are pleasant enough and come with sea views, but the whole place could use some maintenance.

Long-distance buses don't head straight into Perula; they stop at The Super. From there, call a taxi – if you're lucky there will be cheaper shared taxis, or *taxi colectivos* (minibus taxis). It's about a 10-minute drive to Perula.

Playas La Negrita & Chamela
Near the Km 64 highway marker, a dirt road leads to a couple of isolated and relaxing beaches nestled in at the south end of Bahía de Chamela and great for day trips. Chamela beach has a calm shore with small waves and is home to four palapa restaurants and some fishing boats. The feel is small and local, so if you don't want to see any gringos this is a good shot. A five-minute walk from here and just past a rocky point is La Negrita, 50m of tiny cove beach with one small restaurant. Neither of these places is built up, so no accommodation is available (other than possibly camping – ask first).

To find these little havens, take the dirt road just 30m south of yellow 'Chamela principal' bridge. Go about 1km on this road – you'll pass a small village and then a lagoon. Don't follow the fork up to the left, unless you want to see some abandoned condominiums. Where it forks right is Chamela beach; at the stony end just past this fork is La Negrita.

Playa Careyitos
Another small and beautiful beach is Careyitos, sheltered in a dune cove and sloping steeply to the water. Here you'll find only friendly locals, a snack and beer shack and some fishing cooperative boats. A big pink palapa building sits as a landmark on the hillside above.

Careyitos is located 200m down a dirt road just south of the white Careyes bridge (*not* the nearby Careyitos bridge) at Km 52. Look for a bus stop shed.

Hacienda de Cuixmalá

At Km 44, just north of the Río Cuitzmala bridge, is the organic farm and ranch of Mercedes Gargollo, ecologist and homesteader extraordinaire. Her purpose is to educate Mexicans to appreciate and conserve the natural resources and biodiversity of the region. On her lands are agricultural plots, mango orchards, cattle pastures and a small number of buildings, one of which is the B&B **La Casa Azul** (☎ *315-351-02-72;* e *cutzmalan@yahoo.com.mx; singles/doubles with breakfast US$41/66)*. Three simple but comfortable rooms open to a common living room area, great for relaxing. There's a simple kitchen, but no phone or TV. Mercedes provides free access to the beach, and turtle project tours are given during season. On the property are a few short walking trails and some lush jungle. There are plans to build more trails and a café at the farm's entrance; a tiny organic product store already exists here, run by Mercedes' daughters. This is a good place for those in search of peace and tranquility, with a touch of political correctness.

Biologists interested in the nearby **Reserva de la Biosfera Cuixmala-Chamela**, off-limits to the general public, can contact Mercedes for more information.

Playas Las Brisas & La Chica

These two beaches head off in opposite directions from the cute village of **Arroyo Seco**, about 4km down a dirt road from the highway at Km 36.

When you find the school yard with a mural of Snow White, turn right 90 degrees and go 1.5 km past farmland and a red gate. A nice beach with latte-colored sand, no services and few people awaits between two headlands.

To get to Las Brisas, turn left at the schoolyard and right at the fork. Go past farmland about 1.5km and you'll reach the sea. Here too there no services, though camping and RV parking are possible under the palmy area (someone may turn up to

collect a small property use fee). The long, flat beach has very surfable waves and little competition for them.

Playa Tecuán

About 10km off the highway at Km 33 lie the pristine shores of Playa Tecuán. And, high above the beach, is the abandoned resort of Hotel Tucuán, a spooky skeleton of door-less rooms, broken windows and caved-in beamed hallways just waiting to be turned into the snazziest youth hostel in existence. Horror film buffs might know this was the location for the slasher flick *I Still Know What You Did Last Summer*. You can still see steel kitchen freezers and bats in the pantries. It's a cool experience and worth getting to if you've got wheels – but remember to be respectful, as it's still considered private property.

The 2km road going south along Playa Tecuán is actually part of an old landing strip. It passes a private housing complex on the mountain and eventually peters out at the edge of a pretty lagoon.

Tenacatita

The highway Km 30 sign marks the way to Tenacatita, a town on the western promontory of **Bahía Tenacatita** which boasts three separate beaches. As you drive the 8.5km into town from the highway, you pass **Playa Mar Abierto** on the right, which extends for kilometers back to the north towards **Playa Tecuán**. You then hit **Playa Tenacatita** itself, which is lined with palapa seafood restaurants but remains beautiful, wide and calm. And over to the right a bit, just over a small hill and tucked into some headlands in between these larger two beaches, are the tiny twin shores of **Playa Mora**. The snorkeling is great in the crystal-clear waters around the protected rocks here.

A mangrove lagoon backing onto Playa Tenacatita is home to scores of birds and sunning reptiles. Boat tours of El Manglar (the Mangrove) are available; ask at the **Fiesta Mexicana Restaurant**. Trips take one hour and cost US$28 per boatload up to six; each extra person pays US$3 (up to 10 total). Bring insect repellent.

Places to Stay & Eat RVs can try the unofficial **free sites** at Playa Mora – space is limited here, so be considerate. **Camping** is good on the main beach, though you may need to ask permission.

Hotel Paraíso de Tenacatita (*☎ 01-314-353-69-23; doubles US$28*) offers adequate rooms, though there's no hot water. It's the orange building just beyond the last palapa restaurant towards the south.

Las Villetas Suites (*☎ 315-355-53-54 in Barra de Navidad; doubles US$100*) has nine very pleasant suites with kitchen, sofa areas and beach views. There's also a pool and Jacuzzi, but the electricity and water supply don't always function properly here. To find this place, just look for the loudest building on the beach (it's bright pink and 200m further south from Hotel Paraíso de Tenacatita).

If you can't find a room at either of these places, try **Hotel Costa Alegre** (*☎ 351-51-21; doubles US$28*), on the main road in El Rebalsito, the service town between the highway and Tenacatita. It has air-con, hot water and large, modern rooms.

Seafood **palapas** provide most of the nourishment here, though they cater to day-trippers and thus tend to close at 6pm or 7pm. For late meals try **Hotel Paraíso de Tenacatita**.

Boca de Iguanas

Smack in the middle of Bahía Tenacatita lies the wide, long, and very pleasant beach of Boca de Iguanas (Km 19). The surf is mild, the sand is hot and wonderful, and the beach is quite shallow for a long way out, making it good for a swim (just don't go past the rocky point). And the palm-fringed bay curves uninterrupted around all the way to La Manzanilla, making for tranquil hour-long walks along a firm waterline. An abandoned hotel nearby adds visual interest and curiosity (clue: propane explosion).

There's a couple of beachside RV parks, two 'hotels', a restaurant, and the adjacent small lagoon is home to a very large crocodile. Don't let your young 'uns or dogs run amok without checking where the reptile is sunning itself, but don't let him scare you off either – he's a big sweetie, at least from afar.

Places to Stay & Eat Unmemorable accommodation for up to four people can be had at **Entre Palmeras** (*☎ 33-36-13-67-35 in Guadalajara; camp sites per person US$3.50, rooms/bungalows US$22/44*). Camp sites are cheap and OK but not right on the beach. The best thing here is the restaurant, which has views of the small lagoon and sometimes Señor Cocodrilo.

Boca de Iguana Camping & Trailer Park (*camping per person US$5.50, trailer sites US$15*) sits on beach, with pleasant sites under peaceful palms.

Boca Beach Trailer Park (*☎ 317-381-03-93; e bocabeach@hotmail.com; trailer sites US$15, camping per person US$7*) is the biggest of all, complete with more than 60 palmy sites.

Coconuts by the Sea (*☎ 33-38-63-15; e cocos@ciber.net.mx; apartments US$75*) perches itself high on the bluff above the beach, with grand views to the other side of the bay. The two extremely comfortable and charming apartments are very welcoming: both have full kitchens (bring food), cable TV, air-con, king-size beds and patios. Plans are afoot for a third apartment. There's a small pool on a grassy cliff. Getting there is tricky; phone or email beforehand.

La Manzanilla
☎ 315

At the sheltered, southern end of Bahía Tenacatita basks the peaceful, dusty little town of La Manzanilla (Km 13). It's home to some decent restaurants, an agreeable beach, a few expat residents and many more locals. Tourism still hasn't quite caught on here (there's no Internet café yet), but the town has grown mightily during past few years.

At northern end of the main road in town is a lagoon filled with...large crocodiles! They haul themselves up on the sandy beach to sun themselves. Some lurk in the water like sinister logs. A viewing platform is being built over the lagoon and beach area to prevent folks from approaching the crocs too closely and getting munched.

For those who get dragged into the lagoon but manage to escape, there's a **lavandería** (wash & dry per kg US$1; open 9am-2pm & 3pm-5pm Mon-Sat) across the street from Chava's Café.

Get out on the water with **Immersion Adventures** (☎/fax 351-53-41; W www.immersionadventures.com) and go on some cool kayak-snorkeling tours of the area. Half-day/full-day tours cost US$55/95-105 per person and include kayaks, snorkeling gear and a snack or lunch. Surf, mangrove and other custom tours are possible, and all experience levels are accommodated. You can also just rent his kayaks. Dave, the manager's, office is at his home, on the road into town (look for the A-frame sign).

Places to Stay At the northern end of town just past the crocodiles' lagoon, is **RV parking** (sites US$2, no hookups or services). Find a pleasant shady site that appeals, and pay the man snoozing under a palm. **Campamento Ecologico** is a 10-minute walk farther down the beach; Jorge's camp sites will set you back US$3.50 per person and include basic showers and toilets.

Hotel Posada del Cazador (☎ 351-50-00; Asunción 183; singles/doubles US$14/17) is bare-bones, budget and bleak, but basically bearable without breaking the bank.

Hotel La Manzanilla (rooms US$14) sits up the side street around the corner from Hotel Posada del Cazador. Large, clean and spartan rooms surround a slightly funky old courtyard garden. Kitchen use is included.

Hotel Posada Tonalá (☎ 351-54-74; e posadatonalahotel@prodigy.net.mx; Asunción 75; rooms US$45) comes modern and shiny-tile clean, with nice wood details and pleasing architecture. Spacious rooms include TV, fans and whimsically-carved wooden furniture. Most face into a modern palapa patio area where breakfast costs US$3 to US$4. There's Internet access for guests.

Casa Maguey (☎ 351-50-12; W www.casamaguey.com; bungalows US$50-80) has three bungalows, perched above the southern end of the beach and surrounded by a lush, hilly garden, are all charmingly different. Each is like a home and wonderfully decorated with Mexican tiles. RSVP if you want a hope of staying here in high season.

La Casa de Maria (☎ 351-50-44; W www.lamanzanilla.com/maria.html; cnr Los Angeles Locos & Conca Molida; apartments US$45-66) has five peaceful, artistically decorated and very spacious apartments, all with private patios. María is the gracious host and opens her rooftop palapa terrace to community teaching projects such as art, yoga, meditation, cooking or dance (teachers with project ideas can contact her). Her house is one street south of the main road into town.

Palapa Joe's Restaurant & Bungalows (☎ 351-53-48; Asunción 163; bungalows US$66) has two big bungalows in a peaceful backyard garden. The decor is gorgeous, there's cable TV and you can hang out in the cool covered rooftop terrace with Jacuzzi.

Places to Eat For a casual seafood palapa on the beach, try **Restaurant Rincón** (mains US$4.50-11; open 8am-6pm daily). It has, in our opinion, the best shrimp ceviche in Mexico (US$7) and the fish fillet al mojo de ajo (US$4.50) is excellent. Round it all out with a coconut drink (US$1).

Restaurant El Quetzal (☎ 351-52-76; Asunción 13; mains US$4-12; open noon-11pm Mon-Sat) sits underneath a rather gloomy indoor palapa, but the Mexican–quasi-French menu is interesting – it ranges from pozole (a kind of hearty stew) to duck in Dijon sauce.

Palapa Joe's Restaurant & Bungalows (mains US$4-8; open 9am-noon & 6pm-10pm) offers tasty food, like roasted herb chicken or beer-battered shrimp, plus CNN on TV.

Martin's Restaurant (☎ 351-51-06; Playa Blancas; mains US$7-12; open 8:30am-11:30pm daily) prepares some wonderful gourmet seafood, meats, soups, salads and fajitas. The 2nd-floor open palapa is romantically lit at night, and service is first-rate. The restaurant is on the main road at the south end of town.

Chava's Café (Asunción; open 7am-4pm daily) is a tiny but popular place near Hotel Posada Tonalá that caters primarily to breakfasting gringos.

Playa Cuastecomate

About 3km west of Melaque is this pleasant beach with mocha-colored sands and a full line-up of palapa restaurants. It's in a little cove within the Bahía de Cuastecomate – you can hardly see open ocean for all the enclosing mountainsides. Calm waters make for safe swimming and good snorkeling, and you can explore the village and surrounding hills. There's only one hotel, the resort wanna-be **Royale Costa Azul** (☎ 315-355-5730; doubles US$45).

MELAQUE
☎ 315 • pop 8000

Officially named San Patricio-Melaque (the name of two original *haciendas*), Melaque (meh-**lah**-kay) is an area that actually encompasses three different neighborhoods: Melaque, San Patricio and Villa Obregon. To make things easier, though, both locals and tourists generally refer to the whole enchilada as Melaque.

Located approximately 60km southeast of Chamela on lovely and calm Bahía de Navidad, Melaque doesn't have the small-town touristy charm of its southern neighbor Barra de Navidad, though it holds its own as a decent Mexican beach town. A nearby naval base keeps crime low, and its sheltered bay location means warmer temperatures than other surrounding areas. From December to April, the population doubles as snowbird Canadians fly in, and during the school holidays Mexican families snap up hotel rooms. And if you're here in March, witness the town's famous week-long St Patrick's Day celebrations (Fiesta de San Patricio).

And what would a Mexican beach town around here be without its own abandoned hotel? The crumbling ruins of the Casa Grande Hotel, now home to squatter families, are an imposing reminder of the 1995 earthquake and subsequent *maremotos* (tidal waves) that paid the region an expensive visit.

Orientation

Everything in Melaque is within walking distance. Most of the hotels, restaurants and public services are situated on or near east-west Gómez Farías, which parallels the beach, and the north-south street López

Mateos, which exits to Hwy 200. Building numbers on Gómez Farías and some other streets are not consecutive – refer to the map for locations. Barra de Navidad is 5km southeast of Melaque via Hwy 200 or 2.5km by walk along the beach.

Information

Barra's tourist office has some basic information on Melaque.

Banamex (open 9am-3pm Mon-Fri), near the bus terminal on Gómez Farías, has an ATM but doesn't change cash or traveler's checks. For these services go to nearby **Casa de Cambio Melaque** (open 9am-2pm & 4pm-7pm Mon-Sat, 9am-2pm Sun).

The **post office** (cnr Orozco & Corona; open 8am-3pm Mon-Fri, 8am-noon Sat) flies your mail home. There are several **casetas teléfonicas** (public telephone call stations) with fax (cnr Morelos & Hidalgo; open 8am-10pm daily • Corona 65; open 9am-3pm & 4pm-8:30pm Mon-Sat, 9am-2pm Sun).

And for your duds, there's the no-name **lavandería** (Gómez Farías near Vallarta; open 9am-6pm Mon-Sat) and **Lavandería Francia** (Juárez near Hidalgo; open 9am-9pm daily). Both charge about US$1.25 per kilogram for wash and dry.

Internet junkies have quite a few outlets, such as **Centro Virtu@l Internet** (cnr Corona & López Mateos; US$2.50 per hour; open 9am-6pm Mon-Sat, 9am-2pm Sun), **El Navigante** (Gómez Farías 48; US$4 per hour; open 8:30am-2:30pm & 5pm-9pm Mon-Sat, 10am-2pm Sun), **Ciber@Net** (cnr Carranza & Gómez Farías; US$4 per hour; open 9:30am-2:30pm & 4pm-7:30pm Mon-Fri, 9:30am-2:30pm Sat) and **Paris Internet Café** (cnr López Mateos & Morelos; US$2.50 per hour; open 8am-3pm & 6pm-9pm Fri-Wed).

Things to See & Do

Other than your typical beach activities – swimming, relaxing, walking to the next town (in this case, Barra de Navidad) – you can check out the town's *zócalo* (main plaza) and small **market**. A **flea market** (tianguis) is held every Wednesday starting around 8am, on Orozco two blocks east of the plaza.

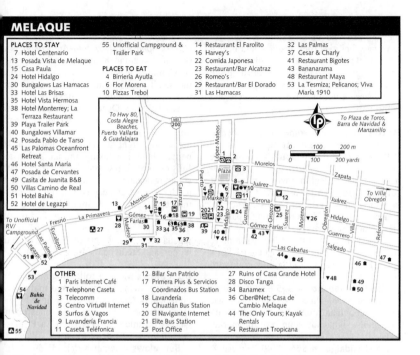

MELAQUE

PLACES TO STAY
7 Hotel Centenario
13 Posada Vista de Melaque
15 Casa Paula
24 Hotel Hidalgo
30 Bungalows Las Hamacas
33 Hotel Las Brisas
35 Hotel Vista Hermosa
38 Hotel Monterrey; La Terraza Restaurant
39 Playa Trailer Park
40 Bungalows Villamar
42 Posada Pablo de Tarso
45 Las Palomas Oceanfront Retreat
46 Hotel Santa María
47 Posada de Cervantes
49 Casita de Juanita B&B
50 Villas Camino de Real
51 Hotel Bahía
52 Hotel de Legazpi

55 Unofficial Campground & Trailer Park

PLACES TO EAT
4 Birriería Ayutla
6 Flor Morena
10 Pizzas Trebol

14 Restaurant El Farolito
16 Harvey's
22 Comida Japonesa
23 Restaurant/Bar Alcatraz
26 Romeo's
29 Restaurant/Bar El Dorado
31 Las Hamacas

32 Las Palmas
37 Cesar & Charly
41 Restaurant Bigotes
43 Bananarama
48 Restaurant Maya
53 La Tesmiza; Pelicanos; Viva María 1910

OTHER
1 Paris Internet Café
2 Telephone Caseta
3 Telecomm
5 Centro Virtu@l Internet
8 Surfos & Vagos
9 Lavandería Francia
11 Caseta Teléfonica

12 Billar San Patricio
17 Primera Plus & Servicios Coordinados Bus Station
18 Lavandería
19 Cihuatlán Bus Station
20 El Navigante Internet
21 Elite Bus Station
25 Post Office

27 Ruins of Casa Grande Hotel
28 Disco Tanga
34 Banamex
36 Ciber@Net; Casa de Cambio Melaque
44 The Only Tours; Kayak Rentals
54 Restaurant Tropicana

If you're adventurous, head out on the trail past the unofficial RV/camping ground area west of town. You'll pass the very visible military terrace (unfortunately off-limits) to various rocky points and **rocky beaches** beyond; some light but potentially dangerous rock-scampering is required at times, and for God's sake keep an eye on the tide levels. Don't plan on swimming back here: the gravel beach is steep and the backwash unforgiving, but there probably won't be too many folks around to share the wonderful beach and cliff views.

For mountain bike rentals go to **The Only Tours** (☎ 355-67-77; Las Cabañas 26), which rents them for US$6/9 a half/full day. Also available here are snorkeling tours (US$14) and Colima tours (US$33).

The town's patron saint, St Patrick, is celebrated in a big way, with weeklong festivities leading up to **St Patrick's Day**, March 17 – parties all day, rodeos, carnival, music, dances and a fiesta with fireworks every

night in the plaza. The 17th begins with a mass and the blessing of the fishing fleet. Take care when the *borrachos* (drunks) take over after dark.

Places to Stay

Rates vary greatly depending on the season; the town fills up with families during Mexican school holidays in July and August, in December and at Semana Santa (Easter), when prices are higher and it's best to reserve ahead. The rest of the year it's pretty quiet, and many hotels will give discounts. Bungalows are common and cheaper by the week.

Camping There are two popular camping options conveniently located in town.

Playa Trailer Park (☎ 355-50-65; Gómez Farías 250; camp sites US$5 per person, full hookups for 2 US$17, US$2 per extra person) has a 45-space beachfront RV park under the radio tower.

The unofficial beachfront **camp ground** at the far west end of La Primavera doesn't have any facilities (buy water – and beer – from trucks that make the rounds), but the price is right: US$2.25 for a RV or camp site in the high season. Nearby palapa restaurants charge a nominal fee for showers and bathrooms.

Hotels You've got some choice when it comes to hotels here in Melaque.

Posada Vista de Melaque (☎ 355-62-19; *per person US$5.50; cnr La Primavera & Madero*) is the best deal in town, especially for solo travelers. The location isn't great (inland on a big street), but rooms are newish and come with TV. Look for the painted sign 'Hotel Economico'.

Casa Paula (☎ 355-50-93; *Vallarta 6; singles/doubles US$11/17*) is a backpacker's special: worn, cheap and homey courtyard rooms with bath.

Hotel Centenario (☎ 355-63-08; *Corona 38; singles/doubles/triples US$11/18/24*) has nine small, clean rooms. It's friendly, with the smells, sights and sounds of the market outside.

Hotel Hidalgo (☎ 355-50-45; *Hidalgo 7; singles/doubles/triples US$17/19/22*) comes with kitchen use and a small central courtyard where washing takes place. Get a brighter upper-level room.

Hotel Bahía (☎ 355-56-81; *Legazpi 5; singles/doubles/triples US$17/22/28*) claims the 'best in town' award for clean, modern, neat, nicely finished rooms. Add friendly management, available kitchen use and closeness to the beach and you'll want to hike it here to the west end.

Hotel Santa María (☎ 355-56-77; *Salgado 85; singles/doubles/quads US$17/25/45*) sits on a dusty street in Villa Obregon. It has fair and spacious but darkish rooms, agreeable if you want the beach *right there*. It's an OK budget choice, and there's a pool.

Hotel de Legazpi (☎/fax 355-53-97; *Las Palmas 3; doubles/triples US$40/44, US$5 extra with kitchenette*) sits near the beach and boasts a swimming pool and 16 large, bright rooms, some with a balcony and sea view. There's a garden and flowery bedspreads too.

Casita de Juanita B&B (☎ 355-62-18; e *casamarr@hotmail.com; Fco Villa 5; rooms US$50; open mid-Nov–mid-April only*) is a private Canadian household offering just two homey, pleasing rooms. Guests can use the small patio, common living room and rooftop terrace with hammocks.

Las Palomas Oceanfront Retreat (☎/fax 355-53-45; w *www.tomzap.com/lapaloma .html; Las Cabañas 13; studios US$70-90*) encompasses eight studio apartments for 16 people. Each is relaxing, unique and tastefully decorated, and some have terraces with stunning ocean views. Luxuries include lush gardens, a great beachside pool, complimentary breakfast, a small library and a shared kitchen. There's an art studio and drawing, painting, basketry and mask-making classes given. Reservations are a must in winter, and credit cards are not accepted.

Bungalows Most of following beachfront digs have swimming pools and multiroom units with kitchens. All are cheaper by the week or month. There are also cheap bungalows on inland streets from La Primavera, on the west side of town.

Bungalows Villamar (☎/fax 355-50-05; *Hidalgo 1; singles/doubles/triples/quads US$17/26/32/43*) exudes a slightly funky feel with its five spacious but worn garden bungalows and a beachfront terrace. The owner Roberto speaks English.

Posada Pablo de Tarso (☎ 355-51-17; *Gómez Farías 408; singles/doubles with aircon US$22/41, bungalows from US$53*) has good, nicely tiled rooms with TV, dark beams and short beds. Common areas are attractive, and the garden leads to the beach.

Bungalows Las Hamacas (☎/fax 355-51-13; *Gómez Farías 13; singles/doubles US$27/36; bungalows from US$57*) is roomy, but nothing special except for the beach, which is very close. Secure parking and an inexpensive restaurant top the deal.

Hotel Monterrey (☎ 355-50-04; *Gómez Farías 27; singles/doubles/triples US$35/40/43*) offers a fair deal in its semimodern and spacious rooms. Beachfront terraces, sea views, a restaurant/bar and parking are a nice touch, too.

Hotel Vista Hermosa (☎ 355-50-02; Gómez Farías 23; singles/doubles US$42/50, bungalows from US$80) isn't a sock knocker-offer, but does have a great beach area, and some of the standard rooms come with a decent view.

Hotel Las Brisas (☎/fax 355-51-08; Gómez Farías 9; singles/doubles/triples US$36/50/70, bungalows from US$70) has OK but unspectacular rooms with fridge, air-con and TV. Surrounding them are very pleasant common areas with kitchen.

Posada de Cervantes (☎/fax 355-65-74; e posadadecervantes@hotmail.com; Salgado 132; bungalows US$66-72) is a pleasant little place, with friendly management and a nice lobby area. Seven bungalows with TV and air-con are well decorated and maintained.

Places to Eat

From 6pm to midnight, **food carts** serve inexpensive Mexican fare a block east of the plaza along Juárez; a bellyfull of *carne asada* (grilled beef) costs around US$3. Lots of little eateries await along Corona in the two market alleys on either side of López Mateos, including **juguerías** (juice stands) that whip up fresh fruit and vegetable drinks.

La Terraza (Gómez Farías 27; breakfast US$3-4; open 8am-11pm daily) is located at Hotel Monterrey and serves a kick-ass breakfast. Try the veggie omelet, French toast and/or bacon. Servings are generous and tasty, and the upstairs open patio is pretty nice too.

Bananarama (cnr Gómez Farías & Orozco; breakfast US$3-4, mains US$4.50-8; open 7am-noon & 5pm-9pm daily) is popular with gringos for breakfast (omelets and waffles) though the coffee is not great. Van Morrison music is likely to entertain you in the large, concrete back patio. Burgers, pastas and specials are served for dinner.

Harvey's (cnr Gómez Farías & Vallarta; breakfast US$4; open 7am-noon daily) sports sidewalk seating and a casual patio out back. Enjoy Western-style breakfasts (fluffy pancakes, bacon) and good coffee.

Paris Internet Café (cnr López Mateos & Morelos; open 8am-3pm & 6pm-9pm Fri-Wed) is a tiny café with Internet access, but it also serves baked goods, coffee (they're trying to fix the espresso machine) and a few lunch items.

Restaurant El Farolito (Vallarta 53; mains US$3.50-8; open 8am-10pm Fri-Wed) is family-run, small and friendly. It also serves breakfast, so if Harvey's is full around the corner consider coming here.

Flor Morena (Juarez s/n; mains US$1-3; open 6pm-11pm Tues-Sun) remains popular for its inexpensive *pozoles*, but tamales, tacos and other Mexican mainstays also arrive fresh and tasty. Vegetarians have some options here too.

Birriería Ayutla (☎ 355-55-70; Corona 40; mains US$3-4; open 8am-3pm Sat-Thur) cooks up some mighty fine *birria de chivo* (goat stew). It's a very casual Mexican joint, with goat skins on the benches and deer heads on the walls.

Comida Japonesa (cnr López Mateos & Corona; mains US$3.50-6.50; open 11am-5pm Tues-Sat) cooks and rolls up teriyaki, gyoza, sushi, curry dishes and generous lunch specials, with quality ingredients that make this 10-seater luncheonette ridiculously popular with both locals and foreigners. The Japanese family busy running this place will make you wonder how (and why) they got to Melaque, of all places. Try the Calpico drink.

Restaurant/Bar Alcatraz (cnr López Mateos & Gómez Farías; mains US$7-9; open 5:30pm-10:30pm daily) perches cheerfully on the 2nd floor under a lofty palapa, serving seafood, kebabs and burgers, along with a few cocktails to swizzle your stick.

Romeo's (☎ 355-68-00; Moreno 9; mains US$7-8; open 5:30pm-10:30pm daily Dec-Apr) is a small Canadian-run restaurant with good Italian food like baked garlic, pizza and pastas. The upstairs patio is intimate and pleasant, and the restaurant has wines from France, Italy, Chile, California and Mexico.

Restaurant Maya (Obregón 1; w www.restaurantmaya.com; mains US$7-14; open noon-3pm & 6pm-10:30pm Tues-Sat, 11:30am-2:30pm & 6pm-10pm Sun) is good for fine cuisine. The open kitchen whips up dishes like Thai prawn curry, prosciutto-wrapped fish fillet and barbecue ribs. Reservations are recommended; email them up to the night before, and check the website for the current menu.

There are several more upmarket bars and restaurants right on the beach.

Cesar & Charly (☎ 355-56-53; Gómez Farías 27A; breakfast US$3-5, dinner US$4.50-9; open 7:30am-10pm daily) serves good, varied fare on the beach, and has a great casual ambience and eager waiters.

Restaurant Bigotes (south end of López Mateos; seafood US$3.50-7; open 8am-10pm daily) relies on seafood and burgers to please its patrons; the 2pm to 9pm happy hour is icing on the cake. Watch soccer on TV while sitting under the casual beachfront palapa, and order an alligator tail, salty dog or dirty mother to keep you company. The piña colada served in a coconut (US$3.50) is especially tasty.

A row of pleasant palapa restaurants stretches along the beach at the west end of town – most are open 9am to 6pm. **Pelicanos** (open to 10pm), **Restaurant La Tesmiza** and **Viva María 1910** are popular and good. The fancy **Restaurant/Bar El Dorado** (open 8am-11pm) has live music on weekends. Nearby, **Las Palmas** and **Las Hamacas** are much more casual and cheaper.

Entertainment

On Sunday nights, the locals gather in the plaza to snack, socialize and enjoy the balmy evening air. During the spring and winter, *corridas de toros* (bullfights) occasionally liven up the bullring off Hwy 200 near the Barra turnoff. Watch for flyers promoting *charreadas* (rodeos), and keep an ear out for cruising cars with megaphones mounted on their roofs scratchily announcing *béisbol* games, *fútbol* matches and the anticipated arrival of the circus during the hot summer months.

Surfos & Vagos (☎ 355-64-13; Juárez 43; open 8pm-2am daily except either Tues or Thur, they couldn't decide) is a bar with one pool table and some board games. It's also energetically managed – if you're a lone woman, at least – and plays some good music. The 2nd-floor open patio is pleasant and intimate.

Billar San Patricio (cnr Juárez & Orozco; tables per hour US$1.35; open 10am-11pm daily) has large tables with smooth felt, and you'll be getting a good look at some sleazy and/or drunk local men.

El Dorado and **La Terraza** (see Places to Eat) are popular nighttime hangouts with live music on the weekends.

Disco Tanga (cnr Gómez Farías & Madero; open 10pm-3am daily high season, 10pm-3am Fri-Sun low season) is Melaque's only dedicated disco. On the beach at the west end of town, **Restaurant Tropicana** puts on a Sunday afternoon dance that's popular with young locals.

Getting There & Away

See the Barra de Navidad Getting There & Away section for air travel information.

Melaque has three bus stations. **Transportes Cihuatlán** and **Primera Plus/Servicios Coordinados** are on opposite sides of Carranza on the corner of Gómez Farías. Both have 1st-class and 2nd-class buses and ply similar routes for similar fares. The buses trundling out of these stations serve the following destinations:

Barra de Navidad US$0.75, 5km, every 15 minutes 6am to 9pm
Guadalajara US$22 1st class, five hours, 294km, frequent; US$18 2nd class, 6½ hours, frequent
Manzanillo US$4.50 1st class, 1½ hours, 65km, nine daily; US$3.75 2nd class, two hours, at least hourly 3am to 11:30pm
Puerto Vallarta US$15 1st class, four hours, 220km, four daily; US$12.75 2nd class, five hours, frequent

The 1st-class **Elite bus station** is a block east on Gómez Farías. Two buses daily head for Puerto Vallarta (US$13, four hours) and continue up the coast all the way to Tijuana. Elite's southbound buses depart from Manzanillo.

Local buses for Villa Obregón and Barra de Navidad ($0.40, 15 to 20 minutes) stop near the plaza every 15 minutes.

A taxi between Melaque and Barra costs around US$4.50; to Playa Cuastecomate it's US$4.

BARRA DE NAVIDAD

☎ 315 • pop 7000

The clean beach resort of Barra de Navidad (usually simply called 'Barra') is charmingly squeezed onto an elephant-snout-looking sandbar extending out between Bahía de Navidad and Laguna de Navidad, about 5km south around the bay from Melaque. More than 400 years ago, Spanish galleons were built on this sandbar for the sole purpose of conquering the Philippines. Today, Canadians sit on the sandbars with the purpose of conquering margaritas.

Local and foreign surfers both come here to ride the rippin' waves, which are a nice size in January. The marina of the Grand Bay Hotel is a popular yachtie destination from November to May, and some of the boats in that marina belong to some filthy rich folk indeed.

Barra is best seen on your own two feet, since everything is compact, streets are narrow and parking very limited in spots. The center is very touristy, much more so than Melaque.

Information

Delegación Regional de Turismo (☎/fax 355-51-00; Jalisco 67; open 9am-5pm Mon-Fri, 9am-5pm Sat-Sun in high season) has free maps and runs an info kiosk on the jetty during the high season.

Barra is now blessed with an air-con **Banamex** ATM, on the southeast corner of the plaza. Change money at **Vinos y Licores Barra de Navidad** (open 9am-11pm daily), on Legazpi near the southwest corner of the plaza, and at the **Casa de Cambio** (Veracruz 212; open 9am-2pm & 4pm-7pm Mon-Fri, 9am-6:30pm Sat), between Michoacán and Guanajuato.

Send mail from the **post office annexe** (cnr Sinaloa & Mazatlán; open 9am-2:30pm Mon-Fri). For telephone and fax services try **Telecomm** (cnr Veracruz & Guanajuato; open 9am-3pm Mon-Fri), **Mini-Market Hawaii** (cnr Legazpi & Sonora; open noon-10pm daily) or the **caseta telefónica** (Veracruz 102; open 9am-10:30pm daily).

Ciber@Money (200 block of Veracruz; US$4 per hour; open 9am-2pm & 4pm-7:30pm

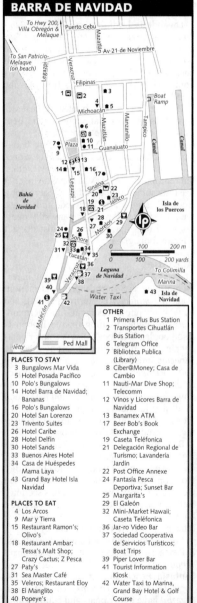

BARRA DE NAVIDAD

OTHER
1 Primera Plus Bus Station
2 Transportes Cihuatlán Bus Station
6 Telegram Office
7 Biblioteca Publica (Library)
8 Ciber@Money; Casa de Cambio
11 Nauti-Mar Dive Shop; Telecomm
12 Vinos y Licores Barra de Navidad
13 Banamex ATM
17 Beer Bob's Book Exchange
19 Caseta Teléfonica
21 Delegación Regional de Turismo; Lavandería Jardín
22 Post Office Annexe
24 Fantasía Pesca Deportiva; Sunset Bar
25 Margarita's
29 El Galeón
32 Mini-Market Hawaii; Caseta Teléfonica
36 Jar-ro Video Bar
37 Sociedad Cooperativa de Servicios Turísticos; Boat Trips
39 Piper Lover Bar
41 Tourist Information Kiosk
42 Water Taxi to Marina, Grand Bay Hotel & Golf Course

PLACES TO STAY
3 Bungalows Mar Vida
5 Hotel Posada Pacífico
10 Polo's Bungalows
14 Hotel Barra de Navidad; Bananas
16 Polo's Bungalows
20 Hotel San Lorenzo
23 Trivento Suites
26 Hotel Caribe
28 Hotel Delfin
30 Hotel Sands
33 Buenos Aires Hotel
34 Casa de Huéspedes Mama Laya
43 Grand Bay Hotel Isla Navidad

PLACES TO EAT
4 Los Arcos
9 Mar y Tierra
15 Restaurant Ramon's; Olivo's
18 Restaurant Ambar; Tessa's Malt Shop; Crazy Cactus; Z Pesca
27 Paty's
31 Sea Master Café
35 Veleros; Restaurant Eloy
38 El Manglito
40 Popeye's

JALISCO COAST & COLIMA

Mon-Fri, 9am-6:30pm Sat) is next to the Casa de Cambio.

Lavandería Jardín *(Jalisco 71; open 9am-2pm & 4pm-7pm Mon-Fri, 9am-noon Sat)* may take longer siestas in the *temporada baja* (low season). Clean, dry clothes will cost you US$1 per kilogram. If nobody's home, try **Mak y Mar** at the Hotel Caribe (see Places to Stay).

If there ever was a bookstore that deserved its own special section, it is **Beer Bob's Book Exchange** *(Mazatlán 61; open noon-3pm Mon-Fri).* You can't buy books here; you can only exchange them on a one-to-one basis. You can also borrow books, but return them before you leave town, or at least 'do someone a good favor' (says Bob). Book donations are accepted, and please read the signs before asking any silly questions – Bob's not grumpy, he just doesn't tolerate fools gladly.

Activities

The beach, shopping and hanging out in restaurant/bars are Barra's prime attraction. Walk the *malecón* (waterfront street), and have your photo taken at the mermaid/merman statue. Boating on the lagoon is also popular. The local *lancha* (motor boat) cooperative, the **Sociedad Cooperativa de Servicios Turísticos** *(Veracruz 40; tours US$15-160; dock open 7am-8pm daily)*, posts prices at their open-air lagoonside office. Tours range from half-hour trips around the lagoon to all-day jungle trips to Tenacatita; prices are for up to eight people. It also offers fishing, snorkeling and diving trips.

Boat tours may also be taken across the lagoon to the village of Colimilla (US$11). Or, you can catch a water taxi to Grand Bay Hotel on Isla de Navidad (US$1 return; see Getting There & Away later in this section). Before you get in the boat, make sure you know whether you're taking a *taxi colectivo* (cheap) or private tour (expensive).

For serious deep-sea fishing expeditions, **Z Pesca** *(☎ 355-60-99; @ crazycactusmx@ yahoo.com; Jalisco 8, at Crazy Cactus)* and **Fantasía Pesca Deportiva** *(☎ 355-68-24; @ fantasia1@terra.com.mx; cnr Jalisco & Legazpi)* have better boats and equipment; a

six-hour trip costs around US$330 including gear (less if split among some buddies).

Surfboards, boogie boards, snorkeling gear, cars, houses and apartments can be rented from English-speaking **Crazy Cactus** *(☎ 355-60-99 Dec-Apr, ☎/fax 355-60-91 all year; @ crazycactusmx@yahoo.com; Jalisco 8; open 9:30am-6pm Mon-Sat).* **Nauti-Mar** *(☎ 355-57-91; Veracruz 204)* is a dive shop that rents gear for fishing, diving, snorkeling, kayaking and windsurfing.

Grand Bay Hotel's 27-hole championship **golf course** *(☎ 355-61-94)* welcomes nonguests; cost is approximately US$150 for 27 holes. A water taxi will drop you there for US$1 return.

Fishing Tournaments

Big-money international fishing tournaments are held annually for marlin, sailfish, tuna and dorado. The most important, the three-day **Torneo Internacional de Pesca**, is held around the third week in January. The second most important is the two-day **Torneo Internacional de Marlin**, held during late May or early June, with another two-day tournament in mid-August. The final tournament of the year is held around Independence Day on September 15 and 16.

Places to Stay – Budget

There are a few decent budget choices in Barra de Navidad.

Casa de Huéspedes Mama Laya *(Veracruz 69; rooms without/with private bathroom US$11-17/14-20)* is a good, simple and clean backpackers' crashpad with some very pleasant sitting areas. You can also pitch a tent on the roof.

Hotel Caribe *(☎ 355-59-52; Sonora 15; singles/doubles US$15/23)* has seen better days, but clean rooms (of different sizes and levels of mustiness) are decent. There's a rooftop terrace, hot water and laundry service.

Hotel Posada Pacífico *(☎ 355-53-59, fax 355-53-49; Mazatlán 136; singles/doubles US$17/22, bungalows with kitchen from US$38)* has tidy, spacious and clean rooms with leafy common areas. It's friendly, has personality, and a few bungalows (sleeping up to four) are available.

Hotel San Lorenzo *(☎/fax 355-51-39;* **e** *lorenzomx@yahoo.com; Sinaloa 7, near Mazatlán; singles/doubles US$17/20)* offers OK rooms (get them upstairs).

Places to Stay – Mid-Range & Top End

You'll have more accommodation choice in Barra if you can dish out a few more pesos.

Hotel Delfín *(☎ 355-50-68, fax 355-60-20;* **w** *www.geocities.com/delfinhotel; Morelos 23; singles/doubles May-Nov US$23/27; Dec-Apr US$35)* is four stories of large, clean, pleasant rooms with shared balconies and, if you're lucky, lagoon views. A good-value breakfast buffet is served poolside.

Trivento Suites *(☎/fax 355-53-78;* **e** *ar turomadrigal@prodigy.net.mx; Jalisco 75; singles/doubles US$28/33)* has nice, new rooms, some with balcony, around a developing courtyard garden. There's a *very* orange/salmon color scheme here, but if you can stand that it's a good deal.

Hotel Sands *(☎/fax 355-50-18,* ☎ *33-36-16-28-59 in Guadalajara for reservations; Morelos 24; singles/doubles with breakfast US$33/43, bungalows with kitchen from US$75)* hosts a poolside party scene at its restaurant/bar (winter happy hour 4pm to 5pm daily). The pretty garden and nearby lagoon make for good atmosphere, and the rooms are great too. Request one away from the adjacent El Galeón disco, and bargain in low season.

Buenos Aires Hotel *(☎/fax 355-69-67;* **e** *hotelbuenosairesmx@yahoo.com.mx; Veracruz 209; doubles US$39-50, suites US$90)* emphasizes safety for its guests, who stay in new, good-sized air-con rooms with balcony. Continental breakfast is extra, and served on the 3rd-floor terrace. It's an intimate place and they speak English.

Polo's Bungalows *(☎ 355-64-10; Veracruz 174; 1/2 bedroom bungalows US$39/60)* is comfortable and modern, but located in a bleak parking lot; try the more intimate annexe up the street.

Bungalows Mar Vida *(☎ 355-59-11;* **w** *www.tomzap.com/marvida.html; Mazatlán 168; 2/4 person apartments US$55/66)* offers five big, attractive apartments (all with

air-con and TV) and a super clean pool. The neighborhood is peaceful, and English is spoken here.

Hotel Barra de Navidad *(☎ 355-51-22, fax 355-53-03;* **w** *www.hotelbarradenavidad.com; Legazpi 250; singles/doubles US$65/74, bungalows from US$127)* comes big, colorful, modern and next to the beach. There's an attractive swimming pool, and the 60 rooms have air-con and cable TV.

Grand Bay Hotel Isla Navidad *(☎ 355-50-50, fax 355-60-71; suites US$322-2925)* sits regally on a peninsula in the lagoon. Golf, tennis and other packages are available (three-night minimum stay).

Places to Eat

Barra has many good restaurants, the most atmospheric of which are on beachfront terraces with beautiful sunset views. Several more overlook the lagoon. Many simple, inexpensive little indoor-outdoor places line Calle Veracruz in the center of town.

Bananas *(☎ 355-55-54; Legazpi 250, at Hotel Barra de Navidad; breakfast US$3-4; open 8am-noon & 6pm-10pm Mon-Sat, 8am-noon Sun)* serves breakfast in a pleasant, airy dining room with a beach view.

Tessa's Malt Shop *(cnr Veracruz & Jalisco; open 9am-11pm Mon-Sat)* is popular with homesick gringos who are longing for burgers and fries (US$4), sandwiches like BLTs (US$4.50), and most important – malts, shakes, root beer floats and sundaes (US$3).

Restaurant Ambar *(cnr Veracruz & Jalisco; dinner US$7-20; open 5pm-midnight daily, Nov-Apr & July-Aug)* offers up stuff like duck paté, roquefort salad and escargots. Imaginative crepes are the house specialty, and there's a good wine list. Head on upstairs.

Paty's *(cnr Jalisco & Veracruz; mains US$4; open 7am-11pm daily)* sits in the middle of Barra, serving lots of cheap Mexican specialties at pleasant street/sidewalk tables.

Los Arcos *(cnr Mazatlán & Michoacán; mains US$3-5; open 9am-11pm daily)* is one of the homiest place you'll eat at, with Mom and Pop cooking and serving you homemade food in a tiny dining area.

Olivo's *(cnr Legazpi & Guanajuato; mains US$9-14)* offers renowned Mediterranean food, including baked lamb and pork fillets, while artwork surrounds diners in a pleasant atmosphere.

Restaurant Ramon's (☎ 355-64-35; Legazpi 260; mains US$7-11; open 7am-11pm daily) has a good, comprehensive menu, and serves it all under a dark palapa with CNN on TV. It's casual and friendly too.

Sea Master Café (Legazpi 146; mains US$7-13; open noon-11pm daily) harbors very colorful and artsy decor. It doesn't serve quite everything, but it has a great selection of international and Mexican dishes on the menu – and it overlooks the beach.

Popeye's (cnr Legazpi & Veracruz; mains US$5-10; open 10am-8pm) whips up margaritas (US$4) that can blow fish out of water. The views are great: watch surfers rip some waves out on the bay while gringos fry on the beach below.

Mar Y Tierra (☎ 355-64-95; Legazpi at the plaza; mains US$8-11; open 10am-6pm Mon, Wed & Thur, 10am-11pm Fri-Sun) swings on the upscale side, with a fancy limited menu served under a big palapa and between colorful adobe walls. A great place to enjoy a whiskey, cognac, vodka or tequila – and there's a relaxing sea view.

El Manglito (Veracruz at the boat dock; mains US$7-9; open noon-7pm daily) has a mangrove tree growing right in the center. There's some unique animal skeleton/painting multimedia artsy-craft stuff going on along the walls, and they'll serve seafood if you ask for it. Nearby, also with fine views overlooking the lagoon on Veracruz, are **Restaurant Eloy** and **Veleros**.

Entertainment

There are lots of bars in which to partake in local alcoholic beverages and meet other tourists. Some bars have live music on occasion. Otherwise, look for those musician groups that play on street corners and ask for spare change, whether you're listening to them or not.

Sunset Bar (open 1pm-2am daily) pours large drinks for its 2pm to 10pm happy hour, and they are especially popular during the sunset-viewing hours.

Palm Fronds, Anyone?

One visit to any laid-back, Mexican beach town and you will notice a peculiar commonality: almost all the open-air restaurants (called *enramadas* and sometimes palapas) on the sands are topped with layers and layers of dried palm tree fronds. This ubiquitous, practical and extremely handy material literally grows on trees.

Each palm tree frond produces its own sprig of coconuts and grows to about 4m in length. Fronds are 'harvested' and are often dried on the ground before being layered onto rooftop support beams, where they'll last four to five years before needing to be replaced. Sit under one during a thunderstorm, and you will realize that they're pretty efficient, inexpensive and protective covering – as well as providing vital shade under which to sip a refreshing margarita.

And, if you ever drive your car onto the beach and get mired in sand, try this little hint: grab yourself a few fronds and stick them under the stuck tire, for traction. Often they're the only material on hand, and can save your ass surprisingly well.

Margarita's (pub fare US$3-8; open noon-2am daily) is a restaurant/sports bar with a 6pm to 11pm happy hour. Order margaritas, daiquiris and piña coladas, along with gin 'n tonics, bloody Marys and Tom Collins. The 2nd-floor palapa with view is snappy.

Piper Lover Bar (☎ 355-67-47; Legazpi near Yucatán; pub fare US$2.50-5.50; open 10am-2am daily) shouldn't be forgotten either, with its tough motorcycle-bar look and loud live music on weekends. Pricey mixed drinks start revving from US$4.50.

Jar-ro Video Bar (Veracruz near Yucatán; open 2pm-3am daily) is a more local place that plays live music at 10pm Thursday to Sunday, and has a pool table and lagoon views. Happy hour is from 2pm to 4pm.

El Galeón (open Nov-Easter), adjacent to Hotel Sands, is a loud disco with a popular bar. The daily happy hour (4pm to 6pm) includes a splash in the pool.

Getting There & Away

Barra de Navidad and Melaque are served by the **Playa de Oro international airport** (ZLO), 25km southeast on Hwy 200, which also serves Manzanillo. To get to town from the airport, take a taxi (US$22; 30 minutes), or a bus 15km to Cihuatlán and a cheaper taxi from there. See the Manzanillo section for flight details.

For bus information, see Melaque earlier in this chapter. Long-distance buses stopping in Melaque also stop here (15 minutes before or after). The **Transportes Cihuatlán bus station** (Veracruz 228) is virtually opposite the **Primera Plus bus station**.

In addition to the long-distance buses, colorful local buses connect Barra and Melaque (US$0.40, every 15 minutes from 6am to 9pm), stopping in Barra at the long-distance bus stations (buses stopping on the southbound side of the road loop round Legazpi and back to Melaque).

Taxis between Barra and Melaque cost about US$4.50.

Water taxis operate from 7am to 7pm from the south end of Veracruz, offering return-trip service to the Grand Bay Hotel (US$1), the marina (US$1), the golf course (US$1.35) and Colimilla (US$1.35).

MANZANILLO

☎ 314 • pop 110,000

Home to the largest Mexican port on the Pacific Ocean, Manzanillo (this name refers to once-common local strands of Manzanillo trees) has also become a major tourist attraction. Its distinct bay, split neatly into two smaller bays (called Bahía de Santiago and Bahía de Manzanillo) by a dangling peninsula, is edged with decent sandy beaches and resort hotels. Between central Manzanillo and these twin bays rests an industrial sector of shipping piers, train tracks and warehouses. Downtown, narrow bustling streets and an active zócalo define an up-and-coming destination poised for even more tourism in the future. A seafront plaza being built next to the zócalo will connect to the current *malecón* – beautifying that will do Manzanillo some good. And, befitting the city's deep-sea fishing reputation, fans call Manzanillo the 'World Capital of Sailfish', and each year fishing tournaments draw hopeful anglers from all around.

Orientation

Central (downtown) Manzanillo is located at the southeastern end of the bay, which curves gracefully to the prominent Juluapán peninsula, 16km to the northwest. Morelos, the city's main drag, turns into Niños Heroes and passes the industrial arm of the city, heading out to business Hwy 200. Here the scene turns to resort hotels, beaches and services, and some smaller sub-towns such as Santiago and Salagua. Walking is not terribly pleasant on this long, built-up coastside stretch, also referred to as Blvd Miguel de la Madrid. Drivers wishing to bypass the Manzanillo area completely should take the *cuota* section of Hwy 200 here, skipping almost 20km of stop lights and traffic for a mere US$3.75.

Note that Km distance markers instead of actual street addresses are used in this section for destinations along business Hwy 200 (the coastal stretch of highway with traffic stoplights, businesses, shops, hotels, restaurants etc).

Information

Tourist Offices The municipal **Departamento de Turismo** (☎ 332-10-02 ext 247; open 9am-7pm daily) operates a sidewalk tourist information desk in front of the Presidencia Municipal office. **Tourist police** are stationed nearby. The state-run **Secretaría de Turismo** (☎ 333-22-77/64; Hwy 200 Km 8.7; open 9am-2pm & 5pm-7:30pm Mon-Fri, 10am-2pm Sat) is near Moustache's Bigotes Restaurant on Hwy 200.

Money Many banks with ATMs are scattered around the city center. Refer to maps for locations.

Banamex open 9am-4pm Mon-Fri and 10am-2pm Sat

Bancomer open 8:30-4pm Mon-Fri and 10am-2pm Sat

Banco Santander open 9am-4pm Mon-Fri and 10am-2pm Sat

Bital open 8am-7pm Mon-Fri and 9am-2:30pm Sat

Cambio Majapara open 9am-2pm and 4:30pm-7pm Mon-Fri and 9am-2pm Sat

Casa de Cambio Km 14.1; open 9am-2pm and 4:30pm-8pm Mon-Sat, 10am-2pm Sun

Post & Communications The post office (*Galindo 30; open 9am-3pm Mon-Fri, 9am-1pm Sat*) is situated 300m south of the zócalo. **Telecomm** (*open 8am-7:30pm Mon-Fri, 9am-12:30pm Sat, Sun & hols*) is on the zócalo while **Computel** has offices at Morelos 144 and México 302 (*both open 7:30am-9:30pm daily*).

Internet Access There are plenty of ways to get online in Manzanillo. **Internet Online** (*Carrillo Puerto 223; US$2 per hour; open 10am-2pm & 5:30pm-8pm Mon-Sat*) is one place to go. Another one (*cnr Juárez & Av 21 de Marzo*), off the zócalo, has funny cartoons in the front window. And don't even

try to look up porn sites at **La Red Internet** (*Carillo Puerto 64; US$2 per hour; open 9am-4pm & 6pm-10pm daily*).

The following places are around the bay. **Café Angelitos Internet** (*Hwy 200 Km 11.3; US$2.75 per hour; open 9am-10pm Mon-Sat, 10am-6pm Sun*) gives all profits to kids programmes. Another place (*Lázaro Cárdenas s/n; open 9:30am-10:30pm daily; US$2.75 per hour*) is at the opposite end of the bay.

Laundry Wash your clothes at **Lavandería Lavimatic** (*cnr Madero near Domínguez*). On Hwy 200, try **Alex Lavandería** (*Km 8.8; open 10am-2pm & 4pm-8pm Wed-Mon*) or **Lavandería** (*Km 14.4; open 9am-noon & 3pm-6pm Mon-Fri, 9am-2pm Sat*), which charges about US$5 for a full load.

Museo Universitario de Arqueología

University of Colima's archaeological museum (*☎ 332-22-56; Niños Héroes at Glorieta*

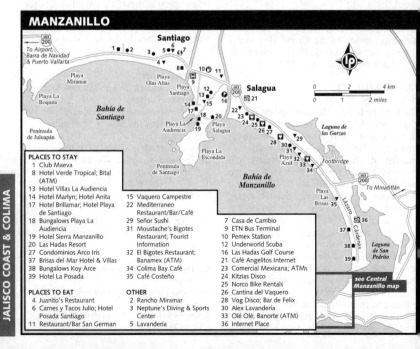

MANZANILLO

PLACES TO STAY
1 Club Maeva
8 Hotel Verde Tropical; Bital (ATM)
13 Hotel Villas La Audiencia
14 Hotel Marlyn; Hotel Anita
17 Hotel Brillamar; Hotel Playa de Santiago
18 Bungalows Playa La Audiencia
19 Hotel Sierra Manzanillo
20 Las Hadas Resort
27 Condominios Arco Iris
37 Brisas del Mar Hotel & Villas
38 Bungalows Koy Arce
39 Hotel La Posada

15 Vaquero Campestre
22 Mediterraneo Restaurant/Bar/Café
29 Señor Sushi
31 Moustache's Bigotes Restaurant; Tourist Information
32 El Bigotes Restaurant; Banamex (ATM)
34 Colima Bay Café
35 Café Costeño

PLACES TO EAT
4 Juanito's Restaurant
6 Carnes y Tacos Julio; Hotel Posada Santiago
11 Restaurant/Bar San German

OTHER
2 Rancho Miramar
3 Neptune's Diving & Sports Center
5 Lavandería

7 Casa de Cambio
9 ETN Bus Terminal
10 Pemex Station
12 Underworld Scuba
16 Las Hadas Golf Course
21 Café Angelitos Internet
23 Comercial Mexicana; ATMs
24 Kitzias Disco
25 Norco Bike Rentals
26 Cantina del Vaquero
28 Vog Disco; Bar de Felix
30 Alex Lavandería
33 Olé Olé; Banorte (ATM)
36 Internet Place

To Airport, Barra de Navidad & Puerto Vallarta

Playa Miramar
Playa La Boquita
Bahía de Santiago
Península de Juluapán
Santiago
Playa Olas Altas
Playa Santiago
Península de Santiago
Playa La Audiencia
Playa La Escondida
Salagua
Playa Salagua
Playa Azul
Bahía de Manzanillo
Laguna de las Garzas
Footbridge
To Minatitlán
Playa Las Brisas
Laguna de San Pedrito

0   2   4 km
0   1   2 miles

see Central Manzanillo map

JALISCO COAST & COLIMA

San Pedrito; admission US$1.25; open 10am-2pm & 5pm-8pm Tues-Sat, 10am-1pm Sun) displays interesting objects from ancient Colima and some other parts of Mexico. There are excellent pottery examples, including two rather, uh, amorous hombres in a compromising position. Check out the shell jewelry and obsidian arrowheads, too. The university art gallery is opposite.

Beaches

Playa San Pedrito, 1km northeast of the zócalo, is the closest beach to town. The next closest stretch of sand, spacious (but at times trashy) **Playa Las Brisas**, caters to a few moderate hotels; part of the beach's view includes awful inland smokestacks. **Playa Azul** stretches up from Las Brisas and meets with **Playa Salagua**, fronting Las Hadas Resort.

On this peninsula and farther northwest are the best beaches in the area: **La Audiencia, Santiago, Olas Altas, Miramar** and **La Boquita**. Playa La Audiencia, on a clean cove at the west side of the Península de Santiago and overlooked by resort hotels and villas, is popular for water-skiing and other noisy motorized water sports. Olas Altas and Miramar are long, wide and flat and have the best surfing waves; surfboards can be rented at Miramar.

Getting to these beaches from the downtown is easy: Local buses that are marked 'Las Brisas', 'Santiago' and 'Miramar' head around the bay and make stops at the beaches. The 'Las Hadas' bus takes a more circuitous, scenic route down the Peninsula de Santiago. They all depart from México near Domínguez and from the main bus station every 10 minutes from 6am to 11pm. Fares are US$0.35 to US$0.70, depending on your destination.

Diving

The scuba diving in Manzanillo can be spectacular, and there are many sites to explore – either off the beach or out on the bay. All sorts of fish and other critters, such as seahorses, moray eels, puffers, whale sharks, mantas, turtles and octopus frequent certain areas. And about 250m off Playa La Boquita, up in the northwestern arm of the bay, lies a sunken cargo ship only 9m underwater. Even snorkelers can easily explore this wreck.

Susan and Carlos have 35 years of diving experience between them at **Underworld Scuba** *(☎ 333-06-42, 044-314-358-50-42, fax 333-36-78; ⓦ www.divemanzanillo.com)*, on the Santiago Peninsula. Their complete PADI dive center charges around US$80 for two tank dives, including equipment. They also do tours of jungle waterfalls and Colima (each seven hours and US$50 per person) and also rent snorkeling/scuba equipment for US$8/39.

Another choice is **Neptune's Diving & Sports Center** *(☎ 334-30-01; ⓦ www.neptunesdiving.com; Hwy 200 Km 14.8)*, which offers similar dives, costs and services. It also operates night dives and snorkeling trips.

Other Water Sports

For deep-sea fishing, try **Ocean Pacific Adventures** *(☎ 335-06-05, 044-314-357-07-17; ⓦ www.gomanzanillo.com/fishing)*. This outfit will take you out for sailfish, marlin, mackarel and red snapper, while supporting a catch-and-release programme. Tours cost US$200 on 26-foot cruisers (one to five people) and US$260 on 40-foot cruisers (one to 10 people); prices are for the whole boat and include gear, drinks and having your fish cooked up for dinner.

Other Activities

Norco Bike Rentals *(☎ 334-11-22; Hwy 200 Km 10.4; open 10am-2pm & 4pm-8pm Mon-Fri, 9am-2pm Sat)* rents bikes for US$11 per 24 hours.

Want to go horse riding on the beach? Look for **Rancho Miramar** *(☎ 044- 314-358-08-44 days, 333-24-33 nights)* palapa shelters on Hwy 200 near Playa de Miramar and ask for Gamaliel; be prepared to sacrifice US$33 for a two-hour tour.

Special Events

May 1 to 10, the **Fiestas de Mayo** celebrate Manzanillo's anniversary by holding sporting competitions and other events. The **Fiesta de Nuestra Señora de Guadalupe** is

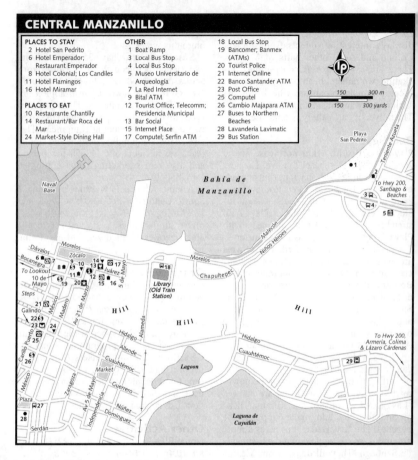

CENTRAL MANZANILLO

PLACES TO STAY
2 Hotel San Pedrito
6 Hotel Emperador;
  Restaurant Emperador
8 Hotel Colonial; Los Candiles
11 Hotel Flamingos
16 Hotel Miramar

PLACES TO EAT
10 Restaurante Chantilly
14 Restaurant/Bar Roca del
  Mar
24 Market-Style Dining Hall

OTHER
1 Boat Ramp
3 Local Bus Stop
4 Local Bus Stop
5 Museo Universitario de
  Arqueología
7 La Red Internet
9 Bital ATM
12 Tourist Office; Telecomm;
  Presidencia Municipal
13 Bar Social
15 Internet Place
17 Computel; Serfin ATM

18 Local Bus Stop
19 Bancomer; Banmex
  (ATMs)
20 Tourist Police
21 Internet Online
22 Banco Santander ATM
23 Post Office
25 Computel
26 Cambio Majapara ATM
27 Buses to Northern
  Beaches
28 Lavandería Lavimatic
29 Bus Station

held from December 1 to 12 in honor of Mexico's revered manifestation of the Virgin Mary, here as elsewhere in Mexico.

Sailfish season runs November to March, with marlin, red snapper, sea bass and tuna also plentiful. The biggest international tournament is held in November, with a smaller national tournament in February.

Places to Stay

Most of central Manzanillo's accommodations are within a block or two of the zócalo and in the budget category. Around the bay, where the better beaches are, hotels tend to be newer and more expensive; Playa Santiago, 30 minutes away by bus, is an exception.

Places to Stay – Budget

Hotel Emperador (☎ 332-23-74; Dávalos 69; singles/doubles US$11-13/13-15) is an old cheapie with small rooms, springy beds and claustrophobic halls. Try for a quieter and brighter top-floor room. The restaurant here is good and inexpensive.

Hotel Flamingos (☎ 332-10-37; Madero 72, cnr Av 10 de Mayo; doubles US$11-15) is a perfectly serviceable budget stop half a block south of the zócalo. Some rooms can be musty; try for one with two beds and an outside window.

Hotel Miramar (☎ 332-10-08; Juárez 122; singles/doubles US$11-13/15) has funky stairways and huge old tiled hallways that could do with some furniture. Old worn rooms sport saggy mattresses but are OK.

Places to Stay – Mid-Range

Hotel Colonial (☎ 332-10-80; Bocanegra 28; singles/doubles with air-con & TV US$26/32) is where you want to be if you're downtown. Big rooms, tiled outdoor hallways and a thick colonial air make this place a gem, and it's centrally located. There's underground parking and a restaurant/bar on the premises.

Hotel San Pedrito (☎/fax 332-05-35, fax 332-60-05; e hotelsanpedrito@hotmail.com; Teniente Azueta 3; rooms US$22) sits next to Playa San Pedrito, the beach nearest downtown. Old tiled rooms are generous in size, but worn and dank – see a few before deciding. A chain-link fence spoils the beach view, and the garden area's a bit too concrete, but it's cheap.

All the following places are on the Manzanillo map.

Hotel Posada Santiago (☎ 333-00-14; Hwy 200 Km 14.3; singles/doubles US$13/22) is on Hwy 200, two blocks west of Santiago town's plaza. The small, basic and dingy rooms are better upstairs.

Bungalows Koy Arce (☎ 333-93-01; Playa Las Brisas; singles/doubles US$20/22) represents good value if you can stand the worn, outdated rooms that aren't spick-'n-span clean, but can be sizable and even harbor sea views. There's a decent pool.

Hotel Verde Tropical (☎ 334-30-14; Hwy 200 Km 14; doubles US$33-44) has a nice pool in a dark palm garden. While the good-sized modern rooms come with TV and decent decor, some can be musty.

The following hotels are on the Santiago peninsula down a curvy but relatively short road. All except Anita have beachfront swimming pools; Marlyn and Playa de Santiago also have restaurant/bars.

Hotel Anita (☎ 333-01-61; singles/doubles/ triples US$13/24/35) has old rooms with

springy, worn beds. The remodelled rooms, however, come with balconies, sea views, bright clean tiles and fans – a super deal for just US$7 more.

Hotel Marlyn (☎ 333-01-07, 33-3613-84-11 in Guadalajara for reservations; rooms from US$44) hosts pleasant rooms with TV and fan. The ones you want have sea views and balconies, and consequently cost more. Six-person kitchen suites are available.

Hotel Brillamar (☎ 334-11-88; rooms US$35, bungalows from US$110) has air-con and TV, though some toilets may be missing their seats – unforgivable. Rooms are otherwise reasonable, but small. Large kitchen bungalows are also available.

Hotel Playa de Santiago (☎ 333-02-70; rooms US$65) is perched at the end of the road and offers comfortable, semimodern rooms with balconies, sea views and decent – though ageing – baths.

Places to Stay – Top End

Manzanillo's upmarket hotels are on or near the beaches on the northern and eastern sides of the bay. All these hotels are on the Manzanillo map.

Brisas del Mar Hotel & Villas (☎ 334-11-97; e hecluna@prodigy.net.mx; Playa las Brisas; singles/doubles US$36/51) has beautiful and generous suites and villas, all modern, clean and colorfully decorated. A nice pool and beachside location round out this good deal.

Condominios Arco Iris (☎/fax 333-01-68; Hwy 200 Km 10; doubles US$51) is home to 20 cottages with kitchens on grassy, palm-shaded grounds. There's a pool, pleasant common areas and secure parking.

Hotel Villas La Audiencia (☎ 333-08-61, fax 333-26-53; Santiago Peninsula; rooms US$53, villas from US$100) has golf course views and is pleasant enough for families or large groups. All the villas come with a kitchen, air-con and satellite TV, and there's a swimming pool and restaurant/bar.

Bungalows Playa la Audiencia (☎ 333-09-55; near Playa la Audiencia; doubles/quads US$66/106) is a good mid-range option for large groups in this area. Rooms don't have views or anything special, but are close to the beach and come with TV, kitchen, and eating and sitting areas. There's also a pool; try asking for discounts.

Hotel La Posada (☎/fax 333-18-99; e po sada@bay.net.mx; Lázaro Cárdenas 201; singles/ doubles with breakfast US$68/78 plus tax) is a charmingly rustic lodge overlooking Playa Las Brisas. There's a pool, some great common areas and comfortable rooms with Dutch doors, antique furniture and brick details.

Club Maeva (☎ 331-08-75, 800-523-8450 in Mexico, 800-466-2382 in the USA & Canada; W www.maevaresorts.com; Playa Miramar; rooms per person all-inclusive from US$80-120) is popular especially with active Canadians; basketball, volleyball, horse riding and water sports are all included, along with food, drink and entertainment. Most of the 500-plus rooms in villas are cute but small; bigger ones have kitchenette and balcony. It's not right on beach, but the pedestrian bridge gives easy access.

Hotel Sierra Manzanillo (☎ 333-20-00, 800-515-4321 in the USA; W www.sidek .com.mx/hotel/ing/sierra.asp; Playa Audiencia; singles/doubles all-inclusive US$176/212) is a blindingly white, sterile hotel beautifully situated above Playa Audiencia. It's not ultra-luxurious, but pleasant enough for most vacationers – most of whom are package tourists from Canada.

Las Hadas Resort (☎ 1-888-559-43-29; W www.brisas.com.mx; Playa Audiencia; rooms from US$247 plus tax) sits like a Moroccan kingdom, so bright and white you'll need sunglasses just walking around. Even the TVs are white. A beautiful pool with waterfall, palm trees and swim-up bar awaits guests out back. Hard-core film buffs may know this is where the film *10*, featuring sexy Bo Derek, was made. There's also a golf course.

Places to Eat

A number of good, inexpensive restaurants surround the zócalo. A market-style **dining hall** (cnr Madero & Cuauhtémoc; open 7am-9pm daily) has cheap food stalls. For some trendier, more sophisticated fare, head out around the bay.

Restaurante Chantilly (☎ 332-01-94; Juárez 44; mains US$3.50-9; open 7:30am-10:30pm Sun-Fri) is a cafeteria-style restaurant on the south side of the zócalo. Reasonably priced meals satisfy a local crowd, as does the *comida corrida* (daily special; US$5.50), espresso and ice cream.

Restaurant/Bar Roca del Mar (☎ 332-03-02; Morelos 225; mains US$4-10; open 7am-10:30pm daily) lies on the east side of the zócalo, offering good service and a regular *comida corrida* (US$5), along with burgers, sandwiches, seafood and Mexican food. Among its specialties is a seafood *comida corrida* (US$9) with seafood soup, rice, fish or shrimp and dessert.

Los Candiles (☎ 332-10-80; Bocanegra 28, at Hotel Colonial; mains US$4-10; open 8am-10:30pm Mon-Sat) has a pleasant covered patio, surf-and-turf fare and – best of all – a full bar. Other highlights include sports on satellite TV.

Restaurant Emperador (☎ 332-23-74; Dávalos 69, at Hotel Emperador; mains US$2-4.50; open 8am-11:30pm daily) rings true for budget-minded locals, who crowd the small, casual space to enjoy the good, cheap food. Highlights include set breakfasts and the seafood *comida corrida* (US$4).

Many more restaurants are spread out around the bay. Note Km markers are approximate. All the following places listed are on the Manzanillo map.

Café Costeño (☎ 333-94-60; Lázaro Cárdenas 1613; breakfast US$3; open 9am-10:30pm Mon-Sat, 9am-1pm & 5pm-10:30pm Sun) is a good start to your day: French toast, hotcakes and omelets are cheerfully served along with espresso and cappuchino. Sit in the shady garden out back.

Colima Bay Café (☎ 333-11-50; Hwy 200 Km 8; mains US$9-17; open 1pm-midnight daily) is a bit pretentious in its decor, trying too hard to be cute. The obnoxious menu has headings such as 'moo moo' and 'oink oink' (for meat selections).

El Bigotes (☎ 334-08-31; Hwy 200 Km 8.4; mains US$9-22; open 1pm-10pm daily) is popular for seafood like 'octopus drunken crazy' or 'snail garlic'. The beachside location is pretty fine, too.

Moustache's Bigotes (☎ 333-12-36; Hwy 200 Km 8.7; mains US$10-19; open noon-10pm daily) cooks seafood and meats, and has lots of tequilas and a beautiful sea view to help wash it all down.

Señor Sushi (☎ 333-09-82; Hwy 200 Km 9; rolls US$4-9; open 1pm-midnight Mon-Fri, 1pm-2am Sat-Sun) satisfies that sushi craving. There's pleasant outdoor umbrella seating, and takeout is available.

Comercial Mexicana Supermarket (Plaza Manzanillo, Km 10.5; open 8am-10pm Sun-Thur, 8am-11pm Fri-Sat) isn't too difficult to find on Hwy 200; just look for the pelican symbol and the large building. There's plenty of food here, including the ready-to-eat variety.

Mediterraneo (Hwy 200 Km 11; mains US$6-12; open 8am-11pm daily) boasts of generous salads, good crepes, pasta and several kinds of stuffed chicken breast. Have tzatziki for an appetizer while enjoying the golf course view.

Vaquero Campestre (☎ 334-14-48; Audiencia near Las Palmas; mains US$8-15; open 2pm-10:30pm Tues-Sat) serves pitchers of margaritas and sangria to help lubricate those servings of grilled beef and seafood. Palapa roofs and a few animal heads and skins surround diners.

Restaurant/Bar San German (☎ 333-94-41; Hwy 200 Km 13; mains US$7-17; open 1pm-11pm Mon-Sat, 1pm-10pm Sun) plays live music daily to help the seafood and meats go down easily. Both the stage and dining room are massive, so don't expect much intimacy. Service is good, and in winter there are weekly performances, such as ballet.

Carnes y Tacos Julio (☎ 334-00-36; Hwy 200 Km 14.3; mains US$3.50-12; open 8am-midnight daily) is near the town of Santiago, and serves excellent, inexpensive meat choices on pleasant sidewalk tables under a green awning.

Juanito's (☎ 333-13-88; Hwy 200 Km 14.5; mains US$2-8; open 8am-11pm daily) is a popular gringo hangout, and it's no wonder: burgers, chili dogs, fajitas and a few salads make them happy. It also offers telephone, fax and Internet service.

Entertainment

If you're in town on a Sunday evening, stop by the zócalo, where multiple generations come out to enjoy the fountains and topiaries while licking an ice-cream cone in the warm evening air. On the most atmospheric of nights, a band belts out traditional music from the gazebo. Sailors from the nearby naval base can often be spotted, adding cultural color to the area. At sunset, listen to the cacophony of the exuberant *zanates* (blackbirds) as they settle into their roosts. And be sure to check out the *golondrinas* (swallows) perching on the wires later in the evening; it's eerily reminiscent of the Hitchcock classic *The Birds*.

Bar Social (open noon-midnight Mon-Sat) sits behind heavy-set doors and blocked windows, a strange bar straight out of *The Twilight Zone*. It has a good, simple atmosphere.

For disco nightlife you'll have to head out around the bay. All places listed are on the Manzanillo map.

Vog (open Fri-Sat nights; Hwy 200 Km 9.2) is a popular disco with live music. It calls itself 'A classy place for classy people'. Next door, **Bar de Felix** (open daily) has no cover charge and many folks like it better for dancing. **Kitzias Disco** (Hwy 200 Km 10.5) is another popular rockin' and rollin' joint. **Ole Ole** (open Thur-Sat nights; Hwy 200 Km 8.2) is *the* destination for swaying to live salsa music.

Cantina del Vaquero (☎ 334-19-69; Hwy 200 Km 10.1; open 6pm-2am daily) features music for dancing. On Playa Miramar at **Club Maeva** (☎ 335-05-96) are **Disco Boom Boom** (adults) and **Tropical Hut** (families), which present theme entertainment mostly on weekends from 10:30pm; during slower times they allow nonguests into the discos (US$17 includes all drinks; phone for reservations).

Fantasy Men's Club and **Sexy Bar table dancing** exist somewhere on Hwy 200, but if you want to peep them out you'll have to find them yourself.

Getting There & Away

Playa de Oro international airport (ZLO) is about 35km northwest of Manzanillo's Zona

Hotelera on Hwy 200. **Aero California, Aeromar** and **Mexicana** fly direct to/from Mexico City. **Aerolitoral** (under Aeroméxico) goes to/from Guadalajara, Ixtapa, Monterrey and Puerto Vallarta. **Aero California** and **Alaska Airlines** both connect to Los Angeles, while **America West** does its thing to Phoenix.

Manzanillo's deficient bus terminal is 1.5km east of the center. Ticket offices, luggage storage, a *caseta telefónica* and small restaurants huddle in a dusty row where a terminal once stood prior to the 1995 earthquake. Destinations include:

Armería US$4, 45 minutes, 5km, 2nd class every 15 minutes, 4am to 10pm, with Autobuses Nuevo Horizonte and hourly, 2am to 10pm, with Autotransportes del Sur de Jalisco

Barra de Navidad US$5 1st class, one to 1½ hours, 60km, at least hourly; US$3.75 2nd class, at least hourly 4:30am to midnight with Transportes Cihuatlán

Colima US$5.25 1st class, 1½ to two hours, 101km, with La Línea Plus; US$4.50 2nd class, every 30 minutes, 2am to 10pm, with Autobuses Nuevo Horizonte, Autotransportes del Sur de Jalisco

Guadalajara US$15 to US$22 1st class, 4½ to eight hours, 325km, 27 daily with La Línea Plus, Transportes Cihuatlán and ETN; US$11 to US$18 2nd class, 19 daily with Transportes Cihuatlán and Autotransportes del Sur de Jalisco

Lázaro Cárdenas US$21 1st class, six hours, 313km, with Elite at 2am and 6am; US$16 2nd class, six daily with Autotransportes del Sur de Jalisco and Galeana

Melaque one to 1½ hours; 65km, same as to Barra de Navidad

Mexico City (Terminal Norte) US$37 1st class with ETN, US$55 deluxe with Elite, 12 hours *via corta* (short route) or via Morelia, 843km, all leave between 7pm to 9:30pm daily

Puerto Vallarta US$19/20 1st class, five to 6½ hours, 285km, at 4pm, 7:30pm & 9:30pm with Elite, 8am & noon with Transportes Cihuatlán; US$16 2nd class, nine daily with Transportes Cihuatlán

ETN (☎ 334-10-50) has its own terminal at Km 13.7; deluxe and 1st-class buses go to Colima (US$8, seven daily), Guadalajara (US$28, six daily) and Mexico City (US$75, 7:30pm daily).

Getting Around

For door-to-door shuttles to/from Playa de Oro airport, try **Transportes Turísticos Benito Juárez** (☎ 334-15-55). Fare is US$28 for *particular* (private) service (for one or two people), or US$10 per person *colectivo* when there are three or more. A taxi from the airport to Manzanillo's center or most resort hotels is US$25.

Local buses heading around the bay depart from México near Domínguez and from the main bus station, every 10 minutes from 6am to 11pm. Fares are US$0.35 to US$0.70, depending on your destination.

Taxis are plentiful in Manzanillo. From the zócalo, it's US$1.50 to the bus station, US$4 to Playa Azul, US$6 to Playa Santiago and US$9 to Playa Miramar. To keep him honest, agree with the driver on the price *before* you get into the cab.

CUYUTLÁN
☎ 313 • pop 1000

The long stretch of fine-grained, black-sand beach here attracts Mexican vacationers like bears to honey. Rickety wooden paths make walking the hot black sands tolerable, there are plenty of seaside restaurants, and hundreds of colorful, rentable beach chairs and umbrellas keep the scorching sun off. Many of the typical beach activities, such as swimming, people-watching and boogie boarding, can be savored on this pleasant flat expanse. Cuyutlán just might be best known, however, for its *ola verde*, a sort of glowing green wave appearing in April and May. It's supposedly caused by little green phosphorescent creatures, but the true reason is a mystery and the subject of much local debate. Even outside those months there's good stuff to check out, though: try the nearby turtle sanctuary and environmental education center, or give the local salt museum (it's one-of-a-kind) a shot.

Orientation & Information

Cuyutlán is near the *salinas* (salt ponds) at the southeast end of Laguna de Cuyutlán, 40km southeast of Manzanillo and 12km west of Armería. El Paraíso is 12km away by road.

Most tourist facilities are clustered near the beach. If you arrive by bus you'll be let off on Hidalgo, on the east side of the zócalo. Walk four blocks toward the ocean on Hidalgo and you'll land right in the middle of the beachfront hotel and restaurant area.

There's a post office in town, but you'll have to visit Armería for a bank and Internet service. Public telephones and *casetas de larga distancia* (long-distance public telephone call stations) live near the zócalo.

Things to See & Do
The beach – it's there, so go. Beach chairs and umbrellas cost US$8 for the day; boogie boards are also available. Get a coconut to sip for just over US$1.

If you like sea turtles, don't miss the **Centro Tortuguero** *(admission US$1.75; open 8:30am-5:30pm Tues-Sun)*, about 4km toward Paraíso. On display are various small pools containing a few of the endearing reptiles as well as some crocodile and iguana enclosures. Guides speak English, and there are educational talks almost hourly. Lagoon trips lasting 45 minutes leave from the premises and cost US$4.50 per person. Bring your swimsuit if you want to splash in the pool. Get there by taxi or walk 4km along the beach.

Back in town, a block north of the plaza and in an old wooden warehouse, the small **Museo de Sal** *(open 8am-5:30pm daily)* depicts the process of salt production in miniature (all signs are in Spanish). Salt was used in silver extraction, among other things. There is also some pottery and historic photos of life around the lagoon. Whale bones and boxes of coconut products add incongruity. Admission is free, but the retired salt workers who act as caretakers appreciate donations.

Places to Stay & Eat
Reserve rooms in advance for Christmas and Semana Santa, when Cuyutlán's hotels are booked solid by Mexican families. During these holidays, many hotels require that you take three meals a day; cost for room and board will be at least US$25 per person. Campers, try the empty sands on either side

Big Waves
A sign at some beaches warns, 'Si Tiembla busque terreno alto': 'If it shakes, seek higher ground'. In other words, don't be looking on the beach for tidal waves when there's an earthquake underfoot; get yourself inland quick before you realize what a stupid thing it would be to get washed away at ground zero.

of the hotels – when in doubt, ask for permission. Several beachfront *enramadas* rent showers. Prices here reflect the winter rates without meals.

Hotel Morelos *(☎ 326-40-13; Hidalgo 185; per person US$13)* gets points for no-frills, spacious rooms with hot water. Some are remodeled, a few have no toilet seat, and others come with old kitchens (take your pick). There's a swimming pool, and the good but greasy restaurant (open 7:30am-10pm daily) has a US$5 *comida corrida.*

Hotel Fénix *(☎/fax 326-40-82; Hidalgo 201, cnr Veracruz; rooms per person US$9-11)* supports small, basic rooms and large, covered halls. Breezier and brighter 2nd-story rooms are worth the extra pesos. English is spoken.

Hotel El Bucanero *(☎ 326-40-05; cnr Hidalgo & Malecón; interior/sea view rooms per person US$9-12 depending on view)* claims high marks for good standard rooms near the beach. Its restaurant is decent and cheap, and has sea views.

Hotel María Victoria *(☎ 326-40-04; Veracruz 10; per person US$23)* spawns a giant mushroom-shaped structure amidst the airy lobby – see it for yourself. Cuyutlán's most luxurious hotel also sits next to the beach, and the spacious rooms have sitting areas. Get one with a view. The restaurant serves fresh typical Mexican fare at high-roller prices.

Hotel San Rafael *(☎ 326-40-15; Veracruz 46; per person US$17)* is just OK despite a remodel. Rooms are small and raggedy for the price, so unless you get a good sea view go somewhere else. At least there's a pleasant swimming pool and beachfront restaurant/bar.

JALISCO COAST & COLIMA

La Puesta del Sol (☎ 326-40-29; *López Mateos 10; singles/doubles US$11/22*) is home to 17 good, plain rooms around a pleasant garden in a quiet neighborhood away from the center. Go one block past the radio towers at the south end of town (about five blocks from Hildalgo); it's a block from the beach on López Mateos.

Hotel Morelos and Hotel Fénix both have good open-air restaurants. **Beachfront restaurants** and snack stands supply seafood and cold drinks. Or grab a snack at one of the simpler places near the zócalo.

Getting There & Away

Cuyutlán is connected to the rest of the world through Armería, a friendly little service center on Hwy 200, 46km southeast of Manzanillo and 55km southwest of Colima. All long-distance buses stop here; you must take a local bus to reach Cuyutlán.

Local buses depart from Armería's market, one block north and one block east of the long-distance bus depots. They leave every 30 minutes from 6am to 7pm (US$0.75, 20 minutes). A taxi from Armería to Cuyutlán costs US$5.50.

The **Autotransportes Nuevo Horizonte** and **Sociedad Cooperativa de Autotransportes Colima Manzanillo** lines both have 'terminals' near Armería's main street at Álvarez. They operate 2nd-class buses to Manzanillo every 15 minutes, 6am to 10pm (US$2.50, 45 minutes) and to Colima every 30 minutes, 5:45am to 10:30pm (US$2.50, 45 minutes). Buses go every 20 minutes to Tecomán (US$0.80, 25 minutes), where you can connect with **Elite**, **Galeana** and other buses heading southeast on Hwy 200 (to Lázaro Cárdenas etc). A couple of doors away, **Flecha Amarilla** runs frequent 2nd-class buses to Mexico City and Guadalajara. Across the street, **Autotransportes del Sur de Jalisco** operates buses to Colima and Manzanillo.

To reach the nearby beach town El Paraíso from Cuyutlán by bus, you must return to Armería. A taxi from Cuyutlán to El Paraíso costs US$5.50.

A driving tip when going south towards Tecomán: Take Hwy 110 towards Colima for a few kilometers to the Tecomán exit (the misleading signs suck).

EL PARAÍSO
☎ 313

As the crow flies, the small, rustic fishing village of El Paraíso is just 6km southeast of Cuyutlán, but by road it's more like 12km. Like its larger neighbor, it harbors a fine, charcoal-colored beach that attracts Mexican families. Unlike its larger neighbor, there are fewer decent places to stay, which this makes for a less crowded and more tranquil beach. An unending line of seafood restaurants sits on the sands, there's good surfing 3km south near **Boca de Pascuales**, and a nearby lagoon provides affordable boat trips to the turtle sanctuary (see Cuyutlán). Not too bad for a laid-back little beach town.

Places to Stay & Eat

As always, expect higher prices and fewer (if any) rooms available during the Christmas and Easter holidays. For free camping try the beach (ask around). Rates quoted here are for winter season.

Campamento Rafles (*per person US$4.50*) has decent sites and services.

Hotel Valencia (☎ 328-80-58; *1/2 beds US$14/28*) thumbs its nose at luxury and safety with eight grungy rooms and one rail-less stairway. Sea views might make staying here worthwhile, but you've got to think spartan.

Parador del Bucanero Hotel (*rooms US$17*) is a better choice than Valencia; go two blocks further north. The pool's half-filled with water and kids, but rooms are tolerable.

Hotel Paraíso (☎ 322-10-32; *singles/doubles US$25/28-35*) is the fanciest hotel here, but that's not saying much. The older wing is next to the beach and has the cheapest rooms, with cold water; the four-story newer wing is set inland and has modern rooms with TV, hot water and balconies. There's a swimming pool and the most expensive seafood restaurant in town.

All of El Paraíso's beachfront **enramadas** serve basically the same food at similar prices; expect to spend US$5 to US$10 per person for a full, fresh meal.

Getting There & Away

As with Cuyutlán, you'll need to pass through Armería to reach El Paraíso. Local buses from Armería to El Paraíso run every 45 minutes from 6am to 7pm (US$0.60, 15 minutes); a taxi sets you back US$4.

For long-distance transport details or for getting to Cuyutlán, see Cuyutlán's Getting There & Away section.

COLIMA

☎ 312 • pop 134,000 • elevation 550m

Colima lives at the mercy of the forces of nature. Volcán de Fuego, clearly visible 30km to the north, has had nine major eruptions in the past four centuries. Of even greater concern are earthquakes; the city has been hit by a series of them over the centuries, the most recent major one occurring in 1941. Because of these devastating natural events, Colima has few colonial buildings, despite having been the first Spanish city in western Mexico.

Today Colima is a small, pleasant city graced by palm trees and ringed by mountains. Not many foreign tourists come here, but there are a number of interesting things to see and do in town and in the surrounding countryside. Though only 45km from the coast, Colima is at a higher elevation and, consequently, is cooler and less humid. The rainy months are July to September.

Orientation

Central Colima spreads around three plazas, with Plaza Principal (also known as Jardín Libertad) at the center of things. Portal Medellín is the row of arches on the north side of the plaza; Portal Morelos is on the south side. Jardín Quintero lies directly behind the cathedral, and three blocks farther east is Jardín Núñez. Street names change at Plaza Principal. Some of the sights are eight or 10 blocks from the city center, so be prepared for some walking.

The shiny modern main bus terminal is about 2km east of the city center, on the Guadalajara–Manzanillo road.

Information

The **state tourist office** (☎ 312-43-60; ⓦ www .visitacolima.com.mx; cnr Hidalgo & Ocampo; open 8:30am-8:30pm Mon-Fri, 10am-2pm Sat) is in a domed white building.

Cartographer wanna-bes will want to check out **Inegi** (☎ 313-99-56; ⓦ www.inegi .gob.mx; Madero 500; open 8:30-4:30 Mon-Fri), where regional maps and other related informational products can be purchased.

Change money at one of the numerous banks around the city center. **Banamex** (Hidalgo; open 9am-4pm Mon-Fri, 10am-2pm Sat), a block southeast of the cathedral, has an ATM. **Banco Serfin** (Jardín Núñez) also has an ATM and keeps similar hours.

Majapara Casa de Cambio (open 9am-2pm & 4:30pm-7pm Mon-Fri, 8:30am-2pm Sat) is at the southwest corner of Jardín Núñez. Other moneychangers are nearby.

The **post office** (Madero 247; open 9am-5pm Mon-Fri, 9am-12:30pm Sat) is at the northeast corner of Jardín Núñez. The **Telecomm office** (open 9am-8pm Mon-Fri, 9am-1pm Sat) sits nearby.

There are two branches of **Computel** (Morelos 236, facing Jardín Núñez; open 7:30am-9:30pm Mon-Fri, 8am-9pm Sat-Sun • Medellín 55, near cnr of Hidalgo; open 7am-10pm daily).

IcepNet (Madero 295; US$2.25 per hour; open 7am-8pm Mon-Fri, 9am-2pm Sat) and **Club Net Internet** (Obregón 25; US$2.50 per hour; open 10am-8pm Mon-Sat) both hook you up to the web.

Lavandería Amana (cnr Domínguez & Morelos; open 8am-9pm Mon-Sat, 9am-3pm Sun) and **Lavandería Tonanzán** (Medina near Allende; open 9am-2pm & 4pm-6pm Mon-Fri, 9am-2pm Sat) both places charge about US$3.50 to wash and dry a 3kg load.

Around Plaza Principal

The **cathedral**, on the east side of Plaza Principal, has been rebuilt several times since the Spanish first built a cathedral here in 1527. The most recent reconstruction dates from just after the 1941 earthquake. Next to the cathedral is the **Palacio de Gobierno**, built between 1884 and 1904. Local artist Jorge Chávez Carrillo painted the murals on

COLIMA

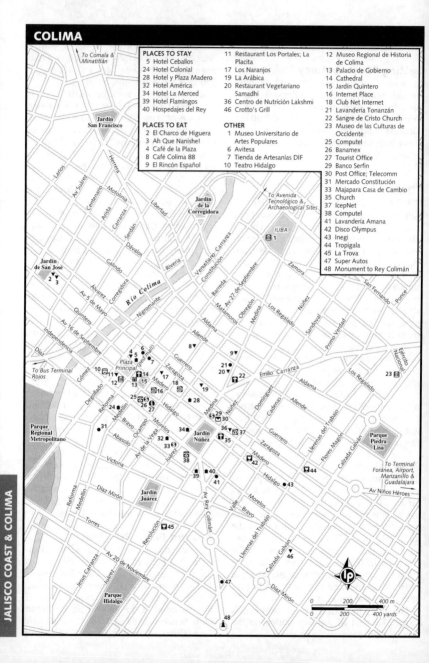

PLACES TO STAY
5 Hotel Ceballos
24 Hotel Colonial
28 Hotel y Plaza Madero
32 Hotel América
34 Hotel La Merced
39 Hotel Flamingos
40 Hospedajes del Rey

PLACES TO EAT
2 El Charco de Higuera
3 Ah Que Nanishe!
4 Café de la Plaza
8 Café Colima 88
9 El Rincón Español

11 Restaurant Los Portales; La Placita
17 Los Naranjos
19 La Arábica
20 Restaurant Vegetariano Samadhi
36 Centro de Nutrición Lakshmi
46 Crotto's Grill

OTHER
1 Museo Universitario de Artes Populares
6 Avitesa
7 Tienda de Artesanías DIF
10 Teatro Hidalgo

12 Museo Regional de Historia de Colima
13 Palacio de Gobierno
14 Cathedral
15 Jardín Quintero
16 Internet Place
18 Club Net Internet
21 Lavandería Tonanzán
22 Sangre de Cristo Church
23 Museo de las Culturas de Occidente
25 Computel
26 Banamex
27 Tourist Office
29 Banco Serfin
30 Post Office; Telecomm
31 Mercado Constitución
33 Majapara Casa de Cambio
35 Church
37 IcepNet
38 Computel
41 Lavandería Amana
42 Disco Olympus
43 Inegi
44 Tropigala
45 La Trova
47 Super Autos
48 Monument to Rey Colimán

the stairway to celebrate the 200th anniversary of the birth of independence hero Miguel Hidalgo, who was once parish priest of Colima. The murals depict Mexican history from the Spanish conquest to independence.

On the south side of the plaza, **Portal Morelos** is a handsome colonnade shading outdoor tables. **Museo Regional de Historia de Colima** (☎ 312-92-28; Portal Morelos 1; admission US$3; open 9am-6pm Tues-Sat, 5pm-8pm Sun) is worth a visit to see well-displayed, quality ceramic vessels and figurines (mostly people and cute Tepezcuintle dogs) unearthed in Colima state. Other permanent displays include costumes and shellwork from the Colima coast and exhibits on the 19th- and 20th-century history of the state.

Teatro Hidalgo (cnr Degollado & Independencia), one block south of Plaza Principal, was built in neoclassical style between 1871 and 1883 on a site originally donated to the city by Miguel Hidalgo. The theater was destroyed by the earthquakes of 1932 and 1941, and reconstruction was undertaken in 1942. It still needs a little help.

Museo de las Culturas de Occidente

This Museum of Western Cultures (☎ 313-06-08; cnr Calzada Galván & Ejército Nacional; admission US$1.75; open 9am-6:30pm Tues-Sun) is located a little over 1km east of the city center. On exhibit are many pre-Hispanic ceramic vessels, figurines and musical instruments from Colima state, with explanations in Spanish. Most impressive are the human figures and Tepezcuintle dogs, but the wide variety of other figures includes mammals, reptiles, fish and birds, depicted with a cartoonlike expressiveness that would make Walt Disney proud.

Museo Universitario de Artes Populares

This museum (☎ 312-68-69; cnr Av 27 de Septiembre & Gallardo; admission US$1, free Sun; open 10am-2pm & 5pm-8pm Tues-Sat, 10am-1pm Sun) is about 900m north of Plaza Principal in the Instituto Universitario de Bellas Artes (IUBA). It displays an excellent collection of folk art from Colima and other states, with a particularly good section of costumes and masks used in traditional Colima dances. Other fascinating exhibits include instruments, gourd art, lacquerware, textiles, basketry, folk art and papier mâché.

Adjacent to the museum, the interesting **Taller de Reproducciones** is a workshop making reproductions of ancient Coliman ceramic figures. Some of these figures may be on sale at the museum shop, which stocks an assortment of inexpensive folk-art souvenirs.

Parks

Parque Regional Metropolitano, a few blocks southwest of the city center, has a small zoo, a swimming pool, a café and a forest with an artificial lake. You can rent bikes to explore the forest paths, or rowboats to cruise the lake.

Towards the east, **Parque Piedra Lisa** (Calzada Galván) is named after its famous Sliding Stone, which is visible from the park entrance (close to the traffic circle where Galván and Aldama meet). Legend says that visitors who slide on this stone will some day return to Colima, either to marry or to die.

Archaeological Sites

On the north side of town are two archaeological sites dating from as early as 1500 BC. Both are still being excavated. **La Campana** (Tecnológico s/n; admission US$2.50, free Sun; open 9am-5pm Tues-Sun) is easily accessible by a No 7 or No 22 bus from the city center. It's about 5km from Colima. Several low, pyramid-like structures have been excavated and restored, along with a small tomb you can look into and a space that appears to be a ball court (very unusual in western Mexico). The structures seem to be oriented due north toward Volcán de Fuego, which makes an impressive backdrop to the site. A taxi from Colima costs US$4.

The other site, **El Chanal** (admission US$2.50, free Sun; open 10am-6pm Tues-Sun), is in the countryside 3km north of Tecnológico about 1.5km before La Campana. Only serious archaeology buffs should visit;

it's not as interesting and more difficult to reach. A taxi from Colima costs US$5.

Special Events

Many masked dances are performed at fiestas in Colima state. The Museo Universitario de Artes Populares has a good display of the masks and costumes worn by the dancers, and plenty of information on the subject. The following festivals take place in or very near Colima city.

Ferias Charro–Taurinas San Felipe de Jesús For 15 days in late January and early February, this celebration takes place in Villa de Álvarez, about 5km north of the city center. Each day of the festival, except Tuesday and Friday, a large crowd parades through the streets, accompanied by giant *mojigangos* (giant puppets of famous Mexicans or Colima celebrities) and groups of musicians. They start at Colima's cathedral and go to Villa de Álvarez, where the celebrations continue with food, music, rodeos and bullfights.

Feria de Todos los Santos Also called the Feria de Colima, the Colima state fair (late October and early November) includes agricultural and handicraft exhibitions, cultural events and carnival rides. About 10 municipalities are represented.

Día de la Virgen de Guadalupe From about December 1 to the actual feast day, on December 12, women and children dress in costume to pay homage at the Virgin's altar in the cathedral. In the evenings the Jardín Quintero behind the cathedral fills with busy food stalls.

Places to Stay

Rooms in budget hotels can vary in size, quality and features, so ask to see a couple before registering.

Hotel Colonial (☎ 313-08-77; *Medellín 142; singles/doubles US$13-18/14-20*) has old and new rooms, all simple, tidy and a bit dark. Small grassy areas outside soften the edges a bit.

Hotel La Merced (☎ 312-69-69; *Juárez 82; singles/doubles US$17/20*) stashes its best rooms, the larger ones with two beds, in the older back section away from the street. It's a decent budget place, and there's off-street parking too.

Hotel Flamingos (☎ 312-25-25; *Rey Colimán 18; singles/doubles US$16/22*) is a good budget choice. Rooms aren't anything to write home about, but are bright and have balconies, TV and fan – the 4th floor even has views, though there's some street noise. Those facing west bake in the afternoon sun.

Hospedajes del Rey (☎/fax 313-36-83; *Rey Colimán 125; 1/2 beds US$29/33*) takes good care of its 13 modern rooms; get one farther back for better sleep. There's cable TV and fan, and it's friendly.

Hotel y Plaza Madero (☎ 330-28-95; *Madero 165; 1/2 beds US$44/55*) is good, pleasant, modern and inside a shopping mall. At least it's quiet at night, when the mall is closed to shoppers.

Hotel Ceballos (☎ 312-44-44, fax 312-06-45; e hceballos@ucnet.com.mx; *Portal Medellín 12; rooms from US$62*) is a stately hotel dating from 1880, and was in its past home to three state governors. Beautifully remodelled rooms come with high ceilings, air-con and TV; the fancier rooms display French windows opening onto small balconies, but the least expensive ones are on the small side.

Hotel América (☎ 312-74-88, fax 314-44-25; e hamerica@prodigy.com.mx; *Morelos 162; rooms/suites US$55/88*) could use a remodel on its standard rooms and hallways, though the suites are large and have indoor or outdoor balconies. Enclosed garden areas surround them all.

Places to Eat

The food is good in Colima, thanks to an abundance of fresh fruit and vegetables, savory seafood and choice coffee. Budget-minded travelers can check out **Mercado Constitución** (cnr Abasolo & Medellín) for juices and snacks. Many small restaurants around Plaza Principal offer good simple fare at outdoor tables.

Café de la Plaza (*Portal Medellín 20; mains US$3.50-7; open 7am-midnight daily*) sits across from the plaza, with high ceilings and a jukebox full of Mexican and Western music. Nothing is high priced, and the menu includes a large traditional US- or Mexican-style breakfast. In the same vein are **Restaurant Los Portales** and **La Placita**, on the opposite side of the plaza.

Ah Qué Nanishe! (☎ 314-21-97; Calle 5 de Mayo 267; mains US$5-7; open 1pm-midnight Wed-Mon) lives up to its name 'How delicious!' Fine Oaxacan specialties like *moles* (thick sauces made with many spices) and *chapulines* (fried grasshoppers) are placed in front of you in an airy, colorful and comfortable environment.

El Charco de Higuera (☎ 313-01-92; Jardín de San José s/n; mains US$6-8; open 7am-midnight daily) has a pretty standard menu, with the usual Mexican soups, *antojitos* (light snacks) and grills, but the outdoor tables and lively atmosphere make it an enjoyable place to sit down and appease those hunger pangs.

El Rincón Español (☎ 044-312-318-34-20; Medina 167; mains US$5-13; open 10:30am-11pm Tues-Sat, 10:30-6pm Sun) offers well-prepared nouvelle cuisine, as well as old standbys, such as tapas and paella, in relaxed indoor spaces and a beautiful elegant courtyard.

Los Naranjos (☎ 312-00-29; Barreda 34; mains US$5-9; open 8am-11:30pm daily) is a bit upscale, serving meat dishes and *antojitos*. Not a bad place to bring your parents, if they're around.

Café Colima 88 (☎ 330-01-08; Av 27 de Septiembre 129; mains US$5-7; open 5pm-midnight Wed-Mon) cooks up Mexican specialties in a leafy, intimate courtyard. 'Sexy' drinks are US$3.50, and there's live music Thursday to Sunday nights at 9:30pm.

Restaurant Vegetariano Samadhi (☎ 313-24-98; Medina 125; mains US$2-3; open 8:30am-6pm Mon-Sat) has passable but not great veggie food such as soy burgers (damp bun) and chicken Caesar salad (iceberg lettuce). The music's insipid, but at least the garden courtyard is pleasant.

Centro de Nutrición Lakshmi (☎ 312-64-33; Madero 265; light meals US$2; open 8am-9:30pm Mon-Sat, 6pm-9:30pm Sun) is mostly a whole-grain bakery and health-products store. A small café serves light breakfasts, soy burgers and yogurt.

La Arábica (☎ 314-70-01; Guerrero 162; coffee from US$1.50; open 8am-3pm Mon-Sat) will do triple shots of espresso without batting an eyelid. Of course, they'll leave you twitchier than a chipmunk in a mustard gas attack, but you'll be sitting pretty in the astroturfed patio out back.

Crotto's Grill (☎ 314-97-97; Calzada Galvan 207; mains US$6-10; open 8am-midnight Tues-Sun) serves shrimp, meat dishes like fajitas, and a load of mixed drinks on its open patios. Live music plays Fridays and Saturdays at 9pm.

Entertainment

Other than a few discos, Colima is basically a quiet city, but there are some things you can do in the evening – hanging around the plaza and lingering over coffee or beer is a well-practiced pastime here. To help with the relaxed mood, the state band plays in Plaza Principal every Thursday and Sunday from 6pm to 8pm.

La Trova (☎ 314-11-59; Revolución 363; open 8pm-2am daily) calls itself a 'bar bohemio', but attracts affluent older couples rather than ragged bohemians. There's live nightly music and a casual courtyard.

Disco Olympus (☎ 313-42-81; Madero s/n; open 9pm-3am Wed-Sat) thumps from a block away. Throngs of local students make this flashy disco popular and *the* place to be seen within walking distance of the city.

Tropigala (☎ 330-65-65; cnr Zaragoza & Llerenas del Trabajo; admission US$8-13; open 9pm-2am Wed-Sat) swings with merengue and salsa beats. There's also a small dance floor, colorful tropical decor and lots of tables for wallflowers.

Argenta (☎ 313-80-12; Sevilla del Río 574; admission free up to US$3; open 10pm-3am Wed-Sat) is a fashionable hot spot for dance and Latin sounds, attracting a mostly well-dressed 20- to 30-something crowd and some very smooth movers. It's about 2km northeast of the city center, so grab a taxi.

Getting There & Away
Air Both Aeromar (☎ 313-55-88) and Aero California (☎ 314-48-50) serve Mexico City daily (with onward connections) and Tijuana several times a week. **Avitesa** travel agency (☎ 312-19-84; cnr Constitución & Zaragoza), a block north of Plaza Principal, can make flight arrangements.

Bus Colima has two bus stations. The main long-distance terminal is **Terminal Foránea**, 2km east of the city center at the junction of Niños Héroes and the city's eastern bypass. The terminal has pay phones, a *caseta telefónica*, luggage keep, a pharmacy and some places to eat. Daily departures include:

Guadalajara US$21 deluxe, 2½ hours, 220km, six with ETN; US$15 1st class, frequent with La Línea and Primera Plus; US$13 1st class, frequent with Ómnibus de México, Servicios Coordinados; US$11.50 2nd class, frequent with Sur de Jalisco

Manzanillo US$8 deluxe, 1½ hours, 101km, seven with ETN; US$5 1st class, many with La Línea, Primera Plus, Servicios Coordinados; US$4.50 2nd class, two hours, frequent with Autobuses Nuevo Horizonte, Autotransportes del Sur de Jalisco (via Tecomán and Armería)

Mexico City (Terminal Norte) US$70 deluxe, 10 hours, 740km, with ETN at 9pm; US$54 1st class, several with Primera Plus, with La Línea at 9:30pm; US$43 1st class, with Flecha Amarilla at 3:30pm and 9pm; US$50 1st class, with Ómnibus de México at 8:30pm and 10pm; US$43 2nd class, two with Autobuses de Occidente

Autobuses de Occidente and others also run many buses daily to Morelia and Uruapan.

The second bus station is **Terminal Rojos**, about 1.5km west of Plaza Principal on the Carretera a Coquimatlán. This is the station for buses to Comala and nearby places, and for 2nd-class **Autobuses Colima-Manzanillo** buses, which travel every 15 minutes to Manzanillo (US$4.50, 1½ hours), Tecomán (US$2.50, 45 minutes) and also to Armería (US$2.50, 45 minutes).

Getting Around

Colima's airport is near Cuauhtémoc, 12km northeast of the city center off the highway to Guadalajara. A taxi to or from the city center is about US$15.

Local buses (US$0.30) run 6am to 9pm daily. Ruta 4 and 5 buses from the **Terminal Foránea** will take you to the city center; to return to the bus station you can catch Ruta 4 on Av 5 de Mayo or Zaragoza. To reach Terminal Rojos, take a Ruta 2 or Ruta 4 bus west along Morelos.

Taxi fares within town are US$1.25 to US$2.50.

Colima's not a bad place to rent a car, and you might want one to explore the volcanoes and the nearby villages. Try **Super Autos** (☎ 313-26-26; Rey Colimán 381; open 8am-9pm Mon-Sat, 9am-2pm Sun), which has Tsurus for US$55 per 24 hours including tax, 300km and 10% deductible insurance.

AROUND COLIMA
Comala
☎ 312 • pop 7700 • elevation 600m

About 9km north of Colima is this darling little town, with great views of the nearby twin volcanoes, Fuego and Nevado. Comala is known for its fine handicrafts, especially wood furniture. Many folks from all around visit on weekends, and on Sunday there are markets for browsing. It's not so small that there isn't an Internet café or *casa de cambio* (exchange house), however.

The leafy plaza has a fine white gazebo, pretty flowering trees and a cute little church with a mix of architectural styles. Under the arches along one side of the plaza are some inviting *centros botaneros*, which are bars where minors are allowed (but not served alcohol) and where each beverage is accompanied by a free snack. They're open from about noon to 6pm. Many people come to Comala just to enjoy these restaurants.

Comala buses leave Colima's Terminal Rojos approximately every 15 minutes; the fare is US$0.60 for the 20-minute ride. In Comala, the buses back to Colima depart from the plaza.

Zona Mágica

Approximately 5km north of Comala there's a stretch of road that seems to slope downhill, but if you let your car roll...hey! It stops, then goes backward. This convincing optical illusion works in both directions: if you're heading south, you can put your car in neutral and it will roll 'uphill'.

Suchitlán
☎ 318 • pop 3200 • elevation 1200m

The village of Suchitlán, 8km northeast of Comala and 1km east of the main road, isn't so off the beaten path that you won't see older, white gringos stumbling around here and there. Suchitlán is otherwise famous for its animal masks and witches. The masks are carved in the village and worn by dancers in the traditional Danza de los Morenos, which takes place here during Semana Santa. The dance commemorates the legend that dancing animals enabled the Marys to rescue Christ's body by distracting the Roman guards. You can ask around for the homes of the mask makers, who often have masks for sale.

Take a break at **Restaurant Portales de Suchitlán** (☎ 395-44-52; Galeana 10; appetizers US$2-6; open 8:30am-6:30pm Tues-Sun). It serves killer handmade corn tortillas and little plates of snacks (including rabbit), along with some alcoholic beverages. It's at the southwest corner of the plaza and popular with locals and tourists alike; pleasant tables are set around a garden and patio, and parrots provide a squawking background.

The walls are decorated with dozens of animal masks, which are available for purchase (US$18 to US$28).

Buses to Suchitlán leave almost hourly from Colima's Terminal Rojos (US$0.85, 45 minutes).

San Antonio, Laguna La María & Carrizalillos

From Suchitlán the road winds about 8.5km north to **El Jacal de San Antonio**, a restaurant where tables under big palapas have an unsurpassed view of Volcán de Fuego. It's worth a stop for lunch, but it's open only on Saturday, Sunday and holidays.

About 5km farther, the paved road ends at **Mahakua – Hacienda de San Antonio** (☎ 312-313-44-11, fax 312-314-37-27; w www .mahakua.com; singles/doubles US$1030/1158, with meals, drinks & activities). This superluxurious resort hotel is a beautifully restored 19th-century casa grande set on a former coffee farm. The suites are nicely

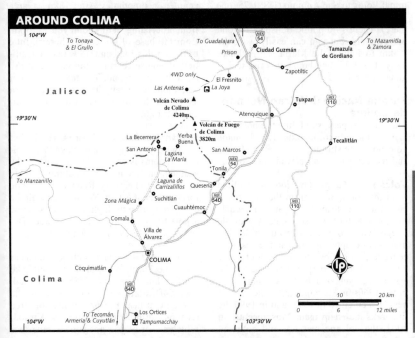

AROUND COLIMA

furnished with tapestries, antiques and original artworks.

A gravel road continues 1km to the small village of **San Antonio**. About 1.5km east of here lies **Laguna La María**, a lovely cool green lake surrounded by hills and lush trees – it's a popular weekend picnic, fishing and camping spot. Admission is US$1 per person, and there are a few rustic stone **houses** (☎ 312-320-88-91) containing simple stoves; rates are US$33 to US$55 for two to eight people. If you want one at holiday times, call ahead to book. Camp sites go for US$1.75 per person.

Laguna de Carrizalillos is back down the main road 7km and east 3.5km along the branch road to Queseria. There are picnic tables (US$1.75) and accommodations (camping sites US$4.50, bungalows US$20), but it's not as nice as La María. Admission costs US$0.75 per person, and horse rentals are available for US$3.50 per half hour.

Three buses daily run from Colima's **Terminal Rojos** to San Antonio (US$1.75, one hour; those saying 'La Becerrera' will go there). There's no public transport beyond San Antonio, but you can easily walk the 1.5km to Laguna La María. Three buses daily (US$1.75, one hour) also run to Laguna Carrizalillos.

Parque Nacional Volcán Nevado de Colima

This national park, straddling the border of Colima and Jalisco, includes two dramatic volcanoes: the still-active Volcán de Fuego and the extinct Volcán Nevado de Colima.

Volcán de Fuego Overlooking Colima from the north, 30km from the city as the crow flies, the steaming Volcán de Fuego de Colima (3820m) is also called Volcán de Fuego (Volcano of Fire) or Fuego de Colima. It has erupted 30 times in the past four centuries, with a big eruption about every 70 years. A major burp in 1913 spelled the end of one cycle of activity. Another began in the 1960s and is ongoing. Some 3km of new lava emerged in 1998, and in 1999 the fireworks started up again. Most recently, in 2002, the volcano was hot and bothered

enough to prompt the evacuation of the nearby pueblo Yerba Buena. Information on the current condition of the volcano is posted (in Spanish) on the University of Colima's website: **W** www.ucol.mx/volcan

If you want to take a closer look, you'll need a four-wheel drive. The fastest way – but more expensive (US$8) – is to take the *cuota* (toll) road, Hwy 54D, from Colima toward Guadalajara and get off at the first exit past the stinky mill town of Atenquique (the exit is marked 'Tuxpan'). Backtrack through Atenquique (you'll now be on the free road, Hwy 54) and keep an eye out for the landmark parabolic church. Go 2.5km uphill past the church, to Km 56, and turn right at the 'RMO Cerro Alto–Telmex' sign onto the 32km dirt track to the volcano. The longer approach is to take the free road, Hwy 54, all the way north to Km 56, turning left at the 'RMO Cerro Alto–Telmex' sign.

On this 32km dirt track, stay on the main route. Expect to brush past bushes and encounter deep potholes. After 18km, a large bump in the road prevents most vehicles from proceeding; at this point you are 14km from the base of the cone. There is little traffic on this road and no water or facilities; if you're fearful your vehicle won't make it, turn around. The track is in poor condition and usually impassable (even for 4WD vehicles) after the July to September/October rains.

Volcán Nevado de Colima The higher and more northerly peak of Nevado de Colima (4240m) is accessible for most of the year, but the best months for climbing it are September to February. Remnants of a pine forest cover most of Nevado, and alpine desert appears at the highest altitudes. Snow is possible on the upper slopes between December and March – *nevado* means 'snowy' or 'snow-covered'.

To access the volcano with your own car (two-wheel drive is OK in dry season), take the fast but expensive (US$8) toll road, Hwy 54D, north about 45 minutes to the Tuxpan exit near Km 63. Or take the free Hwy 54 north about 1½ hours to Km 63. Whichever way you go, you'll come to a confusing roundabout intersection here. An overhead sign says 'Guadalajara Cuota'. Go left around the roundabout and follow another sign that says 'Guadalajara libre'. Take the branch that finally says 'Colima Cuota' and go over the yellow and white bridge. You'll parallel Hwy 54D and eventually cross over it. Head towards Ciudad Guzmán; just before you reach the town, turn left onto El Grullo road (from Km 63, this should be about 15 minutes). For the next 8km you'll go back under the *cuota* highway, past a prison, and past the El Fresnito turnoff. On the left you'll see a good gravel road marked 'Nevado de Colima.' Go 16km on it to reach the volcano.

If you've no car and want some support, the El Fresnito-based family of **Agustín Ibarra** (☎ *313-414-70-03; Montes 85)* does a different approach to the volcano. Contact them in advance for help with transport and organization. Sr Ibarra no longer conducts guided treks up the mountain, but his son is sometimes available to provide 4WD transport up the rough road to Las Antenas (the radio masts; also referred to as *microondas,* the microwave station). It's wise to camp here for a night to acclimatize to the altitude, though there are no facilities. Bring all the supplies you'll need, including water. From Las Antenas it's about a 1½-hour walk to the top on a reasonably well-marked trail.

On your very own without a car, it's possible to walk up from El Fresnito to Las Antenas in six to eight hours. It's about 22km, uphill. The Ibarra family has a couple of basic rooms at their house in El Fresnito to rent to climbers. By bus, take one of the frequent **Autotransportes del Sur de Jalisco** 2nd-class buses from Colima's main bus station to Ciudad Guzmán (US$4, 1½ hours). From there, take another bus to El Fresnito. They are much more frequent during the morning.

Tampumacchay

Some small shaft tombs from about AD 200 perch on the edge of a ravine at Tampumacchay, near the town of Los Ortices about 15km south of Colima. For US$2.50 per person, a guide (who probably doesn't speak English and is only superficially knowledgeable on this subject) will take you around; only budding archaeologists will find these holes in the ground interesting, although the masses of daddy longlegs huddling in the tiny grottoes are worth a shudder. The **hotel** *(doubles US$28)* where you start the tour has a pleasant restaurant and pool to splash around in, along with some picnic spots (both pool and picnic spots cost US$1.75). From the hotel to the tombs it's a hot 1.5km walk or drive.

Buses go from Colima's Terminal Rojos to Los Ortices.

Michoacán Coast

Adventurers looking for desolate expanses of golden sand, tiny rocky beach coves, quiet estuaries harboring a multitude of birdlife, and mostly undeveloped coastal towns will discover them all here along the scenic 250km coast of Michoacán. Hwy 200 traces the shoreline and passes dozens of different beaches; some have gentle lapping waves and are good for swimming, others have big breakers suitable for surfing. Many of the beaches are uninhabited; some have small communities. Overdeveloped mega-resorts are few and far between, nightlife only comes calm and laid back, and just a few towns attract large groups of gringos. Mango, coconut, papaya and banana plantations line the highway, while the green Sierra Madre del Sur mountains form a lush backdrop inland. Cattle pastures peek from between predominantly deciduous tree-covered hillsides, and the odd cactus or weaverbird nest adds visual curiosity.

The Michoacán coast is certainly a gorgeous part of Mexico and wonderful to explore on your own, but, if you're on public transport, you'd better have some time on your hands, as the isolation on this coast makes for slow going at times; you might even be tempted to make hitching part of your daily routine.

Plenty of Michoacán's coves and beaches are not listed in this or any guidebook, and those places will be even more isolated and untouched. They are waiting to be discovered, so see them now.

BOCA DE APIZA
☎ 313

Near the Michoacán–Colima border, at the mouth of the Río Coahuayana, basks this dusty little fishing town lined with egret-filled mangrove lagoons. A 300m line of competing seafood *enramadas* (thatched roof, open-air restaurants) crowd the beach, and on Sunday afternoons hordes of local kids bathe and splash in the river. Gentle waves, hot black sands and general fun-in-the-sun

Highlights

- Enjoying lush, primordial and untouched mountain scenery along the spectacular coast

- Camping on one of the many isolated beaches with very few signs of human development

- Exploring authentic Mexican villages and towns that don't receive many foreign visitors

- Surfing awesome waves at the laid-back communities of Playa La Ticla, Playa Azul or Barra de Nexpa

- Watching sea turtles come ashore in summer and fall, to lay precious eggs at Playa Maruata

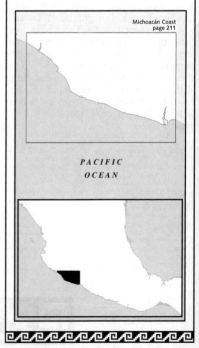

Michoacán Coast
page 211

PACIFIC
OCEAN

activities prevail here, and your big foreign gringo face might even attract the attention of the town drunk, who will pause to practice his English on you. If this sounds like your idea of an adventure, turn off Hwy 200 at the town of Coahuayana (Km 228) and continue about 4km to the beach.

There's another side to Boca de Apiza, literally. Across the river (and across the state border) is where Mexican families have built many *palapas* (thatched-roof shelters) for Sunday picnics. Here a long beach heads northwards, with a sandy access road going inland 6.5km to meet back with the highway. There are no services here, so bring everything if you want to hang out for a little while.

Thinking about sticking around? Try **Hotel Sarahi** *(☎ 327-05-64; 1/2 beds US$11/ 17, bungalows US$39)*, the most decent digs in town, with plain rooms that will do in a pinch. Management is hoping to add TV and air-con, so prices may rise.

SAN JUAN DE ALIMA
☎ 313

About 20km south of Boca de Apiza, near where the highway meets the coast, lie the concrete bumps of San Juan de Alima (Km 211). It's a town still defining itself: half-finished constructions attest to a continuing growth process. A main road of cobbles and concrete keeps dust levels down and heat levels up. However, there are reasons to come: plenty of hotels, small stores and beachfront restaurants service the tourists, and are spread out along the wide, flat and long coast where creamy surfing breakers curl and fall. Be careful of swimming out too far, though, where heavier currents lurk.

Places to Stay & Eat
The restaurants you want to eat at are on the beach, and they're just like the ones up and down the rest of the coast, so don't expect any surprises. There's a choice of slightly atypical hotels, though.

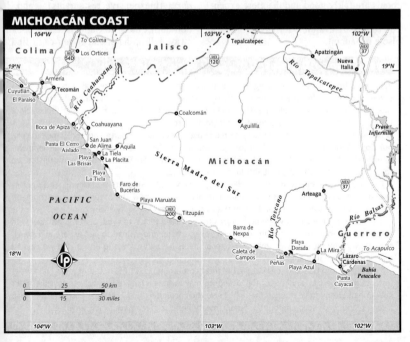

MICHOACÁN COAST

Hotel Puerta del Mar (☎ 327-05-64; *rooms US$17*) comes with clean, bright, good-sized balconied rooms overlooking its own palapa restaurant and the beach. There are small swimming pools to wade in, and the whole thing is 500m north of town.

Hotel Villas de San Juan (☎ 311-25-00; *rooms US$17, bungalows US$33*) is more centrally located and painted an indescribable shade of blue. Inside the high wing, sea view rooms are decent but could use some balconies. Bungalows lining the driveway have kitchens and hold up to four people.

Hotel Coral (☎ 328-80-06; *1/2 beds US$11/17*) has decent, comfortable rooms. The otherwise empty ground floor is marked by supporting pillars, however – giving a bleak, tidal-wave-ready feel to the whole place. Small pink rooms greet you up the concrete stairs, if that's where you want to go.

Hotel Parador (☎ 328-87-12; *rooms US$17-22*) is another tidal-wave-fearing place, but with a much more pleasant ambience. Small rooms are fairly good and the more expensive ones have balconies with views. Air-con rooms are available for US$33; there's also a restaurant.

LAS BRISAS

This tiny community, 1.5km down a dirt road from the highway (Km 207), is accented by just a few palapa restaurants and one big-ass, incongruous mid-range hotel, the only solid building on the beach. It's very peaceful, with swaying palms and a long, wide and flat beach with fine, firm dark sand. The wind tends to kick up (as the name implies) and a nice birdy lagoon stands nearby. Camping and RV parking (no hookups) are reasonably pleasant here.

Unless you camp, you'll be staying at the moderately priced **Hotel Paraíso Las Brisas** (☎ 324-71-20; e war2000@hotmail.com; *1/2 beds US$50/66, suite with Jacuzzi US$88*). There are 30 large, modern, attractive rooms here and they come with cable TV and air-con, and there's even a pool.

LA PLACITA

Here's a cute little highway town (Km 199) with a leafy plaza and surrounding *comedores* (inexpensive restaurants) – and, if you're going south, the last Pemex gas station until Caleta de Campos, about 150km away. Fill up here, and if you can't find a

---

Cocos Frios: 10 Pesos!

What says 'tropical' more than lying on a hammock at the beach, sipping through a straw the transparent and mildly sweet milk from a freshly opened coconut? *Cocos* are available at many beachside restaurants or road stalls; the dead giveaway is a shady pile of them near a chopping block (often a section of palm tree) cleaved by a large machete.

If you're very lucky, the *cocos* will be stored in big freezer-like compartments and come out cold, but sipping coconut milk straight out of a coconut is wonderfully refreshing even at air temperature. And, unlike most of Mexico's tap water, it's safe to drink. Some huge specimens can store up to 1L of liquid, though most probably hold about half that.

First the coconuteer selects a (hopefully) big green coconut, tender at the stalk end. This signifies the coconut is immature, has soft flesh and harbors plenty of milk. The coconuteer then chops off one end (enough to make it stand upright) and proceeds to chip away at the other end: once the outer shell is off, the tender white flesh begins to show. The trick is to avoid piercing this layer with a severe chop that would have liquid spraying everywhere, and instead to just expose and peel it back slowly without losing any milk. Most coconuteers have this down to an art, and we haven't seen any with missing fingers yet.

Prices vary from US$0.50 to US$1.50, but most cost around US$1.25. In tourist areas and fancier restaurants, expect to pay at least this. The price may include a final few whacks to split the fruit's hulk in half after you've finished the milk. Have the coconuteer add chili, lime juice and salt, grab a spoon, and enjoy scooping out the tender, meaty flesh...a great quick snack, anytime!

Hwy 200, Michoacán Style

Be prepared for some slower driving along the stretch of coast from Km 74 to Km 134, somewhere between Faro de Bucerías and Barra de Nexpa. This area isn't the highest priority for Mexican highway funds, and the road is mostly curvy with some minor rough spots. Give yourself a couple more hours of daylight to cover this stretch, and make sure your vehicle is full of gas; there are no Pemex stations between La Placita (Km 199) and Caleta de Campos (Km 50), though you'll pass dinky little towns where signs may offer a few liters for sale. Also, don't expect much solid accommodation when the sun gets low: unless you're camping, you won't run across many places to stay, though there will be a few eateries along the way.

roof to sleep under in nearby Playa La Ticla, try **Hotel Reyna** or **Hotel de la Costa**, two basic cheapies near the highway.

PLAYA LA TICLA

In the early morning, calm seas near the shore give birth to curving arcs of gorgeous, misty-edged waves, simply beautiful to watch – but even better to ride. The quaint pueblo of La Ticla, hiding behind a small coastal mountain, draws mostly foreign surfers with their own vehicles. They also bring their own boards and camping equipment, since beach services are fairly undeveloped and the quiet little town isn't yet geared toward tourism of any sort. A nearby palm-ringed lagoon provides bird-watching possibilities, salt-free swimming and a variation in landscape.

You can **camp** *(sites per person US$1.25)* under flimsy palapa shelters at the northern edge of town. The only other place to stay is **Parador Turistico la Ticla** *(☎ 313-88-665; camp sites per person US$3.50, rooms with shared bathroom US$11, cabanas US$66)*. If you snag a tiny room, don't expect much privacy or peace; the ceiling is shared and your neighbors will be young surfers, dude, so bring earplugs. Perhaps the interesting

burning smells in the air will aid entry into a dreamlike state.

Restaurant Serrano *(mains US$2.50-8)*, nearest the lagoon's mouth, is popular for breakfast and seafood. Camp for free if you eat there often enough.

You have a choice of two dirt roads that lead to Playa La Ticla, at Km 183 or 186. And don't forget your sunscreen and insect repellent.

FARO DE BUCERÍAS

About 2km down another ubiquitous Mexican beach dirt road, at Km 173, lies a calm, perfectly sized cove, which has decent snorkeling and is wonderful for swimming. Known for its clear, pale-blue waters, soft yellow sand and rocky islands, Faro de Bucerías is also good for camping and having a spot of lunch with the Nahua community. A cute square red-and-white lighthouse sits high up on the hill, and there's some good tide-pooling behind the lofty restaurant **Palapa Miramar** – just be careful getting around the rocky point, and never turn your back on those ocean waves.

There are no hotels; either rumble in with your RV or **camp** *(sites US$8)* under one of the palapa shelters. There are a number of open palapa **seafood restaurants**, which constitute the majority of buildings on the beach.

PLAYA MARUATA

About 1km west of Km 150, past the town's sad, bleak plaza, lies this paradise for beach lovers and rustic campers. Playa Maruata is actually three beaches in one – two large, climbable rocky heads, riddled with some small caves and tunnels, separate the three sections of white-sand crescents. Each has a different size and character: the one on the right (northernmost) is about 1km long and has the roughest waters (don't try swimming here); the middle arc is more intimate and OK for strong swimmers; the one on the left is 3km long, fairly wide, decorated with fishing boats and where most camping shelters and their snack sheds lie. There are also shallow, palm-ringed lagoons to explore, often visited by vultures looking for fish scraps (you can get mighty close to them on the ground). A couple of simple **palapa restaurants** and some camping shelters dot the varied landscape here and there, but there are no real concrete structures or hotels. It's not bad as a pleasant and tranquil place to hang out with your sweetie or a large stack of paperbacks.

Maruata is also the principal Mexican beach where black sea turtles lay their eggs – from June to December they come ashore nightly. These and other species of sea turtles are set free here each year by conservation programmes.

Camping shelters are pretty much all the same and most charge US$1.25 per person. Have a look around and find one that appeals. You can also string up a hammock, or rent one at some shelters. Those who need four semisolid walls can try one of the few rustic, two-bed **cabanas** for US$11, and RV drivers have several discreet spots in which to park. For simple groceries such as fruit, ramen, cereal or beer, there's a **small store** at the end of the southernmost beach past all the palapa shelters.

BARRA DE NEXPA
☎ 753

At Km 55.5, just north of Puente Nexpa bridge and 1km from the highway down a dirt road, lies the small community of Barra de Nexpa. The salt 'n' pepper bar of sand here, and a good number of healthy waves – which build up and curl sharply in the mornings – are all that's necessary to bring in surfers from around the world. An inland lagoon empties out at the southern end of the

Scorpions

Many travelers never even see one, but *alacranes* (scorpions) are a common and dangerous pest in many parts of Mexico. There are more than 200 species of this particular arachnid worldwide, all of them poisonous to some degree (though only seven can actually kill a human being). Their habitat ranges widely, from high desert areas to low tropical coastlines.

In Durango, scorpions are collected by the thousands and turned into attractive knick-knacks such as keychains, paperweights and napkin holders. But across other parts of Mexico, the little beasties aren't seen in quite the same light. Scorpions sting more than 200,000 people and kill hundreds of children in the country every year, and intense extermination programmes have successfully been implemented to limit the populations of this 'national pest.'

Scorpions are often seen on the floors, walls or even ceilings of old dwellings, such as wooden beach cabanas, though they also favor trash heaps and rock piles. They often like to hide out in dark, enclosed spaces such as your hiking boots, backpack, clothes and even bedsheets. If staying in rustic abodes, shake out your footwear, clothing and backpack – especially when they've been lying on the ground. Hands and feet are the body parts most often pricked, so don't reach into strange rocky crevices indiscriminately. You shouldn't get overly paranoid, but be aware that the little creatures could lurk in some surprising places.

Young children and feeble elderly folk are most affected by stings. If you're a healthy adult (and not especially allergic to insect bites or stings) you should survive an encounter, though you may experience intense pain, convulsions, sweating, difficulty swallowing, rolling eyes, nausea and heart palpitations. Get yourself to a clinic quickly; it should have an excellent antivenin readily available, which starts working within 20 minutes or so.

But remember: scorpions aren't all that bad, feeding on a variety of insects – including cockroaches! In places where there are many scorpions, cockroach populations are low. So if you see one of these critters, think twice before lowering the boot.

sometimes stony 3km beach, with decent swimming there and beyond. Rustic cabanas, good camp sites and some decent restaurants add comfort to the mix, and the very laid-back feel completes the recipe for a peaceful stay. Keep an eye out for scorpions, though.

Pablo's Palapa, near Chichos restaurant, repairs and rents a surfboard or two. Look for the small palapa building with a broken surfboard as a sign. There's a larger surf shop in the nearby service town of Caleta de Campos; a taxi there costs about US$3.50.

Places to Stay & Eat

Gilberto's Cabañas *(☎ 247-57; camp sites US$2.50, trailer sites with water hookups from US$3.50, most cabanas US$9-22)* offers a variety of cabanas, some more rustic than others, some with kitchen, and most with hammocks (a crucial item here in Nexpa). There's a communal kitchen and shower block for campers and RVs, and Gilberto offers a taxi service to Caleta de Campos. Look for Gilberto's sign on the right side as you enter town.

Marta Mellín *(☎ 602-59; cabanas US$22)* is Gilberto's sister and also rents cabanas; check at her grocery store across from Gilberto's 'office.'

Restaurant Chicho *(☎ 443-437-1323; open 7am-9pm daily)* has tables perched just right for watching surfers cut waves nearby. The food is good, and cabanas here go for US$17 to US$22, with grassy camp sites at US$3 per person.

La Isla Restaurant *(open 7:30am-9pm daily; cabanas & rooms US$11-20)* cooks up the best Western breakfasts around, with good cappuccinos and the largest fruit plate on the coast. A casual book exchange and a taxi service are available.

Noche de Mar Restaurant offers a palapa shelter for free if you eat meals there.

CALETA DE CAMPOS
☎ 753 • pop 3000

A friendly little town on a bluff overlooking a lovely azure bay, Caleta (Km 50) is the region's service center and has two good, clean hotels and several decent places to eat. The paved main drag provides all the essen-

tials, including *casetas teléfonicas* (public telephone call stations), late-night *taquerías* (places to buy tacos), a pharmacy and several *abarrotes* (small groceries). To reach the large cove beach below, take either the dirt and cement road from behind town or the 500m cement road from the highway, past the south end of town. You can swim in the calm waters and grab a bite at one of the many palapa restaurants on the flat beach.

If riding waves is your sport, head to **Surf y Espuma** *(☎ 152-55; open 10am-8pm daily)*, near Hotel Yuritzi, for boogie board or surfboard rentals (US$7 to US$9 per day). It also carries some surfwear, does fishing charters and even washes your laundry (US$1.25 per kilogram).

Caleta's best accommodation is **Hotel Los Arcos** *(☎ 150-38; singles/doubles US$17/22-27, doubles with air-con & hot water US$39)*. Try to get a room with an awesome view of the Bahía de Bufadero blowhole. Or dip into the pool at **Hotel Yuritzi** *(☎ 150-10; Corregidora 10; singles/doubles with fan US$22/27, with air-con & TV US$33/44)*. Rooms are pleasant and spacious, but lack hot water.

Hourly buses depart Caleta for Lázaro Cárdenas from 5am to 7pm (US$3.50, 1½ hours). A taxi between Caleta de Campos and Barra de Nexpa costs US$3.50.

LAS PEÑAS
A small cove at Km 18 is home to eight *enramadas* and one wide but cozy beach, punctuated by rocky headlands. Around the southern point is a much longer beach called **Playa Dorada**, dotted with a few rustic restaurants of its own and stretching as far as you can see. No accommodations are available around here, but camping may be possible – ask around at Playa Dorada or just pick an isloated spot.

PLAYA AZUL
☎ 753 • pop 4000

Some 24km northwest of Lázaro Cárdenas, Playa Azul is a midsized beach resort town backed by lagoons fed by Río Balsas tributaries. It attracts Mexican families during Semana Santa (Holy Week), and during the

Christmas holidays, when all the hotels fill up, prices rise and reservations are necessary. The rest of the time the town is pretty quiet and even desolate-looking, with a trickle of foreign travelers enjoying its very long, flat beach and surfable waves. A strong undertow makes swimming touch-and-go; be very careful, as one man drowned while this author was in town. Also watch out for stray stingrays just under the sand. Swimming is better at Laguna Pichi, 2km east along the beach, where boat trips explore the plant, animal and birdlife that takes refuge in the surrounding mangrove forest. There's also a great big shipwreck just northwest of town that's worth checking out.

Orientation & Information

There are five main streets that run parallel to the beach. The beachside street, usually known as the *malecón* (waterfront street), is officially named Zapata. The second street inland is Carranza, the third one is Madero, the fourth is Independencia and the fifth is Justo Sierra. They are all intersected by Aquiles Serdán, where some good restaurants and a small clothes market are located.

A Pemex station on the corner of Independencia represents the beginning of town and rests 4.5km from the Hwy 200/37 turnoff. It's a major landmark, where buses and Combis gather. The beach is three blocks straight ahead. A few blocks east (left as you face the sea) is a large, bleak plaza. Almost everything you need is somewhere between the plaza and the Pemex station. A long row of seafood *enramadas* stretches along the coast here.

The **post office** *(open 10am-3pm Mon-Fri)* is on Madero behind the Hotel María Teresa, a block off the northeast corner of the plaza. There are several *casetas telefónicas*, including one on Carranza at the market and another near the Pemex.

Activities

Pools provide a safer choice than swimming in the turbulent ocean. Behind Hotel Playa Azul, **Balneario Playa Azul** *(☎ 536-00-91; Malecón; admission US$1.75, free to Hotel Playa Azul guests; open 10am-6pm Sat-Sun)*

has a large swimming pool, a water slide and a restaurant-bar. Hotel Playa Azul and Hotel María Teresa also have courtyard pools with poolside restaurants (see Places to Stay & Eat).

There are seafood restaurants, swimming possibilities and bird-watching boat trips at **Laguna de Pichi**. From the Pemex station go 3.5km east along Independencia. If you don't have a car, you can walk there in 30 minutes, take a taxi (US$3), or try renting a bike at a bike repair shop on Independencia.

To see the shipwrecked remains of the **Norweigan freighter Betula**, head about 2km northwest from town on the coastal road bordering a lagoon. At the end of this dirt track are a parking lot and a few *enramadas*. You'll see the 10-year-old wreck 1km north, buried in sand and looming just offshore. Even if you notice people climbing on the remains, don't be tempted to go out there yourself; the surf is rough and the climb is potentially dangerous. Oyster divers often go out there to harvest beds near the hulk.

If you surf and have no board, check out the bougainvillea-covered shack on the *malecón* near the restaurants Marinera del Pacifico and Pirata del Caribe. It's open from 8am to 6pm daily and rents both **boogie boards** and **surfboards** for the same price: US$2.50 per hour or US$11 per day.

Places to Stay & Eat

You can string up a hammock at most of the beachfront *enramadas;* ask permission from the family running the restaurant, who probably won't mind, especially if you eat there once or twice. If you don't have your own hammock, they may loan you one. A few of the *enramadas* provide public toilets and showers.

Hotel Costa de Oro *(☎ 536-02-51; cnr Madero & Francisco Villa; singles/doubles US$11/17-22)* is a small, friendly and family-run hotel with just more than a dozen spacious rooms.

Hotel María Isabel *(☎ 536-00-16; Madero s/n; singles/doubles US$19/25, 6-bed rooms US$50, TV & air-con US$5.50 extra)* is popular for its swimming pool and 30 good, spacious rooms, some brighter than others.

It's located on the east side of town, past the plaza.

Hotel Playa Azul *(☎ 536-00-91; cnr Carranza & Aquiles Serdán; rooms US$33-39, with TV & air-con US$59, full trailer hookups US$20)* caters to upscale visitors with 73 OK rooms, the best of which are set around the pool. Its restaurant-bar, Las Gaviotas (open 7am to 11pm daily), serves pizza and burgers and has happy hour from 7pm to 8pm; if you eat or drink here, you can use the pool and *balneario* (bathing place) for free.

Hotel María Teresa *(☎ 536-00-05; Independencia 626; singles/doubles with TV & air-con US$39/45)* is great if you can stand the pink-and-blue color scheme. The 42 large and comfortable balconied rooms could use a remodel, but as a whole are a much better deal than Hotel Playa Azul. A poolside palapa restaurant-bar comes with an attractive patio area. Look for this place two blocks north of the plaza.

Playa Azul's **beachfront enramadas** prepare a similar selection of fresh seafood at competitive prices – the fanciest are to the right as you face the beach. Try the *pescado relleno,* a regional specialty – a fried fillet of fish stuffed with seafood.

Two small family restaurants, **Restaurant Galdy** and **Restaurant Familiar Martita**, both on the Aquiles Serdán near Madero, are recommended by locals. Both serve fresh-squeezed juices, good coffee and cheap grub, and are open 7am to 11pm daily. The *comida corrida* (daily special) is US$3, breakfast is less than US$4.

Entertainment
The only disco in town is **Oasis** *(open 9pm Sat only)*, located above beachside *enramada* Silvia, near the plaza. Look for the Rasta colors of red, yellow and green.

Getting There & Away
Combis run every 10 minutes, 5am to 9pm, between Playa Azul and Lázaro Cárdenas (US$1.25, 30 minutes, 24km). They enter Playa Azul and follow Carranza, looping back on Independencia.

Long-distance buses don't pass through Playa Azul; they will drop you off 7km to

the north at the Hwy 200 junction in La Mira. If you're going north, catch a long-distance bus here.

Taxis between Playa Azul and Lázaro Cárdenas cost around US$11.

LÁZARO CÁRDENAS
☎ 753 • pop 76,400
The significant port of Lázaro Cárdenas is Michoacán's largest coastal city. Originally named Melchor Ocampo, its name was changed in 1970 to honor Lázaro Cárdenas, who was Michoacán's reform-minded governor (1928–32) and Mexico's president (1934–40), though he was most famous for nationalizing foreign (mostly US) oil assets during his tenure.

An industrial but not totally unpleasant city, Lázaro has nothing of real interest to travelers – but since it's the terminus of several bus routes, travelers do pass through. Reasons to stop here include changing buses, stocking up on provisions and checking email. If you need to catch some shuteye here, there are several good hotels near the bus stations.

Orientation & Information
The eponymous main drag, Av Lázaro Cárdenas, caters to travelers' needs. Near the bus terminals along Lázaro Cárdenas, the town center is a busy commercial area, with a **Banamex** *(open 9am-1pm Mon-Fri for money exchange)* and a **Bancomer** *(open 8:30am-4pm Mon-Fri, 10am-2pm Sat)* across from each other and sporting ATMs. There are also several travel agencies.

Checking your email? Try **Sin Límite** *(Av Lázaro Cárdenas 1745; US$1.75 per hour; open 9am-9pm Mon-Sat, 10am-2pm Sun)*. **Ciber Tequil@s** *(open 10am-10pm daily)*, at Hotel Viña del Mar (see Places to Stay & Eat), is a lounge act that charges US$1.75 per hour.

The state-run **tourist office** *(☎ 532-15-47; Nicolás Bravo 475; open 8am-5pm Mon-Fri, 8am-2pm Sat)* awaits in front of Hotel Casablanca (see Places to Stay & Eat), four blocks northwest of the Galeana bus station and a block east of Av Lázaro Cárdenas. Its hours can be erratic.

Places to Stay & Eat

Hotel Reyna Pio (☎ 532-06-20; Corregidora 78; singles/doubles with air-con & TV US$16/18) is a good, friendly budget hotel with clean, spacious rooms. It's located on the corner of Av 8 de Mayo, a block west of Av Lázaro Cárdenas and near the bus terminals.

Hotel Viña del Mar (☎ 532-04-15; Javier Mina 352; singles/doubles US$20/26) has a leafy, inviting courtyard with pool, but most darkish rooms are not around it. Still, they're good-sized and come with air-con and TV. It's half a block west of Av Lázaro Cárdenas.

Hotel Casablanca (☎ 537-34-80, fax 537-40-36; e arregala@prodigy.net.mx; Nicolás Bravo 475; singles/doubles US$36/52) caters to business travelers with air-con, TV, pool with Jacuzzi and secure parking. The 56 modern rooms with balconies and wide windows overlook the city or inland mountains. Look for this high-rise a block east of Av Lázaro Cárdenas.

Many restaurants cluster around the bus terminals. Locals recommend **Restaurant El Tejado** (☎ 532-01-40; Lázaro Cárdenas, between Corregidora & Javier Mina; open noon-midnight daily; mains US$5.50-11) for meats, seafood, six styles of frog legs and four pages of drinks.

Getting There & Around

Air Lázaro Cárdenas' airport (LZC) is 6km from the center. It takes only five minutes to get there and costs US$4 by taxi or US$0.50 by colectivo (minibus or car). **Aeromar** hops to Mexico City; **Aero Cuahonte** skips to Uruapan, Morelia and Guadalajara; **Aeropacifico** jumps to Colima and Puerto Vallarta.

Bus Lázaro Cárdenas inconveniently has four separate bus terminals, but all are within a few blocks of each other.

Two companies, **Galeana** (☎ 532-02-62) and **Parhikuni** (☎ 532-30-06), share a terminal on the corner of Av Lázaro Cárdenas 1810 and Constitución de 1814.

Opposite, at Av Lázaro Cárdenas 1791, are **Autobuses de Jalisco**, **Vía Plus** and **Sur de Jalisco** (☎ 537-18-50).

The **Estrella Blanca terminal** (☎ 532-11-71), two blocks west behind the Galeana

terminal at Francisco Villa 65, is also used by **Elite**.

Estrella de Oro (☎ 532-02-75; Corregidora 318) is two blocks southwest of Estrella Blanca.

Acapulco US$16 1st class with Estrella Blanca, six to seven hours, 340km, at 11pm, midnight, 5:30am; US$12 2nd class with Estrella Blanca, at 1pm, 2pm, 4pm, 7:30pm; US$17 1st class with Estrella de Oro, at 6:30am, 3pm; US$13 2nd class with Estrella de Oro, 4:50am to 6:50pm, hourly

Caleta de Campos US$4 2nd class with Galeana, 1½ hours, 65km, every 30 minutes, 5am to 8pm

Colima US$21 with Autobuses de Jalisco, US$15 with Sur de Jalisco, six to 6½ hours, 320km (same buses as to Guadalajara)

Guadalajara US$33 to US$36 1st class with Autobuses de Jalisco, nine to 11 hours, 540km, at 8:45pm, 10:30pm, 12:15am; US$26 2nd class with Sur de Jalisco, at 1pm

Manzanillo US$24 1st class with Elite, six to seven hours, 313km, at 12:13pm, 2:20pm, 11:13pm; US$16 2nd class with Galeana, at 4:30pm, 5:30pm, 10pm, 11:30pm; US$16 2nd class with Sur de Jalisco, at 2:30pm, 5:30pm; US$13 to US$20 to Tecomán with any Tecomán bus, 5½ hours to Tecomán – then take a frequent local bus from Tecomán to Manzanillo

Mexico City (Terminal Sur) US$43 1st class with Estrella Blanca, 10 to 11 hours, 711km, at 8am, 4:30pm, 8:05pm, 9:45pm, 8:05pm; US$39 with Estrella de Oro, frequent; US$44 with Vía Plus, at 8:20pm, 12:15am

Morelia US$22 2nd class with Parhikuni, eight hours, 406km, frequent; US$27 2nd class with Galeana, frequent; US$27 1st class with Vía Plus, at 6:15pm; US$27 1st class with Estrella Blanca, at 3:10pm, 11pm

Uruapan US$17 with Autobuses de Jalisco, six hours, 280km, at 12:15am; US$15 to US$19 for same buses as to Morelia

Zihuatanejo US$5 1st class with Estrella de Oro, two to three hours, 120km, at 6:30am, 7am, 3pm, 8pm, 9pm; US$5.50 1st class with Estrella Blanca, at 6am, 8am, 10am, 11am, noon; or take same buses as to Acapulco

Combi Combis to Playa Azul trawl Av Lázaro Cárdenas every 10 minutes from 5am to 9pm (US$1.25, 30 minutes, 24km) stopping to rebait outside the Autobuses de Jalisco terminal. A taxi between Lázaro Cárdenas and Playa Azul fetches US$13.

Ixtapa, Zihuatanejo & Costa Grande

The Costa Grande, Guerrero's 'Big Coast,' stretches 325km from the Río Balsas at the Michoacán border southeast to Acapulco. In the northeast, around Troncones and Majahua, low hills of tropical deciduous forest sit next to the sea. Around Ixtapa and Zihuatanejo and southeast to Acapulco, coconut plantations dominate the landscape. Just inland, the Sierra Madre del Sur, with its perpetually cloud-covered peaks, is the only reminder that temperatures cool down in other places.

Ixtapa and Zihuatanejo, and to a growing extent Troncones, are the only serious blips on the Costa Grande tourist screen. Troncones is little more than a growing stretch of fabulous B&Bs on a beautiful beach. Ixtapa's the biggie, with dozens of luxury mega-hotels lining a long, wave-pounded beach on the open sea. But with nothing authentically Mexican (except the Mexican tourist industry itself), Ixtapa leans on the nearby 'sister city' Zihuatanejo for its Mexican-ness – and its beaches, and its restaurants, and its scenery. About 8km away, Zihuatanejo is an overgrown fishing village set on a spectacular, tightly curved bay with four beaches that rarely receive a wave big enough to tip a toddler off an air mattress. The beaches and fishing villages southeast of Zihuatanejo make great day trips or overnight stops en route to Acapulco (a four-hour drive from Zihuatanejo), as do the beaches to the north (all under two hours from Zihuatanejo).

History

Archaeological sites near the Río Balsas, at Soledad de Maciel (near Petatlán), and at Puerto Marqués (near Acapulco) show human presence on the Costa Grande as far back as 2500–2000 BC. Ceramic pieces and architecture found on the Costa Grande, which are unlike those found on the coastal areas to the north, indicate the region had

Highlights

- Surfing the astounding lefts of Saladita and Troncones, goofy-footer's paradises
- Renting a kayak and paddling around the mangrove-fringed lagoon of Barra de Potosí
- Stuffing your belly with *pozole*, Guerrero's favorite soup, in Zihuatanejo
- Chartering a boat in Zihuatanejo and deep-sea fishing till the beer's all gone
- Snorkeling among the coral and rocks of Isla Ixtapa
- Perusing the trinkets and jewelry of Petatlán's gold market behind the church

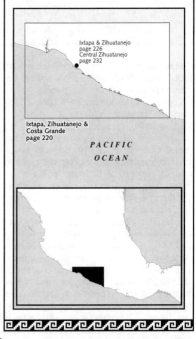

Ixtapa & Zihuatanejo
page 226
Central Zihuatanejo
page 232

Ixtapa, Zihuatanejo &
Costa Grande
page 220

PACIFIC OCEAN

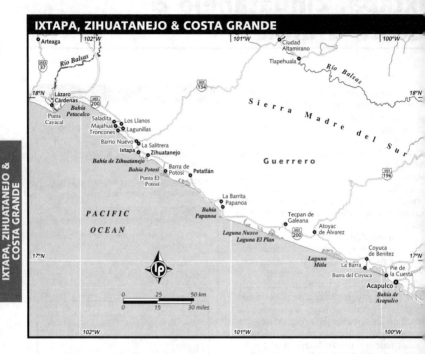

IXTAPA, ZIHUATANEJO & COSTA GRANDE

contact with the Olmecs and later with Teotihuacán. Still, settlements always remained small and widely dispersed.

Tourism, so to speak, goes back a long way. The Tarascos, who ruled present-day Michoacán from the early 15th century until the arrival of the Spanish, had an early king named Calzontzin who liked Bahía de Zihuatanejo enough to have his slaves build a winter 'retreat' on the point at Playa Las Gatas. They constructed a reef (which is still there) to make a natural swimming pool for Calzontzin and his many wives.

When the Spanish arrived in the early 16th century, the region was loosely controlled by the Aztecs. Following the conquest, Hernán Cortés set his sights on developing a maritime route between Mexico and Asia, and in 1523 he established the shipyard and port of Puerto Santiago (present-day Zacatula) on the Río Balsas. Alvaro Saavedra de Cerón sailed from Zihuatanejo in search of a trade route in 1527, never to return. When a return

trade route from Asia was finally discovered in 1565 between Acapulco and Manila (in the Philippines), Zihuatanejo's importance fizzled out to all but a few English and Dutch pirates who occasionally used the bay as a hideout before they attacked treasure-filled galleons en route to Acapulco.

After independence, and the subsequent finish of the Acapulco–Manila maritime route, Zihuatanejo remained a sleepy fishing village – until the 1970s when Fonatur developed Ixtapa.

Ixtapa and Zihuatanejo are now major tourist destinations. Though they're right next door to each other, they still feel worlds apart.

The Ixtapa–Zihuatanejo municipal website (W www.ixtapa-zihuatanejo.com) is packed with useful information in Spanish and English, as are Zihua.net (W www.zihua.net) and ZihuaRob's Travel Guide and Directory (W www.zihuatanejo.net). All three focus primarily on Zihuatanejo and

Ixtapa, but provide information on Troncones and other Costa Grande destinations.

TRONCONES
☎ 755 • pop 1400

About a 25-minute drive northwest of Zihuatanejo, Playa Troncones is a beautiful 3km beach on the open sea, lined (unobtrusively) with B&Bs, guest inns, vacation homes and seafood restaurants. Though accommodations are moderately expensive, the place is addictively laid-back and friendly. It has just two roads: the road coming in from the highway, and another stretching 5km along the beach, with the lovely little Playa Manzanillo toward its northern end.

At the end of the road is the village of Majahua, a friendly village with as many pigs and chickens as people, and a couple of basic seafood restaurants, great for afternoon beer and fried fish.

Families generally fill Troncones' lodgings through the winter, but the place changes face in summer, when prices fall, the waves pick up and surfers roll in from all over.

Orientation & Information
The village of Troncones is about 100m from the beach at the end of a 5km paved road from Hwy 200 – but most of what you'll be interested in is along the beachfront road. From the T-junction where the road from the highway meets the beachfront road, the Burro Borracho is about 1.5km to your left (south), and Playa Manzanillo is about 3.5km to the right (north). Majahua, a 10-minute walk past Playa Manzanillo, is a small village with a 6km dirt road out to the highway.

Abarrotes Gaby (open 7:30am-9pm daily) has the cheapest long-distance telephone service. It's located just off the coast road in Troncones village. For Internet service try the reliable Internet café at Tropic of Cancer Beach Club (☎ 553-28-00; W www.tronconestropic.com; US$3.30 per hour; open 11am-6pm Wed-Mon).

Zihu@Rob's Troncones website (W www.troncones.com.mx) is chock a block full of useful information.

Organized Tours
Dewey McMillin of Jaguar Tours (☎ 553-28-62; W www.jaguartours.net; open Tues-Sun) offers a thrill-packed three-part tour featuring a hike through subtropical forest, exploration of a 300-foot-deep limestone cave, and a 'zipline' canopy tour. (This involves climbing up to platforms in the forest canopy, clicking onto a line and zipping through the trees.) Tours cost US$50 per person, last four hours, and include transport and guide. The office is located across from Casa de la Tortuga, north of the T-junction.

Surfing
Most people bouncing around the vicinity of Troncones are either looking for waves or riding them. With more than a dozen breaks within 20km, short-boarders, long-boarders, rookies and rippers will all find something to ride. As usual, it's best to get out before the breeze picks up (usually around 11am), or around sunset when it gets glassy once again. The waves are biggest May to October.

Troncones itself has several world-class breaks. The beach breaks here can be excellent at summer, but the wave to chase is the left at Troncones Point. When it's small, the takeoff is right over the rocks (complete with sea urchins), but when it's big, it's beautiful, beefy and rolls halfway across the bay.

Saladita, about 7km from Troncones, has a blissfully long, rolling left, perfect for long-boarders. Yet another endless left and some rights can be had at El Rancho, a reef break accessible by car (standard drive OK in dry season) or – easier but pricier – by boat. La Boca, a river mouth just north of Majahua (via the beach and an easy-to-miss dirt track) is best in summertime when the sandbar breaks and both rights and lefts are consistent.

The best place for surfboard rentals is Mike Bensal's surf shop at the Inn at Manzanillo Bay (☎ 553-28-84; fax 553-28-83; W www.manzanillobay.com; Playa Manzanillo). Mike has an excellent selection of short-boards and long-boards (US$15 per day) as well as two wave kayaks (US$6.50 per day) and boogie boards (US$22/42 per half/full day). **Jaguar Tours** (see Organized Tours earlier in this chapter) also has a small selection of boards (US$16 per day) and boogie boards (US$6.50 per day), and offers **surf lessons**.

Other Activities

There's good **snorkeling** at Troncones Point off Playa Manzanillo, and equipment can be rented for US$6.50 per day at both Jaguar Tours and the Inn at Manzanillo Bay. Both shops rent **mountain bikes** for about US$16 per day; a good ride heads north along the beach as far as Saladita. For a trot down Playa Troncones, rent **horses** (about US$20 per hour) at the little Las Palmitas, a small store just north of the Burro Borracho.

Other activities include **fishing**, **hiking**, **bird-watching** and **sea-turtle spotting** – you can observe sea turtles laying their eggs here in the sand on moonlit nights. Planting your ass in the sand is another excellent pastime.

Places to Stay

While still a sleepy hideaway, Troncones has been experiencing a gringo-led building boom since *ejido* land (land held communally) went public in December 1992. Its pristine 5km shoreline now has upwards of 80 beachfront rooms, and Playa Manzanillo and Majahua appear poised to follow a similar development trajectory.

Places to Stay – Budget

If you're hurting for an inexpensive place to stay, try asking at the shops in the village. You can **camp** for free on the municipal beach at Playa Manzanillo or on the beach at Majahua.

At the time of writing, there were plans to open one **Troncones Youth Hostel & Campground** behind Jaguar Tours by 2003; prices were estimated at US$10 to US$15 per person. Until then, the cheapest places to stay are the two plain but clean rooms with small terraces over **Miscelanea Jasmín** *(rooms US$25)*, a shop in the village.

Restaurant La Gaviota *(☎ 553-29-08)* rents three simple rooms with private baths, fan and cold showers for US$15 per person.

Places to Stay – Mid-Range & Top End

Hotel prices include breakfast unless otherwise noted; bungalow prices are for two people. The following accommodations are spread out along the beachfront road. The road from the highway intersects the beach road between Casa Ki (to the right of the T junction) and Tropic of Cancer Beach Club (to the left). The following are listed in north–south order.

Hacienda Edén *(☎ 553-28-02; W www.edenmex.com; Playa Manzanillo; rooms US$65-75, bungalows US$90; open Nov-Apr)*, in the middle of Playa Manzanillo, boasts four stunning bungalows and six private rooms, all with hot water, TV, fans and screens. The entire place exudes relaxation, and the friendly proprietors, Eva and Jim, are gracious hosts.

Posada de Los Raqueros *(☎ 553-28-70; W www.raqueros.com; Playa Manzanillo; rooms US$85, bungalows US$100 & US$125)* offers two split-level bungalows, each with beds above and living room, kitchen and bathroom below. Two other private rooms have a shared kitchen. All are stylishly designed and open onto a sand and grass area leading to the beach.

Inn at Manzanillo Bay *(☎ 553-28-84, fax 553-28-83; W www.manzanillobay.com; Playa Manzanillo; rooms year-round US$88, bungalows Nov–mid-May US$98-108, mid-May-Oct US$64-70)* boasts a prime location facing the surf break at Troncones Point, so surfers can literally check the waves from bed – or from the gorgeous pool, or the gourmet restaurant, or the beachside bar and grill, or.... The Inn is relaxed and thoughtfully designed, and its eight bungalows appeal to everyone from surfers to honeymooners. Amenities include Internet access, fax and copy service, a surf shop, satellite TV at the bar, and one of the best swimming pools around.

Casa de la Tortuga *(☎ 553-28-12; e casa delatortuga@yahoo.com; doubles with shared/ private bathroom US$28/55)* was the first beachfront house at Troncones. With six comfortable rooms – three of which are huge – and a fabulous communal kitchen his modest B&B is one of the beach's best deals. There is a large round dining table conducive to social breakfasts (chatting and how both included in the price), and an attractive beachside patio and self-service beer bar.

Casa Delfín Sonriente (☎ 553-28-03, ☎/fax 831-688-6578 in the USA; **w** www casadelfinsonriente.com; bungalows with shared bathroom US$65, rooms US$85, suites US$119, 40% discount May-Oct) sleeps a total of 12 guests (more by arrangement) between two modest bungalows, two comfortable rooms and two marvelous open-air suites. Perks include a large communal kitchen, a small pool, plenty of vegetation, mosquito nets, hammocks, an artist's workshop, and an owner who keeps up on the surf reports.

Casa Ki (☎ 553-28-15; **w** www.casa-ki com; bungalows US$75-85, house US$165; 20% discount May-Oct) is obviously a work of love with a stunning, fully equipped two-bedroom house (sleeps six) and three delightful bungalows each with a king-size bed, private bathroom, porch and hammock. An exquisite tropical garden keeps everything shady, and a meditation bungalow keeps everyone relaxed. Breakfast is served in a tidy palapa (thatched-roof) kitchen which guests may use the rest of the day.

Canadian expat Anita Lapointe, owner of **Tropic of Cancer Beach Club** (☎ 553-28-00; **e** casacanela@yahoo.com), manages several properties in Troncones, and, with a bit of time, can set you up with anything from an affordable room to a luxurious house. Drop her an email or stop by the Beach Club to let her know what you're after.

La Puesta del Sol (☎ 553-28-18, 323-913-1423 in the USA; **e** troncones@yahoo.com; basic room US$35, room with mountain view US$65, ocean view minisuite with kitchen US$80, penthouse per week only US$1120), an attractive three-story, four-room palapa offers a variety of rooms from a simple 'surfers' room' to a super-luxurious penthouse apartment. From May to October you'll get a 20% to 30% discount.

Burro Borracho (tent sites with bathroom US$5, singles/doubles with breakfast May-Nov US$25/30, Dec-Apr US$50/60) is a popular beachfront restaurant-bar with three attractive stone-wall duplexes (six units), all with relaxing hammocks on beachfront terraces. It is cheaper for longer stays and there's space to pitch a tent. Guests can use boogie boards for free, whip up meals in the communal kitchen and borrow books from the owner's extensive library.

Casas Canela & Canelita (**e** casacanela@yahoo.com; house with kitchen US$100, duplex per unit US$35; 50% discount Dec-Apr) is about the only accommodation that isn't right on the beach, but its good price makes it worth the extra few steps across the beach road. Casa Canela, the house in front, sleeps six and boasts a large kitchen and hammock-strewn front porch. Casa Canelita, the pleasant duplex beneath the palm trees out the back, has a shared kitchen and terrace.

Places to Eat

The cheapest eats are at the taco stands and shop-front restaurants in Troncones village, where you can eat well for less than US$3, or the enramadas (thatch-covered, open-air restaurants) in Majahua.

Good Mexican-owned beachfront restaurants include **Costa Brava**, to the north of the T-junction just across the bridge, and nearby **Enramada Doña Nica** (mains US$4-10; open 8:30am-6pm daily), just to the south of the T-junction. In Majahua, try **Enramada Gladys** (open 7am-9pm), to the left as you approach the beach, where you can get great lobster and fish for under US$10 or a dozen fresh oysters for US$5.50.

La Cocina del Sol (☎ 553-28-02; **w** www .edenmex.com; Playa Manzanillo; mains US$6-14, nightly set-menu dinner US$11-15; open 8am-7pm daily), at Hacienda Edén, is run by a seasoned chef who creates some truly sublime dishes – breakfast, lunch and dinner. The burgers will knock your socks off and the set-menu dinners (reservations recommended) are culinary works of art. Don't miss the Sunday barbecue with ribs, salads and peach cobbler.

Restaurant Playa Manzanillo (mains US$5-15; open 9am-7pm daily), otherwise known as María's, is a popular, laid-back

Mexican *enramada* on Playa Manzanillo. Choose from good fish and shrimp tacos (US$3 to US$5), mouth-watering *huachinango* (red snapper; US$5.50 to US$8); and motorhome-size lobsters (US$13 to US$18).

Inn at Manzanillo Bay *(☎ 553-28-84, fax 553-28-83; Ⓦ www.manzanillobay.com; Playa Manzanillo; mains US$5-12; open 8am-9pm daily)* has an excellent restaurant. It's tough choosing between smoked barbecued pork ribs (US$11), Oaxacan-style chicken in *mole* (chili sauce; US$9.50), aloha duck (US$14), and chef and owner Mike's signature Thai-style shrimp tacos with soy dipping sauce (US$6.50). Out on the sand with views of the surf break, the Inn's **Beach Bar & Grill** *(mains US$4-8; open noon-sunset)* is great for grilled specialties, 'boat drinks' and some truly spectacular sunsets.

Restaurant La Gaviota *(☎ 553-29-08; mains US$4-10; open 9am-6pm)* is a friendly Mexican-owned restaurant that offers tasty seafood and down-home Mexican dishes all at reasonable prices. It's on the beach, just south of the intersection.

Tropic of Cancer Beach Club *(☎ 553-28-00; Ⓦ www.tronconestropic.com; mains US$5-8; open 11am-10pm Wed-Mon)* is a popular bar-restaurant with good burgers, pasta and seafood. There are also rooms and a house for rent.

Burro Borracho *(☎ 553-28-34; open 10am-10pm Tues-Sun; mains US$5-10)*, toward the southern end of the beachfront road, is *the* hangout for travelers, expats and locals alike. The seafood's fresh, the Mexican dishes are delicious and the chicken sandwiches and hamburgers can't be beat. This is also the informal information center for Troncones, with a bulletin board and English-language lending library.

Entertainment

It seems like most people fall asleep shortly after the sun goes down in Troncones – except on Sunday nights. Every Sunday night at the **Burro Borracho** *(performance 7:30pm-10:30pm)*, school kids from Pantla, Buena Vista and Troncones put on a knockout performance of traditional Mexican dances. It's free, though a hat is passed around for tips; all proceeds go directly to the schools. It's a Troncones highlight that shouldn't b missed. (See also the listing under Places t Eat earlier in this chapter.)

The beachside **billiards parlor** in Majahu is likely the coolest pool hall we've ever see – two rickety old tables, a roof, no walls an the ocean breeze. It closes around 10pm.

Getting There & Away

If driving to Troncones from Ixtapa or Zihuatanejo, head northwest on Hwy 200 toward Lázaro Cárdenas. Just north of Km 3 you'll see the marked turnoff for Troncones; follow this winding paved road 5kr west to the beach.

There are no direct buses, but 2nd-class buses heading northwest toward Lázar Cárdenas or La Unión from Zihuatanejo' long-distance terminals will let you off a the turnoff for Troncones (US$1.60, 40 minutes). More La Unión buses depart from th lot a couple of blocks east of the market. As to be let off at the Troncones turnoff.

A *microbús* (minibus) runs between Hw 200 and Troncones every 30 minutes or s in the morning and evening, and every hou or so around siesta time (US$0.65). It i possible to hitch during daylight hours fro the turnoff into Troncones, and vice vers. Flagging down a bus on Hwy 200 for the re turn trip to Zihuatanejo is best done durin daylight hours. You could hitch a ride t Pantla, halfway to Zihuatanejo, then catch *microbús* or 2nd-class bus (both $1.10 from there.

A taxi from Ixtapa or Zihuatanejo airpo costs US$35/50 one way/return. Taxis fro Zihuatanejo to Troncones can be bargaine down to around US$20/35 one way/retur and taxis from Troncones back to Zihuatanejo can be even cheaper.

SALADITA

Around 7km northwest of Troncones, **Saladita** has a long, gentle left, perfect for long boarding. The beach itself, often complete empty, stretches far to the northwest an makes for blissful walks and good campin

Restaurant Jaquelin *(☎ 755-554-45-32* the first restaurant you'll hit on the way i rents **surfboards** and serves mind-blowing lobster (some swear it's the best on the coast), beer and other seafood dishes. Here you will also find Lourdes, who manages the five lovely, beachfront cabanas, once known as **Saladita Surf Camp** (e surfcampmx@aol.com; w www.saladita.com; doubles US$59-89). Each cabana contains a bathroom, screens, fan, coffeemaker, minifridge and a private deck with a hammock. Make reservations far in advance for May to October; you may get lucky simply showing up the rest of the year.

Several restaurants, including the Jaquelin, allow people to **camp** or sleep in a hammock and use their bathrooms and showers for free, provided they eat regularly in the restaurant.

To get there from Troncones, take Hwy 200 north and turn left at the town of Los Llanos (around Km 140); follow the road to the fork near the convenience stores, hang a right and follow the dirt road 5km to the beach. Any northbound 2nd-class bus will drop you at Los Llanos; busing is only feasible if you plan to stay more than a day.

IXTAPA & ZIHUATANEJO
Zihuatanejo ☎ 755 • pop 59,000
Ixtapa ☎ 755 • pop 1500

Not so long ago, Zihuatanejo (see-wah-tah-**nay**-ho) was a small fishing village, and nearby Ixtapa (iks-**stap**-pah) was a coconut plantation. Then in 1970 Fonatur, the Mexican government tourism development organization that built Cancún, decided that the Pacific coast needed a Cancún-like resort to bring more tourist dollars into Mexico. Nowadays, Ixtapa boasts a string of impressive resort hotels spread out along the Bahía del Palmar. The luxurious hotels, restaurants and shops of Ixtapa are expensive, and many travelers cringe at package-travel land created for the gringos.

Zihuatanejo, on the other hand, 8km away, though quite touristy, retains an easygoing, coastal town ambience, and its setting on a small, beautiful bay with several fine beaches makes it a pleasant place to visit. Small-scale fishing is still important to the town's economy; if you walk down on the beach near the pier in the early morning you can join the pelicans in greeting the returning fishermen and see the morning's catch. Needless to say, the seafood in 'Zihua' is magnificent.

Orientation
Though Zihuatanejo's suburbs are growing considerably, spreading around the Bahía de Zihuatanejo and climbing the hills behind the town, the city's center is compressed within a few square blocks. It's difficult to get lost and street names are clearly marked. Ixtapa, 8km away, is easily reached by frequent local buses or by taxi. Most of the services or stores you'll need in Ixtapa are found in the outdoor *centros comerciales* (shopping centers), all within walking distance of each other on the main drag, Blvd Ixtapa.

Information
The only tourist office in Zihuatanejo is the municipal **Dirección de Turismo** (☎/fax 554-23-55, 554-75-23; w www.ixtapa-zihuatanejo.com; Zihuatanejo Poniente s/n, Colonia La Deportiva; open 8am-4pm Mon-Fri), upstairs in the *ayuntamiento* (town hall), about 2km from the town center (local buses between Zihuatanejo and Ixtapa stop in front).

In Ixtapa, the state-run **Sefotur tourist office** (☎/fax 553-19-67/68; Centro Comercial La Puerta 2; open 9am-2pm & 5pm-8pm Mon-Fri, 8am-2pm Sat) is near the tourist police station and opposite the Hotel Presidente Inter-Continental.

Zihuatanejo and Ixtapa both have many banks and *casas de cambio* (exchange houses) where you can change US dollars and traveler's checks. The banks give the best rate of exchange. In Zihuatanejo try **Bancomer** (☎ 554-74-90; Juárez 13), **Banco Serfín** (☎ 554-32-80; cnr Juárez & Bravo), **Bancrecer** (☎ 554-49-00; cnr Juárez & Ejido) and **Banamex** (☎ 554-21-96; cnr Ejido & Guerrero). Banamex changes cash only. All are open from around 9am to 5pm Monday to Friday, 10am to 2pm Saturday, and have ATMs.

The *casas de cambio* give a slightly less favorable rate but they're open longer. In

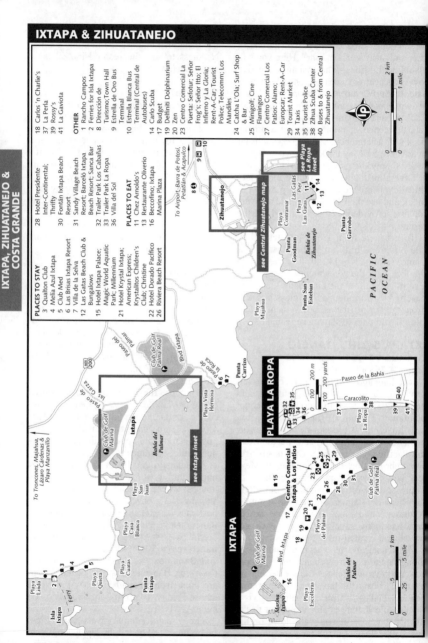

IXTAPA, ZIHUATANEJO & COSTA GRANDE

IXTAPA & ZIHUATANEJO

PLACES TO STAY
3 Qualton Club
4 Melia Azul Ixtapa
5 Club Med
6 Las Brisas Ixtapa Resort
7 Villa de la Selva
12 Las Gatas Beach Club & Bungalows
15 Hotel Ixtapa Palace; Magic World Aquatic Park; Millennium
21 Hotel Krystal Ixtapa; American Express; Krystalitos Children's Club; Christine
22 Hotel Dorado Pacífico
26 Riviera Beach Resort
28 Hotel Presidente Inter-Continental; Thrifty
30 Fontán Ixtapa Beach Resort
31 Sandy Village Beach Resort; Barceló Ixtapa Beach Resort; Sanca Bar
32 Trailer Park Los Cabañas
33 Trailer Park La Ropa
36 Uno del Sol

PLACES TO EAT
11 Chez Arnoldo's
13 Restaurante Oliverio
16 Beccofino; Ixtapa Marina Plaza
18 Carlos 'n Charlie's
37 La Perla
39 Rossy's
41 La Gaviota

OTHER
1 Rancho Campos
2 Ferries for Isla Ixtapa
8 Dirección de Turismo;Town Hall
9 Estrella de Oro Bus Terminal
10 Estrella Blanca Bus Terminal (Central de Autobuses)
14 Carlo Scuba
17 Budget
19 Definiti Dolphinarium
20 Zen
23 Centro Comercial La Puerta: Sefotur; Señor Frog's; Señor Itto; El Infierno y La Gloria; Rent-A-Car; Tourist Police; Telecomm; Los Mandiles
24 Catcha L'Ola; Surf Shop & Bar
25 Minigolf; Cine Flamingos
27 Centro Comercial Los Patios: Alamo; Europcar; Rent-A-Car
29 Tourist Market
34 Taxis
35 Tourist Police
38 Zihua Scuba Center
40 Buses to & from Central Zihuatanejo

PLAYA LA ROPA

IXTAPA

Zihuatanejo try **Casa de Cambio Guiball** (☎ 544-28-00; Galeana 4; open 8am-9pm daily).

American Express (☎ 553-08-53; open 9am-6pm Mon-Sat) is in Ixtapa at the Hotel Krystal Ixtapa.

Zihuatanejo's **post office** (open 8am-3pm Mon-Fri) is a few blocks north of the town center just off Morelos. Several other places in town, near postboxes serviced daily, also sell stamps. Ixtapa lacks a post office, but you can mail letters from any big hotel.

Zihuatanejo's **Telecomm office** (open 8am-7.30pm Mon-Fri, 9am-noon Sat & Sun), with telegram, Mexpost and fax, is beside the post office. Ixtapa's **Telecomm office** (open 9am-3pm Mon-Fri) is behind Sefotur.

Long-distance phone and fax services are available at several casetas teléfonicas (public telephone call stations) in Zihuatanejo, including two on the corner of Galeana and Ascencio, and one at Ejido 14; the last is open from 8am to 10pm daily. They're all marked 'Larga Distancia.'

Zihuatanejo is bursting with Internet cafés. Among them, **Bar-Net** (Ramirez 2; US$1.10 per hour; open 9am-10pm daily) offers comfortable booths and air-con, and **ServiNet** (Cuauhtémoc 128; open 9am-8pm Mon-Sat) has telephone and fax services.

Various agencies provide general travel agency services and also offer local tours. In Zihuatanejo, three of the biggest for local tours are **Turismo Internacional del Pacífico** (TIP; ☎ 554-75-10/11; cnr Juárez & Álvarez, local 2), **América-Ixtamar Viajes** (☎ 554-85-90; cnr Cuauhtémoc & Bravo) and **Viajes Bravo** (☎ 554-88-90; Álvarez 8; open 9am-8pm & 4pm-8pm daily). The last sells Estrella Blanca bus tickets.

Laundromats seem to gravitate toward the intersection of Cuauhtémoc and González, and they all charge about US$1.65 per kilogram with a 3kg minimum. **Lavandería Express** (☎ 554-43-93; Cuauhtémoc 37A; open 8am-8pm Mon-Sat) offers pickup and delivery services, and **Lavandería y Tintorería Premium** (Cuauhtémoc 34; open 9am-8pm Mon- Sat, 9am-1pm Sun) does laundry and dry cleaning. Both these places offer a same-day service.

For medical service, expats swear by English-speaking **Dr Rogelio Grayeb** (☎ 554-33-34, 554-50-41 office, 553-17-11 home; Bravo 71A; office hours 9am-2pm & 4pm-8pm Mon-Fri, 9am-2pm & 5pm-7pm Sat).

Museo Arqueológico de la Costa Grande

At the east end of Zihua's Paseo del Pescador, this small museum (☎ 554-75-52; Paseo del Pescador at Plaza Olof Palme; admission US$0.50; open 9am-7pm Tues-Sun) houses exhibits on the history, archaeology and culture of Guerrero's Costa Grande, the coastal region between Acapulco and the border of Michoacán. It's all in Spanish.

Beaches

Bahía de Zihuatanejo Waves are gentle at all the beaches of Bahía de Zihuatanejo. If you want a thrashing in big ocean waves, you can go to Ixtapa, only a few minutes away by local bus.

On Bahía de Zihuatanejo, fishing pangas (motorized skiffs) line the sands of the **Playa Municipal**, which buzzes with activity when the fishermen haul in their catch in the early morning. The beach is the least appealing for swimming, especially when the seasonal, polluted Agua de Correa Canal is flowing into the bay. Standing on this beach you can see several other beaches spread around the bay, starting with Playa Madera just past the rocky point on your left, then the long white stretch of Playa La Ropa past that. Directly across the bay lies the enticing Playa Las Gatas.

Playa Madera was once isolated from Playa Municipal by a couple of rocky points, but now a walkway over the rocks makes it an easy five-minute walk from town. It's better for swimming than the municipal beach and there are several decent seafood restaurants.

From Playa Madera, walk over the hill along the Camino a Playa La Ropa (about 20 minutes) and you reach the broad, 2km expanse of **Playa La Ropa**, bordered by palm trees and lined with low-level hotels, seafood restaurants and sun beds. It's a pleasant walk, with the road rising up onto

'Las Gatas' Were Not Cats...& Other Tales of Zihuatanejo

Several places around Zihuatanejo and Ixtapa have names rooted in the distant past. The name 'Zihuatanejo' comes from the Náhuatl word *zihuatlán*, meaning 'place of women' (it was occupied solely by women); the Spanish added the suffix '-ejo,' meaning 'small.' 'Ixtapa,' also from the Náhuatl dialect, means 'white place.' It was so named not only for its white sands but also for the white guano left by the seabirds on the rocky islands just offshore.

The beaches around the Bahía de Zihuatanejo also have historical names. Playa Madera (Wood Beach) got its name from the timber that was loaded on boats from its shore and shipped to various parts of the world; at one time there was also a shipyard here. The name of Playa La Ropa (Beach of the Clothes) commemorates an occasion when a cargo of fine silks washed ashore here from a wrecked Spanish galleon coming from the Philippines. Playa Las Gatas (Beach of the Cats) was not actually named for cats, but for the nurse sharks that inhabited the waters here long ago – called 'cats' because of their whiskers.

cliffs offering a fine view over the bay. The first road to the beach is beside La Casa Que Canta hotel. Most restaurants along the beach charge a minimum of US$4 to US$6 for use of their sun beds, but once you hit the minimum, you can stay all day – and feel pretty safe that someone is guarding your goodies while you swim. That said, La Ropa is hardly prone to theft. Arguably the most beautiful beach on the bay, La Ropa is great for swimming, and popular for parasailing, water-skiing and 'banana rides' (this involves being pulled behind a speedboat on a big, long, yellow, rubber banana). You can also hire sailboards, dinghies and small catamarans for about US$20 an hour.

Opposite Zihuatanejo, **Playa Las Gatas** is a protected beach, crowded with sun beds and restaurants. It's excellent for snorkeling (there's coral growth) and as a swimming spot for children, but beware of sea urchins. According to legend, Calzontzin, a Tarascan chief, built a stone barrier here in pre-Hispanic times to keep the waves down and prevent sea creatures from entering, making it a sort of private swimming pool. Beach shacks and restaurants rent snorkeling gear for around US$4 per day.

Boats to Playa Las Gatas depart frequently from the Zihuatanejo pier, 8am to 5pm daily. Tickets (US$3.50 return) are sold at the **ticket booth** at the foot of the pier; one-way tickets can be bought on board. You can also reach Playa Las Gatas by walking from Playa La Ropa; a road takes you half the way, then

there's 10 minutes of mild rock scrambling before you reach Playa Las Gatas.

South of Zihuatanejo About 10km south of Zihuatanejo, halfway between town and the airport, **Playa Larga** has big waves, beachfront restaurants and horseback riding. Nearby **Playa Manzanillo**, a secluded white-sand beach reachable by boat from Zihuatanejo, is said to offer the best snorkeling in the area. Between these two beaches is **Playa Riscalillo**. To reach Playa Larga, take a combi marked 'Coacoyul' from Juárez opposite the market, and ask to get off at the turnoff to Playa Larga. Another combi will take you from the turnoff to the beach, about 3km along a paved road through a coconut plantation.

Ixtapa & Around Situated between Zihuatanejo and Ixtapa, **Playa Majahua**, not to be confused with the village of Majahua northwest of Ixtapa, is an isolated beach that was headed down a development path similar to Ixtapa's until the project was abandoned in its early stages. Accessible by car or boat but rarely visited, it's now an empty beach backed by a sort of gated, overgrown construction site. Facing the open sea, Majahua has large waves and similar conditions to Ixtapa. If you drive, you may have to talk your way past the guard at the gate.

Ixtapa's big hotels line **Playa del Palmar** a long, broad stretch of white sand teeming with families, strolling beach vendors and sunburnt honeymooners. Be very careful if you swim here: the powerful waves crash straight down and there's a powerful undertow. The west end of this beach, just before the entrance to the lagoon, is known as **Playa Escolleras** and is a favorite spot for surfing. Farther west, past the marina, are three small beaches that are among the most beautiful in the area: **Playa San Juan**, **Playa Casa Blanca** and **Playa Cuatas**. Unfortunately, they've all been effectively privatized by new developments, so unless you can gain access by skiff or helicopter they are off bounds – public access, required by Mexican law, appears to have been overlooked.

To the northwest, past Punta Ixtapa, are **Playa Quieta** and the long, wide **Playa Linda**. The latter has several decent seafood *enramadas* and a few shops selling souvenirs, snacks and beer, all at the beach's southern end near the pier.

Isla Ixtapa Just offshore, Isla Ixtapa is a small, wooded island with four pocket-sized beaches and several seafood *enramadas* that feed the island's steady stream of visitors. It's home to deer, raccoons, armadillos, iguanas and numerous species of birds, as well as the flipper-footed humans who migrate here daily for the excellent snorkeling.

Playa Cuachalalate, the main beach, has plenty of restaurants and the island's main pier, but, with fishing boats anchored along the beach and jet skiers zipping around just offshore, it's the least appealing for swimming. No matter, the smaller but equally beautiful **Playa Varadero** is only a short walk away. The best snorkeling is at **Playa Coral**, directly behind Varadero, where you will see numerous species of tropical fish, including blowfish, butterfly fish, angelfish and, as the name suggests, lots of coral. **Playa Carey** is the most isolated beach of all and is accessible only by boat, usually from the pier at Cuachalalate.

Boats zip over to the island every few minutes (less frequently in low season) from the Playa Linda pier and drop visitors at Playa Cuachalalate or Playa Varadero. The return boat ride (five minutes one way) will set you back US$3.50; boats operate 8am to 5pm daily. A boat also goes to Isla Ixtapa from the Zihuatanejo pier, but only when there are eight passengers or more. It departs at 11am, and leaves the island at around 4pm. The trip (US$11 return) takes an hour each way. The ticket office is at the foot of the pier.

Snorkeling & Scuba Diving

The ocean waters here enjoy an abundance of species because of a convergence of currents, and can offer great visibility, sometimes up to 35m. There are more than 30 dive sites nearby, offering conditions for beginners and advanced divers. Migrating humpback whales pass through from December to February, and manta rays can be seen all year, though there's greater likelihood of seeing them in summer, when the water is clearest, bluest and warmest.

A 40-minute boat ride from Zihua, the granite rocks of **Los Morros del Potosí** offer some of the most fascinating diving along the coast, with submarine caves, walls, canals and tunnels; the high currents require experience. Isla Ixtapa offers numerous shallow- and deep-water dives for all skill levels. Experts can explore the nearby **Islas Blancas**, just off Playa del Palmar, with coral-covered walls, caves, canals and abundant sea life.

Snorkeling is good at **Playa Las Gatas** and even better on **Isla Ixtapa**; restaurants and booths at both places rent **snorkel gear** for around US$6 per day. There's also excellent snorkeling at **Playa Manzanillo**, about an hour's boat ride south from Zihuatanejo. Zihua Scuba Center takes snorkeling trips there; the *Tristar* trimaran (see Cruises later in this chapter) also goes there, but only allows about 20 minutes for snorkeling. Or you can hire a boat at the foot of the Zihuatanejo pier, stop at Playa Las Gatas to rent snorkeling gear, and off you go.

The NAUI-affiliated **Zihua Scuba Center** (☎/fax 554-21-47; e divemexico@mail.com; w www.divemexico.com; Hotel Paraiso Real, Playa La Ropa) is Zihuatanejo's most professional dive outfit, offering daily morning and afternoon dives at more than 30 sites. One-/two-tank dives cost US$50/80, night dives cost US$60, and a two-dive trip to Los Morros del Potosí costs US$90; prices include boat, equipment and one dive master per three people. Six-day certification courses are also offered – former-president Ernesto Zedillo was once a student here. Stop by to look at owner Juan Barnard's underwater photos and pose any questions about diving in the area.

On Playa Las Gatas, French-owned **Carlo Scuba** (☎ 554-35-70, 554-60-03; e zih@carloscuba.com) offers a variety of PADI courses in English, French or Spanish, including a refresher for US$60 and open-water certification for US$400. Guided one-/two-tank dives cost US$50/60; one-tank night dives cost US$60. Snorkel gear goes for a wee US$4 per day.

On Isla Ixtapa, the **Escuela de Buceo Oliverio Maciel** (Oliverio Maciel Diving School) is a reliable diving outfit at the far end of Playa Cuachalalate. Now run by Oliverio's amiable son Ignacio, it offers one-hour guided dives (US$50) and one-hour instructional dives (US$50, noncertified). Snorkel equipment goes for US$6.50 per day, and for a small fee, one of the guys will take you out and show you the best spots to snorkel.

Sport Fishing
Lugging a cooler full of beer onto a fishing boat and bringing it home full of fish (or empty of both) is one of Zihua's favorite tourist attractions. Sailfish are caught here year-round; seasonal fish include blue and black marlin (March to May), roosterfish (September to October), wahoo (October), mahimahi (November to December) and Spanish (not holy) mackerel (December). Many captains now maintain a strict catch-and-release policy for billfish (especially sailfish and marlin). Fishing trips are generally six to eight hours long and leave the Zihuatanejo pier no later than 7am.

Three fishing cooperatives are based near Zihuatanejo's pier: the **Sociedad Cooperativa de Lanchas de Recreo y Pesca Deportiva del Muelle Teniente José Azueta** (☎ 559-52-79, ☎/fax 554-20-56) at the foot of the pier; **Servicios Turísticos Acuáticos**

de Zihuatanejo Ixtapa (☎/fax 554-41-62; Paseo del Pescador 6); and **Sociedad Cooperativa Benito Juárez** (☎ 554-37-58; Paseo del Pescador 20-22) next door. Any of these can arrange deep-sea fishing trips for about US$150 for up to four people in a 27-foot boat, US$250 for up to eight people in a 30-footer, and US$300 for up to 10 in a 36-footer. Prices quoted by operators always include equipment and usually include fishing license, bait, beer and water – always ask. You can also walk along the pier and talk with the various fishermen, many of whom speak some English.

Privately owned **Whisky Water World** (☎ 554-01-47, 556-64-88; w www.zihuatanejosportfishing.com; Paseo del Pescador 20) charges US$395 for six to eight lines on a 38-foot boat, US$300 for up to five lines on a 30-footer, and US$170 for three to four lines on a 25-footer. Prices include equipment (always Penn International two-speed reels), beer, soda, bottled water, bait, license and a stop for snorkeling if requested. Trips are seven hours, and French, English and Spanish are spoken.

Hawaiiana (☎ 554-32-91, 554-87-96; e hawaiianomx@yahoo.com.mx; cnr Álvarez & Cuauhtémoc) is run by former Mexican national surf champ Hiram Verboonen. Its prices are similar to those of other operators and negotiable if higher.

There are several tackle and supply shops near the pier. A good one is **Pesca Deportiva** (☎ 554-36-51; Álvarez 66; open 9am-2pm & 4pm-6pm Mon-Fri, 9am-2pm Sat).

Surfing
The best bet for waves in the immediate area is the beach break at **Playa Linda**, directly in front of the parking lot at the end of the Playa Linda road. In winter, when it's pancake-flat everywhere else, it can be chest-high and fun. Further down the beach, the **river mouth** is good during the rainy season after the river breaks through the sandbar. For both spots, take a Playa Linda bus to the pier and walk up the road (or the beach) to the parking lot. Another local favorite for its proximity to town is **Playa Escolleras**, a jetty-side beach break in Ixtapa

favoring rights and, on weekends, crowds. It's at the west end of Playa del Palmar next to (and thanks to) the marina; bring your short-board. The only surf in Zihuatanejo is the point at **Playa Las Gatas**. Just inside the bay, it requires a big swell to break, but when it does, it's reportedly a perfect hollow left, rarely more than five feet; take a boat over from the Zihua pier.

The best surf shop around is **Catcha L'Ola Surf Shop & Bar** (☎ 553-13-80/84; ⓦ www ixtapasurf.com; Centro Comercial Kiosko, Local 12, Ixtapa; open 9am-9pm daily), owned by Masters Division national champ Leon Vargas, who is a great source of information. Behind the movie theater in Ixtapa, it's well stocked and likely your best bet for board repairs. Short-boards and long-boards both rent for US$22 per day or US$90 per week. Leon will drive you out to Playa Linda and back for US$11 or up to Troncones or Saladita for US$55. He also offers three-hour lessons for US$55. The shop is good for cheap beer and gossip.

In Zihuatanejo try **Hawaiiana** (see Sport Fishing earlier in this chapter), run by former Mexican national surf champ Hiram Verboonen. He stocks wax, leashes and other basics, and it's worth stopping in if you have questions on local conditions. Boards rent for US$25 to US$45 per day, and Hiram will set you up for surf trips and lessons.

Cruises

The *Tristar* (☎ 554-26-94, 554-82-70) is a 67-foot trimaran based in the Bahía de Zihuatanejo. Its sailing and snorkeling trip, from 10am to 2.30pm, takes a load of day-trippers outside the bay for about 20 minutes of snorkeling at Playa Manzanillo, about an hour's cruise away. Flying from the spinnaker and plenty of partying are the order of the day. The cost of US$55 per person includes lunch and open bar; snorkel gear costs an additional US$5. Alternatively, a 2½-hour sunset cruise around the bay and out along the coast of Ixtapa costs US$45. Add US$3 for transport to or from any hotel in Ixtapa. Reservations are required; private charters are also available.

The *Nirvana* (☎/fax 554-59-15), a 65-foot Alden Cutter built in Australia and operated by an Australian couple, offers day-sailing trips that include snorkeling, swimming, lunch and open bar for US$65 per person, and sunset cruises with snacks and open bar for US$45 per person. With a maximum capacity of 25 people, cruises on the *Nirvana* are a bit more personal than those aboard the *Tristar*. Private charters are available for US$400 for four hours.

Other Activities

A 15km *ciclopista* (bicycle path) stretches from Playa Linda north of Ixtapa, through the Aztlán Eco Park practically into Zihuatanejo; **mountain bikes** can be rented at several places in and around the Centro Comercial Los Patios in Ixtapa, including both Rent-A-Car locations (approximately US$5.50 per hour or US$22 per day).

Horseback riding is possible on Playa Linda and Playa Larga. At Playa Linda, poke your head in at **Rancho Campos**, the stable just north of the pier. You'll get a horse, saddle and guide for about US$22 an hour, usually long enough to ride the 2km up to the Río Barrio Viejo, head upstream a bit and return.

The new **Delfiniti Dolphinarium** (☎ 553-27-07/08; ⓦ www.delfiniti.com; Blvd Ixtapa 6B; sessions 10am-noon & 4pm-6pm daily) beside Carlos 'n' Charlie's in Ixtapa, offers a chance to get up close – real close – to bottlenose dolphins. After some evolutionary history and a tour, you can swim with the dolphins for 20 minutes (US$66) or 45 minutes (US$120). Child and adult together pay US$99 for 20 minutes. Reservations are recommended.

Magic World (☎ 553-13-59; admission US$4.50; open 10.30am-5.30pm Tues-Sun), an aquatic park beside the Hotel Ixtapa Palace in Ixtapa, has rides, water slides, toboggans and other amusements.

Club de Golf Palma Real (☎ 553-10-62; Blvd Ixtapa s/n) and **Club de Golf Marina** (☎ 553-14-10; Blvd Ixtapa s/n) both have 18 holes, tennis courts and swimming pools. The green fees at Palma Real are US$75 per person and cart and caddie are included.

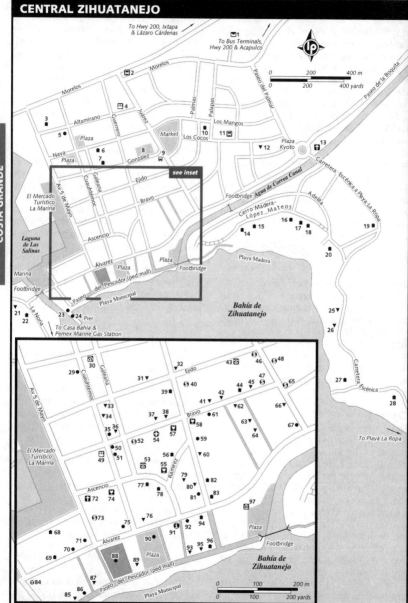

CENTRAL ZIHUATANEJO

CENTRAL ZIHUATANEJO

PLACES TO STAY
3 Hotel Laris
6 Hotel Casa Miriam
   (Casa de Huéspedes Miriam)
7 Hotel Imelda
10 Hotel Posada Coral
14 Casa Adriana
15 Bungalows Pacíficos
16 Bungalows Sotelo
17 Bungalows Ley
18 Hotel Brisas del Mar
19 Bungalows El Milagro
20 Hotel Palacios
22 Hotel Raúl Tres Marías
27 La Casa Que Canta
28 Hotel Sotavento-Catalina
39 Hotel Amueblados Valle
44 Hotel Casa Bravo
56 Hotel Zihuatanejo; Bar-Net
68 Hotel Ulises
69 Hotel Raúl Tres Marías
   Centro; Garrobo's
77 Hotel Cartier
78 Amueblados/Suites Isabel
82 Posada Citlali
83 Hotel Susy
94 Hotel Avila
96 Casa de Huéspedes La Playa

PLACES TO EAT
12 Cocina Económica Doña
   Licha
21 Casa Puntarenas
25 Restaurant Kau-Kan
26 Puesta del Sol
31 Los Braseros
32 Tamales y Atoles Any
33 Restaurant Acacio
34 Cafetería Nueva Zelanda
36 Gondwana

37 Express Oriental
38 Il Paccolo
41 Fonda Económica Susy;
   Taquería Paisanos
42 Pollos Locos
45 Banana's
60 Pizzas Locas
62 Cenaduría Antelia
63 Cenaduría Callita
64 Cenaduría Yola
66 Paul's; El Mascarero
76 La Bocana
79 Panificadora El Buen Gusto
80 Coconuts
85 La Sirena Gorda
87 Casa Elvira; Sport Fishing
   Operators; Garrobo's
89 Café Marina
93 Mariscos Los Paisanos
95 Restaurant/Bar Tata's

OTHER
1 Post Office; Telecomm;
   Mexpost
2 Local Buses to Ixtapa,
   Playa Linda
4 Cinema Zihuatanejo
5 Public Library
8 Mercado de Artesanías
9 'Coacoyul' & 'Correa' Buses
   to Bus Terminals, Playa Larga
   & Airport
11 Buses to Petatlán, La Unión
13 Church
23 Ticket Office for Boats to
   Playa Las Gatas, Isla Ixtapa
24 Harbor Master
29 Lavandería y Tintorería
   Premium
30 ServiNet; Lavandería Express

35 Plata de Taxco
40 Banamex
43 Caseta Telefónica
46 Bancrecer
47 Bancomer
48 Banamex ATM;
   Late-Night Pharmacy
49 Cine Paraíso;
   América-Ixtamar Viajes
50 Alberto's
51 Pancho's
52 Casa de Cambio Guiball
53 Caseta Telefónica
54 Dr Rogelio Grayeb's Office
55 Jungle Bar
57 D'Latino
58 Ventaneando
59 Mexicana
61 Hertz
65 Banco Serfín
67 Turismo Internacional del
   Pacífico (TIP)
70 Aero Cuahonte
71 Aeroméxico
72 Church
73 Bital Air-Con ATM
74 Rick's Bar
75 Hawaiiana
81 Coco Cabaña
84 Public Bathrooms & Showers
86 Sport Fishing Operators;
   Whisky Water World
88 Casa Marina: El Jumil;
   La Zapoteca; El Embarcadero
90 Basketball Court
91 Tourist Office
   (High Season Only)
92 Viajes Bravo
97 Museo Arqueológico de la
   Costa Grande

IXTAPA, ZIHUATANEJO & COSTA GRANDE

The Marina charges US$45 per person and requires players to rent either a cart (US$25) or a caddie (US$15). Children (and certain adults) might enjoy the **minigolf** near Ixtapa's Cine Flamingos cinema.

If you need to ditch the kids for the day, take them to the **Krystalitos Children's Club** (☎ 553-03-33; admission US$16.50; open 10am-4.30pm daily) at the Hotel Krystal Ixtapa. Enroll them at 10am; kids aged between four and 12 will be fed breakfast and lunch, enjoy fun activities all day long and receive a club T-shirt and hat. The club is open to the public.

Organized Tours

Most travel agencies (see Information earlier in this chapter) offer a wide array of tours, including city tours by foot (about US$20), all-day trips to Acapulco (US$130), and day trips southeast of town to Barra de Potosí and Petatlán. One very interesting tour is to La Soledad de Maciel archaeological site, also called 'La Chole.' Another takes you to Pantla, on Hwy 200, 30 minutes northwest of Zihuatanejo, to see bricks being made.

Adventours (☎ 553-02-88/89; e adven toursixt@email.com) is run by biologist Pablo Mendizabal. He speaks English and Spanish and offers several fun tours. On one six-hour adventure you'll bike to Playa Linda, kayak to Isla Ixtapa, snorkel for an hour, kayak back, eat lunch and return to Ixtapa by bike. On another, Pablo (or his fellow guide) takes you for a 12km bike ride down Playa Larga to Barra de Potosí where you can row around the lagoon before returning by car. Both cost US$47 per person. Less-intensive excursions are also offered. Señor Mendizabal was moving to a new office at the time of writing, so give him a ring for the new location.

Places to Stay

The reasonably priced hotels are in Zihuatanejo, and the top-end hotels gravitate toward Playa La Ropa and Ixtapa. Playa Madera is a good middle ground and has some excellent mid-range hotels, many with kitchens, all with great views. If you like to stumble out of your hotel room into the ocean, try Playa La Ropa or Playa Madera; if you like to stumble home from the bar, go for Zihuatanejo.

Unless specified, prices are for the high season (December 15 to mid-April). Prices drop by 20% to 40% between mid-April and mid-December. The busiest times of all are the three weeks around Semana Santa (Holy Week) and the week between Christmas and New Year; at these times you *must* reserve a room and be prepared to pay top peso (often 20% more than quoted high-season rates).

Places to Stay – Budget

There are two small, basic, family-run camping grounds near Playa La Ropa and they offer spaces for trailers and tents.

Trailer Park La Ropa (☎ 554-60-30; *tent sites per person US$3.25, trailers US$15-22*), beside the Mercado de Artesanías (artisan market), has no sign, but it does have tent spaces and about 10 trailer spaces with full hookups. It's a bare-bones place with four showers (which *usually* work), four toilets, a small grocery and a restaurant.

Trailer Park Los Cabañas (☎ 554-47-18; *sites per person US$4.50, trailers US$15.50*), across the street and up the hill from Playa La Ropa, has three small trailer spaces behind the owner's house, and a few spots to

pitch a tent, one being the front lawn. There are two cold showers for everyone and electric hookups (no water) for trailers. It's friendly, secure and usually full of return visitors.

Casa de Huéspedes La Playa (☎ 554-22-47; *Álvarez 6; singles/doubles US$13/22*), facing the beach in Zihuatanejo, is a basic guesthouse with six simple rooms, each with two twin beds, a cold-water bathroom and a lightbulb. There is a laundry basin and a clothesline out back, and English is spoken.

Hotel Ulises (☎ 554-37-51; *Armada de México s/n; singles/doubles US$13/17.50*), a family-run hotel 50m inland from the pier, is appealing for its price tag. Its 16 simple rooms, though slightly claustrophobic, have bathrooms, hot water and fans. Upstairs rooms are brighter.

Casa de Huéspedes Miriam (Hotel Casa Miriam; ☎ 554-39-86; *Nava 16; rooms with bathroom per person US$8.50*) is a cold-water cheapie where the owner's friendliness (Miriam's) blinds you to the fact that the rooms are tiny and the toilets have no seats. Shoot for one of the two in front with a balcony.

Hotel Cartier (☎ 554-50-84; *singles/doubles with bathroom US$16/18*), on Ascencio near Galeana, is a simple place with small rooms and a shared kitchen.

Hotel Laris (☎ 554-37-67; *Altamirano 28; singles/doubles US$16/22*) offers recently refurbished rooms with fan, bathroom and hot water. Though a bit stark and just outside the downtown hub, it's clean and cheap.

Hotel Posada Coral (☎ 554-40-52; *Los Mangos 3; singles/doubles US$16.50/22*), near the market, is great if you need a break from the downtown tourist scene. It's secure and has large spotless rooms with tiled bathrooms and hot water – and the sights, sounds and smells of the market right outside the door.

Hotel Casa Bravo (☎ 554-25-48; *Bravo 12; singles/doubles US$22/27, with air-con US$28/33*) has clean, pleasant rooms with firm beds and TV. Try for an interior room, because traffic outside can be noisy.

Posada Citlali (☎ 554-20-43; *Guerrero 3; singles/doubles May-Nov US$22/27, Dec-Apr US$33/38.50*) is pleasant, with terrace sitting areas and rooms around a courtyard filled with trees and plants. The rooms are comfortable and clean, and the location is excellent.

Hotel Susy (☎ 554-23-39; cnr Guerrero & Álvarez; singles/doubles US$27.50/38.50), next door to Posada Citlali, is a great deal, with cheerful rooms with TV, bath, hot water and fans. The new rooms upstairs get lots of light and have views of the bay from their terraces.

Hotel Raúl Tres Marías (☎ 554-21-91, 554-25-91; e r3mariasnoria@yahoo.com; La Noria 4, Colonia Lázaro Cárdenas; singles/ doubles May-Nov US$17/24, Dec-Apr US$22/ 35) is just across the lagoon from town, over a small footbridge. Many a budget traveler's favorite place to stay in Zihua, most of its 25 rooms open onto large terraces with flowers and views over town and the bay. Rooms have cold-water baths and two or more twin beds.

Places to Stay – Mid-Range

If you're staying more than a few days, consider a place with a kitchen – the money you'll save cooking will offset the cost of the hotel.

Central Zihuatanejo With five large, airy units equipped with everything you need, including full kitchens, **Hotel Amueblados Valle** (☎/fax 544-32-20; Guerrero 33; 1-/2-bed apartments May-Nov US$30/45, Dec-Apr US$40/60) is a good deal. Three- bedroom apartments are also available, and reservations are highly recommended in high season. Ask owner Luis Valle about other apartments in town and on Playa La Ropa, which may be cheaper, especially for longer stays.

Hotel Raúl Tres Marías Centro (☎ 554-67-06, 554-57-29; w www.Ixtapa-zihuatanejo .com/r3marias; Álvarez 214; singles/doubles with air-con US$40/50), above Garrobo's restaurant, has simple but clean rooms that are cheaper if you take them by the week.

Hotel Imelda (☎ 554-76-62; e hotelim elda@prodigy.net.mx; González 70; singles/ doubles US$44/55) has two swimming pools, an elevator, interior parking, and restaurant-bar open in high season. The clean rooms come with air-con and cable TV.

Hotel Zihuatanejo (☎ 554-53-30; w www .ixtapa-zihuatanejo.com/zihuacenter; Ramírez 2; singles/doubles US$71/115), one of the swankier hotels downtown, offers modern rooms with air-con and cable TV. The clean swimming pool is a relief in the summer.

Hotel Avila (☎ 554-20-10; Álvarez 8; singles/doubles without sea view US$66/72, with sea view US$83/94), on the municipal beach, has terraces overlooking the sea, private parking and large, well-equipped rooms with air-con, fan and cable TV.

Amueblados/Suites Isabel (contact Hotel Zihuatanejo for reservations; Ascencio 11; 2/ 3-bed apartments from May-Nov US$93.50/ 104.50, Dec-Apr US$121/143) has fully equipped apartments with air-con, telephone, TV and kitchen. Guests can use the pool at nearby Hotel Zihuatanejo, which manages the Isabel.

Playa Madera Only a five-minute walk from the center of Zihuatanejo, Playa Madera has several good places to stay. Most of them are bungalows with fully equipped kitchens and large terraces offering splendid views of the bay. Nearly all of them are perched up on Cerro Madera, the hill above the beach, and have steps – lots of them – down to the sand. The following are listed from west to east (moving away from town).

Casa Adriana (☎ 554-30-34, 554-26-01; e casa_Adriana@yahoo.com; López Mateos s/n; doubles US$66) is a friendly hotel with small but appealing rooms. Most have a kitchenettes, balconies and there is plenty of bougainvillea around.

Bungalows Pacíficos (☎ 554-21-12; e bungpacificos@cdnet.com.mx; López Mateos 31; doubles & quads Dec-Apr US$88, May-Nov US$66) has six attractive bungalows with ample (sometimes enormous) sea-view terraces and equipped kitchens. Anita Hahner, the Swiss owner, is a gracious and helpful host who speaks English, Spanish and German, and can help you find anything from good restaurants to good bird-watching spots.

Bungalows Sotelo (☎ 554-63-07; López Mateos 13; doubles US$66, 8-person apartment US$176) is another one with huge balconies, although the rooms feel a little bit institutional with their tiled floors and high-sheen walls. The eight-person apartment, however, is great for a group (or a party).

Bungalows Ley (☎ 554-45-63, 554-40-87; e bungalowsley@prodigy.net.mx; López Mateos s/n; bungalow doubles/quads Nov-Apr US$82/120 or US$92/170; May-Oct US$60/85 or US$66/100) offers some lovely rooms, two with open-air kitchens and a shared terrace. The lower two rooms don't have the views, but they've fewer steps to the beach. There's also a beautiful suite with an open-air living room, kitchen, private terrace, luxurious bath and hammocks.

Hotel Brisas del Mar (☎ 554-21-42; w www.brisasdelmar.net; López Mateos s/n; rooms with/without balcony US$57/38, suites with kitchen US$81, master suites US$164) is a pleasant red adobe-style hotel with a large swimming pool, a beachfront restaurant and a hill-top bar with magnificent views of the bay. The cheaper rooms, which is not what the Brisas is about, have a street view and no kitchen. The better rooms contain kitchenettes, TV and exquisite balconies with hammocks.

Hotel Palacios (☎ 554-20-55; Adelita s/n; singles/doubles with fan Dec-Apr US$44/55, with air-con US$50/60) is a colorful family hotel with a modest beachfront terrace and swimming pool. Unlike other Playa Madera hotels, the Palacios is nearly at beach level, so you avoid the post-beach stair climbing. High-season rates include breakfast; low-season rates are US$20 to US$50 less, but meals are not served.

Bungalows El Milagro (☎ 554-30-45; Paseo del Palmar s/n; apartments for 2/4/6 people US$72/83/94), just off the road to Playa La Ropa, is a laid-back place with two floors of fully equipped apartments around a large overgrown courtyard. Each room has a balcony and hammock overlooking the courtyard pool. El Milagro's faithful returnees swear the courtyard trees make cooler shade than others.

Playa Las Gatas There's just one place to stay at Playa Las Gatas. **Las Gatas Beach Club & Bungalows** (☎ 554-83-07; w www.lasgatasbeachclub.com; bungalows per double Dec-Apr US$80, June-Nov US$60) contains five rustic, Polynesian-style bungalows on the peaceful, sandy grounds of King's Point – a location without rival, period. It's accessible only by boat from the Zihuatanejo pier, or by foot via Playa Las Gatas, and the only sounds out here are the surf and the sea breezes rustling through the palms. Bungalow choices include the large Hotel California, which has four double rooms and a communal kitchen and is great for groups; the romantic La Jaula bungalow, which is perfect for two; the private El Rincón, which sleeps up to four and has a kitchen; and El Escondite, which sleeps up to six. It's operated by Owen Lee, an ex-New Yorker who has been living on this beach since 1969 'and loving every minute of it.' The first American diver to work with Jacques-Yves Cousteau, and author of a large book about diving and snorkeling, Owen has also written a useful guidebook to Zihuatanejo and Ixtapa.

Places to Stay – Top End
Nearly all top-end hotels are along Playa La Ropa or in Ixtapa. Playa La Ropa can be as luxurious as Ixtapa, but its hotels are smaller and more relaxed. La Ropa also has better swimming and is a shorter cab ride from Zihua. Ixtapa, admittedly, takes the cake when it comes to sunsets: only here do they set on the water.

Playa La Ropa The beach here boasts some excellent hotels.

Hotel Paraíso Real (☎ 554-81-56, 554-21-47; w www.divemexico.com; Playa La Ropa; doubles Nov 15–Apr 31 US$105, May 1–Nov 14 US$70) offers comfortable, spotless rooms over a large garden and small estuary complete with crocodiles. At the time of writing, air-con was in the works. Owners Juan Barnard and Mago Arizmendi are always around and take excellent care of their guests. Juan, a professional diver and marine photographer, runs Zihua Scuba

Center here and offers hotel-and-dive packages and a wealth of information.

Villa del Sol (☎ 554-22-39, 888-389-2645 in the USA & Canada; W www.hotelvilladel sol.net; Playa La Ropa; doubles Apr-Dec US$280-995, Jan-Mar US$199-527) is a rambling, two-story, adobe-style resort and the most indulgent on Playa La Ropa. With private terraces, even the standard rooms are luxurious; the deluxe rooms and suites are simply sumptuous. Perks include a first-rate gym, four swimming pools and two restaurants. A breakfast-and-dinner plan for an additional US$60 per person is mandatory in winter, optional the rest of the year.

Hotel Sotavento-Catalina (☎ 554-20-32/34; doubles Dec-Apr US$90-150, May-Nov US$45-90), on a hill overlooking Playa La Ropa, is an old favorite and has one of Zihuatanejo's most beautiful settings; its white terraces are visible from all around the bay and they offer incredible views. The price you pay for a room varies, depending on size, view and facilities; children under 12 stay free.

La Casa Que Canta (☎ 554-65-29, 888-523-5050 in the USA; W www.lacasaquecanta .com; doubles high season US$410-749, low season US$333-614), perched high on a cliff between Playa La Ropa and Playa Madera, is where the film *When a Man Loves a Woman* starring Meg Ryan was filmed. Its reddish adobe-style walls and thatched awnings are visible from all around the bay, and the entire bay is visible from its rooms. It's quite likely Zihuatanejo's most exclusive hotel.

Ixtapa Mega-resorts line the long, wide Playa del Palmar. Rates for a standard room can range from around US$70 per double in low season to as much as US$350 per double, all-inclusive, in high season. Double rates almost always mean two children under 12 can stay free. Travel agencies and hotel websites are the best way to compare prices and find the latest package deals.

Hotel Presidente Inter-Continental (☎ 553-00-18; W http://ixtapa.interconti.com; Blvd Ixtapa s/n) is one of the most popular on the beach. It has five restaurants and throws some of the biggest Fiestas Mexicanas around.

Hotel Krystal Ixtapa (☎ 553-03-33, 800-903-3300; W www.krystal.com.mx; Blvd Ixtapa s/n) has some of the best-value rooms on the strip (all of them with ocean views), one of the area's liveliest nightclubs, and a highly regarded children's club, Krystalitos.

Riviera Beach Resort (☎ 553-10-66; W www.riviera.com.mx; Blvd Ixtapa s/n) does not usually dip its prices below around US$155 per double and maintains one hell of a slick lobby to match its higher rates. The pool area is one of the better on the strip.

Barceló Ixtapa Beach Resort (☎ 555-20-00; W www.barcelo.com; Blvd Ixtapa s/n) has especially good pool and patio areas. The Barceló generally maintains all-inclusive rates for advance reservations, meaning three meals, alcoholic beverages, gym use, tennis courts, room service and childcare are all included. Walk-ins can get breakfast-only rates.

Las Brisas Ixtapa Resort (☎ 553-21-21; W www.brisas.com.mx/ixtapa) sits alone on the small Playa Vista Hermosa, essentially laying claim to this lovely beach just southeast of Playa del Palmar.

Other resorts that deal almost entirely in all-inclusive packages are **Sandy Village Beach Resort** (Karisma Aristos; ☎ 553-00-11; www.hacienda-resorts.com/karisma_ixtapa/ index.htm; Blvd Ixtapa s/n), **Fontán Ixtapa Beach Resort** (☎ 553-16-66; Blvd Ixtapa s/n), and, on Playa Linda, **Club Med** (☎ 553-00-40; W www.clubmed.com), **Melía Azul Ixtapa** (☎ 550-00-00) and **Qualton Club** (☎ 552-00-80; W www.qualton.com).

Places to Eat

Seafood in Zihuatanejo is excellent. *Tiritas* (slivers of raw fish quickly marinated in lemon juice, onion and green chili) are a local specialty. The dish originated with local fishermen: it was a quick snack requiring no cooking, easily prepared in the boat or on the beach after a morning at sea. *Tiritas* were just too damn good, however, to remain a treat for the fishermen alone. You can find them at seafood stands in the market and at some of the smaller seafood restaurants around town. They're served cold with soda crackers and *salsa picante* (hot chili sauce) on the side and make a great snack on a hot day.

Guerrero is famous for its *pozole* (see the boxed text 'Holy *Pozole!*' below). On many a menu in town (especially on a Thursday, which is *pozole* day), it's well worth a try.

Central Zihuatanejo There are plenty of popular seafood restaurants along the beachfront walkway Paseo del Pescador, though a few shine more brightly than others. They are listed in west to east order.

La Sirena Gorda (☎ 554-26-87; *Paseo del Pescador 90; mains US$5-12; open 9am-10:30pm Thur-Tues*), near the foot of the pier, is a Zihua institution and a casual open-air place famous for its seafood tacos (US$4.50 to US$8.50). It also has delicious burgers, shrimp and other dishes.

Casa Elvira (☎ 554-20-61; *Paseo del Pescador 8; breakfast US$2-4, lunch & dinner US$8-16; open 8am-10pm daily*) is known for its outstanding seafood, though it also turns out some delicious meat and chicken dishes and has an extensive list of tasty soups.

Café Marina (☎ 554-24-62; *Paseo del Pescador 9; mains US$5-9; open 8am-10pm Mon-Sat, closed June-Sept*) is a pleasant American-owned place facing the fishing beach, and has been attracting the Zihua

---

Holy *Pozole!*

When it comes to flavor, heartiness, healthiness, and getting the most meal for your money, few Mexican dishes can top *pozole*, a hearty stew whose definitive ingredient is hominy. *Pozole* is eaten throughout Mexico, but it's especially popular in Jalisco, Michoacán, Nayarit, Colima and – more than anywhere else – Guerrero. In Guerrero, every Thursday is *pozole* day (called *jueves pozolero*): when restaurants big and small cook up giant batches, and folks migrate to their favorite eateries to relax over a bowl of soup.

The word *'pozole'* comes from the Náhuatl *'pozolli,'* meaning 'foam' or 'froth.' The word was probably used to describe the foam created when corn kernels are treated with lime and water, the traditional process used to remove the skins from the kernels, allowing them to expand into the soft, easily digestible hominy. Now *pozole* is a rich stew with many variations but usually prepared with pork and, perhaps, a few vegetables for good measure.

Eating *pozole* is an art – and a very personal one – that is taken quite seriously. A proper bowl of *pozole* is served with side plates of colorful garnishing (sometimes called *botanas*), which, at the very least, should include avocado, diced onion, sliced radishes, oregano, chili powder and lemon or lime – all of which are carefully added to the soup, according to one's taste, and stirred in gently. A good restaurant will always serve a few fried tortillas and *chicharrones* (fried pork skins) on the side as well.

The traditional *pozole* served on Thursday in Guerrero is *pozole verde* (green *pozole*), which is a bit richer than another popular variation, *pozole blanco* (white *pozole*). Many people who haven't tried *pozole* before prefer the milder *pozole blanco*, so choose accordingly if both are on the menu.

The best part about *pozole* is that it's usually pretty cheap, and one bowl will surely fill you up. In markets and small *cenadurías* (family-style dinner restaurants), where *pozole* is often at its best, a bowl will cost no more than US$2!

Zihuatanejo is loaded with restaurants which serve *pozole* every night of the week, so you don't have to wait until Thursday to indulge. Our favorites are **Cenaduría Antelia** and **Cenaduría Callita** or, for something a little more gourmet, the excellent **Tamales y Atoles Any** (see Central Zihuatanejo under Places to Eat).

Perhaps the grandest of all *pozolerías* (restaurants specializing in *pozole*) is **Pozolería Los Cazadores** in Acapulco (see Places to Eat in the Acapulco & Costa Chica chapter). If you make it down there, stop in on a Thursday or Saturday evening (the only days it's open) and you'll see just how serious *pozole* can be.

regulars for more than 20 years with evening specials like meatloaf and pork chops (and some famous chocolate cake). It also prepares great breakfasts, including one of the biggest waffle and fruit plates on the coast.

Just east of the basketball court on Paseo del Pesacador, menu-wielding waiters will surely invite you into **Mariscos Los Paisanos** and **Restaurant/Bar Tata's**. Both are good value, specialize in seafood and have popular happy hours and shaded beachfront tables with fine views of the bay. They're open from 8am until late in the evening.

Garrobo's (☎ 554-67-06; Álvarez 52; mains US$8-13; open 2pm-10:30pm daily), behind Casa Elvira with its door on Álvarez, is yet another tempting seafood option. Try the paella, a house speciality, for US$17.

You'll find countless other eateries around town, and you don't have to order seafood to get excellent food.

Casa Puntarenas (☎ 554-21-09; La Noria 12; mains US$2.50-5; open 8am-11am & 6pm-9pm daily, Dec-Apr only), just over the footbridge crossing the lagoon, is a delightful, family-run patio restaurant with a small menu and a big reputation for serving large portions of excellent, inexpensive food. For atmosphere, quality and value, it's about the closest you'll come to eating in someone's home.

Casa Bahía (☎ 544-86-66; Paseo del Morro s/n; mains US$9-16; open noon-11pm daily), across the lagoon and left up the road, has an exquisite location overlooking the bay from Punta El Morro. The food is well prepared and mostly Italian, with pastas averaging US$9, seafood US$11 and salads US$5. It's a romantic spot for dinner.

La Bocana (☎ 554-35-45; Álvarez 26; mains US$5-13; open 8am-10pm daily) is known for its carne asada Tampiqueña (sauted, sliced beef marinated in garlic, oil and oregano) served with enchiladas, salad, rice and beans (US$7.70). It does plenty of other good dishes, including a long list of reasonably priced seafood plates and soups, and a variety of breakfast combinations.

Los Braseros (☎ 554-87-36; Ejido 64; mains US$3-9; open 9am-1am daily) is the reigning king of the Zihua taco world; the

tacos al pastor (with sliced, rotisserie-cooked, marinated pork) are its crowning glory. Most tacos cost around US$3 for three (they're the small ones). Some 30 combinations of grilled and skewered meat and veggie dishes are also offered.

Gondwana (☎ 554-60-16; Galeana 15; mains US$7-11; open 8am-11pm Mon-Sat) is a stylish new British-owned curry restaurant, which prepares outstanding madras, korma and balti curries in one of the most handsome kitchens in town. Other dishes you'll want to sink your teeth into include tikka kebabs, mouthwatering spicy coconut mushrooms (US$5.50) and the avocado fan with walnut-and-apple salad (US$4.40). You'll be hard pressed to find Indian food this good anywhere else on the coast.

Tamales y Atoles Any (☎ 554-73-73; Ejido 15; mains US$5-12; open 9am-10:30pm daily) serves some of the most consciously traditional Mexican cuisine in town – and does an outstanding job. It's an excellent place to try pozole (the waiters even explain the art of garnishing it; see the boxed text 'Holy Pozole!' on the previous page) or any of the 16 varieties of homemade tamales. Phone for free delivery.

Il Paccolo (Bravo 38; open 4pm-late daily) kicks out delicious lasagna (US$6.50) as well as reliable pizza, pasta, meats and seafood.

For cheap eats, take a stroll down Calle Nicolas Bravo; the following are all good, often busy, always fresh and always cheap.

Express Oriental (☎ 557-96-92; Bravo 40; mains US$2.50-4; open 2pm-11pm Tues-Sat, 4pm-11pm Sun) offers simple but tasty Chinese dishes such as mixed vegetable Buddha's delight, fried rice, chop suey and imperial chicken. The yummy cheese wantons (US$2.75) make a good appetizer, and the salads are refreshing and interesting.

Fonda Económica Susy (☎ 554-23-49; Bravo 24B; comida corrida US$2.50; open 8am-6pm Mon-Sat) serves some of the cheapest food in town, makes handmade tortillas and has a reliable comida corrida (daily special). **Taquería Paisanos**, the taco stand next door, opens in the evening, serving authentic tacos (US$0.45 each) made from tripa (tripe), cabeza (beef head) or straight up carne (beef). It gets busier through the night when folks stand around on the sidewalk downing their tacos with US$1.30 beers.

Pollos Locos *(Bravo 15; mains US$2-4; open 1pm-10.30pm daily)*, just up the street, is a popular open-air place serving inexpensive wood-grilled chicken, charging about US$4 for a whole bird. Other meats are served as well.

Banana's *(☎ 554-47-21; Bravo 9; breakfast & lunch US$3-6; open 8am-4pm daily)*, a few doors up, serves great egg breakfasts, fruit bowls, *liquados* (fruit shakes) and reliable Mexican standards. The *chilaquiles* (fried tortillas with red sauce, cheese and your choice of egg or chicken) are especially good.

Across the street and down the small Pellicer alleyway, several family-run *cenadurías* (supper restaurants) prepare tasty meals at rock-bottom prices; you can stuff yourself for under US$3.50 – beer included. **Cenaduría Antelia** *(☎ 554-30-91; cnr Bravo & Pellicer; open 5pm-midnight daily)* does fair *antojitos* (light meals), but is best for its hearty bowls of delicious *pozole* for only US$1.65. Next door, **Cenaduría Callita** *(☎ 554-84-88; Pellicer 11; open 6pm-midnight daily)* serves equally good *pozole* (US$1.10 to US$1.50), basic chicken tamales (US$0.55 each) and *atole*, a traditional sweetened corn drink. The next one over, **Cenaduría Yola** *(☎ 554-63-64; Pellicer 7; open 6pm-11pm Mon-Sat, 8am-noon Sun)* serves similar fare, but is known for its big Sunday morning bowls of *panza*, the undisputed Mexican cure-all for hangovers. Also known as *menudo*, *panza* is a hearty stew of cow stomach, hominy and vegetables garnished with lemon, onions and cilantro. If you wish to test its miraculous powers, do so before noon, which is when the pot often goes empty.

Pizzas Locas *(☎ 554-35-69; Guerrero 10; mains US$4-9; open 4pm-11pm Fri-Wed)* bakes good wood-fired pizzas, charging from US$5 for a small cheese to US$9 for a large house special with the works. Pastas, tacos and seafood are also served, and big wood tables make for a homey atmosphere.

Coconuts *(☎ 554-79-80; Ramirez 1; mains US$6-10)* is a well-anchored Zihua standby: good food, great drinks and is a favorite meeting place before a night out. Enter from Ramirez or Guerrero.

Restaurant Acacio *(Galeana 21; mains US$2.50-5; open 10am-midnight Mon-Sat)*, a simple little seafood eatery with shaded streetside tables, is one of the best places in town to get authentic *tiritas*, prepared fresh daily with the catch of the day and costs only US$3.30. There are plenty of other seafood dishes on the menu too, all at unbeatable prices.

Cocina Económica Doña Licha *(☎ 544-39-33; Los Cocos 8; mains US$3-5; open 8am-6pm daily)*, east of the market, attracts locals and tourists alike with its down-home Mexican cooking, casual atmosphere and excellent prices. There are always several *comidas corridas* to choose from including one delicious speciality, *pollo en cacahuate* (chicken in a peanut sauce); they're all US$2.20 and come with rice, beans and handmade tortillas. Breakfasts are huge.

Cafetería Nueva Zelanda *(Cuauhtémoc 23; mains US$3-5; open 7:30am-10pm daily)* has entrances on both Cuauhtémoc and Galeana. It's a clean, popular café where you can get anything on the menu *para llevar* (to go). Here you can get a decent cappuccino and choose from a lengthy list of yummy juices.

Panificadora El Buen Gusto *(☎ 554-32-31; Guerrero 8; bakery goods US$0.10-0.40; open 7.30am-10pm daily)* is a delightful little bakery with fresh Mexican *pan dulce* (sweet bread), chocolate doughnuts and a variety of savory *empanadas* (small pastries with savory or sweet fillings). The attached café has an espresso machine.

Paul's *(☎ 554-65-28; Juárez near Bravo; mains US$10-20; open 3pm-late Mon-Sat)* is a gourmet restaurant named after its Swiss owner-chef, who consistently creates some of Zihua's best fancy food, including good vegetarian options. The adjacent **El Mascarero** piano bar is a rather mellow after-hours hangout.

As in most Mexican towns, inexpensive food is available in the **central market**. Zihua's is on Juárez, opposite González, and most food stalls are open daily from dawn until around 3pm.

Playa Madera & Playa La Ropa Perched on the cliffs high above Playa Madera, **Puesta del Sol** (☎ 554-83-42; *Carretera Escénica s/n; mains US$7-14; open 4pm-11pm daily*) has fabulous sunset views and a menu as flaming as the seven o'clock sky. Roquefort medallion flambe, beef stroganoff flambe and, on the unlit side, fillet of beef heart are just a few of the options. Of course, there's seafood aplenty. People come for the sunset as much as the food, so make a reservation.

Restaurant **Kau-Kan** (☎ 554-84-46; *Carretera Escénica 7; mains US$12-18; open 1pm-midnight daily*) is another gourmet place with the same great view on the scenic road to Playa La Ropa. It's a bit pricier than Puesta del Sol, but the food is tops. Choosing is exhausting when you're faced with choices like stingray in black butter sauce, sauted octopus and grilled beef paillard.

La Casa Que Canta (☎ 554-65-29, 888-523-5050 in the USA; W www.lacasaque canta.com) has the most expensive restaurant in Zihuatanejo with dinner easily costing more than US$60, wine and drinks extra. The public is admitted only for dinner (6.30pm to 10.30pm), and reservations are required. Those who've tried it describe the experience with a watery mouth and faraway eyes.

Playa La Ropa and Playa Las Gatas both have plenty of beachside restaurants specializing in seafood. On La Ropa, **Rossy's** (☎ 554-40-04; *mains US$8-11; open 9am-10pm daily*), **La Perla** (☎ 554-27-00; *mains US$7-11; open 9am-10pm daily*) and, the last one on the beach, **La Gaviota** (☎ 554-38-16; *mains US$7-18; open noon-10pm daily*) are all popular and good.

Restaurants close earlier on Playa Las Gatas, usually before sunset when people are packing up and heading back to their hotels. **Restaurante Oliverio** is a good choice, as are most of the others. The one that gets the raves, however, is **Chez Arnoldo's** (☎ 557-80-69; *open 10am-5:30pm*), the third restaurant from the pier. The restaurant at **Las Gatas Beach Club & Bungalows** (☎ 554-83-07; W www.lasgatasbeachclub.com; mains US$4-

8; *open 8am-5.30pm*) has a peerless location on the point, with dinner by arrangement. It's also great to wander over for an afternoon drink at the bar. The club's taxi provides transport in the evening.

Ixtapa In the Centro Comercial La Puerta (one of Ixtapa's many outdoor malls), **Señor Frog's** (☎ 553-06-92; *mains US$6-13; open 8am-midnight daily*) and **El Infierno y La Gloria** (☎ 553-03-04; *mains US$7-13; open 8am-midnight daily*) both serve giant portions of good, foreigner-friendly Mexican food and show their guests a good time; the latter has live music from 7pm to 10pm. In the same mall, owned by the same conglomerate, **Señor Itto** (☎ 553-02-72) serves Thai and Chinese dishes and has a decent sushi and noodle bar.

Carlos 'n' Charlie's (☎ 553-00-85; *Paseo del Palmar s/n; mains US$6-13; open 8am-late*), further west on Blvd Ixtapa, has the same party-restaurant atmosphere and turns into one of the area's most popular dance club after around 11pm.

Beccofino (☎ 553-17-70; *Veleros Lote 6, Ixtapa Marina Plaza; mains US$8-18*), an indoor-outdoor restaurant at the Ixtapa Marina, has a good reputation for delicious Italian cuisine, especially seafood. Several other recommended restaurants surround the marina.

Villa de la Selva (☎ 553-03-62) is an elegant restaurant in the former home of Mexican president Luis Echeverría. Set on the cliffside near Las Brisas Ixtapa Resort hotel, it overlooks the ocean and has a spectacular sunset view. It's a good place to fire up a romantic evening; reservations are recommended.

Entertainment

Bars People like to knock 'em back when they come to Zihuatanejo, and, though the bars can get boisterous, they usually avoid the riotous, frat-party feel. The following bars are all in Zihuatanejo.

Restaurant/Bar Tata's and **Mariscos Los Paisanos** (sea Places to Eat), side by side on the beach on Zihuatanejo's Playa Municipal, attract a jolly sunset crowd.

The lobby bar on the top terrace of **Hotel Sotavento-Catalina** (☎ 554-20-32/34 bar open 3pm-11pm, happy hour 6pm-8pm), perched on the cliffs above Playa La Ropa, is a great place to watch the sunset, with a magnificent view over the entire bay. The bar at nearby **Puesta del Sol** (☎ 554-83-42; Carretera Escénica s/n) has similarly beautiful views.

The tiny outdoor **street-corner bar** below D'Latino (☎ 554-22-30; cnr Bravo & Guerrero) pours cheap draft beer and tequila from noon until late and is usually buzzing with some hilarious conversation. Across the street, **Ventaneando** (☎ 554-53-90) is a canta-bar (karaoke bar) which brings in a steady crowd of singers, on weekends.

Rick's Bar (☎ 554-25-35; Cuauhtémoc 5; open 10am-10pm daily) is especially popular with the boating crowd. There's always something going on, including live music from 6pm to 10pm most nights. The place gets packed for Monday night football 'pressure night,' when all beers cost only US$1.10 'until someone goes potty.'

Jungle Bar (cnr Ascencio & Ramírez; open noon-late) is a kick-back street-side bar with a great, English-speaking staff and cheap drinks. It's an excellent place to meet others (locals and travelers alike) and get the low-down on town.

Most of Ixtapa's big hotels (see Places to Stay) have bars. **Sanca Bar** at Barceló Ixtapa Beach Resort (see Places to Stay) is popular for Latin music and dancing. The lobby bar at **Las Brisas Ixtapa Resort** is worth checking out.

El Faro (Marina Ixtapa), at the top of a 25m-high lighthouse in the Marina Ixtapa, is great for watching the sunset and has music and dancing as well.

Discos & Shows The only real disco in Zihuatanejo, **D'Latino** (☎ 554-22-30; cnr Bravo & Guerrero; admission US$3-6), attracts the weekend teenyboppers who can't make it over to the clubs in Ixtapa.

If you need a night on the dance floor, you're best off in Ixtapa. All the big hotels have bars and nightclubs, and most have discos to boot.

Christine (☎ 553-04-56; Blvd Ixtapa s/n; admission free Mon; open 10:30pm-late nightly), in front of the Hotel Krystal Ixtapa, is the most popular disco in Ixtapa.

Zen (Blvd Ixtapa s/n; admission around US$10; open 10pm-late nightly Nov-Apr), on the resort strip near the Radisson Hotel, spins a decent mix of lounge, house, trance and acid jazz.

Carlos 'n' Charlie's (☎ 553-00-85; Paseo del Palmar s/n) is a restaurant with a disco; it's one of the top weekend dance floors for tourists and Zihuatanejo kids alike.

Los Mandiles (Centro Comercial La Puerta) is a restaurant-bar with an upstairs disco. **Millennium** (☎ 553-27-10), in the Magic World aquatic park, is another decent disco.

Several of Ixtapa's big hotels hold **Fiestas Mexicanas** in the evening, including **Barceló Ixtapa Beach Resort**, **Hotel Dorado Pacífico**, **Riviera Beach Resort**, **Club Med** and **Melía Azul Ixtapa**. Most include a Mexican buffet, an open bar, and entertainment including traditional Mexican dancing, mariachis, rope dances and bloodless cockfighting demonstrations, as well as door prizes and dancing. The total price is usually around US$40.

Cinemas Zihuatanejo has two cinemas: **Cine Paraíso** (☎ 554-23-18; Cuauhtémoc 21) and **Cinema Zihuatanejo** (☎ 557-02-84). Both are tiny and charge about US$2.50 per person. Ixtapa has a newer, plusher cinema, **Cine Flamingos** (☎ 553-24-90; admission US$4), behind the tourist office and opposite the Plaza Ixpamar and minigolf. All three show two films nightly, usually in English with Spanish subtitles.

Shopping

Mexican handicrafts, including ceramics, clothing, wood carvings, *huaraches* (woven leather sandals), Taxco silver crafts and masks from around the state of Guerrero, are sold everywhere. Ixtapa's **Tourist Market** (open 9am-9pm daily) is situated opposite the Barceló Ixtapa Beach Resort. The best shopping, however, is to be found in Zihuatanejo.

El Mercado Turístico La Marina stretches for nearly three blocks along Av 5 de Mayo in Zihuatanejo. There are more stalls here in one location than anywhere else in town, and many of the booths have quality merchandise, though you have to look carefully. There are also a few stalls in the **Mercado Municipal de las Artesanías** on González near Juárez.

The next three listings are all in the Casa Marina building, which occupies a full block on the east side of the main plaza. The building houses some of the finest crafts shops in town, all of which are open from 10am to 9pm daily.

El Jumil (☎ 554-61-91; Casa Marina, Paseo del Pescador 9) specializes in authentic Guerrero masks. The state is known for its variety of interesting masks and there are some museum-quality ones here, many starting around US$15.

La Zapoteca (☎ 544-23-73; Casa Marina, Paseo del Pescador 9) sells high-quality weavings from Teotitlán del Valle, Oaxaca, and thin-string, *doble tejido* (double-weave) hammocks from Yucatán.

El Embarcadero (Casa Marina, Paseo del Pescador 9) specializes in Mexican *huipiles* (blouses) and other hand-embroidered cotton clothing.

Numerous shops around Zihuatanejo sell silver jewelry from Taxco; several good ones are located near the intersection of Cuauhtémoc and Bravo, including **Plata de Taxco** (☎ 554-42-36; Bravo 6), **Alberto's** (☎ 554-21-61; Cuauhtémoc 12 & 15) and **Pancho's** (☎ 554-52-30; Cuauhtémoc 15). All are open 9am to 9pm Monday to Saturday.

Coco Cabaña (☎ 554-25-18; Guerrero 5; open 9:30am-2pm & 4:30pm-9pm Mon-Sat) deals in select folk art from all over Mexico. Drool-worthy goods include figurines, ceramics, carved boxes and beautiful barkpaper engravings.

Keep your eyes peeled, especially in the central market, for *dulces de tamarindo* (those gooey dark-brown sweets made from tamarind pulp) and *dulces de coco* (coconut sweets, sold in countless shapes and flavors – a speciality of this coconut-producing region).

Getting There & Away

Air The **Ixtapa/Zihuatanejo international airport** (☎ 544-54-08) is 19km from Zihuatanejo, about 2km off Hwy 200 heading toward Acapulco. Airlines serving this airport, and their direct flights, are listed here; all have connections to other centers.

Aero Cuahonte (☎ 554-39-88, 554-70-61) Álvarez 34, Zihuatanejo. Flies from Lázaro Cárdenas to Morelia, Uruapan and Guadalajara

Aeroméxico (☎ 554-20-18/19) Álvarez 34, Zihuatanejo. Flies to Guadalajara, Mexico City

Alaska Airlines (☎ 554-84-57, 001-800-252-7522) Flies to Los Angeles, San Francisco

America West (☎ 001-800-235-9292) Flies to Phoenix

Continental (☎ 554-42-19, 01-800-900-5000) Flies to Houston

Mexicana (☎ 554-22-08/9) Guerrero 32, Zihuatanejo; Hotel Dorado Pacífico, Ixtapa. Flies to Guadalajara, Mexico City

Bus Both long-distance bus terminals are on Hwy 200 about 2km south of the town center (toward the airport). You'll find 1st-class Elite, Futura, Plus and Cuauhtémoc buses at the **Estrella Blanca bus terminal** (☎ 554-34-76/77), called the Central de Autobuses. **Estrella de Oro** (☎ 554-21-75) has its own smaller terminal, across a side road from Estrella Blanca. Buses include those to:

Acapulco US$11 to US$13 1st class with Estrella Blanca, four hours, 239km, 10 daily; US$8 2nd-class with Estrella Blanca, every half hour; US$11 1st class with Estrella de Oro, three daily; US$8 2nd-class with Estrella de Oro, hourly from 7am to 7pm

Lázaro Cárdenas US$5 1st class with Estrella Blanca, two hours, 120km, 11 daily from 1am to 9.30pm; US$3.50 2nd class with Estrella Blanca, hourly from 9am to 10pm; US$3.85 2nd class with Estrella de Oro, every hour or two from 5.40am to 6pm

Manzanillo US$28 1st class with Estrella Blanca, 433km, three daily at approximately 10am, noon and 5pm

Mexico City (Terminal Norte) US$43 1st class with Estrella Blanca, 10 hours, 640km, 6.30pm

Mexico City (Terminal Sur) US$38 1st class with Estrella Blanca, eight to nine hours, 640km, six daily; US$53 one ejecutivo; US$34 to US$53 1st class with Estrella de Oro, 10 daily

Petatlán US$1.25 with Estrella Blanca, 30 minutes 32km, every 30 minutes from 3.45am to 11.20pm; US$1.25 with Estrella de Oro hourly from 7am to 6pm; most buses to Acapulco stop in Petatlán; you can also take a local bus from the bus lot east of the market, in Zihuatanejo

Puerto Escondido US$32 1st class with Estrella Blanca, 12 hours, 628km, several buses daily

Manzanillo-bound buses continue to Puerto Vallarta (US$49, 14 hours, 718km) and Mazatlán (US$75, 24 hours, 1177km). Estrella Blanca offers a daily service to Pochutla (US$38, 13½ hours) and Huatulco (US$41, 14½ hours). All Estrella Blanca buses to and through Puerto Escondido stop in Cuajinicuilapa (US$23, seven hours), Pinotepa Nacional (US$25, nine hours) and Rio Grande (US$30, 11 hours).

Car & Motorcycle The cheapest car rental we found on our visit was US$50 per day with Alamo. Be sure to shop around as prices can fluctuate considerably between companies and seasons. Most companies deliver the car to your hotel the night before your rental period begins. Car rental companies in Zihuatanejo and Ixtapa include:

Alamo (☎ 553-02-06) Centro Comercial Los Patios, Ixtapa; (☎ 554-84-29) airport

Budget (☎ 554-48-37) Centro Comercial Ambiente, Local 10, Ixtapa; (☎ 554-48-37) airport

Econo Franquicia (☎ 554-78-07) airport

Europcar (☎ 553-10-32) Centro Comercial Los Patios, Ixtapa

Hertz (☎ 554-22-55) Bravo 37, Zihuatanejo; (☎ 554-25-90) airport

Rent-A-Car (☎ 553-10-88) Centro Comercial La Puerta, Local 1; (☎ 553-16-30) Centro Comercial Los Patios, Local 61, Ixtapa

Thrifty (☎ 553-00-18 ext 4156) Hotel Presidente Inter-Continental; (☎ 544-57-45) airport

Getting Around

Getting To/From the Airport The cheapest way to the airport (US$0.45) is in a *microbús* or *colectivo* (the white VW vans) marked 'Coacayul' or 'Aeropuerto'; they leave from González near Juárez in Zihua. The same *micros* carry passengers from the airport to town; catch them just outside the parking lot (they cannot enter the airport) on the way out to the freeway (easy). Another *colectivo* van provides transport from inside the airport parking lot to Zihuatanejo or Ixtapa for US$6 per person, but not in the other direction. A taxi *to* the airport costs around US$9 from Zihuatanejo, US$12 from Ixtapa. A taxi *from* the airport costs around US$14 to Zihuatanejo, US$17 to Ixtapa (one cab company enjoys a monopoly on airport passengers).

Bus Local buses run frequently between Zihuatanejo and Ixtapa (US$0.55, 15 minutes) between 6am and 11pm. In Zihuatanejo the buses depart from the 'island' at Juárez and Morelos. In Ixtapa the bus stops all along the main street, in front of all the large hotels.

Some of these buses, the ones marked 'Zihuatanejo–Ixtapa–Playa Linda,' continue through Ixtapa to Playa Linda (US$0.55), stopping near Playa Quieta on the way. These operate from around 7am to 7pm.

To get to the long-distance bus terminals from Zihuatanejo, take a *microbús* marked 'Correa', 'Coacayul' or 'Aeropuerto' from González near Juárez any time between 6am and 9.30pm (US$0.45).

Playa La Ropa buses head south on Juárez in Zihuatanejo and out to Playa La Ropa every half hour from 7am to 8pm (US$0.55, 10 minutes).

To Playa Larga, take any *microbús* marked 'Coacoyul' or 'Aeropuerto' from the stop on González near Juárez (US$0.45); they drop you at the turnoff, from where you must walk the 3km to the beach (pleasant in the morning) or wait for the lone, blue mystery-*microbús* that turns up every couple hours on its route to the beach and back (US$0.35 one way).

Taxi Cabs are plentiful in Ixtapa and Zihuatanejo. Agree on a price before climbing into the cab. Fares between Zihuatanejo and Ixtapa are around US$4.50; to or from Playa La Ropa US$3.50, and to or from Playa Larga, US$8.

Bicycle & Motor Scooter Several places in and around Centro Comercial Los Patios (including both Rent-A-Car locations) rent mountain bikes (around US$5.50 per hour, US$22 per day) and motor scooters (around US$11 per hour, US$45 per day). Renting usually requires a driver's license and credit card. Scooter rentals may not leave the Ixtapa–Zihuatanejo area.

BARRA DE POTOSÍ
☎ 755

About a 40-minute drive from Zihuatanejo, Barra de Potosí is a tiny fishing village visited regularly by folks who come to wander the endless fine-sand beach, eat seafood in the simple beachfront *enramadas,* and explore the mangrove-fringed Laguna de Potosí. In winter, when the waves are small, the ocean makes for sublime swimming outside the breakers, an almost divine experience as you gaze back at the dramatic backdrop of the cloud-capped Sierra Madre del Sur. The beach itself stretches north for miles, unbroken as far as Playa Larga, near Zihuatanejo. Fishermen still string nets by hand in the village, about 100m inland from the beach.

Exploring the lagoon is best in the cool of the morning, when bird-watching is good and the sun is gentle. Single and double **kayaks** and traditional wooden **canoes** can be rented at several restaurants. **Enramada Leticia** *(open 8am-6pm daily),* to the left as you approach the beach, has a good selection, charging US$6 per hour for kayaks and US$5 per day for canoes. **Boat tours** aboard covered fishing *pangas* (skiffs), cost about US$11 for a 30-minute buzz around the lagoon. **Hiking** and **horseback riding** are also popular. Rent horses from Roberto, who usually sets up shop near the restaurants by the beach; he charges around US$14 per hour.

There are several places to stay in Barra de Potosí, either on the beach or in the village, a short walk from the sea.

Casa de Frida *(☎ 556-74-62, 556-39-44; w www.zihuatanejo.net/casafrida; doubles US$70; open Nov-Mar only),* the bright yellow building on the beach, is a stunning Mexican-French-owned B&B with two artistically decorated units – one above and one below. Both are comfortable, and have

mosquito nets, excellent beds and a lovely shared yard. A delicious breakfast is included, eaten in a sheltered dining area which doubles as a shrine to the Mexican painter Frida Kahlo. Reservations are recommended (email being the best method).

Casa del Encanto *(☎ 556-81-99; w www.casadelencanto.com; doubles US$60)* is a knockout B&B with the sort of open-air rooms that, while private, blend interior with exterior to keep them as cool and relaxed as possible. Candles provide the only nighttime light. There are four spacious rooms, all with bathrooms and mosquito nets and plenty of books around to flip through. It's located on the main road back in the village.

Hotel Barra de Potosí *(☎ 554-70-60, 556-89-34; doubles without/with sea view US$55/110, suites with kitchen & sea view US$165)* is a modern five-story hotel with a swimming pool and spotless, tiled rooms with balconies. Discounts of up to 60% are common outside Easter and Christmas weeks.

Down at the beach, there are plenty of **seafood restaurants** that serve generous portions of whatever's fresh. Most are open between 8am or 9am and 7pm (bad for late-night munchies). Basic supplies are available at shops in the village.

To get here from Zihuatanejo, head southeast on Hwy 200 toward Acapulco; turn off at the town of Los Achotes, 25km from Zihua, and head for the sea, another 10km. Any bus heading to Petatlán (see Getting There & Away under Ixtapa & Zihuatanejo, earlier) will drop you at the turnoff. Tell the driver you're going to Barra de Potosí, and you'll be let off where you can catch a *camioneta* (covered truck) going the rest of the way. The total cost is about US$2.50 if you go by bus; a taxi from Zihua will set you back US$40/50 one way/return (but the cost is negotiable).

PETATLÁN
☎ 758

A colonial town 30 minutes southeast of Zihuatanejo, Petatlán is best known for its Santuario Nacional del Padre Jesús de Petatlán, a large, modern sanctuary attracting pilgrims from near and far who leave votive offerings (traditionally the tiny, gold trinkets that have been sold behind the church for decades) to the statue of Christ inside. Legend has it the statue was found floating in a nearby stream shortly after Petatlán's congregation took up a collection to purchase a new one. Gold is still sold cheaply from many little shops beside the church.

Petroglyphs and other pre-Hispanic artifacts are displayed in the center of town, most of them collected from the nearby archaeological site of **Soledad de Maciel**, known as **La Chole**. The site itself is about 5km up a signed road that takes you seaward from Hwy 200, about 6km north of Petatlán; you can visit on your own or go as part of a tour from Zihuatanejo (see Organized Tours under Ixtapa & Zihuatanejo, earlier in this chapter).

During Semana Santa (Holy Week), Petatlán has a traditional fair with food, music and handicrafts exhibitions. Petatlán's religious festival is held on August 6.

Hotel Plaza Cocos (☎ 538-36-89; Vicente Guerrero 2; rooms without/with air-con & TV US$16/27), just off the main plaza, behind Yardas Pizza, is a friendly hotel. There are other hotels around.

Several restaurants flank the plaza, but the best deals are in the **fondas** (small restaurants) beside the church. They all charge around US$2.25 for the *comida corrida* and serve fresh, handmade tortillas to accompany the meal.

Petatlán is on Hwy 200, 32km southeast of Zihuatanejo. For bus information, see Getting There & Away under the Ixtapa & Zihuatanejo section, earlier in this chapter.

LA BARRITA
About an hour south of Zihuatanejo, at Km 187, La Barrita is a shell-size village on an attractive beach. There ain't a thing to do but wear out your legs walking the long empty beach, swim when the waves are gentle, or sit in one of the seafood *enramadas* chewing fresh fish. That is unless you **surf**. La

Barrita has a good beach break that's well worth a peek if you're passing by. There's an even better beach break 3km to the north at **Loma Bonita**. At the village of Loma Bonita (Km 190), take the dirt road (4WD only) about 2km to the cliff and walk down.

There are two places to stay in La Barrita, both of them restaurants with attached accommodations: **Restaurant Maritoña** (☎ 758-538-2963; rooms US$7.50) and **Las Peñitas** (double bed US$6.50, 2 beds US$12, cottage US$33). Both places offer stuffy, bare-bones rooms, but you can escape the evening heat of your room by dozing in the restaurants' hammocks.

Second-class buses heading south from Zihuatanejo or north from Acapulco will drop you at La Barrita.

PLAYA CAYAQUITOS & OJO DE AGUA
At Km 160 (78km from Zihuatanejo), Hwy 200 rolls through the nondescript town of **Papanoa** where you can gas up and purchase basic provisions. At the southern outskirts of town, **Hotel Club Papanoa** (☎ 742-422-01-50; w www.hotelpapanoa.com; Hwy 200, Km 160; doubles without/with air-con & TV US$55/66) overlooks the beautiful, and almost always deserted, Playa Cayaquitos. The hotel, built in 1963 and well worth a few days' stay, has a good **restaurant**, a lovely sundeck and a clean swimming pool; the rooms are spacious and clean.

Even if you don't plan to stay the night, Playa Cayaquitos is a beautiful place to spend the day. The main access is just north of the Hotel Club Papanoa sign. The beach is long and the swimming is good in the winter when the waves are gentle. At the southern end of the beach, a tiny headland separates Cayaquitos from Ojo de Agua, a picture-perfect little cove with several beachfront **seafood enramadas**.

Camping is possible on both beaches, though Ojo de Agua is more sheltered and the restaurants will allow you to use their services if you eat their food.

Acapulco & Costa Chica

Acapulco, city of discos, divers and Holly-wood honeymoons, enchanted the world for decades as Mexico's most glamorous beach resort. The city's uncontrolled growth, how-ever, tarnished its glow, and Acapulco had to step aside for Cancún, which now attracts the most foreign tourists annually to its shore. But Acapulco still has some magic, still has some of the biggest discos around, and still keeps plenty of visitors swearing it's the best resort around.

For some peace and quiet, leave the city and head southeast along Guerrero's Costa Chica, and the glitz and chaos of Acapulco fade like a summer sunset. Coastal Hwy 200 rolls through palm plantations, thorn forest, cattle land and villages and past turnoffs to some truly spectacular beaches. Many of the Costa Chica's inhabitants are Afro-mestizos, or *morenos,* as they refer to themselves – people of mixed African, in-digenous and European decent. Cuajinicuil-apa, the small-town de facto capital of the Costa Chica, is worth a stop for its museum of Afro-mestizo cultures. The beaches of Playa Ventura and Playa La Bocana make adventurous day trips from Acapulco and offer basic accommodations for a few days of quiet relaxation.

PIE DE LA CUESTA
☎ 744

About 10km northwest of Acapulco, Pie de la Cuesta is a narrow 2km strip of land bordered by the beach and ocean on one side and the large, freshwater Laguna de Coyuca on the other. Compared to Acapulco, it's quieter, cleaner, closer to nature and much more peaceful. Swimming in the ocean at Pie de la Cuesta can be dangerous due to a riptide and the shape of the waves. Laguna de Coyuca, three times larger than the Bahía de Acapulco, is better for swimming; in the lagoon are the islands of Montosa, Presido and Pájaros, which is a bird sanctuary.

Pie de la Cuesta has many beachside restaurants specializing in seafood, and it's a

Highlights

- Seeing Acapulco's cliff-divers plunge 45m into the surf below

- Boogying till the break o' dawn in Acapulco's mega-discos

- Drinking a 'coco-loco' at sunset at the famous Hotel Flamingo, once owned by John Wayne

- Exploring the isolated beaches of the Costa Chica

- Visiting the small Museum of Afro-Mestizo Cultures in Cuajinicuilapa

- Taking a sunset 'booze cruise' around Bahía de Acapulco

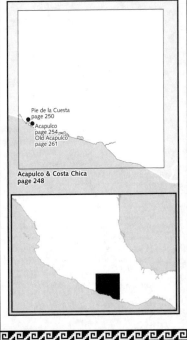

Pie de la Cuesta
page 250

Acapulco
page 254
Old Acapulco
page 261

Acapulco & Costa Chica
page 248

great place for watching the sunset. There's no nightlife, so if you're looking for excitement you may be better off staying in Acapulco.

There's one main road with two names; Av de la Fuerza Aérea Mexicana or Calzada Pie de la Cuesta.

Activities

Pie de la Cuesta has been famous for **water skiing** for decades. The glassy morning waters of the enormous Laguna de Coyuca are perfect for the sport, and several clubs will gladly pull you around the lagoon from

their speedboats. They all charge approximately US$44 per hour, which includes boat, driver and ski equipment.

Cadena X Ski Club (☎ 460-22-83; e ca denax@yahoo.com; Calzada Pie de la Cuesta s/n) is the best equipped for wakeboarding and has the only boat with a wakeboard tower. Owner Fernando Cadena has competed in Florida and Mexico and teaches ski and wakeboard classes in French, English and Spanish.

Other friendly and reliable ski clubs are **Club de Ski Tres Marías** (see Places to Eat), **Club de Ski Acuario** (☎ 447-83-01) and **Club**

ACAPULCO & COSTA CHICA

de Ski Chuy (☎ 460-11-04; Calzada Pie de la Cuesta 74).

Boat tours of the lagoon (which, incidentally, is where *Rambo*, starring Sylvester Stallone, was filmed) are another popular activity, though **bird-watching** en route is often reduced to a minimum by speedboats and jet skis. Still, if you can convince someone to take you early enough, chances are high you'll spot storks, herons, avocets, pelicans, ducks and other waterfowl. Stroll down to the **colectivo boat launch** and you'll be greeted by independent captains ready to take you for a tour. Some operators, like **Hawaii 5-0** (☎ 460-19-58), next to the dock, have set, four-hour afternoon tours for around US$5.50 per person; they usually include a spin around the islands, bird-watching and a stop for swimming, fishing and a bite to eat.

Places to Stay

For accommodation, Pie de la Cuesta is a decent alternative to Acapulco. Every hotel provides safe car parking. High-season dates are approximately December 15 to around Easter.

Camping Pie de la Cuesta proper has two clean, pleasant trailer parks toward the far end of the road from the highway. Both have full hookups and are good for tents and trailers. Take a look at both parks and ask for prices before you choose your spot; most campers have a distinct preference for one or the other. Each place has camping areas on both the beach and lagoon sides of the road.

Trailer Park Quinta Dora (☎ 460-11-38; tent/trailer sites US$11/16) is the smaller of the two, and the lagoon side of the park is shaded by palms.

Acapulco Trailer Park & Mini-Super (☎ 460-00-10; e acatrailerpark@hotmail.com; tent/trailer sites US$11/16) has 60 comfortable spaces shaded by coconut palms, a boat launch and spotless bathrooms with five showers each for both women and men. The handy Mini-Super stocks basic provisions.

KOA (☎ 444-40-62; w www.koa.com; Playa Luces; tent/trailer sites US$14/22, double-size beachfront spaces US$27, rooms US$33), about 4km northwest of Pie de la Cuesta, is a large, 100-space landscaped trailer park. Spaces come with full hookups and have cheaper weekly and monthly rates. Amenities include a large beachfront swimming pool, a restaurant/bar, children's playgrounds and Internet service. The 'Pie de la Cuesta – Playa Luces' bus stops at the gate.

Hotels & Guesthouses The following are listed from east to west.

Hotel & Restaurant/Bar Rocío (☎ 460-10-08; singles/doubles US$33/44) has spiffy beachfront rooms with large balconies that cost the same as some of the other, slightly stuffy doubles. Félix López, the longtime resident bartender, chef and guitarist, provides music and good times.

Villa Nirvana (☎ 460-16-31; w www.lavillanirvana.com; Calzada Pie de la Cuesta 302; rooms low/high season US$22-55/33-66, 4-person room with kitchen US$88/110, double with kitchen US$44/55) offers eight spotless, lovingly decorated rooms with two fans in each and shaded hammocks in front of most. Walk *through* Villa Roxana to get to it. There's a relaxing, shady pool area fronting the beach, and breakfast is served on outdoor tables for an additional price. English is spoken.

Villa Roxana (☎ 460-32-52; Calzada Pie de la Cuesta 302; rooms US$20-30, with kitchen US$55-85) shares a lot (but not the beachfront) with Villa Nirvana and has similarly attractive and spotlessly clean amenities with plenty of hammocks, balconies and shade, a small swimming pool, and a restaurant serving breakfast. Some rooms have fully-equipped kitchens. English is spoken here.

Hotel Quinta Blancas (☎ 460-03-12; doubles with air-con US$44-50, without air-con US$22) has a big swimming pool and 24 spotless rooms.

Hotel Puesta del Sol (☎ 460-04-12; rooms US$33, 4-bed rooms US$55), also known as the Paraíso del Sol, was one of the first hotels on the strip, and has an expansive palm-shaded garden area, a large pool, a beat-up tennis court and a **restaurant/bar**.

ACAPULCO & COSTA CHICA

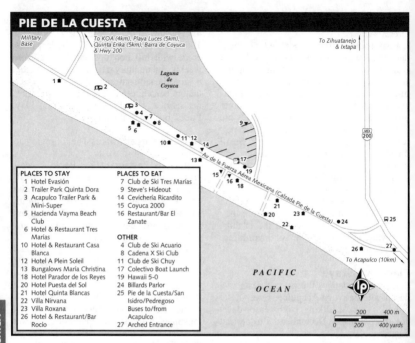

PIE DE LA CUESTA

Military Base

To KOA (4km), Playa Luces (5km), Quinta Erika (5km), Barra de Coyuca & Hwy 200

Laguna de Coyuca

To Zihuatanejo & Ixtapa

MEX 200

Av de la Fuerza Aérea Mexicana (Calzada Pie de la Cuesta)

To Acapulco (10km)

PACIFIC OCEAN

PLACES TO STAY
1 Hotel Evasión
2 Trailer Park Quinta Dora
3 Acapulco Trailer Park & Mini-Super
4 Hacienda Vayma Beach Club
6 Hotel & Restaurant Tres Marías
10 Hotel & Restaurant Casa Blanca
12 Hotel A Plein Soleil
13 Bungalows María Christina
18 Hotel Parador de los Reyes
20 Hotel Puesta del Sol
21 Hotel Quinta Blancas
22 Villa Nirvana
23 Villa Roxana
26 Hotel & Restaurant/Bar Rocío

PLACES TO EAT
7 Club de Ski Tres Marías
9 Steve's Hideout
14 Cevichería Ricardito
15 Coyuca 2000
16 Restaurant/Bar El Zanate

OTHER
4 Club de Ski Acuario
8 Cadena X Ski Club
11 Club de Ski Chuy
17 Colectivo Boat Launch
19 Hawaii 5-0
24 Billards Parlor
25 Pie de la Cuesta/San Isidro/Pedregoso Buses to/from Acapulco
27 Arched Entrance

0   200   400 m
0   200   400 yards

The rooms are small, simple and clean and some have ocean views.

Hotel Parador de los Reyes (☎ 460-01-31; rooms per person US$13) is a reliable and economical choice. It's beside the road, with a small courtyard swimming pool.

Bungalows María Christina (☎ 460-02-62; rooms low/high season US$27/44, 4-person bungalow with kitchen US$70/88), run by a friendly family that speaks English and Spanish, is a clean, well-tended place with a barbecue and a line of hammocks facing the beach. The large beachfront bungalow comes with a kitchen and sleeps up to five people.

Hotel a Plein Soleil (☎ 460-31-51; low season rooms without/with air-con US$33/45) is a lovely, recently renovated place with a fine swimming pool and fabulous terrace on the lagoon. When we last visited, the new owners had plans to serve sushi and Italian food from a patio **restaurant/bar**.

Hotel & Restaurant Casa Blanca (☎ 460-03-24; e casablanca@acanet.com.mx; doubles low/high season US$32/44) is a well-kept, French-owned place on the beachfront, with a homey atmosphere and a good restaurant. The hotel's strongpoint is its outdoor common area with plenty of sofas and hammocks.

Hotel & Restaurant Tres Marías (☎ 460-01-78; 1-/2-bed rooms US$49/55; restaurant mains US$4-7) is a spotless, modern place with a sparse pool area and large, tiled, fan-cooled rooms. Its beachside restaurant serves quality meals.

Hacienda Vayma Beach Club (☎ 460-28-82; Calzada Pie de la Cuesta 378; e vayma@ vayma.com.mx; Sat-Sun & high-season doubles without/with air-con US$44/63, midweek low-season doubles US$33/53, suites low/ high US$143/165) is the snazziest on the strip (though some rooms are tiny and have cold water only). The four suites are luxurious, with private balconies, Jacuzzis, hot water, satellite TV, room service and king-size beds. Petanque is played regularly on the patio next to the swimming pool. The restaurant/bar serves wood-oven pizza and seafood and boasts a good wine list and excellent cocktails.

Hotel Evasión (☎ 444-40-18; e *dianele _blanc@hotmail.com; Calzada Pie de la Cuesta 5; singles/doubles high season US$33/ 38, low season US$22/27)*, the last hotel on the road, is attractively landscaped, with hammocks, swimming pool and a **restaurant**. Some rooms are quite small, but they still represent good value.

Quinta Erika (☎ 444-41-31; Playa Luces; W *www.quintaerika.de.vu; singles/doubles with breakfast US$45/50, bungalow US$120)*, 5km from Pie de la Cuesta (1km past KOA), is a small, quality lodging with five large rooms and one bungalow on two hectares of beautifully landscaped grounds beside the lagoon. The price includes boat tours, as well as use of the hotel's kayaks and small *lancha* (skiff). Quinta Erika takes pride in being private, quiet, restful and attentive. Reservations are highly recommended. German, English and Spanish are spoken.

Places to Eat
Restaurants here are known for their fresh seafood. There are plenty of open-air places on the beach, though some close early in the evening. Food prices tend to be higher here than in Acapulco, so it may be worth bringing some groceries and getting a room with kitchen access, as many local families do on Saturday and Sunday.

Many of Pie de la Cuesta's guesthouses have good restaurants, as do most of the ski clubs.

Roadside **El Zanate** serves a US$2.25 *comida corrida* (daily special). Across the street from El Zanate, around the lagoon at the end of the dirt road, **Steve's Hideout**, built on stilts over the water, has good food and a fine view.

Coyuca 2000 (Calzada Pie de la Cuesta s/n; mains US$4.50-12; open 11am-11pm daily) serves delicious seafood, *ceviche* (raw seafood marinated in lime, onion, chili, garlic and tomato), steak *Tampiqueña* (Tampico style) and barbecued chicken. The spicy *chipotle salsa* (a spicy red chili sauce) is outstanding and is used in several

fish dishes. The owner, Paulino, is known for concocting new cocktails and offers several margaritas and numerous tropical drinks all made with purified water and ice.

Cevichería Ricardito (☎ 474-29-39; Calzada Pie de la Cuesta 359; mains US$2-4; open 10am-8pm daily) serves no-nonsense *antojitos* (snacks or light meals) and does wonders with marinated seafood.

Club de Ski Tres Marías (☎ 460-00-13; Calzada Pie de la Cuesta 375; mains US$7-20; open 8am-7pm daily) is said to have the best food on the strip, though some complain it's getting lax on service. It's a comfy lagoonside restaurant and the closest you'll come to upscale dining in town. The hotel/ restaurant across the road is more economical.

Getting There & Away
From Acapulco, take a 'Pie de la Cuesta' bus from La Costera, opposite the main *correos* (post office) near the *zócalo* (main plaza), on the bay side of the street. Buses go every 15 minutes from 6am until around 8pm (US$0.40, 35 minutes). Buses marked 'Pie de la Cuesta – San Isidro' or 'Pie de la Cuesta – Pedregoso' stop on the highway at the arched entrance to Pie de la Cuesta; those marked 'Pie de la Cuesta – Playa Luces' roll into Pie de la Cuesta, go partway down the hotel strip and continue to Playa Luces and Barra de Coyuca about 6km farther. *Colectivos* (minibuses; US$0.40) continue from Barra de Coyuca back out to Hwy 200.

Colectivos operate 24 hours and charge US$1.25 one way. A taxi costs from US$7 to US$10 one way from Acapulco (more after dark), but typically US$5 to US$6 for the return trip since Acapulco cabbies hate to go home empty handed.

ACAPULCO
☎ 744 • pop 800,000
Acapulco is the granddaddy of Mexican coastal resort cities. Tourism is the number one industry in this city, and has been for decades now. The name Acapulco justifiably evokes images of white-sand beaches, high-rise hotels, glittery nightlife and the divers at La Quebrada gracefully swan-diving into

a narrow chasm with the surf rising and falling below.

Acapulco is a fast-growing city of mixed personalities. Around the curve of the Bahía de Acapulco stretches an arc of beautiful beaches, high-rise hotels, discos, shopping plazas and restaurants with trilingual menus (many French Canadians come here). On the west side of the bay is the not very glamorous commercial center with its tree-filled zócalo, bustling, dirty sidewalks, suicidal taxi drivers and roaring, custom-airbrushed, neon-lit buses. Heading west from the downtown area, the Peninsula de las Playas' sheltered beaches, spectacular cliffs and sunset views offer a nostalgic taste of romantic, old Acapulco.

History

Like the Costa Grande to the north, archaeological finds show humans inhabited the coastal region around Acapulco as far back as 2500 BC. Some of the oldest ceramic pieces in Mexico have been found near Puerto Marqués, just southeast of Acapulco. While large-scale, complex civilizations were developing in the rest of Mesoamerica the coast remained characterized by localized cultures ruled by chieftains or lords. The name 'Acapulco' is derived from ancient Náhuatl words meaning 'where the reeds stood' or 'place of giant reeds.'

Spanish sailors discovered the Bahía de Acapulco in 1512. The area was predominantly inhabited by Yopes, a small number of Tepuztecos, and, on the Costa Chica, Mixtecs and Amuzgos. The Yopes put up fierce resistance to the Spanish (as they did to the Aztecs before them) and Spanish dominance of the area wasn't complete for nearly a decade. Port and shipbuilding facilities were soon established on the bay because of the substantial natural harbor.

During the next 40 years the Spanish Crown financed expeditions in hopes of discovering a return route between Asia and Nueva España (New Spain). Before that route was discovered, Spanish ships, after sailing from Nueva España to Asia and trading American goods for Asian goods, would continue west around Africa's storm-ridden Cape of Good Hope and north to Europe. In 1565 Friar Andrés de Urdaneta successfully navigated from Manila, the Philippines back to Acapulco, establishing the *tornavuelta* (return route). By Spanish decree, Acapulco became the only port in the New World authorized to receive *naos* (Spanish trading galleons, or Manila Galleons) from China and the Philippines – Urdaneta's *tornavuelta* would remain the only trade route between Neuva España, Asia and Spain for the next 200 years. Only one galleon sailed into Acapulco each year, spawning the annual springtime Acapulco Fair, an enormous event that lasted up to two months and brought traders from Mexico City, Manila and Peru.

By the 17th century, trade with Asia was flourishing, and English and Dutch pirate ships were thriving in the Pacific and along the mainland Mexican and Baja Californian coastlines. To fend off freebooters, the Fuerte de San Diego was built atop a low hill overlooking the Bahía de Acapulco. It was not until the end of the 18th century that Spain permitted its American colonies to engage in free trade, ending the monopoly of the *naos* and the Manila-Acapulco trade route.

Upon gaining independence, Mexico severed most of its trade links with Spain, and Acapulco declined as a port city. It remained relatively isolated from the rest of the world until a paved road finally linked it with Mexico City in 1927 (you can still see the older green signs along La Costera). As Mexico City flourished, its citizens began vacationing on the Pacific coast. A new international airport was built, Hollywood filmed a few flicks here and by the 1950s Acapulco was on its way to becoming a glitzy resort.

Orientation

Acapulco is on a narrow coastal plain along the 11km shore of the Bahía de Acapulco. Reached by Hwy 200 from the east and west and by Hwys 95 and 95D from the north, it is 400km south of Mexico City and 240km southeast of Zihuatanejo and Ixtapa.

Acapulco's tourist industry divides the city into three parts: 'Acapulco Naútico'

(Nautical Acapulco), 'Acapulco Dorado' (Golden Acapulco) and 'Acapulco Diamante' (Diamond Acapulco). To everyone else, Acapulco Naútico is simply 'el centro.' It's the old part of town on the west side of the bay. The Malecón is the strip of waterfront facing Playa Tlacopanocha south of the zócalo. Acapulco Dorado, usually called the 'Zona Dorada,' wraps around the bay from Playa Hornos to the Icacos naval base. 'Acapulco Diamante' (Diamond Acapulco), is the relatively new, luxury resort area that stretches 10km from the peninsula on the southern tip of Puerto Marqués – a bay situated about 18km southeast of Acapulco proper – down Playa Revolcadero to the international airport.

At the west end of Bahía de Acapulco, the Peninsula de las Playas juts south from central Acapulco. South of the peninsula is the popular Isla de la Roqueta. From Playa Caleta on the southern edge of the peninsula, Av López Mateos climbs west and then north to Playa La Angosta and Playa La Quebrada before curling east back toward the city center.

Playa Caleta also marks the beginning of Av Costera Miguel Alemán. Known simply as 'La Costera' or as 'Miguel Alemán,' it's Acapulco's principal bayside avenue. From Playa Caleta, La Costera cuts north-north-west across the Peninsula de las Playas and then hugs the shore all the way around the bay to the Icacos naval base at the east end of the city. Most of Acapulco's major hotels, restaurants, discos and other points of interest are along or just off La Costera. After the naval base, La Costera becomes La Carretera Escénica (the Scenic Highway) and, after 9km, intersects the road to Hwy 200 on the left and the road to Puerto Marqués on the right. The airport is about 2.5km past this intersection.

Information
Tourist Offices In the yellow building on the front grounds of the Centro de Convenciones (a large complex on the north side of La Costera, east of the golf course), **Procuraduría del Turista** (☎/fax 484-44-16, 484-45-83; La Costera 4455; open 9am-11pm

daily), offers tourist information and assistance for all manner of tourist needs, problems or complaints. It offers free medical care for tourists, money exchange and handicrafts for sale, and there is usually someone around who speaks English. It also sells tickets for local attractions and for bus and air travel.

Secretaría de Fomento Turístico del Estado de Guerrero (Sefotur; ☎ 484-24-15, fax 481-11-60; @ sefotur@yahoo.com; open 8am-3:30pm Mon-Fri), inside the Centro de Convenciones, provides basic information on Acapulco and the state of Guerrero.

Immigration You can extend visas for free at **Migración** (☎ 484-90-14, 484-90-21; cnr La Costera & Elcano; open 8am-2pm Mon-Fri).

Money You can change money at many places around Acapulco; but banks give the best rates. The casas de cambio (exchange houses) pay a slightly lower rate but are open longer hours and are less crowded; shop around, as rates vary. There are plenty of both near the zócalo and along La Costera. Hotels will also change money, but their rates are usually painful. **American Express** (☎ 485-99-08; Gran Plaza, La Costera 1628; open 10am-7pm Mon-Fri, 10am-3pm Sat) changes AmEx traveler's checks at bank rates, minus the crowds.

Post & Communications The main post office (☎ 483-53-63; La Costera 125; open 8am-6pm Mon-Fri, 9am-1pm Sat) is in the Palacio Federal beside the Sanborns department store, a couple of blocks east of the zócalo. In the same building, **Telecomm** (open 8am-7pm Mon-Fri, 9am-noon Sat & Sun) has telegraph, telex and fax services.

Another **post office** (Cuauhtémoc; open 8am-3pm Mon-Fri, 9am-1pm Sat) and **Telecomm office** (Cuauhtémoc; open 8am-7.30pm Mon-Fri, 9am-noon Sat, Sun & hols) are at the Estrella de Oro bus station, on the corner of Massieu, upstairs on the outside right corner of the building.

Long-distance phone calls can be made from Telmex (Ladatel) pay phones – plentiful throughout the city – or from casetas de

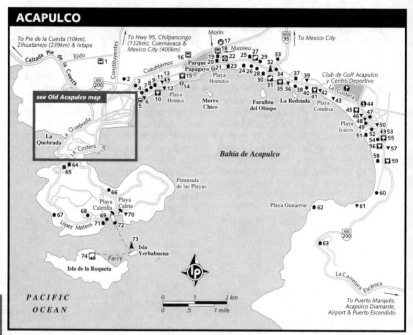

teléfono (public telephone call stations) – look for signs saying 'larga distancia'. Telephone and fax services are available at **Caseta Alameda** (☎ 483-86-95; La Paz s/n; open 9am-8pm Mon-Fri, 9am-7pm Sat), half a block off the west side of the zócalo, and other casetas are around the center and along La Costera.

Internet services are abundant. Above Video Juegos Johnny just off the zócalo, **ezocalo.com** (☎ 482-35-25; Juárez 3; US$1.30 per hour; open 9am-11pm daily) is stuffy but convenient. For fast connection and air-con, try **Tequila.com** (☎ 482-29-53; La Costera 326; US$1 per hour; open 9am-midnight Mon-Sat, noon-midnight Sun). **Compufin** (☎ 482-33-79; cnr Hidalgo & Valle; US$1.10 per hour; open 8am-11pm Mon-Fri, 10am-10pm Sat & Sun) is slow but has air-con. Both **GDS Internet** (☎ 480-01-16; Mina 3C; US$1.10 per hour; open 9am-9pm Mon-Sat, 9:30am-9pm Sun) and **SGD Internet** (☎ 483-41-45; Galeana 13; US$0.90 per hour; open 10am-11pm daily)

have quick connections and plenty of computers. Internet cafés proliferate in the shadows of the large hotels all along La Costera in the Zona Dorada.

Bookstores You can almost always find a small selection of books and magazines in English at **Sanborns** department stores; the branch (☎ 484-20-44; La Costera 3111; open 7am-1am daily) a few blocks east of CICI water-sports park, has a better selection than the location (☎ 482-61-67; La Costera 209; open 7am-11pm daily) east of the zócalo. Both stock good road and city maps for all of Mexico. **Comercial Mexicana**, on La Costera opposite CICI, has some magazines in English, and **Wal-Mart** (La Costera), farther east, keeps a small supply of English-language books and magazines on hand. The bookstore in the **Fuerte de San Diego** (see that section later) maintains the best supply of art, architecture and history books, though most are in Spanish.

ACAPULCO

PLACES TO STAY
9 Hotel Playa Suave;
   Playa Suave Trailer Park
19 Hotel Ritz
20 Hotel Jacqueline;
   Hotel del Valle
23 Hotel Monaco; Hertz
24 Costa Club Acapulco;
   Aerolíneas Internacionales
25 Hotel Club del Sol;
   American Airlines
30 Hotel Continental Emporio
   Acapulco; Tony Roma's;
   Shotover Jet; US Consulate
37 Romano Palace Hotel
51 Hotel Quinta Mica;
   Suites Selene
58 Hyatt Regency Acapulco;
   Mexicana Airlines
62 Radisson Resort
63 Las Brisas Acapulco
64 Hotel Lemarliz
65 Hotel Villa Romana
67 Hotel Los Flamingos;
   100% Natural
71 Hotel Boca Chica

PLACES TO EAT
6 100% Natural
11 100% Natural;
   Banamex ATM
12 El Amigo Miguel III
36 Pancho's
39 Carlos 'n Charlie's
42 VIPS; Sanborns
43 El Gaucho
46 Mariscos Pipo's
48 Hard Rock Café

50 Fersato's; Immigration Office
   (Migración); German
   Consulate
57 24-hour VIPS; Wal-Mart;
   Swedish Consulate
61 Señor Frog's
70 La Cabaña de Caleta

OTHER
1 Estrella Blanca 1st-Class Bus
   Station (Central Ejido)
2 Unidad Deportiva Acapulco
3 Mercado Central
4 Aeroméxico; Bital &
   Banamex ATMs
5 Local Bus Stops
7 Mercado de Artesanías
   Noa Noa
8 Mercado de Artesanías
   Papagayo
10 Tropicana; Copacabana
13 Banamex
14 Public Bathrooms
15 Tequila's Le Club
16 Estrella Blanca 1st-Class Bus
   Station (Central Papagayo)
17 Pemex Gas Station
18 Estrella de Oro Bus Station;
   Post Office; Telecomm; ATM
21 Public Bathrooms
22 Centro Commercial La Gran
   Plaza; VIPS; American
   Express; Estrella Blanca Bus
   Ticket Office; ATM
26 Centro Commercial Plaza
   Bahía; Museo Histórico Naval
   de Acapulco
27 Dutch Consulate

28 Quick Car Rental
29 Mercado de Artesanías Dalia
31 Canadian Consulate
32 Diana Statue (La Diana)
33 Sam's Club
34 Mercado de Artesanías La
   Diana; Pemex Gas Station
35 Disco Beach
38 Hackett Bungee Paradise;
   Acapulco Scuba Center;
   Fiesta Americana Condesa
40 Budget Car Rental
41 Bedroom
44 Centro de Convenciones;
   Procuraduría del Turista;
   Sefotur; Casa Consular;
   French Consulate
45 Nina's Tropical
47 Comercial Mexicana
49 CICI & Acapulco Mágico
52 Casa de la Cultura
53 Bancomer ATM;
   Saad Rent-A-Car
54 Sanborns; Alamo
   Rent-A-Car; Salon Q
55 Baby 'O
56 Andromedas
59 El Alebrije
60 Icacos Naval Base
66 Yacht Club
68 Plaza de Toros
69 Mercado de Artesanías La
   Caletilla
72 Mágico Mundo Marino;
   Boats to Isla de la Roqueta
73 La Capilla Submarina
   (Underwater Chapel)
74 Zoo

Laundry A couple of blocks west of the zócalo, **Lavandería Lavadín** (☎ 482-28-90; cnr La Paz & Iglesias; open 8am-10pm Mon-Sat) offers pickup and delivery service for about US$3. **Lavandería Azueta** (☎ 546-69-49; Azueta 14A; open 9:30am-6pm Mon-Sat), below Hotel Paola, charges US$1 per kilogram for wash and dry. **Lavandería Coral** (☎ 480-0735; Juárez 12; open 9am-noon & 4pm-7pm Mon-Fri, 9am-2pm Sat), next door to Casa de Huéspedes Sutter, charges about the same and offers dry cleaning. Several more laundries are along La Costera, including **Lavandería del Sol** at the Hotel Club del Sol (see Places to Stay).

Emergency Operated by Sefotur, **Locatel** (☎ 481-11-00) is a 24-hour contact for all types of emergencies; the office is in the Centro de Convenciones, on La Costera. There's also the **tourist police** (☎ 480-02-10).

Fuerte de San Diego

This handsomely restored, five-sided fort was built in 1616 atop a hill just east of the zócalo to protect the *naos* (galleons) that conducted trade between the Philippines and Mexico from marauding Dutch and English buccaneers. Thanks in no small part to the fort's effectiveness, the trade route – which was a crucial link between

Europe, Nueva España and Asia – lasted until the early 19th century. It was also strong enough to forestall independence leader Morelos' takeover of the city in 1812 for four months. The fort had to be rebuilt after a 1776 earthquake damaged most of Acapulco, fort included. It remains basically unchanged today. The view of the bay from the ramparts is fabulous and, best of all, free of charge.

The fort is now home to the 15-room **Museo Histórico de Acapulco** (☎ 482-32-28; *Hornitos y Morelos s/n; adult/child US$3.30/ free, free Sun & hols; open 9:30am-6:30pm Tues-Sun).* The first few rooms explain the story of the Yopes and Tepuztecos, the native inhabitants at the time of Spanish arrival in the early 16th century. Most of the museum recounts Acapulco's historical importance as a port, with exhibits explaining the *tornavuelta* (the fastest return route from Manila to Nueva España), the galleons and the treasure they carried, and the famous buccaneers who tried to capture that treasure and take the booty home to England or to the Netherlands.

The new **Casa de las Máscaras** *(open 10am-6pm Mon-Sat)* mask museum is nearby on the pedestrian portion of Morelos, just downhill past the parking lot through the fort's front entrance gate.

Museo Histórico Naval de Acapulco

This small but fascinating naval museum (☎ 463-29-84; *La Costera 125, Local 48, 2nd floor, Centro Comercial Plaza Bahía; admission US$1.10; open 10am-2pm & 5pm-10pm daily)* will dazzle anyone even slightly interested in historic sailing ships such as clippers and galleons. The museum contains several 1:25 scale models built entirely by hand with an intricacy that is truly mind boggling. Each model takes more than six months to build, not including research time; they're built from the ship's original plans! There's usually a model in progress, and the friendly folks who run the place walk you through, explaining everything. There are photos, maps and other small exhibits as well.

La Quebrada Divers

Visiting Acapulco without seeing the famous cliff divers *(admission US$1.65; diving times 12:45pm, 7:30pm, 8:30pm, 9:30pm & 10:30pm daily)* is like visiting Pisa without checking out the Leaning Tower. These guys (and their predecessors) have been amazing visitors since 1934, diving and flipping with graceful finesse from heights of 25m to 45m into the rising and falling ocean swells below. Understandably, the divers pray at small cliff-top shrines before leaping over the edge (as did Elvis Presley in the 1963 film *Fun in Acapulco).* At least three and often five or six *clavadistas* (divers) perform at each diving time; those at night dive with torches. Most of the money collected for admission makes its way to the divers themselves, who literally risk their lives (and slowly collapse their vertebrae) diving for the crowds. Don't miss it.

To get to La Quebrada you can either walk up the hill from the zócalo on Calle La Quebrada or take a taxi; get there at least 30 minutes early to get a spot on the edge. La Quebrada is also an excellent place to watch the sunset.

Views are just as good from the terrace of Hotel Plaza Las Glorias' cliffside **Restaurant La Perla** (see Places to Eat), though they come at a price.

Parque Papagayo

Across the Costera from Playas Hornos and Hornitos, this 52-hectare amusement park (☎ 485-71-77; *open 8am-8pm daily, mechanical rides section open 4pm-11pm daily)* is full of trees and has a 1150m 'interior circuit' pathway, great for jogging and walking. Its other attractions, for kids and adults, include a roller-skating rink, skateboard area, a lake with paddleboats, a children's train, quadricycles, mechanical rides, sports fields, animal enclosures with deer, rabbits, crocodiles and turtles, an aviary and a hill affording an excellent view. Park admission is free; ride, attraction and rental rates vary.

Casa de la Cultura

Set around a garden east of CICI, this complex (☎ 484-23-90, 484-38-14 for schedules;

A Mexican teenager proudly shows off his ray fish (top left); Carnaval in Mazatlán, when people dress in colorful costumes and paint their faces, is a time for celebration (top right); folk dancers in native costume dance up a storm in Oaxaca state (bottom).

STUART WASSERMAN

JOHN NEUBAUER

NEIL SETCHFIELD

The famous (and slightly mad?) cliff divers of Acapulco (top left); Puerto Vallarta's Fiesta Americana hotel, perfect for a relaxing day beside the pool (top right); getting hot and sweaty on the sand, Puerto Vallarta (bottom).

La Costera 4834; open 10am-6pm Mon-Sat), houses an innovative art gallery, quality handicrafts stalls and the **Salon de Fama de los Deportistas de Guerrero** *(Guerrero Sports Hall of Fame; admission free)*. There's also an open-air theater and an indoor auditorium.

CICI

On the east end of the Costera, the Centro Internacional de Convivencia Infantil *(CICI; ☎ 484-19-70, 484-80-33; 🆆 www.cici.com .mx; La Costera s/n; admission US$6.60; open 10am-6pm daily)* is a family water-sports park. Dolphin, seal and diving shows are presented several times daily, and there's a small tide pool aquarium to poke around in. If captive marine life doesn't thrill you there are various 90m waterslides or a wave-pool that might. Lockers are available for US$1, and the required inflatable tubes for the to-boggan slides cost US$2.

The latest CICI attraction is **swimming with dolphins**. Though it's a bit more like bobbing with dolphins, it's a great way to get up close to these playful marine mammals. A half-hour frolic costs US$58 and an hour in the water costs US$105; be sure to call ahead for reservations.

Any local bus marked 'CICI,' 'Base' or 'Puerto Marqués' will drop you here.

Mágico Mundo Marino

This aquarium-cum-water park *(☎ 483-12-15; adult/child US$3.25/1.75; open 9am-6pm daily)* occupies a rocky spit between Playas Caleta and Caletilla on the west side of town, and is busy with local families on weekends. Highlights include a sea lion show, the feeding of crocodiles, piranhas and turtles, swimming pools, waterslides and an oceanographic museum. There are also small restaurants and a bar.

Isla de la Roqueta

In addition to a popular beach and snorkeling and diving possibilities, Isla de la Roqueta has an obviously underfunded **zoo** *(admission US$0.65; open 10am-5pm daily)* with lots of exotic cats (pumas, jaguars, leopards etc) and other jungle critters in small cages. Snorkeling gear, kayaks and

That Lucky Old Sun (Did it Set Already?)

All those beaches stretching around the Bahía de Acapulco, and not a single sunset – over the water anyway. If you're achin' to watch the sun sink slowly into the sea, you'll have to pick your spot carefully. First off, think Old Acapulco. The only place you can sit on the sand (within the city limits) and watch the sun set on the water is Playa La Angosta (see Beaches), a sliver of a beach on the Peninsula de las Playas. Plaza La Quebrada, where the divers perform, is another great spot – arrive early for the 7:30pm dives and you'll catch the sunset too. One of the finest views of all can be had at the small Sinfonía del Mar (Symphony of the Sea), a stepped plaza built on the edge of the cliffs just south of La Quebrada. It's sole purpose is giving folks a magical view. The nostalgic clifftop bar at the Hotel Los Flamingos (see Places to Stay), perched high on the peninsula's western cliffs, is pretty darn romantic, and here you can knock back a few cold ones to the fading sun. If you really feel like chasing the sunset, head over to Pie de La Cuesta (see that section earlier), about a 30-minute ride northwest of Acapulco. It's long, wide beach and hammock-clad restaurants are famous for spectacular sunsets.

other water sports gear are available for hire on the beach.

Every 20 minutes or so, between 9am and 5pm, boats make the 10-minute buzz out to the island (US$2.75 return), leaving from the small dock between playas Caleta and Caletilla. A less direct glass-bottomed boat (US$5.50 return) departs from the same spot but passes over **La Capilla Submarina (Underwater Chapel)**, a submerged bronze statue of the Virgen de Guadalupe. The return takes about an hour, or you can alight on the island and take a later boat back.

Beaches

Visiting Acapulco's beaches tops most visitors' lists of things to do here. During the December-April high season, you can bank on the beaches being Speedo-to-Speedo, with rental chairs, umbrellas, vendors, sun-soakers, jet-skis and parasailers dominating the view. But that's Acapulco.

Zona Dorada The beaches heading east around the bay from the zócalo are the most popular. If you jump on a bus in the old town and head east, the first beach you'll pass is **Playa Hornos**, a narrow strip of sand crowded with fishing boats and families. In the morning it's abuzz with activity as the fishermen haul in their catch, but the Costera sits right on its shoulder, making it noisy in the afternoon. At **Playa Hornitos** the beach widens, and from here east it's flanked by high-rise hotels and restaurants. The beach narrows in front of Parque Papagayo before opening up again at **Playa Condesa**, the trendiest of Acapulco's beaches, where you go to show it all off – and watch others do the same. It's also home to Acapulco's most outwardly gay beach, primarily the area near Beto's restaurant. **Playa Icacos** is the east-ernmost stretch of sand on the bay, backed by more hotels and restaurants. Nearly all the beaches east of Playa Hornos are good for swimming and great for sunbathing, and various entrepreneurs set up stands to rent chaise lounges and umbrellas. These are also the beaches where you can **parasail**, ride **banana boats** and **waterski**; mobile outfitters set up shop all down the beach. City buses constantly ply La Costera, the beachside avenue, making it easy to get up and down this long arc of beaches.

Peninsula de las Playas The beaches on the southwestern shores of the Bahía de Acapulco have a markedly different feel than those to the east; they're smaller, more sheltered, lack the glitz of the Zona Dorada, and are often even more crowded due to their smaller size. They're well worth a visit for their old-time feel. Playas **Caleta** and **Caletilla** are two small, protected beaches beside one another in a cove on the south side of the Peninsula de las Playas. They're lined end-to-end with cheap seafood *enramadas* (thatch-covered, open-air restaurants). During Sunday afternoons they're a

spectacle of family fun, the shallow water chaotic with splashing children, anchored fishing *pangas* (small skiffs), and paddling vendors selling trinkets. Music blares over it all from Mágico Mundo Marino, an aquarium on the spit of land separating the two beaches. Boats leave frequently from near the aquarium to Isla de la Roqueta.

All buses marked 'Caleta' heading down La Costera stop here, though it's a pleasant 30-minute walk; take the *malecón* (water-front street) from the zócalo and then follow the Costera and the signs from there.

Playa La Angosta ('Narrow Beach') is in a thin, protected cove nestled between two high cliffs on the west side of the peninsula. It has a few seafood *enramadas* and the only stretch of sand in Acapulco with a view of the sunset on the water. From the zócalo it takes about 30 minutes to walk there, either along the Costera (go as far as the Hotel Avenida and turn right and walk another block); or along the cliffside walkway heading downhill from La Quebrada, a more strenuous but also more scenic route. The latter takes you past the **Sinfonía del Mar**, perhaps the best spot in Acapulco for sunsets.

Outer Beaches Other good beaches are farther afield, but can be easily reached by bus or taxi and make good day trips from Acapulco proper.

Laden with seafood restaurants, the beach at **Puerto Marqués** lies on a striking little bay of the same name about 18km southeast of old Acapulco. It's a madhouse on weekends when families pour in to devour seafood prepared in the countless **restaurants** which have come to be Puerto Marqués' main attraction. Midweek it can be quiet. Beyond Puerto Marqués lies the long, wide **Playa Revolcadero**, home to Acapulco's grandest luxury resorts. They're spread out, however, so you rarely feel crowded here. It has the only **surf** in Acapulco; though it's best as a big-wave break, there are people out chasing waves all year.

If you're going to Puerto Marqués from La Costera, take an eastbound 'Puerto Marqués' bus (US$0.45) from the west end of Playa Hornos; they pass every 30 minutes or so, less frequently on weekends. The other option is a 'Colosio' bus (from anywhere along the Costera) to 'La Glorieta', the junction east of town where you turn right to Puerto Marqués (or left to Hwy 200). From La Glorieta, take a shared taxi (US$0.55) to the beach or walk (20 minutes). To Revolcadero, take a private taxi (about US$1.50).

Your best chance of finding a relatively quiet beach is to head to **Pie de la Cuesta** (see that section earlier this chapter), about 10km northwest of Acapulco. There are plenty of places to stay, though it's great to head over for a day on the beach, catch the spectacular sunset from one of the beachside restaurants, and head back to Acapulco for a night on the town.

Water Sports

Just about everything that can be done on, under or above the water is done in Acapulco. On Bahía de Acapulco, water-skiing, boating, 'banana-boating' and *paracaida* (parasailing) are all popular activities. To partake in any of these, walk along the Zona Dorada beaches and look for the kiosks (they're usually orange) run by **Fadap**, the local cooperative. They're usually open between 10am and 6pm and charge around US$20 per person for an approximate five-minute **parasailing** flight. The smaller Playas Caleta and Caletilla have sailboats, fishing boats, motorboats, pedal boats, canoes, snorkel gear, inner tubes and water bicycles for rent.

For a fast, white-knuckle boat ride on the Río Papagayo, contact **Shotover Jet** (☎ 484-11-54/55/56; 🔲 www.shotoverjet.com; La Costera 121) in front of the Hotel Continental Emporio Acapulco. The trip costs US$55 per person and takes about four hours, including transport time (all included in the price), with about 35 minutes spent rocketing down the river at about 80km/h.

Though Acapulco isn't quite a scuba destination in itself, there are some decent dive sites nearby if you're itching to get wet. Several outfitters offer quality services. **Acapulco Scuba Center** (☎ 484-67-47; 🔲 www.acapulcoscuba.com; La Costera 101), below Hacket Bungee Paradise, has PADI and NAUI certified instructors and offers several certification courses and guided day trips. All prices include guide, gear, boat and refreshments. Prices range from about US$60 for a beginning level dive, to US$350 for a five-day PADI open water certification. A guided, two-tank dive catering to experienced divers costs US$70. **Aqua Mundo Diving School** (☎ 482-10-41; La Costera 100; office open 9am-6pm daily), just west of the marina in the old town, has instruction only and is certified by FMAS (Federación Mexicana de Actividades Subacuáticas, a government certification similar to PADI). Classes are held in shallow ocean and cost US$38.

The best **snorkeling** is off Isla de la Roqueta (see that section earlier), though Playas Caleta and Caletilla have some decent spots; gear can be rented onsite at both places.

Sport fishing is very popular in Acapulco and several companies offer six- to seven-hour fishing trips; book at least a day in advance and figure on a 6am or 7am departure time. **Aqua Mundo** (see previous section), **Divers de México** (☎ 482-13-98; 🇪 eiiliee 1999@infosel.com; La Costera 100) and **Fish-R-Us** (☎ 487-87-87, 482-82-82; 🔲 www.fish-r-us.com; La Costera 100) all offer fishing trips. The cost for a six-hour trip aboard a four- to six-line boat is around US$250 for the entire boat. If you don't have a group large enough to cover the boat, both Fish-R-Us and Divers de Mexico can usually add one or two people to an existing group for US$55 to US$70 per person. The local fishing cooperative **DARH** (☎ 482-96-81, 480-04-65; La Costera 211), which faces Playa Tlacopanocha on the *malecón*, offers trips for six to eight people for US$200.

Other Activities

Acapulco has squash courts, tennis courts, public swimming pools, gymnasiums, tracks and facilities for other sports. The tourist office stays abreast of most sport-related opportunities and events and is a good source of information.

Unidad Deportiva Acapulco (☎ 486-10-33; Chiapas s/n, Colonia Progreso; open noon-6pm Tues, 9am-6pm Wed-Sun) has an

ACAPULCO & COSTA CHICA

Olympic-size pool (admission US$1), a children's pool (US$0.50), stadium track (US$0.30), gymnasium, sports courts and fields.

For tennis, try **Club de Golf Acapulco** (☎ 484-12-25, La Costera s/n), **Club de Tenis Hyatt** (see Hyatt Regency Acapulco in Places to Stay), **Villa Vera Racquet Club** (☎ 484-03-33; Lomas del Mar 35) or **Acapulco Princess Hotel** (see Places to Stay).

The 50m-high bungee tower at **Hackett Bungee Paradise** (☎ 484-75-29; La Costera 107; open 4pm-1am daily), is easy to spot on the Costera, and for US$60 you can throw yourself (bungee included) from its platform – especially exhilarating after several midnight tequilas at the bar next door.

Acapulco has three 18-hole **golf courses**: the **Club de Golf Acapulco** (☎ 484-65-83; La Costera s/n) next to the convention center on the Costera; **Tres Vidas** (☎ 444-51-26) in Acapulco Diamante near the airport; and at the **Acapulco Princess Hotel** (see Places to Stay), also in Diamante. Those in Diamante front Playa Revolcadero and have spectacular views.

Cruises

Various boats and yachts offer cruises, which depart from the *malecón* near the zócalo. Cruises are available day and night and range from 'booze cruises' aboard multilevel boats with blaring salsa music and open bars to yachts offering quiet sunset cruises. All take basically the same route – they leave from the *malecón*, go around the Peninsula de las Playas to Isla de la Roqueta, pass La Quebrada to see the cliff divers, cross over to Puerto Marqués and then come back around the Bahía de Acapulco. Most offer a lunchtime cruise (around 11am to 3:30pm) and a sunset cruise (around 4:30pm to 7pm, later in winter). Some, like the *Aca Tiki* offer moonlight cruises (10:30pm to 2am), complete with dancing.

The *Hawaiano* (☎ 482-21-99, 482-07-85), the *Fiesta* **and** *Bonanza* (☎ 483-18-03), and the large catamaran *Aca Tiki* (☎ 484-61-40, 484-67-86) are all popular; make reservations by calling them directly, or through any travel agency and most large hotels. **Divers**

de México (see Water Sports earlier) also offers cruises. Rates range from US$25 to US$60 depending on the duration of the cruise and the inclusion of food and/or drink.

Special Events

Acapulco hits its height of merry-making during the three weeks around **Semana Santa**, when the city fills with tourists, the discos stay packed every night of the week, and the beaches are crammed.

The city's music festival, the **Festival de Acapulco** is held for one week in May with Mexican and international music at many venues around town. International film festivals include the **Festival de Cine Negro** (Black Film Festival) held during the second week of June, and the **Festival de Cine Francés** (French Film Festival) held for a week in late November. The city celebrates Mexico's patron saint, the **Virgen de Guadalupe**, all night on December 11 and all throughout the following day, with street processions, marching bands, fireworks and folk dances, all converging on the cathedral in the zócalo, where children dressed in costumes congregate.

Places to Stay

Acapulco has a plethora of hotels (more than 30,000 rooms) in every category imaginable. What part of town you choose to stay in depends on your budget and your interests. The cheapest hotels are near the zócalo and uphill along Calle La Quebrada. This also happens to be the part of town with the most historical character, cheaper restaurants, and easily accessible services and bus lines. The Zona Dorada hotels are more expensive, but are on or near the beaches and closer to the clubs and bars. Some of the hotels on the Peninsula de las Playas are extremely relaxing and offer a romantic, old-time Acapulco feel, but they are a fair distance from other restaurants and services.

Rooms are priciest from mid-December until a week or so after Semana Santa, and through the July and August school holidays. Reservations are recommended between Christmas and New Year's Day and

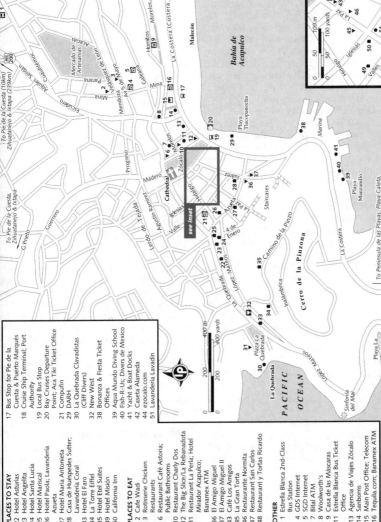

OLD ACAPULCO

PLACES TO STAY
22 Hotel Asturias
23 Hotel Angelita
24 Hotel Santa Lucia
25 Hotel Mariscal
26 Hotel Paola; Lavandería
   Azueta
27 Hotel María Antonieta
28 Casa de Huéspedes Sutter;
   Lavandería Coral
33 Hotel El Faro
34 La Torre Eiffel
35 Hotel Etel Suites
49 Hotel Misión
50 California Inn

PLACES TO EAT
2 Cafe Wadi
3 Rotisserie Chicken
   Restaurants
6 Restaurant Café Astoria;
   Public Bathrooms
10 Restaurant Charly Dos
12 The Big Slice/La Rebanadota
31 Restaurant La Perla; Hotel
   Mirador Acapulco;
   Banamex ATM
36 El Amigo Miguel
37 El Amigo Miguel II
43 Café Los Amigos
45 La Gran Torta
46 Restaurante Normita
47 Restaurant San Carlos
48 Restaurant y Tortas Ricardo

OTHER
1 Estrella Blanca 2nd-Class
   Bus Station
4 GDS Internet
5 SGD Internet
7 Bital ATM
8 Woolworth's
9 Casa de las Máscaras
11 Estrella Blanca Bus Ticket
   Office
13 Agencia de Viajes Zócalo
14 Sanborns
15 Main Post Office; Telecom
16 Tequila.com; Banamex ATM

17 Bus Stop for Pie de la
   Cuesta & Puerto Marqués
18 Cruise Ship Terminal; Port
   Authority
19 Local Bus Stop
20 Bay Cruises Departure
   Point; Aca Tiki Ticket Office
21 Compufin
29 DARH
30 La Quebrada Clavadistas
   (Cliff Divers)
32 New West
38 Bonanza & Fiesta Ticket
   Offices
39 Aqua Mundo Diving School
40 Fish-R-Us; Divers of Mexico
41 Yacht & Boat Docks
42 Caseta Alameda
44 ezzocalo.com
51 Lavandería Lavadin

ACAPULCO & COSTA CHICA

around Semana Santa. Unless specified, the following prices are high season although they'll drop 10% to 40% when things aren't very busy.

Places to Stay – Budget

In a prime location only a block from Playa Hornos, **Playa Suave Trailer Park** (☎ 485-18-85; La Costera 276; tent and trailer sites for 2 people US$16.50, additional person US$4) has 38 well-kept tent and trailer spaces with full hookups. The entrance is on Vasco Nuñez de Balboa, between Mendoza and Malaespina, a block behind La Costera. Reservations are recommended.

Trailer Park Diamante (☎ 466-02-00; Copacabana 8, Fraccionamiento Playa Diamante; tent & trailer sites US$15), southeast of town in the Diamante area, is 3km from the beach but has two swimming pools; spaces come with full hookups.

Three other **trailer parks** are at Pie de la Cuesta (see that section earlier); it's a 30-minute drive or bus ride west of town.

Hotel Santa Lucía (☎ 482-04-41; López Mateos 33; rooms per person US$8) is a no-frills, family run place with some of the cheapest rooms around.

Casa de Huéspedes Sutter (☎ 482-23-96; Juárez 12; rooms per person US$9), a large two-story hotel, offers simple, cement-floor rooms around an empty courtyard. Some rooms get good light, others are dark.

California Inn (☎ 482-28-93; La Paz 12; rooms per person US$11) is a popular place with pleasant rooms set around a plain courtyard.

Hotel Mariscal (☎ 482-00-15; La Quebrada 35; singles/doubles US$11/15), next door to the Angelita, rents basic rooms that come cheaper by the week. The bare-bones private bathrooms have hot showers and seatless toilets.

Hotel Maria Antonieta (☎ 482-50-24; Azueta 17; rooms per person without/with air-con & hot water US$10/13), is a clean, well-liked place near the zócalo with a shared kitchen. Rooms upstairs have the best views and catch the most breeze, though they lack hot water and air-con. These perks are in the lower rooms, which

also happen to be a bit darker. Overall, it's a great deal.

Hotel Paola (☎ 482-62-43; Azueta 16; rooms per person US$14) is a plain, clean five-story hotel. Outside rooms have small private balconies; interior rooms are quieter.

Hotel Angelita (☎ 483-57-34; La Quebrada 37; singles/doubles US$15/20) is an excellent deal, with clean spacious rooms, each with two fans and hot-water bathrooms. There's free drinking water, plenty of plants and a small TV room in front.

Hotel Asturias (☎ 483-65-48; La Quebrada 45; doubles US$25-30) is very popular, with mostly pleasant rooms on a small courtyard, outside tables and a small swimming pool and sunning area.

Up the hill at the top of Calle La Quebrada is Plaza La Quebrada, overlooking the sea. The large attended parking lot here is a safe place to park, but it gets busy and loud in the evening when the cliff divers perform. The hotels here are somewhat cooler than places down the hill toward the zócalo, since they catch the sea breeze.

Hotel El Faro (☎ 482-13-65; La Quebrada 83; singles/doubles US$11/20, Dec–mid-Apr US$11/22), on the plaza parking lot, has large, rundown rooms with private bathrooms and occasional hot water. Its strongest point is the large communal balcony facing the ocean with a fabulous sunset view.

La Torre Eiffel (☎ 482-16-83; Inalámbrica 110; singles/doubles low season US$11/16.50), perched on a hill above Plaza La Quebrada, has a small swimming pool and huge balconies with sitting areas facing the sea. The rooms are bright and airy, and the sunset views are excellent. Although it shows its age in the details, it's a good deal and very popular.

Places to Stay – Mid-Range

The title of 'oldest hotel in Acapulco' goes to **Hotel Misión** (☎ 482-36-43; e hotelmision@hotmail.com; Valles 12; rooms per person US$27.50), a relaxing place in a colonial building near the zócalo. The fresh, comfortable rooms have artful tile work and heavy Spanish furniture and are set around a shady courtyard. There's no air-con, but fans and large windows keep the heat down. Continental or complete breakfasts (US$3 or US$5.50 respectively) are served beneath the trees on the patio.

Peninsula de las Playas The Peninsula de las Playas has several quiet hotels.

Hotel Villa Romana (☎ 482-39-95, fax 483-85-19; Lopez Mateos 185; doubles US$55) is an outstanding nine-room hotel with a small rooftop swimming pool and a sun terrace complete with lounge chairs, bougainvilleas and a marvelous ocean view. Each room has a beautifully tiled kitchenette, good beds, air-conditioning and its own balcony facing the ocean (and the spectacular sunsets). It's on the cliff-side Av Adolfo Lopez Mateos, about a 15-minute downhill walk southwest of La Quebrada.

Hotel Lemarliz (☎/fax 482-54-20; Lopez Mateos 183; doubles without/with balcony US$46/61), Villa Romana's bigger neighbor, offers clean, modern, fan-cooled rooms; those with balconies have a great ocean view. There's also a large rooftop terrace with more fabulous views but little shade.

Hotel Los Flamingos (☎ 482-06-90/91/92; e flamingo@acabtu.com.mx; Lopez Mateos s/n; doubles Dec 16–Apr 15 US$65-125, Apr 16–Dec 15 US$50-100, 'Round House' low/high season US$275/385) is a living landmark to Acapulco's golden years. John Wayne and his Hollywood pals owned the place through the 1950s, and it exudes, even today, a strong sense of that glamorous past. Perched 135m over the ocean on the highest cliffs in Acapulco, this single-story, bright pink beauty also boasts one of the finest sunset views in town. The rooms themselves are modest and comfortable, and most have terraces with period-proper lounge chairs and hammocks. The Duke himself lived in the 'Round House' in back, a two-room circular house surrounded by trees with a private entry and a stone walkway down to a tiny parapet on the cliff's edge; ask a caretaker to take a peek if no one is renting it – or rent it yourself. The Flamingo's bar is sublime for sunsets and worth a visit even if you don't stay. There's a **restaurant** too. On the southwest tip of

Peninsula de las Playas, the hotel is a good 45-minute walk from the zócalo; a taxi is the easiest way out.

Hotel Boca Chica (☎ 483-63-88; w www .acapulco-bocachica.com; Playa Caletilla s/n; singles/doubles with breakfast Dec-Apr US$99/121, May-Nov US$88/99) is a lovely, one-of-a-kind hotel tucked into the rocks at the end of Playa Caletilla. The tranquil, crystal-clear ocean water, only a few steps from the patio, is the Boca Chica's de facto private swimming pool, and Isla de la Roqueta, across the channel, is its backyard view. It has a small, open-air **restaurant/ bar**, and modest air-conditioned rooms with fine vistas.

Hotel Etel Suites (☎ 482-22-40/41; Cerro de la Pinzona 92; doubles low/high season US$30/40, furnished suites from US$40/50), high on the hill overlooking Old Acapulco, offers good-value, spotless suites with expansive terraces and views of La Quebrada and the bay. Amenities include kitchens, swimming pools and well-kept gardens.

La Costera Most of the Zona Dorada hotels are on the beach or across the busy Costera. You pay for the convenience, but it sure makes teetering home with sunstroke a lot easier.

Hotel Monaco (☎ 485-64-67; La Costera 137; singles/doubles US$51/66) has a good swimming pool, simple but clean rooms, lots of nearby activity on the Costera, and reasonable prices considering its desirable location on Playa Hornitos.

Hotel Playa Suave (☎ 485-12-56; La Costera 253; rooms without/with air-con US$33/44) is a small, motel-style place with a swimming pool and an economical **restaurant** in front that opens onto the busy Costera. It's cheap for the area and has a laid-back feel.

Hotel Jacqueline (☎ 485-93-38; Morín 205; rooms low/high season US$44/55), on the east side of Parque Papagayo, near La Costera and Playa Hornitos, has 10 rooms around a pleasant little garden. Each has TV and air-con.

Hotel del Valle (☎ 485-83-36/88; Espinosa 8; rooms with fan/air-con US$51/64), next door to Hotel Jacqueline, has a small pool and good, clean rooms with shared balconies. Use of the fully-equipped shared kitchens costs an extra US$6.50 per day. The nearest street sign indicates Morín (which actually starts a block north).

Hotel Ritz *(☎ 482-40-78, 485-52-42; Av Wilfrido Massieu; rooms US$55)*, half a block from Playa Hornitos, is a well worn six-story hotel with indoor parking. Rooms come with air-con, cable TV, carpet and private balconies overlooking the swimming pool.

Near CICI and Playa Icacos are a number of hotels, most them swanky top-enders. The following two, however, are excellent deals and have large apartments, swimming pool, parking, air-con and fully equipped kitchens.

Suites Selene *(☎ 484-29-77; e suitesselene@hotmail.com; Colón 175; singles/doubles US$45/50, apartments with kitchenette US$64)*, one door frowm Playa Icacos, rents clean rooms and attractive apartments. Ask for a sea-view room as they have spacious balconies and cost no more.

Hotel Quinta Mica *(☎ 484-01-21/22; Colón 115; apartments Dec-Apr US$88, May-Nov US$55)* has simpler apartments than the Selene but they're fine.

The high-rise hotels along La Costera tend to be expensive.

Romano Palace Hotel *(☎ 484-77-30; W www.romanopalace.com.mx; La Costera 130; 2-bed rooms low/high season US$65/105)*, across La Costera from Playa Condesa, is one of the more economical luxury hotels. It has 20 floors of comfortable, but slightly worn rooms with private balconies and floor-to-ceiling windows and great views of Acapulco.

Hotel Club del Sol *(☎ 485-66-00; La Costera at Ascencio; rooms Dec-Apr US$218-283, May-Nov US$53-111)* is a large hotel with four swimming pools (including two for children), a 60m water slide, a gym, squash, volleyball, aerobics, sauna, Jacuzzi, game room, disco, restaurant, bar and a 24-hour supermarket. The rooms all come with air-con, cable TV, kitchenette and private balcony.

Places to Stay – Top End

If you are craving luxury hotels with multipool sun patios, elegant restaurants, grand lobbies, in-house discos and beachside service, Acapulco's your answer. The city has countless Grand Tourism (the rank above five stars) and super-*lujo* Special Category (top of the tops) hotels; the most extravagant are in Acapulco Diamante, east of Puerto Marqués, though there are plenty along the Costera in the Zona Dorada (which is also where you'll find the best nightlife and a broader choice of restaurants). Travel agencies abroad and throughout Mexico usually offer package deals and promotions that can be ideal, aside from turning up in the lobby in the dead of September.

Hotel Continental Emporio Acapulco *(☎ 469-05-05; La Costera 121; doubles US$168-504)*, formerly Continental Plaza, has a giant pool area with poolside bars and a great location on the hip Playa Condesa. It's one of the best on this stretch of the Costera.

Hyatt Regency Acapulco *(☎ 469-12-34; W www.hyatt.com; La Costera 1; doubles high season US$187-286, low season from US$88)* is one of the swankiest Special Category hotels in Acapulco's Zona Dorada.

Two more Special Category resorts are on the southeast side of the bay on the road to Puerto Marqués: **Las Brisas Acapulco** *(☎ 469-69-00, fax 446-53-28; W www.brisas.com.mx; Carretera Escénica s/n)* and, after that, the **Camino Real Acapulco Diamante** *(☎/fax 435-10-10/20; W www.caminoreal.com; Carretera Escénica Km 14)*.

Impressive Grand Tourism hotels include **Costa Club Acapulco** *(☎ 485-90-50; La Costera 123)*, **Villa Vera Health Spa** *(☎ 484-03-34, fax 484-74-79; Lomas del Mar 35)*, **Radisson Resort** *(☎ 446-65-65; W www.radisson.com; Costera Guitarrón 110)* and **Fiesta Americana Condesa** *(☎ 484-28-28; W www.fiestaamericana.com; La Costera 97)*.

The following hotels are at Acapulco Diamante/Playa Revolcadero.

The Fairmont Acapulco Princess *(☎ 469-10-00; W www.fairmont.com; Playa Revolcadero s/n; doubles high season US$329-1530, low season US$165-1375)*, boasts five restaurants, four swimming pools, plush rooms and nearly every service imaginable. The pool layout is excellent.

The Fairmont Pierre Marqués (☎ 466-10-00; Playa Revolcadero s/n; doubles high season US$403-539, low season US$170-316), just up the beach, is smaller and a bit more restrained and lacks the fabulous landscaping of its nearby big sister. The Pierre's attractions are its private bungalows.

Vidafel Mayan Palace (☎ 800-366-6600; W www.mayanpalace.com; Playa Revolcadero s/n; rooms/suites US$231/403) is palatial, yes. Mayan? In a Las Vegas, Nevada sort of way. This over-the-top Special Category hotel is probably Acapulco's most extravagant, occupying 20 acres of landscaped grounds with lakes, an 18-hole golf course, 12 tennis courts and plenty of swimming pools.

Places to Eat

For inexpensive, down-home Mexican cooking, the eateries around the zócalo offer the best pop for your peso. For finer dining and a more celebratory atmosphere, try something on the Costera – many serve outstanding food.

Old Acapulco On the east side of the zócalo, **The Big Slice/La Rebanadota** (☎ 482-55-55; mains US$2-6; open 8am-1am daily) is a popular place, with tasty, economical food and attractive tables both out on the zócalo (great for people-watching) and inside where it's air-conditioned. The kitchen specializes in pasta, salads, and, as the name suggests, big slices of pizza.

Restaurant Café Astoria (☎ 482-29-44; Edificio Pinios 4C; mains US$2-3; open 8am-11pm daily), hidden away at the back of the zócalo east of the cathedral, has outdoor tables in a pleasant, shady, quiet spot. It has economical prices and serves tall glasses of excellent horchata (a cold, sweetened rice drink), delicious juices and giant lattes and cappuccinos. The comida corrida is served 1pm to 4pm.

Restaurant Charly Dos (mains US$2-3; open 7.30am-11pm daily), on Morelos just east of the zócalo, has shady sidewalk tables and a long list of cheap comidas corridas (US$2.80 each). One tasty vegetarian option is the nopal relleno de champiñones, a nopal cactus paddle stuffed with mushrooms.

Restaurant y Tortas Ricardo (☎ 482-11-40; Juárez 9; mains US$3-4; open 8am-midnight daily) is another good choice for cheap comidas corridas (US$3) and tasty house specials like camarones en ajo (shrimp with garlic) or pollo en salsa de cacahuete (chicken in peanut sauce).

Restaurant San Carlos (☎ 482-64-59; Juárez 5; mains US$3-4; open 8am-10:30pm daily) has an open-air patio, casual atmosphere and good prices. The menu has an endless list of Mexican standards, including green and white pozole (a hearty pork and hominy soup).

El Amigo Miguel (☎ 483-69-81; Juárez 31; mains US$3-7; open 10:30am-9pm daily) is one of the most patronized of several good seafood restaurants near the intersection of Juárez and Azueta, a few blocks west of the zócalo. It's an open-air place with an long menu of reasonably priced dishes including huachinango (red snapper), shrimp platters and seafood soups. The house special is fillet miguel (US$5.50), baked Spanish sierra (mackerel) stuffed with a medley of seafood. **El Amigo Miguel II** (☎ 483-23-90; Juárez 16), across the street, has the same menu.

Café Los Amigos (La Paz 10; mains US$3-5; open 8:30am-9pm daily) is the place to go for North American egg-and-bacon style breakfasts. Every morning its outdoor tables are full of hungry gringos devouring tasty set breakfasts which include eggs (however you want them), toast with jam, juice, beans or potatoes, and a bottomless cup of coffee all for US$3.50.

Café Wadi (☎ 482-09-14; Mina 18; open 8am-8pm Mon-Sat) serves excellent espresso drinks made from its own fresh roasted coffee. Its standing-only espresso bar is a great morning stop before visiting the nearby artisans market.

Restaurante Normita (La Paz 7-13; breakfast US$2.75, comida corrida US$3; open 8am-8pm daily), one block over on La Paz, dishes out no-nonsense comida casera (homestyle cooking) with good set breakfasts and a succinct selection of antojitos and mariscos (shellfish).

La Gran Torta (☎ 483-84-76; La Paz 6; mains US$2.50-3.50; open 7am-11:45pm *daily)* is an excellent value with a dozen *co-midas corridas* (US$2.80 each) and countless menu items (average US$3) to choose from. Breakfasts are good and the *tortas* (sandwiches) are delicious.

For eat-in or takeout rotisserie roasted chicken sold at rock-bottom prices, try one of the **several rotisseries**, all side by side on Av 5 de Mayo near the Mercado de Artesanías.

Restaurant La Perla *(☎ 483-11-55; Plaza La Quebrada; open 7pm-11pm daily)*, at the Plaza Las Glorias Hotel Mirador Acapulco, has outstanding views of the Quebrada divers, but the purchase-as-you-enter prix fixe dinner (US$37 with two drinks) doesn't quite measure up to the view (or the price). The cliff-side candlelit terraces are, however, an indisputably special spot to dine. If you opt out on dinner, the only other way to watch the divers from this terrace is by paying a US$20 cover which includes two drinks.

La Costera The restaurants situated along La Costera tend to be pricier than those around the zócalo.

100% Natural *(mains US$4-7)*, a national vegetarian chain, has several restaurants in Acapulco. The food is usually fresh, the prices are decent, and the fare covers everything from sandwiches, soy burgers and soups to healthful takes on traditional Mexican dishes. The fruit plate with yogurt, granola and honey (US$3 or US$4) is great for breakfast. The location on the pier at Playa Hornitos *(☎ 480-14-50; La Costera s/n; open 7am-11pm daily)* is the best and busiest and has outdoor tables over the beach. There's a 24-hour branch *(☎ 485-39-82; La Costera 200)* farther east and another one *(☎ 486-20-33; La Costera 248)* located east of Parque Papagayo.

El Amigo Miguel III *(☎ 486-28-68; La Costera s/n; open 11am-8pm daily)* serves the same delicious seafood as its counterparts in the old town (see Places to Eat, Old Acapulco).

Hotel Club del Sol *(see Places to Stay; breakfast buffet 9am-noon Mon-Thur, dinner buffet 6pm-10pm Mon-Sat)* serves a popular breakfast and dinner buffet. Breakfast costs US$8 and dinner costs US$15; both prices include drinks.

Tony Roma's *(☎ 484-3343; La Costera s/n; mains US$8-15; open 1pm-midnight Mon-Thur, 1pm-1am Sat, 1pm-11pm Sun)*, at the Hotel Continental Emporio Acapulco near the La Diana traffic circle, serves the same tasty ribs it does in its restaurants up north – damn good onion rings too. Figure on US$18 for a plate of baby-backs and a drink.

Pancho's *(☎ 484-10-96; La Costera 109; mains US$6-15; open 6pm-midnight daily)*, an open-air restaurant on Playa Condesa, is reasonably priced and serves tasty Mexican and international food, especially grilled and barbecued meats. This stretch of the Costera is lined with festive **beachfront restaurants**, all of them open day and night, and they're especially fun at night.

Carlos 'n Charlie's *(☎ 484-00-39; La Costera 999, Local 6; mains US$10-20; open 1pm-1am daily)*, shows diners a good time (as it does in just about every resort town in Mexico) with rowdy music and a reliable, quirky, bilingual menu of tourist-friendly fish, burgers and steaks.

Señor Frog's *(☎ 446-57-34; Carretera Escénica 28, Centro Commercial La Vista)*, run by the same Grupo Anderson, has a similar scene with similar food and prices. It's on the east side of the Bahía de Acapulco and has a great view.

VIPS *(☎ 486-85-74; Gran Plaza, cnr La Costera & Massieu; mains US$5-9; open 7am-midnight Sun-Thur, 7am-2am Fri & Sat)* is that big, bright, air-conditioned chain diner that always seems more popular with locals than tourists. It has two other locations on the Costera besides this one in the Gran Plaza shopping center.

El Gaucho *(☎ 484-17-00; La Costera s/n, Hotel Presidente; mains US$12-20; open 5pm-11pm daily)* is one of the top joints in town for a steak, but you pay dearly for it. A *bife de chorizo* (thick sirloin) goes for US$23 and a *bife de lomo* (tenderloin) will set you back US$20. All the meat is grilled in the true Argentine style.

Mariscos Pipo's *(☎ 484-01-65; cnr La Costera & Nao Victoria; mains US$10-20; open*

1pm-9.30pm daily) used to be known as one of Acapulco's best *marisquerías* (shellfish and seafood restaurants), but it's far from the best value on the beach. The combination seafood plate (US$14/17 small/large) serves two if you're not famished.

Hard Rock Café (☎ 484-00-47; *La Costera 37; mains US$8-18; open noon-midnight daily)*, that old reliable break from the local cuisine, serves the same food you ate in the last Hard Rock: burgers, sandwiches, steaks and, wow! tacos. The bar stays open until 2am, and the food's always hot.

Fersato's (☎ 484-39-49; *La Costera 44; mains US$5-10; comida corrida US$4.40; open 8am-midnight daily)*, is a long-standing family establishment with delicious Mexican food at reasonable prices, two qualities that are rare for this area around the Casa de la Cultura and CICI.

Fast-food chains are ubiquitous along the Costera, especially toward the east end. If you're doing your own food shopping, your best bet is the **Mercado Central** (see Shopping later), several blocks north of the Costera.

Elsewhere Playas Caleta and Caletilla have numerous inexpensive, open-air **seafood restaurants**, either under the big trees behind the beaches or facing them with chairs and tables out on the sand.

La Cabaña de Caleta (☎ 482-50-07; *Playa Caleta s/n; mains US$5-8; open 9am-2pm daily)* is the longest running establishment on the beach and it's always busy. The food is fresh, the service good and the prices reasonable.

The attractive open-air restaurant at **Hotel Boca Chica** (see Places to Stay; *buffets US$10-15; lunch buffet 12:30pm-2:30pm daily, dinner buffet 7:30pm-10pm daily)* on the west end of Playa Caletilla, sits under a high *palapa* (thatched-roof shelter) with a view across to Isla de la Roqueta.

Pozolería Los Cazadores (☎ 482-51-29; *cnr Calle 6 & Mexico, Colonia Cuauhtémoc; open 2pm-midnight Thur & Sat only)*, in a residential area north of the zócalo, takes the spirit of pozole to amazing heights. Every Thursday and Saturday a squad of kids out front begins directing traffic, parking cars and opening taxi doors for the slew of people who come to fill Los Cazadores' two floors of tables, devour its *pozole* and listen to the loud live bands that kick in around 4pm. A large bowl of *pozole verde* (green) or *blanco* (white and more mild) will set you back US$2.20. Though it costs an extra US$3 for the 'regular' size *botana* (a side plate of avocado, tortilla chips, lemon, fried pork rinds, quesadillas, cheese, a stuffed chile and more), it's enough for two bowls of *pozole* and a must if you want to enjoy your soup properly. Admittedly it isn't the most gourmet *pozole* in town, but the experience is incomparable, especially when folks take to the floor to dance off their meal. A taxi from the zócalo costs US$3.

Entertainment

The stretch of the Costera along Playa Condesa (just east of La Diana traffic circle) is a hotbed of hip bars and is a perfect place to kick off the night.

Discos Acapulco's nightlife compares to its beaches as the city's main attraction, and often comes up smiling. New discos pop up to challenge the old, but the established mega-discos pretty much dominate the club scene. Most discos open around 10pm and stay relatively empty until well after midnight. They charge anywhere from US$10 to US$35 to get in, though the price almost always includes an open bar. (Only six or seven tequilas and you've made up the cover.) Discos usually enforce an informal dress code (no shorts, beach thongs, sneakers, dirty Che Guevarra T-shirts). Women can get in for a fraction of the cover on 'Ladies Nights' which are common at all discos from Monday to Friday. Monday to Thursday nights are cheaper for everyone.

Palladium (☎ 446-54-90; *Carretera Escénica s/n, Las Brisas; admission around US$25)* is hailed by many as Acapulco's best disco, and its location on the east side of the bay with fabulous views from giant windows certainly can't be beat. House, hip-hop and their nameless variations are the primary grooves. Dress up and expect a wait.

Enigma (☎ 446-57-11; Carretera Escenica s/n, Las Brisas; admission around US$25) sits on the same cliffs as the Palladium, has the same outstanding views and is owned by the same people. It's a sort of Egyptian extravaganza with waterfalls, endless lightshows and a house/techno takeoff point. The club alternates nights with the Palladium so if one's closed, try the other.

Andromedas (☎ 484-88-15; La Costera s/n; admission around US$25) is a huge castle-like structure on the Costera that gets busy with the rest of them. The interior takes a nautical theme, complete with scantily clad mermaids swimming in giant aquariums near the dance floor.

Baby 'O (☎ 484-74-74; La Costera 22; admission US$15-30) attracts a younger crowd, has always been popular, has regular Wednesday night theme parties and it usually spins a poppy soundtrack.

El Alebrije (☎ 484-59-02; La Costera 3308; admission from US$25) is a disco/concert hall which bills itself as 'one of the largest and most spectacular discos in the world.' The cover's more mind-blowing than the disco, but it's guaranteed to be packed, and it's definitely big. The music is a middle-of-the-road mix of Latin dance and rock and pop *nuevas* (recent hits).

Salon Q (☎ 481-01-14; La Costera 23 admission from US$25) is the place to go for Latin rhythms and live shows. There are plenty of tables to sit around if you don't feel like dancing, though you won't hear a word your friend is saying.

Disco Beach (☎ 484-82-30; La Costera s/n; admission for women before/after 12:30am US$5.50/23, men US$30), tucked into the lively strip along Condesa Beach, throws absurd foam parties every Wednesday and Saturday night and is the only disco right on the sand. There's no admission charge if you want to drink in the streetside Rock 'n' Roll bar upstairs.

If you don't feel up to a disco (or their exorbitant covers), most of the big hotels along La Costera have bars with some sort of lounge act, be it quiet piano music or a live band. Chain restaurants like **Hard Rock Café**, **Carlos 'n Charlie's** and **Señor Frog's** (see Places to Eat) have bars and live music or low-key dancing.

Clubs & Bars Show bars are everywhere in Acapulco, and men (of all sexual persuasions) tend to get the better end of the stick. One show that cuts across genders and sexual bents (though it's predominantly gay) is the famous *travesti* (transvestite) show at **Tequila's Le Club** (☎ 485-86-23, 483-82-36; Urdaneta 29; admission US$10-12). Shows are from 11.30pm to 1am Monday to Saturday during the high season and Thursday to Saturday during low season, with an international show at 11.15pm and a Latin show at 1.30am. Women get their due on Thursday nights with a women-only, male stripper show presented from 8:45pm to 11pm. Reservations are recommended.

Bedroom (☎ 481-17-67; La Costera 91, Local 1; admission free; open 9pm-late Mon-Sat) is a small, hip and chillingly minimalist martini bar that gets positively packed on weekends. Friday nights are 'Ladies Night' when women can pay US$5.50 for a *barra libre* (open bar).

Nina's Tropical (☎ 484-24-00; La Costera 2909; admission around US$25; open 10pm-4am daily) is the place you should go for live Latin music (salsa, cumbia, cha cha cha, merengue) and a heated dance floor.

Tropicana and **Copacabana** (admission free, US$4.50 minimum drink charge), next door to each other on Playa Hornos, are two fast routes out of the glitzy disco scene and into the world of norteña, ranchera and banda, the most popular music styles in Mexico (country stuff despised by the most fashionable clubbers). But if you want a party...

New West (☎ 483-10-82; La Quebrada 81; open 8pm-late nightly), in old Acapulco, is a popular local bar with a sawdust floor, a mechanical bull (fun to watch, painful to ride), beer on tap, rodeo videos and a jukebox blaring norteño, banda, tejano and a smattering of US country-western hits.

Dance & Theater Every Wednesday and Friday night, from 7pm to 10pm, the **Centro de Convenciones** (☎ 484-71-52, 484-70-98;

La Costera 4455; admission with buffet US$49, show & bar only US$22) holds a **Fiesta Mexicana**, featuring regional dances from many parts of Mexico, *mariachi* (small ensemble of street musicians) bands, a rope performer and the famous *voladores de Papantla* (fliers of Papantla who, suspended by a rope tied to their ankles, fly around a tall pole). The full price includes a sumptuous Mexican buffet, an open bar and the show. You can skip the buffet and come for drinks and the two-hour show at 8pm.

Other theaters at the Centro de Convenciones present plays, concerts, dance and other cultural performances, as does the **Casa de la Cultura** (see Casa de la Cultura section earlier); phone or stop by for current schedules.

Spectator Sports

Bullfights are held at the Plaza de Toros, southeast of La Quebrada and northwest of Playas Caleta and Caletilla, every Sunday at 5.30pm from December to March; tickets are sold at the **bullring ticket office** *(☎ 482-11-82, 483-95-61)* after 4.30pm and at travel agencies; both have details. The 'Caleta' bus passes near the bullring.

Shopping

Acapulco's main craft market, the 400-stall **Mercado de Artesanías** *(open 9am-8pm daily)*, is a few blocks east of the zócalo between Av Cuauhtémoc and Vicente de León. Paved and pleasant, it's a good place to get better deals on everything you see in the hotel shops – sarapes, hammocks, jewelry, huaraches, clothing and T-shirts. Bargaining is definitely the rule. Other artisan markets include the **Mercados de Artesanías Papagayo**, **Noa Noa**, **Dalia** and **La Diana**, all on La Costera, and the **Mercados de Artesanías La Caletilla** at the western end of Playa Caletilla.

Mercado Central *(Diego H de Mendoza s/n; open dawn-dusk daily)*, several blocks north of the Costera on the east side of the street, is a sprawling indoor-outdoor market where you'll find everything from peat moss and piñatas to chainsaws and child-salvation booths (not to mention sandals,

T-shirts, leather goods, food products and souvenirs). Any eastbound 'Pie de la Cuesta' or 'Pedregoso' marked bus will drop you in front; when the sidewalk turns to covered stalls, you know you're there.

Getting There & Away

Air Acapulco's busy **airport** *(airport code ACA; ☎ 466-94-34)* has many international flights; most connect through Mexico City or Guadalajara, both short hops from Acapulco. Airlines serving Acapulco and their direct flights, all with connections to other cities, include:

Aeroméxico/Aerolitoral (☎ 485-16-25, 485-16-00) La Costera 286; (☎ 466-92-04, 800-021-26-22) airport. Flies to Mexico City and Guadalajara
Aerolineas Internacionales (☎ 486-56-30, 486-00-02) La Costera 127, Local 9. Flies to Cuernavaca
America West (☎ 466-92-75, 800-235-92-92) airport. Flies to Phoenix
American Airlines (☎ 481-01-61, 800-904-60-00) La Costera 116, Local 109, Plaza Condesa. Flies to Dallas
Continental Airlines (☎ 466-90-46/63, 800-900-50-00) airport. Flies to Houston
Mexicana (☎ 486-75-85/86/87/90, 466-91-21, 800-502-20-00) La Gran Plaza, La Costera 1632, Hyatt Regency, ground floor. Flies to Mexico City
Northwest (☎ 800-900-08-00) airport. Flies to Minneapolis (one Saturday flight, December to April)

Bus Acapulco has two major long-distance bus companies: Estrella Blanca and Estrella de Oro, but there are several terminals. The main **Estrella de Oro terminal** *(☎ 485-87-05; cnr Cuauhtémoc & Wilfrido Massieu)* has 1st- and 2nd-class service. Estrella Blanca has two 1st-class terminals with some 2nd-class departures: **Central Papagayo** *(☎ 469-20-80; Cuauhtémoc 1605)*, opposite Parque Papagayo, and **Central Ejido** *(☎ 469-20-28/30; Ejido 47)*. Estrella Blanca also has a **2nd-class terminal** *(☎ 482-21-84; Cuauhtémoc 97)*, which sells tickets for all terminals but only has buses travelling to nearby towns.

Estrella Blanca tickets are sold at the terminals and at several agencies around town, including **Agencia de Viajes Zócalo** (☎ 483-58-88; La Costera 207, Locales 1 & 2; open 8am-10pm daily) a **ticket office** (Ignacio de la Llave 3; open 9am-9pm Mon-Fri, 10am-6pm Sat & Sun) one block east of the zócalo, and another in the **Procuraduría del Turista** (see Tourist Offices under Information earlier) in the Centro de Convenciones. There's an **Estrella de Oro ticket office** among the craft shops just east of the bay cruises departure point on the Costera in old Acapulco.

Both bus companies offer frequent services to Mexico City, with various levels of luxury; journey durations depend on whether they use the new, faster *autopista* (Hwy 95D) or the old federal Hwy 95. Both lines have buses to the Terminal Sur and Terminal Norte in Mexico City.

Destinations include:

Bahías de Huatulco US$26, 10 hours, 515km, three 1st-class Estrella Blanca buses daily
Chilpancingo US$5.50, 1½ to two hours, 132km, hourly 1st-class and semi-directo Estrella de Oro buses from 6am to 9:30pm; US$5.75 to US$6.50, seven 1st-class Estrella Blanca buses daily from Central Papagayo; US$4.50, three hours, half-hourly 2nd-class Estrella Blanca buses from 5am to 7pm departing from 2nd-class terminal
Lázaro Cárdenas US$11 to US$18.50, six hours, 360km, three 1st-class Estrella de Oro buses daily; US$12.75, hourly 2nd-class Estrella Blanca buses from Central Ejido
Mexico City (Terminal Norte) US$26, six hours, 400km, with Estrella de Oro; Estrella Blanca: US$25, Futura buses daily, US$39, Ejecutivo buses daily all leaving from Central Papagayo; US$23, Económico buses daily, US$24, Futura buses daily all leaving from Central Ejido
Mexico City (Terminal Sur) Estrella de Oro: US$25, five hours, 400km, 20 Plus-class buses daily, US$25.50 daily Crucero buses, US$38, six Diamante buses daily; Estrella Blanca: US$25, hourly Futura buses from 7am to midnight, US$36, four Ejecutivo buses from Central Papagayo; US$24, five Primera from Central Ejido, US$25, eight Futura buses from Central Ejido
Mazatlán US$56, 18 hours, 1410km, 1st-class Estrella Blanca buses at 6:15am and 5pm daily from Central Ejido

Puerto Escondido US$14.50 to US$18, seven hours, 400km, three Primera class Estrella Blanca buses daily from Central Ejido
Zihuatanejo US$11, four hours, 239km, three 1st-class Estrella de Oro buses daily; US$8.50, hourly 2nd-class Estrella de Oro buses; US$11, 15 Primera buses daily, US$14, two Futura buses from Central Ejido

Second-class Estrella Blanca buses leave from Central Ejido about every half-hour to Costa Chica destinations south of Acapulco along Hwy 200, including Copala (US$4.80, two hours), Marquelia (US$5, 2½ hours) and Cuajinicuilapa (US$7, 3½ hours).

Car Most car rental agencies have offices at the airport as well as in town, and many offer free delivery to your hotel. As always, it's a good idea to shop around to compare prices. Rental companies include:

Alamo (☎ 484-33-05) La Costera 2148; (☎ 466-94-44) airport
Avis (☎ 466-91-90, 462-00-75)
Budget (☎ 481-24-33) La Costera 93, Local 2, Hotel Torres Gemelas; (☎ 466-90-03) airport
Europcar (☎ 466-02-46, 466-07-00)
Galgo (☎ 484-30-66, 484-35-47)
Hertz (☎ 485-68-89, 485-89-47) La Costera 137, Hotel Monaco; (☎ 466-91-72) airport
Quick (☎ 485-86-99, 486-34-20) La Costera 127, Local 12
Saad (☎ 484-34-45, 484-53-25) La Costera 28; (☎ 466-91-79) airport; local driving only (between Pie de la Questa and Revolcadero)

The local **Angeles Verdes** (Green Angels; ☎ 483-84-70) offer roadside assistance as

---

Drivers Beware (Bridge Bummer)

If you're driving southeast of Acapulco, you cannot connect to Hwy 200 via the Barra Vieja coastal road on the south side of Laguna Tres Palos (the one running past the junction to Puerto Marqués and past the airport). Road maps fail to show that a bridge is out just past Barra Vieja, after the road hooks north. It has been out for years and there are no signs of future repair.

far south as the Oaxacan border and north to Zihuatanejo.

Getting Around

Acapulco's airport is 23km southeast of the zócalo, beyond the junction for Puerto Marqués. Arriving by air, buy a ticket for transport into town from the *colectivo* desk before you leave the terminal; it's around US$9 per person for a lift directly to your hotel.

Leaving Acapulco, telephone **Móvil Aca** (☎ 462-10-95) or **Shuttle** (☎ 462-10-95) 24 hours in advance to reserve transport back to the airport. They'll pick you up 1½ hours before your flight for domestic flights, two hours for international flights; the cost is US$8.25 per person. Taxis from the center to the airport cost around US$20 if hailed in the street; 'hotel rates' are higher.

Acapulco has a good city bus system (especially good when you get an airbrushed beauty with a bumping sound system). The buses operate from 5am to 11pm daily and cost US$0.35 to US$0.45. From the zócalo area, the bus stop opposite Sanborns department store on La Costera, two blocks east of the zócalo, is a good place to catch buses – it's the beginning of several bus routes so you can usually get a seat. The most useful city routes include:

Base-Caleta From the Icacos naval base at the southeast end of Acapulco, along La Costera, past the zócalo to Playa Caleta

Base-Cine Río-Caleta From the Icacos naval base, cuts inland from La Costera on Av Wilfrido Massieu to Av Cuauhtémoc, heads down Cuauhtémoc through the business district, turning back to La Costera just before reaching the zócalo, continuing west to Caleta

Puerto Marqués–Centro From opposite Sanborns, along La Costera to Puerto Marqués

Zócalo–Playa Pie de la Cuesta From opposite Sanborns, to Pie de la Cuesta; Buses marked 'Playa' or 'Luces' go all the way down the Pie de la Cuesta beach road; those marked 'San Isidro' or 'Pedregoso' stop at the entrance to Pie de la Cuesta

Blue and white VW cabs are as plentiful as they are noisy in Acapulco, and drivers are happy to take gringos for a ride, especially for fares higher than the official rates. Ask locals the going rate for your ride and make sure you agree on the fare with the cabby before you climb in.

COSTA CHICA

When Guerrero state tourist brochures refer to the Costa Chica ('small coast') they're usually referring to the coast of Guerrero from Acapulco southeast to the border of Oaxaca. The Costa Chica actually stretches as far south as Puerto Angel in Oaxaca, though even that boundary varies depending on who you talk to, what you read, or what radio station you're tuned into. This section covers the Costa Chica as far as the Oaxacan border. The coast south of there is described in the Oaxaca chapter.

Guerrero's Costa Chica is far less traveled than its Costa Grande (the stretch of coast from Acapulco northwest to the border of Michoacán), though it has some spectacular beaches. Afro-mestizos – people of mixed African, indigenous and European decent – make up a large portion of the population; the region was a safe-haven for Africans who escaped slavery, some from the interior, others (it's believed) from a slave-ship that sank just off the coast.

San Marcos & Cruz Grande

San Marcos (pop 12,000), 60km east of Acapulco, and Cruz Grande (pop 12,000), about 40km past that, are both unremarkable towns, but they provide basic services including banks, gas and simple hotels. They're the only two towns of significant size before Cuajinicuilapa near the Oaxacan border.

Playa Ventura

☎ 744

About 2½ hours southeast of Acapulco, Playa Ventura is a long, beautiful beach with soft white and gold sand, decent swimming, and a number of simple beachfront fish restaurants and places to stay. From Playa Ventura you can walk or drive about 1.5km southeast through the tiny village of **Juan Álvarez** to an even more spectacular beach, Playa La Piedra ('stone beach') so named for the golden, wave-sculpted rock formations at its north end and the jagged rocks that accent its long, sandy shoreline as it disappears from sight to the south. The rock formations are known as La Casa de Piedra ('house of stone'). On weekdays it's possible to have both beaches all to yourself, a blissful condition that makes leaving extremely difficult.

Most restaurants will allow you to **camp** beneath their beach *ramadas* (palm-frond shelters) and use their toilet and shower (if they have one), provided you patronize their restaurant. If you plan to cook your own food, bring it with you; there are only two little *mini-supers* (convenience stores). Some in town (one in the village, one over near La Casa de Piedra) and they stock little beyond snacks, cold drinks and, on a good day, fruit.

There are several good places to stay, all of them cheaper in the May-to-November low season and midweek during high season. All of them offer clean rooms with private baths and cold showers.

Las Hermanas Pacheco *(1-/2-bed rooms high season US$19/27)* the baby-blue place and the first as you approach the beach, has spotless rooms and friendly owners who allow you to camp for free and use their showers if you eat in their restaurant (it's very good).

La Perla de Coacoyul *(☎ 438-61-45; doubles high season US$22)* offers firm beds, friendly owners and a restaurant. Nearby **Hotel Tommy** *(☎ 501-81-72; doubles high season US$27)*, the big, bright yellow place, is clean but catches some serious afternoon sun; you can camp here too.

It's worth walking into the village to have a cold beer at the outdoor, standing-only **bar** simply because it's there.

You won't find Playa Ventura on any map – on maps it's called **Juan Álvarez**, though sometimes that doesn't even figure. To get there from Acapulco, take a bus heading southeast on Hwy 200 to **Copala** (US$4.80, two hours, 120km; see Bus under Getting There & Away in the Acapulco section earlier), a small town on Hwy 200. Ask the driver to drop you there or at *el crucero,* the

turnoff to Playa Ventura just southeast of town. In Copala, *combis* (microbuses) and *camionetas* (pickup trucks) depart for Playa Ventura six times a day (US$0.75, 20 minutes, 10km). If you're driving, the signed turnoff to Playa Ventura is at Km 124, about 3km past (southeast of) Copala.

Playa La Bocana
Some 20km east of Playa Ventura is Playa La Bocana, another endless, course-sand beach and a perfect spot for a few days of sun-filled felicity. Here the Río Marquelia meets the sea, forming a small lagoon that attracts rich birdlife and makes for great morning exploration and bird-watching. If you have a kayak or canoe, you're golden. Except during large swells, ocean swimming is excellent outside the breakers. The turnoff to La Bocana is at **Marqelia** (Km135), another small town on Hwy 200, 20km southeast of Copala. Marquelia provides basic services, including cheap hotels.

There are ample camping opportunities, either on the beach or beneath one of the restaurant *ramadas* (provided you eat in their restaurant). Bring supplies if you plan to do your own cooking.

Palapa Benny *(☎ 741-416-01-67; cabanas with shared bathroom low/high season US$10/ 15)*, to the left as you approach the beach, is the only established lodging, with four tiny, clean, sand-floor cabanas behind its excellent **restaurant**. Basic toilets and showers are shared but clean, and the cabanas have fans and light.

To get there from Acapulco, take a 2nd-class or semi-directo Estrella Blanca bus to Marquelia (US$5, 2½ hours; see Bus under Getting There & Away in the Acapulco section earlier). From there take a *s* (US$0.40) to Playa La Bocana.

Cuajinicuilapa
☎ 741 • pop (estimated) 15,000
Cuaji (**kwah**-hee), as everyone in their right mind calls Cuajinicuilapa (kwah-**hee**-nee-kwee-**lah**-pah), is the nucleus of Afro-mestizo culture on the Costa Chica and well worth a stop if you're at all interested the mixed African-indigenous heritage that is

unique, in nearly all of Mexico, to this region. Hwy 200 is the main drag in Cuaji, and gas, food and lodging are all available right off its dusty shoulders.

If you're only stopping for a few hours, be sure to visit the interesting **Museo de las Culturas Afromestizas** *(Museum of Afromestizo Cultures;* ☎ *414-03-10; cnr Manuel Zárate & Cuauhtémoc; admission US$1.50; open 10am-2pm & 4pm-7pm Tues-Sun)*, a tribute to the history of African slaves in Mexico and, specifically, to local Afro-mestizo culture. Behind the museum are three examples of *casas redondas,* the round houses typical of West Africa which were built around Cuaji until as late as the 1960s. The museum is across from the municipal building, behind the basketball courts on the inland side of the highway.

Hotel Lozano *(*☎ *414-07-08; Ignacio Zaragoza 19A; doubles US$14-30)* is the best hotel in town, owned by the amiable Dr Enrique, the local dentist. It's half a block inland from Hwy 200.

Las Siete Flores, near the bus terminal on the inland side of the highway, is a great, rickety palapa restaurant serving inexpensive daily specials for breakfast, lunch and dinner. The Thursday bowls of *pozole* are huge and delicious.

Coming from Acapulco, 2nd-class buses to Cuaji depart hourly, 3:30am to 6:30pm (US$7, 3½ hours, 200km) from Estrella Blanca's Central Ejido terminal.

Punta Maldonado

The last beach worth checking out before crossing the Oaxacan border is at Punta Maldonado (also known as **El Faro**), a remote fishing village about 31km down a partially paved road from Hwy 200. It's a ramshackle little place, almost eerie in its isolation, at the base of dramatic cliffs on a small bay. The swimming is good, and the **surfing**, on occasion, is excellent; the break is a reef/point favoring lefts. Punta Maldonado has a few seafood **restaurants** on the beach and two small **hotels**, both far from beautiful.

To reach Punta Maldonado by bus, you first must get to Cuajinicuilapa (see previous section). Then take one of the *camionetas* that leave Cuaji every two hours or so (US$1.50, 45 minutes). A Taxi from Cuaji is also possible. If you're driving, the turnoff from Hwy 200 is just past Cuaji; the road is accessible in a standard-drive vehicle all year.

Oaxaca

The rugged southern state of Oaxaca (wah-**hah**-kah) enjoys a slow, sunny existence and a magical quality that has something to do with its dry, rocky landscape, its remoteness, its bright southern light and its large indigenous population. The state capital, Oaxaca city, is a major travel destination, yet remains beautiful and artistic. It's a long-standing handicrafts center and has a blossoming art scene – indigenous people are the driving force behind both. Around the city, in the Valles Centrales (Central Valleys), are thriving village markets and spectacular ruins of pre-Hispanic towns such as Monte Albán. On the beautiful Oaxaca coast, Mexico's newest tourist resort is growing up on the lovely Bahías de Huatulco, while Puerto Escondido and the Puerto Ángel area are older beach destinations that remain small-scale and laid back.

Situated in a region where temperate and tropical climatic zones and several mountain ranges meet, Oaxaca has spectacularly varied landscapes and a biodiversity greater than any other Mexican state. The inland highlands still have cloud forests and big stands of oak and pine, while lower-lying areas and Pacific-facing slopes support deciduous tropical forest.

History

The Valles Centrales have always been the hub of Oaxacan life, and the pre-Hispanic cultures reached heights rivaling those of central Mexico. The hilltop city of Monte Albán here became the center of the Zapotec culture, which extended its control over much of Oaxaca by conquest, peaking between AD 300 and AD 700. Monte Albán declined suddenly; by about AD 750 it was deserted, as were many other Zapotec sites in the Valles Centrales. From about 1200, the surviving Zapotecs came under growing dominance by the Mixtecs, renowned potters and metalsmiths from Oaxaca's northwest uplands. Mixtec and Zapotec cultures became entangled in the Valles Centrales

Highlights

- Spotting sea turtles and crocodiles on the tropical beaches and lagoons near Mazunte
- Bird-watching at Manialtepec and Lagunas de Chacahua coastal lagoons
- Visiting artisans and viewing their crafts in the tiny villages around Pinotepa Nacional
- Seeing or surfing the wild waves of Puerto Escondido (and tasting the fabulous food while you're there)
- Exploring the colonial streets and spectacular churches of Oaxaca city
- Indulging in Oaxaca city's fabulous cuisine – *moles* (sauces), chocolate, grasshoppers and more

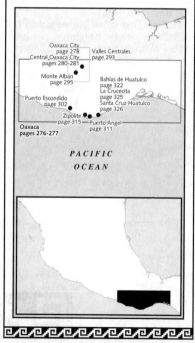

Oaxaca City page 278
Central Oaxaca City pages 280-281
Valles Centrales page 293
Monte Albán page 295
Bahías de Huatulco page 322
La Crucecita page 325
Santa Cruz Huatulco page 326
Puerto Escondido page 302
Zipolite page 315
Puerto Ángel page 311
Oaxaca pages 276-277

PACIFIC OCEAN

before the Aztecs conquered them in the 15th and early 16th centuries.

The Spaniards had to send at least four expeditions before they felt safe enough to found the city of Oaxaca in 1529. Cortés donated large parts of the Valles Centrales to himself and was officially named Marqués del Valle de Oaxaca. In colonial times, the indigenous population dropped disastrously. The population of the Mixteca region in the west is thought to have fallen from 700,000 at the time of the Spanish arrival to about 25,000 in 1700. Rebellions continued into the 20th century, but the indigenous peoples rarely formed a serious threat.

Benito Juárez, the great reforming leader of mid-19th-century Mexico, was a Zapotec. He served two terms as Oaxaca state governor before being elected Mexico's president in 1861.

Through the close of the 19th century tobacco planters set up virtual slave plantations in northern Oaxaca, and indigenous communal lands were commandeered by foreign and *mestizo* (person of mixed ancestry) coffee planters. After the Mexican Revolution plantations were dissolved and about 300 *ejidos* (peasant land-holding cooperatives) were set up, but land ownership remains a source of conflict even today. With little industry, Oaxaca is one of Mexico's poorest states, and many of its residents leave to work in the cities or the USA. The situation is made worse in some areas, notably the Mixteca, by deforestation and erosion. Tourism is thriving in Oaxaca city and nearby villages and in a few places on the coast, but in the backcountry underdevelopment is prevalent.

Geography & Climate

The Sierra Madre del Sur (average height 2000m) runs parallel to the Pacific coast. It meets the Sierra Madre de Oaxaca (average height 2500m), which runs down from Mexico's central volcanic belt, roughly in the center of the state. Between them lie the three Valles Centrales, which converge at the city of Oaxaca.

The Valles Centrales are warm and dry, with most rain falling between June and

Oaxaca Bus Companies

The following abbreviations for 2nd-class bus companies are used in this chapter:

AVN	Autotransportes Valle del Norte
EB	Estrella Blanca
ERS	Estrella Roja del Sureste
EV/OP	Estrella del Valle/Oaxaca Pacífico
FYPSA	Fletes y Pasajes
TOI	Transportes Oaxaca-Istmo

September. The coast and low-lying areas are hotter and a bit wetter.

Population & People

Oaxaca's population of 3.4 million includes 15 indigenous groups, numbering somewhere between one million and two million people in total. Each group has its own language, but most also speak Spanish. Colorful traditional costumes are seen less than they used to be, but you will still notice a strong indigenous presence in the villages and markets and strong indigenous influence on festivals. Indigenous land and housing are usually the poorest in the state.

The approximately 400,000 Zapotecs live mainly in and around the Valles Centrales and on the Isthmus of Tehuantepec in eastern Oaxaca. You're sure to come into contact with Zapotecs, though there are few obvious identifying signs. Most are farmers, but they also make and trade handicrafts, mezcal and other products. Many emigrate temporarily for work.

About 300,000 Mixtec people are spread around the mountainous borders of Oaxaca, Guerrero and Puebla states, with more than 2000,000 residing in Oaxaca. You will surely encounter Mixtecs if you spend any time around the coastal towns of Pinotepa Nacional and Jamiltepec. The Amuzgos and the Chatinos, both numbering between 20,000 and 25,000, are also indigenous to Oaxaca's coastal region.

Internet Resources

Oaxaca's Tourist Guide (W *oaxaca-travel .com*) is an excellent photo-filled website with everything from information pertaining to beaches and hotels to regional recipes and biographies of famous Oaxacans. **Oaxaca's Forum** (**w** *bbs.oaxaca.com*) is a bulletin board where you can look for rented accommodation or shared transport or ask any old question. **Oaxaca's Index** (**w** *index.oaxaca.com*) has listings of language schools and lodgings.

Dangers & Annoyances

Buses and other vehicles traveling along isolated stretches of highway, including the coastal Hwy 200 and Hwy 175 from Oaxaca city to Pochutla, are occasionally stopped and robbed. The best way to avoid this risk is not to travel at night.

Oaxaca City

☎ 951 • pop 257,000 • elevation 1550m

The state's capital city has a Spanish-built heart of straight and narrow streets that are liberally sprinkled with lovely colonial stone buildings. Oaxaca's atmosphere is relaxed but energetic, remote but cosmopolitan. The city's dry mountain heat, manageable scale, old buildings, broad shady plazas and leisurely cafés help slow the pace of life, while the diverse Oaxacan, Mexican and international cultures help create a current of excitement.

Head first for the *zócalo* (main plaza) to get a taste of the atmosphere. Then give yourself time to ramble and discover markets, handicrafts, galleries, cafés and festivities. There are also many fascinating places in the Valles Centrales within day-trip distance of Oaxaca.

The original Aztec settlement here was Huaxyacac (meaning 'In the Nose of the Squash'), from which 'Oaxaca' is derived. The Spanish laid out a new town around the existing zócalo in 1529, which quickly became the most important place in southern Mexico.

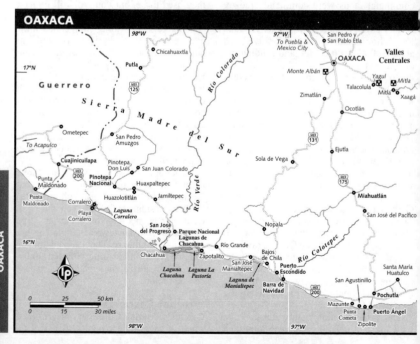

Orientation

Oaxaca centers around the zócalo and the adjoining Alameda de León in front of the cathedral. Calle Alcalá, running north from the cathedral to the Iglesia de Santo Domingo (a famous Oaxaca landmark), is mostly for pedestrians only.

The blocks north of the zócalo are smarter, cleaner and have less traffic than those to the south and, particularly, the southwest, where cheap hotels and some markets congregate.

The road from Mexico City and Puebla winds around the slopes of the Cerro del Fortín, then runs east across the northern part of Oaxaca as Calzada Niños Héroes de Chapultepec. The 1st-class bus station is on this street, 1.75km northeast of the zócalo. The 2nd-class bus station is 1km west of the center, near the Central de Abastos market.

Information

The **Oaxaca state tourist office** *(Sedetur; ☎ 516-01-23; ⓦ oaxaca.gob.mx/sedetur; In-dependencia 607; open 8am-8pm daily)* is across from the Alemeda. A **branch office** *(☎ 511-50-40)* is at the airport.

There are plenty of banks and ATMs around the center. The best exchange rates for US dollars (cash or traveler's checks) are often at **Casa de Cambio Puebla** *(García Vigil 106-L; open 9am-6pm Mon-Fri, 9am-2pm Sat)*. Banks with reasonable exchange rates include **Scotiabank** *(Independencia 101; Window 1; open 9am-5pm Mon-Fri, 10am-3pm Sat)*, **Banamex** *(Valdivieso at Hidalgo • cnr Hidalgo & Armenta y López)*, and **Bital** *(Armenta y López)*, one block east of the zócalo.

The **main post office** *(open 8am-7pm Mon-Fri, 9am-1pm Sat)* is on the Alameda.

There are many *casetas telefónicas* (public telephone call stations) scattered about; those on Independencia and Trujano, on our Central Oaxaca map, offer fax service too.

For reliable Internet connections try **C@fé Internet** *(Hidalgo 616; US$1.10 per hour; open 8am-8pm daily)* facing the Alameda,

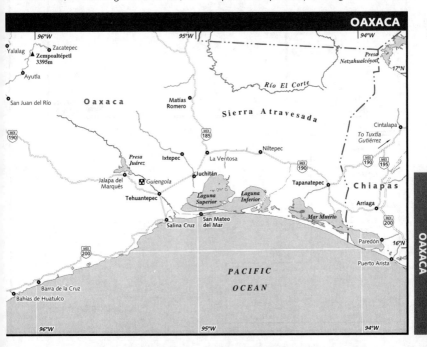

OAXACA

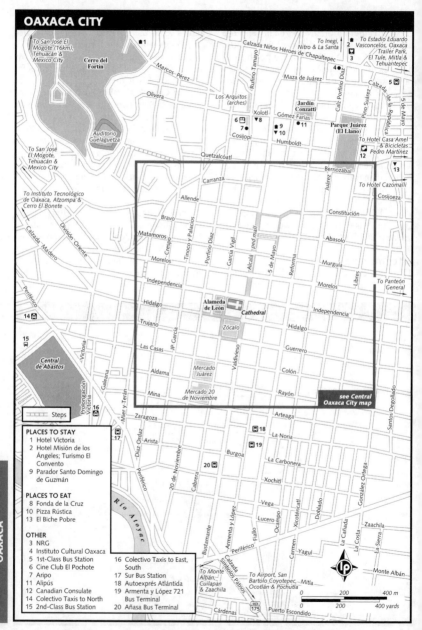

OAXACA CITY

To San José El Mogote (16km), Tehuacán & Mexico City

Cerro del Fortín

Marcos-Pérez

Olivera

Los Arquitos (arches)

Auditorio Guelaguetza

To San José El Mogote, Tehuacán & Mexico City

To Instituto Tecnológico de Oaxaca, Atzompa & Cerro El Bonete

Calzada Madero

División Oriente

Periférico

Calzada Niños Héroes de Chapultepec

Rufino Tamayo

Maza de Juárez

Jardín Conzatti

Xolotl

Gómez Farías

Cosijopí

Humboldt

Quetzalcóatl

Carranza

Allende

Bravo

Matamoros

Morelos

Independencia

Hidalgo

Trujano

Las Casas

Aldama

Mina

Zaragoza

Crespo

Timoco y Palacios

Porfirio Díaz

García Vigil

Alcalá

ped mall

JP García

5 de Mayo

Reforma

To Inegi, Nitro & La Santa

To Estadio Eduardo Vasconcelos, Oaxaca Trailer Park, El Tule, Mitla & Tehuantepec

Calz Porfirio Díaz

Pino Suárez

Calzada de la República

5 de Mayo

Parque Juárez (El Llano)

To Hotel Casa Amel & Bicicletas Pedro Martínez

Berriozábal

Juárez

To Hotel Cazomalli

Cosijoeza

Constitución

Abasolo

Murguía

Morelos

Libres

To Panteón General

Independencia

Hidalgo

Guerrero

Colón

Rayón

see Central Oaxaca City map

Alameda de León

Cathedral

Zócalo

Mercado Juárez

Mercado 20 de Noviembre

Santos Degollado

Arteaga

La Noria

La Carbonera

Burgoa

Xochitl

Vega

Lucero

Zaachila

La Cañada

La Costa

González Ortega

Doblado

Xicoténcatl

Ocampo

Carmen

Yagul

La Sierra

Monte Albán

Díaz Ordaz

Arista

20 de Noviembre

Cabrera

Periférico

Armenta y López

Periférico

Fiallo

Bustamante

Calzada Símbolos Patrios

Río Atoyac

Central de Abastos

Galeana

Victoria

Prolongación Victoria

Mier y Terán

Steps

To Monte Albán, Cuilapan & Zaachila

To Airport, San Bartolo Coyotepec, Ocotlán & Pochutla

To Mitla

Cárdenas

Puerto Escondido

MEX 175

0   200   400 m
0   200   400 yards

PLACES TO STAY
1 Hotel Victoria
2 Hotel Misión de los Ángeles; Turismo El Convento
9 Parador Santo Domingo de Guzmán

PLACES TO EAT
8 Fonda de la Cruz
10 Pizza Rústica
13 El Biche Pobre

OTHER
3 NRG
4 Instituto Cultural Oaxaca
5 1st-Class Bus Station
6 Cine Club El Pochote
7 Aripo
11 Alipús
12 Canadian Consulate
14 Colectivo Taxis to North
15 2nd-Class Bus Station
16 Colectivo Taxis to East, South
17 Sur Bus Station
18 Autoexprés Atlántida
19 Armenta y López 721 Bus Terminal
20 Añasa Bus Terminal

OAXACA

La Gran Plaza (☎ 516-38-07; Guerrero 100; US$1.10 per hour; open 7:30am-9:30pm daily), or Café Internet Plus (☎ 516-53-23; Trujano 300; US$1.10 per hour; open 9am-9pm Mon-Sat, 10am-8:30pm Sun). Inter@ctive (Alcalá 503; US$1.30 per hour; open 9am-9pm daily) has a very fast connection.

Inside the Plaza Alcalá, Amate Books (☎ 516-69-60; e corazon@spersaoaxaca.com.mx; Alcalá 307-302; open 10:30am-2:30pm & 3:30pm-7:30pm Mon-Sat) is probably the best English-language bookstore in Mexico, stocking almost every Mexico-related title in print in English. Oaxaca's Inegi map sales center (Calzada Porfirio Díaz 241; open 8am-8pm Mon-Fri), north of the town center, sells an outstanding range of topographical maps.

Two free monthly English-language papers aimed at tourists, Oaxaca Times and Oaxaca, are available around town and have some useful practical information. Guía Cultural, free at the tourist offices, is a comprehensive listing of cultural events, classes and entertainment around town.

Same-day wash-and-dry laundry service is available at Lavandería Azteca (☎ 514-79-51; Hidalgo 404; open 8am-8pm Mon-Sat, 10am-2pm Sun) and Superlavandería Hidalgo (☎ 514-11-81; cnr Hidalgo & JP García; open 8am-8pm Mon-Sat). Both charge US$5.50 for up to 3.5kg. Lavandería Antequera (☎ 516-56-94; Murguía 408; open 8:30am-2pm & 4pm-8pm Mon-Sat) charges US$4.50 for up to 3kg.

There are several English-speaking doctors at Clínica Hospital Carmen (☎ 516-26-12; Abasolo 215; open 24 hrs daily).

For any emergency service, you can call ☎ 066. The Centro de Protección al Turista (Ceprotur; ☎ 514-21-55, 516-01-23; Independencia 607), in the tourist office, helps tourists with legal problems. Report complaints and lost or stolen documents or items here.

Zócalo, Alameda & Around

Shady, traffic-free and surrounded by portales (arcades) sheltering several cafés and restaurants, the zócalo is the perfect place to relax and watch the city go by. The adjacent Alameda, also traffic-free although without the cafés, is another popular local gathering place.

The south side of the zócalo is occupied by the Palacio de Gobierno, whose stairway mural by Arturo García Bustos depicts famous Oaxacans and Oaxacan history. The city's cathedral, begun in 1553 and finished (after several earthquakes) in the 18th century, stands just north of the zócalo.

Fine carved facades adorn two nearby colonial churches: Iglesia de La Compañía, just off the southwest corner of the zócalo; and the popular Iglesia de San Juan de Dios (Aldama at Av 20 de Noviembre), which dates from 1526 and is the oldest church in Oaxaca.

Heading north from the zócalo, the pedestrian-only Alcalá makes a fine route to the Iglesia de Santo Domingo, where many colonial-era stone buildings have been cleaned up or restored.

Iglesia de Santo Domingo

Santo Domingo (cnr Alcalá & Gurrión; open 7am-1pm & 4pm-8pm daily), four blocks north of the cathedral, is the most splendid of Oaxaca's churches. It was built mainly between 1570 and 1608, for the city's Dominican monastery. The finest artisans from Puebla and elsewhere helped with its construction. Like other large buildings in this earthquake-prone region, it has immensely thick stone walls. During the 19th-century wars and anticlerical movements it was used as a stable and warehouse.

Museums

The excellent Museo de las Culturas de Oaxaca (Museum of Oaxacan Cultures; ☎ 516-29-91; admission US$2, free Sun; open 10am-8pm Tues-Sun) occupies the beautifully restored Ex-Convento de Santo Domingo, adjoining the Iglesia de Santo Domingo. These old monastery buildings were used as military barracks for more than 100 years until 1994, when they were handed over to the city of Oaxaca. The museum, opened in 1998, takes you through the history and cultures of Oaxaca state up to the present day. Behind the museum lies the Jardín Etnobotánico, a fascinating landscaped display of Oaxaca state plants, most of them cacti.

OAXACA

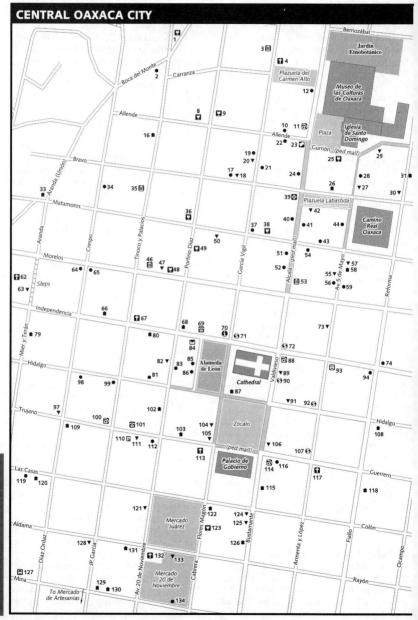

CENTRAL OAXACA CITY

118 Magic Hostel
120 Posada Las Casas
122 Hotel Trébol
126 Hotel Aurora
129 Hotel Mina
130 Hotel Pasaje
131 Hotel El Chapulín

PLACES TO EAT
18 Nuevo Mundo
20 La Brew
27 Coffee Beans
29 Los Pacos; Galería Quetzalli
30 Café La Antigua
42 El Topil
47 Restaurant Flor de Loto
50 Panini
55 Coffee Beans
57 Decano
63 Neverías
73 1254 Marco Polo
82 Los Girasoles
89 El Sagrario
91 El Mesón
95 El Buen Gourmet
97 Café Alex
104 La Cafetería
105 El Asador Vasco
106 Terranova Café
111 Restaurante El Naranjo
121 La Fonda Mexicana
124 Mariscos La Red
125 Mariscos La Red
128 Don Pollo
133 La Rana Feliz

BARS
1 La Caracola
8 La Resistencia
9 Club 502
13 El Sol y La Luna
25 La Divina
36 La Cucaracha
38 La Tentación
45 Candela
48 Hipótesis
49 La Nueva Bábel
123 La Casa del Mezcal

PLACES TO STAY
6 Las Mariposas
15 La Casa de mis Recuerdos
16 Hotel Las Golondrinas
26 Posada Margarita; Hertz
31 Las Bugambilias; Café La Olla
33 Hotel Azucenas
58 Hotel Principal
66 Hotel Posada del Centro
68 Hotel Antonio's
75 Hotel Santa Clara
76 Hostel Luz de Luna Nuyoo
79 Hostal Santa Isabel
80 Youth Hostel Plata/Gelatina
87 Hotel Marqués Del Valle; Turismo Marqués Del Valle
102 Hotel Francia
103 Hotel Las Rosas
108 Casa de Sierra Azul
109 Casa Paulina
115 Hotel Gala

OTHER
2 Tierraventura
3 Casa Juárez
4 Templo & Ex-Convento del Carmen Alto
5 Tierra Dentro
7 Aviacsa
10 Galería Índigo
11 Inter@ctive
12 Instituto de Artes Gráficas de Oaxaca
14 Virtuali@
17 Becari Language School
19 Bicicletas Bravo
21 Expediciones Sierra Norte; Ángel Azul
22 Galería Punto y Línea
23 Centro Commercial Plaza Santo Domingo; US Consulate
24 El Cactus
28 Plaza Gonzalo Lucero (Cantera Tours; Café Gecko; Axis Internet)
32 Clínica Hospital Carmen
34 Centro de Esperanza Infantil
35 Museos Comunitarios del Estado de Oaxaca
37 Casa de las Artesanías de Oaxaca
39 Plaza Alcalá (Corazón del Pueblo; Amate Books; La Crêpe; Hostería de Alcalá)
40 Oaxaca Lending Library
41 Centro Cultural Ricardo Flores Magón
43 Arte de Oaxaca
44 Budget
46 Museo Rufino Tamayo
51 La Mano Mágica
52 Aerotucán
53 Museo de Arte Contemporáneo de Oaxaca
54 Casa Cantera
56 Alamo
59 MARO
60 Centro Fotográfico Álvarez Bravo
61 Lavandería Antequera
62 Basílica de la Soledad
64 Alianza Francesa
65 Fonart
67 Templo de San Felipe Neri
69 Caseta Telefónica
70 Tourist Office (Sedetur)
71 Casa de Cambio Puebla
72 Scotiabank
74 Proveedora Escolar
77 Cuba Sol
78 Amigos del Sol
81 Aeroméxico
83 Ticket Bus
84 Post Office
85 Transportes Aeropuerto
86 Hotel Monte Albán; Aerovega
88 C@fe Internet
90 Banamex
92 Banamex
93 Teatro Macedonio Alcalá
94 Mexicana; Aerocaribe
96 Iglesia de La Merced
98 Lavandería Azteca
99 Superlavandería Hidalgo
100 Café Internet Plus
101 Caseta Telefónica
107 Bital
110 Estacionamiento Trujano
112 Viajes Turísticos Mitla; Hostal Santa Rosa
113 Iglesia de La Compañía
114 La Gran Plaza
116 Librería Universitaria
117 Iglesia San Augustín
119 El Rey de los Mezcales
127 Autobuses Turísticos (to Monte Albán); Viajes Turísticos Mitla; Hotel Rivera del Ángel
132 Iglesia de San Juan de Dios
134 Chocolatería La Soledad; Posada Chocolate

OAXACA

Free guided tours are given at 1pm and 5pm Tuesday to Saturday; get tickets at the museum's ticket desk.

Museo de Arte Contemporáneo de Oaxaca (☎ 514-10-55; Alcalá 202; admission US$1, free Sun; open 10:30am-8pm Wed-Mon), occupies a lovely colonial house on the Alcalá, which was built around 1700. It exhibits recent art from around the world and work by leading modern Oaxacan artists such as Rufino Tamayo, Francisco Toledo, Rodolfo Morales, Rodolfo Nieto and Francisco Gutiérrez.

Casa Juárez (Juárez House Museum; ☎ 516-18-60; García Vigil 609; admission US$3, free Sun & holidays; open 10am-7pm Tues-Sat, 10am-5pm Sun), opposite the Templo del Carmen Alto, is where Benito Juárez found work as a boy with bookbinder Antonio Salanueva. The renovated house shows how the early-19th-century Oaxacan middle class lived.

Museo Rufino Tamayo (☎ 516-47-50; Morelos 503; admission US$1.50; open 10am-2pm & 4pm-7pm Mon & Wed-Sat, 10am-3pm Sun), an excellent museum of Mexican Pre-Hispanic art, was donated to Oaxaca by its most famous artist, the Zapotec Rufino Tamayo (1899–1991).

Galleries

As capital of a state that has produced many top-notch Mexican artists, Oaxaca attracts artists and dealers from far and wide. Several of the city's commercial galleries display some of the best contemporary Mexican art, free of charge. One, **Arte de Oaxaca** (☎ 514-09-10, W www.artedeoaxaca.com.mx; Murguía 105; open 10am-2pm & 5pm-8pm Mon-Fri, 10am-2pm Sat), is part of the Fundación Cultural Rodolfo Morales, set up in 1990 by Morales, a native of Ocotlán and one of Mexico's leading 20th-century artists, to foment the arts, education, heritage and social welfare of Oaxaca's Valles Centrales. The gallery includes a room devoted to the work of Morales himself.

Galería Quetzalli (☎ 514-26-06; W www .quetzalli.com; Constitución 104; open 10am-2pm & 5pm-8pm Mon-Sat) handles some of the biggest names in Oaxacan art. **Galería**

Punto y Línea (☎ 516-09-18; Allende 107; open 10am-2pm & 4pm-8pm daily) and **Galería Índigo** (☎ 514-38-89; Allende 104; open 10am-2pm & 4:30pm-8:30pm Mon-Sat, noon-6pm Sun) are two other galleries well worth a look. **Centro Fotográfico Álvarez Bravo** (☎ 516-19-33; Murguía 302; open 9.30am-8pm Tues-Sun) puts on good photographic exhibitions and has a library of photography books.

Basílica de la Soledad

The image of Oaxaca's patron saint, the Virgen de la Soledad (Virgin of Solitude), resides in this 17th-century church, about four blocks west of the Alameda along Independencia. The church, with a rich carved stone baroque facade, stands where the image is said to have miraculously appeared in a donkey pack a few centuries ago. In the mid-1990s, the virgin's 2kg gold crown was stolen, along with the huge pearl and many of the 600 diamonds with which she was adorned. The adjoining convent buildings contain a **religious museum** (☎ 516-50-76; admission US$2.20; open 10am-2pm daily).

Courses

Oaxaca is a wonderful place to study, and the following schools have received rave reviews from some of our readers. The language schools can arrange accommodation.

Amigos del Sol (☎ 514-34-84; W www .oaxacanews.com/amigosdelsol.htm; Libres 109) maintains a maximum class size of five. Tuition is US$75 per week with three hours' instruction each day. Students may start any Monday.

Instituto Cultural Oaxaca (☎ 515-34-04; W www.instculturaloax.com.mx; Juárez 909) offers four-week 'total-immersion' courses for US$400 and has experienced, qualified teachers. Its courses include culture, arts and crafts workshops, cooking and dance lessons and lectures. It's possible to enroll for less than the full four weeks. There's a US$50 registration fee.

Seasons of My Heart (☎/fax 518-77-26; W www.seasonsofmyheart.com; postal address: Rancho Aurora, Apartado Postal 42, Admon 3, Oaxaca 68101) has English-language classes in Mexican and Oaxacan cooking – we've heard glowing reports.

Organized Tours

'Turismo alternativo' (alternative tourism) and 'ecoturism' are loose terms gaining currency in Mexico and used to refer to a broad span of activities from hiking, biking and climbing to spotting birds or chatting with *curanderos* (traditional medical practitioners) in remote villages. All foster close contact with Mexican nature or Mexican communities and most reach destinations that few other visitors get to.

Bicicletas Pedro Martínez (☎ 518-44-52; W *www.bicicletaspedromartinez.com; Hidalgo 100 A, Colonia Jalatlaco; open 10am-3pm & 4:30pm-9pm Mon-Fri, 10am-9pm Sat)*, run by the amiable Pedro Martínez, offers excellent bicycle day rides for a minimum of two people in the Valles Centrales, Sierra Norte and Mixteca regions of Oaxaca. Half-day trips cost around US$33 per person without a support vehicle (US$66 with a vehicle), and full-day trips to more remote destinations cost around US$110. Two-day trips cost US$120 per person. A four-day Oaxaca–Puerto Escondido expeditions costs US$600 (US$550 with your own bike), with a minimum of three people; the price includes a support vehicle to carry all your gear. Bicycles are available for hire (US$12 per day).

Italian/American owned **Bicicletas Bravo** (☎ 516-09-53; W *www.bikeoaxaca.com, García Vigil 409C)* gets consistent hurrahs for its day rides in the Valle Centrales (US$27 to US$33) and the Sierra Norte (US$44 to US$66). The enthusiastic owners also offer two-day bike trips (around US$80 per person), one-day hiking trips (US$27 to US$55) and bike-hike combos. Spanish, English and Italian are spoken, and all levels are catered to. Rental bikes are available for hire here for US$12 per day.

Museos Comunitarios del Estado de Oaxaca (☎/fax 516-57-86; W *www.umco .org; Tinoco y Palacios 311, Depto [Office] No 12; open 10am-6pm Mon-Fri)* is composed of about 15 Oaxacan villages that have established community museums to help foster their unique cultures and attempt to keep archaeological and cultural treasures 'at home'. A programme of day tours with villager guides is organized around the museums, including lunch with a family; activities such as horse or bicycle rides or walks to little-known archaeological sites; and craft, cooking or agricultural demonstrations. Groups of three to five can usually arrange a tour at one day's notice (US$21 to US$32 per person). English-speaking guides need to be arranged a few days ahead; there's rarely an English-speaker at the office.

Tierra Dentro (☎ 514-92-84; W *www.tier radentro.com; Reforma 528B)* offers climbing for beginners near Oaxaca and Yagul (US$34 to US$45 per half day), seven-hour birding trips (around US$70) and mountain bike trips.

Tierraventura (☎ 514-38-43; W *www.tier aventura.com; Boca del Monte 110)*, run by a multilingual Swiss and German couple, takes groups of up to six on trips in the Valles Centrales, Sierra Norte, Mixteca or along the Pacific coast. Some fairly remote destinations are included and the focus is on hiking, nature, crafts, meeting locals, traditional medicine, working with local communities and using local guides where possible. Tour prices range from US$45 to US$65 per person per day.

Several companies offer day trips to places in the Valles Centrales. A typical three- or four-hour trip to Monte Albán, or to El Tule, Teotitlán del Valle and Mitla, costs around US$17. Agencies with a wide choice of itineraries include **Turismo Marqués Del Valle** (☎ 514-69-62; Portal de Clavería s/n), at Hotel Marqués del Valle, and **Viajes Turísticos Mitla**, with offices at Hotel Rivera del Ángel (☎ 514-31-52; Mina 518) and Hostal Santa Rosa (☎ 514-78-00; Trujano 201).

Special Events

All major national festivals are celebrated in Oaxaca; unique fiestas include:

Virgen del Carmen The streets around the Templo del Carmen Alto, on García Vigil at Carranza, become a fairground for a week or more before the day of the Virgen del Carmen, July 16. The nights are lit by processions and fireworks.

OAXACA

Guelaguetza A brilliant feast of Oaxacan folk dance, takes place in the big open-air Auditorio Guelaguetza on Cerro del Fortín on the first two Mondays after July 16. (The only time the dates vary is when July 18, the anniversary of Benito Juárez's death, falls on a Monday. Guelaguetza is then celebrated on July 25 and August 1.) Thousands of people flock into the city, and a festive atmosphere builds for days beforehand. On the appointed days, known as Los Lunes del Cerro (Mondays on the Hill), the whole hill comes alive with hawkers, food stalls and picnickers. From about 10am to 1pm, magnificently costumed dancers from the seven regions of Oaxaca perform a succession of dignified, lively or comical traditional dances to live music, tossing offerings of produce to the crowd as they finish. Excitement climaxes with the incredibly colorful pineapple dance by women of the Papaloapan region, and the stately, prancing Zapotec Danza de las Plumas (Feather Dance), in which men wearing glorious feather headdresses perform a symbolic reenactment of the Spanish conquest.

Seats in the amphitheater (it holds about 10,000) are divided into four *palcos* (areas). For the two palcos nearest the stage, tickets (around US$40 and US$33) go on sale months in advance at the tourist office on Independencia. Nearer festival time they're also available at other outlets in the city. Tickets guarantee a seat, but you should still arrive before 8am if you want one of the better ones. The two much bigger rear palcos are free and fill up early – if you get in by 8am you'll get a seat, but by 10am you'll be lucky to get even standing room.

For all areas take a hat and something to drink, as you'll be sitting under the naked sun for hours.

Blessing of Animals Pets are dressed up and taken to Iglesia de La Merced, on Independencia, at 5pm on August 31.

Christmas Events December 16 is the first of nine nights of *posadas*, neighborhood processions of children and adults symbolizing Mary and Joseph's journey to Bethlehem. December 18, Día de la Virgen de la Soledad, sees processions and traditional dances, including Danza de las Plumas, at Basílica de la Soledad. On Noche de los Rábanos (Night of the Radishes), December 23, amazing figures carved from radishes are displayed in the zócalo. You're supposed to eat *buñuelos* (crisp fried pastries), then make a wish while throwing your bowl in the air. On December 24, evening processions called *calendas* leave from churches and converge on the zócalo at 10pm, bringing music, floats and fireworks.

Places to Stay

The tourist high seasons in Oaxaca are from about mid-December to mid-January, mid-July to mid-August, a week each side of Easter, and a week each side of Día de los Muertos. The following rates apply in the high season. Low-season rates can be 10% to 25% lower, especially if you pay cash.

Places to Stay – Budget

Hostels are the cheapest way to go, though there are plenty of bargain hotels, especially on the noisy, crowded streets south and west of the zócalo. Streetside rooms everywhere tend to be noisy.

About 3.5km northeast of the center, **Oa-xaca Trailer Park** (☎ 515-27-96; *Violetas at Heroica Escuela Naval Militar; car or van plus 2 people US$10, trailer with hookups for 1/2 people US$11.50/17*) is fairly well shaded but slightly shabby too. Turn north at the 'Colonia Reforma' sign on Calzada Niños Héroes de Chapultepec, 500m east of the 1st-class bus station, and go about seven blocks.

Oaxaca's hostels offer something for all tastes, from big, hip and hectic to small and quiet. The following have shared bathrooms and guest kitchens unless stated.

Hostel Luz de Luna Nuyoo (☎ 516-95-76; e *mayoraljc@hotmail.com;* w *www.geocities.com/luznuyoo; Juárez 101; dorm beds without/with breakfast US$5.50/7*) is a spotless, friendly hostel owned and operated by two young Oaxacan musician brothers who converted their grandmother's former home. It sleeps 26 people in four co-ed and women-only dorm rooms, each with a private bathroom. We've received quite a few glowing recommendations too – and not just for the US$0.80 beers and free coffee.

Magic Hostel (☎ 516-76-67; w *www.magichostel.com.mx; Fiallo 305; dorm beds US$6.50, doubles/triples US$15/23*) is a busy place and a serious hangout for international hostel hoppers. Cigarettes and coffee are the dominant theme in the eclectic café-cum-common area. It has about 45 beds in women-only and mixed dorms, 11 rooms holding from two to five people, a beer bar next to the kitchen and a roof lounge.

Casa Paulina (☎ 516-20-05; ⓔ hpaulina@ prodigy.net.mx; Trujano 321; dorm beds US$8, singles/doubles with shared bathroom US$10/ 19) is impeccably clean, and has an ultra-modern interior, comfortable beds (five to 11 per room), lockers and five showers each for men and women. It has a pretty little interior garden and a cafeteria, but no guest kitchen.

The following hotels have private bathrooms unless stated.

Posada Las Casas (☎ 516-23-25; Las Casas 507; singles & doubles with shared/ private bathroom US$8.50/15) is a bare-bones place, but the rooms are clean enough (and dark enough); they all have fans, and the water's hot.

Posada Chocolate (☎ 516-57-60; Mina 212; singles/doubles US$11/16), above Choc-olatería La Soledad, offers clean, comfy rooms with TV, shared bathroom and the perpetual scent of Oaxacan chocolate from below.

Hotel Mina (☎ 516-49-66; Mina 304; singles/doubles with shared bathroom US$11/ 14) has cheerful but matchbox-size rooms. There are four communal showers for about a dozen rooms.

Hotel El Chapulín (☎ 516-16-46; ⓔ hotel chapulin@hotmail.com; Aldama 317; singles/ doubles US$15/18), is a new family-run hotel with about 10 simple rooms with private, hot-water baths. It has a laundry basin and clothes lines. The entrance hall is covered in guests' comments – wall-to-wall proof that they loved it.

Hotel Pasaje (☎ 516-42-13; Mina 302; singles/doubles US$13/18-23) has small but clean, comfortable rooms around a plant-filled interior. It's good value with friendly management.

Hotel Aurora (☎ 516-41-45; Bustamante 212; singles/doubles US$16.50/24), close to the zócalo, has 30 bare but decent rooms with hot water and clean bathrooms. The management is friendly.

Posada Margarita (☎ 516-28-02; Plazuela Labastida 115; singles/doubles with shared bathroom US$12/16, with private bathroom US$19/23) has 12 simple, plain, clean rooms. Its location, a stone's throw from Alcalá and Santo Domingo, is its main plus.

Hotel Casa Arnel (☎ 515-28-56; ⓦ www .oaxaca.com.mx/arnel; Callejón Aldama 404; singles/doubles with shared bath US$12.50/ 25, singles/doubles/triples with private bath-room from US$28/28/31; suites US$56-84) is in quiet, cobbled Colonia Jalatlaco, a five-minute walk south from the 1st-class bus station and 20 minutes northeast from the city center. This is a long-running travelers hangout. The clean but smallish rooms mostly surround a big, leafy, bird-inhabited courtyard. Casa Arnel has a fabulous roof-top terrace, breakfast and evening snacks, a travel agency, and a laundry basin.

Places to Stay – Mid-Range
Rooms in this range all have private bath-rooms unless stated.

Hotel Las Rosas (☎ 514-22-17; Trujano 112; singles/doubles/triples US$32/40/48) has clean, fan-cooled rooms on two levels around a pleasant courtyard. The hotel has a TV area, a place to wash clothes and free drinking water, tea and coffee.

Hotel Principal (☎ 516-25-35; ⓔ jdbrena@ spersaoaxaca.com.mx; Av 5 de Mayo 208; singles/doubles US$27/31-36) is an old trav-elers haunt providing good rooms at rea-sonable prices. Most rooms are large and surround a sunny, empty courtyard.

Hotel Las Golondrinas (☎ 514-32-98; ⓔ las golon@prodigy.net.mx; Tinoco y Palacios 411; singles US$32-40, doubles US$40-50, triples US$48), an excellent place lovingly tended by friendly owners and staff, has about 18 rooms opening onto a trio of leafy courtyards. It's often full, so book ahead. Good breakfasts (not included in room rates) are served from 8am to 10am.

Hotel Azucenas (☎ 514-79-18; Aranda [for-merly Unión] 203; singles/doubles US$38/44) is a 10-room colonial home, recently con-verted into a delightful little hotel by its Canadian owners who take wonderful care of their guests. The highlight is the roof-top terrace where a tasty breakfast, complete with warm bread, is served (additional US$2.50). There's free coffee all day.

Hotel Posada del Centro (☎ 516-18-74; Independencia 403; ⓦ www.mexonline.com/ posada.htm; singles with shared bathroom

OAXACA

US$13-21, doubles with shared bathroom US$25-30, singles/doubles with private bathroom US$39/44) is an attractive colonial building with two interior patios complete with plants, tables and chairs. It has a roof terrace and Internet service for guests. Rooms lack windows but are still cheerful.

Hotel Francia (☎ 516-48-11; Av 20 de Noviembre 212; singles/doubles/triples US$40/45/56), a venerable, 65-room hotel, has moderate-sized rooms with fan, phone and TV. This is a clean, amiable place (and DH Lawrence stayed here!).

Hotel Trébol (☎ 516-12-56; e hotrebol@prodigy.net.mx; Flores Magón 201; singles & doubles US$49), almost hidden opposite the Mercado Juárez, has sizable, bright, clean, well-furnished rooms with fan and TV all around a modern-colonial courtyard.

Hotel Gala (☎ 514-22-51; e galaoax@prodigy.net.mx; w www.gala.com.mx; Bustamante 103; singles/doubles US$61/82), half a block south of the zócalo, has a convenient restaurant and carpeted rooms with cable TV, phone and fan. Rooms facing the street are biggest and brightest; interior rooms are slightly stuffy. Overall, it's an elegant place.

Hotel Marqués Del Valle (☎ 514-06-88, 800-849-9936; e hmarques@prodigy.net.mx; Portal de Clavería s/n; singles/doubles with fan US$79/98, with air-con US$84/103) boasts an incomparable location right on the zócalo. It's an old building with four floors of spotless, modern, comfortable rooms. Some have superb views over the plaza, and all have TV, phone and fan or air-con.

Oaxaca's so-called B&Bs are actually attractive guesthouses; the next three listings fall into this category. More B&Bs are advertised in the *Oaxaca Times* and *Oaxaca* newspapers and on the Internet.

La Casa de mis Recuerdos (☎ 515-56-45; Pino Suárez 508; w www.misrecuerdos.net; singles US$41-52, doubles US$60-74) is a welcoming guesthouse with nine attractive rooms, seven with private bathroom. The best of them overlook a central garden. A big Oaxacan breakfast is served at a large table in the family dining room.

Las Bugambilias (☎ 516-11-65; w www.mexonline.com/bugambil.htm; singles US$42-

72, doubles US$66-138) is a beautifully decorated guesthouse with a good location just southeast of the Iglesia de Santo Domingo. Its eight colorful rooms surround a grassy garden and are adorned with regional crafts. A traditional breakfast is served at a communal table.

Las Mariposas (☎/fax 515-58-54; w www.mexonline.com/mariposas.htm; Pino Suárez 517; singles/doubles US$28/39, studio apartments US$39-50) offers six studio apartments (with small kitchens) and four rooms along a pretty patio. It's a tranquil and friendly place with an open-air guest kitchen as well.

Places to Stay – Top End

Retaining much of its old-time charm, **Casa de Sierra Azul** (☎ 514-84-12; w www.mexonline.com/sierrazul.htm; Hidalgo 1002; singles/doubles/triples US$103/128/154) is a thoroughly remodeled, 200-year-old home. It has a large, columned patio and 12 luxurious rooms with TV, telephone and great bathrooms.

Hotel Victoria (☎ 515-26-33, fax 515-24-11; w www.hotelvictoriaoax.com.mx; Lomas del Fortín 1; singles & doubles US$175, villas for up to 4 US$210, suites for up to 5 from US$250) stands on the lower slopes of Cerro del Fortín. Many of the 150 large rooms and suites overlook the city, and the hotel has an Olympic-size pool in big gardens. Its restaurant gets good reports too. The hotel runs a free shuttle to/from the city center.

Camino Real Oaxaca (☎ 516-06-11; w www.caminoreal.com; Av 5 de Mayo 300; singles & doubles US$234-292), four blocks northeast of the zócalo, is Oaxaca's ultimate hotel for colonial atmosphere. The entire 16th-century convent of Santa Catalina, which takes up a whole city block, was converted in the 1970s to create this unique hotel. The old chapel is a banquet hall, one patio contains an enticing swimming pool, and the bar is lined with books on otherworldly devotion. Thick stone walls – some still bearing original frescoes – keep the place nice and cool. If you can, choose a room upstairs and away from the street and kitchen noise.

Places to Eat

Cheap *oaxaqueño* (Oaxacan) meals can be had in the **Mercado 20 de Noviembre**, south of the zócalo. Most of the many small *comedores* (inexpensive restaurants) here serve up local specialties such as chicken in *mole negro*. Few post prices, but a typical main dish is about US$1.50. Pick a *comedor* that's busy – those are the best. Many stay open until early evening, but their fare is freshest earlier in the day. More *comedores* can be found in the big **Central de Abastos** (see Shopping, later in this section).

The **ice-cream stands** *(neverías)* in front of the Basílica de la Soledad are great for an afternoon book and a *bola* (scoop) of home-made ice cream. For live music to dine to, see the Entertainment section.

Cafés & Breakfast The two branches of **Coffee Beans** *(Av 5 de Mayo 114 • Av 5 de Mayo 411)* offer a range of good coffee fixes, as does the popular **Café La Antigua** *(☎ 516-57-61; Reforma 401; open 9:30am-11pm Mon-Sat)*.

Nuevo Mundo *(Bravo 206; open 8am-8pm Mon-Sat)* is a slick little café serving fabulous espresso drinks, muffins, cinnamon rolls and bagels. The owner roasts his own coffee every day!

Café Alex *(☎ 514-07-15; Díaz Ordaz 218; mains US$3-6; open 7am-9pm Mon-Sat, 7am-12:30pm Sun)* is well worth a visit for the delicious, good-value breakfasts, served until noon. The *comida corrida* (daily special) is usually top-rate and costs US$3.30. The servings are generous, the service is quick, and the patrons are a mix of locals and foreigners.

La Brew *(☎ 514-96-73; García Vigil 409B; mains US$2-4; open 8am-8pm Mon-Sat, 8am-2pm Sun)* is a cozy café serving waffles (US$3.30), sandwiches, yogurt and granola, homemade brownies, banana bread, and, if you're lucky, bagels with cream cheese.

Ángel Azul *(☎ 514-84-76; García Vigil 406; mains around US$3; open 8am-9pm Mon-Thur, 8am-11pm Fri & Sat)* is a relaxed café-cum-bar with interior and courtyard tables – the latter being perfect for killing a few hours with a book. Breakfasts,

Oaxaqueña Cuisine

Good *oaxaqueño* (Oaxacan) regional cooking is 'spicily' delicious, and the seven traditional Oaxacan *moles* (sauces) are renowned. Specialities include:

Amarillo (con pollo) – a yellow-orange cumin and chili *mole* (with chicken)

Chapulines – grasshoppers! They come fried, often with chili powder, onion and garlic; high in protein and good with a squeeze of lime – vendors sell them from baskets in the zócalo and you can find them in food markets too

Chíchilo – a dark, rich *mole* made with varied chilies

Colorado – a dark red *mole*

Coloradito – a brick-red chili-and-tomato *mole*, usually served over pork or chicken

Manchamanteles – 'tablecloth-stainer': a *mole* made with pineapple and bananas

Memelitas – small tortillas with varied toppings

Mole negro – the monarch of Oaxacan moles, sometimes called just *mole* oaxaqueño: a dark, spicy, slightly sweet sauce made with many ingredients including chilies, bananas, chocolate, pepper and cinnamon; usually served with chicken

Picadillo – spicy minced or shredded pork, often used for the stuffing in chiles rellenos

Tamal oaxaqueño – a tamal with a *mole* and (usually) chicken filling

Tasajo – a thin slice of pounded beef, usually grilled

Tlayuda or tlalluda – a big crisp tortilla, traditionally served with salsa and chili but now topped with almost anything, making it into a kind of pizza

Quesillo – Oaxacan stringy cheese

Verde (con espinazo) – a green *mole* (with pork back) made from beans, chilies, parsley and epazote (goosefoot or wild spinach)

sandwiches and light meals are all good. There's Internet access too.

Café Gecko *(☎ 516-22-85; Av 5 de Mayo 412, Plaza Gonzalo Lucero; mains US$2-3; open 8:30am-8:30pm Mon-Sat)* serves good hotcakes, croissants, sandwiches, snacks and about 20 types of coffee. The music's mellow and the patio's pleasant.

Decano *(Av 5 de Mayo 210; mains US$3-5; open 8am-midnight daily)* satisfies a range of food needs, from breakfast to a good *menú del día* (menu of the day) and tasty light eats. In the evening it's a popular spot for young oaxaqueños to down a beer or two.

The cafés and restaurants beneath the zócalo arches are great spots for watching Oaxaca life. These places are generally mediocre, but they're worth it just for the setting. The following are two of the best.

La Cafetería *(☎ 514-76-16; Portal de Flores 3; mains US$4-8; open 7am-11:30pm daily)*, on the west side of the zócalo, concentrates on *especialidades oaxaqueñas* (Oaxacan specialties) and *antojitos* (light meals, literally 'little whims'). Its prices are some of the best on the park. The giant yogurt, fruit and granola plate (US$3.75) is excellent.

Terranova Café *(☎ 514-05-33; Portal Juárez 116; mains US$5-8)*, on east side of the zócalo, is one of the best (and priciest) places on the square. Breakfast is served until 1pm (with a US$7.50 unlimited buffet on Sunday), and there's a big range of *antojitos*, baguettes and other light eats, as well as lunches and dinners.

Oaxacan & Mexican With a pleasant courtyard setting **Restaurante El Naranjo** *(☎ 514-18-78; Trujano 203; mains US$7-11; open 1pm-10pm Mon-Sat)* features sublime *oaxaqueño* food prepared with a modern touch. One of the seven Oaxacan moles is served each day, with chicken breast or pork fillet. The five different *chiles rellenos* (chilies stuffed with cheese, meat or other foods, fried and baked in sauce) are yum.

Fonda de la Cruz *(☎ 513-91-60; García Vigil 716A; mains US$3.50-5.50; open 1pm-10pm Mon-Sat)* is a cool, little wooden-table hideaway specializing in Oaxacan and Yucatán dishes. Try the *pan de cazón* (a thick pancake with fish and a piquant tomato sauce) or *panuchos* (corn pizzas with pork and onion in a spicy sauce).

El Topil *(☎ 514-16-17; Plazuela Labastida 104; mains US$4-6; open 7:30am-11:30pm*

daily) serves dishes with a touch of home cooking; *tasajo* (thinly sliced grilled beef) with guacamole and frijoles is one specialty. The menu also offers soups, *tlayudas*, *chiles rellenos* and some good *antojitos*.

El Biche Pobre *(☎ 513-46-36; Calzada de la República 600; mains US$4-6; open 1pm-9pm daily)*, 1.5km northeast of the zócalo, is an informal place with about a dozen long tables and a wide variety of reasonably priced Oaxacan dishes. For an introduction to the local cuisine, you can't beat the US$5 *botana surtida*, a dozen assorted little items that add up to a tasty meal.

La Rana Feliz *(Aldama 207; mains US$2.50; open 8am-9pm daily)*, on the north side of the Mercado 20 de Noviembre, is hard to beat for cheap Oaxacan food like tlayudas smothered in black beans, *huaraches* (a long corn tortilla covered with beans and cheese), enchiladas, *entomatadas* (enchiladas made with a tomato-chili sauce), and *enfrijoladas* (enchiladas made with a black bean sauce). Nothing costs over US$2.50.

La Fonda Mexicana *(☎ 514-31-21; Av 20 de Noviembre 208; mains US$3-4; open 8am-5pm daily)* serves healthy portions of down-home Oaxacan food in a busy family atmosphere. The *comida corrida* is a deal at US$3.30.

El Mesón *(☎ 516-27-29; Hidalgo 805; mains US$3-6)*, just off the zócalo, prepares tasty, mainly charcoal-grilled Mexican food. Tacos and quesadillas are the specialties, mostly at US$2 to US$3 for two or three. Decent breakfast, lunch and dinner buffets all cost US$5.50.

Seafood With two locations around the corner from each other, **Mariscos La Red** *(☎ 514-88-40; Bustamante 200 • ☎ 514-68-53; Las Casas 101; mains US$6-11; open noon-9pm daily)* whips out excellent seafood to a packed house every day. There are 12 different shrimp dishes for about US$11 each and the various filets cost US$7 to US$11. Both locations have the same menu, but the Las Casas location is more casual.

1254 Marco Polo *(☎ 514-43-60; Av 5 de Mayo 103; mains US$6-11; open 8am-8:30pm Mon-Sat)* is another excellent fish and

So much choice at the Mercado Juárez, Oaxaco city (top left); decaying colonial architecture in Oaxaca city (top right); anyone is entitled to an ice-cream break when they are collecting for charity, near Guadalajara, Jalisco (bottom).

Mezcal is an alcoholic drink made from the sap of the maguey plant. First the sap is obtained from the plant (top left), then it's made into mezcal and bottled (top right) and then it can be sold in *cantinas* (usually men-only drinking establishments) like Le Casa del Mezcal in Oaxaca city (bottom).

seafood restaurant. Soups and seafood cocktail starters cost US$4 to US$5. Complete breakfasts cost about US$2.50.

Vegetarian Many restaurants have vegetarian options, but the following have more than most.

Café La Olla (☎ 516-66-88; Reforma 402; mains US$3-9; open 9am-11pm Mon-Sat) serves a mouth-watering array of wholegrain *tortas* (sandwiches), salads, pastas, seafood, meat dishes and regional specialities all cooked with natural ingredients and a whole lot o' love. Breakfast (US$3 to US$4) is good too.

Panini (Matamoros 200A; mains & sandwiches US$2-3) makes more than a dozen *tortas* on delicious ciabatta bread, as well as imaginative salads. They treat their produce with an 'organic citrus based disinfectant.'

Restaurant Flor de Loto (Morelos 509; mains US$3-6) takes a reasonable stab at pleasing a range of palates from vegan to carnivore. The US$3.75 *comida corrida*, with a veggie version available, is a real meal.

Other Places to Eat One of Oaxaca's swankiest eateries, the courtyard restaurant **Hostería de Alcalá** (☎ 516-20-93; Alcalá 307; mains US$6-10; open 8am-11pm daily) is known for its delectable Oaxacan dishes; steaks are also a specialty; wines start around US$20 a bottle.

Los Pacos (☎ 516-17-04; Constitución 104; mains US$5-10; open 8:30am-10pm Mon-Sat) is a stylish (one might say artsy) restaurant/bar with a tantalizing menu of Oaxacan and international dishes. Low lighting, mixed drinks, paintings on the walls and good service make it an enjoyable place.

El Asador Vasco (☎ 514-47-55; Portal de Flores 11; mains US$9-14; open noon-11:30pm Mon-Sat), upstairs on the southwest corner of the square, serves good Spanish, Mexican and international food. Steaks and *brochetas* (kebabs) are among the best choices. For a table overlooking the zócalo, book early in the day.

Pizza Rústica (☎ 516-75-00; Alcalá 303; pizzas US$6-10; open 1pm-11pm or midnight daily), set in a lovely courtyard, serves

top-notch pizzas, tasty salads and several pasta dishes with a big choice of sauces. Wine too? Absolutely.

Don Pollo (cnr Aldama & JP García; mains US$2-4; open 8am-5pm daily) is all about chicken – roasted, breaded and fried, or in sandwiches, tacos and tostadas. It's cheap too: a quarter bird with fries and spaghetti will only set you back US$2.

Entertainment

Live Music The state marimba ensemble or state band usually give free **concerts** in the zócalo around 7pm Monday to Saturday. The city orchestra usually chimes in at noon on Sunday.

Candela (☎ 514-20-10; Murguía 413; admission US$3-4; open 1pm-1:30am Tues-Sat) draws foreigners and locals with its writhing salsa band and colonial-house setting. Arrive fairly early (9:30pm to 10:30pm) to get a good table, and either learn to dance or learn to watch. Candela is great for lunch and dinner too.

El Sol y La Luna (☎ 514-80-69; Reforma 502; admission US$2; open 8pm-12:30am or 1am Mon-Sat) offers jazz starting at 10pm Thursday to Saturday and has good food, including crepes (US$3), pasta (US$4) and pizza or meat for more.

La Nueva Bábel (Porfirio Díaz 224; admission free; open 5pm-11pm Mon-Sat) has live music Thursday to Saturday. Music can be anything from *trova* (ballad-based folk music) to loud rock and *loco* salsa jams. It's a small place with tables and a good vibe.

Bars & Clubs If you feel the need to make the acquaintance of a few typical Mexican beverages, try **La Cucaracha** (Porfirio Díaz 301A), a specialist bar with 40 varieties of mezcal and 100 versions of tequila costing around US$1.75 to US$5 a shot. Everyone's welcome (it's not a cantina), food is available, and there's live Latin music and a lively atmosphere on weekends.

La Casa del Mezcal (☎ 516-21-91; Flores Magón 209; open 9am-1am daily) is one of Oaxaca's oldest bars, serving good mezcal for US$1 to US$4.50 a shot. It has a roaring juke box, tables at the back and a rowdy, cantina-like atmosphere (women are welcome).

Hipótesis (☎ 514-74-08; Morelos 511; open 6pm-2am daily) is a laid-back café/piano bar with dim lighting, low ceilings, a tiny area upstairs and a bohemian air – great for disappearing over a few beers.

Club 502 (☎ 516-60-20; Porfirio Díaz 502; admission US$4.50; open 11pm-dawn Thur-Sat) is Oaxaca's only overground gay nightclub and probably offers the best house music in town. It's the only club downtown with a late-opening license. Ring the bell to enter, and be prepared for a strict door policy.

La Divina (☎ 582-05-08; Gurrión 104; open 12:30pm-1am Tues-Sun), across from Santo Domingo, draws a mixed-nationality crowd generating a warm dance-friendly atmosphere that spills out into the street on a good night.

Cinema & Theatre Tucked behind Los Arquitos (the ruins of a 17th century arched Dominican aqueduct just north of downtown) the **Cine Club El Pochote** (☎ 514-11-94; Garcia Vígil 817; admission by donation) is a 120-seat movie theater showing international films in their original language. Screenings are at 6pm Tuesday and at 6pm and 8pm Wednesday to Sunday. It's usually standing-room-only for late arrivals. Shows are listed in the Guía Cultural.

Centro Cultural Ricardo Flores Magón (☎ 514-03-95; Alcalá 302) puts on varied musical, dance and theater shows most nights. Many events are free; drop by to see the programme or check the Guía Cultural.

Casa Cantera (☎ 514-75-85; Murguía 102; admission US$10) stages a lively mini-Guelaguetza (see Special Events) at 8pm nightly. Food and drinks are available. To book, phone or stop by during the afternoon.

Shopping

The state of Oaxaca has probably the richest, most inventive folk art scene in Mexico, and the city is the chief clearinghouse for the products. The best work is generally in shops, but prices are lower in the markets. You might pay similar prices for crafts in the city as you would in the villages where most

---

Mezcal

Central Oaxaca state produces probably the best mezcal in Mexico (and therefore the world). Just like its cousin tequila, mezcal is made from the maguey plant and is usually better when reposado or añejo (aged). There are also some delicious crema varieties with fruit or other flavors.

Several Oaxaca shops southwest of the zócalo specialize in mezcal. Try **El Rey de los Mezcales** (☎ 514-16-22; Las Casas 509; open 9am-8pm daily). For US$10 you can buy a decent bottle but some US$3 mezcals are also fine. For fancy export mezcals (up to US$45 a bottle), head for **Alipús** (☎ 515-23-35; Gómez Farías 212B), north of the center.

---

of them are made, but if you buy in the city a lot of your money usually goes to intermediaries. Some artisans have grouped together to market their own products directly.

Though many traditional techniques remain alive – back-strap and pedal looms, hand-turning of pottery – new product forms frequently appear in response to the big international demand for Oaxaca crafts. The brightly painted wooden animals and monsters known as alebrijes were developed only a few years ago from toys that Oaxacans had been carving for their children for centuries.

Special crafts to look out for include the distinctive black pottery from San Bartolo Coyotepec; blankets, rugs and tapestries from Teotitlán del Valle; huipiles and other indigenous clothing from around the state; the creative pottery figures made by the Aguilar sisters of Ocotlán; and stamped and colored tin from Oaxaca itself.

The vast main market, the **Central de Abastos** (Supplies Center), is on the Periférico in the western part of town, next to the 2nd-class bus station. Saturday is the big day, but the place is a hive of activity daily. If you look long enough, you can find almost anything, including handicrafts. Each type of product has a section to itself. Nearer the city center, the indoor **Mercado**

Juárez, a block southwest of the zócalo, concentrates on food (more expensive than at the Central de Abastos) but also has flowers and some crafts. The **Mercado 20 de Noviembre**, one block farther south, is mainly *comedores*. The **Mercado de Artesanías** *(Handicrafts Market)*, a block southwest of the Mercado 20 de Noviembre, gets fewer customers because it's a bit off the beaten track – so you may pick up some bargains. It's strong on pottery, rugs and textiles.

The highest-quality crafts are found in the smart stores on and near Alcalá and Av 5 de Mayo.

MARO (☎ 516-06-70; *Av 5 de Mayo 204; open 9am-8pm daily*) is an outstanding, sprawling store run by a cooperative of women artisans from around the state who are dedicated to the preservation of traditional crafts. The money goes to the makers.

La Mano Mágica (☎ 516-42-75; *Alcalá 203; open 10:30am-3pm & 4pm-7:30pm Mon-Sat*) sells outstanding crafts, including weavings by one of its owners, the Teotitlán del Valle master weaver Arnulfo Mendoza.

Corazón del Pueblo (☎ 514-18-08; *Alcalá 307-309, 2nd floor; open 10:30am-2:30pm & 3:30pm-7:30pm Mon-Sat*), in the Plaza Alcalá, sells beautiful, carefully chosen crafts from around the country.

Casa de las Artesanías de Oaxaca (☎ 516-50-62; *Matamoros 105; open 9am-9pm Mon-Sat, 10am-6pm Sun*) is the outlet for this organization of more than 80 *oaxaqueño* artisans. Quality is high and money goes to the artists.

Getting There & Away

Air Most international flights to Oaxaca city (airport code OAX) connect through Mexico City.

Over the years a variety of airlines have offered flights over the Sierra Madre del Sur to Puerto Escondido and Bahías de Huatulco on the Oaxaca coast – a spectacular 30-minute hop for about US$100. If you dread the bus journey it's a great alternative.

Airlines with direct flights to/from Oaxaca, most with connections to other cities, include:

Aerocaribe (☎ 516-02-66, 516-02-29) Fiallo 102; daily flights to Bahías de Huatulco, Tuxtla Gutiérrez, Villahermosa and Mérida

Aeroméxico (☎ 516-10-66, 516-71-01) Hidalgo 513; flies to Mexico City three times daily

Aerotucán (☎ 501-05-30) Alcalá 201, Interior 204; flies daily to Bahías de Huatulco and Puerto Escondido

Aerovega (☎ 516-49-82) Hotel Monte Albán, Alameda de León 1; Aerovega flies a seven-seat Cessna at 8am daily to Puerto Escondido

Aviacsa (☎ 518-45-55), Pino Suárez 604; flies once daily to Mexico City

Cuba Sol (☎ 514-79-30) Independencia 1103; flies a seven-seat Cessna to Puerto Escondido, Huatulco and Acapulco; departures at anytime from 8am to 7pm daily, by arrangement (three-person minimum)

Mexicana (☎ 516-84-14, 516-73-52) Fiallo 102; flies four times daily to Mexico City

Bus The **1st-class bus station** (*Calzada Niños Héroes de Chapultepec 1036*), used by UNO, ADO and Cristóbal Colón, is 1.5km northeast of the zócalo. The **2nd-class bus station** is 1km west of the zócalo along Trujano or Las Casas; the main long-distance companies using it are EV/OP, FYPSA and TOI. Unless otherwise noted, buses mentioned in this section use one of these two main stations.

It's advisable to book a day or two in advance for the less frequent services to the coast, especially in high season. **Ticket Bus** (☎ 514-66-55; *Av 20 de Noviembre 103D; open 8am-10pm Mon-Sat, 9am-4pm Sun*), in the city center, sells tickets for UNO, ADO, Colón and a few other 1st-class companies.

To get to the Pacific coast, there are three basic options: 2nd-class buses head down Hwy 175 through Miahuatlán and Pochutla; 1st-class buses take Hwy 190 via Salina Cruz then turn west along the coast (a longer way round though the roads are in better condition); and a few 2nd-class buses take Hwy 131 (paved but in bad condition) direct to Puerto Escondido.

To Pochutla (the jumping-off point for Puerto Ángel, Zipolite and other nearby beaches), it's 245km and about seven hours by Hwy 175 (a spectacular, winding, downhill ride), or 450km and nine to 10 hours via

OAXACA

Salina Cruz. Puerto Escondido is 65km (1½ hours) west of Pochutla, by the coastal Hwy 200, or 200km from Oaxaca (eight to nine hours) by Hwy 131.

All in all, Hwy 175 is the happy medium. At the time of writing the best service on Hwy 175 was EV/OP's *directo* 2nd-class service (at 10am, 2:30pm and 10:45pm) to Pochutla (US$10) and Puerto Escondido (US$11) from a terminal at Armenta y López 721, 500m south of the zócalo. The 10am bus is best of all because it's safest to travel in daylight. EV/OP also runs hourly *ordinarios* to Pochutla (US$8, 7½ hours) and Puerto Escondido (US$9, 8½ hours) and a 10pm *directo* to Santa Cruz Huatulco (US$12, 7½ hours), all by Hwy 175.

Cristóbal Colón (1st-class) takes the Salina Cruz route with two buses daily to Bahías de Huatulco (US$18, eight hours), Pochutla (US$18, nine hours) and Puerto Escondido (US$19, 10½ hours).

Services by Hwy 131 to Puerto Escondido are from the 2nd-class bus station by ERS (US$9 to US$10, four daily) and Transol (US$9 to US$13, seven daily).

Minivan An increasingly popular (and faster) alternative to bussing to the coast is the air-con Chevy vans of **Autoexprés Atlántida** (☎ 514-70-77; *La Noria 101*). They head to Pochutla (US$13, five hours) via Hwy 175 six times daily; three of these continue to Puerto Escondido (US$17.50, six hours).

Mexbus (☎ 800-523-9412; ⓦ *www.mexbus .net*), a backpackers' shuttle service, runs daily between Mexico City and Oaxaca for US$27.50, stopping at hostels in both cities. Call for reservations or book at any hostel listed in Places to Stay.

Car Driving Hwys 175 and 131 to the coast is best done during the day. Toll-road Hwy 190 via Salina Cruz is the smoothest, albeit longest way down. See the previous Bus section for more road information to the coast.

Car tolls from Mexico City to Oaxaca on highways 150D and 135D total US$30; the trip takes about six hours. The 135D is also numbered 131D for some stretches. The main

toll-free alternative, via Huajuapan de León on Hwy 190, takes several hours longer.

The best deals we found were at Budget (VW Bugs for US$60 a day with unlimited kilometers). The airport desks may come up with offers. Rental agencies include:

Alamo (☎ 514-85-34) Av 5 de Mayo 203A; (☎ 511-62-20) airport
Avis (☎ 511-57-36) airport
Budget (☎ 516-44-45) Av 5 de Mayo 315A
Hertz (☎ 516-24-34) Plazuela Labastida 115, Local 4; (☎ 511-54-78) airport

Getting Around

Oaxaca airport is 6km south of the city, 500m off Hwy 175. Transporte Terrestre vans from the airport will take you to anywhere in the city center for US$2.25. A taxi costs about US$8.

Transportes Aeropuerto (☎ *514-43-50; Alameda de León 1G*) will shuttle you from your hotel to the airport, getting you there one hour before your flight for US$2.50. Reservations must be made in person from the office facing the cathedral.

Most points of interest in the city are within walking distance of each other, but you might want to use city buses (US$0.30) to and from the bus stations.

From the 1st-class bus station, a westbound 'Juárez' or 'Av Juárez' bus takes you down Juárez and Ocampo, three blocks east of the zócalo. A 'Tinoco y Palacios' bus goes down Tinoco y Palacios, two blocks west of the zócalo. To return to the bus station from downtown, take an 'ADO' or 'Gigante' bus north up Xicoténcatl or Pino Suárez, four blocks east of the zócalo, or up Díaz Ordaz or Crespo, three blocks west of the zócalo.

Buses between the 2nd-class bus station and the center pass slowly along congested streets; it's almost as quick to walk. 'Centro' buses head toward the center along Trujano, then turn north up Díaz Ordaz. Going out to the 2nd-class bus station, 'Central' buses head south on Tinoco y Palacios, then west on Las Casas.

A taxi anywhere within the central area, including the bus and train stations, costs about US$2.50.

You can rent mountain bikes for US$12 a day at Bicicletas Pedro Martínez or Bicicletas Bravo; see Organized Tours, earlier, for details.

Valles Centrales

Three valleys radiate from the city of Oaxaca: the Valle de Tlacolula, stretching 50km east; the Valle de Etla, reaching about 40km north; and the Valle de Zimatlán, stretching about 100km south.

In these Valles Centrales (Central Valleys), all within day-trip distance of Oaxaca city, you'll find pre-Hispanic ruins, craft-making villages and thronged country markets. The people are mostly Zapotec.

The Oaxaca state tourism department, Sedetur, runs nine small self-catering units called *tourist yú'ùs* in the Valles Centrales. (Yú'ù, pronounced 'you,' means 'house' in the Zapotec language.) Most sleep about six people in bunks or on mattresses. Bedding, towels, showers and an equipped kitchen are provided. The cost is US$5 for one person or US$20 for a family of five or six. Some have space for camping at US$2.50 per person. It's advisable to book ahead, either at one of Oaxaca city's two main tourist offices (which can also give you information on the villages where the yú'ùs are) or by calling the individual yú'ùs directly.

Most of the places in the Valles Centrales are accessible by 2nd-class buses from Oaxaca. An alternative to traveling by bus – still cheap, though it will cost you twice as much – is to take a *colectivo* taxi. These run to places north of Oaxaca (such as Atzompa and San José el Mogote) from the street on the north side of the 2nd-class bus station; and to places east, south and southwest (including El Tule, Teotitlán del Valle, San Bartolo Coyotepec, Ocotlán, Arrazola, Cuilapan and Zaachila) from Prolongación Victoria just east of the Central de Abastos market. They leave when full (five or six people).

MONTE ALBÁN

The ancient Zapotec capital Monte Albán (**monh**-teh ahl-**bahn**), which means White Mountain, stands on a flattened hilltop, 400m above the valley floor, just a few kilometers west of Oaxaca. The views from here are spectacular.

History

The site was first occupied around 500 BC, probably by Zapotecs from the outset, with early cultural connections with the Olmecs to the northeast.

Archaeologists divide Monte Albán's history into five phases. The years up to about 200 BC (Monte Albán I) resulted in the leveling of the hilltop, the building of temples and probably also the palaces, and the growth of a town of 10,000 or more people on the hillsides. Between 200 BC and about AD 300 (Monte Albán II) the city came to dominate more and more of Oaxaca. Buildings were typically made of huge stone blocks and had steep walls.

The city was at its peak around AD 300 to AD 700 (Monte Albán III), when the

VALLES CENTRALES

96°45'W

To Lachatao, Guelatao, Ixtlán & Tuxtepec

Guadalupe Etla
San José el Mogote

Atzompa
La Nevería

To Puebla & Mexico City
San Felipe del Agua

Cerro El Bonete

OAXACA
El Tule

Monte Albán
Santa Cruz Xoxocatlán
Teotitlán del Valle

Arrazola
18°15'N
Airport
Tlacochahuaya
San Sebastián Abasolo
Dainzú

Cuilapan
San Bartolo Coyotepec
Valle de Tlacolula

Zaachila

Zimatlán
San Martín Tilcajete
Santo Tomás Jalieza

0   5   10 km
0   3   6 miles

San Pablo Huixtepec

To Puerto Escondido
Ocotlán
To Ejutla, Miahuatlán, San José del Pacífico & Pochutla

96°45'W

OAXACA

main and surrounding hills were terraced for dwellings, and the population reached about 25,000. Most of what we see now dates from this time.

Monte Albán was the center of a highly organized, priest-dominated society, which dominated the extensively irrigated Valles Centrales, home to at least 200 other settlements and ceremonial centers. Many Monte Albán buildings were plastered and painted red, and *talud-tablero* (a style of building with sloped walls and a flat, over-hanging table-top roof) architecture indicates influence from Teotihuacán. Nearly 170 underground tombs from this period have been found, some of them elaborate and decorated with frescoes. Monte Albán's people ate tortillas, beans, squashes, chilies, avocados and other vegetarian fare, plus the odd deer, rabbit or dog.

Between AD 700 and AD 950 (Monte Albán IV), the place was abandoned and fell into ruin. Monte Albán V (950 to 1521) received minimal activity, except for the old tombs that Mixtecs arriving from northwestern Oaxaca reused to bury their own dignitaries.

Information

At the entrance to the site *(☎ 951-516-12-15; admission US$4, free Sun; open 8am to 6pm daily)* has a worthwhile museum (with explanations in Spanish only), a cafeteria and a good bookstore. It's worth asking at the ticket office if any tombs are open – none were open when we last visited. Official guides offer their services in Spanish, English, French and Italian, outside the ticket office (around US$20 for a small group).

Gran Plaza

The Gran Plaza, about 300m long and 200m wide, was the center of Monte Albán. Its visible structures are mostly from the peak Monte Albán III period. Some were temples, others residential. The following description takes you clockwise around the plaza.

The stone terraces of the deep, I-shaped **Juego de Pelota** (Ball Court) were probably part of the playing area, not stands for spectators. The **Pirámide** (Edificio P) was top-ped by a small pillared temple. From the altar in front of it came a well-known jade bat-god mask, now in the Museo Nacional de Antropología in Mexico City. The **Palacio** (Palace) has a broad stairway and, on top, a patio surrounded by the remains of typical Monte Albán III residential rooms. Under the patio is a cross-shaped tomb.

The big **Plataforma Sur** (South Platform), with its wide staircase, is still good for a panorama of the plaza. **Edificio J**, an arrowhead-shaped Monte Albán II building riddled with tunnels and staircases (unfortunately you can't go in), stands at an angle of 45° to the other Gran Plaza structures and, once upon a time, is believed to have been an observatory.

The front of **Sistema M**, dating from Monte Albán III, was added, like the front of Sistema IV, to an earlier structure in an apparent attempt to conceal the plaza's lack of symmetry.

Edificio L is an amalgam of the Monte Albán I building that contained the famous Danzante carvings and a later structure built over it. The **Danzantes** (Dancers), some of which are seen around the lower part of the building, are thought to depict captives and Zapotec leaders. Hieroglyphs accompanying them are the earliest known true writing in Mexico.

Sistema IV, the twin to Sistema M, combines typical Monte Albán II construction with overlays from Monte Albán III and IV.

Plataforma Norte

The North Platform, constructed over a rock outcrop, is almost as big as the Gran Plaza. It was rebuilt several times over the centuries. The chambers on either side of the main staircase contained tombs, and columns at the top of the stairs supported the roof of a hall. On top of the platform is a ceremonial complex built between AD 500 and AD 800; it's composed of Edificios D, VG and E (which were topped with adobe temples) and the Templo de Dos Columnas. Also atop the platform is the **Patio Hundido** (Sunken Patio), with an altar at its center.

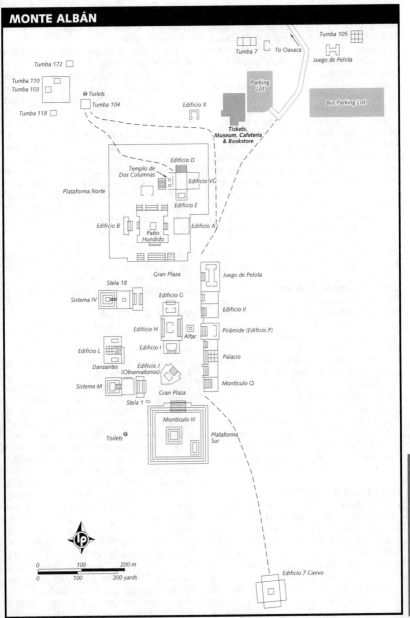

MONTE ALBÁN

Tumba 172

Tumba 110
Tumba 103
Tumba 118

Tumba 7   To Oaxaca

Tumba 105

Juego de Pelota

Parking Lot

Bus Parking Lot

Toilets

Tumba 104

Edificio X

Tickets, Museum, Cafeteria & Bookstore

Edificio D

Templo de Dos Columnas

Edificio VG

Plataforma Norte

Edificio E

Edificio B

Patio Hundido

Edificio A

Gran Plaza

Juego de Pelota

Stela 18

Edificio G

Sistema IV

Edificio II

Edificio H

Pirámide (Edificio P)

Altar

Edificio L

Edificio I

Palacio

Danzantes

Edificio J (Observatorios)

Monticulo Q

Sistema M

Gran Plaza

Stela 1

Monticulo III

Toilets

Plataforma Sur

0   100   200 m
0   100   200 yards

Edificio 7 Ciervo

OAXACA

Tombs

Dating from AD 500 to AD 700, **Tumba 104** is the tomb that you have most chance of finding open, though on our last visit it was closed indefinitely. Above its underground entrance stands an urn in the form of Pitao Cozobi, the Zapotec maize god, wearing a mask of Cocijo, the rain god whose forked tongue represents lightning.

Tumba 7, just off the parking lot, dates from Monte Albán III, but in the 14th or 15th century it was reused by Mixtecs to bury a dignitary, along with two sacrificed servants. It also had one of the richest ancient treasure hoards in the Americas, now housed in the Museo de las Culturas de Oaxaca in Oaxaca city.

Tumba 105, on the hill called Cerro del Plumaje (Hill of the Plumage), features decaying Teotihuacán-influenced murals showing figures that may represent nine gods of death or night, and their female consorts.

Getting There & Away

From Hotel Rivera del Ángel in Oaxaca, **Autobuses Turísticos** (☎ 951-516-53-27; Mina 518) runs buses to the site (US$2.50 return, 20 minutes). They usually leave every 30 minutes from 8:30am to 2pm, and at 3pm, 3:30pm and 4pm. The fare includes a return trip at a designated time, giving you about two hours at the site. If you want to stay longer, you must hope for a spare place on a later return bus, and pay a further US$1.25. The last buses back leave at 5pm and 6pm.

A taxi from Oaxaca to Monte Albán costs about US$7, but returning to Oaxaca you may have to pay more. Walking up from the city center takes about 1½ hours.

VALLE DE TLACOLULA

The unremarkable village of **El Tule** (population 6800), 10km east of Oaxaca along Hwy 190, draws crowds of visitors for one reason: **El Árbol del Tule** (the Tree of El Tule), which is claimed to be the biggest single biomass in the world. This vast *ahuehuete* tree (a type of cypress), 58m around and 42m high, towers in the village churchyard (admission US$0.30; open 9am-5pm daily), dwarfing the 17th-century church. Its

age is even more impressive; the tree is officially reckoned to be between 2000 and 3000 years old.

The famous weaving village of **Teotitlán del Valle** (population 4600) is 4km north of Hwy 190, about 25km from Oaxaca. Blankets, rugs and sarapes wave at you from houses and showrooms along the road into the village (which becomes Av Juárez as it approaches the center), and signs point to the central **Mercado de Artesanías**, where yet more are on sale. The weaving tradition here goes back to pre-Hispanic times.

From Oaxaca's 2nd-class bus station, AVN buses go to El Tule every 10 minutes (US$0.30). AVN buses go depart for Teotitlán (US$0.60, 50 minutes, hourly) from Gate 29, from 7am to 9pm (less frequently on Sunday). The last bus back from Teotitlán leaves at about 7pm. Any Mitla- or Tlacolula-bound bus will drop you at the signposted Teotitlán turnoff (US$0.70) on Hwy 190; catch a local bus or a *colectivo* taxi (US$0.40) to the village from there.

VALLE DE ETLA

Atzompa (pop 9180), 6km northwest of Oaxaca, is a village with many potters. Much of their attractive, colorful work is sold for excellent prices in the **Mercado de Artesanías** (Libertad 303; open daily), on the main road entering the village from Oaxaca. From the church up in the village center, a 2.5km road (mostly dirt) leads south up **Cerro El Bonete**, the top of which is dotted with unrestored pre-Hispanic ruins.

About 14km northwest of central Oaxaca on Hwy 190, a westward turnoff signposted to Guadalupe Etla leads about 2km to **San José el Mogote**, a tiny village indicated by a 'Museo Comunitario Ex-Hacienda El Cacique' sign. Long ago, before Monte Albán became important, Mogote was the major settlement in Oaxaca. It was at its peak between 650 BC and 500 BC, and flourished again between 100 BC and AD 150. Its zócalo was almost as big as Monte Alban's. The major surviving structures (partly restored) are a ball court and a sizable pyramid-mound on the village periphery. The interesting **community museum**

(☎ 951-521-44-66; village center; admission US$1; open 9am-6pm daily) is in the former landowner's hacienda. If you find it closed (as you probably will), either wander around and look lost or ask someone to find the keeper – both work.

Choferes del Sur, at gate 39 of Oaxaca's 2nd-class bus station, runs buses every few minutes to Atzompa (US$0.30). *Colectivo* taxi is a fairly easy way to get to Mogote: see the Valles Centrales Getting There & Away section.

VALLE DE ZIMATLÁN
Arrazola, Cuilapan & Zaachila
Below the west side of Monte Albán and about 4km off the Cuilapan road, **Arrazola** (pop 1000) produces many of the colorful copal *alebrijes* (wooden animals) that are sold in Oaxaca. You can see and buy them in artisans' homes.

Cuilapan (pop 11,200), 12km southwest of Oaxaca, is one of the few Mixtec enclaves in the Valles Centrales. It's the site of a beautiful, historic Dominican monastery, the **Ex-Convento de Santiago Apóstol** (admission US$2.50; open 9am-5pm daily), whose pale stone seems almost to grow out of the land. It's a perfect spot for a picnic especially after a bike ride from the city.

The part-Mixtec, part-Zapotec village of **Zaachila** (pop 12,000), 6km beyond Cuilapan, has a busy Thursday market. Zaachila was a Zapotec capital from about 1400 until the Spanish conquest. There are half a dozen pre-Hispanic monoliths as well as the village church standing on the main plaza. Up the road behind the church, then along a path to the right, the **Zona Arqueológica'** (admission US$2.50, free Sun & holidays; open 8am-5pm daily) has mounds containing at least two tombs used by the ancient Mixtecs.

From Oaxaca, Añasa runs buses to Zaachila and Cuilapan (US$0.40) about every 15 minutes from its terminal at Bustamante 604, five blocks south of the zócalo.

San Bartolo Coyotepec
All the polished, black, surprisingly light pottery you find around Oaxaca comes from San Bartolo Coyotepec (pop 2800), a small village about 12km south of the city. Several families make and sell the *barro negro* (black ware). The method of burnishing it with quartz stones for the distinctive shine was invented by Real Mateo (1900–80). Look for the signs to her family pottery workshop **Alfarería Doña Rosa** (☎ 951-551-00-11; Juárez 24; open 9am-6.30pm daily), a short walk east off the highway.

Buses run to San Bartolo Coyotepec (US$0.50, 20 minutes) every few minutes from the terminal at Armenta y López 721, 500m south of the Oaxaca zócalo.

San Martín Tilcajete
This village, just west of Hwy 175 about 27km south of Oaxaca, is the main source of many of the bright copal *alebrijes* seen in Oaxaca. You can see and buy them in makers' houses.

Ocotlán
The bustling Friday market at Ocotlán (pop 11,500), 32km south of Oaxaca, dates back to pre-Hispanic times and is one of the biggest in the Valles Centrales. Ocotlán's most renowned artisans are the four **Aguilar sisters** and their families, who create whimsical, colorful pottery figures of women with all sorts of unusual motifs. The Aguilars' houses are together by the highway before you get into the town center, and are identified by the pottery women on the wall.

Buses to Ocotlán (US$1, 45 minutes) leave every few minutes from the terminal at Armenta y López 721 in Oaxaca.

SAN JOSÉ DEL PACÍFICO
The small village of San José del Pacífico, about an hour south of Miahuatlán on Hwy 175 to Pochutla, is just outside the Valles Centrales but en route to the coast. It's famed for its magic mushrooms, but is also a good base for walks through the cool mountain pine forests.

You can get basic rooms at **Cabañas Rayito del Sol** (singles/doubles with shared bath US$6.75/13.50) in the village, and better rooms and cabanas at **Cabañas y Restaurante Puesta del Sol** (singles US$23, room for 2-4 people US$45) on Hwy 175, 500m

OAXACA

north of the village. Book both by calling the **caseta telefónica** (☎ 951-572-01-11).

All Hwy 175 buses between Oaxaca and Pochutla stop at San José.

Oaxaca Coast

A laid-back spell on the beautiful Oaxaca coast is the perfect complement to the inland attractions of Oaxaca city and the Valles Centrales. The trip down Hwy 175 from Oaxaca is spectacular: South of Miahuatlán you climb into pine forests, then descend into ever lusher and hotter tropical forest.

In the last 20 years, newly paved roads and scheduled flights to Puerto Escondido and Bahías de Huatulco have brought this once remote area closer to the rest of Mexico. As a result, the fishing villages and former coffee ports of Puerto Escondido and Puerto Ángel have turned into minor resorts, but they remain small and relaxed – Puerto Ángel especially so. Puerto Escondido has famous surf, while Puerto Ángel is at the center of a series of wonderful beaches with plenty of low-cost accommodations – among them that fabled backpackers' hangout, Zipolite. To the east, a new tourist resort on the Bahías de Huatulco is being developed with *some* respect for the area's lovely surroundings.

West of Puerto Escondido, nature lovers can visit the lagoons of Manialtepec and Chacahua, teeming with birdlife.

The coast is hotter and much more humid than the highlands. Most of the year's rain falls between June and September, turning everything green. From October the landscape starts to dry out, and by March many of the trees – which are mostly deciduous – are leafless. May is the hottest month.

The coast is described from west to east, except for the areas around Pochulta (including Puerto Ángel, Zipolite and Mazunte) which are easiest described as they radiate from that transport hub.

Internet Resources

The website for the **Pacific Coast of Oaxaca** (W *www.tomzap.com*) is a mine of information about the coast.

Accommodations

The peak tourism seasons on this coast are from mid-December to mid-January, Semana Santa, and the months of July and August. At other times hotel prices may come down anywhere between 10% and 50% from the prices we list.

Getting There & Away

If you're coming from Guerrero (Acapulco usually), Pinotepa Nacional will be the first major town you'll pass on Hwy 200. From Oaxaca, you'll either hit Pochutla from Hwy 175, Puerto Escondido from Hwy 131 and Bahías de Huatulco from Hwy 190/Hwy 200. See Getting There & Away in the Oaxaca City section for routes from Oaxaca city.

PINOTEPA NACIONAL

☎ 954 • pop 25,100

Pinotepa is the biggest town between Puerto Escondido (145km) and Acapulco (260km). It's an important market town and urban center for indigenous Mixtecs and Amuzgos who live here and in outlying villages. Though there's little to do *in* Pinotepa, there is lots to do *around* the town, and many of the nearby villages, most of them Mixtec, make good day trips.

Walk out of the Estrella Blanca bus terminal and the main plaza will be two blocks to the right (east). Two banks on the main drag, **Bancomer** and **Bancrecer**, change traveler's checks and have ATMs.

The following hotels are friendly and clean and have private bathrooms with hot water.

Hotel Marissa (☎ 543-21-01; *Juárez 134; singles & doubles US$11.50, rooms with 2 beds US$16*), a block east of the central zócalo, has small rooms with windows.

Hotel Carmona (☎ 543-22-22; *Porfirio Díaz 127; singles/doubles with fan US$18/ 23, with air-con US$26/36*), on the main road west of the bus terminal, is the sharpest hotel in town and has a pool.

Tacos Orientales (*Av Pérez Gasga s/n; open 6pm-2am daily*) serves 16 combinations of delicious tacos, including a creative *vegetariano* version. All are US$2.50 to US$3 for a filling plate.

Aside from buses along Hwy 200, 1st-class Cristóbal Colón buses and 2nd-class Fypsa and TOI buses travel north on Hwy 125 through the Mixteca Alta, some reaching Oaxaca city that way.

AROUND PINOTEPA NACIONAL
Playa Corralero
Southwest of Pinotepa, Playa Corralero is a fine beach near the mouth of **Laguna Corralero**. You can stay in *palapas* (thatched-roof shelters) at Corralero village. To get there from Pinotepa by car go about 25km west on Hwy 200, then some 15km southeast. Two *camionetas* (pickups) run there daily from Pinotepa.

East of Pinotepa Nacional
About a 20-minute drive east of Pinotepa the village of **Huazolotitlán** is famous for its colorful wooden Carnaval masks; the village maestro is **José Luna Lopez**, and anyone can point you to his home. Another long-time carver to ask for is **Florencio Gallardo Sanchez**. There are many others.

The mainly Mixtec town of **Jamiltepec** (pop 19,000), 30km east of Pinotepa Nacional on Hwy 200, holds a colorful Sunday market below the *plaza central*. Many Mixtec women here wear their colorful *pozahuancos*. Pozahuancos are horizontally striped, purple wraparound skirts traditionally dyed with purpura (a purple dye made from the shells of sea snails from near Huatulco) and cochineal (a red dye made from tiny insects living on the prickly pear cactus in the Mixteca Alta). Mixtec women traditionally wear nothing above the waist, but now often don a small white cloth draped loosely over their shoulders as a nod to the mestizo culture. Mixteca men dress mostly in white.

Buses to both places leave from a small terminal on Pinotepa's main drag just east of the zócalo.

North of Pinotepa Nacional
It's a refreshing 45-minute drive into the foothills northeast of Pinotepa Nacional to the Mixtec town of **Pinotepa Don Luis**. This is by far the most important Carnaval town

on the coast. Each February the town fills with wildly costumed dancers who perform traditional *danzas* (dances) for eight days before Carnaval, and the celebration finally culminates with a giant *asado* (barbeque) and plenty of merrymaking. Don Luis is also known for the colorfully embroidered napkins, placemats and *rebozos* (shawls) that are sold around the village and throughout the state. If you're seriously interested in purchasing these types of crafts (including *pozahuancos*) contact **Marcela Franco** (☎ 954-542-00-37; Hidalgo 27), who lives a block off the zócalo.

About a 15-minute drive above Don Luis is the even tinier village of **San Juan Colorado**, another important Carnaval town. It's known for its wooden masks carved from the dark brown heartwood of the *guanacastle* or *parota*. Ask around for the workshops of master-carver **Marciano Hernandez Reyes**, his son **Emiliano Hernandez Nicolas** or **Margarito Tapia Cosio**, all of whom carve masks and just about anything else you might be interested in, and will sell from their homes. Or ask anyone to point you to a *fábrica de máscaras* (mask-maker); there are many in town.

About a 1½-hour's drive north of Pinotepa Nacional on Hwy 125, **San Pedro Amuzgos** is known for its fine *huipiles* (colorfully embroidered shawls).

Colectivos to Don Luis leave Pinotepa Nacional's main drag near the corner of Calle 21a Sur, about five blocks west of the main plaza (US$1.65, 45 minutes). From Don Luis, get another *colectivo* from the main plaza to San Juan Colorado (US$0.75, 15 minutes).

PARQUE NACIONAL LAGUNAS DE CHACAHUA
The area around the coastal lagoons of Chacahua and La Pastoría forms the beautiful Parque Nacional Lagunas de Chacahua. Birds from Alaska and Canada migrate here in winter. Mangrove-fringed islands harbor cormorants, wood storks, herons, egrets, ibis and roseate spoonbills, as well as mahogany trees, crocodiles and turtles. El Corral, a mangrove-lined waterway filled with

OAXACA

countless birds, connects the two lagoons. Both **Hidden Voyage Ecotours** and **Ana's Ecotours** (see Organized Tours in the Puerto Escondido section) offer day trips out here from Puerto once a week.

Zapotalito

About 60km from Puerto Escondido, a 5km road leads south from Hwy 200 to Zapotalito, a small fishing village with a few simple restaurants on the eastern edge of La Pastoría lagoon. A cooperative here runs three- to four-hour **boat tours** of the lagoons (US$80 for a boatload up to 10 people). The trips visit islands, channels to the ocean, and the fishing village of Chacahua at the western end of the park.

You can travel straight to Chacahua village by a *colectivo* boat/truck combination (see Getting There & Away), that departs about 300m further round the shore beyond the *lancha* (motor boat) tour departure point.

Chacahua

Chacahua village straddles the channel that connects the west end of Chacahua lagoon to the ocean; half the village is on the inland side of the lagoon and half is on the ocean side. The ocean side of the village, fronting a wonderful beach, is a perfect place to bliss out for the day, or longer. The waves here can be good for surfing, but there are sometimes strong currents; check where it's safe to swim. Besides having the village's only bar – **California Uno** – the inland half of the village contains a **crocodile-breeding center** with a sad-looking collection of creatures kept for protection and reproduction. Chacahua's croc population (not human-eating) has been decimated by hunters.

Places to Stay & Eat Accommodation is simple but enjoyable in Chacahua and the seafood is always fresh.

Restaurant & Cabañas 7 Mares (mains US$5-12) is the restaurant closest to the lagoon and still on the sand. It's open for breakfast and lunch and cooks up some truly mind-blowing *sierra al mojo de ajo* (Spanish mackerel cooked with garlic) and huge plates of lobster. Breakfasts are hearty.

The **cabanas** (1-4 people US$8-13) are just down the beach and have sand floors, fans, mosquito nets and electric lighting. There are two shared toilets and a well for bathing.

Cabañas Los Almendros (cabanas US$11-14) is a friendly little place facing the lagoon with three very creative cabanas and very friendly owners. One of the upstairs cabanas is open-air and overlooks the lagoon, and another is literally over the water (you often get your feet wet entering). There are a few other rooms too, but they're rather claustrophobic.

Other restaurants on the beach will let you **camp** for free if you eat in their restaurant, or you can just wander down the beach and throw out your tent or blanket.

Getting There & Away From Puerto Escondido, you first have to get to the town of Rio Grande, 50km west on Hwy 200. Rio Grande-bound microbuses (US$1.50, one hour) leave from Calle 2 Norte just east of the Carretera Costera (Hwy 200), in the upper part of Puerto, about every half-hour. All EB buses between Puerto Escondido and Acapulco stop at Rio Grande too. From the bus stop in Rio Grande, cross the road and get a *colectivo* taxi (US$0.70) to Zapotalito, 14km southwest.

The cheapest way to Chacahua from Zapotalito is by boat/bus combo: go to the *colectivo* boat dock about 300m past the boat tours departure docks. Boats leave daily at 7:45am, 9:15am, 11am, 1:30pm, 3:30pm, and 5:30pm and make the 15-minute zip (US$1.10) across part of the lagoon to meet a *camioneta* (pickup truck) which then takes you to Chacahua (US$1.10, 30 minutes). It's US$30 to US$45 to hire a boat and go by water all the way to Chacahua – more scenic.

The inland side of Chacahua village is linked to San José del Progreso, 29km north on Hwy 200, by a sandy track that is impassable in the wet season. Locals say a daily *colectivo* runs out to San José and back a few times a day.

PUERTO ESCONDIDO

☎ 954 • pop 50,000

Known to surfers since before paved roads reached these parts, Puerto Escondido (the

Hidden Port) remains relatively small, laid-back and inexpensive. Puerto Escondido has several beaches, a range of reasonable accommodations, excellent restaurants and some nightlife.

Orientation

Puerto Escondido rises above the small, south-facing Bahía Principal. Hwy 200 runs across the hill halfway up, dividing the upper town where the locals live and work, and buses arrive, from the lower, tourism-dominated part. The heart of the lower town is the pedestrianized section of Av Pérez Gasga, known as El Adoquín (*adoquín* is Spanish for paving stone). The west end of Pérez Gasga winds up the slope to meet Hwy 200 at an intersection known simply as El Crucero.

Bahía Principal curves around, at its east end, to the long surf beach Playa Zicatela, which is backed by loads more places to stay and eat. Other beaches line a series of bays to the west.

Information

The very helpful **tourist information office** (*e* ginainpuerto@yahoo.com; open 9am-2pm & 4pm-6pm Mon-Fri, 10am-2pm Sat) is at the west end of the Adoquín and is run almost exclusively by the multilingual Gina Machorro, probably the most enthusiastic tourist information officer on the entire coast. The **main tourist office** (☎ 582-01-75) is about 2.5km west of the center on the road to the airport, at the corner of Blvd Juárez.

There's a handy **Bital ATM** on the Adoquín next to Restaurant Los Crotos. **Banamex** (cnr Pérez Gasga & Unión), changes US and Canadian dollars and US dollars traveler's checks from 9am to noon Monday to Friday. **Bancrecer** (Hidalgo 4), **Bancomer** (Calle 3 Poniente) and **Bital** (Calle 1 Norte), all in the upper part of town, change money from 9am to noon Monday to Friday and can be faster. All these banks have ATMs.

The town's *casas de cambio* (exchange houses) give worse rates than the banks but are open longer hours. Try **Centro Cambiario del Puerto** (Pérez Gasga 905H; open 10am-3pm & 4pm-9pm Mon-Sat, 10am-2pm & 5pm-8pm Sun) at Hotel Casa Blanca, or **Condig Money Exchange** (Pérez Gasga s/n; open 9am-2pm & 4pm-9pm Mon-Sat).

The **post office** (Oaxaca at Calle 7 Norte; open 9am-4pm Mon-Fri, 9am-1pm Sat) is a 20- to 30-minute uphill walk from the seafront, or you can take a 'Mercado' bus or *colectivo* taxi up Av Oaxaca.

Pay phones and a couple of *casetas telefónicas* are on the Adoquín.

Internet cafés are easy to find. On the Adoquín try **Servinet** (Pérez Gasga 705; US$1.10 per hour; open 9am-midnight daily) or **Cofee Net** (US$1.50 per hour; open 8am-10pm daily), with one location on El Adoquín and another at Hotel Surf Olas Altas (see Places to Stay).

The free bimonthly paper *El Sol de la Costa*, in Spanish and English, is full of information about what to do. It's on the web at **w** www.puertoconnection.com. Canadian Helena Szustka (aka Lucy Sonido) DJs a Spanish/English radio show on 94.1 FM from 3pm to 5pm Wednesday, 11am to noon on Saturday, and 8pm to 10pm Sunday. She plays an eclectic music set and covers what's going on in Puerto.

Get your clothes washed (they need it) for US$1.50 per kilo at **Lavamática del Centro** (Pérez Gasga 405A; open 8am-8pm Mon-Sat, 8am-5pm Sun).

Puerto Escondido has had an up-and-down reputation with regard to safety. To minimize risks, avoid isolated or empty places, and stick to well-lit areas at night (or use taxis). Especially take care at night on the beach at Playa Zicatela and in the rocks area between Zicatela and Playa Marinero. It's probably best to avoid altogether the coastal walkway passing the lighthouse.

Beaches

Bahía Principal (or Playa Principal) is the main town beach and is long enough to accommodate restaurants at its west end, sun worshipers at the east end and beached fishing *pangas* (small skiffs) in the middle. Boats bob on the swell, and a few hawkers wander up and down, offering textiles, hammocks and necklaces. The smelly water entering the bay at times from the inaptly

OAXACA

OAXACA

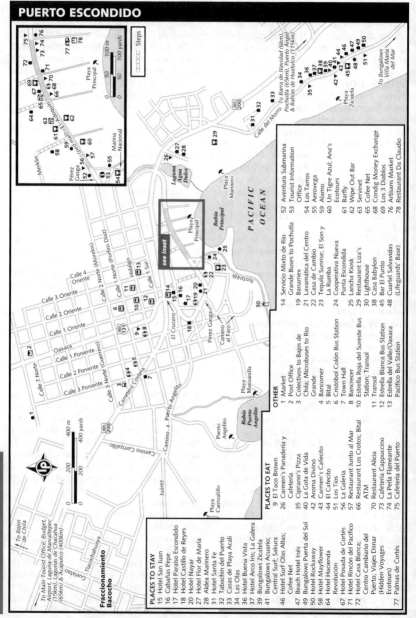

PUERTO ESCONDIDO

Steps

To Main Tourist Office, Budget, Airport, Laguna de Manialtepec (15km), Laguna de Chacahua (65km) & Acapulco (400km)

Fraccionamiento Bacocho

To Bajos de Chila

Cuatlao

Juárez

Tlacochahuaya

To Bajos de Chila

Playa Carrizalillo

Bahía Puerto Angelito

Puerto Angelito

Playa Manzanilla

Bahía Principal

Playa Principal

see inset

PACIFIC OCEAN

Playa Marinero

Laguna Agua Dulce

Playa Zicatela

To Barra de Navidad (6km), Pochutla (65km), Puerto Ángel & Bahías de Huatulco (115km)

To Bungalows Villa María del Mar

Calle del Morro

Calle 4 Oriente

Calle 3 Oriente

Calle 2 Oriente

Calle 1 Oriente

Oaxaca

Calle 1 Poniente

Calle 2 Poniente

Calle 3 Poniente

Calle 7 Norte

Calle 3 Norte (Guerrero)

Calle 2 Norte (Morelos)

Calle 1 Norte (Porfirio Díaz)

Hidalgo

El Crucero

Pérez Gasga

Camino al Faro

Carretera Costera

Camino a Puerto Angelito

Camino Carrizalillo

Marina Nacional

Pérez Gasga

Av Alfonso Pérez Gasga

Merklin

Playa Principal

PLACES TO STAY
15 Hotel San Juan
16 Cabañas Pepe
17 Hotel Paraíso Escondido
18 Hotel Castillo de Reyes
20 Hotel Nayar
27 Hotel Flor de María
28 Aldea Marinero
31 Hotel Santa Fe
32 Tabachín del Puerto
33 Casas de Playa Acali
34 Las Olas
36 Hotel Buena Vista
37 Hotel Arco Iris; La Galera
39 Bungalows Zicatela
41 Bungalows Acuario;
    Central Surf, Sakura
46 Hotel Surf Olas Altas;
    Cofee Net
47 Beach Hotel Inés
49 Bungalows Puerta del Sol
50 Hotel Rockaway
58 Hotel Mayflower
64 Hotel Hacienda
    Revolución
67 Hotel Posada de Cortés
71 Hotel Rincón del Pacífico
72 Hotel Casa Blanca;
    Centro Cambiario del
    Puerto; Viajes Dimar
    (Hidden Voyages)
    Ecotours)
77 Palmas de Cortés

PLACES TO EAT
9 El Taco Brown
26 Carmen's Panadería y
    Cafetería
35 Cipriano's Pizza
40 La Gota de Vida
42 Aroma Divino
43 Carmen's Cafecito
44 El Cafecito
51 Los Tíos
56 La Galería
57 Restaurant Junto al Mar
66 Restaurant Los Crotos; Bital
    ATM
70 Restaurant Alicia
73 Cafetería Cappuccino
74 La Perla Flameante
75 Cafetería del Puerto

OTHER
1 Market
2 Post Office
3 Colectivos to Bajos de
    Chila; Microbuses to Río
    Grande
4 Bancomer
5 Bital
6 Cristóbol Colón Bus Station
7 Town Hall
8 Bancrecer
10 Estrella Roja del Sureste Bus
    Station; Transol
11 Transol
12 Estrella Blanca Bus Station
13 Estrella del Valle/Oaxaca
    Pacífico Bus Station
14 Servicio Mixto de Río
    Grande Buses to Pochutla
19 Banamex
21 Lavamática del Centro
22 Casa de Cambio
23 Tequila Sunrise; El Son y
    La Rumba
24 Cooperativa Nueva
    Punta Escondida
25 Lancha Kiosk
29 Restaurant Liza's
30 Lighthouse
38 Casa Babylon
45 Bar El Punto
48 Cuartel Salvavidas
    (Lifeguards' Base)
52 Aventura Submarina
53 Tourist Information
    Office
54 Los Tarros
55 Aerovega
59 Álamo
60 Un Tigre Azul; Ana's
    Ecotours
61 Barfly
62 Wipe Out Bar
63 Servinet
65 Cofee Net
68 Condig Money Exchange
69 Los 3 Diablos
76 Artisans Market
78 Restaurant Da Claudio

named Laguna Agua Dulce (Sweetwater Lagoon) will put you off dipping anywhere other than **Playa Marinero**, a good swimming beach beginning near the rocks at the east end of the Bahía Principal.

Playa Zicatela still remains Mexico's legendary, board-snapping, ego-taming surf beach and it stretches several kilometers west from Playa Marinero and begins after a short walk along the sand from Bahía Principal. The 'Mexican Pipeline,' as it's called, is best left for surfers, however, as its lethal undertow and powerful waves tend to make mincemeat of swimmers. Lifeguards rescue several careless people most months (their base, the Cuartel Salvavidas, is in front of Hotel Surf Olas Altas).

The sheltered bay of **Puerto Angelito**, about 1km west of the Bahía Principal as the crow flies, has two small beaches separated by a few rocks. **Playa Manzanilla**, the more easterly of the two, is quieter because vehicles can't reach it. **Playa Carrizalillo**, a small beach just west of Puerto Angelito, is in a rockier cove but is OK for swimming. It has a bar with a few palapas for shade. *Lanchas* will whisk you from Bahía Principal to these beaches (see Getting Around later).

Playa Bacocho is a long, straight beach on the open ocean west of Carrizalillo; it has a dangerous undertow.

Activities

More than anything, Puerto is known for surfing. The main break is Zicatela (see Beaches earlier) and it's at its biggest from late-April to August. When it's big it's unforgiving, offering serious punishment to all but the most experienced surfers. If you're a beginner, try **La Punta**, a rolling left point at the far end of Playa Zicatela. When swells are really pumping, Carrizalillo shapes up with some soft lefts and fast rights out over the reef.

You are able to rent **surfboards** and **boogie boards** from shops along Calle del Morro at Playa Zicatela. The best selection can be found at **Central Surf** (☎ 582-22-85; w *www.centralsurf.com; Morro s/n; open 9am-2pm & 4pm-7pm daily*), located in the

Hotel Acuario building. Shortboards cost US$11 to US$13 per day and long-boards go for US$15. Central Surf also offers surfing lessons for US$27 per hour.

Lanchas from the west end of Bahía Principal will take groups of four or five people out for about an hour's **turtle-spotting** (and, in winter, sometimes dolphin-spotting) for around US$33, with a drop-off at Puerto Angelito or Playa Carizalillo, if you like.

Local marlin fishers and sailfishers will take two to four people **fishing** with them for three hours for about US$100. Ask at the *lancha* kiosk at the west end of Bahía Principal or at the **Cooperativa Nueva Punta Escondida** (☎ 582-16-78; *Marina Nacional s/n*). The price usually includes cooking up some of the catch for you at one of the seafood restaurants in the town.

Diving is another possibility. Owned by PADI instructor Jorge Bravo, **Aventura Submarina** (☎ 582-23-53; *Pérez Gasga 601A; open 9am-2pm & 6pm-9:30pm daily*) offers PADI certification courses and dive trips for all levels. It's a professional operation receiving heaps of praise. One-/two-tank dive trips cost US$39/60 per person, and a four-day, open-water certification course costs US$350.

Organized Tours

Nearby Laguna de Manialtepec (see that section later) makes an excellent day trip – especially if you're a bird-watcher. Canadian ornithologist Mike Malone, owner of **Hidden Voyage Ecotours** (☎ 582-07-34, 582-15-51; w *www.wincom.net/~pelewing*), offers outstanding, early-morning birding excursions on the lagoon for US$37 per person, December to April only. He also does a sunset cruise on Manialtepec which incorporates swimming and a bottle of wine on the beach at sundown. His office is inside **Viajes Dimar** (*Pérez Gasga 905; open 7:30am -10pm*) on El Adoquín.

Ana's Ecotours (☎ 582-29-54; w *www .anasecotours.com; Pérez Gasga s/n*) provides similar tours year-round. It also offers four-hour kayaking trips on Manialtepec and nearby Los Naranjos lagoon, southeast of town (both US$33 per person).

OAXACA

Special Events

Semana Santa is a big week for local partying; a local surf carnival is held at this time. At least two international surf contests are held on Zicatela each year, usually in August or September, and the national surfing championships happen on the last weekend of November.

November is a big month in other ways too: the **Festival Costeña de la Danza**, a fiesta of Oaxaca coastal dance, and a sailfish-fishing contest and art exhibitions all take place over the second and/or third weekends of the month. Puerto recently started up a February **Carnaval** celebration, but it's still pretty low key.

Places to Stay

The two main accommodation zones are El Adoquín and the surf beach Playa Zicatela. Playa Marinero is basically the western extension of Zicatela. In the peak seasons the most popular places will probably be full. Any breath of breeze can be at a premium in Puerto, and you're more likely to get one in a place up on a hill.

Several apartments and houses are available for short and long stays. Apartments start from around US$400/800 a month in low/high season; houses overlooking the beach are around US$675/1350. Ask at the tourist information office on El Adoquín.

El Adoquín & Around The only official camping ground in the area is **Palmas de Cortés** (☎ 582-29-17; *Bahía Principal; camp sites per person US$3.50 plus US$3.50 per vehicle*). It's a friendly, palm-shaded place on Bahía Principal, just off El Adoquín. Amenities include showers, electrical hook-ups, fireplaces and 24-hour supervision.

Hotel Mayflower (☎ 582-03-67; *Andador Libertad s/n;* ⓔ *minnemay7@hotmail.com; dorm beds US$6, private rooms for up to 3 US$20-27*), up a flight of steps from the west end of El Adoquín, has a few fan-cooled dorms and some very spacious private rooms, some with balconies. Rates include filtered water and use of a fridge, microwave and pool table. There's a roof-top pizzeria and a bar open in the evening.

Cabañas Pepe (☎ 582-20-37; *Merklin 201; singles US$11, doubles, triples & quads US$16.50*), just below El Crucero, is a laid back, family-run place with basic rooms around a dirt parking area. Top-floor rooms are best: they have hammocks outside and some have good views. All have private, cold-water baths.

Hotel Castillo de Reyes (☎/fax 582-04-42; *Pérez Gasga 210; singles/doubles US$16/20*) is a good-value hotel with 18 sizable and clean rooms, each with two double beds, fans and bathrooms.

Hotel Hacienda Revolución (☎/fax 582-18-18; *Andador Revolución 21; singles/doubles US$16/27*) up a flight of stairs from the Adoquín, has 11 modest, quiet rooms with attractively tiled bathrooms, decent furniture and colorful paintwork. Most have a patio and hammock.

Hotel San Juan (☎ 582-05-18; ⓦ *www.hotelsanjuan.cjb.net; Merklin 503; doubles US$22-33*), a friendly place just below El Crucero, has 30 good rooms with hot water and mosquito screens; the more expensive rooms are bigger, with private terraces and good views. The hotel has a swimming pool and a roof-top sitting area.

Hotel Posada de Cortés (☎ 582-07-74; ⓔ *cortes@ptoescondido.com.mx; Pérez Gasga 218; singles & doubles without/with air-con US$30/38*) is built around a pleasant patio/garden just above El Adoquín. The standard rooms ('bungalows') come with a kitchen. There are also more expensive 'suites.'

Hotel Rincón del Pacífico (☎ 582-00-56; ⓔ *rconpaci@prodigy.net.mx; Pérez Gasga 900; singles/doubles with fan US$26/33, with air-con US$44/55*), on El Adoquín, has 20 or so rooms with big windows set around a palm courtyard. It has its own beachside café/restaurant.

Hotel Casa Blanca (☎ 582-01-68; *Pérez Gasga 905; singles/doubles US$30/38*) is a popular, spotless place on El Adoquín with a small pool. It's friendly and fills up quickly. The best of its 21 large rooms have balconies overlooking the street.

Hotel Nayar (☎ 582-01-13; *Pérez Gasga 407; doubles with fan/air-con US$33/42*) gets a good breeze in its wide sitting areas and has a pool. Its 40-odd rooms have hot water, TV and small balconies. Some have sea views.

Hotel Paraíso Escondido (☎ 582-04-44; *Unión 10; singles/doubles US$98/108)* is owned by a group of architects and designers. A rambling whitewash-and-blue hotel, it's decorated with lots of tile, pottery, stained glass and stone sculpture by well-known Mexican artists. The 20 clean, moderately sized rooms have air-con, and there's an attractive restaurant/bar/pool area.

Playa Marinero On a small lane going back from Playa Marinero, **Aldea Marinero** (*1a Entrada a Playa Marinero; singles/doubles US$6/8)* has cabanas with canvas beds, mosquito nets, hammocks out front and clean, shared bathrooms.

Hotel Flor de María (☎ 582-05-36; w www .mexonline.com/flordemaria.htm; *singles & doubles US$38-50)*, on a little lane behind Playa Marinero, has a small rooftop pool and bar, a TV room and a restaurant. Its 24 ample, nicely decorated rooms, each with two double beds, are set around a courtyard.

Casas de Playa Acali (☎ 582-07-54; *cabanas US$33, with kitchen US$40, with kitchen & air-con US$71)* has 15 wooden cabanas of various sizes. All have private bathroom and mosquito netting. The two priciest have two rooms each, air-con and large kitchens. The rest (except for one kitchenless double) have two double beds and a smaller kitchen. Other amenities include a swimming pool and a bar. Almost all sleep up to four.

Tabachín del Puerto (☎ 582-11-79; w www .tabachin.com.mx; *rooms US$55-82)*, up a short lane behind Hotel Santa Fe, offers six stunning studio rooms of various sizes, all with kitchen, air-con, TV and phone. The decor and furniture range from folksy Mexican to classical fine-art; most have balcony access. Some rooms can take up to four people. The vegetarian breakfast, which includes organically grown coffee and fruits from the owners' mountain farm, is a big bonus.

Hotel Santa Fe (☎ 582-01-70; w www.ho telsantafe.com.mx; *singles/doubles US$82/ 99,*

bungalows US$95/111), behind the rocky outcrop dividing Playa Marinero and Playa Zicatela, has 51 attractive rooms set around small terraces and a palm-fringed pool. Rooms vary in size and view, but good design makes most of them agreeable. Many have air-con. Also available are eight appealing bungalows with kitchens. The restaurant is superb.

Playa Zicatela The following places are along Calle del Morro, either on or across this street from the beach.

Las Olas (☎ 582-09-19; e zazielucassen@ hotmail.com; *Morro 15; singles/doubles/ triples US$23/23/34)* has seven good cabanas and bungalows, each with a private bathroom, fan, screens and a fridge; some have stoves and most have a TV.

Hotel Buena Vista (☎ 582-14-74; e bue navista101@hotmail.com; *singles & doubles US$11-27)*, on the steep hillside above Calle del Morro, has 16 plain, reasonably sized rooms, all with mosquito screens or nets. The cheapest are at the top and have a shared cement terrace with hammocks and incredible views; the most expensive units have kitchenettes, air-con and fewer stairs to climb.

Hotel Arco Iris (☎ 582-04-32; e arcoiris@ ptoescondido.com.mx; *singles & doubles US$40-49, triples & quads with kitchen US$54)* has 32 big, clean rooms with balconies or terraces looking straight out to the surf, plus a large pool and a good upstairs restaurant/bar open to the breeze.

Bungalows Zicatela (☎ 582-07-98; *doubles US$50, bungalow doubles US$55-77)*, next door to Arco Iris and behind its own restaurant, has 12 spacious bungalows that are squeezed around a small, sociable pool area. All have mosquito-netted windows, are solidly built, and some have kitchenettes. A couple of two-story blocks hold more rooms, each with two double beds.

Bungalows Acuario (☎ 582-10-27; e bun acuario@hotmail.com; *rooms with fan/air-con US$51/60, cabanas without/with view US$51/ 88)* has 30 units that range from cramped rooms to wooden cabanas to spacious upstairs rooms with terrace and beach view. All have mosquito nets and there's a good pool.

Hotel Surf Olas Altas (☎ 582-23-15; **w** www
.surfolasaltas.com.mx; Morro 310; singles/
doubles/triples US$77/99/110) is a large,
modern place with 60 immaculate rooms,
all with TV, air-con and telephone. The
hotel has a pool, a restaurant and an Internet café.

Beach Hotel Inés (☎ 582-07-92; **w** www
.hotel-ines.com; singles/doubles US$42/50)
has a sort of nouveau-colonial feel with
fresh, spacious rooms and a beautiful tree-
shaded pool area. There's plenty of 'ham-
mockry' and chill-zones and there's also an
excellent open-air café.

Bungalows Puerta del Sol (☎ 582-29-22;
Morro s/n; singles & doubles US$54) offers
spacious, breezy rooms, all with private,
cold-water baths and most with hammocks.
It has a great communal outdoor kitchen, a
decent courtyard and a good pool.

Hotel Rockaway (☎ 582-06-68; singles/
doubles/triples/quads US$12/17/23/28), to-
ward the far end of Zicatela, has good, solid
cabanas with showers, nets and fans, around
a pool. There's a bar and a handy grocery
to boot.

Bungalows Villa María del Mar (☎ 582-
10-91; singles/doubles US$11/16), on the
south end of Calle del Morro after it turns
to dirt, has about nine spacious, agreeable
rooms around a swimming pool. It's removed from the hubbub of Zicatela, but
right on the beach.

Places to Eat
Puerto has some excellent restaurants, and
vegetarians are well catered to. The main
produce market, the mercado central, is in
the upper part of town.

For cheap taquerías you'll have to head
up the hill as well; there's a good one, **El
Taco Brown** (open 6pm-midnight), on Av
Oaxaca just up from El Crucero, where you
can get five tacos al pastor (tacos made
with rotisserie pork) for US$2.75.

El Adoquín On the Adoquín, the established **Restaurant Los Crotos** (☎ 582-00-25;
mains US$6-9; open 7am-11pm daily) and
Restaurant Junto al Mar (☎ 582-12-72; Pérez
Gasga 600; mains US$6-9; open 8am-11pm

daily) have terraces opening onto the beach
and serve fresh seafood at reasonable prices.

La Galería (☎ 582-20-39; Pérez Gasga s/n;
mains US$4-10; open 8:30am-11pm daily)
opposite the Junto al Mar, is one of the most
popular Italian joints in town, serving good
thin-crust pizza (US$4.50 to US$5.50),
soups, fresh salads and imaginative pastas.

Restaurant Alicia (mains US$2-4; open
8am-11pm daily), around the middle of the
Adoquín, offers good value, with multiple
spaghetti variations, seafood cocktails and
good fish dishes. It does cheap breakfasts too.

Cafetería Cappuccino (☎ 582-01-90;
mains US$3-5; open 8am-11pm) is best for
egg or pancake breakfasts, but serves other
fare too, ranging from crepes and salads to
steaks and seafood.

Cafetería del Puerto (Pérez Gasga 609;
mains US$3.30-6.50; open 5:30pm-11pm
daily) is an unpretentious Italian eatery with
a small menu of reliable meat, seafood and
pasta dishes. It's great for a cheap plate of
pasta.

La Perla Flameante (☎ 582-01-67; mains
US$4-8; open 5pm-1am daily), a deluxe
bamboo palapa overlooking the Adoquín,
serves excellent seafood fillets (dorado,
tuna, yellow-tail, barracuda, sierra, shark...)
with 12 sauces to choose from; they'll set
you back about US$8. It also serves soups,
fish tacos, antojitos and has a full bar.

Playa Marinero The breezy restaurant at
Hotel Santa Fe (mains US$6-14; open 7am-
10:30pm daily) serves up some delicious
vegetarian and vegan Mexican dishes at
comfortable, candlelit tables. Some of the
appetizers make meals in themselves and
there's tofu, great seafood and a full bar.

Carmen's Panadería y Cafetería (1ª Entrada a Playa Marinero; open 7am-3pm Mon-
Sat, 7am-noon Sun), on the little lane behind
Playa Marinero, is a brilliant place for
breakfast or lunchtime snacks, with a small
fan-cooled palapa-style café and a tree-
shaded terrace. You can get a big serving of
fruit salad, yogurt and granola, or whole
wheat French toast with butter, honey and
lots of fruit. Coffee refills are free, and a
bakery section sells great baked goods.

Playa Zicatela Zicatela has a few small grocery stores, including a 24-hour one at Hotel Rockaway.

Cipriano's Pizza (☎ 582-25-88; pizzas US$5-6.50, breakfast US$2.50-3.50; open 8am-midnight daily) makes good brick-oven pizzas with a thin, crisp base and plenty of excellent cheese. The only size available is enough for two. The restaurant also serves breakfasts and Mexican main courses at moderate prices.

Restaurant Bungalows Zicatela (open 8am-10:30pm daily) is great for burgers (meat, soy or fish) for about US$2.50 including salad and fries.

La Gota de Vida (open 8am-11pm daily) is an outstanding vegetarian restaurant with creative salads and crepes, tempeh, tofu, stir-fry and imaginative tortas. The beverage and juice list is out of this world – that's the gota de vida (drop of life).

Carmen's Cafecito (☎ 582-05-16; open 6am-10pm; mains US$2-6) does a roaring trade morning, noon and night. Great pastries, croissants and cakes cost about US$0.75, coffee refills are free, and tortas go for around US$2.50. A monstrous breakfast of three hotcakes, bacon, eggs and potatoes costs only US$2.30. Homemade lunch and dinner dishes, including Mexican options, cost US$3 to US$7. **El Cafecito** (open 7:30am-10pm), next door, has the same owners and menu, plus a breezy upstairs area.

Aroma Divino (☎ 582-34-27; Playa Zicatela; mains US$2-5; open 6:30am-8:30pm Mon-Sat) has a prime site on the sands looking straight out to the surf break. Run by a Christian surfers' group, it serves an array of burritos, tortas, tacos, egg dishes, salads, and chicken and prawn dishes. Devise your own juice combination for about US$2.

Sakura (mains US$4.50-10; open 10am-11pm daily), on Calle del Morro, has a mouthwatering menu of Japanese plates, including tofu and teriyaki dishes, curries, veggie spring rolls, sushi and soups. It's Japanese-owned and the food is always fresh.

Los Tíos (☎ 582-28-79; Playa Zicatela; mains US$3-6; open 9am-10pm Wed-Mon) is a long-time favorite with a great location on the sand and a casual open-air atmosphere.

The food – mostly Mexican – is all fresh and averages US$3; seafood plates are more. It's an excellent night time hangout.

Entertainment

On El Adoquín, **Un Tigre Azul**, **Wipe Out Bar** and **Los 3 Diablos** all fill up with revelers most weekends, though none of them really kick in until after 11pm. **Barfly** is probably the hippest on the strip; it's a small place with good, loud music and a friendly atmosphere. Across the street, on the corner of Marina Nacional and the Adoquín, **Los Tarros** can be another fun one. Most of these have two-for-one happy hours between 9pm and 10pm.

El Son y La Rumba (Marina Nacional 15) has a good salsa/Latin band playing several nights a week on an outdoor patio to a usually seated crowd. The drinks here are pricey though.

Tequila Sunrise (admission US$2; open 10pm-late Tues-Sun) is the only disco below El Crucero and it's definitely hit-or-miss.

A few bars overlooking the sea, such as **Restaurant Liza's** on Playa Marinero or **Hotel Arco Iris** on Zicatela, have happy hours from about 5pm to 7pm to help you enjoy Puerto's spectacular sunsets.

Casa Babylon (open 10:30am-2pm & 6pm-late daily), also on Zicatela, is a laid-back travelers bar with board games and a big selection of second-hand books to sell or exchange.

Bar El Punto, on the Zicatela sands, plays cool music and has a bit of space to dance. It sort of warms up around 2am.

The 1992 Italian travel-and-crime movie *Puerto Escondido* is shown at 8pm nightly at **Restaurant Da Claudio**, just off El Adoquín. Directed by Gabriele Salvatores, the film has given Puerto near cult status among Italians and is worth seeing, even if it makes the place seem more remote than it really is.

Getting There & Away

Air See the Oaxaca City section for details on flights to/from Oaxaca. **Aerocaribe** (☎ 582-20-24; Puerto Escondido airport) flies direct to Mexico City daily (one hour). You can buy air tickets at agencies such as **Viajes Dimar** (☎ 582-15-51; *Pérez Gasga 905B)*. **Aerovega** (☎ 582-01-51) is on Marina Nacional, just off the Adoquín. **Aerotucán** (☎ 582-22-92) has its office at the airport.

Bus The bus terminals are all in the upper part of town, a couple of blocks above El Crucero. **Estrella Blanca** (☎ 582-04-27) is entered from Calle 1 Oriente; **EV/OP** (☎ 582-00-50), **Transol** and **ERS** (☎ 582-06-03) are on Av Hidalgo; and **Cristóbal Colón** (☎ 582-10-73) is on Calle 1 Norte. The only true 1st-class services are Colón's and a couple of the EB Mexico City runs.

It's advisable to book ahead for Colón buses and the better services to Oaxaca. Estrella Blanca tickets can be purchased at **Viajes Dimar** on El Adoquín.

Oaxaca city See Getting There & Away in the Oaxaca City section, earlier, for an explanation of the three possible routes between Oaxaca and Puerto Escondido. If you're taking a 2nd-class night bus, bring warm clothing. Daily departures from Puerto are:

Via Hwy 131 US$9 to US$13, eight to 10 hours, five ERS (three overnight) and six Transol buses daily

Via Hwys 200 & 175 US$9 to US$9.50, eight hours; 11 EV/OP, six ordinario and five 5 directo buses daily

Via Hwys 200 & 190 (Salina Cruz route) US$19, 10 to 11 hours, two Colón buses daily

Coastal Destinations Keep an eye on your bags when going to or departing from Acapulco and get a ticket for any bags placed in the hold. Daily departures include:

Acapulco US$14/19 ordinario/semi-directo, seven hours, 400km, nine EB 1st-class buses daily

Bahías de Huatulco US$4 to US$6, 2½ hours, 115km, nine Colón, eight ordinario and semi-directo EB buses daily

Mexico City US$44 to US$46, 12 to 16 hours, 870km, three EB 1st-class, one Colón bus daily

Pinotepa Nacional US$5, three hours, 151km, three EB ordinaries daily

Pochutla US$3.25 with Colón, 1½ hours, 65km, nine daily; US$2.50/4 ordinario/semi-directo with EB, eight daily; US$2, with Servicio Mixto

de Río Grande from El Crucero every 20 minutes from 5am to 7pm

Zihuatanejo US$32, 12 hours, 640km, 1 EB at 10:45pm daily

Estrella Blanca 2nd-class *económicos* leave every hour to Acapulco and will drop you anywhere you want to get off along coastal Hwy 200.

Car A VW bug costs about US$70 a day, limited kilometers, with **Alamo** (☎ 582-30-03; *Pérez Gasga s/n)*. **Budget** (☎ 582-03-12) has a rental office opposite the tourist office on Blvd Juárez.

Getting Around
The airport is about 4km west of the town center on the north side of Hwy 200. A taxi into town (and vice versa) costs around US$3; the best place to hail one from the airport is out on the main road. *Colectivo* shuttles (US$4 per person) will drop you anywhere in town.

Taxis wait at each end of the Adoquín and charge a fairly set rate (US$1.65) to Playa Zicatela or Puerto Angelito. *Lanchas* shuttle folks between the Playa Principal and Playa Manzanillo (US$2.20 one way) and Carrizalillo (US$3.30 one way); they're run by the **Cooperativa Nueva Punta Escondida** (☎ 582-16-78), which has an office on Marina Nacional and a kiosk on Playa Principal.

AROUND PUERTO ESCONDIDO
Laguna de Manialtepec
This lagoon, 6km long, begins about 15km west of Puerto Escondido along Hwy 200. It's home to ibis, roseate spoonbills, parrots and several species of hawks, falcons, ospreys, egrets, herons, kingfishers and iguanas. The birds are best seen in the early morning, but even in the middle of the day in January birders we know logged 40 species. The lagoon is mainly surrounded by mangroves, but tropical flowers and palms accent the ocean side. It makes an excellent day trip from Puerto Escondido.

The best (practically only) way to see the lagoon is by boat. Two outfits based in

Puerto Escondido offer outstanding tours for about US$36 per person: **Hidden Voyage Ecotours** and **Ana's Ecotours** (for both see Organized Tours in the Puerto Escondido section). Hidden Voyage uses roofless boats to enable you to see more birds and creep through the mangroves.

To see the lagoon independently, take a bus or drive to any of the four, well-marked restaurants that sit on the inland side of the lagoon just off Hwy 200. Three of them have docks and their own boat operators (usually fishers) who offer *paseos en lanchas* (boat tours). They're listed here in east-to-west order.

Las Hamacas (☎ 951-505-99-01; open 9am-8pm daily) is the snappiest place on the lagoon, renting single- and double-seat kayaks for US$5.50 per hour. The food's good too. Boat tours cost US$50 for four to five people.

La Alejandría doesn't do many boat tours but rents basic cabanas if you feel like spending the night with the mosquitoes.

Isla del Gallo (open 8am-7pm Tues-Sun) offers well-received, two-hour boat trips including an ocean-beach stop for US$44 for up to eight people. Good grilled fish is available in the comfortable restaurant for around US$6.

Las Negras is what everyone calls the last restaurant, though its actual name is **La Flor del Pacífico** (open 8am-6pm daily); Las Negras is the name of the village (ask for it if you're bussing). The restaurant itself is a women's coop that changes hands each year. It's a good embarkation point with competent boat operators (ask for Lalo) who know their birds.

From Puerto Escondido, take any Rio Grande-bound microbus from Calle 2 Norte just east of the Carretera Costera (Hwy 200), in the upper part of town; they leave about every 30 minutes. West-bound 2nd-class EB buses will also stop at the lagoon.

Los Naranjos & Palmazola Lagoons

These coastal lagoons, near the village of **Barra de Navidad** (6km southeast of Puerto Escondido on Hwy 200), offer another chance to get close to the abundant birdlife of the Oaxaca coast – and to the local crocodile population. Villagers have formed a society to protect the lagoons and offer **guided visits** (US$12) lasting about 1¼ hours, including a 30-minute boat ride. It's best to go in the early morning or late afternoon. Unaccompanied visits are not permitted. Barra de Navidad is a short walk south from Hwy 200 on the east side of the Rio Colotepec bridge. From Puerto, take a 'La Barra' *colectivo* from the highway at the east end of Pérez Gasga.

POCHUTLA
☎ 958 • pop 10,300
This bustling, sweaty market town is the starting point for transportation to the nearby beach spots Puerto Ángel, Zipolite, San Agustinillo and Mazunte. It also has the nearest banks to those places.

Orientation & Information
Hwy 175 passes through Pochutla as Lázaro Cárdenas, the narrow north-south main street; Hotel Izala marks its approximate midpoint. Bus stations cluster on Cárdenas 500m to 1km south of the Izala. The main square, Plaza de la Constitución, is a block east of the Izala along Juárez. There are two markets: one on Cárdenas a little north of the bus stations; the other east off Cárdenas two blocks north of the Izala.

Bital (Cárdenas 48; open 8am-6pm Mon-Fri, 8am-2pm Sat) is one block north of Hotel Izala. There are several other banks on this street with exchange services and ATMs.

The **post office** (Progreso; open 8am-7pm Mon-Fri, 9am-1pm Sat) is behind the main square. For Internet access, try **Café Internet Pochutla** (Cárdenas s/n; US$1.50 per hour; open 8am-6pm Mon-Sat, 8am-2pm Sun), two blocks north of the bus terminals, or the pricier **Caseta Cybatel** (Cárdenas 62; open 7am-10pm daily), about a block further up; the latter offers long-distance phone service.

Places to Stay & Eat
The following hotels have private bathrooms and fans.

OAXACA

Hotel Santa Cruz (☎ 584-01-16; *Cárdenas 88; rooms per person US$10*) is convenient, tolerable and cheap.

Hotel Izala (☎ 584-01-15; *Cárdenas 59; singles with fan US$14, singles/doubles with air-con US$22/27*) has clean rooms with TV and hot water around an open-air patio.

Hotel Costa del Sol (☎ 584-03-18; *Cárdenas 47; singles/doubles with fan US$22/24, with air-con US$27/30*) is Pochutla's best hotel. It is 1½ blocks north of the Izala and has a good rooftop **restaurant/taquería**.

Getting There & Away

The three main bus stations, in north-south order along Cárdenas, are **Estrella Blanca** *(EB;* ☎ *584-03-80)* situated on the west side of the street, **EV/OP** *(☎ 584-01-38)* on the east side, and **Cristóbal Colón** *(☎ 584-02-74)* on the west side.

Oaxaca city Oaxaca is 245km away by Hwy 175 (six to eight hours) or 450km by the better Hwys 200 and 190 (via Salina Cruz, nine to 10 hours). At the time of research Colón had two daily buses via Salina Cruz. The 13 daily EV/OP buses take Hwy 175 (US$8/10 ordinario/directo). **Autoexprés Atlántida** *(☎ 584-01-16)* based at Hotel Santa Cruz runs five daily air-con Chevy vans by Hwy 175 (US$13.50, 5½ hours).

Puerto Ángel, Zipolite & Mazunte Ever-changing transportation services to the nearby coast make about as much sense as an aerated kayak. When things are going well, frequent buses, microbuses and *colectivo* taxis run along the paved road from Pochutla to Puerto Ángel, Zipolite, San Agustinillo and Mazunte, usually starting at the EV/OP station or nearby on Cárdenas. But at the time of writing these services had been suspended for several months because of a turf battle among the area's drivers. From about 7am to 7pm, frequent *colectivo* taxis to Puerto Ángel (US$1, 20 minutes, 13km) were still leaving from a stand on Cárdenas, 200m north of the EB bus station. But vehicles from Pochutla could not carry passengers beyond Puerto Ángel to Zipolite, San Agustinillo or Mazunte. For these

destinations, you either had to change to another vehicle at Puerto Ángel or – longer but easier – take one of the camionetas leaving frequently between about 7am and 7pm from beside Ferretería RoGa on Cárdenas, 300m north of the Hotel Izala. These roll down Cárdenas then head to Mazunte (US$1, 30 minutes, 20km), San Agustin-illo (US$1, 35 minutes, 21km) and Zipolite (US$1, 45 minutes, 25km), via San Antonio on Hwy 200 northwest of Mazunte (not via Puerto Ángel).

Other Destinations Daily bus departures include:

Acapulco US$17/23.50 1st-class/ordinario, eight to 10 hours, 465km, six EB buses daily
Bahías de Huatulco US$2.25, one hour, 50km, seven Colón and three EB buses daily; US$1.50, Transportes Rápidos de Pochutla buses every 15 minutes from 5:30am to 8pm, from yard opposite EB
Puerto Escondido US$3.25 with Colón, 1½ hours, 65km, six daily; US$4/2.50 semi-directo/ordinario with EB, six daily; US$2, Servicio Mixto de Río Grande buses every 20 minutes from 5am to 7pm, from Allende, one block south and half a block east of Hotel Izala
Zihuatanejo US$35.50, 12 to 14 hours, 710km, one EB bus daily at 7:15pm

All three main companies go to Mexico City (about US$50, 15 hours).

PUERTO ÁNGEL
☎ 958 • pop 2500

The small fishing town, naval base and travelers' hangout of Puerto Ángel (**pwair-toh ahn**-hel) straggles around a picturesque bay between two rocky headlands, 13km south of Pochutla. Many travelers prefer to stay on the beaches a few kilometers west at Zipolite, San Agustinillo or Mazunte, but the fishing village atmosphere of Puerto Ángel makes it a good base too. It offers its own little beaches and has some excellent places to stay.

Orientation & Information

The road from Pochutla emerges at the east end of the small Bahía de Puerto Ángel. The road winds around the back of the bay, over an often-dry *arroyo* (creek) and up a hill. It then forks to the right leading to Zipolite and Mazunte, and then left down to Playa del Panteón.

The **post office** (*Principal; open 8:30am-3pm Mon-Fri*) is at the east end of town.

The nearest bank is in Pochutla, but several accommodations and restaurants will change cash or traveler's checks. **Gelnet** (*Vasconcelos 3; per hour US$2.20; open 7am-10pm daily*) has telephone, fax and Internet, plus a travel agency that can make flight reservations from Puerto Escondido and Bahías de Huatulco. The **Caseta Teléfonica Lila's** (*Uribe; open 7am-10pm Mon-Sat, 7am-8pm Sun*) also has phone and fax service. The best Internet rates are at **G@l@p@gos** (*open 8am-10pm daily*), in Casa de Huéspedes Anahi, for US$1.10 per hour.

Foreign residents recommend **Dr Constancio Aparicio** (☎ 584-30-58) for a local doctor; ask for him in **Farmacia El Ángel** on Vasconcelos.

Watch your back on the Zipolite road at night – robbery has been a problem.

Beaches

On the west side of Bahía de Puerto Ángel, **Playa del Panteón** is shallow and calm, and the water is cleaner than those near the fishers' pier across the bay.

About 500m north along the road to Pochutla, a sign points right along a path to **Playa Estacahuite** 700m away. The three tiny, sandy bays here are all great for snorkeling, but watch out for jellyfish. A couple of shack restaurants serve good, reasonably priced seafood or spaghetti, and may rent snorkel gear. There's one place to stay (see Palapa Paraíso Escondido under Places to Stay).

The coast northeast of Estacahuite is dotted with more good beaches, none of them very busy. A good one is **Playa La Boquilla**, on a small bay about 5km from town; it's the site of the Bahía de la Luna bungalows and restaurant (see Places to Stay). To get to

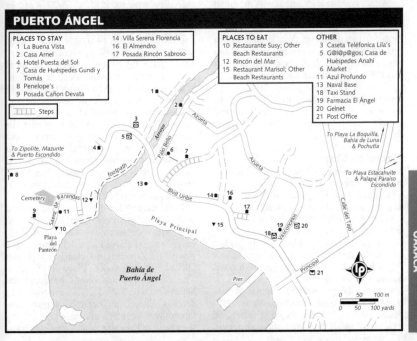

PUERTO ÁNGEL

PLACES TO STAY				PLACES TO EAT		OTHER
1 La Buena Vista	14 Villa Serena Florencia			10 Restaurante Susy; Other		3 Caseta Teléfonica Lila's
2 Casa Arnel	16 El Almendro			Beach Restaurants		5 G@l@p@gos; Casa de
4 Hotel Puesta del Sol	17 Posada Rincón Sabroso			12 Rincón del Mar		Huéspedes Anahi
7 Casa de Huéspedes Gundi y				15 Restaurant Marisol; Other		6 Market
Tomás				Beach Restaurants		11 Azul Profundo
8 Penelope's						13 Naval Base
9 Posada Cañon Devata						18 Taxi Stand
						19 Farmacia El Ángel
⊞⊞ Steps						20 Gelnet
						21 Post Office

To Zipolite, Mazunte & Puerto Escondido

To Playa La Boquilla, Bahía de Luna & Pochutla

To Playa Estacahuite & Palapa Paraíso Escondido

Cemetery

footpath

Arroyo

Palo Bravo

Azueta

Blvd Uribe

Saenz de Barandas

Playa Principal

Calle del Tajo

Vasconcelos

Playa del Panteón

Bahía de Puerto Ángel

Pier

Principal

0   50   100 m
0   50   100 yards

OAXACA

the beach, take a turnoff 4km out of Puerto Ángel on the road toward Pochutla and then follow the road for 3.5km. A taxi from Puerto Ángel costs around US$6, but more fun is to go by boat – you can get a fisher to take a few people from Playa Panteón or from the pier for around US$12 per person, including a return trip at an agreed time.

Activities

Snorkeling and **fishing** are popular around Puerto Ángel, and **diving** is also an option. The drops and canyons out to sea from Puerto Angel are suitable for very deep dives; a nearby shipwreck, dated 1870, is a popular site.

Some of the café/restaurants on Playa del Panteón rent snorkel gear (US$2.75/6.75 per hour/day). **Byron Luna** (☎ 584-31-15) offers snorkeling and fishing trips to four beaches, and provides equipment and transport from your hotel. Two- to three-hour trips will set you back US$11 per person. Look for Byron at his home across the street from Hotel La Cabaña.

Azul Profundo (☎ 584-31-09, *Playa del Panteón*) is a well-run dive shop offering similar deals on snorkeling and fishing trips, plus dives at all levels. One-tank dives cost US$44.50 and four-tank dives US$123. A first-timer session costs US$50 and seven-day PADI courses are US$389. Both Byron and Azul Profundo are great fun and always include dolphin-, orca- and turtle-spotting on their trips.

Places to Stay

Accommodations with an elevated location are more likely to catch any breeze, and mosquito screens are a big plus too. Some places develop a water shortage now and then.

El Almendro (☎ 584-30-68; e gundtoma@ hotmail.com; *low season singles/doubles US$11/16.50*) is set amidst a lovely garden with tables and chairs, and has large, colorful rooms with bath and fan. There's a good outdoor bar-and-grill too.

Casa de Huéspedes Gundi y Tomás (☎ 584-30-68; w www.reisen-mexiko.de; *singles US$9, doubles US$15-25*) offers a good variety of rooms, all with fans and mosquito nets and/or screens. The pricier ones have private bathrooms. In an emergency you can hang or rent a hammock for US$4.40. There's a good vegetarian restaurant, pleasant sitting areas, a safe for valuables, no shortage of hammocks and good views. Gundi will exchange cash or traveler's checks.

Posada Rincón Sabroso (☎ 584-30-95; *Uribe s/n; singles/doubles US$11/17.50*), a shaded hotel, is up a flight of stairs from the main street. It has 10 fan-cooled rooms, each with bathroom, terrace and hammock.

Posada Cañon Devata (☎ 584-31-37; *off Saenz de Barandas; singles/doubles with fan & bath US$13/16, 2-room 4-bed units US$35 plus US$3 per extra adult; open Jul-Apr*), above Playa del Panteon, is a friendly place with a variety of attractive accommodations scattered among hillside foliage. It's a good place for those seeking a quiet retreat. Fine, mainly vegetarian food is available.

Hotel Puesta del Sol (☎ 584-30-96; w www .puertoangel.net; *singles/doubles/triples with shared bathroom US$11.50/18/22, doubles with private bathroom US$30-34, triples with private bathroom US$34-37*), to the right just past the *arroyo*, has 14 sizable, clean rooms with fans and screens. The more expensive rooms have their own terraces. The hotel has a sitting room with videos, a small library, satellite TV and a breezy terrace with hammocks. Breakfast is offered.

Casa Arnel (☎ 584-30-51; *singles/doubles/ triples US$17/23/26*), up the lane past the central market, is owned by relatives of the owners of Hotel Casa Arnel in Oaxaca. It has five spotless rooms with bathrooms and fan, a laundry basin, a breezy hammock area and Internet service (US$1.60) for guests. Breakfast is available.

Penelope's (☎ 584-30-73; *3ª Curva Camino a Zipolite; singles/doubles/triples US$17/28 /34*), with four rooms, is set in a quiet, leafy neighborhood above Playa del Panteón. It's just off the Zipolite road, clearly signposted 200m beyond the fork to Playa del Panteón. The clean, spacious rooms have private bathrooms with hot water, fan and mosquito screens. There's an attractive terrace restaurant with economical meals, prepared by the attentive Penelope, and a small library.

Villa Serena Florencia (☎ 584-30-44; ⓔ vi llaserenaoax@hotmail.com; Uribe s/n; singles/doubles/triples US$27/38/49) has 13 pleasant but smallish rooms with private bathroom, fan and screens. Air-con rooms cost an extra US$3. It has a cool sitting area, an attractive restaurant and a friendly owner.

La Buena Vista (☎/fax 584-31-04; ⓦ www .labuenavista.com; doubles US$34-45) is an alluring hotel with a dozen or so big rooms and a couple of excellent mud-brick bungalows. Everything's kept scrupulously clean. Rooms have private bathrooms, fans, mosquito screens and breezy balconies with hammocks. There's a fine restaurant and lots of shade. To get there turn right just past the arroyo, then go a short way up the first track on the left.

Bahía de la Luna (☎ 584-86-38; ⓔ bahia-de-la-luna@usa.net; singles/doubles/triples with bathroom US$46/53/69, 5-person bungalow US$55, 8-person house US$208), a Canadian-owned hotel at Playa La Boquilla (see Beaches earlier), has nice adobe bungalows and a good beachside restaurant-café with moderate prices. On offer are personal development workshops in yoga, astrology, stress control and dream interpretation.

Palapa Paraíso Escondido (doubles US$11), all alone on Playa Estacahuite (see Beaches earlier), has two tiny, brick-floor cabanas with fans, nets and a simple shared bathroom. The cabanas also share an excellent little terrace that overlooks the beach. It's above one of the little comedores (inexpensive restaurants).

Places to Eat

Many of Puerto Ángel's restaurants are in hotels. **El Almendro** (dinner US$5) fires up the grill every night and offers a choice of barbecued chicken, fish or pork. The food's fresh and is accompanied by house potatoes and a small, all-you-can-eat salad bar.

La Buena Vista (☎/fax 584-31-04; ⓦ www .labuenavista.com; breakfast US$3-4, dinner US$5-6; open 8am-11am & 6:30pm-10pm Mon-Sat), on an airy terrace overlooking the bay, offers well-prepared Mexican and American fare, from hotcakes to tamales and chiles rellenos.

Posada Cañon Devata ((☎ 584-31-37; off Saenz de Barandas; dinners US$9.50; breakfast 8:30am-noon, dinner 7:30pm) is another guesthouse where all are welcome. It serves a good three-course dinner at long tables in a lovely palm-roofed, open-sided dining room. Fare is Mexican and vegetarian. It's best to book early in the day. Healthy veggie breakfasts are served in the morning.

Rincón del Mar (mains US$3-6), above the walkway to Playa Panteon, has great views from its cliffside location, reached by steps up from the walkway leading to Playa del Panteón. The food is good too. The fish specialty, filete a la cazuela, is prepared with olives, peas, onions and tomatoes. Other choices include octopus, prawns or verduras al vapor (steamed vegetables).

Villa Serena Florencia (mains US$3-7), a comfortable Italian restaurant, cooks good pasta (be sure to try the pesto) and serves pizza, seafood, Mexican fare and inexpensive breakfasts. Wine goes for US$11 to US$14 a bottle and there are over 100 cocktails (US$2 to US$4) on the list.

The restaurants on Playa del Panteón offer fish and seafood for US$8 to US$10, plus cheaper fare such as antojitos or eggs. Be careful about the freshness of seafood in the low season. The setting is exquisite after dark. **Restaurante Susy** (☎ 584-30-19) is one of the better ones.

Several eateries hug the main town beach near the pier. They are economical but none is very well frequented. **Restaurant Marisol** is one place that has good-value food, beer for US$0.80 and margaritas for US$1.50.

Getting There & Away

See the Pochutla section for details on transportation from that town. A taxi to or from Zipolite costs US$0.60 colectivo, or US$3 for the whole cab (US$4.50 after dark and even more after 10pm). You can find cabs on Blvd Uribe; there's a stand at the corner of Vasconcelos.

A taxi to Bahías de Huatulco airport costs around US$35 and US$45 to Puerto Escondido airport.

OAXACA

ZIPOLITE

☎ 958 • pop 1000

The beautiful 1.5km stretch of pale sand, called Zipolite, begins about 2.5km west of Puerto Ángel, and is fabled as southern Mexico's perfect place to lie back and do as little as you like, *in* as little as you like, *for* as little as you like (well, almost).

Once just a small fishing settlement with a few comedores, Zipolite has grown a lot in recent years. Cheap restaurants and accommodations now line nearly the whole beach, but most are still reassuringly ramshackle and wooden. Zipolite is as great a place as ever to take it easy, with a magical combination of the pounding sea and the hot sun; open-air sleeping, eating and drinking; some unique scenery; and the travelers' scene. It's the kind of place where you may find yourself postponing departure over and again. The cluster of larger establishments toward the beach's west end is the hub of Zipolite for many, but there's plenty of room elsewhere if you're looking to really chill out.

Theft can be a problem at Zipolite, and it's inadvisable to walk along the Puerto Ángel–Zipolite road after dark.

Orientation & Information

The eastern end of Zipolite (nearest Puerto Ángel) is called Colonia Playa del Amor, the middle part is Centro, and the western end (divided from Centro by a narrow creek-cum-lagoon, often called *el arroyo*) is Colonia Roca Blanca. The few streets behind the beach are mostly nameless.

The nearest banks are in Pochutla, but some accommodations may change US cash. Internet access is available in Colonia Roca Blanca at **Caseta Oceana** *(US$1.50 per hour; open 8am-10pm daily)* on Roca Blanca, a block back from the beach, and **Zipolnet** *(US$1.50 per hour; open 9am-9pm daily)* around the corner. They both provide a long-distance phone service. **Lola's** (see Places to Stay) has another telephone caseta.

Lavandería Yamile, on the main road east of Casa de Huéspedes Lyoban, offers same-day laundry service for US$1.50 per kilo.

Deadly Surf

The Zipolite surf is deadly, literally. It's fraught with rip tides, changing currents and a strong undertow. Locals don't swim here, and going in deeper than your knees can mean risking your life. Most years several people drown here. Local voluntary lifeguards *(salvavidas)* have rescued many, but they don't maintain a permanent watch. If you do get swept out to sea, swim calmly parallel to the shore to get clear of the current pulling you outward.

Places to Stay

Nearly every building on the beach rents simple rooms or cabanas and/or hammocks. It's easy to wander along and pick one that suits. It makes sense to choose one where your belongings can be locked up. Unless noted, assume that bathrooms are shared and basic. Prices fluctuate according to demand. The following is a selection of many options, starting at the low-key east end (nearest Puerto Ángel) and moving west.

Fernando's Trailer Park *(Carretera Puerto Ángel–Zipolite; space per tent or vehicle US$1.75-2.25, per person US$1.25)*, along the road from Puerto Ángel before you enter Zipolite, has a grassy plot edged with trees. It has electricity, clean showers and toilets, washing water and 24-hour caretaking.

Solstice Yoga Center *(☎ 584-30-70; w www .solstice-mexico.com; dorm beds US$11, studios US$30, bungalows US$35)* is an exquisite little Dutch-owned yoga center with a few beautifully designed bungalows and smaller 'studios' and dorm rooms. Accommodation is usually available (except when the place is taken over by a retreat group), but call in advance. Readers rave about the week-long yoga courses and drop-in sessions. And you should see the yoga studio!

Chololo's *(☎ 584-32-01; rooms with shared/ private bath US$8/17)*, the easternmost place on the beach, is friendly, with good food and just a few simple rooms.

Next door, **Lola's** *(☎ 584-32-01; singles/ doubles US$12/15)* has comfy rooms with bathrooms, fan and nets.

Casa de Huéspedes Lyoban (☎ 584-31-77; W www.lyoban.com.mx; hammocks US$4.40, singles/doubles/triples with shared bath US$11/15/19, double with private bath US$33) is well built with clean rooms, a 2nd-floor balcony of hammocks, and foosball, ping-pong and pool tables. The lockers are solid and the bar is well stocked.

Posada María (hammocks US$3, singles/doubles US$8/9) offers box-sized but breezy wooden rooms, and has a lockup baggage store. Inexpensive food is available; such as fish filet, rice, salad and tortillas (US$4).

Palapa Katy (hammocks US$3, cabanas US$6.50-11) has a few sand-floor palapas and two raised cabanas. Well-priced Italian food is available, with spaghetti, pizza and salad all between US$2.25 and US$3.50.

Palapa Aris (hammocks US$2-3, ground-floor singles/doubles US$6.50/9, raised cabanas US$11) rents three decent sand-floor cabanas and two excellent upper-level cabanas which share a balcony overlooking the beach.

Posada La Habana (hammocks US$2.20, ground-floor cabanas US$6.50, raised cabanas US$11) has four solid, raised cabanas with small terraces and hammocks. It's a clean place, and cheap chow is prepared for guests.

La Choza (☎ 584-31-90; Colonia Roca Blanca; rooms for 1-4 persons with shared/private bath US$16/20) is a large (massive by Zipolite standards), 14-room hotel. It has clean, spacious rooms, with mosquito nets or screens.

Tao (☎ 584-31-95; Colonia Roca Blanca; rear cabanas US$11, lower/upper-level cabanas US$13/16) offers four excellent, upper-level cabanas and several comfortable ground-level rooms. The friendly crew keeps everything clean and it has a great beach-side breakfast café.

Restaurant Posada San Cristóbal (☎ 584-31-91, Colonia Roca Blanca; doubles with shared/private bath US$11/16.50) provides bare accommodations with double bed, net and fan, alongside a leafy garden. Its annex,

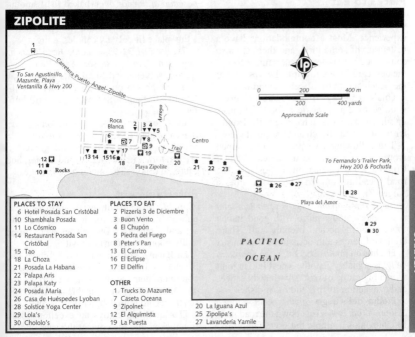

ZIPOLITE

To San Agustinillo, Mazunte, Playa Ventanilla & Hwy 200

Carretera Puerto Ángel–Zipolite

Roca Blanca

Centro

Playa Zipolite

Rocks

To Fernando's Trailer Park, Hwy 200 & Pochutla

Playa del Amor

PACIFIC

OCEAN

0   200   400 m
0   200   400 yards
Approximate Scale

PLACES TO STAY
6 Hotel Posada San Cristóbal
10 Shambhala Posada
11 Lo Cósmico
14 Restaurant Posada San Cristóbal
15 Tao
18 La Choza
21 Posada La Habana
22 Palapa Aris
23 Palapa Katy
24 Posada María
26 Casa de Huéspedes Lyoban
28 Solstice Yoga Center
29 Lola's
30 Chololo's

PLACES TO EAT
2 Pizzería 3 de Diciembre
3 Buon Vento
4 El Chupón
5 Piedra del Fuego
8 Peter's Pan
13 El Carrizo
16 El Eclipse
17 El Delfín

OTHER
1 Trucks to Mazunte
7 Caseta Oceana
9 Zipolnet
12 El Alquimista
19 La Puesta
20 La Iguana Azul
25 Zipolipa's
27 Lavandería Yamile

OAXACA

the **Hotel Posada San Cristobal** (*Colonia Roca Blanca; singles/doubles US$12/17*), is just across the main drag and has rooms with two beds, bathrooms, fan and nets.

Lo Cósmico (*hammocks US$3.30, cabanas US$11-20*) is a rambling place built around a tall rock outcrop near the west end of the beach. The pricier cabanas have two floors, decks and nets and are simply exquisite. Those in the back are stuffy and lack the great views. The hammock area is high on a cliff side with spectacular views over the beach.

Shambhala Posada (*Casa Gloria; hammocks US$2, singles US$5.50, doubles US$6.50-9*) is an eclectic, long-established place that climbs the hill at the west end of the beach, with great views back along it. The single and double 'monks' rooms,' as they're called, are small, dark and clean and have nets. There's a meditation area and a restaurant, and the place is usually full of eccentric, fun-lovin' folks.

Places to Eat

Eating and drinking in the open air a few steps from the surf is an inimitable Zipolite experience. Most accommodations have a restaurant of some kind, and there are also some good stand-alone restaurants. Most of the best eateries are towards the west end of the beach and in the streets behind it.

Lola's (*☎ 584-32-01; mains US$3-7*) serves good seafood and Mexican food and mixes up some tasty juices. It has one of the lengthier menus on the beach and has good views.

The following five places are grouped around the intersection at the east end of Colonia Roca Blanca on, or just off, the road heading out to the main Puerto Ángel–Zipolite road.

Buon Vento (*mains US$3-6; open 8am-late*) is a clean, mellow place with good Italian food, great music and friendly staff. There are board games and occasional live music.

El Chupón (*mains US$3-6; open 6pm-2am daily*) is arguably Zipolite's best Italian joint with a big range of pastas with tasty sauces and a selection of fish and meat dishes.

Piedra del Fuego (*mains US$3-4; open 2:30pm-11pm daily*), east down the road from El Chupón, is a simple but good family-run

place, where you'll get a generous serving of whatever they're offering (fish, prawns, chicken...) with rice, salad and tortillas. Big jugs of *agua de fruta* are US$1.50.

Pizzería 3 de Diciembre (*pizzas US$2-5; open 7pm-2am Wed-Sun*) serves good pastry pies, including vegetarian options such as cauliflower-and-parmesan or baked spinach – and excellent pizzas as well.

Peter's Pan (*breakfasts US$1.75-4; open 7am-noon Mon-Sat, 8am-1pm in summer*) is good for breakfast, and the whole-grain or white bread from the bakery inside go well with a visit to Zipolnet next door.

The next few places are west along Roca Blanca's main drag.

El Eclipse (*Colonia Roca Blanca; Mains US$4-9*) midway down the main drag, does very good Italian fare, such as pasta and pizza (US$4 to US$5.75); seafood and meat cost a bit more. There's even wine (US$3/12 a glass/bottle).

El Delfín (*mains US$3-5*) does an excellent *pescado al horno* (oven-baked fish) smothered in tomatoes and onions for US$5 and whips out some tasty wood-fired pizzas. It's a tiny place lit only by candles at night.

Tao (*☎ 584-31-95; Colonia Roca Blanca; open 8am-4pm low season, 8am-10pm high season*) serves good breakfasts year-round and, in high season, offers a US$4.50 buffet breakfast and US$6.50 mixed-grill buffet dinner.

La Choza (*☎ 584-31-90; Colonia Roca Blanca; mains US$2-7; open 7am-10pm or midnight*) is very popular and great for crepes, *tortas* (sandwiches) and strong, hot espresso drinks. The menu here is huge.

Entertainment

Zipolite's beachfront restaurant-bars have unbeatable locations for drinks around sunset and after dark. Two places were especially popular on our last visit.

La Iguana Azul, about midway down the beach near the lagoon, is the kind of lazy bar you return home to dream about. Drinks are cheap, the setting's unbeatable and the tunes run the record from dub to Michelle Shocked.

El Alquimista enjoys an excellent location tucked into the cove at the west end of the beach. The lighting's low, the music is varied and the drinks slide down easily.

For slightly more active nightlife Zipolite has two open-air *discotecas* (discos), where nothing much happens before midnight (nothing much may happen after midnight either, but you might as well have a look...). **La Puesta** is next door to Zipolnet in Colonia Roca Blanca; **Zipolipa's** opens onto the beach next to Casa de Huéspedes Lyoban.

Getting There & Away

See the Pochutla and Puerto Ángel sections for details on transportation from those places. The *camionetas* between Pochutla, Mazunte, San Agustinillo and Zipolite terminate on the main road at the far west end of Zipolite. *Colectivo* taxis from Puerto Ángel (US$0.60) will go to the same spot too, but pass along the length of Zipolite en route, so are probably a better bet if you're heading for the east end of the beach.

After dark, a non-*colectivo* taxi is your only option for travelling to Puerto Ángel or San Agustinillo. The trip will cost around US$4.50 until about 10pm, and a little more after that.

SAN AGUSTINILLO
☎ 958

West from Zipolite, other glorious beaches stretch almost unbroken all the way to Puerto Escondido. Long, straight **Playa Aragón** – in the Zipolite mold, but almost empty – stretches west from the headland at the west end of Zipolite to the tiny village of San Agustinillo. The footpaths behind Shambhala Posada cross the headland from Zipolite, or you can take the road, which loops inland then comes back down to San Agustinillo (4km from Zipolite).

San Agustinillo is set on a small curved bay, with waves that are perfect for **boogie-boarding** and good for **surfing** when a swell comes in. There are several relaxed little places to stay and a line of open-air beach comedores serving mainly seafood. You can rent boogie boards at **México Lindo y qué Rico!** for US$3.50 an hour. Palapa Olas Altas has *lancha* trips at US$39 an hour for **turtle-viewing** (and occasionally dolphin

viewing) or **fishing** (see Places to Stay & Eat for details on these places).

The coast between Zipolite and Puerto Escondido is a major sea turtle nesting ground (see the boxed text 'Mexico's Turtles' on the following page). Until hunting and killing sea turtles was banned in Mexico in 1990, San Agustinillo was the site of a gruesome slaughterhouse (now demolished) where some 50,000 turtles were killed per year for their meat and shells.

Places to Stay & Eat

Palapa de Evelia (*west end Playa San Agustinillo; rooms US$17; mains around US$5.50*), the third place along from the west end of the beach, has a few basic but clean rooms with bathrooms, a fan and mosquito net. The food is some of the best on the beach, with straightforward but well-prepared fish and seafood and great guacamole.

México Lindo y qué Rico! (*e fafinyleila@ latinmail.com; west end Playa San Agustinillo; rooms US$22; mains around US$5.50*), next door to Evelia's, has the four best rooms in San Agustinillo – especially the breezy upstairs pair under the tall palapa roof. The large rooms have double beds, bathrooms, fan, and net. The owners, Fausto and Leila, are young, friendly and serve good food.

Palapa Olas Altas (*☎ 583-97-60; east end Playa San Agustinillo; hammocks US$3, rooms US$11; mains US$5-8*) has 13 upstairs rooms – only one with a sea view but all with mosquito nets. The restaurant serves decent food.

Cabañas Sol y Mar (*☎ 584-07-56; west end Playa Aragón; hammocks US$3, rooms US$9*) has rooms on both sides of the road, plus breezy upstairs hammocks on the beach side. Cookers are available to cut your eating costs. There's also a roadside spot to park your camper or van for US$3 per person.

Two places have stunning positions atop the steep slope backing Playa Aragón. Both are reachable by drivable tracks from the road or by paths up from the beach.

Rancho Hamacas (*☎ 584-05-49; e b_Sil va_Mendez@hotmail.com; Playa Aragón; hammocks US$3, cabanas US$28*) has a couple of adobe cabanas with double bed, mosquito net, fridge and cooker. There's a separate

OAXACA

patio for hammock-hanging. The owners make beautiful, strong hammocks (around US$100).

Rancho Cerro Largo *(fax 584-30-63;* e *ran chocerrolargomx@yahoo.com; Playa Aragón; single/double cabanas US$56/67)*, on the hilltop farther east from Rancho Hamacas, has just a handful of superior, fan-cooled cabanas. The price includes an excellent breakfast and dinner.

Getting There & Away

See the Pochutla section for information on transportation from there. *Camionetas* to or from Zipolite or Mazunte cost US$0.50.

MAZUNTE
☎ 958 • pop 500

Like San Agustinillo, Mazunte, 1km further west, grew up around the turtle industry. When this was banned in 1990, many villagers turned to slash-and-burn cultivation, threatening nearby forests. Encouraged by a Mexico City-based environmental group, Ecosolar, in 1991 Mazunte declared itself an ecological reserve, attempting to preserve the environment while creating a sustainable economy. The projects included printing and natural cosmetics workshops, construction of ecological toilets, and garbage separation. A key element was tourism, which the government-funded Centro Mexicano de la Tortuga, opened in 1994, was also intended to encourage. After Hurricane Pauline in 1997, which caused great damage at Mazunte, Ecosolar's influence waned, but by then the village was well established on the tourism map, and today it's a travelers' hangout almost as popular and hip as Zipolite. The waters of the fine, curving, sandy beach are generally safe, though the waves can be quite big.

Mexico's Turtles

Of the world's eight sea turtle species, seven are found in Mexican waters, and six of those in the Pacific. Their nesting sites are scattered along the entire coast.

Female turtles usually lay their eggs on the beaches where they were born, some swimming huge distances to do so. They come ashore at night, scoop a trough in the sand and lay 50 to 200 eggs in it. Then they cover the eggs and go back to the sea. Six to 10 weeks later, the baby turtles hatch, dig their way out and crawl to the sea at night. Only two or three of every 100 make it to adulthood. Turtle nesting seasons vary, but July to September are peak months in many places.

Playa Escobilla, just east of Puerto Escondido, is one of the world's main nesting grounds for the small **olive ridley turtle** (*Lepidochelys olivacea*; tortuga golfina to Mexicans), the only sea turtle species that is not endangered. Between May and January, about 700,000 olive ridleys come ashore here in about a dozen waves – known as *arribadas* – each lasting two or three nights, often during the waning of the moon. Playa Escobilla's turtles are guarded by armed soldiers, and there is no tourist access to the beach.

The rare **leatherback** (*Dermochelys coriacea*; to Mexicans, tortuga Laúd or tortuga de altura) is the largest sea turtle – it grows up to 3m long and can weigh one ton and live 80 years. One leatherback nesting beach is Playa Mermejita, between Punta Cometa and Playa Ventanilla, near Mazunte. Another is Barra de la Cruz, east of Bahías de Huatulco.

The **green turtle** (*Chelonia mydas;* tortuga verde) is a vegetarian that grazes on marine grasses. Most adults are about 1m long. For millennia, the green turtle's meat and eggs have provided protein to humans in the tropics. European exploration of the globe marked the beginning of the turtle's decline. In the 1960s, the Empacadora Baja California in Ensenada, Baja California, was canning as many as 100 tons of turtle soup a season.

The **loggerhead turtle** (*Caretta caretta;* tortuga caguama), weighing up to 100kg, is famous for the vast distances it crosses between its feeding grounds and nesting sites. Loggerheads born in Japan and even, it's thought, Australia, cross the Pacific to feed off Baja California. Females later return to their birthplaces – a year-long journey – to lay their eggs.

Orientation

The paved road running west from Zipolite to Hwy 200 passes through the middle of Mazunte. The Centro Mexicano de la Tortuga is beside this main road towards the east end of the village. Three sandy lanes run from the road to the beach (about 500m). The western one is sometimes called Camino al Rinconcito, as the west end of the beach is known as El Rinconcito.

Things to See & Do

The **Centro Mexicano de la Tortuga** *(Mexican Turtle Center;* ☎ *584-30-55; admission US$2.25; open 10am-4:30pm Tues-Sat)* is a turtle aquarium and research center with specimens of all seven of Mexico's marine turtle species, on view in large tanks. It's enthralling to get a close-up view of these creatures, some of which are *big*. Visits are guided (Spanish) and every 10 to 15 minutes.

Cosméticos Naturales *(☎ 583-96-56; open 9am-4pm daily)* is a natural cosmetics workshop and store by the roadside toward the west end of the village. This small co-operative makes shampoo and cosmetics from natural sources such as maize, coconut, avocado and sesame seeds. It also sells organic coffee, peanut butter, natural mosquito repellents and handicrafts made elsewhere.

Temazcal, a traditional herbal steam bath (a kind of pre-Hispanic sauna!) are available at Cabañas Balamjuyuc (see Places to Stay & Eat). They cost US$16.50 per person, including dinner. For US$22 you can also receive a 1½-hour **massage**, including acupressure and aromatherapy.

Cabañas Balamjuyuc takes small groups on 2½ hour **boat trips** to see turtles and dolphins for US$5.75 per person.

Punta Cometa, the rocky cape jutting out from the west end of Mazunte beach, is the

Mexico's Turtles

The **hawksbill turtle** (*Eretmochelys imbricata;* tortuga de carey) nests along both of Mexico's coasts and can live 50 years. The coast's sixth species, the **black turtle** (*Chelonia agassizi;* tortuga negra or tortuga prieta), sticks to the Pacific.

The smallest and most endangered sea turtle, the **Kemp's ridley**, or parrot turtle (*Lepidochelys kempii;* tortuga lora), lives only in the Gulf of Mexico.

Despite international conservation efforts, turtle flesh and eggs continue to be eaten, and some people still believe the eggs to be aphrodisiacs. Turtle skin and shell are used to make clothing and adornments. The world's fishing boats kill many turtles by trapping and drowning them in nets. In Mexico, hunting and killing sea turtles was officially banned in 1990, but the illicit killing and egg-raiding still goes on – a clutch of eggs can be sold for more than a typical worker makes in a week.

To help the turtles that use Mexican beaches – and most people who have seen these graceful creatures swimming at sea will want to do that – follow these tips if you find yourself at a nesting beach:

- Try to avoid nesting beaches altogether between sunset and sunrise.
- Don't approach turtles emerging from the sea, or disturb nesting turtles or hatchlings with noise or lights (lights on or even near the beach can cause hatchlings to lose their sense of direction on their journey to the water).
- Keep vehicles, even bicycles, off nesting beaches.
- Don't build sand castles or stick umbrellas into the sand.
- Never handle baby turtles or carry them to the sea – their arduous scramble is vital to their development.
- Boycott shops or stalls selling products made from sea turtles or any other endangered species.

See the Turtle Trax Internet site at **W** www.turtles.org for more fascinating turtle facts.

southernmost point in the state of Oaxaca and a fabulous place to be at sunset, with great long-distance views in both directions along the coast. You can walk there in 20 to 30 minutes over the rocks from the end of Mazunte beach, or take the Camino a Punta Cometa, a path that starts through the woods almost opposite the entrance to Cabañas Balamjuyuc (see Places to Stay & Eat).

Playa Ventanilla

Some 2.5km along the road west from Mazunte, a sign points left to Playa Ventanilla, 1.2km down a dirt track. The settlement here comprises a handful of simple homes, a couple of comedores and the palapa of **Servicios Ecoturísticos La Ventanilla**, a local cooperative providing interesting canoe trips on the **Estero de la Ventanilla**, a mangrove-fringed lagoon a few hundred meters along the beach. You'll see river crocodiles (there are about 200 in the lagoon), lots of water birds (most prolific in July and August) and, in an enclosure on an island in the lagoon, a few white-tailed deer. The tours (US$4/1.75 per adult/child) last 1½ hours and are offered between 6am and 6pm daily. Servicios Ecoturísticos also offers three-hour **horseback rides** for US$17 to another lagoon further west, where more boat trips (US$5.75) are available.

Frequent *camionetas* run from Mazunte to the Playa Ventanilla turnoff for US$0.50.

Places to Stay & Eat

Most places along the beach have basic rooms or cabanas and hammocks to rent. Most places will let you pitch a tent for the same price as a hammock rental. Prices rise or fall according to season and demand. December is the busiest time; May and June are quiet. The following beachfront places are listed in east-to-west order; accommodations have shared bathrooms unless specified.

La Dulce Vita *(main road, east of Cosméticos Naturales; mains US$4-8)* serves Italian food and is one of Mazunte's best eateries.

Aldea Cocos *(main road, west of turtle center; breakfast US$1.75-3, mains US$3-5)* serves some of Mazunte's most economical meals. A lunch of soup, rice, a main dish

with beans and tortillas, coffee and dessert is just US$3.25.

Cabañas Ziga *(singles/doubles/triples US$11/15/23)*, on a breezy beachside elevation just west of the turtle center, has decent little rooms with fan and mosquito net, and a good, open-air restaurant with views along the beach.

Restaurant Yuri *(hammocks US$3, rooms US$11, cabana with bath US$22)* has plain but adequate rooms and one dark cabana.

Restaurante El Arbolito *(hammocks US$3, cabanas US$9)*, has a decent restaurant and a couple of tiny raised cabanas with good balconies.

Palapa El Mazunte *(hammocks US$3.50, singles/double cabanas US$5.50/9)* is a popular, well-kept place; the cabanas are dark but have good mattresses.

Palapa El Pescador *(hammocks US$3)* has a small hammock area (US$3) and one of the best **restaurants** on the beach. Fish and seafood goes for US$5 to US$6.75, lighter eats such as quesadillas, tacos, fruit salad and eggs cost US$2.25 to US$3, and tortas are around US$1.50.

Backpackers Youth Hostel Carlos Einstein *(just off Camino al Rinconcito; hammocks US$4, dorm bed US$5.50, cabanas US$8 per person)* is squeezed between a sluggish creek and a large rock west of Palapa El Pescador. The accommodations have fresh air but are pretty tightly packed: the beds are small and hard but have mosquito nets. You can use the kitchen for US$0.60 a day (free if you're sleeping in a bed), and accommodation prices include breakfast. Nonguests are welcome for dinner – usually grilled fresh fish for about US$4.

La Posada del Arquitecto *(e laposadadelarquitecto@yahoo.com; El Rinconcito; hammocks US$4.50, cabanas with shared bath per person US$9, with private bath per person US$11.50-13.50)*, on a rocky outcrop near the west end of the beach, consists of seven cabanas cleverly constructed around the natural features of the land, using predominantly natural materials. Hammocks are available in dry season only.

El Agujón *(El Rinconcito; single/double cabanas US$6.75/13.50)*, across the street from the Posada del Arquitecto, has 10 small but clean cabanas on the hillside. Just below it, its **restaurant** serves a range of excellent French-bread tortas (US$2 to US$2.25), crepes (US$1.50 to US$3.25) and fish (US$5 to US$6). Pizzas (US$4.50 to US$6.75) are baked in the evening.

Cabañas Balamjuyuc (e *balamjuyuc@ hotmail.com; Camino a Punta Cometa; hammocks US$4, cots US$5.50; double cabanas low season US$11-17, high season US$22-27*) is perched on a hilltop above the west end of the beach with superb views. It uses solar electricity, and is run by a friendly, alternative-minded couple. The half-dozen cabanas are large, airy and mosquito-netted. Breakfast and dinner are available. Monthly rates, including use of the kitchen, are US$200. Balamjuyuc is 400m up from Camino al Rinconcito (signposted); you can also get there by steps up from El Rinconcito beach.

Alta Mira (☎/fax 584-31-04; **w** *www .labuenavista.com; Camino a Punta Cometa; doubles with bath US$36-42*) is next door to Cabañas Balamjuyuc and has the same approach routes. Its 10 or so rooms, with nice tiled bathrooms, mosquito nets and terrace with hammock, are Mazunte's classiest and comfiest. They're strung beside steps leading steeply up the hillside, and most catch breezes and magnificent views. There's a restaurant serving breakfast and dinner.

Posada Lalo's (*singles/doubles US$5.50/9*), about 750m inland from the beach, is a quiet, palm-shaded spot with friendly young owners. Its few simple rooms have mosquito nets and the price includes kitchen usage. Take the dirt track beside the *arroyo* (creek) from midway down the main road in Mazunte.

Entertainment
La Barra de Mazunte (*off Camino al Rinconcito*) is set deep among the trees on a minor track east of Camino al Rinconcito. It's the place to check out if you're after mellow, late-night music.

Getting There & Away
See the Pochutla section for information on transportation from Pochutla. *Camionetas*

between Mazunte and San Agustinillo or Zipolite cost US$0.50.

BAHÍAS DE HUATULCO
☎ 958 • pop 18,000

Mexico's newest big coastal resort is arising along a series of beautiful sandy bays, the Bahías de Huatulco (wah-**tool**-koh), 50km east of Pochutla. Until the 1980s this stretch of coast had just one small fishing village and was known to just a few lucky people as a great place for a quiet swim in translucent waters. Huatulco's developers appear to have learned some lessons from other modern Mexican resorts. Pockets of development are separated by tracts of unspoiled shoreline. The maximum building height is six stories, and no sewage goes into the sea. For now, Huatulco is still an enjoyable, relatively uncrowded resort with a succession of lovely beaches lapped by beautiful water and backed by forest. You can have a pretty active time here – agencies offer all sorts of energetic pursuits from rafting and horseback riding to diving and kayaking. Huatulco is not a place to stay long on a tight budget, however.

The Parque Nacional de Huatulco, declared in 1998, protects 119 sq km of land, sea and shoreline west of Santa Cruz Huatulco, but is under pressure as developers seek to open up new areas.

Orientation
A divided road leads about 5km down from Hwy 200 to La Crucecita, the service town for the resort. La Crucecita has the bus stations, the market, most of the shops and the only cheap accommodations. One kilometer south, on Bahía de Santa Cruz, is Santa Cruz Huatulco, site of the original village (no trace remains), with some hotels and a harbor. The other main developments so far are at Bahía Chahué, 1km northeast of Santa Cruz, and Tangolunda, 4km farther northeast.

The Huatulco bays are strung along the coast about 10km in each direction from Santa Cruz. From west to east, the main ones are: San Agustín, Chachacual, Cacaluta, Maguey, El Órgano, Santa Cruz, Chahué, Tangolunda and Conejos.

Bahías de Huatulco airport is 400m north of Hwy 200, 12km west of the turnoff to La Crucecita.

Information

Sedetur Oaxaca state tourist office (☎ 581-01-76; e sedetur6@oaxaca.gob.mx; Juárez; open 9am-5pm Mon-Fri, 9am-1:30pm Sat) is in Tangolunda, on the left as you roll in, behind La Pampa Argentina (see Places to Eat). **Bahías de Huatulco National Park administration** (☎ 587-04-46, 587-08-49; e pnh uatulco@mexico.com) didn't have an office at the time of writing, but feel free to call.

In La Crucecita, there's a **Bancrecer ATM** on the south side of Plaza Principal. **Bancrecer** (Bugambilias 1104) and **Bital** (Bugambilias 1504; open 8am-6pm Mon-Sat) change cash and traveler's checks. **Banamex** (open 9am-4pm Mon-Fri, 10am-2pm Sat) and **Bancomer** (open 8:30am-4pm Mon-Fri), both on Blvd Santa Cruz in Santa Cruz, change cash and traveler's checks and have ATMs.

La Crucecita's **post office** (Blvd Chahué s/n; open 8am-7pm Mon-Fri, 9am-1pm Sat) is 400m east of the Plaza Principal.

You can use the Internet at **Mare 2000** (Guanacastle 203; open 10am-9pm Mon-Fri, 10am-4pm Sat), in La Crucecita, for US$2 an hour. **Café Porticos** (☎ 587-01-65; Gardenia 902) has much better computers with faster access but it's more expensive at US$3.30 per hour. However, it has the best coffee in town!

In La Crucecita, **Lavandería Estrella** (cnr Flamboyan & Carrizal; open 8am-9pm Mon-Sat) will wash 3kg of laundry for US$3.85 with same-day service. **Lavandería Escorpión** (Gardenia 1403; open 7am-8:30pm Mon-Sat, 7am-noon Sun) is marginally cheaper.

Some doctors speak English at the **Hospital IMSS** (☎ 587-11-84; Blvd Chahué), halfway between La Crucecita and Bahía Chahué. The big hotels all have English-speaking doctors on call.

You can fuel up at the Pemex gas station just east of the intersection of Guamuchil and Blvd Chahué.

Beaches

Huatulco's beaches are sandy with clear waters (though boats and jet skis leave an oily film here and there). As throughout Mexico, all beaches are under federal control, and anyone can use them even when hotels like to treat them as private property.

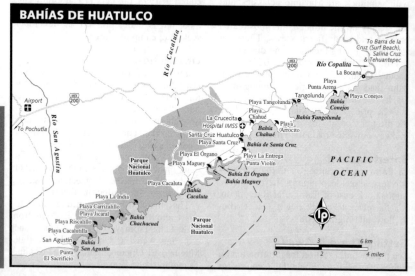

Some beaches have coral offshore and excellent snorkeling, though visibility can be poor in the rainy season.

Lanchas will whisk you out to most of the beaches from the Santa Cruz harbor. Taxis can also get you to most beaches for less money, but a boat ride is more fun. See Getting Around for information on both.

Bahía de Santa Cruz At Santa Cruz Huatulco, the small **Playa Santa Cruz** is kept pretty clean but is inferior to most Huatulco beaches.

Playa La Entrega lies toward the outer edge of Bahía de Santa Cruz, a five-minute *lancha* trip or 2.5km by paved road from Santa Cruz. This 300m-long beach, backed by a line of seafood palapas, can get crowded, but it has calm water and good snorkeling in a large area from which boats are cordoned off. 'La Entrega' means 'The Delivery': here in 1831, Mexican independence hero Vicente Guerrero was betrayed to his enemies by an Italian sea captain for 50,000 pieces of gold. Guerrero was taken to Cuilapan, near Oaxaca, and shot.

West of Bahía de Santa Cruz Some of the western bays are accessible by road. A 1.5km paved road diverges to **Bahía Maguey** from the road to La Entrega about half a kilometer out of Santa Cruz. Maguey's fine, 400m beach curves around a calm bay between forested headlands. It has a line of seafood palapas but is less busy than La Entrega. There's good snorkeling around the rocks at the left (east) side of the bay. **Bahía El Órgano**, just east of Maguey, has a 250m beach. You can reach it by a narrow 10-minute footpath that heads into the trees halfway along the Santa Cruz–Maguey track, where that track briefly broadens out. El Órgano has calm waters good for snorkeling, but it lacks comedores.

The beach at **Bahía Cacaluta** is about 1km long and protected by an island, though there can be undertow. Snorkeling is best around the island, and swimming is best at the east end of the beach. Behind the beach is a lagoon with birdlife. A narrow track that's just drivable in dry conditions heads

west 200m above the Maguey parking area and winds 2.5km, mostly through forest, to Cacaluta. Part of it follows a sandy riverbed, however, and cars have gotten stuck even in the dry season.

Bahía Chachacual, inaccessible by land, has a headland at each end and two beaches: The easterly **Playa La India** is one of Huatulco's most beautiful and is excellent for snorkeling and beach camping.

About 13km down a dirt road from a crossroads on Hwy 200, 1.7km west of the airport, is **Bahía San Agustín**. After 9km the road fords a river, which can be tricky after rains. The beach is long and sandy, with a long line of palapa comedores, some with hammocks to rent overnight. It's popular with Mexicans on weekends and holidays, but it's mostly quiet during other times. Usually the waters are calm and the snorkeling is good (some of the comedores rent equipment).

East of Bahía de Santa Cruz A paved road runs all the way to the eastern bays from La Crucecita and Santa Cruz, continuing eventually to Hwy 200. **Bahía Chahué** has a beach at its west end and another beach at its eastern end, along with a new harbor. **Bahía Tangolunda** is the site of the major top-end hotel developments to date. The sea is sometimes rough here, and you should beware of currents and heed the colored-flag safety system. Tangolunda has an 18-hole **golf course** too. About 3km farther east is the long sweep of **Playa Punta Arena**, on Bahía Conejos. Around a headland at the east end of Bahía Conejos is the more sheltered **Playa Conejos**, unreachable by road.

About 2km to 3km beyond Bahía Conejos, the road runs down to the coast again at **La Bocana**, at the mouth of the Río Copalita, where you'll find a handful of seafood comedores and a long, driftwood-strewn beach stretching to the east.

The small fishing village of **Barra de la Cruz**, at the mouth of the Río Zimatán, has good surf. Access is by a 1.5km dirt road from Hwy 200, around 20km east of Santa Cruz. A taxi from La Crucecita costs US$10 to the village and about US$17 all the way to the beach. East-bound 2nd-class buses will drop you at the crossroad from where it's a pleasant half-hour walk to the beach.

Activities

Snorkeling & Diving You can rent **snorkeling gear** beside the *lancha* kiosk at Santa Cruz harbor for US$5.75 a day. At Playa Maguey you can rent a snorkel, mask and fins for US$4.50 a day. These prices may rise in high season.

Buceo Sotavento *(Leeward Dive Center; ☎ 587-21-66; e scubahector@huatulco.net.mx; Plaza Oaxaca, Local 18, La Crucecita)* is owned and operated by the friendly Hector Lara who is both PADI and FMAS certified. Three-hour guided snorkeling trips (lots of fun) cost US$17 per person. An instructional dive costs US$71. Certified divers pay US$50/77 for guided one-/two-tank dives. Five-day PADI Open-Water (US$330) and 10-day Dive Master (US$500) certifications are also offered. He'll rent just about any dive equipment you need.

Hurricane Divers *(☎ 587-11-07; w www.hurricanedivers.com; Playa Santa Cruz)* is operated by an international group of divers who speak several languages between them and offer well-received tours, educational programs and all levels of DAN and PADI certifications and instructor courses. They're on Playa Santa Cruz, 50m from the harbor.

Triton Dive Center *(☎ 587-08-44; harborside, Santa Cruz)* is another reliable operator with similar offerings.

Rafting Near Huatulco, the **Copalita** and **Zimatán Rivers** have waters ranging from class 1 to class 4/5 in rafting terms. They're at their biggest in the rainy season, between July and November. Rafting and kayaking trips are operated out of La Crucecita by three outfitters:

Copalita River Tours *(☎ 587-05-35; Posada Michelle, Gardenia 8)* offers four-hour beginner and family outings for US$33 per person. Longer, more challenging trips cost US$66.

Turismo Conejo *(☎ 587-00-09; e turismoconejo@hotmail.com; Plaza Conejo, Guamuchil 208)* charges from US$17 per person for mellow bird-watching and family-style trips, to US$82 for rapid-packed runs.

Aventuras Piraguas *(☎ 587-13-33; w www.piraguas.com; Local 19, Plaza Oaxaca)* has a four-hour trip for US$50 and a full day tour for US$90.

Other Activities For full-day **rappelling, canyoning** and **ropes courses** (all around US$65 per person) contact Aventuras Piraguas or Turismo Conejo (see Rafting).

Buceo Sotavento (see Snorkeling & Diving) offers two- to eight-hour **fishing trips** for US$88 to US$220 for a maximum of six people. If you're fishing on your own (a fun way to supplement your food while camping on those isolated beaches) you can purchase equipment, including hand-spools, at **Implementos El Pescador** *(cnr Gardenia & Macuil)* in La Crucecita. Get your bait at the market.

Action Sports Marina *(☎ 581-00-55; w www.barcelo.com; Barceló Resort, Blvd Juárez s/n, Tangolunda; open daily)* rents sea kayaks, sailboats and catamarans costing US$17 to US$33 per hour.

Agritur *(☎ 587-18-10; Ocotillo 312, La Crucecita)* is a cooperative of fishermen-turned-papaya farmers who were displaced from their land by Huatulco resort development. They're now attempting another transition to ecotourism, offering **horseback rides** through the papaya plantation, the forest and out to Playa Cacaluta. Rides cost US$38 per person for 1½-hours.

Places to Stay

Where you sleep in Huatulco depends largely on your pocketbook. La Crucecita has all the budget and mid-range hotels, and Santa Cruz, Tangolunda and Bahía Chahué have nearly all the top-enders.

Most Huatulco room rates vary with the seasons. Prices given in this section, unless specified, are for the high season between early January and Easter.

Camping within the national park is US$11 per person per night; enforcement is lax. If you wish to acquire forms and pay the fee, contact the **Bahías de Huatulco National Park** office administration by telephone (see

Information earlier). One of the two administrators will tell you where their new (or temporary) office is and will explain in Spanish the complex process of paying the fee. That process goes something like this: you purchase a SAT-05 form at a *papelería* (stationary store), fill it out, take it to a bank, and pay the camping fee to the bank. The bank clerk stamps your SAT-05 form, which you must then bring to the park administrators who will give you a permit.

La Crucecita The following hotels all have fans and private bathrooms.

Hotel Posada Del Parque (☎ 587-02-19; *Flamboyan 306; low season singles/doubles US$16.50/22, with air-con US$22/27*), a good deal on the main plaza, has fairly comfortable and sizable rooms. The pricier ones have TV.

Posada Michelle (☎ 587-05-35; *Gardenia 8; singles & doubles US$22*) is next to the EB bus station and can be noisy. But it's a friendly place, and the dozen or so rooms are reasonable.

Hotel Busanvi I (☎ 587-00-56; *Carrizal 601; rooms with fan/air-con US$22/44*) offers clean rooms with good beds and great showers. Two have balconies.

LA CRUCECITA

To Hwy 200 & Pochutla

0   50   100 m
0   50   100 yards

Sabali
Gardenia
Jazmin
Pochote
Palo Verde
Palma Real
Ocotillo
Macuil
Macuil
Macuhitle
Guarumbo
Guanacastle
Priv Tamarindo
Plaza Principal
Flamboyan
Flamboyan
Chacah
Colorin
Laurel
Canal
Cocotillo

Av Bugambilias
Carrizal
Blvd Chahué
Blvd Chahué

Parque Ecológico Rufino Tamayo

Av Oaxaca
Blvd Chahué
Guamuchil
Guamuchil
Market

To Santa Cruz Huatulco

To Hospital IMSS, Posada Chahué, Bahía Chahué & Tangolunda

PLACES TO STAY
5 Hotel Benimar
7 Posada Michelle; Copalita River Tours
16 Misión de los Arcos; Café Porticos
17 Hotel Flamboyant
27 Hotel Plaza Conejo; Turismo Conejo
33 Hotel Posada Del Parque
36 Hotel Suites Begonias
38 Hotel Busanvi I
40 Hotel Arrecife

PLACES TO EAT
13 Taquería Safari
15 Restaurant Portalitos
19 Pizzería Don Wilo
23 Comedores
25 Los Portales
28 Panificadora San Alejandro
34 Cactus Bar & Grill
35 Café Oasis

OTHER
1 Microbuses to Salina Cruz
2 Transportes Rápidos de Pochutla Bus Stop
3 Park Entrance
4 Bital
6 Lavandería Escorpión
8 Estrella Blanca Bus Station
9 Cristóbal Colón Bus Station
10 Budget
11 Agritur
12 Bancrecer
14 Implementos El Pescador
18 La Crema; La Tropicana
20 Mare 2000
21 Park Entrance
22 Parroquia de Guadalupe
24 Bahías Plus
26 La Selva
29 Colectivo Taxi & Microbus Stop
30 Pemex
31 Bancrecer (ATM)
32 Plaza Oaxaca (Buceo Sotavento; Aventuras Piraguas)
37 Lavandería Estrella
39 Post Office

OAXACA

Hotel Arrecife (☎ 587-17-07; *Colorín 510; singles US$23, doubles & triples US$28-39, with air-con US$45*) has varied rooms, the best of which are sizable and have air-con, balcony and TV; the worst are small and open straight onto the street. All have private bath, but some are outside the room.

Hotel Benimar (☎ 587-04-47; *Bugambilias 1404; singles/doubles/triples US$27/33/44*) is a family-run hotel with plain but cheerful rooms.

Hotel Plaza Conejo (☎ 587-00-09; e *tur ismoconejo@hotmail.com; Guamuchil 208; singles/doubles US$49/60*) is a friendly hotel in Plaza Conejo. The five tidy, bright rooms have fan, telephone and TV.

Misión de los Arcos (☎ 587-01-65; w *www .misiondelosarcos.com; Gardenia 902; rooms with fan/air-con US$44/50, suites with kitchen US$104*) is Huatulco's angelic love pad. Its 15 plush rooms are cloud-white from floor to ceiling, making for a *romantic* holiday. The suite has a kitchen and the junior suite has a balcony. Yum.

Hotel Flamboyant (☎ 587-01-13; e *flam boyant@huatulco.net.mx; Plaza Principal; singles & doubles US$68*), a big pink hotel with a courtyard, pool and restaurant, offers 70 comfortable rooms with TV, telephone and air-con. It runs free transportation to Playa La Entrega, and up to two children under 12 stay free.

Santa Cruz Huatulco Santa Cruz has quality hotels, though none of them are right on the beach.

Hotel Marlin (☎ 587-00-55, 800-712-73-73; *Mitla 107; rooms US$80-100*) has spacious rooms with TV and air-con. The restaurant is good.

Hotel Castillo Huatulco (☎ 587-01-44; e *castillo@huatulco.net.mx; Blvd Santa Cruz 303; low-season rooms US$66-77, high-season US$110-150*) has a decent pool, a restaurant and 112 good-size air-con rooms with TV. Transportation to Castillo's beach club on Bahía Chahué is free.

Hotel Marina Resort (☎ 587-09-63; w *www.hotelmarinaresort.com; Tehuantepec 112; singles/doubles US$98/115*) is on the east side of the harbor with 50 spacious rooms, many with balconies. It has three pools and offers extras like temazcal, massage and skin-treatment with mud.

Hotel Meigas Binniguenda (☎ 587-00-77; e *binniguenda@huatulco.net.mx; Blvd Santa*

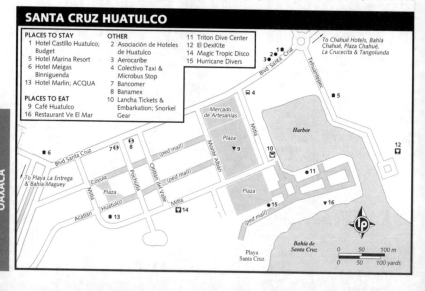

SANTA CRUZ HUATULCO

PLACES TO STAY
1 Hotel Castillo Huatulco; Budget
5 Hotel Marina Resort
6 Hotel Meigas Binniguenda
13 Hotel Marlin; ACQUA

PLACES TO EAT
9 Café Huatulco
16 Restaurant Ve El Mar

OTHER
2 Asociación de Hoteles de Huatulco
3 Aerocaribe
4 Colectivo Taxi & Microbus Stop
7 Bancomer
8 Banamex
10 Lancha Tickets & Embarkation; Snorkel Gear
11 Triton Dive Center
12 El DexKite
14 Magic Tropic Disco
15 Hurricane Divers

To Chahué Hotels, Bahía Chahué, Plaza Chahué, La Crucecita & Tangolunda

Blvd Santa Cruz

Tehuantepec

Mercado de Artesanías

Mitla

Harbor

Plaza

(ped mall)

Monte Albán

Blvd Santa Cruz

Coyula

Pochula

Ojitlán del Valle

Mitla

Plaza

Huatulco

Acatlán

To Playa La Entrega & Bahía Maguey

Plaza

(ped mall)

Bahía de Santa Cruz

Playa Santa Cruz

0   50   100 m
0   50   100 yards

OAXACA

Cruz 201; low-season rooms US$66, high-season US$132) is Huatulco's oldest hotel, dating from all of 1987. It has a garden, a relaxing pool area, a restaurant and 195 aircon rooms with TV. It's a good deal in the low season.

Tangolunda & Bahía Chahué If you want a holiday in a top-end Huatulco hotel, right on the beach, a package is your best bet. If you're already in Mexico, ask a travel agent. Around US$700 could buy two people return flights from Mexico City and three nights in a top hotel. Many of Tangolunda's hotels are all-inclusive, meaning you eat, sleep and drink at your hotel (so get you're money's worth – drink heavily).

Hotel Plaza Huatulco *(☎ 581-00-35; e plazahuatulco@hotmail.com; Blvd Juárez 23; singles/doubles US$50/56, suites US$100-150)* is a small place across the street from the Barceló Resort in Tangolunda. All units have air-con and cable TV; the suites also have terraces and kitchenettes.

Quinta Real *(☎ 581-04-28; W www.quintareal.com; Paseo Juárez 2; suites from US$280)* is a luxurious hotel with a hilltop location at the west end of Tangolunda. It has 27 suites only, all with Jacuzzis and splendid ocean views. The grounds extend down to the beach, with an excellent pool area near the sand.

Barceló Resort *(☎ 581-00-55; W www.barcelo.com; Blvd Juárez s/n; all-inclusive rates per double per night US$225)*, east of the Quinta Real, has more than 300 rooms, all with ocean view. Its big pool sits in a beachside garden, and you'll find all the amenities you'd expect – restaurants, bars, tennis courts, gymnasium, water sports, shops and nightly mariachi entertainment. Packages for two people including meals are sometimes available for around US$165. The resort requires a minimum stay of three nights.

Hotel Gala *(☎ 581-00-00; W www.galaresorts.com.mx, Blvd Juárez s/n; all-inclusive singles/doubles US$180/360)* next door to the Barceló, has four pools, a disco and 300 aircon rooms. Prices include all meals, drinks, land and water sports and entertainment.

Camino Real Zaashila *(☎ 581-04-60; W www.caminoreal.com/zaashila; Blvd Juárez 5; rooms US$200-250)*, a little farther around the bay from the Gala, is tranquil and attractive, with an excellent pool and beautiful gardens. The more expensive rooms have their own small pool.

Casa del Mar *(☎ 581-02-03; W hotels .baysofhuatulco.com.mx/casadelmar/; Balcones de Tangolunda 13; suites US$132)*, 1km past the Zaashila, is an elegant hotel with 25 air-con suites and a beautifully sited pool.

Hotel Villablanca *(☎ 587-06-06; W www .villablancahotels.com.mx; Blvd Juárez at Zapoteco; rooms US$91, suites US$108)*, about 250m back from the beach on Bahía Chahué, has a good pool and a spacious patio area complete with a volleyball court. It offers pleasant, air-con rooms with satellite TV, and the restaurant cooks up good food at reasonable prices.

Places to Eat

If you're off to the beach for the day, you'll find decent seafood palapas at playas La Entrega, Maguey, San Agustín and La Bocana. A whole grilled *huachinango* (red snapper) will cost US$6 to US$9.

La Crucecita The very clean market has several comedores serving up fish or shrimp platters for US$4 to US$5 and enfrijoladas or entomatadas for US$2.75. Get your baked goods at **Panificadora San Alejandro** *(Flamboyan 213; open 6:30am-10pm daily)*.

Café Porticos *(☎ 587-01-65; Gardenia 902; open 8am-11:30pm daily)* serves the best coffee and espresso drinks in town. They have ice cream, malts and *liquados* (fruit shakes), and Internet service to boot.

Café Oasis *(☎ 587-00-45; Plaza Principal; mains US$2.50-5; open 7am-midnight daily)* serves good, moderately priced fare, from tortas to *filete de pescado* (fish fillet), steaks and Oaxacan specialities. The whopping yoghurt, fruit and granola plate with a bottomless cup of coffee make an excellent breakfast.

Los Portales *(☎ 587-00-70; Bugambilias 603; mains US$3.50-5)* is also good, with offerings such as an *alambre de pechuga de* *pollo* (chicken breast kebab) with bell peppers and onions or a *farolado de pollo* (two flour tortillas with chicken, bacon and cheese). Burgers run US$4 to US$5, and there are vegetarian options as well.

Cactus Bar & Grill (☎ 587-06-48; Flamboyan 304; mains US$3-10; open noon-late daily) serves flavorful seafood dishes and, thanks to its popular saddle-seat bar, has a good-time feel.

Pizzería Don Wilo (☎ 587-06-23; Guanacastle 307; mains US$4-7; open noon-11pm daily), on the plaza, serves pizza, but it's more popular for its Oaxacan specialties like tlayudas and tamales.

Restaurant Portalitos (Carrizal 1008; open 6pm-2am daily) is a cool *rancho*-style taquería serving plates of four good tacos for less than US$2.

Taquería Safari (Macuil; open 5pm-11pm daily) is great for cheap eats: authentic tacos, alambres and tlayudas all cost under US$2.50. Five *tacos de barbacoa* cost only US$1.60. Beer is also cheap.

Santa Cruz Huatulco Food at the restaurants on Playa Santa Cruz is mostly average.
Restaurant Ve El Mar (☎ 587-03-64; Playa Santa Cruz; mains US$6-15; open 8am-10pm daily) is the exception to the rule. How does filet mignon (US$10) or squid cooked in its own ink sound? It's all fresh and delicious, the margaritas pack a wallop, and the beachside location can't be beat.

Café Huatulco (☎ 587-12-28; drinks average US$2; open 8am-11:30pm daily) smack in the middle of the central plaza, serves good, local Pluma coffee in many different ways. Nine varieties of tamales cost between US$0.75 and US$3 each.

Tangolunda The big hotels offer a choice of expensive bars, coffee shops and restaurants. The **Casa del Mar** (☎ 581-02-03; w hotels .baysofhuatulco.com.mx/casadelmar/; Balcones de Tangolunda 13) has one of the best restaurants, with a great view. You'll spend US$30 to US$50 for a full dinner with wine.

There are also a few restaurants, medium to expensive in price, along Tangolunda's two streets.

La Pampa Argentina (☎ 581-01-75; Blvd Juárez s/n; mains US$11-20; open 1pm-1am daily), opposite the golf course, serves delicious grilled meats. Staking out a good table is usually easy.

La Casa de la Nona (☎ 581-00-35; Blvd Juárez s/n; mains US$4-15), opposite the Barceló Resort, is an Italian/Argentine restaurant offering good-priced pastas, steaks, pizzas and salads.

Entertainment

La Crema (☎ 587-07-02; Plaza Principal, La Crucecita; open 7pm-3am daily), an upstairs bar entered from Gardenia, pulls a cool crowd. A shot of tequila starts at US$2. Pizzas are available too.

La Selva (☎ 587-10-63; Bugambilias 601, La Crucecita) is a laid-back, open-air bar overlooking the Plaza Principal.

Santa Cruz has a couple of nightspots, open from around 10pm, Thursday to Sunday. Cover charges are typically US$7 per person, but different nights have different deals. **ACQUA**, beside Hotel Marlin, is decent and **Magic Tropic Disco** plays *cumbia*, merengue and *tropical*. **El DexKite** (☎ 587-09-71; harborside) is *the* hottest place in Huatulco, where the fun goes on all night, assisted by drinks-by-the-liter.

Noches Oaxaqueñas (☎ 581-00-01; Blvd Juárez s/n, Tangolunda; admission US$17), beside the Tangolunda traffic circle, presents a Guelaguetza regional dance show Friday, Saturday and Sunday evenings (drinks and/or dinner cost extra).

Getting There & Away
Air Two to four flights daily to/from Mexico City are offered by **Mexicana** (☎ 587-02-23, Plaza Chahué, Local 3, Blvd Juárez, Tangolunda; ☎ 581-90-08, airport). Cheap charters from Canada and the US are occasionally available. Huatulco's airport code is HUX.

Aerocaribe (☎ 587-12-20, Blvd Santa Cruz; ☎ 581-90-30, airport) has an office near the Hotel Castillo Huatulco in Santa Cruz; it flies daily to Oaxaca city (about US$100). The travel agency **Bahías Plus** (☎ 587-09-32; Carrizal 704), in La Crucecita, can help with air tickets.

Bus The main bus stations are on Gardenia in La Crucecita. Some buses coming to Huatulco are marked 'Santa Cruz Huatulco,' but they still terminate in La Crucecita. Make sure your bus is *not* travelling to Santa María Huatulco, which is a long way inland.

Cristóbal Colón (☎ 587-02-61) is on Gardenia at Ocotillo and has 1st-class buses. Many of its buses are *de paso* (en route), meaning tickets are sold when the bus arrives; get there early. If bussing to Oaxaca in peak season, purchase your ticket as much as five days in advance to guarantee yourself a seat. **Estrella Blanca** (☎ 587-01-03), on Gardenia at Palma Real, has 1st- and 2nd-class services.

Daily departures include:

Acapulco 1st-class/ordinario US$25/19, 10 to 12 hours, 515km, five EB buses daily
Oaxaca city US$19, 7½ hours, 405km via Salina Cruz; two Colón buses overnight
Pochutla US$1.50 one hour, 50km, Transportes Rápidos de Pochutla every 15 minutes to about 8:30pm, from Blvd Chahué opposite Bugambilias; US$1.75 to US$2.25, five EB buses daily; US$2.25, nine Colón buses daily
Puerto Escondido US$4.25 to US$5.50, 2½ hours, 115km, five EB buses and nine Colón buses daily
Salina Cruz US$3.50, 2½ hours, 145km, microbuses every 20 minutes from street one block north of Blvd Chahué; US$6.50, three EB buses daily; US$7, five Colón buses daily

For coastal destinations west of Huatulco, take an Acapulco–bound EB bus; the 2nd-class buses will stop just about anywhere along Hwy 200. Colón and EB travel to Mexico City.

Car & Motorcycle VW beetles cost around US$60 a day to rent with unlimited kilometers, taxes and insurance; other cars start around US$85. Auto rental agencies include:

Alamo (☎ 581-00-58) Juárez s/n, Tangolunda; (☎ 581-90-74) airport
Budget (☎ 587-00-10) Ocotillo at Jazmín, La Crucecita; (☎ 587-01-35) Hotel Castillo Huatulco, Santa Cruz; (☎ 581-90-00) airport

Getting Around

Colectivo combis from the airport are provided by **Transportación Terrestre** (☎ 581-90-14, 581-90-24) for US$7.50 per person to La Crucecita, Santa Cruz or Bahía Chahué, and for US$8.75 to Tangolunda. Get tickets at the company's airport kiosk. For a private cab, walk just outside the airport gate, where one will be there waiting for you for US$10 to La Crucecita, Santa Cruz or Tangolunda – or US$13.50 to Pochutla. You could, walk 400m down to Hwy 200 and get a microbus for US$0.60 to La Crucecita or US$1.25 to Pochutla. Those heading to La Crucecita are marked 'Santa Cruz' or 'Bahías Huatulco'.

Colectivo taxis and a few microbuses provide transportation between La Crucecita, Santa Cruz Huatulco and Tangolunda. In La Crucecita catch them on Guamuchil at Carrizal. In Santa Cruz they stop by the harbor, and in Tangolunda at the traffic circle outside the Hotel Gala. Fares are the same in either type of vehicle: from La Crucecita to Santa Cruz US$0.35, to Tangolunda and Bahia Chahué US$0.45.

For mountain bike rentals contact **Eco Discover** (☎ 581-00-02; Juárez s/n, Plaza Las Conchas 6, Tangolunda) or **La Tropicana** (☎ 587-09-12; Guanacastle 311) opposite the main plaza in La Crucecita.

From La Crucecita you will pay around US$1.50 for a taxi to Santa Cruz, US$2.25 to Tangolunda and US$6.25 to Bahía Maguey.

Lanchas take passengers from Santa Cruz to nearby beaches between 8am and 4pm or 5pm, and return to collect you by dusk; tickets are sold at a hut beside the harbor. Round-trip rates for up to 10 people include: Playa La Entrega, US$12; Bahía Maguey or Bahía El Órgano, US$35.

OAXACA

Language

LANGUAGES OF MEXICO

The predominant language of Mexico is Spanish. In cities, towns and larger villages you'll almost always find someone who speaks at least some English. All the same, if you take the time to learn a few words and phrases in Spanish, the response you'll get from Mexicans will generally be far more positive.

About 50 indigenous languages are spoken as a first language by seven million or more people in Mexico, of whom about 15% don't speak Spanish.

For a more in-depth guide to the Spanish of Mexico, get a copy of Lonely Planet's *Latin American Spanish phrasebook*.

SPANISH

Mexican Spanish is unlike the variety of the language spoken in Spain in two main respects: in Mexico the Castilian lisp has more or less disappeared and numerous indigenous words have been adopted.

Pronunciation

Most of the sounds in Spanish have equivalents in English, and there is a clear and consistent relationship between pronunciation and spelling.

Vowels

Spanish has five vowels: **a**, **e**, **i**, **o** and **u**. They have a uniform pronunciation more or less as in the following English examples:

a	as in 'father'
e	as in 'met'
i	as in 'feet'
o	as in the British 'hot'
u	as in 'put'

Consonants

c	as the 's' in 'sit' before **e** or **i**; elsewhere as 'k'
ch	as in 'choose'
g	as in 'gate' before **a**, **o** and **u**; before **e** or **i** it's a harsh, breathy sound as the 'h' in 'hit.' Note that when **g** is followed by **ue** or **ui** the **u** is silent, unless it has a dieresis (**ü**), in which case it functions much like English 'w', eg, *guerra* – '**geh**-rra', *güero* – '**gweh**-ro'.
h	always silent
j	a harsh, guttural sound similar to the 'ch' in the Scottish *loch*
ll	as the 'y' in 'yard'
ñ	nasal sound like the 'ny' in 'canyon'
q	as the 'k' in 'kick'; always followed by a silent **u**
r	a very short rolled 'r'
rr	a longer rolled 'r'
x	like the English 'h' when followed by **e** or **i**; otherwise as in 'taxi'. In many Indian words (particularly Mayan ones) 'x' is pronounced like English 'sh'.
z	the same as English 's'; never as English 'z'

Stress

There are three general rules regarding stress:

- For words ending in a vowel, **n** or **s**, the stress falls on the penultimate (next-to-last) syllable, eg, *naranja* – 'na-**rahn**-ha', *joven* – '**ho**-ven', *zapatos* – 'sa-**pa**-tos'

- For words ending in a consonant other than **n** or **s**, the stress falls on the final syllable, eg, *estoy* – 'es-**toy**', *ciudad* – 'syoo-**dahd**', *catedral* – 'ka-teh-**dral**'

- If a word has an accented vowel, the stress will always fall on that syllable, eg, *México* – '**meh**-hee-ko', *mudéjar* – 'moo-**deh**-har, *Cortés* – 'cor-**tess**'

Gender

Nouns in Spanish are either masculine or feminine; nouns ending in 'o,' 'e' or 'ma' are usually masculine, and nouns ending in 'a,' 'ión' or 'dad' are usually feminine. Some nouns take either a masculine or feminine form, depending on the ending, eg, *viajero* is a male traveler, *viajera* is a female traveler.

Greetings & Civilities

Hello/Hi.	*Hola.*
Good morning/ Good day.	*Buenos días.*
Good afternoon.	*Buenas tardes.*
Good evening/ Good night.	*Buenas noches.*
See you.	*Hasta luego.*
Good-bye.	*Adiós.*
Pleased to meet you.	*Mucho gusto.*
Please.	*Por favor.*
Thank you.	*Gracias.*
You're welcome.	*De nada.*
Excuse me.	*Perdóneme.*

People

I	*yo*
you (informal)	*tú*
you (polite)	*usted*
you (pl, polite)	*ustedes*
he/it	*el*
she/it	*ella*
we	*nosotros*
they	*ellos/ellas* (m/f)
Sir/Mr	*Señor*
Madam/Mrs	*Señora*
Miss	*Señorita*

my ...	*mi ...*
wife	*esposa*
husband	*esposo/marido*
sister	*hermana*
brother	*hermano*

Useful Words & Phrases

Yes.	*Sí.*
No.	*No.*
I understand.	*Entiendo.*
I don't understand.	*No entiendo.*
Please speak slowly.	*Por favor hable despacio.*
What did you say?	*¿Mande?* (colloq) or *¿Cómo?*
Where is ...?	*¿Dónde está ...?*

good/OK	*bueno*
bad	*malo*
better	*mejor*
best	*lo mejor*
more	*más*
less	*menos*
very little	*poco/poquito*

Nationalities

Where are you from?	*¿De dónde eres?*

I'm ...	*Yo soy ...* (m/f)
American	*(norte)americano/a*
Australian	*australiano/a*
British	*británico/a*
Canadian	*canadiense*
English	*inglés/inglesa*
French	*francés/francesa*
German	*alemán/alemana*

Getting Around

I'm looking for ...	*Busco ...*
the bus station	*la terminal de autobuses/ la central camionera*
the train station	*la estación del ferrocarril*
the airport	*el aeropuerto*
the ticket office	*la taquilla*
the waiting room	*la sala de espera*
the baggage check-in	*(recibo de) equipaje*
a toilet	*un sanitario*

When does the ... leave/arrive?	*¿A qué hora sale/llega ...*
bus	*la camión/el autobús*
minibus	*el (colectivo/combi/ micro)*
plane	*la avión*
train	*el tren*

taxi	*taxi*
departure	*salida*
arrival	*llegada*
platform	*andén*
left-luggage room/ checkroom	*guardería/guarda de equipaje*

How far is ...?	*¿A qué distancia está ...?*
How long? (How much time?)	*¿Cuánto tiempo?*
street	*calle*
avenue	*avenida*
road	*camino*
highway	*carretera*
corner (of)	*esquina (de)*
corner/bend	*vuelta*
block	*cuadra*
to the left	*a la izquierda*
to the right	*a la derecha*
forward, ahead	*adelante*
straight ahead	*todo recto* or *derecho*
north	*norte (Nte)*
south	*sur*
east	*este*
east (in an address)	*oriente (Ote)*
west	*oeste*
west (in an address)	*poniente (Pte)*

Car Travel

gasoline/petrol	*gasolina*
fuel/petrol station	*gasolinera*
unleaded	*sin plomo*
fill the tank	*llene el tanque/ llenarlo*
full	*lleno/ful*
oil	*aceite*
tire	*llanta*
puncture	*agujero*

How much is a liter of gasoline?
¿Cuánto cuesta el litro de gasolina?
My car's broken down.
Se me ha descompuesto el carro.

Signs

Entrada	**Entrance**
Salida	**Exit**
Información	**Information**
Abierto	**Open**
Cerrado	**Closed**
Prohibido	**Prohibited**
Comisaria	**Police Station**
Servicios/Baños	**Toilets**
Hombres	**Men**
Mujeres	**Women**

Highway Signs

Though Mexico mostly uses the familiar international road signs, you should be prepared to encounter these other signs as well:

Camino en Reparación	road repairs
Conserve Su Derecha	keep to the right
Curva Peligrosa	dangerous curve
Derrumbes	landslides/ subsidence
Despacio	slow
Desviación	detour
Disminuya Su Velocidad	slow down
Escuela (Zona Escolar)	school (zone)
Hombres Trabajando	men working
No Hay Paso	road closed
No Rebase	do not overtake
Peligro	danger
Prepare Su Cuota	have toll ready
Puente Angosto	narrow bridge
Topes/Vibradores	speed bumps
Tramo en Reparación	road under repair
Vía Corta	short route (often a toll road)
Vía Cuota	toll highway

I need a tow truck.
Necesito un remolque.
Is there a garage near here?
¿Hay un garaje cerca de aquí?

Border Paperwork

birth certificate	*certificado de nacimiento*
border (frontier)	*la frontera*
car-owner's title	*título de propiedad*
car registration	*registración*
customs	*aduana*
driver's license	*licencia de manejar*
identification	*identificación*
immigration	*migración*
insurance	*seguro*
passport	*pasaporte*
temporary vehicle import permit	*permiso de importación temporal de vehículo*
tourist card	*tarjeta de turista*
visa	*visado*

Mexican Slang

Style your conversations with a little slang and you'll do your street cred no harm at all. You'll hear many of these slang words and phrases all over Mexico.

¿Qué onda?
  What's up?, What's happening?
¿Qué pasión? (Mexico City only)
  What's up?, What's going on?
¡Qué padre!
  How cool!
fregón
  really good, way cool, awesome
buena onda
  good vibe, cool
estar de pelos
  to be super, awesome
alipús
  booze
Echamos un alipús/trago.
  Let's go for a drink.
tirar la onda
  try to pick someone up, flirt
ligar
  to flirt
irse de reventón
  go partying
¡Vámonos de reventón!
  Let's (go) party!
reven
  a 'rave' – huge party, lots of loud music and
  wild atmosphere
un desmadre
  a mess
Simón.
  Yes.
Nel.
  No.
No hay tos.
  No problem. (literally 'There's no cough.')
¡Órale! (positive meaning)
  Sounds great! (responding to an invitation)
¡Órale! (negative meaning)
  What the #$*£!? (taunting exclamation)
Órale
  OK, fine (responding to a statement)

¿Te cae?
  Are you serious?
Me late.
  Sounds really good to me.
Me vale.
  I don't care. Whatever.
Sale y vale.
  I agree. Sounds good.
¡Paso sin ver!
  I can't stand it! No thank you!
¡Guácatelas! ¡Guácala!
  How gross! That's disgusting!
¡Bájale!
  Don't exaggerate! Come on!
¡Te sales! ¡Te pasas!
  That's it! You've gone too far!
¿Le agarraste?
  Did you understand? Do you get it?
un resto
  a lot
lana
  money, dough
chela
  beer
brodi, carnal
  brother
cuate, cuaderno
  buddy
chavo
  guy, dude
chava
  girl, gal
jefe
  father
jefa
  mother
la tira, la julia
  the police
chapusero
  a cheater (at cards, for example)
chingón
  bad-ass, tough, cool, macho

Accommodation

I'm looking for ... Busco ...
  a guesthouse una casa de
                  huéspedes

a hotel un hotel
an inn una posada
a room un cuarto/
          una habitación

LANGUAGE

I'd like (a) ...	Quisiera ...
Do you have (a) ...	¿Tiene ...?
room with one bed	un cuarto sencillo
room with two beds	un cuarto doble
room for one	un cuarto para una persona
room for two	un cuarto para dos personas
double bed	una cama matrimonial
twin beds	camas gemelas

with bath	con baño
shower	ducha/regadera
hot water	agua caliente
air-conditioning	aire acondicionado
blanket	manta/cobija
towel	toalla
soap	jabón
toilet paper	papel higiénico
the check (bill)	la cuenta

What's the price?
  ¿Cuál es el precio?
Does that include taxes?
  ¿Están incluidos los impuestos?
Does that include service?
  ¿Está incluido el servicio?

Around Town

Where is ...?	¿Dónde está ...?
I'm looking for ...	Estoy buscando ...
a bank	un banco
an exchange bureau	una casa de cambio
an ATM	una caja permanente or un cajero automático
the post office	el correo

money	dinero
traveler's checks	cheques de viajero
credit card	tarjeta de crédito
exchange rate	tipo de cambio

I'd like to change some money.
  Quiero/quisiera cambiar dinero.
What's the exchange rate?
  ¿Cuál es el tipo de cambio?
Is there a commission?
  ¿Hay comisión?

Emergencies

Help!	¡Socorro!/¡Auxilio!
Fire!	¡Fuego!
Call a doctor!	¡Llama a un médico!
Call the police!	¡Llama a la policía!
I'm ill.	Estoy enfermo/a. (m/f)
I'm lost.	Estoy perdido/a. (m/f)
Go away!	¡Váyase!

letter	carta
parcel	paquete
postcard	postal
stamps	estampillas, timbres
airmail	correo aéreo
telephone	teléfono
telephone call	llamada
telephone number	número telefónico
telephone card	tarjeta telefónica
local call	llamada local
long-distance call	llamada de larga distancia
person to person	persona a persona
collect (reverse charges)	por cobrar
busy	ocupado

(Don't) Hang up.   (No) Cuelgue.

Shopping

How much is it?	¿Cuánto cuesta? or ¿Cuánto se cobra?
I want ...	Quiero ...
I don't want ...	No quiero ...
I'd like ...	Quisiera ...
Give me ...	Déme ...
Do you have ...?	¿Tiene ...?
Is/are there ...?	¿Hay ...?

Times & Dates

yesterday	ayer
today	hoy
tomorrow (also at some point, or maybe)	mañana
morning	mañana
tomorrow morning	mañana por la mañana
afternoon	tarde
night	noche
What time is it?	¿Qué hora es?

Monday	*lunes*
Tuesday	*martes*
Wednesday	*miércoles*
Thursday	*jueves*
Friday	*viernes*
Saturday	*sábado*
Sunday	*domingo*

Numbers

0	*cero*
1	*un/uno* (m), *una* (f)
2	*dos*
3	*tres*
4	*cuatro*
5	*cinco*
6	*seis*
7	*siete*
8	*ocho*
9	*nueve*
10	*diez*
11	*once*
12	*doce*
13	*trece*
14	*catorce*
15	*quince*
16	*dieciséis*
17	*diecisiete*
18	*dieciocho*
19	*diecinueve*
20	*veinte*
21	*veintiuno*
22	*veintidós*
30	*treinta*
31	*treinta y uno*
32	*treinta y dos*
40	*cuarenta*
50	*cincuenta*
60	*sesenta*
70	*setenta*
80	*ochenta*
90	*noventa*
100	*cien*
101	*ciento uno*
143	*ciento cuarenta y tres*
200	*doscientos*
500	*quinientos*
700	*setecientos*
900	*novecientos*
1000	*mil*
2000	*dos mil*
one million	*millón*

FOOD
Eating Out

Note that *el menú* can mean either the menu or the special fixed-price meal of the day. If you want the menu, ask for *la carta*.

fork	*tenedor*
knife	*cuchillo*
spoon	*cuchara*
plate	*plato*
cup	*taza*
glass	*vaso*
wineglass	*copa*
napkin	*servilleta*
waiter	*mesero/a*
check (bill)	*cuenta*
tip	*propina*

Menu Decoder
Antojitos

Antojitos – literally 'little whims' – can refer to anything from snacks to light meals. They can be eaten any time, on their own or as part of a larger meal. There are countless varieties, but here are some of the more common ones:

burrito – any combination of beans, cheese, meat, chicken or seafood seasoned with salsa or chili and wrapped in a wheat-flour tortilla – especially popular in northern Mexico

chilaquiles – fried tortilla chips with sauce or scrambled eggs, often with grated cheese on top

chiles rellenos – chilies stuffed with cheese, meat or other foods, deep fried and baked in sauce

empanada – small pastry with savory or sweet filling

enchilada – ingredients similar to those used in burritos and tacos rolled up in a tortilla, dipped in sauce and then baked or partly fried; *enchiladas Suizas* (Swiss enchiladas) come smothered in a blanket of thick cream

enfrijolada – soft tortilla in a frijole sauce with cheese and onion on top

entomatada – soft tortilla in a tomato sauce with cheese and onion on top *gordita* – fried maize dough filled with refried beans, topped with cream, cheese and lettuce

guacamole – mashed avocados mixed with onion, chili, lemon, tomato and other ingredients

quesadilla – flour tortilla topped or filled with cheese and occasionally other ingredients and then heated

queso fundido – melted cheese served with tortillas

sincronizada – a lightly grilled or fried flour-tortilla 'sandwich,' usually with a ham and cheese filling

sope – thick patty of corn dough lightly grilled then served with *salsa verde* or *salsa roja* and frijoles, onion and cheese

taco – the Número Uno Mexican snack: soft corn tortilla wrapped or folded around the same fillings as a burrito

tamal – corn dough stuffed with meat, beans, chilies or nothing at all, wrapped in corn husks or banana leaves and then steamed

torta – Mexican-style sandwich in a roll

tostada – crisp-fried, thin tortilla that may be eaten as a nibble while you're waiting for the rest of a meal or can be topped with meat or cheese, tomatoes, beans and lettuce

Soups

birria – a spicy-hot soup (practically stew) of meat, onions, peppers and cilantro, served with tortillas

caldo – broth *(caldo tlalpeño* is a hearty chicken, vegetables and chili variety)

gazpacho – chilled vegetable soup spiced with hot chilies

menudo/panza – tripe soup made with the spiced entrails of various four-legged beasts

pozole – a hearty stew of hominy and meat, garnished with spices, avocado, lemon, onion, served with chicharrones and tortilla chips.

sopa – soup

Eggs

huevos estrellados – fried eggs
huevos fritos – fried eggs

huevos mexicanos – eggs scrambled with tomatoes, chilies and onions (representing the red, green and white of the Mexican flag)

huevos rancheros – fried eggs on tortillas, covered in salsa

huevos revueltos – scrambled eggs

huevos poches – poached eggs

Fish & Seafood

Fish after being caught is *pescado,* while a fish in the water is a *pez. Mariscos* can mean 'seafood' or 'shellfish.'

abulón – abalone
almejas – clams
calamar – squid
callos – scallops
camarones – shrimp
camarones gigantes – prawns
cangrejo – large crab
caracol – snail
ceviche – raw seafood marinated in lime and mixed with onion, chili, garlic and tomato
coctel – cocktail appetizer such as *coctel de camarón* (shrimp cocktail)
corvina – bass
dorado – dolphinfish, mahimahi
filete de pescado – fish filet
huachinango – red snapper
jaiba – small crab
langosta – lobster
mariscos – shellfish
mojarra – sunfish/bluegill
ostiones – oysters
pez espada – swordfish
pulpo – octopus
salmón (ahumada) – (smoked) salmon
sierra – mackerel
trucha – trout

Meat & Poultry

bistec – beefsteak; usually beef *(de res),* sometimes fish or poultry
cabra – goat
carne – meat, usually beef
carnitas – deep-fried pork
cerdo – pork
chicharrón – deep-fried pork rind; pigskin cracklings

chorizo – spicy pork sausage
chuleta – chop (such as a pork chop)
conejo – rabbit
cordero – lamb
costillas – ribs
faisán – pheasant; turkey
guajolote – turkey
hamburguesa – hamburger
hígado – liver
jamón – ham
pato – duck
pavo – turkey
pechuga – chicken breast
pollo – chicken
puerco – pork
res – beef
salchicha – spicy pork sausage
ternera – veal
tocino – bacon
venado – deer (venison)

Cooking Methods

Meat, poultry and fish are prepared in a number of ways. Try as many as possible.

a la parrilla – grilled, perhaps over charcoal
a la plancha – 'planked': grilled on a hotplate
a la tampiqueña – 'Tampico style': sautéed, thinly sliced meat, officially also marinated in garlic, oil and oregano
al carbón – charcoal-grilled
al horno – baked
al pastor – 'shepherd-style': roasted on a stake or spit
alambre – shish kebab, 'en brochette'
asada – grilled
barbacoa – literally 'barbecued,' but meat is usually covered and placed under hot coals
cocido – boiled
empanizado – breaded
frito – fried

Vegetables, Legumes & Grains

aceitunas – olives
aguacate – avocado
arroz – rice
calabaza – squash or pumpkin

cebolla – onion
champiñones – mushrooms
chícharos – peas
ejotes – green beans
elote – corn on the cob
ensalada (verde) – (green) salad
espinaca – spinach
frijoles – beans, usually black
lechuga – lettuce
lentejas- lentils
nopales – green prickly-pear cactus ears
papas – potatoes
verdures – vegetables
zanahoria – carrot

Fruit

coco – coconut
fresa – strawberry or other berry
fruta – fruit
guanabana – green pearlike fruit
guayaba – guava (better yellow than pink)
higo – fig
limón – lime or lemon
manzana – apple
melón – melon
naranja – orange
papaya – papaya
pera – pear
piña – pineapple
plátano – banana
toronja – grapefruit
uva – grape

Desserts

Most *postres* (desserts) are small afterthoughts to a meal. Here's a handful of standards:

flan – custard; crème caramel
galletas – cookies/biscuits
gelatina – Jell-O (jelly)
helado – ice cream
nieve – sorbet
paleta – flavored ice on a stick (Popsicle)
pastel – pastry or cake

Other foods

azúcar – sugar
chipotle – chilies dried, then fermented in vinegar; makes an excellent sauce for meat and fish

cilantro – fresh coriander leaf
crema – cream
leche – milk
mantequilla – butter
margarina – margarine
mole – traditional spicy sauce from Oaxaca made with chilies and other ingredients (sometimes including chocolate), often served over poultry
pan integral – (whole-grain) bread
pimienta – pepper
queso – cheese
sal – salt

salsa roja/verde – red/green sauce made with chilies, onions, tomato, lemon or lime juice and spices
sandwich – toasted sandwich

Coffee & Tea

café americano – black coffee
café con crema/leche – coffee with cream or milk
café negro – black coffee
té de manzanilla – chamomile tea
té negro – black tea, to which you can add *leche*

Glossary

For food, drink and general terms, see the Language chapter; for transportation terms, see the Getting Around chapter.

abarrote – small grocery
agave – family of plants the including *maguey*
alfarería – potter's workshop
amate – paper made from tree bark
antojitos – light meals or snacks; literally 'little whims'
Apdo – abbreviation for Apartado (Box) in addresses; hence Apdo Postal means Post Office Box
arroyo – brook, stream
artesanías – handicrafts, folk arts

bahía – bay
balneario – bathing place, often a natural hot spring
barrio – neighborhood of a town or city, often a poor neighborhood
billete – bank note
boleto – ticket
brujo, -a – witch doctor, shaman; similar to *curandero, -a*

caballeros – literally 'horsemen,' but corresponds to 'gentlemen' in English; look for it on toilet doors
cabana – cabin, simple shelter
calle – street
callejón – alley
camión – truck or bus
camioneta – pickup truck
campesino, -a – country or rural person, peasant
casa de cambio – exchange house; place where currency is exchanged
caseta de larga distancia, caseta de teléfono, caseta telefónica – public telephone call station
cazuela – clay cooking pot; usually sold in a nested set
cerro – hill
charreada – Mexican rodeo
charro – Mexican cowboy

chingar – literally 'to fornicate'; it has a wide range of colloquial usages in Mexican Spanish equivalent to those in English
Churrigueresque – Spanish late-baroque architectural style; found on many Mexican churches
cigarro – cigarette
clavadistas – the cliff divers of Acapulco and Mazatlán
colectivo – minibus or car that picks up and drops off passengers along a predetermined route; can also refer to other types of transport, such as boats
colonia – neighborhood of a city, often a wealthy residential area
comedor – inexpensive restaurant
comida corrida – set lunch or dinner special
completo – no vacancy, literally 'full up'; a sign you may see at hotel desks
conquistador – early Spanish explorer-conqueror
cordillera – mountain range
correos – post office
criollo – Mexican-born person of Spanish parentage; in colonial times considered inferior by peninsular Spaniards
crudo – hangover
cuota – toll; a *vía cuota* is a toll road
curandero, -a – literally 'curer'; a medicine man or woman who uses herbal and/or magical methods and often emphasizes spiritual aspects of disease

damas – ladies; the sign on toilet doors
dársena – pier; dock

edificio – building
ejido – communal landholding
embarcadero – jetty, boat landing
encomienda – a grant made to a *conquistador* of labor by or tribute from a group of indigenous people; the conquistador was supposed to protect and convert them, but usually treated them as little more than slaves
enramada – literally a bower or shelter, but it generally refers to a thatch-covered, open-air restaurant

enredo – wraparound skirt
escuela – school
esq – abbreviation of *esquina* (corner) in addresses
ex-convento – former convent or monastery

faja – waist sash used in traditional indigenous costume
feria – fair or carnival, typically occurring during a religious holiday
ficha – locker token available at bus terminals

gringo, -a – US or Canadian (and sometimes European, Australasian etc) visitor to Latin America; can be used derogatorily
gruta – cave, grotto
guarache – also *huarache*; woven leather sandal, often with tire tread as the sole
guardería de equipaje – room for storing luggage, eg, in a bus station
güero, -a – fair-haired, fair-complexioned person; a more polite alternative to *gringo*

hacienda – estate; Hacienda (capitalized) is the Treasury Department
hombres – men; sign on toilet doors
huarache – see *guarache*
huipil, -es – indigenous woman's sleeveless tunic, usually highly decorated; can be thigh-length or reach the ankles

iglesia – church
INAH – Instituto Nacional de Antropología e Historia; the body in charge of most ancient sites and some museums
indígena – indigenous, pertaining to the original inhabitants of Latin America; can also refer to the people themselves
INI – Instituto Nacional Indígenista; set up in 1948 to improve the lot of indigenous Mexicans and to integrate them into society; sometimes accused of paternalism and trying to stifle protest
ISH – *impuesto sobre hospedaje*; lodging tax on the price of hotel rooms
isla – island
IVA – *impuesto de valor agregado*, or 'ee-bah'; a 15% sales tax added to the price of many items
jai alai – the Basque game *pelota*, brought to Mexico by the Spanish; a bit like squash, played on a long court with curved baskets attached to the arm
jefe – boss or leader, especially political

lancha – fast, open, outboard boat
latifundio – large landholding; these sprang up after Mexico's independence from Spain
latifundista – powerful landowner who usurped communally owned land to form a *latifundio*
lleno – full, as with a car's fuel tank

machismo – Mexican masculine bravura
maguey – a type of agave; tequila and *mezcal* are made from its sap
malecón – waterfront street, boulevard or promenade
mariachi – ensemble of street musicians playing traditional ballads on guitars and trumpets
marimba – wooden xylophone-type instrument, popular in the south
mercado – market
Mesoamerica – the region inhabited by the ancient Mexican and Mayan cultures
mestizo – person of mixed (usually indigenous and Spanish) ancestry, ie, most Mexicans
metate – shallow stone bowl with legs, for grinding maize and other foods
mezcal – an aolcoholic drink made from the sap of the maguey plant
mirador, -es – lookout point(s)
Montezuma's revenge – Mexican version of Delhi-belly or travelers' diarrhea
mordida – literally 'little bite,' a small bribe to keep the wheels of bureaucracy turning; that which you pay to a cop to get off the hook
mota – marijuana
mujeres – women; seen on toilet doors
municipio – small local-government area; Mexico is divided into 2394 of them

Nafta – North American Free Trade Agreement – see *TLC*
Náhuatl – language of the Nahua people, descendants of the Aztecs
Nte – abbreviation for *norte* (north), used in street names

Ote – abbreviation for *oriente* (east), used in street names

pachanga – party
palacio municipal – town or city hall, headquarters of the municipal corporation
palapa – thatched-roof shelter
panga – fiberglass skiff for fishing, excursions and transport
parada – bus stop, usually for city buses
parque nacional – national park
paseo – boulevard, walkway or pedestrian street; also the tradition of strolling in a circle around the plaza in the evening
Pemex – government-owned petroleum extraction, refining and retailing monopoly
periférico – ring road
petate – mat, usually made of palm or reed
peyote – a hallucinogenic cactus
piñata – clay pot or papier-mâché mold decorated to resemble an animal, pineapple, star etc; filled with sweets and gifts and smashed open at fiestas
playa – beach
plaza de toros – bullring
plazuela – small plaza
Porfiriato – Porfirio Díaz's reign as president-dictator of Mexico for 30 years, until the 1910 revolution
portales – arcades
presidio – fort or fort's garrison
PRI – Partido Revolucionario Institucional (Institutional Revolutionary Party); the political party that ruled Mexico for most of the 20th century
propina – tip; different from a *mordida*, which is closer to a bribe
Pte – abbreviation for *poniente* (west), used in street names
puerto – port

Quetzalcóatl – plumed serpent god of pre-Hispanic Mexico

ramada – thatched shelter
rebozo – long woolen or linen shawl covering the head or shoulders
reserva de la biósfera – biosphere reserve; an environmentally protected area where human exploitation is steered towards ecologically unharmful activities

retablo – altarpiece; or painting on wood, tin, cardboard, glass etc, in a church to give thanks for miracles, answered prayers etc
río – river

s/n – *sin número* (without number); used in street addresses
sanitario – toilet, literally 'sanitary place'
sarape – blanket with opening for the head, worn as a cloak
Semana Santa – Holy Week, the week from Palm Sunday to Easter Sunday; Mexico's major holiday period, when accommodations and transport get very busy
servicios – toilets
sierra – mountain range
sitio – taxi stand; place
supermercado – supermarket
Sur – south; often seen in street names

taller – shop or workshop; a *taller mecánico* is a mechanic's shop, usually for cars; a *taller de llantas* is a tire-repair shop
tapatío, -a – person born in Jalisco state
taquilla – ticket window
telar de cintura – backstrap loom
templo – church; anything from a wayside chapel to a cathedral
tianguis – indigenous people's market
tienda – store
típico, -a – characteristic of a region; particularly used to describe food
TLC – Tratado de Libre Comercio, the North American Free Trade Agreement (Nafta)
topes – speed bumps; found on the outskirts of many towns and villages
trova – folk music; ballad

UNAM – Universidad Nacional Autónoma de México (National Autonomous University of Mexico)

viajero, -a – traveler

zócalo – main plaza or square; a term used in some (but not all) Mexican towns
Zona Dorada – literally 'Pink Zone'; an area of expensive shops, hotels and restaurants in Mazatlán and Acapulco frequented most by the wealthy and tourists; by extension, a similar area in another city

Lonely Planet Guides by Region

Lonely Planet is known worldwide for publishing practical, reliable and no-nonsense travel information in our guides and on our Web site. The Lonely Planet list covers just about every accessible part of the world. Currently there are 16 series: Travel guides, Shoestring guides, Condensed guides, Phrasebooks, Read This First, Healthy Travel, Walking guides, Cycling guides, Watching Wildlife guides, Pisces Diving & Snorkeling guides, City Maps, Road Atlases, Out to Eat, World Food, Journeys travel literature and Pictorials.

AFRICA Africa on a shoestring • Botswana • Cairo • Cairo City Map • Cape Town • Cape Town City Map • East Africa • Egypt • Egyptian Arabic phrasebook • Ethiopia, Eritrea & Djibouti • Ethiopian Amharic phrasebook • The Gambia & Senegal • Healthy Travel Africa • Kenya • Malawi • Morocco • Moroccan Arabic phrasebook • Mozambique • Namibia • Read This First: Africa • South Africa, Lesotho & Swaziland • Southern Africa • Southern Africa Road Atlas • Swahili phrasebook • Tanzania, Zanzibar & Pemba • Trekking in East Africa • Tunisia • Watching Wildlife East Africa • Watching Wildlife Southern Africa • West Africa • World Food Morocco • Zambia • Zimbabwe, Botswana & Namibia
Travel Literature: Mali Blues: Traveling to an African Beat • The Rainbird: A Central African Journey • Songs to an African Sunset: A Zimbabwean Story

AUSTRALIA & THE PACIFIC Aboriginal Australia & the Torres Strait Islands •Auckland • Australia • Australian phrasebook • Australia Road Atlas • Cycling Australia • Cycling New Zealand • Fiji • Fijian phrasebook • Healthy Travel Australia, NZ & the Pacific • Islands of Australia's Great Barrier Reef • Melbourne • Melbourne City Map • Micronesia • New Caledonia • New South Wales • New Zealand • Northern Territory • Outback Australia • Out to Eat – Melbourne • Out to Eat – Sydney • Papua New Guinea • Pidgin phrasebook • Queensland • Rarotonga & the Cook Islands • Samoa • Solomon Islands • South Australia • South Pacific • South Pacific phrasebook • Sydney • Sydney City Map • Sydney Condensed • Tahiti & French Polynesia • Tasmania • Tonga • Tramping in New Zealand • Vanuatu • Victoria • Walking in Australia • Watching Wildlife Australia • Western Australia
Travel Literature: Islands in the Clouds: Travels in the Highlands of New Guinea • Kiwi Tracks: A New Zealand Journey • Sean & David's Long Drive

CENTRAL AMERICA & THE CARIBBEAN Bahamas, Turks & Caicos • Baja California • Belize, Guatemala & Yucatán • Bermuda • Central America on a shoestring • Costa Rica • Costa Rica Spanish phrasebook • Cuba • Cycling Cuba • Dominican Republic & Haiti • Eastern Caribbean • Guatemala • Havana • Healthy Travel Central & South America • Jamaica • Mexico • Mexico City • Panama • Puerto Rico • Read This First: Central & South America • Virgin Islands • World Food Caribbean • World Food Mexico • Yucatán
Travel Literature: Green Dreams: Travels in Central America

EUROPE Amsterdam • Amsterdam City Map • Amsterdam Condensed • Andalucía • Athens • Austria • Baltic States phrasebook • Barcelona • Barcelona City Map • Belgium & Luxembourg • Berlin • Berlin City Map • Britain • British phrasebook • Brussels, Bruges & Antwerp • Brussels City Map • Budapest • Budapest City Map • Canary Islands • Catalunya & the Costa Brava • Central Europe • Central Europe phrasebook • Copenhagen • Corfu & the Ionians • Corsica • Crete • Crete Condensed • Croatia • Cycling Britain • Cycling France • Cyprus • Czech & Slovak Republics • Czech phrasebook • Denmark • Dublin • Dublin City Map • Dublin Condensed • Eastern Europe • Eastern Europe phrasebook • Edinburgh • Edinburgh City Map • England • Estonia, Latvia & Lithuania • Europe on a shoestring • Europe phrasebook • Finland • Florence • Florence City Map • France • Frankfurt City Map • Frankfurt Condensed • French phrasebook • Georgia, Armenia & Azerbaijan • Germany • German phrasebook • Greece • Greek Islands • Greek phrasebook • Hungary • Iceland, Greenland & the Faroe Islands • Ireland • Italian phrasebook • Italy • Kraków • Lisbon • The Loire • London • London City Map • London Condensed • Madrid • Madrid City Map • Malta • Mediterranean Europe • Milan, Turin & Genoa • Moscow • Munich • Netherlands • Normandy • Norway • Out to Eat – London • Out to Eat – Paris • Paris • Paris City Map • Paris Condensed • Poland • Polish phrasebook • Portugal • Portuguese phrasebook • Prague • Prague City Map • Provence & the Côte d'Azur • Read This First: Europe • Rhodes & the Dodecanese • Romania & Moldova • Rome • Rome City Map • Rome Condensed • Russia, Ukraine & Belarus • Russian phrasebook • Scandinavian & Baltic Europe • Scandinavian phrasebook • Scotland • Sicily • Slovenia • South-West France • Spain • Spanish phrasebook • Stockholm • St Petersburg • St Petersburg City Map • Sweden • Switzerland • Tuscany • Ukrainian phrasebook • Venice • Vienna • Wales • Walking in Britain • Walking in France • Walking in Ireland • Walking in Italy • Walking in Scotland • Walking in Spain • Walking in Switzerland • Western Europe • World Food France • World Food Greece • World Food Ireland • World Food Italy • World Food Spain **Travel Literature:** After Yugoslavia • Love and War in the Apennines • The Olive Grove: Travels in Greece • On the Shores of the Mediterranean • Round Ireland in Low Gear • A Small Place in Italy

Lonely Planet Mail Order

Lonely Planet products are distributed worldwide. They are also available by mail order from Lonely Planet, so if you have difficulty finding a title please write to us. North and South American residents should write to 150 Linden St, Oakland, CA 94607, USA; European and African residents should write to 10a Spring Place, London NW5 3BH, UK; and residents of other countries to Locked Bag 1, Footscray, Victoria 3011, Australia.

INDIAN SUBCONTINENT & THE INDIAN OCEAN Bangladesh • Bengali phrasebook • Bhutan • Delhi • Goa • Healthy Travel Asia & India • Hindi & Urdu phrasebook • India • India & Bangladesh City Map • Indian Himalaya • Karakoram Highway • Kathmandu City Map • Kerala • Madagascar • Maldives • Mauritius, Réunion & Seychelles • Mumbai (Bombay) • Nepal • Nepali phrasebook • North India • Pakistan • Rajasthan • Read This First: Asia & India • South India • Sri Lanka • Sri Lanka phrasebook • Tibet • Tibetan phrasebook • Trekking in the Indian Himalaya • Trekking in the Karakoram & Hindukush • Trekking in the Nepal Himalaya • World Food India **Travel Literature:** The Age of Kali: Indian Travels and Encounters • Hello Goodnight: A Life of Goa • In Rajasthan • Maverick in Madagascar • A Season in Heaven: True Tales from the Road to Kathmandu • Shopping for Buddhas • A Short Walk in the Hindu Kush • Slowly Down the Ganges

MIDDLE EAST & CENTRAL ASIA Bahrain, Kuwait & Qatar • Central Asia • Central Asia phrasebook • Dubai • Farsi (Persian) phrasebook • Hebrew phrasebook • Iran • Israel & the Palestinian Territories • Istanbul • Istanbul City Map • Istanbul to Cairo • Istanbul to Kathmandu • Jerusalem • Jerusalem City Map • Jordan • Lebanon • Middle East • Oman & the United Arab Emirates • Syria • Turkey • Turkish phrasebook • World Food Turkey • Yemen **Travel Literature:** Black on Black: Iran Revisited • Breaking Ranks: Turbulent Travels in the Promised Land • The Gates of Damascus • Kingdom of the Film Stars: Journey into Jordan

NORTH AMERICA Alaska • Boston • Boston City Map • Boston Condensed • British Columbia • California & Nevada • California Condensed • Canada • Chicago • Chicago City Map • Chicago Condensed • Florida • Georgia & the Carolinas • Great Lakes • Hawaii • Hiking in Alaska • Hiking in the USA • Honolulu & Oahu City Map • Las Vegas • Los Angeles • Los Angeles City Map • Louisiana & the Deep South • Miami • Miami City Map • Montreal • New England • New Orleans • New Orleans City Map • New York City • New York City City Map • New York City Condensed • New York, New Jersey & Pennsylvania • Oahu • Out to Eat – San Francisco • Pacific Northwest • Rocky Mountains • San Diego & Tijuana • San Francisco • San Francisco City Map • Seattle • Seattle City Map • Southwest • Texas • Toronto • USA • USA phrasebook • Vancouver • Vancouver City Map • Virginia & the Capital Region • Washington, DC • Washington, DC City Map • World Food New Orleans **Travel Literature:** Caught Inside: A Surfer's Year on the California Coast • Drive Thru America

NORTH-EAST ASIA Beijing • Beijing City Map • Cantonese phrasebook • China • Hiking in Japan • Hong Kong & Macau • Hong Kong City Map • Hong Kong Condensed • Japan • Japanese phrasebook • Korea • Korean phrasebook • Kyoto • Mandarin phrasebook • Mongolia • Mongolian phrasebook • Seoul • Shanghai • South-West China • Taiwan • Tokyo • Tokyo Condensed • World Food Hong Kong • World Food Japan **Travel Literature:** In Xanadu: A Quest • Lost Japan

SOUTH AMERICA Argentina, Uruguay & Paraguay • Bolivia • Brazil • Brazilian phrasebook • Buenos Aires • Buenos Aires City Map • Chile & Easter Island • Colombia • Ecuador & the Galapagos Islands • Healthy Travel Central & South America • Latin American Spanish phrasebook • Peru • Quechua phrasebook • Read This First: Central & South America • Rio de Janeiro • Rio de Janeiro City Map • Santiago de Chile • South America on a shoestring • Trekking in the Patagonian Andes • Venezuela **Travel Literature:** Full Circle: A South American Journey

SOUTH-EAST ASIA Bali & Lombok • Bangkok • Bangkok City Map • Burmese phrasebook • Cambodia • Cycling Vietnam, Laos & Cambodia • East Timor phrasebook • Hanoi • Healthy Travel Asia & India • Hill Tribes phrasebook • Ho Chi Minh City (Saigon) • Indonesia • Indonesian phrasebook • Indonesia's Eastern Islands • Java • Lao phrasebook • Laos • Malay phrasebook • Malaysia, Singapore & Brunei • Myanmar (Burma) • Philippines • Pilipino (Tagalog) phrasebook • Read This First: Asia & India • Singapore • Singapore City Map • South-East Asia on a shoestring • South-East Asia phrasebook • Thailand • Thailand's Islands & Beaches • Thailand, Vietnam, Laos & Cambodia Road Atlas • Thai phrasebook • Vietnam • Vietnamese phrasebook • World Food Indonesia • World Food Thailand • World Food Vietnam

ALSO AVAILABLE: Antarctica • The Arctic • The Blue Man: Tales of Travel, Love and Coffee • Brief Encounters: Stories of Love, Sex & Travel • Buddhist Stupas in Asia: The Shape of Perfection • Chasing Rickshaws • The Last Grain Race • Lonely Planet ... On the Edge: Adventurous Escapades from Around the World • Lonely Planet Unpacked • Lonely Planet Unpacked Again • Not the Only Planet: Science Fiction Travel Stories • Ports of Call: A Journey by Sea • Sacred India • Travel Photography: A Guide to Taking Better Pictures • Travel with Children • Tuvalu: Portrait of an Island Nation

LONELY PLANET

You already know that Lonely Planet produces more than this one guidebook, but you might not be aware of the other products we have on this region. Here is a selection of titles that you may want to check out as well:

Mexico
ISBN 1 74059 028 7
US$24.99 • UK£14.99

Healthy Travel Central & South America
ISBN 1 86450 053 0
US$5.95 • UK£3.99

Latin American Spanish phrasebook
ISBN 0 86442 558 9
US$6.95 • UK£4.50

Mexico City
ISBN 1 86450 087 5
US$14.99 • UK£8.99

Belize Guatemala & Yucatán
ISBN 1 86450 140 5
US$19.99 • UK£13.99

World Food Mexico
ISBN 1 86450 023 9
US$11.95 • UK£6.99

Yucatán
ISBN 1 74059 456 8
US$17.99 • UK£12.99

San Diego & Tijuana
ISBN 1 86450 218 5
US$16.99 • UK£10.99

Baja California
ISBN 1 86450 198 7
US$16.99 • UK£10.99

Diving & Snorkeling Cozumel
ISBN 0 86442 574 0
US$14.95 • UK£8.99

Read This First: Central & South America
ISBN 1 86450 067 0
US$14.99 • UK£8.99

Green Dreams
ISBN 0 86442 523 6
US$12.95 • UK£6.99

Available wherever books are sold

Index

Text

Bold indicates maps.

Boxed Text

MAP LEGEND

ROUTES

City	Regional	
		.........Freeway
		.........Tollway
		.........Primary Road
		.........Secondary Road
		.........Tertiary Road
		.........Dirt Road

..........Pedestrian Mall
..........Steps
..........Tunnel
..........Trail
..........Walking Tour
..........Path

TRANSPORTATION

..........Train
..........Metro
..........Bus Route
..........Ferry

HYDROGRAPHY

..........River; Creek
..........Canal
..........Lake
..........Spring; Rapids
..........Waterfalls
..........Dry; Salt Lake

ROUTE SHIELDS

MEX 2 Highway
MEX 15D Toll Highway

BOUNDARIES

..........International
..........State

AREAS

..........Beach
..........Building
..........Campus
..........Cemetery
..........Forest
..........Garden; Zoo
..........Golf Course
..........Park
..........Plaza
..........Reservation
..........Sports Field
..........Swamp; Mangrove

POPULATION SYMBOLS

✪ NATIONAL CAPITAL ....National Capital
◉ STATE CAPITAL ....State Capital
● Large City ....Large City
● Medium City ....Medium City
● Small City ....Small City
● Town; Village ....Town; Village

MAP SYMBOLS

● ....Place to Stay
▼ ....Place to Eat
● ....Point of Interest

..........Airfield	..........Church	..........Museum	..........Skiing - Downhill
..........Airport	..........Cinema	..........Observatory	..........Stately Home
..........Archeological Site; Ruin	..........Dive Site	..........Park	..........Surfing
..........Bank	..........Embassy; Consulate	..........Parking Area	..........Synagogue
..........Baseball Diamond	..........Footbridge	..........Pass	..........Tao Temple
..........Battlefield	..........Gas Station	..........Picnic Area	..........Taxi
..........Bike Trail	..........Hospital	..........Police Station	..........Telephone
..........Border Crossing	..........Information	..........Pool	..........Theater
..........Buddhist Temple	..........Internet Access	..........Post Office	..........Toilet - Public
..........Bus Station; Terminal	..........Lighthouse	..........Pub; Bar	..........Tomb
..........Cable Car; Chairlift	..........Lookout	..........RV Park	..........Trailhead
..........Campground	..........Mine	..........Shelter	..........Tram Stop
..........Castle	..........Mission	..........Shipwreck	..........Transportation
..........Cathedral	..........Monument	..........Shopping Mall	..........Volcano
..........Cave	..........Mountain	..........Skiing - Cross Country	..........Winery

Note: Not all symbols displayed above appear in this book.

LONELY PLANET OFFICES

Australia
Locked Bag 1, Footscray, Victoria 3011
☎ 03 8379 8000 fax 03 8379 8111
email: talk2us@lonelyplanet.com.au

USA
150 Linden St, Oakland, CA 94607
☎ 510 893 8555 TOLL FREE: 800 275 8555
fax 510 893 8572
email: info@lonelyplanet.com

UK
10a Spring Place, London NW5 3BH
☎ 020 7428 4800 fax 020 7428 4828
email: go@lonelyplanet.co.uk

France
1 rue du Dahomey, 75011 Paris
☎ 01 55 25 33 00 fax 01 55 25 33 01
email: bip@lonelyplanet.fr
www.lonelyplanet.fr

**World Wide Web: www.lonelyplanet.com *or* AOL keyword: lp
Lonely Planet Images: www.lonelyplanetimages.com**